SUBJECT GUIDE TO BIBLE STORIES

Compiled by
George Frederick Garland

BRADDOCK
PUBLISHEF

Library of Congress catalog card number: 69-19012

ISBN: 978-0-578-68451-2

ROBERT H. SOMMER, PUBLISHER
Harrington Park, N.J. 07640

Printed in the United States of America

First Printing, September 1969
Second Printing, December 1970
Third Printing, December 1972
Fourth Printing, December 1973
Fifth Printing, June 1974
Sixth Printing, June 1976
Seventh Printing, September 1979
Eighth Printing, February 1986
Ninth Printing, August 1990
Tenth Printing, August 1996
Eleventh Printing, May 2002
Twelfth Printing, June 2006
Thirteenth Printing, April 2012

BRADDOCK H. BULL, PUBLISHER

Fourteenth Printing, June 2020

CONTENTS

INTRODUCTION

Modern readers, like people all through the ages, are looking to the Scriptures for inspiration and strength. The stories of the Bible have enduring appeal and are often the easiest passages to understand. They may describe life and customs unfamiliar to us today, yet the lessons and spiritual truths these stories teach are equally valid in our time.

Bible stories reveal the nature of God and both the noble and flawed nature of mankind. They also illustrate divine power acting on the human experience.

The Bible touches on an astoundingly wide variety of topics. It is hard to name a subject upon which it does not shed some light. Answers to even so-called modern problems can be found in Biblical literature. Is not the human fear of war, for instance, the same whether the weapon is an arrow or an atom?

The purpose of this book is to help the researcher locate more easily Bible stories according to their themes. With each story the compiler had to ask himself, "Is this an inspiring story?" and "How should it be classified as to its subject matter?" At the outset, it must be admitted that some Bible stories are so complex and have so many facets that a given story may be used to illustrate different lessons. Some stories thus are listed in more than one place and under several topics.

The intent of this work is to suggest where to find a story that makes a desired point, but not to limit the reader's independent study. A researcher is encouraged to compare a Bible story of their own choosing against this book's list to help decide if they have arrived at the most appropriate narrative for their subject.

This concordance locates Biblical comment on a vast number of familiar topics, but because of its compactness it cannot include all possible subjects. There may be special circumstances in a congregation or new issues in world affairs for which the reader may want to find an appropriate Biblical story, and where this concordance may not offer sufficient help. In that case, perhaps a word synonymous with a reader's topic may be found in this book's list, and its stories may be pertinent to that special subject.

Those who are sensitive to the needs of the group they are addressing will probably choose their subject by inspiration rather than by rote adoption of one of the subjects listed in this book. This concordance should serve less as a guide to the selection of topics and more as a guide to possible references once the topic has been chosen.

Norwalk, Conn., 1969   George Frederick Garland

How to Use the Subject Guide to Bible Stories

The purpose of this Subject Guide is to aid the reader in finding Biblical passages illustrating a chosen subject for a congregation, a Sunday School class, a Bible study group, a church committee, some other type of body, or even a family. The Guide will also be a help to every Bible student in their individual research and study.

PART ONE
The Subject Guide

Topical Concordance If you have chosen a particular subject or idea you wish to illustrate with a Bible story, look in Part One, the topical concordance of stories. There you may find several suitable references under your subject. For instance, you may be looking for a story to illustrate the topic "abundance." Under this subject are listed "Elijah, food supplied," "Elisha, the widow's pot of oil," "Jesus, 5,000 fed," "Jesus, Peter's net filled," and other selections. The exact Bible citation for each always immediately follows the entry. You can choose the one which best brings out the point you wish to share. Turning to the citation, you then have the story in its original form, instead of having to use a Bible story book which retells a Scriptural story in a particular author's words and possibly biased point of view.

PART TWO
The Character Guide

Leading Characters Perhaps you have in mind a leading Bible character for your study such as Moses and want to find stories about him. In Part Two, the Character Guide, look for his name in the alphabetical list. Under his name you will then find capsule summaries of a number of inspiring stories about him. For instance, some listings for Moses are: "Burning bush; the nature of god revealed," "Complains of speaking ability," and "Water from rock." Beside each summary appears the book, chapter, and verses (Bible citation) where you will find the complete story as told in the original words of your Bible. Now you can select the story about Moses that is most suitable for your purpose.

New Testament Since there are so many stories in the New Testament about Jesus, it is useful to divide them into categories such as parables, great works, and the last Passover week. Then the stories under each category are listed with their book, chapter and verses.

Alternates   If you have in mind both a subject and a good story illustration
to go with it, you can still use the Subject Guide as a check
to determine if the story you selected is the most appropriate for the occasion.

Remember, this is a topical concordance of stories only. To clarify your subject, you may want to embellish your chosen story with individual verses or groups of verses of a non-narrative character such as are found in Psalms, Proverbs, and other books. You may identify these by using an exhaustive Bible concordance.

The reader may question the difference between a complete word concordance of the Bible and Part One which is a topical concordance of Bible stories. A Bible word concordance lists the occurrence of every word of the Bible and gives the verse where each appears. A topical concordance of the Bible lists single verses related to a given subject. This Subject Guide is a topical concordance, but it goes further. It classifies whole stories according to their subject. A topical Bible concordance helps you find non-narrative text for your subject; but what about a story that best illustrates that text? For this purpose you will use the Subject Guide.

ABBREVIATIONS

O.T.	Old Testament	N.T.	New Testament
Gen.	Genesis	Mat.	Matthew
Exod.	Exodus	Mark	Mark
Lev.	Leviticus	Luke	Luke
Num.	Numbers	John	John
Deut.	Deuteronomy	Acts	Acts
Josh.	Joshua	Rom.	Romans
Judges	Judges	1 Cor.	I Corinthians
Ruth	Ruth	2 Cor.	II Corinthians
1 Sam.	I Samuel	Gal.	Galatians
2 Sam.	II Samuel	Eph.	Ephesians
1 King.	I Kings	Phil.	Philippians
2 King.	II Kings	Col.	Colossians
1 Chron.	I Chronicles	1 Thess.	I Thessalonians
2 Chron.	II Chronicles	2 Thess.	II Thessalonians
Ezra	Ezra	1 Tim.	I Timothy
Neh.	Nehemiah	2 Tim.	II Timothy
Esther	Esther	Titus	Titus
Job	Job	Philemon	Philemon
Psal.	Psalms	Heb.	Hebrews
Prov.	Proverbs	Jas.	James
Eccl.	Ecclesiastes	1 Pet.	I Peter
Song Sol.	Song of Solomon	2 Pet.	II Peter
Isa.	Isaiah	1 John	I John
Jer.	Jeremiah	2 John	II John
Lam.	Lamentations	3 John	III John
Ezek.	Ezekiel	Jude	Jude
Dan.	Daniel	Rev.	Revelation
Hos.	Hosea		
Joel	Joel		
Amos	Amos		
Obad.	Obadiah		
Jonah	Jonah		
Mic.	Micah		
Nahum	Nahum		
Hab.	Habakkuk		
Zeph.	Zephaniah		
Haggai	Haggai		
Zech.	Zechariah		
Mai.	Malachi		

PART I

THE SUBJECT GUIDE

An alphabetical listing
of selected topics
under which Bible stories
are classified

A

AARON

See Part II, Aaron

ABEL

See Part II, Cain and Abel

ABIDE

Enoch walked with God *Gen 5:18, 21-24, Heb 11:5*
Jacob's dream of angels *Gen 28:10-22*
Moses and the chosen people *Deut 7:6-26*
Moses on "Choose ye" *Deut 30:11-20*
Ruth stays with Naomi *Ruth 1:1-22*
David's song, "Dwell in the house of the Lord" *Psal 23:1-6*
David's song, "Under the shadow of the Almighty" *Psal 91:1-16*
Jesus on prodigal son's elder brother *Luke 15:25-32*
Jesus on source of his great works *John 5:17-47*
Jesus on bread of life *John 6:26-65*
Jesus on unity with Christ *John 8:12-59*
Jesus on the door and the good shepherd *John 10:1-33*
Jesus on the true vine *John 15:1-17*
Jesus on oneness with the Father *John 17:18-26*

See also dwelling, home, house, patience

ABILITY

Joseph demonstrates his ability *Gen 39:21-23, 40:1-23*
Moses questions his own ability *Exod 3:9-12*
Jesus' parable of talents *Mat 25:14-30, Luke 19:11-28*
Jesus on the source of his great works *John 5:17-47*
Paul on diversity of abilities *1 Cor 12:1-31*
Paul says he is least of apostles *1 Cor 15:9-11*

See also energy, power, skill, strength, talent

ABOMINATION

See sin, hatred

ABRAHAM

See Part II, Abraham

ABSOLUTION

Abraham released by angel from sacrificing Isaac *Gen 22:1-19*
Aaron obtains remission through the scapegoat *Lev 16:1-28*
Moses heals Miriam of leprosy *Num 12:1-16*
David's song, "Create in me a clean heart" *Psal 51:1-19*
Jesus on two debtors *Luke 7:36-50*
Jesus on prodigal son *Luke 15:11-24*
Jesus forgives sin of paralytic before healing him *Mat 9:2-8, Mark 2:1-12, Luke 5:17-26*
Peter given keys to kingdom *Mat 16:13-20, Mark 8:27-30, Luke 9:18-21*

See also atonement, death, forgiveness, pardon, priest, sacrament, sin

ABSTINENCE

Adam and Eve forbidden tree of good and evil *Gen 2:16, 17, 3:1-5*
Lot, but not wife, escapes Sodom and Gomorrah *Gen 19:1, 15-29*
Abraham tempted to sacrifice Isaac *Gen 22:1-19*
Joseph refuses Potiphar's wife *Gen 39:1-20*
Moses hears complaint of Israelites *Exod 16:1-16, Num 11:5-15*
Moses gives Second Commandment *Exod 20:1-6*
Moses finds worship of Golden Calf *Exod 32:1-24*
Moses' forty days on mount *Exod 34:27, 28*
Moses forbids abominations *Deut 18:9-14*
Joshua uncovers sin of Achan *Josh 7:1-26, 8:14-21*
David fasts for life of child *2 Sam 12:13-23*

Elijah in desert *1 King 17:1-16, 19: 1-8*

Isaiah and the pride of women *Isa 3:16-26*

Daniel and boys refuse king's wine and meat *Dan 1:1-21*

John the Baptist in desert *Mat 3: 1-12, Mark 1:1-8, Luke 3:1-18*

Jesus' forty days without food *Mat 4:1-11, Luke 4:1-13*

Jesus turns water to wine *John 2: 1-11*

Jesus has meat disciples know not of *John 4:31-38*

James' sermon on temptation *Jas 1:1-27*

See also appetite, temperance, temptation

ABUNDANCE

Creation of teeming universe *Gen 1:1-31*

Abraham proves abundance for all *Gen 13:1-18*

Joseph interprets Pharaoh's dream *Gen 41:1-46*

His brethren come to Egypt for food *Gen 42:1-8*

Moses, food in wilderness *Exod 16: 1-26, Num 11:1-15, 31, 32*

Aaron, God's promises to faithful *Lev 26:1-20*

Joshua and Caleb scout Canaan *Num 13:1-33; 14:1-11, 23-39, Deut 1:19-38*

Moses on blessings of obedience *Deut 28:1-14*

Solomon builds temple *1 King 6:1-38, 7:1-51, 2 Chron 3:1-17, 4:1-22, 5:1-14*

Elijah, food supplied *1 King 17:1-16*

Elisha, widow's pot of oil *2 King 4:1-7*

Elisha, 100 men fed *2 King 4:42-44*

Elisha, drop in price of flour *2 King 7:1-18*

Isaiah, the desert to bloom *Isa 35: 1-10*

Malachi, reward of tithing *Mal 3: 10, 4:1, 2*

Jesus' parable of sower *Mat 13:2-23, Mark 4:1-20, Luke 8:4-15*

Jesus, Peter's net filled *Luke 5:1-11, John 21:1-11*

Jesus' parable of rich man and barns *Luke 12:15-21*

Jesus, 5000 fed *Mat 14:15-21, Mark 6:35-44, Luke 9:12-17*

Jesus, 4000 fed *Mat 15:32-39, Mark 8:1-10*

Paul on how to achieve abundance *2 Cor 8:11-15, 9:6-15*

See also blessing, supply

ACCESS

See Christ, Jesus, mediator

ACCIDENT

Ahaziah fails to recover from fall *2 King 1:1-8*

Elisha recovers axe head *2 King 6:1-7*

Job's cattle and children lost *Job 1:13-22*

Jesus on house built on sand *Mat 7:24-29, Luke 6:48, 49*

Jesus on tower of Siloam that fell on 18 *Luke 13:1-5*

Paul heals Eutychus after fall from window *Acts 20:7-12*

Paul saved from shipwreck *Acts 27: 1-44*

Paul escapes viper sting *Acts 28: 1-6*

See also adversity

ACHIEVEMENT

God creates the perfect universe and man in his image *Gen 1:1-31*

Enoch "walks with God" and is translated over death *Gen 5:18, 21-24, Heb 11:5*

Noah builds the ark and is floated to safety *Gen 6:5-22, 7:1-24*

Tower of Babel built to reach heaven *Gen 11:1-9*

Joseph becomes governor of Egypt *Gen 42:1-8*

Moses leads people out of slavery *Exod 15:1-19, Deut 32:1-47*

Moses gives people Ten Commandments *Exod 20:1-19, Deut 5:1-24*

Joshua leads people into promised land *Josh 1:10-18, 3:1-17*

Joshua takes Jericho *Josh 6:1-27*

David becomes king *2 Sam 2:1-4, 5: 1-5*

Solomon builds the temple *1 King 6:1-38, 7:1-51, 2 Chron 3:1-17, 4: 1-22, 5:1-14*

Elijah is translated *2 King 2:1-11*

Zerubbabel rebuilds temple *Ezra 3:8-13, 6:1-3, 7, 8, 14, 15*

Nehemiah rebuilds the wall *Neh 4:1-23*

Three Hebrews survive fiery furnace *Dan 3:1-30*

Daniel survives the lions' den *Dan 6:1-28*

Jesus' parable of builders on rock and sand *Mat 7:24-27, Luke 6: 48, 49*

Jesus' parable of the talents *Mat 25:14-30, Luke 19:11-28*

Jesus' parable on counting the cost *Luke 14:25-33*

Jesus' healings and great works *(See Part II, Jesus Christ: Great Works)*

Jesus on the source of his great works *John 5:17-47*

Peter and John heal man lame from birth *Acts 3:1-11*

Paul heals Eutychus of accident *Acts 20:7-12*

Paul on the prize for a race *1 Cor 9:24-27*

See also building, fulfillment, progress, success

ACKNOWLEDGE

Enoch walks with God *Gen 5:18, 21-24, Heb 11:5*

Moses' song of deliverance *Exod 15:1-19*

Joshua sets up twelve stones *Josh 4:1-24*

Deborah's song of victory *Judg 5: 1-20*

David comes to Goliath in name of Lord *1 Sam 17:38-52*

David's song of thanksgiving *2 Sam 22:1-51*

Solomon's dedication of the temple *1 King 8:21-66, 2 Chron 6:1-42*

Elijah thanks God for sacrificial fire *1 King 18:17-40*

David's praise to God *Psal 8, 19, 23, 33, 66, 90, 91, 100, 107, 139*

Job acknowledges God's greatness *Job 42:1-17*

Isaiah praises God *Isa 6, 11, 25, 33, 35, 51, 59*

Ezekiel on God's care *Ezek 34:1-31*

Jesus called Christ by wise men *Mat 2:1-12*

Jesus called Christ by Peter *Mat 16:13-20, Mark 8:27-30, Luke 9:18-21*

Jesus at Gethsemane *Mat 25:30, 31-46, Mark 14:26, 32-42, Luke 22: 39-46*

Jesus called Christ by Simon and Anna *Luke 2:21-38*

Jesus heals woman bowed together *Luke 13:11-17*

Jesus heals ten lepers, one acknowledges it *Luke 17:11-19*

Jesus called Christ by John Baptist *John 1:15-34*

Jesus called Christ by Samaritan woman at Jacob's well *John 4:1-30, 39-42*

Jesus on source of his works *John 5:17-47*

Jesus raises Lazarus *John 11:1-46*

Jesus called Christ by Thomas *John 20:24-29*

See also confession, confirmation, praise, testify, thanksgiving

ACTIVITY

Moses commands to "go forward" through Red Sea *Exod 14:5-31*

Moses and Israelites don't listen to Caleb's call for action now *Num 13:1-33, 14:1-11, Deut 1:19-38*

Moses' farewell address "choose ye" *Deut 30:11-20*

Moses charges Joshua with leadership *Deut 31:7-23, Josh 1:1-9*

Ruth gleans in the field *Ruth 2: 1-23*

David visits army and challenges Goliath *1 Sam 17:17-37*

Solomon builds temple *1 King 6:1-38, 7:1-51, 2 Chron 3:1-17, 4:1-22, 5:1-14*

Nehemiah rebuilds wall *Neh 1:1-11, 2:1-20, 4:1-23*

Isaiah, desert blossoms *Isa 35:1-10*

Ezekiel, resurrection of dry bones *Ezek 37:1-28*

Jonah flees action *Jonah 1:1-17, 2:1-10*

Jesus' golden rule for action *Mat 7:12-14*

Jesus and centurion's servant *Mat 8:5-13, Luke 7:1-10*

Jesus heals paralytic let down through roof *Mat 9:1-8, Mark 2:1-12, Luke 5:17-26*

Jesus' parable of leaven *Mat 13:33, Luke 13:20, 21*

Jesus and epileptic boy *Mat 17:14-21, Mark 9:14-29, Luke 9:37-43*

Jesus' parable of two sons ordered to work *Mat 21:28-32*

Jesus' parable of ten virgins *Mat 25:1-13*

Jesus' parable of talents *Mat 25:14-30, Luke 19:11-28*

Nets filled by Jesus *Luke 5:1-11*

Jesus' parable of good Samaritan *Luke 10:25-37*

Jesus' parable of unwilling friend *Luke 11:5-13*

Jesus' parable of faithful steward *Luke 12:41-48*

Jesus' parable of barren fig tree *Luke 13:6-9*

Jesus heals woman bowed together *Luke 13:11-17*

Jesus' parable of serving the master *Luke 17:7-10*

Jesus' parable of judge and widow *Luke 18:1-8*

Jesus and impotent man at pool *John 5:1-16*

Peter must speak out *Acts 4:1-23*

Paul on charity *1 Cor 13:1-13*

Paul on how Christians should act *Col 3:1-17*

Paul on precepts *2 Tim 4:1-8*

John's letters to churches *Rev 2:1-29, 3:1-22*

See also force, occupation, omni-action, service, work

ADAM

See Part II, Adam and Eve

ADMINISTRATION

See government, guidance, problem-solving

ADOPTION

Moses adopted by Egyptian princess *Exod 2:1-10*

Moses tells Israelites they are chosen by God *Deut 7:6-26*

Esther adopted by Mordecai *Esther 2:5-23*

Paul on becoming heirs of God *Rom 8:14-39, Gal 4:1-9*

John on the sons of God *1 John 3:1-3*

See also children, conversion, sonship

ADULTERY

Joseph resists Potiphar's wife *Gen 39:1-20*

Moses gives Second and Seventh Commandments *Exod 20:1-19*

Moses returns to find Golden Calf *Exod 32:1-24*

Moses warns against enticers to idolatry *Deut 13:1-18*

David takes Uriah's wife *2 Sam 11:1-27*

David hears Nathan's parable of ewe lamb *2 Sam 12:1-10*

Jesus on Commandments on a mental basis *Mat 5:21-32, 9:38-50*

Jesus' parable of two debtors told while adulteress anointed his feet *Luke 7:36-50*

Jesus saves an adulteress *John 8:1-11*

See also idolatry, purity

ADVANCEMENT

Enoch walked with God and was translated *Gen 5:18, 21-24*

Tower of Babel, false advance to heaven *Gen 11:1-9*

Abraham's riches grow *Gen 13:1-6*

Abraham and Sarah receive new names *Gen 17:1-9, 15-22*

Jacob wrestles with angel and receives new name *Gen 32:1-32*

Joseph is made governor of Egypt *Gen 41:1-46*

Moses talks with the Lord face to face *Exod 33:7-23*

Moses' face covered with veil *Exod 34:29-35*

Joshua given command by Moses *Josh 1:1-9*

Jotham, parable of the trees *Judg 9:1-15*

Samuel anoints Saul to be king *1 Sam 10:1-8*

David made king *2 Sam 2:1-4, 5:1-5*

Elijah taken to heaven directly *2 King 2:1-11*

Isaiah's vision of office of the Christ *Isa 42:1-12, 16, 18*

Daniel's advancement is envied *Dan 6:1-28*

Jesus instructs twelve and sends them to heal *Mat 9:36-38, 10:1-42, Mark 3:13-21, Luke 6:13-19*

Jesus' parable of wise and foolish virgins *Mat 25:1-13*

Jesus' parable of the talents *Mat 25:14-30, Luke 19:11-28*

Jesus' parable of sheep and goats *Mat 25:31-46*

Jesus overcomes death *Mat 28:1-8, Mark 16:1-8, Luke 24:1-12, John 20:1-10*

Jesus ascends *Mark 16:19, 20, Luke 24:50, 51, Acts 1:9-12*

Jesus' parable of new wine in old bottles *Luke 5:36-39*

Jesus instructs 70 to heal *Luke 10:1-24*

See also evolution, growth, progress

ADVERSARY

Eve deceived by serpent *Gen 3:1-5*

Cain and Abel *Gen 4:1-16*

Abraham's strife with Lot *Gen 13:1-18*

Isaac's herdsmen's strife over wells *Gen 26:12-31*

Jacob wrestles with angel *Gen 32:1-32*

David and Goliath *1 Sam 17:38-52*

David and Saul *1 Sam 24:1-22*

Hezekiah and Sennacherib *2 King 18:1-37, 2 Chron 31:20, 21, 32:1-23*

Esther and Mordecai vs. Haman *Esther 6:1-14*

Job and Satan *Job 1:1-12*

Nehemiah and Sanballat *Neh 6:1-19*

Three Hebrews and Persian courtiers *Dan 3:1-30*

Daniel and courtiers *Dan 6:1-28*

Jesus and Satan *Mat 4:1-11, Luke 4:1-13*

Jesus and Pharisees *Mat 12:22-30, 38-45, 21:12, 13, 23:1-39, John 8:33-59, 10:22-42*

Paul and Christians *Acts 8:1-4, 9:1-22*

Paul's advice to Timothy on enemies *2 Tim 3:1-17*

John's vision of woman and dragon *Rev 12:1-17*

See also enemy, hatred, opposition

ADVERSITY

Abraham sends Hagar and child away *Gen 21:9-21*

Joseph's trials in Egypt *Gen 39:1-20*

Moses finds water in desert *Exod 15:22-27, 17:1-7*

Gideon oppressed by Amalekites *Judg 6:1-40*

Ruth gleans in field of Boaz *Ruth 2:1-23*

Elijah in wilderness *1 King 17:1-16*

Job's trials *Job 1:13-22, 2:1-10*

David's song of ever-presence *Psal 139:1-24*

Ecclesiastes, "all is vanity" *Eccl 1:1-18, 2:1-26*

Isaiah promises help in trials *Isa 43:1-28, 44:1-24*

Jeremiah promises release *Jer 29:8-14, 31:1-14, 31-34*

Jeremiah in prison *Jer 32:2, 6-27, 37-44*

Ezekiel sees God's care of flock *Ezek 34:1-31*

Jesus heals woman with twelve-year hemorrhage *Mat 9:20-22, Mark 5:25-34, Luke 8:43-48*

Jesus' parable of unwilling friend *Luke 11:5-13*

Jesus heals woman ill 18 years *Luke 13:11-17*

Jesus' parable of judge and widow *Luke 18:1-8*

Jesus heals man impotent for 38 years *John 5:1-16*

Peter imprisoned *Acts 5:17-42*

Stephen persecuted *Acts 6:5-15*

Paul relates his hardships *2 Cor 11:21-33*

See also accident, comfort, persecution, trials

ADVICE

Adam and Eve advised by serpent *Gen 3:1-5*

David warned by Jonathan *1 Sam 18:1-16*

Saul consults familiar spirit *1 Sam 28:3-20*

David hears Nathan's parable *2 Sam 12:1-10*

Rehoboam, human advice not good *1 King 12:1-18, 1 Chron 10:1-19*

Elisha's advice finally followed by Naaman *2 King 5:1-14*

Nehemiah does not follow advice to hide *Neh 6:1-19*

Job advised by friends *Job 2:11-13, Job 4:1—37:24*

Preacher advises all is vanity *Eccl 1:1-18, 2:1-26*

Jesus on counting cost before taking action *Luke 14:25-33*

Paul warned not to go to Jerusalem *Acts 21:8-15*

Paul on how Christians should act *Col 3:1-17, 1 Thess 5:1-28*

Paul on duty of a disciple *2 Tim 2:1-26*

Paul's charge to the faithful *2 Tim 4:1-8*

See also instruction, teaching

ADVOCATE

Abraham, ally of Melchizedek *Gen 14:8-20, Heb 6:20, 7:1-28*

Abraham, a city is spared by righteous men *Gen 18:20-33*

Jehoshaphat hears battle is Lord's *2 Chron 20:1-32*

Job aided by Elihuh *Job 32:1—37:24*

David's song, "The Lord is my shepherd" *Psal 23:1-6*

Jesus saves adulteress from mob *John 8:1-11*

Peter defended by Gamaliel *Acts 5:33-40*

John on Jesus as an advocate *1 John 2:1-6*

See also comforter, defense, healing, law, opposition

AFFECTION

Abraham prepared to sacrifice his dear son *Gen 22:1-19*

Joseph reveals himself to his brothers *Gen 43:1, 2, 45:1-11*

Ruth stays with Naomi *Ruth 1:1-22, 2:1-23*

David and Jonathan as friends *1 Sam 18:1-16*

David's and Bathsheba's child dies *2 Sam 12:13-23*

Elisha follows Elijah to see his translation *2 King 2:1-11*

Isaiah's peaceable kingdom *Isa 11:1-12*

Ezekiel shows God's affection for his flock *Ezek 34:1-31*

Jesus' parable of lost sheep *Mat 18:12-14, Luke 15:1-7*

Jesus' head anointed by woman *Mat 26:6-13, Mark 14:3-9*

Jesus' last supper with disciples *Mat 26:26-29, Mark 14:22-25, Luke 22:14-30*

Jesus' feet anointed by a woman *Luke 7:36-50, John 12:3-8*

Jesus as friend of Martha and Mary *Luke 10:38-42*

Jesus' parable of good shepherd *John 10:1-18*

Jesus' friendship for Lazarus *John 11:1-46*

Jesus on cross, gives John care of his mother *John 19:25-27*

Jesus asks Peter, "lovest thou me?" *John 21:12-19*

Paul encourages his disciple *2 Tim 2:1-26*

See also brotherhood, heart, love

AFFIRMATION

God creates spiritual universe *Gen 1:1-31*

Adam and Eve sent forth from garden *Gen 3:6-24*

Moses orders, "go forward" *Exod 14:5-31*

Aaron hears God's promise to faithful *Lev 26:1-20*

Caleb and Joshua report on Canaan *Num 13:1-33, 14:1-11, 23-39, Deut 1:19-38*

Moses' farewell address *Deut 30:11-20*

Elijah and 450 prophets of Baal
  1 King 18:17-40
Elisha hears Shunammite affirm
  truth   *2 King 4:8-37*
Job hears voice of thunder declare
  God's nature   *Job 38:1—41:34*
David's song on law of Lord   *Psal
  19:1-14*
David's song on rejoicing   *Psal 66:
  1-20, 100:1-5*
Isaiah on God's promises   *Isa 35:
  1-10*
Isaiah, "comfort ye"   *Isa 40:1-31*
Isaiah, the Lord's hand   *Isa 59:1-21*
Jeremiah on good and bad figs   *Jer
  24:1-10*
Jesus on Beatitudes   *Mat 5:1-12,
  Luke 6:17-26, 36*
Jesus on how to pray   *Mat 6:5-15,
  Mark 11:23-26, Luke 11:1-13*
Jesus on "seek ye first"   *Mat 6:
  25-34*
Jesus on petitions   *Mat 7:6-11*
Jesus sends disciples forth   *Mat 10:
  1-42, Mark 6:7-13, Luke 9:1-6*
Jesus' parable of tares and wheat
  Mat 13:24-30, 36-43
Jesus' parable of dragnet   *Mat 13:
  47-50*
Jesus denied by Peter   *Mat 26:31-
  35, 57, 58, 69-75, Mark 14:27-31,
  66-72, Luke 22:31-34, 54-62, John
  13:36-38, 18:13-18, 25-27*
Jesus on door and sheep   *John 10:
  1-38*
Paul and Silas freed from prison
  Acts 16:19-40
Paul on spirit and flesh   *Rom 8:1-39*
Paul on thinking on good things
  Phil 4:1-23
John's vision of white horse   *Rev
  19:11-21*

See also denial, opposition, watch

AFFLICTION

David shows kindness to crippled
  son of Jonathan   *2 Sam 9:1-13*
Nehemiah has news of Jerusalem's
  misery   *Neh 2:1-11*
Job's trials   *Job 1:13-22, 2:1-10*
Job's nightmare of fear   *Job 4:13-21*
David's song, "Why are thou cast
  down, O my soul?"   *Psal 42:1-11*

David's song, "Whither shall I go
  from thy spirit?"   *Psal 139:1-24*
Isaiah foretells the sorrows of
  Christ   *Isa 53:1-12*
Jeremiah promises release from
  captivity   *Jer 29:8-14*
Jesus heals paralytic let down
  through roof   *Mat 9:2-8, Mark
  2:1-12, Luke 5:17-26*
Jesus heals withered hand   *Mat
  12:9-13, Mark 3:1-5, Luke 6:6-11*
Jesus foretells his death and resurrection   *Mat 16:21-28, 17:22, 23,
  Mark 8:31-38, 9:30-32, Luke 9:20-
  27, 9:43-45*
Jesus heals epileptic boy   *Mat 17:
  14-21, Mark 9:14-29, Luke 9:37-43*
Jesus at Gethsemane   *Mat 26:30,
  36-46, Mark 14:26, 32-42, Luke 22:
  39-46*
Jesus is scourged and mocked by
  soldiers   *Mat 27:27-31, Mark 15:
  16-20, John 19:1-16*
Jesus restores dead son to his moth-
  er   *Luke 7:11-17*
Jesus' parable of rich man and beg-
  gar   *Luke 16:19-31*
Jesus heals impotent man at pool
  John 5:1-16
Jesus heals man born blind   *John
  9:1-41*
Stephen is stoned   *Acts 7:51-60*
Paul reviews his trials as a Christian
  Acts 20:17-38
Paul's hardships to establish church
  2 Cor 11:21-33
James on how to bear our cross   *Jas
  1:1-27*

See also adversity, disease, evil,
grief, mourning, pain

AFRICA

Joseph sold into Egypt   *Gen 37:
  1-36*
Joseph's brethren come to Egypt
  for food   *Gen 42:1-8*
Jacob and all his children emigrate
  to Egypt   *Gen 45:25-28, 46:2-7*
Moses sees Israelites oppressed
  Exod 1:8-14
Moses and Israelites escape   *Exod
  14:5-31*
Solomon visited by Queen of Sheba
  1 King 10:1-12, 2 Chron 9:1-12

Philip converts African eunuch *Acts 8:26-40*

AGE
Early man lives to advanced age *Gen 5:1-32*

Elderly Isaac deceived by Jacob and his mother *Gen 27:1-44*

Elderly Jacob prophesies future of his sons *Gen 49:1-28, Deut 33:1-29*

Elderly Moses' sight not dim *Deut 34:7*

Caleb ready for war at advanced age *Josh 14:6-15*

Elijah ready to give up *1 King 19:1-8*

Daniel's vision of meeting angel Gabriel *Dan 9:20-23, 10:4-21*

Jesus heals centurion's paralyzed servant *Mat 8:5-13, Luke 7:1-10*

Jesus heals Peter's mother-in-law *Mat 8:14-17, Mark 1:29-34, Luke 4:38, 39*

Jesus talks with Moses and Elijah *Mat 17:1-13, Mark 9:2-13, Luke 9:28-36*

At twelve years Jesus questions rabbis *Luke 2:41-52*

Jesus on eternity of the Christ *John 8:12-59*

Paul heals Publius' father of hemorrhage *Acts 28:7-10*

See also growth, immortality, life, maturity, ripeness, time

AGGRESSION
Cain kills Abel, first murder *Gen 4:1-16*

Gideon repels the Amalekites *Judg 7:1-25*

David defeats the challenger Goliath *1 Sam 17:1-52*

David pacified by Abigail *1 Sam 25:2-42*

Jehoshaphat assured battle is Lord's *2 Chron 20:1-32*

Elisha besieged by Syrians *2 King 6:8-23*

Hezekiah attacked by Sennacherib *2 King 18:1-37, 2 Chron 31:20, 21, 32:1-23, Isa 36:1-22, 37:1-38*

Hezekiah shows treasure and is attacked *2 King 20:12-21, Isa 39:1-8*

Nehemiah outwits conspiracy *Neh 6:1-19*

Esther and Mordecai attacked by Haman *Esther 3:1-15, 4:1-17, 5:1-14*

Jesus accused by Pharisees *Mat 12:22-30, Mark 3:22-30, Luke 11:14-23, John 8:33-39, 10:22-42*

Jesus on how to handle aggression *Mat 18:15-22*

Jesus reproves Pharisees *Mat 23:1-39, Mark 12:38-40, Luke 20:45-47, 11:37-54*

Peter and John on trial *Acts 4:1-23*

Stephen stoned *Acts 7:51-60*

Paul persecutes Christians *Acts 8:1-4*

John's vision of woman and child attacked by dragon *Rev 12:1-17*

See also attack, injury, invasion, offense, war

AGREEMENT
Noah hears God's covenant *Gen 9:1-17*

Zelophehad's daughters sue for inheritance *Num 27:1-11, 36:5-13*

Moses tells chosen people God has set them apart *Deut 7:6-26*

Jesus' parable of laborers in the vineyard *Mat 20:1-16*

Jesus' parable of those who refuse rent *Mat 21:33-46, Mark 12:1-12, Luke 20:9-19*

Jesus' birth announced to Mary *Luke 1:26-38*

Jesus sends disciples to preach and heal *Luke 10:1-16*

Jesus charges Peter, "Feed my sheep" *John 21:12-19*

Peter agrees to accept Gentiles *Acts 10:1-48, 11:1-18*

See also cause, contract, cooperation, covenant, harmony, mind

AGRICULTURE
In the spiritual creation the plant appears before the seed *Gen 1:1-31*

In the material creation the plants come out of the ground *Gen 2:9-17*

Abraham's riches grow *Gen 13:1-18*

Joseph solves the problem of plenty and scarcity *Gen 41:1-46*

Moses urges offering of the first fruits *Deut 26:1-19*

Ruth gleans in the field of Boaz *Ruth 2:1-23*

David the shepherd anointed by Samuel *1 Sam 16:1-13*

Elijah finds Elisha plowing *1 King 19:19-21*

David's song "The Lord is my shepherd" *Psal 23:1-6*

Isaiah's vision of the desert blossoming *Isa 35:1-6*

Ezekiel's vision of God's care over his flock *Ezek 34:1-31*

Jesus' parable of lost sheep *Mat 8: 12-14, Luke 15:1-7*

Jesus' parable of the sower *Mat 13: 3-23, Mark 4:1-20, Luke 8:4-15*

Jesus' parable of wheat and tares *Mat 13:24-30, 36-43*

Jesus' parable of seed, blade, ear, full corn *Mark 4:26-29*

Jesus' parable of mustard seed *Mat 13:31, 32; Mark 4:30-32, Luke 13: 18, 19*

Jesus' parable of the dragnet *Mat 13:47-50*

Jesus' parable of the Good Shepherd *John 10:1-18*

Jesus' parable of laborers in vineyard *Mat 20:1-16*

Jesus' parable of sheep and goats *Mat 25:31-46*

Jesus' parable of the vine and branches *John 15:1-17*

Jesus fills Peter's net *Luke 5:1-11, John 21:1-11*

Paul on fruits of the Spirit *Gal 5: 1-26*

See also farming, harvest, seed, sheep

AIMS

God's aim for man, his image, dominion *Gen 1:26, 27*

Noah builds the ark to save mankind *Gen 6:5-22*

Abraham begins search for promised land *Gen 11:31, 32, 12:1-9*

Moses learns of God's purpose to free his people *Exod 3:1-18*

Caleb fails to persuade people to enter promised land *Num 13:1-33, 14:1-11, 23-39, Deut 1:19-38*

Moses urges choice between life and death *Deut 30:11-20*

David promises to build a house for God *2 Sam 7:1-29*

Elisha asks for a double portion of Elijah's spirit *2 King 2:1-12*

Isaiah foretells birth of Messiah *Isa 7:10-16, 9:2-7*

Jeremiah predicts captivity will be turned *Jer 29:8-14*

Ezekiel's vision of truth encompassing the universe *Ezek 47:1-12*

Jesus instructs twelve disciples to heal *Mat 10:1-42, Mark 3:13-21, Luke 9:1-6*

Jesus speaks only in parables *Mat 13:10-17, 34, 35, Mark 4:10-12, 33, 34*

Jesus' parable of talents *Mat 25: 14-30, Luke 19:11-28*

Jesus' parable of good Samaritan *Luke 10:25-37*

Jesus' parable of rich man and bigger barns *Luke 12:15-21*

Jesus' parable of watchful servants *Luke 12:35-48*

Jesus' parable of rich man and the beggar *Luke 16:19-31*

Jesus' parable of Pharisee and publican *Luke 18:9-14*

Jesus as the light of the world *John 1:1-14, 8:12-32*

Jesus heals man lame 38 years *John 5:1-16*

Paul on "put on the new man" *Col 3:1-17*

James on faith without works *Jas 2:14-26*

John's vision of the new heaven and earth *Rev 21:1-27*

See also ambition, guidance, motive, plan, purpose

ALLEGORY

See parable

ALLIANCE

Abraham joins the war of kings *Gen 14:8-20*

Balak hires Balaam to curse Israel *Num 22:1-41, 23:1-30, 24:1-25*

Jonathan befriends David *1 Sam 18:1-16*

Solomon gets help from King Hiram

to build temple   *1 King 6:1-38,
7:1-51, 2 Chron 3:1-17, 4:1-22, 5:
1-14*
Solomon visited by Queen of Sheba
1 King 10:1-13
Asa is supported in war by allies
1 King 15:9-24, 2 Chron 14:1-7
Judas settles the price to betray
Jesus   *Mat 26:14-16, Mark 14:10,
11, Luke 22:1-6*
John's vision of woman and dragon
(earth helped woman)   *Rev 12:
1-17*

ALL-KNOWING
See omniscience

ALLNESS
God's (Spirit's) whole creation   *Gen
1:1-31, 2:1-5*
Moses and the nature of God   *Exod
3:1-18*
Solomon's selection of proper values
1 King 3:5-15, 2 Chron 1:7-12
Job hears God describe Himself
Job 38:1—41:34
David's song, "earth is full of the
goodness of the Lord"   *Psal 33:
1-22*
David's song, "Whither shall I go
from thy spirit?"   *Psal 139:1-24*
Isaiah on the salvation of all   *Isa
59:1-21*
Jeremiah's parable of potter and
clay   *Jer 18:1-6*
Jesus teaches the Lord's Prayer to
cover all needs   *Mat 6:5-15, Mark
11:25, 26, Luke 11:1-4*
Jesus calms wind and seas   *Mat 8:
23-27, Mark 5:35-41, Luke 8:22-25*
Jesus' parable of the leaven   *Mat
13:33, Luke 13:20-21*
Jesus' parable of treasure in field
Mat 13:44
Jesus' parable of pearl of great price
Mat 13:45, 46
Jesus' transfiguration controls time
*Mat 17:1-13, Mark 9:2-13, Luke
9:28-36*
Jesus' parable of marriage feast
Mat 22:1-14
Jesus at Gethsemane   *Mat 25:30,
36-46, Mark 14:26, 32-42, Luke 22:
35-46*

Peter's vision of great sheet   *Acts
11:1-18*
See also ever-presence, infinity,
omni-action, omnipotence, omniscience, oneness

ALMIGHTY
See omnipotence

ALTAR
Aaron sacrifices scapegoat   *Lev 16:
1-28*
Gideon throws down altar of Baal
Judg 6:1-40
Elijah causes fire on the altar
1 King 18:17-40
David eats shewbread on altar   *Mat
12:1-8, Mark 2:23-28, Luke 6:1-5*
See also communion, Eucharist, sac-
rifice

AMBASSADOR
Lot entertains and protects two
angels   *Gen 18:1-18*
Joseph's brethren come to Egypt
for food   *Gen 42:1-8*
Hezekiah unwisely shows Babylonian ambassadors all his trea-
sures   *2 King 20:12-21, Isa 39:1-8*
Elihu represents himself as a messenger from God   *Job 33:1-6*
Wise men visit "King of Jews"
Mat 2:1-12
John Baptist as forerunner of Mes-
siah   *Mat 3:1-12, Mark 1:1-8,
Luke 3:1-18*
Jesus heals the centurion's servant
absently   *Mat 8:5-13, Luke 7:1-10*
John Baptist sends to Jesus for his
credentials   *Mat 11:2-19, Luke 7:
18-35*
Peter acknowledges Jesus as Son
of God   *Mat 16:13-20, Mark 8:27-
30, Luke 9:18-21*
Jesus' parable of landlord who sent
servants to collect rent   *Mat 21:
33-46, Mark 12:1-12, Luke 20:9-19*
Angel announces Jesus' birth to
Mary   *Luke 1:26-38*
Jesus' parable of the unjust steward
Luke 16:1-14
Jesus Christ sent as a light to the
world   *John 1:1-14, 8:12-32*

Paul on "ambassadors for Christ" *2 Cor 5:17-21*

See also angel, government, herald, messenger, signs

AMBITION

Tower of Babel   *Gen 11:1-9*
Jacob buys Esau's birthright   *Gen 25:24-34*
Jacob deceives Isaac for blessing *Gen 27:1-44*
Gideon's son's parable of trees   *Judg 9:1-15*
Samuel called by the Lord   *1 Sam 3:1-10, 19-21*
Uzziah's heart lifted up   *2 Chron 26:1-23*
David's song, "the good man"   *Psal 1:1-6*
David's song, "Mark the perfect man"   *Psal 37:1-40*
Isaiah on the pride of women   *Isa 3:16-26*
Jesus saves Peter from the sea   *Mat 14:22-33, John 6:15-21*
Jesus' disciples contend who shall be greatest   *Mat 18:1-11, Mark 9: 32-37, Luke 9:46-50, 22:24-30*
Jesus refuses request of mother of James and John   *Mat 20:20-28, Mark 10:35-45*
Jesus betrayed by Judas   *Mat 26: 14-16, 27:3-10, Mark 14:10-11, Luke 22:1-6*
Jesus asks Peter to feed sheep *John 21:12-19*
Paul advises his disciple   *2 Tim 2:1-26*
See also plan, power, purpose

AMEN

See truth

AMPUTATION

Woman made from rib   *Gen 2:21-25*
Malchus' ear restored   *Luke 22:50, 51*
See also restoration

ANALYSIS

Joseph interprets Pharaoh's dream *Gen 41:1-46*
Moses separates God's law into Ten Commandments   *Exod 20:1-19, Deut 5:1-24*
Caleb and Joshua scout Canaan *Num 13:1-33, 14:1-11, 23-29, Deut 1:19-38*
Samuel discovers his mistake about Saul   *1 Sam 5:7-26*
Solomon determines the true mother *1 King 3:16-28*
Elijah examines nature of God *1 King 19:9-13*
Elisha diagnoses Naaman's problem and heals him   *2 King 5:1-14*
Job's friends discuss the nature of God and man   *Job 4: 1—37: 24*
Psalmist outlines nature of man *Psal 8:1-9*
Solomon on nature of a virtuous woman   *Prov 31:1-31*
Isaiah analyzes the pride of woman *Isa 3:16-26*
Daniel interprets king's dream   *Dan 2:1-49*
Jesus gives example of right and wrong prayer   *Luke 18:9-14*
Jesus heals insane man   *Mat 8:28-34, Mark 5:1-20, Luke 8:26-39*
Jesus explains what defiles a man *Mat 15:1-20, Mark 7:1-23*
Jesus saves the adulteress   *John 8:1-11*
Jesus puts some commandments on a mental basis   *Mat 5:21-32, Mark 9:38-50*
Paul on source of spiritual gifts *1 Cor 12:1, 4-21*
Paul on source of supply for all *2 Cor 8:11-15*
Paul on putting on the new man *Col 3:1-17*
Paul on substance of religion   *Heb 11:1-40*
James on relation of faith and works *Jas 2:14-26*
See also problem-solving, psychiatry, separation

ANARCHY

Cain kills Abel from envy   *Gen 4: 1-16*
Isaac strives with herdsmen over wells   *Gen 26:12-31*
See also confusion, government, law, power

ANCESTRY

God creates man in his image *Gen 1:26-27*

Early man lived to advanced age *Gen. 5:1-32*

Zelophehad's daughters sue for inheritance *Num 27:1-11, 36:5-13*

Ruth and Boaz, great grandparents of David *Ruth 4:1-22*

Ezekiel, vision of children's teeth on edge *Ezek 18:1-32*

Jesus teaches the Lord's prayer *Mat 6:5-15, Mark 11:25, 26, Luke 11:1-4*

The Christ, whose son is he? *Mat 22:41-46, Mark 12:35-37, Luke 20:41-44*

Jesus' birth announced to Mary *Luke 1:26-38*

Jesus contrasts himself with Pharisees *John 8:48-59*

Paul on eternity of the Christ *Heb 6:20, 7:1-28*

See also birth, father, heredity

ANGEL

Angel announces future of Ishmael at his birth *Gen 16:1-16*

Abraham entertains angels *Gen 18:1-18*

Lot shelters two angels from mob *Gen 19:1-14*

Jacob's vision of angels on ladder *Gen 28:10-22*

Jacob wrestles with angel *Gen 32:1-32*

Joshua meets "captain of the host" *Josh 5:10-15*

Samson's mother visited by angel *Judg 13:1-25*

Daniel visited by Gabriel *Dan 9:20-23, 10:4-21*

Joseph advised by angel to protect Mary *Mat 1:18-25*

Jesus ministered to by angels after temptation *Mat 4:1-11*

At Jesus' resurrection angels inform women and disciples *Mat 28:1-8, Mark 16:1-8, Luke 24:1-12, John 20:1-10*

Annunciation of John's birth to Elizabeth *Luke 1:5-25*

Annunciation of Jesus' birth to Mary *Luke 1:26-38*

Jesus' birth heralded by angels *Luke 2:8-20*

Peter imprisoned but released by angel *Acts 5:17-42, 12:1-17*

John's vision of angel with little book *Rev 10:1-11*

John's vision of war in heaven *Rev 12:1-17*

See also guard, messenger

ANGER

Adam and Eve fall from grace *Gen 3:6-24*

Noah saved from flood *Gen 6:5-22*

Lot saved from destruction of Sodom and Gomorrah *Gen 19:1, 15-29*

Joseph angers Potiphar's wife *Gen 39:1-20*

David plays harp to calm Saul *1 Sam 16:14-23*

David pacified by Abigail *1 Sam 25:2-42*

Job turns on his "comforters" *Job 16:1-22*

Jesus' parable of debtor unmerciful to fellows *Mat 18:23-35*

Jesus whips traders out of temple *Mat 21:12, 13, Mark 11:15-17, Luke 19:45, 46, John 2:13-25*

Jesus' parable of husbandmen who refuse to pay the rent *Mat 21:33-46, Mark 12:1-12, Luke 20:9-19*

Jesus' parable of marriage feast refused *Mat 22:1-14*

Jesus castigates Pharisees *Luke 11:37-54*

See also adversary, hatred, irritation, resentment

ANIMAL

Creation of animals on fifth and sixth day *Gen 1:20-25, 2:18-20*

Abel sacrifices animals, not vegetables *Gen 4:1-16*

Noah's ark *Gen 7:1-24, 8:1-22*

Abraham finds ram to sacrifice *Gen 22:1-19*

Moses objects to golden calf *Exod 32:1-24*

Aaron atones through the scapegoat *Lev 16:1-28*

Moses heals bites of fiery serpents
Num 21:4-9

Balaam's ass refuses to go *Num 22: 22-35*

Elijah fed by ravens *1 King 17: 1-16*

David's sheep *Psal 23:1-6*

Isaiah, the peaceable kingdom *Isa 11:1-12*

Ezekiel's sheep *Ezek 34:1-31*

Daniel in lions' den *Dan 6:1-28*

Jonah and the big fish *Jonah 2: 1-10*

Jesus' parable of lost sheep *Mat 18:12-14, Luke 15:1-7*

Jesus rides ass' foal into Jerusalem *Mat 21:1-11, 14-17, Mark 11: 1-11, Luke 19:29-44, John 12:12-19*

Jesus' parable of sheep and goats *Mat 25:31-46*

Peter's vision of animals in great sheet *Acts 11:1-18*

See also magnetism

ANNUNCIATION

Abraham is promised a son *Gen 15:1-21*

Moses is charged with release of his people *Exod 3:9-12*

Samson's birth announced to his mother *Judg 13:1-25*

Isaiah foretells the birth of Messiah *Isa 7:10-16, 9:2-7*

Jesus says a prophet is without honor in his own country *Mat 13:53-58, Mark 6:1-6, Luke 4:22-24, John 4:43-45*

Jesus foretells his own death and resurrection *Mat 17:22, 23, Mark 9:30-32, Luke 9:43-45*

Birth of John Baptist announced *Luke 1:5-25*

Jesus' birth announced to Mary *Luke 1:26-38*

Angels announce birth to shepherds *Luke 2:8-20*

Jesus promises the Comforter *John 14:1-31*

John's vision of new heaven and earth *Rev 21:1-27*

See also angel, messenger, prophet

ANOINTING

Aaron as chief priest by Moses *Lev 8:1-13*

Saul as king by Samuel *1 Sam 10:1-8*

David a boy anointed by Samuel *1 Sam 16:1-13*

David as king of Judah *2 Sam 2:1-4*

David as king of Israel *2 Sam 5: 1-5*

Zechariah's two anointed ones *Zech 4:1-14*

David's song, "The Lord is my shepherd" *Psal 23:1-6*

Jesus' head anointed by a woman *Mat 26:6-13, Mark 14:3-9*

Jesus' feet anointed by a woman *Luke 7:36-50*

Jesus anoints eyes of blind with clay *John 9:1-41*

Jesus' feet anointed by Mary, Martha's sister *John 12:3-8*

See also consecration, dedication, king, oil

ANTICHRIST

Judas betrays Jesus *Mat 26:14-16, Mark 14:10-11, Luke 22:1-6*

Paul before his conversion *Acts 8:1-4, 9:1-9*

Paul on armor that protects the Christian *Eph 6:10-17*

Paul defines enemies of the truth *2 Tim 3:1-17*

John defines antichrist *1 John 2: 18-22*

The dragon attacks the woman with child *Rev 12:1-17*

See also devils, evil

ANXIETY

Jacob wrestles with his fear of his brother *Gen 32:1-32*

Samuel concerned because Saul unfit *1 Sam 15:7-26*

David prays for his sick child *2 Sam 12:13-23*

Nehemiah concerned for Jerusalem's misery *Neh 2:1-20*

Esther concerned for her people *Esther 3:1-15, 4:1-17*

Job expresses his woe *Job 3:1-26*

David's song, "Fret not thyself" *Psal 37:1-40*

David's song, "Why art thou cast down?" *Psal 42:1-11*

David's song, "My soul longeth for the courts" *Psal 84:1-12*

David's song of security *Psal 91: 1-16*

Jesus heals Jairus' daughter *Mat 9:18, 19, 23-26, Mark 5:22-24, 35-43, Luke 8:41, 42, 49-56*

Jesus heals the epileptic *Mat 17: 14-21, Mark 9:14-29, Luke 9:37-43*

Jesus' parable of rich man and the beggar *Luke 16:19-31*

See also fear, mind, oppression, pain

APATHY

Hagar and son give up trying *Gen 21:9-21*

Moses' reluctance to lead overcome *Exod 3:9-12*

Gideon has to be encouraged to resist *Judg 6:1-40*

Nehemiah hears of Jerusalem's misery *Neh 2:1-20*

David's song, "Why art thou cast down?" *Psal 42:1-11*

Jesus has to remind disciples of his great works *Mat 16:5-12, Mark 8:13-21*

Rich young ruler discouraged by Jesus *Mat 19:16-30, Mark 10:17-31, Luke 18:18-30*

Jesus' parable of barren fig tree *Luke 13:6-9*

Jesus heals man at pool 38 years *John 5:1-16*

After Jesus' sermon on bread of life many disciples leave him *John 6:66-71*

Jesus denounces Pharisees for lack of understanding *Mat 23:1-39*

See also hypnotism, magnetism, mesmerism, sleep, zealous

APOSTLE

Elijah selects Elisha to follow him *1 King 19:19-21*

Jesus selects his disciples *Mat 4: 17-22, 9:9, Mark 1:14-20, Luke 5: 1-11, John 1:35-42*

Jesus teaches his apostles to heal and preach *Mat 9:36-38, 10:1-42, Mark 3:13-21, Luke 6:13-19, 9:1-6*

Jesus seen after resurrection by apostles *Mark 16:14, Luke 24: 36-49, John 20:19-23*

Jesus promises the Comforter *John 14:1-31*

Paul meets Jesus and is appointed *Acts 9:1-9*

Paul named a chosen vessel *Acts 9:10-22*

See also disciple, witness

APPETITE

Adam and Eve eat of tree of knowledge of good and evil *Gen 3: 6-24*

Joseph resists Potiphar's wife *Gen 39:1-20*

Moses supplies starving people with manna. People then demand meat *Exod 16:1-36, Num 11:1-15, 31, 32*

In absence of Moses people worship golden calf *Exod 32:1-24*

Moses forbids abominations *Deut 18:9-14*

Samson is betrayed by sensuality *Judg 16:4-30*

David takes wife of Uriah *2 Sam 11:1-27*

Elisha's servant's greed punished *2 King 5:15-27*

Jesus' parable of the prodigal son *Luke 15:11-24*

Jesus accused of being a glutton and winebibber *Mat 11:18, 19, Luke 7:33, 34*

Jesus saves adulteress and tells her to sin no more *John 8:1-11*

See also abstinence, body, diet, food, temptation

APPOINTING

Noah selected to build an ark of safety *Gen 6:5-22*

Abraham called to find the promised land *Gen 11:31, 32, 12:1-9*

Joseph appointed governor of Egypt *Gen 41:1-46*

Moses selected to lead people out *Exod 3:1-18*

Moses appoints judges to help him *Exod 18:13-27*

Aaron and sons appointed by Moses
Lev 8:1-13

The chosen people set apart as God's
own *Deut 7:6-26*

Moses transfers command to Joshua
Josh 1:1-9

Jotham's parable of the trees *Judg
9:1-15*

Samuel appoints Saul as king
1 Sam 10:1-8

Samuel anoints David *1 Sam 16:
1-13*

Elijah selects Elisha *1 King 19:
19-21, 2 King 2:1-15*

Jonah appointed to preach to Nineveh *Jonah 1:1-17*

Peter appointed leader by Jesus
*Mat 16:13-20, Mark 8:27-30, Luke
9:18-21, John 21:12-19*

Jesus' parable of the talents *Mat
25:14-30, Luke 19:11-28*

Jesus' parable of the unjust steward
Luke 16:1-14

Jesus as the light of the world *John
1:1-14*

Mathias elected to Judas' place *Acts
1:15-26*

Seven deacons chosen to govern
church *Acts 6:1-4*

Paul appointed a chosen vessel *Acts
9:10-22*

See also anointing, authority, calling, election, office, power

APPRECIATION

God saw what he had made and it
was very good *Gen 1:31*

Balaam refuses to curse Israel *Num
24:1-25*

Samuel's mother dedicates him to
Lord *1 Sam 1:1-28*

Solomon dedicates temple to the
Lord *1 King 8:22-66, 2 Chron 6:
1-42*

The widow realizes Elijah is a man
of God *1 King 17:17-24*

David's song, "The Lord is my
shepherd" *Psal 23:1-6*

David's song, "Rejoice in the Lord"
Psal 33:1-22

David's song, "Make a joyful noise"
Psal 66:1-20, 100:1-5

David's song, "Bless the Lord" *Psal
103:1-22*

David's song, "Praise the Lord for
his goodness" *Psal 107:1-43*

Zephaniah's vision of salvation
promised *Zeph 3:14-17*

Wise men visit King of Jews *Mat
2:1-12*

Jesus blames three cities for lack of
appreciation *Mat 11:20-24*

Jesus' parable of the unmerciful
debtor *Mat 18:23-35*

Jesus' parable of two sons ordered
to work *Mat 21:28-32*

Jesus's parable of the talents *Mat
25:14-30, Luke 19:11-28*

Jesus anointed by a woman *Mat
26:6-13, Mark 14:3-9, Luke 7:36-
50, John 12:3-8*

Jesus' parable of two debtors forgiven *Luke 7:36-50*

Jesus' parable of the prodigal's elder
brother *Luke 15:25-32*

Jesus heals ten lepers *Luke 17:
11-19*

Paul on why we owe Christ *Heb 2:
1-18*

See also senses, thanksgiving, value

ARGUMENT

Jacob wrestles with angel *Gen 32:
1-32*

Moses reluctant to lead *Exod 3:
9-12*

Caleb urges entrance into promised
land *Num 14:1-11, 23-39, Deut
1:19-28*

Daughters of Zelophehad sue for
inheritance *Num 27:1-11, 36:5-13*

Moses urges obedience *Deut 11:
1-32*

Moses lists blessings of obedience
Deut 28:1-14

Joshua offers choice of good or evil
Josh 24:1-25

David pacified by Abigail's gentleness *1 Sam 25:2-42*

Nathan's parable of ewe lamb makes
David repent *2 Sam 12:1-10*

Jehoshaphat urges reliance on God
in war *2 Chron 20:1-32*

Nehemiah not interrupted by conspiracy *Neh 6:1-19*

Job's friends fail to persuade him
Job 2: 11-13, 4: 1—37: 24

Job hears Infinite speak to man *Job 38:1—41:34*

John Baptist's question of Christ answered 'y Jesus *Mat 11:2-19, Luke 7:18-35*

Jesus' parable of rich man and beggar *Luke 16:19-31*

Peter and John tried before the council *Acts 4:1-23*

Paul on Jesus as the Messiah *Acts 13:16-52*

Paul on the unknown God *Acts 17:15-34*

Paul defends himself before King Agrippa *Acts 26:1-32*

See also evidence, logic, mind, proof, reason

ARISTOCRACY

Moses delegates authority to judges *Exod 18:13-27*

Aaron and sons consecrated as priests *Lev 8:1-13*

Jesus dines with a Pharisee *Luke 7:36-50*

Jesus' conflict with scribes and pharisees *Mat 23:1-39, Mark 11: 18, 19, 12:38-40, Luke 20:45-47, John 8:33-59*

See also democracy, government, state, supremacy

ARK

Noah builds to avoid flood *Gen 6: 5-22, 7:1-24, 8:1-22, 9:1-17, Heb 11:7*

Moses as baby in ark of bullrushes *Exod 2:1-10*

Joshua's ark of covenant at Jordan *Josh 3:1-17*

Joshua's ark of covenant at Jericho *Josh 6:1-27*

Uzzah steadies the ark *2 Sam 6:1-19*

David dances before the ark *2 Sam 6:5, 12-23*

David orders ark placed in temple *1 Chron 28:2-10*

See also covenant, safety, sea, ship

ARMAGEDDON

Deborah and Barak defeat Canaanites *Judg 4:1-17*

Gideon defeats Midianites *Judg 7:1-25*

Death of Saul and Jonathan *1 Sam 31:1-13, 1 Chron 10:1-14*

John's revelation of war in heaven *Rev 12:7-13*

ARMOR

David sees Goliath's armor *1 Sam 17:1-16*

David tries on Saul's armor *1 Sam 17:17-37*

Ezekiel's vision of army from dry bones *Ezek 37:1-28*

Nehemiah arms his wall builders *Neh 4:1-23*

Jesus helps centurion's servant *Mat 8:5-13, Luke 7:1-10*

Jesus causes guards to fall backward *John 18:4-6*

Paul on whole armor of God *Eph 6:10-17*

See also clothing, defense, protection, temptation, war

ART

Moses discovers the healing arts *Exod 4:1-9*

Moses finds worship of golden calf *Exod 32:1-24*

Solomon uses art to construct temple *1 King 6:1-38, 7:1-51, 2 Chron 3:17, 4:1-22, 5:1-14*

David's song, "Let the beauty of the Lord our God be upon us" *Psal 90:1-17*

Hezekiah shows ambassadors all his treasures *Isa 39:1-8, 2 King 20: 12-21*

Isaiah describes the making of an idol *Isa 40:18-31*

Wise men bring precious gifts to Jesus *Mat 2:1-22*

Jesus on true treasures *Mat 6:19-21*

Jesus' parable of pearl of great price *Mat 13:45, 46*

Jesus' parable of the householder's treasure *Mat 13:51, 52*

Jesus explains the art of healing difficult cases *Mat 17:14-21, Mark 9:14-29, Luke 9:37-43*

Paul on the statue "To the Unknown God" *Acts 17:15-34*

Paul attacked by the idol silversmith for spoiling his business *Acts 19:23-29*

See also beauty, healing, image, science, skill

ASA (one of the kings)
See Part II, Asa

ASCENSION
Enoch translated to spirit *Gen 5: 18, 21-24, Heb 11:5*
Jacob sees ladder with angels ascending *Gen 28:10-22*
Elijah translated *2 King 2:1-11*
Moses ascends mount to talk with God and receive Ten Commandments *Exod 19:1-9, 33:7-23, Deut 4:1-15*
David ascends throne of Judah and Israel *2 Sam 2:1-4, 5:1-5*
Jesus transfigured on mount *Mat 17:1-13, Mark 9:2-13, Luke 9:28-36*
Jesus' parable of wise and foolish virgins *Mat 25:1-13*
Jesus on the coming resurrection *Mat 26:31-35*
Jesus' final ascension *Mark 16:19, 20, Luke 24:50-53, Acts 1:9-12*
Jesus' parable of rich man and beggar *Luke 16:19-31*
Jesus on unity and eternality of Christ *John 8:12-59*
Jesus on oneness with Father *John 10:22-42*

See also heaven, mountain, translation

ASSOCIATION
Joseph's brethren plot against him *Gen 37:1-36*
Asa calls on allies instead of God *1 King 15:9-24, 2 Chron 14:1-7*
Isaiah, vision of the peaceable kingdom *Isa 11:1-12*
Jesus calls his disciples *Mat 4:17-22, Mark 1:14-20, Luke 5:1-11, John 1:35-42*
Jesus hears scribe offer to follow him *Mat 8:18-22*
Jesus eats with publicans and sinners *Mat 9:10-13, Mark 2:13-17, Luke 5:27-32*
Jesus keeps his mother and brethren waiting *Mat 12:46-50, Mark 3:31-35, Luke 8:19-21*
Jesus' parable of wheat and tares *Mat 13:24-30, 36-43*
Jesus' parable of dragnet *Mat 13:47-50*
Jesus' parable of wedding garment *Mat 22:1-14*
Jesus' parable of sheep and goats *Mat 25:31-46*
Jesus followed by people like sheep *Mark 6:30-34*
Jesus' parable of vine and branches *John 15:1-17*
Peter and apostles receive Holy Ghost *Acts 2:1-13*
Peter causes growth of early church *Acts 4:24-37*
Peter and others choose seven deacons *Acts 6:1-4*
Paul converts Lydia *Acts 16:7-15*
Paul on unity *Eph 4:1-32, 1 Thess 5:1-28, 2 Thess 3:1-17*

See also church, conspiracy, fellowship

ASSURANCE
Noah assured of safety *Gen 6:5-22*
Abraham directed by God to promised land *Gen 11:31, 32, 12:1-9*
Jacob promised God's presence *Gen 28:10-22*
Moses promised God's presence to lead people *Exod 3:9-12*
Moses complains of his speaking ability *Exod 4:10-17*
People guided by pillars of cloud and fire *Exod 13:20-22, Num 9:15-23*
Moses lists blessings of obedience *Deut 28:1-14*
Prophet assures Jehoshaphat that battle is the Lord's *2 Chron 20:1-32*
David's song, "The Lord is my shepherd" *Psal 23:1-6*
David's song, "The secret place of the most high" *Psal 91:1-16*
David's song, "The safety of the godly" *Psal 121:1-8*
David's song "Whither shall I go from thy spirit?" *Psal 139:1-24*
Isaiah predicts war no more *Isa 2:1-5, Mic 4:1-8, 13*

Isaiah describes Christ's peaceable kingdom *Isa 11:1-12*

Isaiah's vision "Comfort ye" *Isa 40:1-31*

Isaiah's promise, God's help in trials *Isa 43:1-28, 44:1-24*

Jeremiah foretells release from captivity *Jer 29:8-14*

Jeremiah foretells new covenant *Jer 31:1-14, 31-34*

Ezekiel's vision of escape from heredity *Ezek 18:1-32*

Ezekiel's vision of God's care for his people *Ezek 34:1-31*

Daniel's vision of God's care *Dan 9:20-23, 10:4-21*

Hosea's vision of God's care *Hos 11:1-4*

Jesus on "Seek ye first" *Mat 6:25-34*

John Baptist sends to Jesus for proof of the Christ *Mat 11:2-19, Luke 7:18-35*

Jesus' parable of mustard seed *Mat 13:31, 32, Mark 4:30-32, Luke 13:18, 19*

Jesus' parable of lost sheep *Mat 18:12-14, Luke 15:1-7*

Jesus' parable of the talents *Mat 25:14-30, Luke 19:11-28*

Jesus' parable of seed, blade, ear, full corn *Mark 4:26-29*

Jesus answers Martha's complaints *Luke 10:38-42*

Jesus' parable of prodigal's older brother *Luke 15:25-32*

Jesus the Christ *John 7:14-40*

Jesus assures Martha and the people of the healing power of the Christ *John 11:1-46*

Jesus on the Comforter *John 14:1-31*

Jesus on comfort in tribulation *John 16:1-33*

Jesus proves to Thomas his resurrection *John 20:19-29*

Paul on Jesus as Messiah *Acts 13:16-52*

Paul on Jesus' resurrection *1 Cor 15:1-58*

Paul on abundance for all *2 Cor 8:11-15*

John on God as love *1 John 4:1-21*

John's vision of new heaven and earth *Rev 21:1-27*

See also conviction, covenant, doubt, ever-presence, fear, promise, safety, salvation

ASTROLOGY

God creates stars as an element of the perfect universe *Gen 1:7, 8, 14-19*

Joshua at Ajalon, sun and moon stand still *Josh 10:6-15*

Sisera defeated by stars and Deborah *Judg 5:1-20*

David's song, "The heavens declare the glory of God" *Psal 19:1-14*

Wise men follow star to Bethlehem *Mat 2:1-12*

See also night

ATMOSPHERE

Jacob finds he has been in God's presence *Gen 28:10-22*

Moses is told he is standing on holy ground *Exod 3:1-18*

Joshua sees sun and moon stand still *Josh 10:6-15*

David plays harp to calm Saul *1 Sam 16:14-23*

Elijah finds God in still small voice not in wind or fire *1 King 19:9-13*

David's song, "The heavens declare the glory" *Psal 19:1-14*

Isaiah's vision of the desert in blossom *Isa 35:1-10*

Jesus heals few in his own country "because of their unbelief" *Mat 13:53-58*

Jesus' birth attended by heavenly host *Luke 2:8-20*

Jesus escapes hostile intentions of crowd *Luke 4:28-31*

Guards fall backward at the sight of Jesus *John 18:4-6*

Disciples at descent of Holy Ghost *Acts 2:1-13*

John sees new heaven and new earth *Rev 21:1-27*

See also influence, storm

ATONEMENT

Cain set apart, as punishment *Gen 4:1-16*

Abraham plans to sacrifice his son *Gen 22:1-19*

Aaron atones through scapegoat *Lev 16:1-28*

Aaron stays plague by atoning *Num 16:3-5, 44-50*

David and Bathsheba's child dies *2 Sam 12:13-23*

David's song, "Create in me a clean heart" *Psal 51:1-19*

Isaiah's promises to the penitent *Isa 58:1-14*

Jonah atones for disobedience *Jonah 2:1-10*

Jesus' parable of lost sheep *Mat 18:12-14, Luke 15:1-7*

Jesus' last supper *Mat 26:26-29, Mark 14:22-25, Luke 22:14-30, 1 Cor 11:23-35*

Judas hangs himself *Mat 27:2-10, Acts 1:15-20*

Jesus crucified *Mat 27:32-56, Mark 15:21-41, Luke 23:26-49, John 19:17-30*

Jesus' parable of prodigal son *Luke 15:11-24*

Jesus' parable of Pharisee and publican *Luke 18:9-14*

Jesus advises adulteress to sin no more *John 8:1-11*

Jesus on oneness with Father *John 10:22-42*

Jesus advises impotent man to sin no more *John 5:1-16*

Jesus' last breakfast with disciples *John 21:1-14*

Paul on atonement *Heb 10:1-39*

See also baptism, cross, pardon, purity, reconciliation, reformation, repentance, sacrifice

ATTACK

Cain kills Abel for religious motive *Gen 4:1-16*

Isaac solves strife between herdsmen *Gen 26:12-31*

Miriam and Aaron speak against Moses *Num 12:1-16*

Sisera invades Israel *Judg 4:1-17*

Amalekites invade Israel *Judg 6:1-40, 7:1-25*

Saul in envy throws javelin at David *1 Sam 18:1-16*

Jehoshaphat defends Israel *2 Chron 20:1-30*

Sennacherib invades Israel *2 King 18:17-37, 19:1-27, 2 Chron 31:20, 21, 32:1-23*

Esther defends the Jews from persecution *Esther 3:1-15, 4:1-17, 5:1-14*

David's song, "God is our refuge and strength" *Psal 46:1-12*

David's song, "Secret place of the most High" *Psal 91:1-16*

David's song "God the preserver of man" *Psal 121:1-8*

A poor wise man saved his city *Eccl 9:3-18*

Jesus' sermon on treatment of enemies *Mat 5:38-48, Luke 6:27-36*

Jesus heals boy in midst of epileptic attack *Mat 17:14-21, Mark 9:14-29, Luke 9:37-43*

Jesus' parable of the husbandmen *Mat 21:33-46, Mark 12:1-12, Luke 20:9-19*

Paul is stoned to death but recovers *Acts 14:19, 20*

John's vision of the woman attacked by dragon *Rev 12:1-17*

See also aggression, enemy, invasion, offense, war

ATTRACTION

Joseph appeals to Egyptians *Gen 39:1-23, 40:1-23, 41:1-46*

Moses appealed to for judgment *Exod 18:13-37*

Ruth's qualities attract Boaz *Ruth 2:1-23*

Samuel selects Saul by mistake *1 Sam 10:1-8*

Samuel selects David as future king *1 Sam 16:1-13*

David befriended by Jonathan *1 Sam 18:1-16*

Solomon receives Queen of Sheba *1 King 10:1-13, 2 Chron 9:1-12*

Elisha sticks by Elijah *2 King 2:1-11*

Jesus hears a scribe volunteer to *3:6-12* follow him *Mat 8:18-22*

All men seek Christ *Mat 12:14-21, 15:29-31, 19:1, 2, Mark 1:35-49,*

Jesus' parable of pearl of great price *Mat 13:45, 46*

Jesus risen, opens scripture to two disciples *Luke 24:13-35*

Jesus on faith in Christ *John 12: 44-50*

Jesus asks Peter if he loves him *John 21:12-19*

Peter's shadow heals *Acts 5:12-16*

Paul and Barnabas worshipped by people *Acts 14:11-18*

Paul on unity *Eph 4:1-32*

AUTHORITY

Moses learns source of eloquence *Exod 4:10-17*

Moses' hands upheld *Exod 17:8-16*

Moses delegates judges *Exod 18: 13-27*

Moses communes with God before Commandments *Exod 19:1-9*

Moses receives Ten Commandments *Exod 20:1-19, Deut 5:1-24*

Aaron and sons anointed by Moses *Lev 8:1-13*

Moses' authority challenged by Miriam *Num 12:1-16*

Moses charges Joshua with leadership *Deut 31:7-23, Josh 1:1-9*

Samuel declares Saul unfit and anoints David *1 Sam 15:7-26, 16: 1-13*

Elisha takes up Elijah's mantle *2 King 2:1-15*

Nehemiah gets Cyrus' authority and rebuilds the wall of Jerusalem *Neh 1:1-11, 2:1-20*

Esther's life and all Jews put in hands of Haman *Esther 3:1-15*

Job hears the voice of thunder *Job 38:1-41*

David's song, "The law of the Lord is perfect" *Psal 19:1-19*

David's song, "Be still and know that I am God" *Psal 46:1-11*

Isaiah, "the Lord's hand is not shortened" *Isa 59:1-21*

Daniel reads handwriting on wall *Dan 5:1-31*

Jonah disobeys God's command *Jonah 1:1-17*

Jesus heals centurion's servant absently *Mat 8:5-13, Luke 7:1-10*

Jesus controls storm *Mat 8:23-27, Mark 4:35-41, Luke 8:22-25*

Jesus sends forth twelve with authority to heal *Mat 10:5-42, Mark 6:7-13, Luke 9:1-6*

Jesus on "a prophet . . . without honor" *Mat 13:53-58, Mark 6:1-6, Luke 4:22-24, John 4:43-45*

Jesus talks with Moses (law) and Elias (prophets) *Mat 17:1-13, Mark 9:2-13, Luke 9:28-36*

Jesus challenged by chief priests to give source of his authority *Mat 21:23-27, Mark 11:27-33, Luke 20: 1-8*

Jesus in temple speaks with authority *Mark 1:21-28, Luke 4:33-37*

Jesus at twelve years talks on equality with rabbis *Luke 2:41-52*

Jesus has authority over death *Luke 7:11-17*

Jesus' parable of chief seats at wedding *Luke 14:7-14*

Jesus opens Scriptures at Emmaus *Luke 24:13-32*

See also dominion, eloquence, law, power, rebellion

AWAKENING

Adam awakes from sleep to find Eve *Gen 2:21-25*

Isaiah, "Awake, Jerusalem is redeemed" *Isa 52:1-15*

Isaiah, "Arise, shine" *Isa 60:1-5*

Jesus awakes Jairus' daughter from death *Mat 9:18, 19, 23-26, Mark 5:22-24, 35-43, Luke 8:41, 43, 49-56*

Jesus awakens disciples at Gethsemane *Mat 26:30, 36-46, Mark 14: 26, 32-42, Luke 22:39-46*

Jesus says Lazarus sleepeth and raises him *John 11:1-46*

See also birth, regeneration, watch

B

BACKSLIDING

See fallen man, morality, reversal

BAPTISM

Abraham blessed by Melchizedek *Gen 14:8-20, Heb 6:20, 7:1-28*

Abram receives a new name *Gen 17:1-9, 15-22*

Jacob receives new name—Israel *Gen 32:24-32*

Elisha heals Naaman the leper by dipping in Jordan seven times *2 King 5:1-14*

David's song, "The fountain of life" *Psal 36:1-12*

David's song, "Create in me a clean heart" *Psal 51:1-19*

Isaiah's vision, "look unto the rock" *Isa 51:1-12*

John baptizes in Jordan *Mat 3:1-12, Mark 1:1-8, Luke 3:1-18*

John baptizes Jesus *Mat 3:13-17, Mark 1:9-11, Luke 3:21, 22*

Jesus' parable of new wine in old bottles *Luke 5:36-39*

John says his baptizing differs from Jesus' *John 3:22-36*

Jesus heals man born blind by washing in pool *John 9:1-41*

Peter and apostles at Pentecost *Acts 2:1-13*

Peter on baptism *Acts 2:38-47*

Peter and church growth through healing *Acts 4:24-37, 5:12-16*

Philip baptizes Simon *Acts 8:5-13*

Philip baptizes Ethiopian *Acts 8:25-40*

See also atonement, consecration, purity, sacrament, spirit, water

BARRENNESS

Noah and his covenant with God *Gen 9:1-17*

Abraham heals Abimelech and his wife *Gen 20:1-7, 17*

Abraham and Sara promised a son *Gen 21:1-8*

Samson's mother promised a son *Judg 13:1-25*

Samuel's mother, Hannah, promised a son *1 Sam 1:1-28*

Elisha prophesies drop in price of flour *2 King 6:24, 25, 7:1-18*

Isaiah prophesies desert will bloom *Isa 35:1-10*

John Baptist lives in desert *Mat 3:1-12, Mark 1:1-8, Luke 3:1-18*

Jesus' 40 days in wilderness *Mat 4:1-11, Mark 1:12, 13, Luke 4:1-13*

Jesus on "Seek ye first" *Mat 6:25-34*

Jesus on know them by fruits *Mat 7:15-20, Luke 6:43-45*

Jesus' parable of the sower (on stony ground) *Mat 13:1-23, Mark 4:1-20, Luke 8:4-15*

Jesus and barren fig tree *Mat 21:18-22, Mark 11:12-14, 20-24, Luke 13:6-9*

Jesus fills Peter's net with great draught *Luke 5:1-11, John 21:1-11*

See also fruits, multiply, wilderness

BEACON

The pillars of cloud and fire *Exod 13:20-22, Num 9:15-23*

Moses' hands upheld during battle *Exod 17:8-16*

Solomon builds the temple *1 King 6:1-38, 7:1-51, 2 Chron 3:1-17, 4:1-22, 5:1-14*

Zerubbabel proclaims rebuilding of temple *Ezra 1:1-4*

Rebuilding of temple starts *Ezra 3:8-13*

Wise men follow the star to Bethlehem *Mat 2:1-12*

Jesus on "Let your light so shine" *Mat 5:13-16, Luke 8:16-18*

The cross *Mat 27:32-56, Mark 15:21-41, Luke 23:26-49, John 19:17-30*

Jesus Christ as the light of the world *John 1:1-14, 8:12-32*

The temple to be raised in three days *John 2:19-22*

Paul on the example left by Jesus *Heb 12:1-29*

See also guidance, leader, light, signs, teaching, watch, way

BEATITUDE

God tells Noah "be fruitful and multiply" *Gen 9:1-17*

Abraham blessed by Melchizedek *Gen 14:8-20, Heb 6:20, 7:1-28*

Promises to Abraham and Isaac extended to Jacob *Gen 35:9-15*

Aaron's rod blossoms *Num 17:1-11*

Chosen people set apart *Deut 7:6-11*

Moses outlines blessings of obedience *Deut 8:1-14*

Job's state before his trials   *Job 1:1-5*

David's song "Make a joyful noise" *Psal 66:1-20, 100:1-5*

Isaiah on blessed state of new Jerusalem   *Isa 65:17-25*

Daniel's meeting with Gabriel   *Dan 9:20-23, 10:4-21*

Jesus' parable of the talents   *Mat 25:14-30, Luke 19:11-28*

Jesus' parable of the true vine   *John 15:1-17*

Jesus' baptism, the voice from heaven   *Mat 3:13-17, Mark 1:9-11, Luke 3:21-22*

Jesus' transfiguration   *Mat 17:1-13, Mark 9:2-13, Luke 9:28-36*

Jesus' birth announced by angels   *Luke 2:8-20*

Jesus opens Sermon on the Mount   *Mat 5:1-12, Luke 6:17-26, 36*

See also benediction, blessing, happiness, sermon

BEAUTY

Jacob's love of Joseph and the coat of many colors   *Gen 37:1-36*

Joseph's appeal to Potiphar's wife   *Gen 39:1-20*

Moses' face veiled   *Exod 34:29-35*

Samson betrayed by Delilah's beauty   *Judg 16:4-30*

Samuel selects David for beauty of character   *1 Sam 16:1-13*

David has Uriah killed for Bathsheba's beauty   *2 Sam 11:1-27*

Esther advanced by her beauty   *Esther 2:5-23*

David's song on Soul   *Psal 84:1-12*

David's song on beauty of the Lord upon us   *Psal 90:1-17*

Isaiah on the ornaments of women   *Isa 3:16-26*

Daniel eats pulse and remains fair   *Dan 1:1-21*

Jesus on take no thought for the body   *Mat 6:25-44*

Jesus heals deformity   *Mat 12:9-13, Mark 3:1-5, Luke 6:6-11*

Jesus transfigured   *Mat 17:1-13, Mark 9:2-13, Luke 9:28-36*

Jesus loves the rich, young ruler   *Mat 19:16-30, Mark 10:17-31, Luke 18:18-30*

Jesus' parable of wedding garment   *Mat 22:1-14*

Jesus anointed by woman   *Mat 26:6-13, Mark 14:3-9*

Jesus' parable of rich and poor man   *Luke 16:19-31*

Jesus heals Malchus' amputated ear   *Luke 22:50, 51*

See also art, body, decay, grace, perfection

BEGGAR

Jesus' parable of rich man and beggar   *Luke 16:19-31*

Jesus heals blind beggar   *Luke 18:35-43*

Jesus heals blind Bartimaeus, begging   *Mark 10:46-52*

Peter and John heal lame man who asks alms   *Acts 3:1-11*

See also giving

BEGINNING

God creates universe   *Gen 1:1-31*

Lord God creates material man and universe   *Gen 2: 6—3: 24*

Prophecy by Isaiah of the coming Messiah   *Isa 7:10-16, 9:2-7*

Jesus' parable of sower   *Mat 13:3-23, Mark 14:1-20, Luke 8:4-15*

Jesus' parable of mustard seed   *Mat 13:31, 32, Mark 4:30-32, Luke 13:18, 19*

Jesus' parable of seed, blade, ear   *Mark 4:26-29*

The birth of Jesus   *Luke 2:1-7*

Jesus on "Ye must be born again"   *John 3:1-21*

Paul on Melchizedek and Christ   *Heb 6:20, 7:1-28*

See also cause, creation, origin, principle, space, time

BEING

See life, reality

BELIEF

Noah builds the ark   *Gen 6:5-22*

Abraham willing to sacrifice his son   *Gen 22:1-19*

Isaac trusts his father *Gen 22:1-19*

Moses' First Commandment *Exod 20:1-5*

Joshua and Caleb disbelieved by Israelites *Num 13:1-33, 14:1-11, 23-39, Deut 1:19-38*

Gideon's faith built by signs from God *Judg 6:1-40*

Ruth puts her faith in Naomi's God *Ruth 1:1-6*

David's trust in God defeats Goliath *1 Sam 17:17-37*

Asa places faith in physicians *2 Chron 16:11-24*

Elijah supplies rain by praying *1 King 18:41-46*

Elisha develops faith of Shunammite woman *2 King 4:8-37*

Elisha heals Naaman despite his disbelief *2 King 5:1-14*

Hezekiah trusts ambassadors unwisely *2 King 20:12-21, Isa 39: 1-8*

Job blesses God in his suffering *Job 2:1-10*

David's song of faith in God *Psal 46:1-11*

Isaiah says God a help in troubles *Isa 43:1-28, 44:1-24*

Jeremiah prophesies end of captivity *Jer 29:8-14, 31:1-14, 31-34*

Jeremiah demonstrates his confidence in God while in prison *Jer 32:2, 6-27, 37-44*

Daniel's companions in fiery furnace *Dan 3:1-30*

Daniel in lion's den *Dan 6:1-28*

Jesus' birthplace visited by wise men *Mat 2:1-12*

Jesus calls his disciples *Mat 4:17-22, Mark 1:14-20, Luke 5:1-11, John 1:35-42*

Jesus heals centurion's servant *Mat 8:5-13, Luke 7:1-10*

Jesus heals Jairus' daughter *Mat 9:18, 19, 23-26, Mark 5:22-24, 35-43, Luke 8:41, 42, 49-56*

Jesus heals woman of issue of blood *Mat 9:20-22, Mark 5:25-34, Luke 8:43-48*

Jesus heals woman's daughter *Mat 15:21-28, Mark 7:24-30*

Jesus reminds disciples of his great works *Mat 16:5-12, Mark 8:13-21*

Jesus heals epileptic boy *Mat 17: 14-21, Mark 9:14-29, Luke 9:37-43*

Jesus sought by all men *Mark 1: 35-39*

Jesus' parable of seed, blade, ear, full corn *Mark 4:26-29*

Jesus' parable of unwilling friend *Luke 11:5-13*

Jesus heals woman bowed together *Luke 13:11-17*

Jesus on faith *Luke 17:1-6, John 12:44-50*

Jesus' parable of judge and widow *Luke 18:1-8*

Jesus seen by apostles, then by Thomas *Luke 24:36-49, John 20: 19-29*

Jesus heals nobleman's son *John 4:46-54*

Jesus' parable of true vine *John 15: 1-17*

Paul on Christian's armor *Eph 6: 10-17*

Paul on faith *Heb 11:1-40*

See also confidence, faith, understanding, trust

BENEDICTION

God saw all his creation and it was very good *Gen 1:31*

Abraham blessed by Melchizedek *Gen 14:8-20, Heb 6:20, 7:1-28*

Jacob deceives Isaac and obtains blessing *Gen 27:1-44*

Balaam, hired to curse, can only bless *Num 23:1-30, 24:1-25*

Solomon dedicates temple and blesses people *1 King 8:22-66, 2 Chron 6:1-42*

David's song, "Bless the Lord, O my soul" *Psal 103:1-22*

Isaiah's vision of Christ's peaceable kingdom *Isa 11:1-12*

Daniel's meeting with Gabriel *Dan 9:20-23, 10:4-21*

Zephaniah promises salvation *Zeph 3:14-17*

Zechariah's vision of two olive trees *Zech 4:1-14*

Jesus blesses Peter when he acknowledges him as Christ *Mat 16:13-20, Mark 8:27-30, Luke 9: 18-21*

Jesus' parable of the talents *Mat 24:14-30, Luke 19:11-28*

Jesus blesses bread and wine at last supper *Mat 26:26-29, Mark 14: 22-25, Luke 22:14-30, 1 Cor 11: 23-25*

See also blessing, grace, happiness, prayer

BENEVOLENCE

Joseph supplies his brothers with food *Gen 43:1, 2, 45:1-11, 25-38*

David shows kindness to Jonathan's son to repay Jonathan *2 Sam 9: 1-13*

David's song, "The Lord is my shepherd" *Psal 23:1-6*

Elisha captures his enemies and sends them home *2 King 6:8-23*

Isaiah's vision of Christ's promises, "Ho, everyone that thirsteth" *Isa 55:1-13*

Ezekiel's vision of God's care of his flock *Ezek 34:1-31*

Jesus urges benevolence in secret *Mat 6:1-4*

Jesus' parable of the lost sheep *Mat 18:12-14, Luke 15:1-7*

Jesus' parable of good Samaritan *Luke 10:25-37*

Jesus' parable of prodigal's elder brother *Luke 15:15-32*

Jesus' parable of the good shepherd *John 10:1-18*

Paul's sermon on charity *1 Cor 13: 1-13*

See also generosity, goodness, kindness, love, happiness, healing

BEREAVEMENT

See consolation

BETRAYAL

Adam and Eve deceived by serpent *Gen 3:1-5*

Jacob and his mother deceive Isaac *Gen 27:1-44*

Moses on mount betrayed by golden calf *Exod 32:1-24*

Joshua's spies concealed by Rahab in Jericho *Josh 2:1-24*

Samson betrayed to Philistines *Judg 16:4-30*

David sends Uriah to his death *2 Sam 11:1-27, 12:1-10*

Isaiah says hypocrisy will be punished *Isa 29:11-24, 30:1-3, 20, 21*

Jesus' parable of sheep and goats *Mat 25:31-46*

Jesus foretells his betrayal *Mat 26: 20-25, Mark 14:18-21, Luke 22:21, 22, John 13:21-35*

Jesus betrayed by Judas *Mat 26: 47-56, 69-75, Mark 14:43-52, Luke 22:47-53, John 18:1-12*

Jesus denied by Peter *Mat 26:57, 58, 69-75, Mark 14:66-75, Luke 22: 54-62, John 18:13-18, 25-27*

Jesus' betrayer hangs himself *Mat 27:3-10, Acts 1:15-20*

Jesus on hypocrisy *Luke 12:1-15*

Paul on enemies of the truth *2 Tim 3:1-17*

John's revelation of the woman and the dragon *Rev 12:1-17*

See also conspiracy, deceit, duplicity, plot

BIBLE

Moses received Ten Commandments *Exod 20:1-19, Deut 5:1-24*

Moses received second tablet *Exod 34:1-8, Deut 10:1-4*

Ezra reads Book of Law to people *Neh 8:1-12*

David's song, "The law of the Lord is perfect" *Psal 19:1-14*

Solomon's proverbs on wisdom *Prov 3:13-26, 4:1-13, 8:1-36*

Jesus hears Satan quote scripture *Mat 4:1-11, Luke 4:1-13*

Jesus fulfills prophecy *Mat 4:12-16*

Jesus' parable of sower (of gospel) *Mat 13:1-23, Mark 4:1-20, Luke 8: 4-15*

Jesus' parable of leaven *Mat 13:33, Luke 13:20, 21*

Jesus summarizes Ten Commandments to two disciples *Mat 22: 34-40, Mark 12:28-34*

Jesus reads scripture and casts out unclean spirit *Mark 1:21-28, Luke 4:33-37*

Jesus opens scripture after he is risen *Luke 24:13-35*

Jesus heals woman and discusses Fourth Commandment *Luke 13: 11-17*

Philip explains scripture to eunuch *Acts 8:26-40*

John describes the sealed book *Rev 5:1-14*

John describes angel with little book *Rev 10:1-11*

See also book, Christian, scripture

BIOLOGY

God creates spiritual universe *Gen 1:1-31*

Lord God puts life into dust *Gen 2:6-8, 18-20, 21-25*

Moses' rod becomes a serpent *Exod 4:1-9*

Ezekiel's vision of children's teeth on edge *Ezek 18:1-32*

Ezekiel's vision of resurrection of dry bones *Ezek 37:1-28*

Jesus' parable of barren fruit tree *Luke 13:6-9*

Jesus feeds 5000 *Mat 14:15-21, Mark 6:35-44, Luke 9:12-17, John 6:5-14*

Jesus feeds 4000 *Mat 15:32-39, Mark 8:1-10*

Jesus' parable of seed, blade, ear, full corn *Mark 4:26-29*

Jesus on man "must be born again" *John 3:1-21*

Paul on "The fruits of the Spirit" *Gal 5:1-26*

Paul on the grafted or natural branch of the olive tree *Rom 11: 17-24*

See also cause, evolution, growth, life, organic, physiology

BIRTH

Adam created from dust *Gen 2:6-8*

Eve created from rib *Gen 2:21-25*

Abraham promised a son despite his age *Gen 15:1-21*

Esau sells his birthright *Gen 25: 24-34*

Moses escapes infanticide *Exod 2: 1-10*

Samson's birth foretold by angel *Judg 13:1-25*

Samuel's miraculous birth *1 Sam 1:1-28*

Elisha foretells Shunammite's child *2 King 4:8-17*

David's song, "The fountain of life" *Psal 36:1-12*

Isaiah prophesies Messiah's birth *Isa 7:10-16, 9:2-7*

Isaiah says "Look unto the rock" *Isa 51:1-12*

Jeremiah, the potter and the clay *Jer 18:1-6*

Jesus' coming birth announced to Joseph *Mat 1:18-25*

Jesus visited by wise men *Mat 2: 1-12*

Jesus' cousin, John Baptist's birth foretold *Luke 1:5-25*

Jesus' coming birth announced *Luke 1:26-38*

Jesus' mother visits Elizabeth *Luke 1: 39-56*

John Baptist born *Luke 1:57-80*

Jesus' birth *Luke 2:1-7*

Jesus' birth announced to shepherds *Luke 2:8-20*

Jesus tells Nicodemus he must be born again *John 3:1-21*

Jesus heals man blind from birth *John 9:1-41*

Peter and John heal man lame from birth *Acts 3:1-11*

Paul on "put on the new man" *Col 3:1-17*

John's vision of woman with child *Rev 12:1-17*

See also awakening, beginning, Christmas, conversion, creation, new

BLASPHEMY

Jesus accused because he forgave sin of palsied man *Mat 9:2-8, Mark 2:1-12, Luke 5:17-26*

Jews attempt to stone Jesus for blasphemy *John 10:22-42*

Jesus condemned to death by priests *Mat 26:59-68, Mark 14:55-65, Luke 22:63-71, John 18:19-24*

BLESSING

God creates all, calls it good, blesses seventh day *Gen 1:1-31, 2:1-5*

Abraham blessed by Melchizedek

after war of kings *Gen 14:8-20, Heb 6:20, 7:1-28*

Isaac blesses Jacob by mistake *Gen 27:1-44*

Jacob blessed by angel he wrestles with *Gen 32:24-32*

Moses on blessings to the good *Lev 26:1-20, Deut 28:1-14, Josh 23:1-16*

Elisha asks Elijah for double portion of spirit *2 King 2:1-11*

Isaiah's vision of peaceble kingdom *Isa 11:1-12*

Isaiah's praise to God for benefits *Isa 25:1, 4, 6-10*

Micah's vision of Lord's house *Mic 4:1-8, 13*

Jesus' Beatitudes *Mat 5:1-12, Luke 6:17-26, 36*

Jesus blesses Peter for calling him Christ *Mat 16:13-20, Mark 8:27-30, Luke 9:18-21*

Paul's advice to his disciple *2 Tim 2:1-26*

See also benediction, happiness, holiness, promise

BLINDNESS

Samson's blindness and death *Judg 16:4-30*

Jesus' parable of the mote and the beam *Mat 7:1-5, Luke 6:37-42*

Jesus heals two blind men *Mat 9:27-31*

Jesus against three cities who disregard his works *Mat 11:20-24*

Jesus heals man blind and dumb *Mat 12:22-30, Luke 11:14-23*

Jesus heals blind Bartimaeus *Mat 20:29-34, Mark 10:46-52*

Jesus heals blind man in two treatments *Mark 8:22-26*

Jesus castigates the Pharisees and lawyers *Luke 11:37-54*

Jesus heals blind beggar *Luke 18:35-43*

Jesus heals man born blind *John 9:1-41*

Paul blinded *Acts 9:1-9*

Paul healed of blindness *Acts 9:10-22*

Paul relates his healing *Acts 22:1-30*

Paul repeats his healing for King Agrippa *Acts 26:1-32*

See also eye, sight, understanding

BLOOD

Cain sheds Abel's blood *Gen 4:1-16*

Blood of pascal lamb struck on posts *Exod 12:1-14*

Aaron uses blood of animals to atone *Lev 16:1-28*

Jesus heals woman's issue of blood *Mat 9:20-22, Mark 5:25-34, Luke 8:43-48*

Jesus foretells the shedding of his blood *Mat 26:26-29, Mark 14:12-16, Luke 22:14-30*

Jesus' crucifixion *Mat 27:32-56, Mark 15:21-41, Luke 23:26-49, John 19:17-30*

Peter cuts off Malchus' ear, Jesus heals it *Luke 22:50, 51*

Stephen is martyred *Acts 7:51-56*

Paul on atonement *Heb 10:1-39*

See also atonement, communion, dedication, flesh, life, sacrifice, sin, wine

BODY

Creation from dust *Gen 2:6-8*

Creation from rib *Gen 2:21-25*

Cain born of man and woman *Gen 4:1-4*

Enoch's body not found *Gen 5:18, 21-24, Heb 11:5*

Isaiah says culture of body in vain *Isa 3:16-26*

Jeremiah's sermon on the potter and the clay *Jer 18:1-6*

Ezekiel sees resurrection of army of dry bones *Ezek 37:1-28*

Daniel's body sustained by eating pulse *Dan 1:1-21*

Daniel's friends' bodies not consumed by fiery furnace *Dan 3:1-30*

Jesus raises Jairus' daughter *Mat 9:18, 19, 23-26, Mark 5:22-24, 35-43, Luke 8:41, 42, 49-56*

Jesus' body placed in tomb *Mat 27:57-66, Mark 15:42-47, Luke 23:50-56, John 19:31-42*

Jesus' body ascends *Mark 16:19, 20, Luke 24:50-53, Acts 1:9-13*

Jesus raises son of widow of Nain *Luke 7:11-17*

Jesus raises body of Lazarus *John 11:1-46*

Jesus proves to Thomas that his body was raised *John 20:24-29*

Paul on spirit and flesh *Rom 8:1-39*

Paul on absent from the body and present with the Lord *2 Cor 4: 14—5:21*

See also atonement, beauty, communion, flesh, mind, resurrection, sacrifice

BOILS

Hezekiah healed by Isaiah *2 King 20:1-11, Isa 38:1-22*

Job's health restored *Job 2:7-10, 42: 1:17*

BONDAGE

Joseph sold into slavery in Egypt *Gen 37:1-36*

Prologue to bondage in Egypt— emigration of Israel *Gen 46:2-7*

Oppression of slaves in Egypt *Exod 1:8-14*

Bricks without straw *Exod 5:7-19*

Passover and release from bondage *Exod 11:4-10, 12:1-14, 21-41, Deut 16:1-22*

Moses' song of deliverance *Deut 32:1-47*

Jehoiachin well treated as captive *2 King 25:27-30*

People in captivity persecuted by Haman *Esther 3:1-15, 4:1-17*

Jeremiah foretells restoration *Jer 29:8-14*

Jeremiah foretells new covenant of release *Jer 31:1-14, 31-34*

Daniel as boy captive refuses king's meat *Dan 1:1-21*

James on equality of man *Jas 2: 1-13*

See also captivity, persecution, prison, slavery

BONES

Making of Eve *Gen 2:21-25*

Jacob's hip out of joint *Gen 32: 24-32*

Ezekiel's vision of resurrection of dry bones *Ezek 37:1-28*

Jesus heals withered hand *Mat 12: 9-13, Mark 3:1-5, Luke 6:6-11*

Jesus heals woman with spinal disorder *Luke 13:11-17*

Peter and John heal man lame from birth *Acts 3:1-11*

Philip heals lameness *Acts 8:9-13*

Paul heals lameness *Acts 14:8-10*

See also lameness, matter, strength

BOOK

The Ten Commandments written on tablets of stone *Exod 20:1-19, Deut 5:1-24*

Book of law read to people *Neh 8: 1-12*

The sealed book opened by the Lamb *Rev 5:1-14*

The angel with the little book *Rev 10:1-11*

See also Bible, law, scripture, study

BREAD

Adam must earn bread by sweat *Gen 3:6-24*

Joseph's brother came to Egypt for food *Gen 42:1-8*

Moses finds manna in wilderness *Exod 16:1-36, Num 11:1-15, 31, 32*

Ruth gleans in field *Ruth 2:1-23*

Elijah fed by ravens and widow *1 King 17:1-16*

Elisha feeds 100 men with 20 rolls *2 King 4:42-44*

Elisha prophesies drop in price of flour (famine ends) *2 King 6: 24, 25, 7:1-18*

Isaiah's vision of desert as blossoming *Isa 35:1-10*

Daniel eats pulse *Dan 1:1-21*

Jesus considers turning stones into bread *Mat 4:3, 4*

Jesus' disciples don't fast *Mat 9: 14-17, Mark 2:18-22, Luke 5:33-39*

Jesus' disciples pluck corn on sabbath *Mat 12:1-8, Mark 2:23-28, Luke 6:1-5*

Jesus' parable of the leaven *Mat 13: 33, Luke 13:20, 21*

Jesus feeds 5000 men and families with few loaves *Mat 14:15-21, Mark 6:35-44, Luke 9:12-17, John 6:5-14*

Jesus' last supper with disciples *Mat 26:26-29, Mark 14:22-25, Luke 22:14-30, 1 Cor 11:23-25*

Jesus' disciples recognize him at Emmaus *Mark 16:12, 13, Luke 24: 13-35, 1 Cor 15:15*

Jesus on the bread of life *John 6: 26-65*

Jesus' breakfast with disciples in Galilee *John 21:1-14*

See also food, hunger, life, manna, passover, word

BREAKFAST

Jacob buys Esau's birthright *Gen 25:24-34*

Moses supplies manna and quail *Exod 16:1-36, Num 11:1-15, 31, 32*

Elijah fed by ravens *1 King 17:1-7*

Elijah fed in a dream *1 King 19: 1-8*

Elisha feeds 100 men with 20 rolls *2 King 4:42-44*

David's song, "The Lord is my shepherd" *Psal 23:1-6*

Jesus has breakfast with disciples after resurrection in Jerusalem *John 21:1-14*

See also bread, communion, fasting, food, reformation, repentance

BREAST

Aaron wears Urim and Thummim of holiness and purity *Exod 28: 29-36*

Jesus' parable of Pharisee and publican *Luke 18:9-14*

John leans on Jesus' breast *John 13:21-30*

Paul on armor—breastplate of righteousness *Eph 6:10-17*

BREATH

Lord God breathes into Adam's nostrils *Gen 2:6-8*

Elisha puts his mouth to dead boy's mouth *2 King 4:29-37*

See also Holy Spirit, inspiration, life, spirit

BRIDE, BRIDEGROOM

Creation of Eve from part of Adam *Gen 2:21-25*

Ruth as bride of Boaz *Ruth 4:1-22*

Esther's true beauty makes her queen *Esther 2:5-23*

Jesus at wedding makes water into wine *John 2:1-11*

Jesus' parable of marriage feast and wedding garment *Mat 22:1-14*

Jesus on marriage and resurrection *Mat 22:23-33, Mark 12:18-27, Luke 20:27-40*

Jesus' parable of ten virgins *Mat 25:1-13*

John's vision of holy city as a bride *Rev 21:1-27*

See also Christ, church, marriage, purity

BROTHERHOOD

Cain murders Abel *Gen 4:1-16*

Abraham parts amicably from Lot *Gen 13:1-18*

Abraham rescues his nephew Lot *Gen 14:8-20*

Jacob steals Esau's blessing *Gen 27:1-44*

Jacob is forgiven by Esau *Gen 33: 1-11*

Joseph sold into Egypt by brothers *Gen 37:1-36*

Joseph forgives his brothers *Gen 43:1, 2, 45:1-11*

Moses heals Miriam, his rebellious sister *Num 12:1-16*

Ruth cleaves to her mother-in-law's religion *Ruth 2:1-23*

David befriended by Jonathan *1 Sam 18:1-16*

David shows kindness to Jonathan's son *2 Sam 9:1-13*

Elijah frees hostile Syrians *2 King 6:8-23*

Esther risks danger to save her people *Esther 3:1-15, 4:1-17, 5: 1-14*

Job's friends no help, but he prays for them *Job 42:1-11*

Isaiah's vision of the peaceable kingdom *Isa 11:1-12*

Union of two sticks *Ezek 37:15-28*

Jesus on anger *Mat 5:21-32, Mark 9:38-50*

Jesus on treatment of enemies *Mat 5:38-48, Luke 6:27-36*

Jesus' golden rule for actions *Mat 7:12-14*

Jesus' mother and brothers wait for him *Mat 12:46-50, Mark 3:31-35, Luke 8:19-21*

Jesus' disciples contend who shall be greatest *Mat 18:1-11, Mark 9: 33-37, Luke 9:46-50*

Jesus' parable of unmerciful debtor *Mat 18:23-25*

Jesus' parable of laborers in vineyard *Mat 20:1-16*

Jesus' crucifixion *Mat 27:32-56, Mark 15: 21-41, Luke 23:26-49, John 19:17-30*

Jesus' parable of good Samaritan *Luke 10:25-37*

Jesus' friend Martha complains of her sister *Luke 10:38-42*

Jesus' parable of those bidden to great supper *Luke 14:15-24*

Jesus' parable of prodigal's elder brother *Luke 15:25-32*

Jesus washes his disciples' feet *John 13:1-20*

Jesus charges Peter, "Feed my sheep" *John 21:12-19*

Stephen forgives those who stone him *Acts 7:51-60*

Philip converts Ethiopian *Acts 8: 26-40*

Paul healed by Ananias *Acts 9: 10-22*

Peter accepts Cornelius, a Gentile *Acts 10:1-48, 11:1-18*

Paul on unity of all *Eph 4:1-32*

James on no respect of persons *Jas 2:1-13*

John on love *1 John 4:1-21*

See also family, fellowship, love, neighbor

BUILDING

God creates perfect universe *Gen 1:1-31, 2:1-5*

Moses sees Israelites make bricks without straw *Exod 5:7-19*

David promises to build house of God *2 Sam 7:1-29*

David told his son shall build temple *1 Chron 17:1-27*

David receives liberal offerings *1 Chron 29:6-19*

Solomon builds temple *1 King 6: 1-38, 7:1-51, 2 Chron 3:1-17, 4:1-22, 5:1-14*

Elisha helps sons of prophet build dwelling *2 King 6:1-7*

Zerubbabel gets permission to rebuild temple *Ezra 1:1-11*

Zerubbabel starts rebuilding *Ezra 3:8-13*

Zerubbabel's adversaries block the work *Ezra 4:1-5*

Zerubbabel gets work started again *Ezra 6:1-3, 7, 8, 14, 15*

Ezra receives king's letter to proceed *Ezra 7:11-26*

Nehemiah gets permission to rebuild wall *Neh 2:1-20*

Nehemiah starts building *Neh 4: 1-23*

Nehemiah foils conspiracy to halt work *Neh 6:1-19*

David's song, "Our dwelling place" *Psal 90:1-17*

Isaiah's vision of the church comforted *Isa 54:1-6, 11-17*

Jesus' parable of builders on rock and sand *Mat 7:24-27, Luke 6: 48, 49*

Jesus' parable of two sons ordered to work *Mat 21:28-32*

Jesus' parable of rich man's bigger barns *Luke 12:15-21*

Jesus' parable of counting cost of building tower *Luke 14:25-33*

Jesus' parable of temple raised in three days *John 2:19-22*

Paul on building *1 Cor 3:4-17*

See also church, creator, house, shelter, structure, temple

BURDEN

Cain's burden too heavy to bear *Gen 4:1-16*

Oppression of Israelites in Egypt *Exod 1:8-14*

Elijah's life becomes a burden to him *1 King 19:1-8*

Elisha takes up the mantle of Elijah *2 King 2:12-15*

David's song, "Why art thou cast down?" *Psal 42:1-11*

David's song, "Make a joyful noise" *Psal 66:1-20, 100:1-5*

Jesus heals woman with issue of blood twelve years *Mat 9:20-22, Mark 5:25-34, Luke 8:43-48*

Jesus says his burden is light *Mat 11:25-30*

Jesus heals woman bowed together 18 years *Luke 13:11-17*

Jesus' promise, the Comforter *John 14:1-31*

Jesus offers disciples comfort in tribulations *John 16:1-33*

James on how to bear our cross *Jas 1:11-27*

See also care, healing, responsibility, weary

BURIAL

Jesus halts funeral procession and raises dead *Luke 7:11-17*

Jesus raises Lazarus four days in tomb *John 11:1-46*

Jesus is placed in the tomb *Mat 27: 57-66, Mark 15:42-47, Luke 23:50-56, John 19:31-42*

Jesus' body raised from the tomb *Mat 28:1-8, Mark 16:1-8, Luke 24: 1-12, John 20:1-10*

See also death, grief, matter

BURNT OFFERING

See atonement

BUSINESS

Abraham's riches grow *Gen 13:1-18*

Isaac's herdsmen fight over wells for cattle *Gen 26:12-31*

Joseph prospers in slavery in Egypt *Gen 39:1-6*

Joseph prospers in prison *Gen 39: 20-23, 40:1-23*

Joseph solves economic problems of Egypt *Gen 41:1-46*

Joseph's success causes emigration to Egypt *Gen 45:25-28, 46:2-7*

Moses delegates authority *Exod 18:13-27*

Balak hires Balaam to curse Hebrews *Num 22:1-41, 23:1-30, 24:1-25*

Moses on sure rewards *Deut 28:1-14*

Solomon dedicates construction of temple *1 King 8:22-66, 2 Chron 6:1-42*

Elijah prays for rain *1 King 18: 41-46*

Elijah converts Elisha from farming *1 King 19:19-21*

Elisha supplies water for an army *2 King 3:16-20*

Elisha supplies oil for widow to sell *2 King 4:1-7*

Isaiah prophesies drop in price of flour *2 King 6:24, 25, 7:1-18*

Rebuilding temple in Jerusalem *Ezra 3:8-13*

Rebuilding wall of Jerusalem *Neh 4:1-23*

Job loses all his possessions *Job 1: 13-22*

Job's possessions restored *Job 42: 1-17*

David's song, the prosperity of the good man *Psal 1:1-6*

David's song, shepherd *Psal 23:1-6*

David's song, "the fountain of life" *Psal 37:1-40*

David's song, God a present help *Psal 46:1-11*

David's song, security *Psal 91:1-16*

David's song, safety of the godly *Psal 121:1-8*

Proverbs on wisdom *Prov 3:13-26*

Proverbs on virtuous woman *Prov 31:1-31*

Ecclesiastes on vanity *Eccl 1:1-18, 2:1-26*

Isaiah on "O Lord, thou art my God" *Isa 25:1, 4, 6-10*

Isaiah's sermon, hypocrisy will be punished *Isa 29:11-24, 30:1-3, 20, 21*

Isaiah on the desert will blossom *Isa 35:1-10*

Isaiah on "Fear not" *Isa 43:1-28, 44:1-24*

Isaiah on reward of the good *Isa 65:17-25*

Jeremiah's vision of the potter and the clay *Jer 18:1-6*

Ezekiel's vision of God's care *Ezek 34:1-31*

Jesus on take no thought for things *Mat 6:25-34*

Jesus on golden rule *Mat 7:12-14*

Jesus' parable of builders upon rock and sand *Mat 7:24-27, Luke 6: 48, 49*

Jesus' disciples pluck corn on sabbath *Mat 12:1-8, Mark 2:23-28, Luke 6:1-5*

Jesus accused of working on sabbath *Mat 12:9-13*

Jesus' parable of sower *Mat 13:3-23, Mark 4:1-20, Luke 8:4-15*

Jesus' disciples contend who shall be greatest *Mat 18:1-11, Mark 9:33-37, Luke 9:46-50*

Jesus' parable of laborers in the vineyard *Mat 20:1-16*

Jesus casts traders out of temple *Mat 21:12, 13, Mark 11:15-17, Luke 19:45, 46, John 2:13-25*

Jesus' parable of two sons ordered to work *Mat 21:28-32*

Jesus' parable of the talents *Mat 25:14-30, Luke 17:11-28*

Jesus' disciple, Judas, settles the price to betray him *Mat 26:14-16, Mark 14:10-11, Luke 22:1-6*

Jesus' disciple, Judas, hangs himself *Mat 27:3-10, Acts 1:15-20*

Jesus' parable of seed, blade, ear *Mark 4:26-29*

Jesus fills Peter's net *Luke 5:1-11, John 21:1-11*

Jesus' parable of rich man building bigger barns *Luke 12:15-21*

Jesus' parable of the faithful steward *Luke 12:41-48*

Jesus' parable of barren fig tree *Luke 13:6-9*

Jesus' parable of the unjust steward *Luke 16:1-14*

Jesus' parable of rich man and beggar *Luke 16:19-31*

Jesus' parable of servant before he sups *Luke 17:7-10*

Jesus visits Zacchaeus who gives large sums *Luke 19:1-10*

Jesus says his works have their source in the Father *John 5:17-47*

Jesus' parable of abiding in the vine *John 15:1-17*

Peter and others choose seven deacons to manage affairs *Acts 6:1-4*

Peter rejects Simon's offer to buy Holy Ghost *Acts 8:14-25*

Paul attacked by silversmith as bad for business *Acts 19:23-29*

Paul on spiritual gifts from God *1 Cor 12:1, 4-31*

Paul on love as the highest value *1 Cor 13:1-13*

John on love *1 John 4:1-21*

See also activity, calling, employment, labor, place, position, problem-solving, supply, work

C

CAIN (son of Adam)
See Part II, Cain and Abel

CALLING

Cain and Abel are farmers *Gen 4:1-16*

Abraham called to promised land *Gen 11:31, 32, 12:1-9*

Abraham's promise renewed to Isaac *Gen 26:1-5*

Joseph's boyhood dreams of advancement *Gen 37:1-36*

Moses commanded to lead Hebrews *Exod 3:9-12*

Moses anoints Aaron and sons *Lev 8:1-13*

Moses charges Joshua with leadership *Deut 31:7-23, Josh 1:1-9*

Gideon demands signs from God *Judg 6:1-40*

Samuel the child called by the Lord *1 Sam 3:1-10*

Samuel calls David to be king *1 Sam 16:1-13*

David's charge to Solomon *1 Chron 22:6-19, 23:1, 28:2-10, 20*

Elijah calls Elisha from plowing *1 King 19:19-21*

Elisha takes up mantle of Elijah *2 King 2:12-15*

Isaiah called to prophecy *Isa 6:1-13*

Jonah called to Nineveh, disobeys *Jonah 1:1-17*

Jonah called again, obeys *Jonah 3:1-10*

Jesus calls Peter, Andrew, James, John and Matthew *Mat 4:17-22, Mark 1:14-20, Luke 5:1-11, John 1:35-42*

Jesus on let your light shine *Mat 5:13-16, Luke 8:16-18*

Jesus hears his position compared to a centurion *Mat 8:5-11, Luke 7:1-10*

Jesus chooses twelve and sends them forth *Mat 9:36-38, 10:1-42, Mark 3:13-21, Luke 6:13-19*

Jesus on the charge to preach and heal *Mat 10:5-42, Luke 10:1-16*

Jesus' parable, the pearl of great price *Mat 13:45, 46*

Jesus' parable, two sons ordered to work *Mat 21:28-32*

Jesus' parable, marriage feast and wedding garment *Mat 22:1-14*

Jesus chooses 70 and sends them

Jesus' parable, on counting the cost of a war *Luke 14:25-33*

Jesus' parable, the prodigal's elder brother *Luke 15:25-32*

Jesus calls Philip and Nathaniel *John 2:43-51*

Jesus says his great works have their source in the Father *John 5:17-47*

Jesus' parable, the true vine *John 15:1-17*

Jesus charges Peter "Feed my sheep" *John 21:12-19*

Paul called, healed, converted *Acts 9:1-22*

Paul repeats the story of his conversion *Acts 22:1-30, 26:1-32*

Paul on to come out and be separate *2 Cor 6:1-18*

Paul on advice to disciple *2 Tim 2:1-26*

See also business, church, disciple, mission, work

CAPACITY

God creates man as his own image *Gen 1:26, 27*

Early man lived to advanced age *Gen 5:1-32*

Jacob's nature changed by wrestling with angel *Gen 32:1-32*

Joseph solves the problem of the whole country *Gen 41:1-46*

Moses complains of his inabilities *Exod 3:9-12, 4:10-17*

Moses talks with God on Sinai *Exod 33:7-23*

Moses charges Joshua with leadership *Deut 31:7-23, Josh 1:1-9*

Caleb tells his abilities at advanced age *Josh 14:6-15*

Jotham's parable of the trees as leaders *Judg 9:1-15*

Samuel declares Saul unfit and anoints David *1 Sam 15:7-26*

David kills Goliath *1 Sam 17:38-52*

Elisha asks for double Elijah's spirit, gets it *2 King 2:1-15*

David's song, the Lord is our refuge and strength *Psal 46:1-11*
out *Luke 10:1-16*

The activities of a good wife and mother *Prov 31:1-31*

Isaiah's vision of the office of the Christ *Isa 53:1-12*

Jesus' parable of the sower *Mat 13:3-23, Mark 4:1-20, Luke 8:4-15*

Jesus walks on water *Mat 14:22-33, John 6:15-21*

Jesus talks with Moses and Elias *Mat 17:1-13, Mark 9:2-13, Luke 9:28-36*

Jesus' parable of the talents *Mat 25:14-30, Luke 19:11-28*

Jesus teaches 70 to heal and preach *Luke 10:1-24*

Jesus on the Christ *John 7:14-40*

Jesus heals man born blind *John 9:1-41*

Paul's hardships to establish church *2 Cor 11:21-33*

Paul on putting off old, putting on new man *Col 3:1-17*

See also ability, dominion

CAPTIVITY

Joseph sold into slavery *Gen 37:1-36*

Joseph in prison *Gen 39:21-23, 40:11-23*

Moses sees Hebrews try to make bricks without straw *Exod 5:7-19*

Moses leads them out of Egypt *Exod 11:4-10, 12:1-14, 29-41, Deut 16:1-22*

Samson captured by Philistines *Judg 16:4-30*

Esther and Mordecai prosper in captivity *Esther 6:1-14, 7:1-10, 8:1-8*

Jehoiachin as captive well treated *2 King 25:27-30*

Zerubbabel permitted to rebuild temple *Ezra 1:1-11*

Zerubbabel returns after captivity *Ezra 3:8-13*

Jeremiah promises end of captivity after 70 years *Jer 29:8-14*

Jeremiah acts on his prophecy from prison *Jer 32:2, 6-27, 37-44*

David's song, "Why art thou cast down?" *Psal 42:1-11*

Isaiah's vision of fall of Babylon *Isa 14:4-8, 12-17, 25-27*

Daniel and others prosper in captiv-

ity *Dan 1:1-21, 2:1-49, 3:1-30, 6: 1-28*
Jesus betrayed and made prisoner *Mat 26:47-56, Mark 14:43-54, Luke 22:47-53, John 18:1-12*
Jesus heals woman whom Satan has bound 18 years *Luke 13:11-17*
Peter escapes from prison *Acts 4: 24-37, 5:17-42*
Paul and Silas imprisoned *Acts 16: 19-40*

See also bondage, prison, slavery

CARE

Cain asks if he is his brother's keeper *Gen 4:1-16*
Noah's covenant of safety with God *Gen 6:5-22*
Abraham's story of the man who saved the city *Gen 18:20-23*
Hagar and her child preserved in desert *Gen 21:9-21*
Abraham's covenant renewed to Isaac *Gen 26:1-5*
Jacob's dream of God's care of him *Gen 28:10-22*
Moses follows pillars of cloud or fire *Exod 13:20-22, Num 9:15-23*
Aaron receives God's promises *Lev 26:1-20*
Moses on the chosen people *Deut 7:6-11*
Moses on blessings of obedience *Deut 11:1-32, 28:1-14*
Moses' song of deliverance *Deut 32:1-47*
Elijah fed by ravens *1 King 17:1-16*
Elisha helps widow earn her living *2 King 4:1-7*
David's song of God's care *Psal 23: 1-6*
David's song of safety *Psal 91:1-16*
David's song on God, the preserver of man *Psal 121:1-8*
David's song on ever-presence *Psal 139:1-24*
Isaiah's comfort to the church *Isa 54:1-6, 11-17*
Ezekiel's vision of God's care of his flock *Ezek 34:1-28*
Daniel's vision of Gabriel *Dan 9: 20-23, 10:4-21*
Hosea's vision of God's care *Hos 11:1-4*

Zephaniah's promise of salvation *Zeph 3:14-17*
Jesus calms storm *Mat 8:23-27, Mark 4:35-41, Luke 8:22-25*
Jesus' parable of good Samaritan *Luke 10:25-37*
Jesus' parable of the great supper *Luke 14:15-24*
Jesus' parable of prodigal's elder brother *Luke 15:26-32*
Jesus' parable of good shepherd *John 10:1-18*
Jesus on Christ is door and shepherd *John 10:1-33*
Jesus washes disciples' feet *John 13:1-20*
Jesus charges John with care of mother *John 19:25-27*
Jesus charges Peter "feed my sheep" *John 21:12-19*
Paul on charity *1 Cor 13:1-13*
Paul's protection during hardships *2 Cor 11:21-33*
Peter to cast care on God *1 Pet 5:1-11*
John's sermon that God is love *1 John 4:1-21*
John's revelation of the city foursquare *Rev 21:1-27*
John's revelation of the river and tree of life *Rev 22:1-21*

See also covenant, keeper, love, protection

CAUSE

God as cause of spiritual universe *Gen 1:1-31, 2:1-5*
Lord God as cause of material universe *Gen 2:6-25*
Abraham promised a son at advanced age *Gen 15:1-21*
God as source of eloquence *Exod 4:10-17*
Job hears voice of thunder *Job 38: 1-41*
David's song, "He spake, and it was done" *Psal 33:1-22*
David's song, the fountain of life *Psal 36:1-12*
Jesus' parable of mustard seed *Mat 13:31, 32, Mark 4:30-32, Luke 13: 18, 19*
Jesus' parable of seed, blade, ear, etc. *Mark 4:26-29*

Jesus' birth announced to Mary
Luke 1:26-38

Jesus says his great works have
their source in the Father John
5:17-47

Paul on spiritual gifts 1 Cor 12:1,
4-31

Paul on creator Rom 1:17-25

See also beginning, creation, creator,
motive, soul

CENSURE

Lord God remands man of dust to
till soil Gen 3:6-24

Lord God disapproves Cain Gen 4:
1-16

Moses censured by people for lack
Exod 16:1-36, Num 11:1-15, 31, 32

Moses criticized by Miriam and
Aaron Num 12:1-16

Balaam refuses to curse Israelites
Num 22:1-41, 23:1-30, 24:1-25

Nathan uncovers David's sin 2 Sam
12:1-10

The vanity of mortal life Eccl 1:
1-18, 2:1-26

Isaiah's vision of war condemned
Isa 2:1-5, Mic 4:1-8, 13

Isaiah's vision of the fall of Babylon
Isa 14:4-8, 12-17, 25-27

Jesus excoriates three cities for disregarding him Mat 11:20-24

Jesus rebukes Peter Mat 16:21-28,
Mark 8:31-38, Luke 9:20-27

Jesus' parable of unmerciful debtor
Mat 18:23-35

Jesus' parable of husbandmen who
won't pay rent Mat 21:32-46,
Mark 12:1-12, Luke 20:9-19

Jesus castigates Pharisees and lawyers Luke 11:37-54

Paul describes enemies of the truth
2 Tim 3:1-17

See also condemnation, criticism,
rebuke

CERTAINTY

Abraham asks how much righteousness needed for deliverance Gen
18:20-33

Moses' reluctance overcome by
promise of God's presence Exod
3:9-12

Pillar of cloud and fire Exod 13:
20-22, Num 9:15-23

Moses' song of mercy and deliverance Deut 32:1-47

Song of Deborah Judg 5:1-20

Elisha heals Shunammite's son
2 King 4:8-37

David's song, "The Lord is my shepherd" Psal 23:1-6

David's song, "The secret place of
the most High" Psal 91:1-16

David's song, "God the preserver of
man" Psal 121:1-8

David's song, "Whither shall I flee
from thy presence" Psal 139:1-24

Isaiah's reassurance to all, "Comfort ye" Isa 40:1-31

John Baptist sends to Jesus for
proof of Christ Mat 11:2-19, Luke
7:18-33

Jesus' parable of the leaven Mat 13:
33, Luke 13:20, 21

Peter says Jesus is Christ Mat 16:
13-20, Mark 8:27-30, Luke 9:18-21

How to inherit eternal life Mat 19:
16-30, Mark 10:17-31, Luke 10:25-
28, 18:18-30

Jesus' parable of wise and foolish
virgins Mat 25:1-13

Jesus' parable of seed, blade, ear,
full corn Mark 4:26-29

Proofs by healing (*See* Part II, Jesus
Christ: Great Works)

See also assurance, conviction, doubt,
reality, truth

CHAINS

Joseph in prison Gen 39:21-23, 40:
1-23

Bondmen in Egypt Exod 1:8-14, 5:
7-19

Jehoiachin well treated in Babylon
2 King 25:27-30

Jeremiah foretells release from
captivity Jer 29:8-14

Jeremiah in prison buys a field in
Israel Jer 32:2, 6-27, 37-44

Daniel as captive refuses king's meat
Dan 1:1-21

Three Jews bound and thrown in
fiery furnace Dan 3:1-30

Jesus heals Gadarene who broke his
chains Mat 8:28-34, Mark 5:1-20,
Luke 8:26-39

Jesus imprisoned and scourged *Mat 27:27-31, Mark 15:16-20, John 19:1-16*

Peter released from prison by angel *Acts 5:17-42*

Peter in prison again *Acts 12:1-17*

Paul and Silas imprisoned in stocks *Acts 16:19-40*

Paul seized at Jerusalem *Acts 22:1-30*

Paul travels to Rome as prisoner *Acts 27:1-44*

See also captivity, prison, slavery

CHALLENGE

Isaac's strife with herdsmen over wells *Gen 26:12-31*

Jacob wrestles with angel *Gen 32:24-32*

Moses and Aaron challenged by Egyptian sorcerers *Exod 7:1-12*

Moses' authority challenged by Aaron and Miriam *Num 12:1-16*

Moses charges people to choose whom they will serve *Deut 30:11-20*

Saul's army challenged by Goliath *1 Sam 17:1-16*

Elijah challenges 450 prophets of Baal *1 King 18:17-40*

Esther challenges Haman *Esther 4:1-17, 5:1-14*

Job's faith challenged by Satan *Job 1:1-22*

Daniel refuses king's meat *Dan 1:1-21*

Daniel refuses to stop praying *Dan 6:1-28*

Jesus challenged by Satan *Mat 4:1-11, Mark 1:12, 13, Luke 4:1-13*

John Baptist sends to Jesus for proof he is Christ *Mat 1:2-19, Luke 7:18-35*

Jesus reproves scribes and Pharisees *Mat 23:1-39, Mark 12:38-40, Luke 20:45-27*

Jesus castigates Pharisees and lawyers *Mat 23:1-39, Luke 11:37-54*

Jesus challenges Herod to stop him from healing *Luke 13:31-35*

Jesus challenged by Thomas to prove body raised *John 20:19-29*

Peter and John challenge the council *Acts 4:1-23*

Paul urged not to return to Jerusalem *Acts 21:8-15*

John's vision of war in heaven *Rev 12:1-17*

See also defiance

CHANCE

The vanity of human things *Eccl 1:1-18, 2:1-26*

Jesus' parable of laborers in vineyard *Mat 20:1-16*

Election of Mathias by lot *Acts 1:15-26*

See also accident, cause, fortune, opportunity

CHANGE

Enoch is translated to spirit *Gen 5:18, 21-24*

Abram and Sarai get new names (natures) *Gen 17:1-9, 15-22*

Jacob's nature is changed *Gen 32:1-32*

Gideon drives off invaders *Judg 7:1-25*

Ruth reverses her lack *Ruth 2:1-23*

David pacified by Abigail *1 Sam 25:2-42*

Elisha captures his captors and sends them home *2 King 6:8-33*

Elisha predicts change in price of flour *2 King 6:24, 25, 7:1-18*

Job's prosperity is reversed *Job 1:13-22*

Jonah changes from disobedience to obedience *Jonah 1:1-17, 2: 1-10, 3:1-10*

Jesus' parable of debtor unmerciful to his fellow servant *Mat 18:23-35*

Jesus saddens the rich young ruler by asking too much *Mat 19:16-30, Mark 10:17-31, Luke 18:18-30*

Peter vows never to deny Jesus, then does it *Mat 26:57, 58, 69-75, Mark 14:66-72, Luke 22:54-62, John 18:13-18, 25-27*

Jesus' parable of the unwilling friend *Luke 11:5-13*

Jesus' parable of rich man and beggar *Luke 16:19-31*

Jesus' parable of judge and widow *Luke 18:1-8*

Jesus reforms Zacchaeus *Luke 19: 1-10*

Peter changes mind after vision of great sheet *Acts 11:1-18*

Philip converts Simon *Acts 8:9-13*

Paul, the persecutor, becomes Paul, the Christian evangelist *Acts 8: 1-4, 9:1-22*

See also conversion, reversal

CHAOS

The flood wipes out civilization *Gen 7:1-24*

The tower of Babel falls *Gen 11: 1-9*

Moses returns from Sinai to find worship of the golden calf *Exod 32:1-24*

Moses warns against false leaders *Deut 13:1-18*

Nehemiah learns of Jerusalem's misery *Neh 1:1-11*

See also confusion, matter, government

CHARACTER

Abraham blessed by Melchizedek *Gen 14:8-20, Heb 6:20, 7:1-28*

Abraham learns it only takes one righteous man to save a whole city *Gen 18:20-33*

Abraham willing to sacrifice his son *Gen 22:1-19*

Joseph refuses Potiphar's wife *Gen 39:1-20*

Moses receives Ten Commandments —basis of all law *Exod 20:1-19, Deut 5:1-24*

Moses' face concealed by veil *Exod 34:29-35*

Aaron's rod blossoms *Num 17:1-11*

A chosen people set apart as God's *Deut 7:6-11*

Gideon refuses to be king *Judg 8: 22, 23*

Ruth is loyal to her mother-in-law's religion *Ruth 1:1-22*

David's character recognized by Samuel *1 Sam 16:1-13*

David's character recognized by Jonathan *1 Sam 18:1-16*

David appeased by Abigail's character *1 Sam 25:2-42*

Solomon's choice of gifts valued by

God *1 King 3:5-15, 2 Chron 1: 7-12*

Elijah's goodness recognized by Elisha *2 King 2:1-11*

Elisha's greatness appreciated by Shunammite *2 King 4:8-37*

Josiah's good reign *2 King 23:1-22, 2 Chron 34:1-8, 29-33*

Esther's best nature appealed to by Mordecai *Esther 3:1-15, 4:1-17*

Job's integrity left intact by trials *Job 3:1-26*

David's song, "Mark the perfect man" *Psal 37:1-40*

The virtuous woman *Prov 31:1-31*

Isaiah is called to prophesy *Isa 6: 1-13*

Isaiah's vision of office of Christ *Isa 42:1-12, 16, 18, 61:1-11, 62: 1-12*

Daniel refuses king's meat *Dan 1: 1-21*

Hebrews refuse to worship image *Dan 3:1-30*

Daniel refuses to worship image *Dan 6:1-28*

Jesus' character testified by voice from heaven *Mat 3:13-27, 17:1-13, Mark 1:9-11, 9:2-13, Luke 3:21, 22, 9:28-36*

Jesus finds centurion exceptional *Mat 8:5-13, Luke 7:1-10*

Jesus' character testified by Peter *Mat 16:13-20, Mark 8:27-30, John 9:18-21*

Jesus' character recognized at early age *Luke 2:41-52*

Jesus' character testified by John *John 1:15-34*

Jesus on "I am the bread of life" *John 6:26-65*

Peter and John speak with boldness *Acts 4:1-23*

Seven deacons chosen to divide labor *Acts 6:1-4*

Peter on the ideal of church members *1 Pet 2:1-25*

Paul on how minister should conduct himself *2 Cor 6:1-18*

Paul on how Christians should act *Col 3:1-17*

Paul on advice to a disciple *2 Tim 2:1-26*

James on how to bear our cross *Jas 1:1-27*

James on need for works *Jas 2:14-26*
John finds one to open the sealed book *Rev 5:1-14*

See also conscience, goodness, integrity, name, nature

CHARITY

Moses heals Miriam of leprosy after her rebellion *Num 12:1-16*
David shows kindness to Jonathan's son *2 Sam 9:1-13*
Jesus on benevolence *Mat 6:1-4*
Jesus on not judging others *Mat 7:1-5, Luke 6:37-40*
Jesus on Golden Rule *Mat 7:12-14*
Jesus on go heal and teach *Mat 28:16-20, Mark 16:15-18*
Jesus' parable of good Samaritan *Luke 10:25-37*
Martha complains to Jesus about her sister *Luke 10:38-42*
Jesus saves the adultress from stoning *John 8:1-11*
Jesus on Christ the good shepherd *John 10:1-33*
Jesus washes disciples' feet *John 13:1-20*
Jesus charges Peter "Feed my sheep" *John 21:12-19*
Paul on charity *1 Cor 13:1-13*
James on faith without works *Jas 2:14-26*
John on "God is Love" *1 John 4:1-21*

See also affection, benevolence, care, compassion, love

CHASTEN

See discipline, punishment, purity

CHASTITY

Spiritual creation of male and female by God *Gen 1:26, 27*
Joseph resists Potiphar's wife *Gen 39:1-20*
Moses breaks up worship of golden calf *Exod 32:1-24*
Moses forbids abominations *Deut 18:9-14*
Moses lists blessings of obedience *Deut 28:1-14*
Moses bids Israelites "Choose ye" *Deut 30:11-20*

Samson betrayed by mistress *Judg 16:4-30*
David's song on the happiness of the godly *Psal 1:1-6*
The virtuous woman *Prov 31:1-31*
Annunciation of immaculate conception to Mary *Mat 1:18-25*
Jesus puts commandments on mental basis *Mat 5:21-32*
Jesus' sermon on what defiles a man *Mat 15:1-20, Mark 7:1-23*
Jesus' parable of wise anad foolish virgins *Mat 25:1-13*
Jesus saves woman taken in adultery *John 8:1-11*
Paul on spirit vs. flesh *Rom 8:1-39*
Paul on come out and be separate *2 Cor 6:1-18*
Paul on Christian's armor *Eph 6:10-17*
James on temptation *Jas 1:1-27*

See also adultery, childlikeness, innocence, lamb

CHEER

See comfort, encouragement, joy, rejoicing

CHEMISTRY

Lord God makes man from dust *Gen 2:1-5*
Gideon and the fleece of wool *Judg 6:36-40*
Elisha and widow's pot of oil *2 King 4:1-7*
Uzziah's heart lifted with pride *2 Chron 26:1-23*
Jesus feeds multitude with loaves and fishes *Mat 14:15-21, 15:32-39, Mark 6:35-44, 8:1-10, Luke 9:12-17, John 6:5-14*
Jesus' body is reconstructed after death *Mat 28:1-8, Mark 16:1-8, Luke 24:1-12, John 20:1-10*
Virgin birth announced to Mary *Luke 1:26-38*
Jesus turns water to wine *John 2:1-11*

See also matter, organic, science, substance

CHERUB

See angel, innocence

CHILDLIKENESS

Isaac completely trusts his father *Gen 22:1-19*

Joseph tells his boyhood dreams *Gen 37:1-11*

Samuel as a child called by the Lord *1 Sam 3:1-10, 19-21*

David pacified by Abigail's gentleness *1 Sam 35:2-42*

Elisha heals Naaman *2 King 5:1-14*

Isaiah's vision of Christ's peaceable kingdom *Isa 11:1-12*

Daniel refuses to eat king's meat *Dan 1:1-21*

Hosea's vision of Israel as a child of God *Hos 11:1-4*

Jesus on qualities that make a Christian *Mat 5:1-12, Luke 6:17-26, 36*

Jesus on gospel revealed to babes *Mat 11:25-30, Luke 10:21, 22*

Jesus gives the example of a little child *Mat 18:1-11, Mark 9:33-37, Luke 9:46-50*

Jesus' parable of the lost sheep *Mat 18:12-14, Luke 15:1-7*

Jesus blesses little children *Mat 19:13-15, Mark 10:13-16, Luke 18:15-17*

Jesus' parable of two sons ordered to work *Mat 21:28-32*

Jesus at twelve with doctors in temple *Luke 2:41-52*

Jesus' parable of chief seats at the wedding *Luke 14:7-14*

Peter's sermon on milk of the word *1 Pet 2:1-25*

See also education, innocence, trust

CHILDREN

Hagar and son cast out *Gen 21:9-21*

Abraham tempted to sacrifice his son, Isaac, who is obedient and trustful *Gen 22:1-19*

Jacob buys Esau's birthright for pottage *Gen 25:24-34*

Joseph's boyhood dreams provoke envy *Gen 27:1-36*

Moses as baby is preserved from death *Exod 2:1-10*

Zelophehad's daughters sue for inheritance *Num 27:1-11, 36:5-13*

Gideon's son's parable of trees *Judg 9:1-15*

The boy Samuel called by God *1 Sam 3:1-10, 19-21*

David selected from among Jesse's sons *1 Sam 16:1-13*

David plays harp to calm Saul *1 Sam 16:14-23*

David shows kindness to Jonathan's son *2 Sam 9:1-13*

David's and Bathsheba's child dies *2 Sam 12:13-23*

Solomon judges who owns the baby *1 King 3:16-28*

Elijah heals son of widow of Zarephath *1 King 17:17-24*

Elisha heals son of Shunammite *2 King 4:8-37*

Solomon's advice to children on wisdom *Prov 3:13-26, 4:1-13, 8:1-36*

The virtuous woman and mother *Prov 31:1-31*

Ezekiel's vision on heredity *Ezek 18:1-32*

Daniel refuses to eat king's meat *Dan 1:1-21*

Hosea's vision, "when Israel was a child" *Hos 11:1-4*

Jesus raises Jairus' daughter *Mat 9:18, 19, 23-26, Mark 5:22-24, 35-43, Luke 8:41, 42, 49-56*

Jesus heals Syrophenician's daughter *Mat 15:21-28, Mark 7:24-30*

Jesus heals epileptic boy *Mat 17:14-21, Mark 9:14-29, Luke 9:37-43*

Jesus blesses little children *Mat 19:13-15, Mark 10:13-16, Luke 18:15-17*

Jesus' parable of two sons ordered to work *Mat 21:28-32*

Jesus at twelve years old astonishes the rabbis *Luke 2:41-52*

Jesus raises son of widow of Nain *Luke 7:11-17*

Jesus heals nobleman's son *John 4:46-54*

See also family, father, innocence, mother, sonship

CHILDREN OF ISRAEL

Children of Israel (Jacob) escape revenge of their uncle Esau *Gen 33:1-11*

Jacob (Israel) and his sons' families emigrate to Egypt for food *Gen 46:2-7*

Their future predicted *Gen 49:1-28, Deut 33:1-29*

Persecution in Egypt *Exod 1:8-14, 15-22, 5:7-19*

Moses leads them out of Egypt *Exod 11:4-10, 12:1-14, 29-41, Deut 16:1-22*

Moses' song of deliverance *Exod 15:1-19*

Moses leads through wilderness *Exod 15:22-27, 16:1-36, 17:1-7*

Moses gives them Ten Commandments *Exod 20:1-19, Deut 5:1-24*

Aaron helps them worship golden calf *Exod 32:1-24*

Moses tells them they are the chosen people *Deut 7:6-11*

Joshua leads them into promised land *Josh 1:1-9, 3:1-17*

David made king of Judah and Israel *2 Sam 2:1-4, 5:1-5*

Zerubbabel rebuilds temple of Jerusalem *Ezra 3:8-13*

Isaiah promises them Messiah *Isa 7:10-16, 9:2-7*

Jehoiachin and all people taken captive *Jer 29:8-14*

Nehemiah rebuilds wall of Jerusalem *Neh 4:1-23*

Jesus commends centurion's faith above Israel *Mat 8:5-13, Luke 7:1-10*

Jesus sends his disciples to lost sheep of house of Israel *Mat 10:1-42*

Paul on circumcision *Rom 2:23-29, Gal 5:1-14, 6: 12-18*

See also circumcision, chosen people

CHOICE

Eve, deceived by serpent, makes wrong choice of fruit *Gen 3:1-5*

Moses urges choice of life, not death *Deut 30:11-20*

Joshua bids people choose God or gods *Josh 24:14-25*

Gideon chooses not to be king *Judg 8:22, 23*

Ruth chooses to follow her mother-in-law *Ruth 1:1-22*

Samuel chooses David *1 Sam 16:1-13*

Elijah and prophets of Baal *1 King 18:17-40*

Daniel chooses pulse rather than defile himself *Dan 1:1-21*

Jonah disobeys at first *Jonah 1:1-17*

Jonah eventually obeys *Jonah 3:1-10*

Jesus calls disciples *Mat 4:17-22, Mark 1:14-20, Luke 5:1-11, John 1:35-42*

Jesus on two masters *Mat 6:22-24*

Jesus on "take no thought," "seek ye first" *Mat 6:25-34*

Jesus insists on a choice between him and the world *Mat 8:18-22*

Jesus' parable of virgins *Mat 25:1-13*

Matthias elected to replace Judas *Acts 1:15-26*

Philip converts the Ethiopian *Acts 8:26-40*

James, show faith by works, not without *Jas 2:14-26*

See also chosen people

CHOSEN PEOPLE

God makes man in his image and likeness *Gen 1:26, 27*

Noah, the righteous, promised safety *Gen 6:5-22*

Abraham called by God to find promised land *Gen 11:31, 32, 12:1-9*

Promise to Abraham renewed to Isaac *Gen 26:1-5*

Jacob's dream of angels on ladder *Gen 28:10-22*

Jacob on future of his sons *Gen 49:1-28, Deut 33:1-29*

Moses tells Israelites they are set apart as God's chosen people *Deut 7:6-11*

Rahab in Jericho protects the spies because God's children must win *Josh 2:1-24*

Ezekiel on God's care over His flock *Ezek 34:1-31*

Jesus heals daughter of woman of Canaan *Mat 15:21-28, Mark 7:24-30*

Jesus' discourse with Samaritan woman *John 4:1-30*

Peter accepts Gentiles as Christians *Acts 10:1-48, 11:1-18*

See also children of Israel, choice, circumcision, election

CHRIST, EVIDENCE OF

To John Baptist *Mat 3:13-17, 11:2-19-11, Mark 1:9-11, Luke 7:18-35, John 1:15-34, 3:22-36*

By fulfillment of prophecy *Mat 4: 12-16*

To disciples *Mat 16:5-12, Mark 8: 13-21, John 10:17-24*

As Son of David *Mat 22:41-46, Mark 12:35-37, Luke 20:41-44*

By resurrection *Mat 28:1-8, Mark 16:1-8, Luke 24:1-12, John 20:1-10*

Expressed by Jesus *John 7:25-53*

By Peter on how lame man was healed *Acts 2:12-37*

By Paul on resurrection *1 Cor 15: 1-58*

Jesus' healings and great works (*See* Part II, Jesus Christ: Great Works)

See also fulfillment, proof

CHRIST HEALING

See Part II, Jesus Christ: Great Works

See also healing, Messiah

CHRIST, PROPHECY OF

Melchizedek, the forerunner of Christ *Gen 14:8-20, Heb 6:20, 7:1-28*

Christ foreshadowed again *Deut 18: 15-22*

Messiah promised by Isaiah *Isa 2: 1-5, Mic 4:1-8, 13*

Birth of the Messiah foretold *Isa 7:10-16, 9:2-7*

Christ's kingdom of peace *Isa 11: 1-12*

Christ causes the desert to blossom *Isa 35:1-10*

The office of Christ *Isa 42:1-12, 16, 18*

Description of the Messiah *Isa 53: 1-12*

Promises of the Messiah *Isa 55: 1-13*

On being Christ-like *Isa 60:1-5*

The works of Christ *Isa 61:1-11, 62:1-12*

Jesus' parable of the leaven *Mat 13:33, Luke 13:20,21*

Jesus' parable of the treasure in field *Mat 13:44*

Jesus' parable of the pearl of great price *Mat 13:45, 46*

Jesus' parable of the lost sheep *Mat 18:12-14, Luke 15:1-7*

Jesus' parable of the sheep and goat *Mat 25:31-46*

Jesus' parable of the seed, blade, ear *Mark 4:26-29*

See also Jesus, manifestation, Messiah

CHRIST, RECOGNIZED, OR BELIEF IN

His lineage *Mat 1:1-17, Luke 3: 23-29*

At birth of Jesus, wise men and shepherds *Mat 2:1-12, Luke 2: 8-20*

By John Baptist *Mat 3:13-17, Mark 1:9-11, Luke 3:21, 22, John 1:15-34, 3:22-36*

By Peter *Mat 16:13-20, Mark 8:27-30, Luke 9:18-21*

By Zebedee's wife *Mat 20:20-28, Mark 10:35-45*

Jesus' parable of farmers who refused to pay rent *Mat 21:33-46, Mark 12:1-12, Luke 20:9-19*

By a woman with ointment *Mat 26: 6-13, Mark 14:3-9*

By Mary Magdalene after risen *Mark 16:9-11, John 20:11-18*

At temple by Simon and Anna *Luke 2:21-38*

By Rabbis at twelve years old *Luke 2:41-52*

By Zacchaeus *Luke 19:1-10*

Jesus on the Scriptures about Christ *Luke 24:25-35*

By John as light of world *John 1:1-14, 8:12-32*

By Nicodemus at night *John 3:1-21*

By woman at Jacob's well *John 4: 1-42*

Jesus' sermon that he is Christ *John 7:14-40, 8:12-32*

Jesus on oneness with Father *John 10:22-42*

Jesus on faith in Christ *John 12: 44-50*

By Thomas after risen *John 20:
24-29*

By Paul near Damascus *Acts 9:
1-9*

Paul on history of Messiah *Acts
13:16-41*

CHRISTIAN

Isaiah on being Christ-like *Isa 60:
1-5*

Forty-seven parables by Jesus, teaching Christian principles *(See* Part
II, Jesus Christ: Parables)

Fifty-two healings and great works
by Jesus as examples of Christian
healing and dominion *(See* Part II,
Jesus Christ: Great Works)

Fifty-two discourses by Jesus ex-
plaining Christian precepts *(See*
Part II, Jesus Christ: Teachings)

Jesus chooses his disciples and
sends them forth *Mat 9:36-38,
10:1-42, Mark 3:13-21, Luke 6:13-
19, John 10:1-24*

Jesus founds his church *Mat 16:13-
20, Mark 8:27-30, Luke 9:18-21*

The cross as the symbol of the Christian *Mat 27:32-56, Mark 15:21-41,
Luke 23:26-49, John 19:17-30*

The church grows and develops
Acts 4:24-37

Peter outlines the ideal of a Christian *1 Pet 2:1-25*

Paul on the Christian's armor *Eph
6:10-17*

Paul on Christian qualities *Heb 12:
1-29, Col 3:1-17, 1 Thess 5:1-28,
2 Tim 2:1-26, 4:1-8*

John's letters to Christian churches
Rev 1:4-20, 2:1-29, 3:1-22

See also belief, disciple, example,
follower, profession

CHRISTMAS

Isaiah on coming of Christ's kingdom *Isa 2:1-5*

Isaiah prophesies birth of Messiah
Isa 7:10-16, 9:2-7

Isaiah prophesies Christ's peaceable kingdom *Isa 11:1-12*

Isaiah reassures the people *Isa 40:
1-31*

Isaiah on the office of Christ *Isa
42:1-12, 16-18*

Isaiah describes the Messiah *Isa
53:1-12*

Isaiah lists promises of Christ *Isa
55:1-13*

Isaiah inspires to be Christ-like *Isa
60:1-5*

Micah on coming of Christ's kingdom *Mic 4:1-8, 13*

Angel appears to Joseph *Mat 1:
18-25*

Jesus visited by wise men *Mat 2:
1-12*

Joseph, Mary and baby flee to
Egypt *Mat 2:13-23, Luke 2:39, 40*

Jesus' love of little children *Mat
19:13-15, Mark 10:13-16, Luke 18:
15-17*

Jesus' birth announced to Mary
Luke 1:26-38

Mary's visit to Elizabeth *Luke 1:
39-56*

Jesus born in Bethlehem *Luke 2:
1-7*

His birth announced to shepherds
Luke 2:8-20

See also birth, giving, Jesus, Messiah

CHURCH

Cain and Abel sacrifice differently
Gen 4:1-16

Abraham plans to sacrifice his son
Gen 22:1-19

The boy Samuel serves in the temple
1 Sam 3:1-10

Solomon builds temple *1 King 6:
1-38, 7:1-51, 1 Chron 3:1-17, 4:1-22,
5:1-14*

Solomon dedicates temple *1 King 8:
22-26, 2 Chron 6:1-42*

Elijah brings fire to the altar
1 King 18:17-40

Nathan reveals to David that his
son will build the Lord's house
1 Chron 17:1-27

David receives liberal offerings for
the temple *1 Chron 29:6-19*

Uzziah desecrates temple and is
punished *2 Chron 26:1-23*

Zerubbabel starts rebuilding temple
Ezra 3:8-13

Ezra reads book of the law to people
Neh 8:1-12

Isaiah's vision of mountain of Lord's house *Isa 2:1-5, Mic 4:1-8, 13*

Isaiah comforts church *Isa 54:1-6, 11-17*

Ezekiel's vision of dry bones *Ezek 37:1-14*

Ezekiel's vision of holy waters *Ezek 47:1-12*

Jesus' parable of mustard seed *Mat 13:31, 32, Mark 4:30-32, Luke 13: 18, 19*

Jesus founds his church *Mat 16:13-20, Mark 8:27-30, Luke 9:18-21*

Jesus casts out traders from temple *Mat 21:12, 13, Mark 11:15-17, Luke 19:45, 46, John 2: 2-25*

Jesus' first reading in temple heals unclean spirit *Mark 1:21-28, Luke 4:33-39*

Jesus' parable of vine and branches *John 15:1-17*

Peter and John cause church growth *Acts 4:24-37*

Seven deacons chosen *Acts 6:1-4*

Paul and church *Acts 11:19-26, 2 Cor 11:21-33*

Paul on building church *1 Cor 3: 4-17*

Peter's sermon on ideal of church members *1 Pet 2:1-25*

John's letters *Rev 1:4-11, 2:1-29, 3:1-22*

See also building, house, temple, worship

CIRCUMCISION

God's covenant with Abraham *Gen 17:9-14*

Moses orders people to circumcise the heart *Deut 10:12-22*

David accepts challenge of uncircumcised Philistine *1 Sam 17: 17-37*

Jesus heals Gentile centurion's servant *Mat 8:5-13, Luke 7:1-10*

Jesus heals daughter of woman of Canaan *Mat 15:21-28, Mark 7: 24-30*

Jesus' parable of the good Samaritan *Luke 10:25-37*

Peter permits conversion of Gentiles *Act 10:1-48, 11:1-18*

Paul on the law *Rom 2:24-29*

Paul on "neither circumcision availeth any thing, nor uncircumcision" *Gal 5:1-14, 6:12-18*

See also children of Israel, chosen people, Christian, purity

CITIZEN

Abraham asks how many righteous men it takes to save a city *Gen 18:20-33*

A poor wise man saves his city *Eccl 9:13-18*

Jesus pays his taxes *Mat 22:15-22, Mark 12:13-17, Luke 20:20-26*

Paul includes Gentiles in the church *Eph 2:11-22*

John describes nations of the heavenly city *Rev 21:24-27*

See also city, fellowship, membership

CITY

Abraham is told that the city is saved by its righteous men *Gen 18:20-33*

Lot escaped the evil city of Sodom *Gen 19:1, 15-29*

Jericho encompassed seven times *Josh 6:1-27*

Elisha heals the waters of a city *2 King 2:16-22*

Jerusalem besieged by Sennacherib *2 King 18:17-37, 2 Chron 31:20, 21, 32:1-23, Isa 36:1-22*

Nehemiah rebuilds walls of Jerusalem *Neh 4:1-23*

The poor man who saved his city *Eccl 9:13-18*

Daniel prophesies destruction of city by handwriting on wall *Dan 5:1-31*

Jonah preaches to Nineveh *Jonah 3:1-10*

Jesus excoriates three cities for disregarding his mighty works *Mat 11:20-27*

Jesus born in the city of David *Luke 2:1-7*

Jesus sets his face toward Jerusalem *Luke 9:51-56*

John's vision of Babylon fallen *Rev 14:8-13*

John's vision of city foursquare *Rev 21:1-27*

See also Jerusalem, Zion

CLEANSING

Aaron and sons anointed by Moses as priests *Lev 8:1-13*

Aaron's atonement through the scapegoat *Lev 16:1-28*

Miriam cleansed of leprosy and rebellion by Moses *Num 12:1-16*

David's song, "Create in me a clean heart" *Psal 51:1-19*

Jesus' parable of unclean spirit and seven others *Mat 12:43-45, Luke 11:24-26*

Jesus heals man in temple of unclean spirit *Mark 1:21-28, Luke 4:33-37*

Jesus heals ten men of leprosy *Luke 17:11-19*

Jesus visits Zaccheus, the publican *Luke 19:1-10*

Jesus' parable of the true vine purged *John 15:1-17*

Peter accepts the uncircumcised *Acts 10:1-48, 11:1-18*

Paul on remission of sin *Heb 10: 1-39*

See also atonement, baptism, priest, purity, spirit

CLOTHING

Adam asked, "Who told thee that thou wast naked?" *Gen 3:6-24*

Jacob changes clothes to deceive Isaac *Gen 27:1-44*

Joseph's coat gets him into trouble *Gen 37:1-36*

Moses ordered to remove shoes *Exod 3:1-18*

Aaron's garments include Urim and Thummim *Exod 28:29-36*

David refuses Saul's armor *1 Sam 17:17-37*

David cuts Saul's skirt while sleeping *1 Sam 24:1-22*

Garments made by the virtuous woman *Prov 31:10-26*

Garments worn by proud women *Isa 3:16-26*

Jesus on take no thought for raiment *Mat 6: 25-34*

Jesus, healing follows touching hem of his garment *Mat 9:20-22, Mark 5:24-34, Luke 8:43-48*

Jesus' parable about the wedding garment *Mat 22:1-14*

Jesus' parable about new cloth in old garment *Luke 5:36-39*

Jesus' parable of the prodigal reclothed *Luke 15:11-24*

Jesus girded with a towel to wash disciples' feet *John 13:1-20*

Soldiers cast lots for Jesus' garments *John 19:17-30*

Paul describes Christian's armor *Eph 6:10-17*

James on clothing the naked *Jas 2:14-26*

See also armor

COMFORT

Abraham hears God's promises *Gen 15:1-21*

Isaac hears God's promises *Gen 26: 1-5*

Aaron lists God's promises *Lev 26: 1-20*

The blessings of obedience *Deut 28:1-14*

Moses encourages Joshua to take over leadership *Deut 31:7-23, Josh 1:1-9*

Joshua encourages the people *Josh 3:1-10*

Samson's birth announced to his mother *Judg 13:1-25*

Samuel's birth announced to Hannah *1 Sam 1:1-28*

David plays harp for Saul *1 Sam 16:14-23*

David shows kindness to his enemy's grandson *2 Sam 9:1-13*

Reliance on God in war *2 Chron 20: 1-32*

Elijah's discouragement overcome *1 King 19:1-8*

Job's friends no comfort *Job 16: 1-22*

The Lord is my shepherd *Psal 23: 1-6*

"Why art thou cast down?" *Psal 42:1-11*

"Be still, and know that I am God" *Psal 46:1-11*

Ever-presence of God *Psal 139:1-24*

"All is vanity" *Eccl 1:1-18, 2:1-26*

Isaiah, "Comfort ye" *Isa 40:1-31*

Isaiah, "Fear not" *Isa 43:1-28, 44: 1-24*

Isaiah, "Sing, O barren" *Isa 54:1-6, 11-17*

Jeremiah prophesies release *Jer 29:8-14, 31:1-14, 31-34*

Ezekiel on God's care of His flock *Ezek 34:1-31*

Zephaniah promises salvation *Zeph 3:14-17*

Jesus restores daughter to Jairus *Mat 9:18, 19, 23-26, Mark 5:22-24, 35-43, Luke 8:41, 42, 49-56*

Jesus' parable of lost sheep *Mat 18:12-14, Luke 15:1-7*

Jesus after death is restored to his disciples *Mat 28:2, 9, 10, Mark 16:9-11, Luke 24:1-13, 33-49, John 20:11-31*

Jesus restores son to widow of Nain *Luke 7:11-17*

Jesus' parable of prodigal's elder brother *Luke 15:25-32*

Jesus restores Lazarus to his family *John 11:1-46*

Jesus on comfort in tribulation *John 16:1-33*

Jesus washes his disciples' feet *John 13:1-20*

Jesus' parable of the true vine *John 15:1-17*

Descent of Holy Ghost at Pentecost *Acts 2:1-13*

Paul's sermon on charity *1 Cor 13:1-13*

John's sermon on love *1 John 4:1-21*

John's vision of river of life and tree of life *Rev 22:1-21*

See also adversity, encouragement, strength

COMFORTER

Isaiah's reassurance "comfort ye" *Isa 40:1-31*

Jesus' parable of good Samaritan *Luke 10:25-37*

Jesus teaches that truth will make free *John 8:12-32*

Jesus promises the Comforter *John 14:1-31, 15:1-27*

Jesus promises comfort in tribulation *John 16:1-33*

Peter and apostles receive the Holy Spirit (Ghost) *Acts 2:1-13*

Peter tells Simon Holy Spirit (Ghost) not for sale *Acts 8:14-25*

Paul explains Holy Spirit (Ghost) *Acts 19:1-10*

See also healing, Holy Spirit (Ghost), Pentecost, Trinity

COMMANDMENT

Adam and Eve told "Ye shall not eat of it" *Gen 3:1-5*

Moses talks with God on Mt. Sinai *Exod 19:1-9*

Moses delivers Ten Commandments *Exod 20:1-19, Deut 5:1-24*

Moses breaks tablet of Ten Commandments *Exod 32:1-24*

Moses listens to God again *Exod 33:7-23*

Moses delivers second set of tablets *Exod 34:1-8, Deut 10:1-4*

Joshua exhorts to obedience *Josh 23:1-16*

Ezra reads the book of the law *Neh 8:1-12*

David's song, "The law of the Lord is perfect" *Psal 19:1-14*

Jesus puts some commandments on mental basis *Mat 5:21-32, Mark 9:38-50*

Jesus expands Third Commandment *Mat 5:33-37*

Jesus' parable of two sons ordered to work *Mat 21:28-32*

Jesus answers question on greatest commandment *Mat 22:34-40, Mark 12:28-34*

Jesus saves woman taken in adultery *John 8:1-11*

Jesus promises a new commandment *John 13:31-35, 1 John 2:8-11*

John explains the command to love *1 John 4:1-21*

See also authority, law, obedience, power

First Commandment

Creation of God commanded to have dominion *Gen 1:26-28*

Abraham willing to sacrifice Isaac *Gen 22:1-19*

Moses at burning bush *Exod 3:1-18*

First Commandment *Exod 20:3, Deut 5:7*

Three Hebrews go to fiery furnace *Dan 3:1-30*

Daniel goes to lions' den   *Dan 6: 1-28*

Jesus' parable, the pearl of great price   *Mat 13:45, 46*

Jesus' temptations   *Mat 4:1-11, Luke 4:1-13*

Jesus on two masters   *Mat 6:22-24*

Rich young ruler and eternal life   *Mat 19:16-30, Mark 10:17-31, Luke 18:18-30*

Jesus names two great commandments   *Mat 22:34-40, Mark 12:28-34*

Jesus' parable, the rich fool   *Luke 12:15-21*

Jesus' oneness with Father   *John 10:22-40*

See also God, gods, monotheism

Second Commandment

Second Commandment   *Exod 20:4-6, Deut 5:8-10*

Moses and the golden calf   *Exod 32:1-24*

Daniel interprets king's dream   *Dan 2:1-49*

Three Hebrews refuse to worship image   *Dan 3:1-30*

See also image, jealousy

Third Commandment

Man, "God's image," created from dust   *Gen 2:6-8*

God's nature revealed at burning bush   *Exod 3:1-18*

The Third Commandment   *Exod 20:7, Deut 5:11*

Worship of golden calf   *Exod 32: 1-24*

Jonah refuses to obey   *Jonah 1: 1-17*

Jesus expands on Third Commandment   *Mat 5:33-37*

Jesus casts traders out of temple   *Mat 21:12, 13, Mark 11:15-17, Luke 19:44, 45, John 2:13-25*

John's sermon, "God is love"   *1 John 4:1-21*

See also name, vanity

Fourth Commandment

Creation finished in seven days   *Gen 1:1-31*

Fourth Commandment   *Exod 20:8-11, Deut 5:12-15*

Jericho falls on seventh day   *Josh 6:1-27*

Jesus' disciples pluck corn on sabbath   *Mat 12:1-8, Mark 2:23-28, Luke 6:1-5*

Jesus, Son of man, is Lord of sabbath   *Mat 12:1-8*

Jesus heals on sabbath:
  Withered hand   *Mat 12:9-13, Mark 3:1-5, Luke 6:6-11*
  Impotent man at pool   *John 5:1-16*

See also holiness, labor, rest, sabbath, servant, work

Fifth Commandment

God creates man in His image   *Gen 1:26, 27*

Isaac submits to his father   *Gen 22: 1-19*

Jacob deceives his father   *Gen 27: 1-44*

Fifth Commandment   *Exod 20:12, Deut 5:16*

Absalom's conspiracy against David   *2 Sam 15:1-23, 18:6-33*

Jesus' parable of two sons   *Mat 21: 28-32*

Jesus obeys his mother and returns from Jerusalem   *Luke 2:41-52*

Jesus' prayer, "Our Father"   *Mat 6:5-15, Mark 11:25, 26, Luke 11:1-4*

Paul urges obeying Fifth Commandment   *Eph 6:1-3*

See also father, God, honor, life, mother

Sixth Commandment

See kill

Seventh Commandment

See adultery

Eighth Commandment

See stealth

Ninth Commandment

See deceit, lie, witness

Tenth Commandment

See covetousness

COMMUNICATION

Adam asked "Where art thou?" *Gen 3:6-24*

Cain asked, "Where is Abel thy brother?" *Gen 4:1-16*

Enoch walked with God and was translated *Gen 5:18, 21-24, Heb 11:5*

Abraham promised a son and his own land *Gen 15:1-21*

Abraham given a new name *Gen 17: 1-9, 15-22*

Abraham entertains angels *Gen 18: 1-18*

Isaac receives same promise as Abraham *Gen 28:1-5*

Jacob dreams of a ladder of angels *Gen 28:10-22*

Jacob receives new name *Gen 32: 1-32*

Moses at burning bush *Exod 3:1-18*

Moses, rod and leprosy transformed *Exod 4:1-9*

Moses learns source of eloquence *Exod 4:10-17*

Moses at Red Sea told to go forward *Exod 14:5-31*

Moses on Mt. Sinai *Exod 19:1-9, Deut 4:10-15*

Moses receives Ten Commandments *Exod 20:1-19, Deut 5:1-24*

Joshua meets captain of the host *Josh 5:10-15*

Gideon tests God three times *Judg 6:19-40*

Samuel as a child called by the Lord *1 Sam 3:1-10*

Samuel told to anoint a new king *1 Sam 16:1-13*

Elijah and the still small voice of God *1 King 19:9-13*

Job hears voice of thunder *Job 38: 1—41:34*

Jesus' baptism noted by God *Mat 3:13-17, Mark 1:9-14, Luke 3:21, 22*

See also communion, contagion, messenger, prayer

COMMUNION

First passover in Egypt *Exod 11: 4-10, 12:1-14, 21-41, Deut 16:1-22*

Jesus casts traders from temple *Mat 21:12, 13, Mark 11:15-17, Luke 19: 45, 46, John 2:13-25*

Jesus' parable of wedding feast *Mat 22:1-14*

Jesus' parable of ten virgins *Mat 25:1-13*

Jesus orders passover prepared *Mat 26:17-19, Mark 14:12-16, Luke 22: 7-13*

Jesus at Last Supper *Mat 26:26-29, Mark 14:22-25, Luke 22:14-30, 1 Cor 11:23-25*

Jesus atones on the cross *Mat 27: 32-56, Mark 15:21-41, Luke 23: 26-49, John 19:17-30*

Jesus, arisen, at breakfast with disciples *Mat 28:16-18, John 21: 1-14*

Jesus with two disciples at Emmaus *Mark 16:12, 13, Luke 24:13-25*

Jesus' parable of great supper *Luke 14:15-24*

Jesus turns water to wine *John 2: 1-11*

Jesus' sermon on bread of life *John 6:26-65*

Jesus' parable of the true vine *John 15:1-17*

Apostles receive Comforter *Acts 2:1-13*

Paul and his church receive Comforter *Acts 19:1-10*

Paul's teaching on reconciliation with God *2 Cor 5:14-21*

Paul on unity *Eph 4:1-32*

See also blood, bread, flesh, Holy Spirit (Ghost), Last Supper, reconciliation, sacrament, wine

COMPANIONSHIP

Lord God creates Eve as helpmate for Adam *Gen 2:21-25*

A proper wife is found for Isaac *Gen 24:1-67*

Ruth returns with Naomi from Moab *Ruth 1:1-22*

David and Jonathan *1 Sam 18:1-16*

Jesus on "Who is my mother? . . . my brethren?" *Mat 12:46-50*

Jesus' parable of prodigal's elder brother *Luke 15:25-32*

Jesus' parable of the true vine *John 15:1-17*

Jesus promises the Comforter *John 14:1-31*

Paul works with Barnabas to establish church *Acts 11:19-26*

See also association, family, fellowship, friendship, marriage, relation

COMPASSION

Joseph feeds his brothers in Egypt *Gen 42:1-8*

Moses on the blessings of obedience *Deut 28:1-14*

Moses on God's care of Israel *Deut 32:1-47*

David pacified by Abigail *1 Sam 25:2-42*

David shows kindness to Mephibosheth *2 Sam 9:1-13*

Elisha sends invaders home safe *2 King 6:8-23*

David's song about shepherd and sheep *Psal 23:1-6*

The activities of a good woman *Prov 31:1-31*

Isaiah's vision "Comfort ye" *Isa 40:1-31*

Ezekiel's vision of God's care of his flock *Ezek 34:1-31*

Daniel's vision of meeting with angel *Dan 9:20-23, 10:4-21*

Hosea's vision, "When Israel was a child *Hos 11:1-4*

Zephaniah's promise to daughter of Zion *Zeph 3:14-17*

Jesus' sermon on benevolence in secret *Mat 6:1-4*

Jesus' golden rule for actions *Mat 7:12-14, Luke 6:41, 42*

Jesus raises Jairus' daughter *Mat 9:18, 19, 23-26, Mark 5:22-24, 35-43, Luke 8:41, 42, 49-56*

Jesus heals multitudes *Mat 14:14, 15:29-32, Luke 22:50, 51*

Jesus' parable of lost sheep *Mat 18:12-14, Luke 15:1-7*

Jesus' parable of debtor unmerciful to fellows *Mat 18:23-35*

Jesus raises son of widow of Nain *Luke 7:11-17*

Jesus' parable of good Samaritan *Luke 10:25-37*

Jesus' parable of the prodigal's father *Luke 15:11-32*

Jesus saves the woman taken in adultery *John 8:1-11*

Jesus' parable of rich man and beggar at his gate *Luke 16:19-31*

Jesus' parable of good shepherd *John 10:1-18*

Jesus on Christ as the good shepherd *John 10:1-38*

Paul on charity *1 Cor 13:1-13*

John on love one another *1 John 4:1-21*

See also comforter, fellowship, grace, love, mercy, pity

COMPETITION

Cain and Abel compete for God's favor *Gen 4:1-16*

Abraham refuses to compete with Lot *Gen 13:1-18*

Isaac's herdsmen strive over wells *Gen 26:12-31*

Jacob intercepts the blessing intended for Esau *Gen 27:1-44*

Moses hears Eldad and Medad prophesy *Num 11:16-30*

Moses attacked by his brother and sister *Num 12:1-16*

Saul is jealous of David's success *1 Sam 18:1-16*

Esther helps Mordecai defeat Haman *Esther 3:1-15, 6:1-14, 7:1-10*

Job is the prize between God and Satan *Job 1:1-12, 2:1-10*

Daniel is attacked by courtiers *Dan 6:1-28*

Jesus' disciples contend who shall be greatest *Mat 18:1-11, Mark 9:33-37, Luke 9:46-50, 22:24-30*

Jesus' parable of laborers in vineyard *Mat 20:1-16*

Jesus approached by Zebedee's wife for her sons *Mat 20:20-28, Mark 10:35-45*

Jesus' parable of ten virgins *Mat 25:1-13*

Jesus hears Martha complain of her sister *Luke 10:38-42*

Jesus' parable of chief seats at wedding *Luke 14:7-14*

Jesus' parable of prodigal and elder son *Luke 15:25-32*

Jesus' parable of Pharisee and publican *Luke 18:9-14*

Paul's sermon on envy and strife *1 Cor 3:1-17*

John's vision of war in heaven *Rev 12:1-17*

See also adversary, business, envy, jealousy, war

COMPLAINT

Moses complains of his speaking ability *Exod 4:10-17*

Moses watches Israelites make bricks without straw *Exod 5:7-19*

Moses hears murmurs on lack of food *Exod 16:1-36, 17:1-7, Num 11:1-15, 31, 32*

Zelophehad's daughters' complaint about inheritance *Num 27:1-11, 36:5-13*

Nathan complains to David about Uriah's death *2 Sam 12:1-10*

Elijah complains of discouragement *1 King 19:1-8*

Job complains of his suffering *Job 3:1-26*

The Preacher complains of vanity *Eccl 1:1-18, 2:1-26*

Ezekiel answers complaint of heredity *Ezek 18:1-32*

Jonah complains of God's treatment of him *Jonah 4:1-11*

Jesus' parable of workers in vineyard *Mat 20:1-16*

Jesus hears Martha complain about Mary *Luke 10:38-42*

Jesus' parable of elder brother *Luke 15:25-32*

Jesus' parable of judge and widow *Luke 18:1-8*

See also condemnation, grief, joy, pain, rejoicing

COMPROMISE

Adam and Eve eat of the knowledge of good an evil *Gen 3:1-24*

Moses returns to find people worshipping golden calf *Exod 32:1-24*

Moses offers people choice—good or evil *Deut 30:11-20*

Joshua offers same choice *Josh 24:1-25*

Samuel resists people's demand for a king and then accepts *1 Sam 8:1-22, 10:1-8*

David to obtain Bathsheba, has her husband killed *2 Sam 11:1-27*

Daniel refuses to compromise his principles *Dan 1:1-21, 6:1-28, 9:20-23, 10:4-21*

Jesus accepts baptism by John *Mat 3:13-17, Mark 1:9-11*

Jesus shows no man can serve two masters *Mat 6:22-24, Luke 16:13, 14*

Jesus' parable of wheat and tares *Mat 13:24-30, 36-43*

Jesus' parable of dragnet *Mat 13:47-50*

Peter breaks his vow and denies he knows Jesus *Mat 26:57, 58, 69-72, Mark 14:66-72, Luke 22:54-62, John 18:13-18, 25-27*

Jesus heals a deaf mute *Mark 7:32-37*

Jesus heals man born blind *John 9:1-41*

See also agreement, character, danger, idolatry, principle, righteousness

CONDEMNATION

Adam condemned to work *Gen 3:6-24*

Cain condemned to wander *Gen 4:1-16*

Moses condemns Israel for worship of golden calf *Exod 32:1-24*

Balak hires Balaam to curse Israel *Num 22:1-41, 23:1-30, 24:1-25*

Jotham's parable of trees *Judg 9:1-15*

Samuel declares Saul unfit to be king *1 Sam 15:7-26*

David blamed by Nathan's parable *2 Sam 12:1-10*

Hezekiah reproached for showing his treasure *2 King 20:12-21, Isa 39:1-8*

Nehemiah reproaches conspirators *Neh 6:1-19*

Job reproached by God *Job 38:1-41*

Isaiah's parable of wild grapes *Isa 5:1-8*

Isaiah rebukes hypocrisy *Isa 29:11-24, 30:1-3, 20, 21*

Daniel reads handwriting on wall *Dan 5:1-31*

Jonah's disobedience rebuked by trials *Jonah 1:1-17*

Jesus reproves three cities *Mat 11:20-30*

Jesus admonishes Peter *Mat 16:21-28, Mark 8:31-38, Luke 9:20-27, John 21:20-22*

Jesus' parable of farmers who refused rent *Mat 21:33-46, Mark 12:1-12, Luke 20:9-19*

Jesus' parable of wedding garment *Mat 22:1-14*

Jesus reproves Pharisees *Mat 23:1-39, Mark 12:38-40, Luke 11:37-54, 20:45-47, John 8:33-59*

Jesus' parable of foolish virgins *Mat 25:1-13*

Jesus' parable of talents *Mat 25:14-30, Luke 19:11-28*

Jesus' parable of sheep and goats *Mat 25:31-46*

Jesus reproves Peter with a look *Luke 22:54-62*

Judas condemns himself *Mat 27:3-10, Acts 1:15-20*

Jesus' parable of unjust steward *Luke 16:1-14*

Jesus' parable condemns Pharisee's prayer *Luke 18:9-14*

Jesus does not condemn adulteress *John 8:1-11*

Peter rebukes Simon for his offer to buy healing power *Acts 8:14-25*

See also complaint, guilt, judgment, rebuke

CONFESSION

Adam and Eve confess disobedience *Gen 3:6-24*

Cain avoids confession of murder *Gen 4:1-16*

David repents of killing Uriah *2 Sam 12:1-10*

Jeroboam repents *1 King 12:32, 33, 13:1-10*

Preacher confesses mortal life is vain *Eccl 1:1-18, 2:1-26*

Jonah confesses his disobedience *Jonah 2:1-10*

Peter acknowledges Jesus as Christ *Mat 16:13-20, Mark 8:27-30, Luke 9:18-21*

Jesus' parable of two debtors forgiven *Luke 7:36-50*

Jesus' parable of prodigal son *Luke 15:11-24*

Jesus' parable of prayer of publican *Luke 18:9-14*

John Baptist testifies that Jesus is Christ *John 1:15-34*

John Baptist confesses difference of Jesus' preaching *John 3:22-36*

Thomas acknowledges Jesus as risen *John 20:24-29*

Ethiopian eunuch acknowledges Jesus as Son of God *Acts 8:26-40*

See also acknowledge, church, denial, remorse, revelation, sin

CONFIDENCE

Noah builds the ark of safety *Gen 6:5-22*

Isaac trusts his father *Gen 22:1-19*

Jacob's fear is overcome *Gen 32:1-32*

The people trust Moses to lead them through the Red Sea *Exod 14:5-31*

Gideon develops confidence in God's direction *Judg 6:19-40*

David runs to meet Goliath *1 Sam 17:38-52*

Shunammite in distress still says, "It is well" *2 King 4:8-37*

Job refuses to blame God *Job 2:1-10*

David's song, "The Lord is my shepherd" *Psal 23:1-6*

David's song, put trust under his wings *Psal 36:1-12*

David's song, "The secret place of the most High" *Psal 91:1-16*

David's song, The safety of the godly *Psal 121:1-8*

In prison Jeremiah buys a field in Israel *Jer 32:2, 6-27, 37-44*

Jesus heals centurion's servant, admires his faith *Mat 8:5-13, Luke 7:1-10*

Jesus heals Syrophenician's daughter *Mat 15:21-28, Mark 7:24-30*

Jesus on the coming resurrection *Mat 26:31-35*

Jesus on unity and eternity of Christ *John 8:12-59*

Jesus' parable of the good shepherd *John 10:1-18*

Paul heals Eutychus of accidental fall *Acts 20:7-12*

Paul's sermon on source of supply *2 Cor 8:11-15, 9:6-15*

See also belief, comfort, doubt, expectation, **faith**, fear, trust, understanding

CONFIRMATION

Noah sends forth the raven and the dove *Gen 8:1-22*

The covenant is repeated to Noah *Gen 9:1-17*

The rainbow as a token to Noah *Gen 9:12-17*

Abram and Sarai receive new names *Gen 17:1-9, 15-22*

Covenant with Abraham and Isaac renewed to Jacob *Gen 35:9-15*

Moses' song of mercy confirms God's care *Deut 32:1-47*

Gideon asks for signs from Lord God *Judg 6:19-40*

John Baptist sends to Jesus for proof he is Christ *Mat 11:2-19, Luke 7:18-35*

Jesus confirms his words with the resurrection *Mat 28:1-8, Mark 16:1-8, Luke 24:1-12, John 20:1-14*

At Pentecost the promised Holy Ghost descends *Acts 2:1-13*

Paul on Jesus' resurrection proves our resurrection *1 Cor 15:1-58*

See also acknowledge, assurance, confession, proof, strength, truth

CONFLICT

See competition, struggle

CONFUSION

Tower of Babel falls *Gen 11:1-9*

Isaac takes Jacob to be Esau *Gen 27:1-44*

Moses' leadership is challenged by Miriam and Aaron *Num 12:1-16*

Saul's troubled spirit *1 Sam 16:14-23*

Elijah flees to juniper tree *1 King 19:1-8*

Solomon looks to source of wisdom *Prov 3:13-26, 4:1-13, 8:1-36*

Isaiah's vision of fall of Babylon *Isa 14:4-8, 12-17, 25-27*

John Baptist sends to Jesus for proof *Mat 11:2-19, Luke 7:18-35*

Herod thinks Jesus is John returned *Mat 14:1-13, Mark 6:14-29, Luke 9:7-9*

Jesus when risen is not recognized *Mark 16:9-11, Luke 24:13-35, John 20:11-18*

Peter returns to his vocation *Mat 28:16-18, John 21:1-14*

Paul and Barnabas worshipped as gods *Acts 14:11-18*

See also defeat, error, language, order

CONGREGATION

Israelites complain for lack of food *Exod 16:1-36, Num 11:1-15, 31, 32*

People worship the golden calf *Exod 32:1-24*

The chosen people to be set apart as God's own *Deut 7:6-11*

Solomon dedicates the temple for the congregation *1 King 8:27-66, 2 Chron 6:1-42*

Book of the law read to people in the street *Neh 8:1-12*

Jesus heals withered hand before congregation *Mat 12:9-13, Mark 3:1-5, Luke 6:6-11*

Jesus reads scripture to congregation *Mark 1:21-28, Luke 4:14-24*

See also church, worship

CONQUEROR

Enoch overcomes death by translation *Gen 5:18, 21-24, Heb 11:5*

Abraham blessed after victory over kings *Gen 14:8-20*

Aaron's rod swallows sorcerers' rods *Exod 7:1-12*

Jericho falls to children of Israel *Josh 6:1-27*

Gideon routs enemy *Judg 7:1-25*

David kills Goliath *1 Sam 17:38-52*

Elijah defeats 450 prophets of Baal *1 King 18:17-40*

Jehoshaphat learns "battle is not your's, but God's" *2 Chron 20:1-32*

Isaiah on Christ's peaceable kingdom *Isa 11:1-12*

Jesus shows mastery by raising Lazarus *John 11:1-46*

Jesus' own resurrection *Mat 28:1-8, Mark 16:1-8, Luke 24:1-12, John 20:1-10*

See also defeat, master, obstacle, power, tyranny, victory

CONSCIENCE

Adam and Eve hide from the Lord
Gen 3:6-24

Cain has no conscience about murder
Gen 4:1-16

Moses appoints judges to help him
Exod 18:13-27

David mourns the sickness of his
child   2 Sam 12:13-23

David's song on the happiness of the
godly   Psal 1:1-6

Solomon's wisdom   Prov 3:13-26, 4:
1-13, 8:1-36

Jesus' parable of the mote and the
beam   Mat 7:3-5, Luke 6:37-42

Jesus' parable of the unclean spirit
returning   Mat 12:42-45, Luke 11:
24-26

Jesus mistaken for John Baptist by
Herod   Mat 14:1-13, Mark 6:14-
29, Luke 9:7-9

Jesus tells what defiles a man   Mat
15:1-20, Mark 7:1-23

Peter denies Jesus   Mat 26:57, 58,
69-72, Mark 14:66-72, Luke 22:54-62,
John 18:13-18, 25-27

Pilate washes his hands   Mat 27:15-
26, Mark 15:6-15, Luke 23:13-25

Jesus sees widow cast in her mite
Mark 12:41-44, Luke 21:1-4

Jesus' parable of the prodigal son
Luke 15:11-24

Jesus casts traders out of temple
John 2:13-25

Jesus saves the woman taken in
adultery   John 8:1-11

Peter and John demand to be heard
Acts 4:1-23

Stephen martyred for his beliefs
Acts 7:51-60

Paul persecutes Christians as a matter of conscience   Acts 8:1-4

Peter accepts Gentiles   Acts 10:1-48,
11:1-18

Paul's sermon to come out and be
separate   2 Cor 6:1-18

See also character, goodness, heart,
morality, remorse, soul

CONSCIOUSNESS

God creates man in his image   Gen
1:26, 27

Moses at the burning bush   Exod
3:1-18

Moses demands a choice by the
people   Deut 30:11-20

Job asks why the good man should
suffer   Job 3:1-26

David's song, "What is man?"   Psal
8:1-9

David's song, "Why art thou cast
down?"   Psal 42:1-11

The vanity of human things   Eccl
1:1-18, 2:1-26

Mortal events all within time   Eccl
3:1-15

Isaiah's vision of God's glory   Isa
6:1-13

Isaiah urges man to fear not   Isa
43:1-28, 44:1-24

Jesus on taking thought   Mat 6:
25-34

Jesus on being born again   John
3:1-21

Jesus' discourse with woman of Samaria   John 4:1-30

Jesus' parable of the true vine   John
15:1-17

The conversion of Paul   Acts 8:1-4,
9:1-22

Paul's teaching, "Put on the new
man"   Col 3:1-17

See also awakening, man, psychology

CONSECRATION

Aaron and sons consecrated to
priesthood   Lev 8:1-13

Samuel consecrated to Lord by his
mother   1 Sam 1:1-28, 3:1-10

David promises a temple   1 Chron
17:1-27

Solomon dedicates temple   1 King
8:22-66, 2 Chron 6:1-42

Solomon's proverb on the work of
a good woman   Prov 31:1-31

Isaiah envisions the office of Christ
Isa 42:1-12, 16-18, 61:1-11, 62:
1-12

Zechariah's vision of two anointed
ones   Zech 4:1-14

Jesus overcomes temptation by Satan
Mat 4:1-11, Luke 4:1-13

Jesus on letting light shine   Mat 5:
13-16, Luke 8:16-18

Jesus, "Seek ye first"   Mat 6:25-34

A scribe volunteers to follow Jesus
Mat 8:18-22

Jesus' parable of pearl of great price
Mat 13:45, 46

Jesus' transfiguration *Mat 17:1-13, Mark 9:2-13, Luke 9:28-36*

Jesus' parable of ten virgins *Mat 25:1-13*

Peter vows never to deny Jesus *Mat 26:31-35, Mark 14:27-31, Luke 22: 31-34, John 13:36-38*

Simon and Anna watching for the Christ *Luke 2:21-38*

Jesus' parable of watchful servants *Luke 12:35-40*

Jesus' parable of faithful steward *Luke 12:41-48*

Jesus' parable on counting the cost *Luke 14:25-33*

Jesus on being born again *John 3:1-21*

Jesus sets example by washing disciples' feet *John 13:1-20*

Jesus' parable of true vine *John 15:1-17*

Jesus charges Peter, "feed my sheep" *John 21:12-19*

A new apostle consecrated by election *Acts 1:15-26*

Paul on cost of establishing church *Acts 20:17-38, 2 Cor 11:21-33*

Paul on faithfulness *2 Cor 6:1-28*

Paul on many Christian precepts *1 Thess 5:1-28*

Paul on advice to disciple *2 Tim 2:1-26*

Paul on charge to faithful *2 Tim 4: 1-8*

Paul on atonement *Heb 10:1-39*

Paul on example left by Jesus *Heb 12:1-29*

See also anointing, church, dedication, sacrament

CONSENT

See agreement, harmony

CONSISTENCY

Two stories of creation differ *Gen 1:1-31, 2:6-25*

The rod of Aaron, the chief priest, blossoms *Num 17:1-11*

Balaam cannot curse whom God has blessed *Num 22:1-41, 23:1-30, 24: 1-25*

Gideon's faith built by signs of God *Judg 6:19-40*

Job refuses to blame God *Job 2: 1-10*

Jeremiah in prison but he buys a field in Israel for he has foretold the restoration *Jer 32:2, 6-27, 37-44*

Three Jews refuse to worship an image *Dan 3:1-30*

Jesus' parable of the mote and the beam *Mat 7:1-5, Luke 6:37-42*

John Baptist sends to Jesus for proof of Christ *Mat 11:2-19, Luke 7:18-35*

Jesus' parable of the unmerciful debtor *Mat 18:23-35*

Jesus' parable of hiring laborers *Mat 20:1-16*

Peter vows never to deny Jesus, but breaks his word *Mat 26:31-35, 57, 58, 69-75, Mark 14:27-31, 66-72, Luke 22:31-34, 54-62, John 13:36-38, 18:13-18, 25-27*

Jesus' last words to preach to all the world and signs will follow *Mark 16:15-18*

Jesus' parable of new wine in new bottles *Luke 5:36-39*

Jesus' discourse that God is Spirit and must be worshipped spiritually *John 4:1-30, 39-42*

Paul's sermon, on Jesus' resurrection proving our resurrection *1 Cor 15:1-58*

See also agreement, harmony, logic, proof

CONSOLATION

Jacob is promised God's presence *Gen 28:10-22*

Caleb's reward 40 years later *Josh 14:6-15*

Ruth consoles her mother-in-law *Ruth 1:1-22*

Job's friends no help to him *Job 16:1-22*

David's song, "The Lord is my shepherd" *Psal 23:1-6*

Isaiah promises birth of Messiah *Isa 7:10-16, 9:2-7*

Isaiah's promise of desert blossoming *Isa 35:1-10*

Isaiah's promise of comfort *Isa 40: 1-31*

Jeremiah's promise of Jerusalem restored *Jer 31:1-14, 31-34*

Ezekiel's vision of God's care *Ezek 34:1-31*

Daniel's vision of meeting with Gabriel *Dan 9:20-23, 10:4-21*

Jesus raises son of widow of Nain *Luke 7:11-17*

Jesus' parable of prodigal's elder brother *Luke 15:25-32*

Jesus' parable of good shepherd *John 10:1-18*

Jesus promises Holy Spirit (Ghost) *John 14:1-31*

Jesus' prayer for his disciples and their disciples *John 17:1-26*

Descent of Holy Spirit (Ghost) *Acts 2:1-13*

John's sermon, "God is love" *1 John 4:1-21*

See also comfort, grief, loss, mourning, repentance

CONSPIRACY

Eve persuaded by serpent to disobey *Gen 3:1-5*

Jacob and his mother deceive Isaac *Gen 27:1-44*

Joseph's brother plan his destruction *Gen 37:1-36*

Aaron and Miriam plan to overthrow Moses *Num 12:1-16*

Conspirators against Nehemiah fail *Neh 6:1-19*

Esther foils plot of Haman against Mordecai *Esther 6:1-14, 7:1-10*

Jesus denounces scribes and Pharisees *Mat 23:1-39*

Judas betrays him *Mat 26:14-16, Mark 14:10, 11, Luke 22:1-6*

Jesus rebukes Pharisees' plot against him *Luke 12:1-15*

Caiaphas urges council to put Jesus to death *John 11:47-54*

Paul on enemies of the truth *2 Tim 3:1-17*

See also alliance, betrayal, plot, rebellion

CONSTITUTION

See body, government

CONTAGION

Moses commands to put lepers out *Lev 13:1-59*

Moses heals plague in wilderness *Num 16:3-5, 44-50*

Elisha heals Naaman the leper *2 King 5:1-14*

Elisha is disobeyed by Gehazi who catches leprosy *2 King 5:15-27*

Hezekiah saved by epidemic among besiegers *2 Chron 31:20, 21, 32: 1-23, Isa 36:1-22, 37:1-38*

Jesus touches leper and heals him *Mat 8:1-4, Mark 1:40-45, Luke 5: 12-16*

Jesus on what defiles *Mat 15:1-20, Mark 7:1-23*

Jesus heals ten lepers *Luke 17:11-19*

Pentecost—contagion of good *Acts 2:1-13*

Peter's success causes church growth *Acts 4:24-37*

See also communication, disease, infection, plague

CONTENTMENT

God saw his creation was very good *Gen 1:31*

Noah sees rainbow a token that God is pleased *Gen 9:12-17*

Moses' song of deliverance *Deut 32:1-47*

Caleb content with his portion of land *Josh 14:6-15*

Deborah's song of rejoicing *Judg 5:1-20*

David's song of thanksgiving *2 Sam 22:1-51, 1 Chron 16:17-36*

Solomon receives Sheba's praise *1 King 10:1-12, 2 Chron 9:1-12*

Job before and after his trials *Job 1:1-12, 42:1-17*

David's song of the good man *Psal 1:1-6*

David's song of goodness of the Lord *Psal 33:1-22*

David's song, "make a joyful noise" *Psal 66:1-20, 100:1-5*

Isaiah's vision of the peaceable kingdom *Isa 11:1-12*

Micah's vision of glory of church *Mic 4:1-8, 13*

Jesus on letting your light shine *Mat 5:13-16, Luke 8:16-18*

Jesus on taking no thought for things *Mat 6:25-34*

Jesus' parable of laborers in vineyard   *Mat 20:1-16*

Jesus' prayer is answered at Gethsemane   *Mat 25:30, 36-46, Mark 14:26, 32-42, Luke 22:39-46*

Mary magnifies the Lord for coming birth   *Luke 1:26-38*

Simon content to die after seeing Christ child   *Luke 2:21-38*

Jesus' parable of prodigal's elder brother   *Luke 15:25-32*

Jesus' parable of rich man at ease in matter   *Luke 16:19-31*

Jesus' parable of servant   *Luke 17:7-10*

Paul content despite his trials   *Acts 20:17-38*

Paul on rejoicing   *Phil 4:1-23*

John's vision of tree of life and twelve fruits   *Rev 22:1-21*

See also complaint, happiness, joy, satisfaction

CONTINGENCY

Noah prepares for the flood   *Gen 7:1-24*

Jacob fears retribution by his brother   *Gen 32:1—33:11*

Joseph prepares for famine   *Gen 41:1-46*

Food supplied in wilderness   *Exod 16:1-36, Num 11:1-15, 31, 32*

Moses warns against idolatry   *Deut 13:1-18*

David selects five stones for his sling   *1 Sam 17:38-52*

Nehemiah arms builders of wall   *Neh 4:1-23*

Job's integrity tested   *Job 1:1-22*

Isaiah's vision of Christ's peaceable kingdom   *Isa 11:12, 35:1-10*

Jesus foresees raising temple in three days   *John 2:19-22*

Jesus' plan for tares among wheat   *Mat 13:24-30, 36-43*

Jesus' advice on healing difficult cases   *Mat 17:14-21, Mark 9:14-29, Luke 9:37-43*

Jesus' parable of lost sheep   *Mat 18:23-35, Luke 15:1-7*

Jesus' parable of good Samaritan   *Luke 10:25-37*

Jesus' parable of unwilling friend   *Luke 11:5-13*

Jesus' parable of rich fool   *Luke 12:15-21*

Jesus' parable on counting the cost   *Luke 14:25-33*

Paul on supply and demand as reciprocal   *2 Cor 8:11-15*

Paul on qualities that protect   *Eph 6:10-17*

Paul warns against enemies of the truth   *2 Tim 3:1-17*

Paul on true sacrifice to save from sin   *Heb 10:1-39*

James on how to bear our cross   *Jas 1:12-27*

James on faith without works   *Jas 2:14-26*

See also accident, chance, possibility, preparation, reward

CONTRACT

Jacob buys Esau's birthright   *Gen 25:24-34*

Joseph appointed to save Egypt from famine   *Gen 41:1-46*

Moses promises salvation by obeying Ten Commandments   *Exod 20:1-19, Deut 5:1-24*

Gideon agrees to trust on basis of signs   *Judg 6:19-40*

Soul of Jonathan knit with David   *1 Sam 18:1-16*

David promises to build a house for God   *2 Sam 7:1-29*

Elijah assures Elisha of double his spirit   *2 King 2:1-15*

The Lord and Satan wager on Job   *Job 1:1-12*

Jeremiah in prison but he buys a field in Israel   *Jer 32:2, 6-27, 37-44*

Daniel makes pact with Melzar for ten days   *Dan 1:1-21*

Malachi urges tithing for rewards   *Mal 3:10, 4:1, 2*

Satan offers Jesus reward for obeisance   *Mat 4:1-11, Mark 1:12, 13, Luke 4:1-13*

Jesus' parable of unmerciful debtor   *Mat 18:23-35*

Jesus' parable of laborers in the vineyard   *Mat 20:1-16*

Jesus' parable of husbandmen who refuse rent   *Mat 21:33-46, Mark 12:1-12, Luke 20:9-19*

God fulfills his promise to Simon and Anna   *Luke 2:21-38*

Jesus' parable of the unjust steward   *Luke 16:1-14*

See also agreement, covenant, marriage, promise

CONTROL

Joseph overcomes temptation   *Gen 39-1-20*

Israelites escape, directed by pillars of cloud and fire   *Exod 13:20-22, Num 9:15-23*

Moses' hands upheld to win battle   *Exod 17:8-16*

Joshua encompassed Jericho   *Josh 6:1-27*

Joshua sees sun and moon stand still   *Josh 10:6-15*

Gideon demands signs of God's control   *Judg 6:19-40*

Jehoshaphat says battle is the Lord's   *2 Chron 20:1-32*

Elijah prays for rain   *1 King 18:41-46*

Elijah divides water of Jordan   *2 King 2:8*

Elisha divides water of Jordan   *2 King 2:12-15*

Elisha causes iron to swim   *2 King 6:1-7*

David's song, "The law of the Lord is perfect"   *Psal 19:1-14, 46:1-11*

Isaiah's vision of Christ's peaceable kingdom   *Isa 11:1-12*

Isaiah's vision that the desert will blossom   *Isa 35:1-10*

Isaiah's vision, "The Lord's hand is not shortened"   *Isa 59:1-21*

Jeremiah, the potter and the clay   *Jer 18:1-6*

Ezekiel sees resurrection of dry bones   *Ezek 37:1-14*

Jonah disobeys, is corrected and turned in God's direction   *Jonah 1:1-17, 2:1-10, 3:1-10*

Jesus is tempted   *Mat 4:1-11, Mark 1:12, 13, Luke 4:1-13*

Jesus calms wind and sea   *Mat 8:23-27, Mark 4:35-41, Luke 8:22-25*

Jesus on son of man as Lord of the sabbath   *Mat 12:1-8*

Jesus' parable of wheat and tares   *Mat 13:24-30, 36-43*

Jesus' parable of dragnet   *Mat 13:47-50*

Jesus walks on water   *Mat 14:22-33, John 6:15-21*

Jesus' control over time   *Mat 17:1-13, Mark 9:2-13, Luke 9:28-36*

Jesus appears after resurrection   *Mat 28:16-20, Mark 16:1-18, John 21:12-25*

Jesus puts ship at destination at once   *Mark 6:32-45, John 6:21*

Jesus delivered by passing through enemies   *Luke 4:28-32*

Jesus turns water to wine   *John 2:1-11*

Jesus reveals his great works have their source in the Father   *John 5:17-47*

James on temptation and trials   *Jas 1:1-27*

James on faith without works   *Jas 2:14-26*

See also government, guidance, reconciliation

CONVENTION

See custom

CONVERSION

Esau after hating Jacob forgives him   *Gen 33:1-11*

Moses complains of inability to persuade the Israelites   *Exod 4:10-17*

Moses' success after passover   *Exod 11:4-10, 12:1-14, 21-41, Deut 16:1-22*

Rahab converted to help Israelites   *Josh 2:1-24*

Gideon's faith developed by three signs   *Judg 6:19-40*

Ruth follows her mother-in-law's religion   *Ruth 1:1-22*

Nathan's parable turns King David   *2 Sam 12:1-10*

Elijah finds Elisha plowing   *1 King 19:19-21*

David's song, the law of the Lord that converts the soul   *Psal 19:1-14*

Isaiah's vision of Jerusalem redeemed   *Isa 52:1-15*

Jeremiah's vision of restoration of Israel *Jer 31:1-14, 31-34*

Jonah finally obeys God *Jonah 2: 1-10, 3:1-10*

Jesus calls his disciples *Mat 4:17-22, Mark 1:14-20, Luke 5:1-11, John 1:35-42*

Jesus' parable of the lost sheep recovered *Mat 18:12-14, Luke 15: 1-7*

Jesus' parable of prodigal son *Luke 15:11-24*

Jesus causes Zacchaeus to repent *Luke 19:1-10*

Jesus on being born again *John 3: 1-21*

Jesus recognized as Christ by woman of Samaria *John 4:1-42*

Jesus convinces Thomas he has risen *John 20:24-29*

Peter's experience causes growth of church *Acts 4:24-37*

Paul from Jew to Christian *Acts 8:1-5, 9:1-9, 10-22*

Philip converts Simon *Acts 8:9-13*

Philip converts Ethiopian *Acts 8: 26-40*

Peter converts Cornelius a Roman *Acts 10:1-48*

Peter defends conversion of Gentiles *Acts 11:1-18*

Paul converts Lydia *Acts 16:7-15*

Paul and Silas convert their jailer *Acts 16:19-40*

Paul tells of his own conversion *Acts 22:1-30, 26:1-32*

See also birth, chance, purity, redemption, repentance, sin

CONVICTION

Noah convinced of a coming flood, builds ark *Gen 6:5-22*

Moses overcomes self-depreciation at God's word *Exod 3:9-12, 4: 1-9*

Moses persuades Israelites to go forward through the Red Sea *Exod 14:5-31*

Gideon convinced by God he can defeat Midianites *Judg 6:19-40*

Elisha hears Shunammite say, "It is well" *2 King 4:8-37*

Elisha heals Naaman despite his resistance *2 King 5:1-14*

David psalm of trust in God *Psal 36:1-12*

Jeremiah in prison buys field in Israel *Jer 32: 2, 6-27, 37-44*

Jeremiah prophesies captivity will be turned *Jer 29:8-14*

Hebrew boys enter fiery furnace without fear *Dan 3:1-30*

Daniel goes to lions' den calmly *Dan 6:1-28*

Jonah convinced he must do God's word *Jonah 2:1-10*

John Baptist sends to. Jesus for proof *Mat 11:2-19, Luke 7:18-35*

Peter acknowledges Jesus as Christ *Mat 16:13-20, Mark 8:27-30, Luke 9:18-31*

Jesus appears after crucifixion *Mat 28:16-20, Mark 16:12-18, Luke 24: 13-49*

Jesus seen by two disciples at Emmaus *Mark 16:12, 13, Luke 24:13-35, 1 Cor 15:15*

Peter's net filled *Luke 5:1-11*

Jesus convinces woman of Samaria he is Christ *John 4:1-30, 39-42*

Jesus heals man born blind *John 9:1-41*

Doubting Thomas convinced *John 20:24-29*

Peter and John speak the word and risk prison *Acts 4:24-37*

Philip's healings convince witnesses *Acts 8:9-13*

See also belief, doubt, faith, proof, understanding

COOPERATION

Moses' hands upheld by Aaron and Hur *Exod 17:8-16*

Rahab cooperates with spies in Jericho *Josh 2:1-24*

Deborah and Barak work together to defeat Sisera *Judg 4:1-17*

Gideon's 300 men cooperate to defeat host *Judg 7:1-25*

Ruth and Naomi try to reestablish themselves *Ruth 2:1-22*

Jonathan protects David *1 Sam 18: 1-16*

Nehemiah's workers build the wall *Neh 4:1-23*

Esther works with her uncle to defeat his enemy *Esther 5:1-14, 6:1-14, 7:1-10*

Malachi urges tithing *Mal 3:10, 4: 1, 2*

Jesus' oneness with Father *Mat 6: 22-24, John 5:17-47*

Peter calls for help to get the fish ashore *Luke 5:1-11*

Jesus' parable of good Samaritan *Luke 10:25-37*

Jesus hears Martha complain of Mary's lack of cooperation *Luke 10:38-42*

Jesus' parable of faithful steward *Luke 12:41-48*

Jesus promises Holy Ghost *John 14:1-31*

Early Christians hold things in common *Acts 2:14-47*

Paul and Barnabas establish church at Antioch *Acts 11:19-26*

Paul and Silas free themselves from prison *Acts 16:19-40*

Paul's sermon on unity of us all *Eph 4:1-32*

John's vision of earth helping the woman *Rev 12:1-17*

See also association, work

CORNERSTONE

Abraham promised that he will be the founder of a new nation *Gen 15:1-21*

Isaac receives the same promises *Gen 26:1-5*

Jacob calls sons to hear prophecy of tribes *Gen 49:1-28, Deut 33: 1-29*

Moses receives Ten Commandments on tablet of stone *Exod 20:1-19, Deut 5:1-24*

Solomon builds temple *1 King 6: 1-38, 7:1-51, 2 Chron 3:1-17, 4:1-22, 5:1-14*

Zerubbabel starts to rebuild temple *Ezek 3:8-13*

Jesus' parable of builders on rock and sand *Mat 7:24-27, Luke 6: 48, 49*

Simon renamed Peter (stone) *Mat 16:13-20, Mark 8:27-30, Luke 9: 18-21*

Jesus rolls away stone at tomb *Mat 28:2, Mark 16:1-4, Luke 24:1-3, John 20:1, 2*

Jesus on stone which builders rejected *Mark 12:10*

Jesus says he will raise temple in three days *John 2:19-22*

Paul on the master builder *1 Cor 3:4-17*

Paul on Christ, "The chief cornerstone" *Eph 2:15-22*

Peter on "I lay in Sion a chief corner stone" *1 Pet 2:1-9*

See also building, Christ, origin, purity, structure

CORPOREAL

Lord God makes man of dust *Gen 2:6-8*

Lord God makes woman from rib *Gen 2:21-25*

Moses finds people worshipping the golden calf *Exod 32:1-24*

Aaron seeks atonement through scapegoat *Lev 16:1-28*

David's song, "What is man?" *Psal 8:1-9*

David's song, "Why art thou cast down, O my soul?" *Psal 42:1-11*

The vanity of mortal life *Eccl 1: 1-18, 2:1-26*

Body culture is in vain *Isa 3:16-26*

The fall of Babylon *Isa 14:4-8, 12-17, 25-27*

Ezekiel's vision of children's teeth on edge *Ezek 18:1-32*

Daniel eats pulse instead of king's meat *Dan 1:1-21*

Daniel interprets dream of great image *Dan 2:1-49*

Daniel interprets dream of great tree *Dan 4:1-27*

Jesus heals withered hand *Mat 12: 9-13, Mark 3:1-5, Luke 6:6-11*

Jesus' parable of unclean spirit and seven others *Mat 12:43-45, Luke 11:24-26*

Jesus walks on water *Mat 14:22-33, John 6:15-21*

Jesus talks with Moses and Elijah *Mat 17:1-13, Mark 9:2-13, Luke 9: 28-36*

Jesus crucified *Mat 27:32-56, Mark 15:21-41, Luke 23:26-49, John 19: 17-30*

Resurrection *Mat 28:1-8, Mark 16: 1-8, Luke 24:1-12, John 20:1-10*

Jesus heals impotent man at pool
John 5:1-16

Risen body confirmed by Thomas
John 20:24-29

Paul's sermon on flesh vs. spirit
Rom 8:1-39

See also body, matter

CORRECTION

See discipline, punishment

CORRUPTION

The material view of creation *Gen
2:6-8, 3:1-24*

Noah alone is righteous *Gen 6:5-22*

Lot escapes Sodom *Gen 19:1, 15-29*

Moses finds Israelites worshipping
golden calf *Exod 32:1-24*

Moses warns of enticers *Deut 13:
1-18*

Moses forbids abominations *Deut
18:9-14*

Moses gives choice of good or evil
Deut 30:11-20

Rehoboam corrupted by wrong advice *1 King 12:1-18, 2 Chron 10:
1-19*

Elijah destroys 450 prophets of Baal
1 King 18:17-40

Preacher views the vanity of human
life *Eccl 1:1-18, 2:1-26*

Preacher views mortal events within time *Eccl 3:1-15*

Isaiah's parable of wild grapes *Isa
5:1-8*

Isaiah's vision of fall of Babylon
Isa 14:4-8, 12-17, 25-27

Isaiah's vision of hypocrisy punished
Isa 29:11-24, 30:1-3, 20, 21

Jeremiah's vision of good and bad
figs *Jer 24:1-10*

Jesus not corrupted by temptations
Mat 4:1-11, Luke 14:1-13

Jesus and the swine that are
drowned *Mat 8:30-34*

Jesus excoriates three wicked cities
Mat 11:20-24

Jesus' parable of unclean spirit *Mat
12:43-45, Luke 11:24-26*

Jesus' parable of wheat and tares
Mat 13:24-30, 36-43

Jesus on what defiles *Mat 15:1-20,
Mark 7:1-23*

Jesus casts traders out of temple
*Mat 21:12, 13, Mark 11:15-17, Luke
19:45, 46, John 2:13-25*

Jesus foretells destruction of temple
and Jerusalem *Mat 24:1-41, Mark
13:1-37, Luke 21:5-36*

Jesus' parable of sheep and goats
Mat 24:31-46

Judas settles price of betrayal *Mat
26:14-16, Mark 14:10, 11, Luke 22:
1-6*

Judas hangs himself *Mat 27:3-10,
Acts 1:15-20*

Jesus on corrupt men *Luke 11:
37-54*

Stephen reviews persecution of
prophets *Acts 7:1-53*

Peter refuses to sell Simon ability
to lay on hands *Acts 8:14-25*

Paul on anti-Christians *2 Tim 3:1-17*

See also adultery, crime, decay, sin

COUNSEL

See advice

COURAGE

Moses leads Israelites through Red
Sea *Exod 14:5-31*

Moses encourages Joshua to replace
him *Deut 31:7-23, Josh 1:1-9*

Joshua leads people through Jordan
into promised land *Josh 3:1-17*

Deborah leads her people to resist
Sisera *Judg 4:1-17*

David accepts Goliath's challenge
1 Sam 17:1-52

Nathan uncovers David's sin *2 Sam
12:1-10*

Elijah destroys 450 prophets of
Queen Jezebel *1 King 18:17-40*

Hezekiah urges resistance to invaders *2 King 18:17-37, 19:1-27,
2 Chron 32:1-23, Isa 36:1-22, 37:
1-38*

David's song on safety in God *Psal
91:1-16*

David's songs of encouragement
Psal 42:1-11, 46:1-11

Esther risks all to save her people
Esther 5:1-14

Daniel refuses portion of king's
food *Dan 1:1-21*

Hebrews face fiery furnace *Dan
3:1-30*

Daniel faces lions' den *Dan 6:1-28*

Jesus denounces scribes and Pharisees *Mat 23:1-39*

Peter lacks courage to acknowledge Jesus *Mat 26:57, 58, 69-75, Mark 14:66-72, Luke 22:54-62, John 18: 13-18, 25-27*

Jesus sets face towards Jerusalem and death *Luke 9:51-56, John 7: 1-13*

Jesus' parable on counting the cost *Luke 14:25-33*

Peter and John, free from prison, go back to preaching again *Acts 4:1-23*

Ananias, fearless of Paul, heals him *Acts 9:10-22*

Paul's review of trials shows his courage *Acts 20:17-38*

Paul's hardships show cost of establishing church *2 Cor 11:21-33*

Paul on Christian's armor *Eph 6: 10-17*

John's vision of war between woman and dragon *Rev 12:1-17*

See also danger, encouragement, fear, heart, spirit

COVENANT

Noah receives God's covenant *Gen 9:1-17*

Noah sees rainbow as token *Gen 9: 12-17*

Abraham receives God's pomises *Gen 15:1-21*

Isaac receives renewal of promise to Abraham *Gen 26:1-5*

Jacob and promise of ever-presence *Gen 28:13-15*

Moses is promised God's presence *Exod 3:9-12*

Israelites set apart as God's chosen people *Deut 7:6-11*

David and Jonathan swear friendship *1 Sam 18:1-5*

Jeremiah foretells end of captivity *Jer 29:8-14*

Jeremiah gives God's new covenant —to write laws in their hearts *Jer 31:1-14, 31-34, Heb 8:8-13*

Jesus gives his blood as cup of the new covenant *Mat 26:20-29, Mark 14:18-25, Luke 22:14-30, 1 Cor 11:20*

See also agreement, care, contract, promise

COVETOUSNESS

Tenth Commandment by Moses *Exod 20:17*

David covets Uriah's wife *2 Sam 11:1-27*

David is punished for his sin *2 Sam 12:13-23*

Ahab covets Naboth's vineyard *1 King 21:1-27*

Zebedee's wife requests seats next to Jesus for her sons *Mat 20:20-28, Mark 10:35-45*

Judas betrays Jesus *Mat 26:14-16, Mark 14:10, 11, Luke 22:1-6*

Jesus' parable of chief seats at wedding *Luke 14:7-14*

John's sermon on love *1 John 4:1-21*

See also envy, greed, jealousy, love, stealth

CREATION

God creates spiritual universe *Gen 1:1-31, 2:1-5*

Lord God creates material universe *Gen 2:6-25*

Abraham at 99 is promised a son *Gen 15:1-21*

Samson's birth announced to his mother *Judg 13:1-25*

Samuel's miraculous birth *1 Sam 1:1-28*

Job hears God explain creation *Job 38:1-41*

David's songs on the nature of God's universe *Psal 8:1-9, 33:1-22*

Jesus feeds 5000 *Mat 14:15-21, Mark 6:35-44, Luke 9:12-17, John 6:5-14*

Jesus feeds 4000 *Mat 15:32-39, Mark 8:1-10*

Jesus' resurrection *Mat 28:1-8, Mark 16:1-8, Luke 24:1-12, John 20:1-10*

Jesus says he is light of the world *John 1:1-14*

Jesus' birth announced by angel to Mary *Luke 1:26-38*

Jesus tells Nicodemus man must be born again *John 3:1-21*

Jesus on God as Spirit *John 4:1-30, 39-42*

Jesus on source of great works *John 5:17-47*

Jesus heals man born blind *John 9:1-41*

Paul's sermon on Unknown God *Acts 17:15-34*

Paul on creation *Rom 1:17-25*

John's vision of new heaven and earth *Rev 21:1-27*

See also building, cause, father, life, man, universe

CREATOR

The spiritual creation *Gen 1:1-31, 2:1-5*

The material creation *Gen 2:6—3:24*

At 99 years Abraham promised a son by God *Gen 15:1-21*

Moses meets great I Am at burning bush *Exod 3:1-18*

Samuel's miraculous birth *1 Sam 1:1-28*

David's song, "The earth is the Lord's" *Psal 24:1-10*

David's song, "Create in me a clean heart" *Psal 51:1-19*

Jesus one with the Father *Mat 6: 22-24, John 10:22-40*

Birth of Jesus announced to Mary *Luke 1:26-38*

In the beginning was the Word *John 1:1-14*

Destroyed temple to be raised in three days *John 2:19-22*

Jesus on being born again *John 3:1-21*

Paul on creator *Rom 1:17-25*

See also building, cause, evolution, father, God, life, word

CREED

Moses' farewell address on proper choices *Deut 30:11-20*

Book of the law read to the people *Neh 8:1-12*

Job continues to trust God *Job 2:1-10*

Jeremiah foresees restoration *Jer 31:1-14, 31-34*

Jesus' parable of the temple raised in three days *John 2:19-22*

Jesus' discourse that God is Spirit *John 4:1-30, 39-42*

Jesus on the bread of life *John 6: 26-65*

Jesus teaching that he is Christ *John 7:14-40*

Peter on resurrection and baptism *Acts 2:14-47*

Paul teaching that Jesus is Messiah *Acts 13:16-52*

Paul on love as highest value *1 Cor 13:1-13*

Paul on Jesus' resurrection proves our resurrection *1 Cor 15:1-58*

James on faith without works *Jas 2:14-26*

John on God is love *1 John 4:1-21*

See also belief, church, confession, doctrine, principle

CRIME

Cain murders Abel *Gen 4:1-16*

Joseph's brothers as juvenile delinquents *Gen 37:1-36*

Moses defines crime *Exod 20:1-19, Deut 5:1-24*

David arranges Uriah's death *2 Sam 11:1-27*

Nathan's parable uncovers crime *2 Sam 12:1-10*

Jesus on Golden Rule *Mat 7:12-14, Luke 6:41, 42*

John Baptist beheaded *Mat 14:3-12, Mark 6:17-29*

Jesus' parable of unclean spirit and seven others *Mat 12:43-45, Luke 11:24-26*

Jesus on defilement *Mat 15:1-20, Mark 7:1-23*

Jesus' parable of farmers who refuse rent *Mat 21:33-46, Mark 12:1-12, Luke 20:9-19*

Jesus betrayed by Judas *Mat 26: 14-16, Mark 14:10, 11, Luke 22:1-6*

Judas hangs himself *Mat 27:3-10, Acts 1:15-20*

Pilate offers Barabbas or Jesus to the crowd *Mat 27:15-26, Mark 15: 6-15, Luke 23:13-25, John 18:39, 40*

Jesus escapes enemies *Luke 4:28-31*

Caiaphas urges council to put Jesus to death *John 11:47-59*

Jesus causes guards to fall backwards *John 18:4-6*

Steven stoned but forgiving *Acts 7:51-60*

Four horsemen of Apocalypse *Rev 6:1-17*

John's vision of the dragon *Rev 12:1-17*

See also commandment, corruption, evil, law, sin

CRIPPLE

David shows kindness to Mephibosheth *2 Sam 9:1-13*

Jeroboam's withered hand healed *1 King 12:32, 33, 13:1-10*

Ezekiel's vision of resurrection of dry bones *Ezek 37:1-14*

Jesus heals withered hand *Mat 12:9-13, Mark 3:1-5, Luke 6:6-11*

Jesus heals group, maimed, lame, etc. *Mat 15:29-31*

Jesus heals woman bowed together *Luke 13:11-17*

Jesus heals Malchus' ear *Luke 22:50, 51*

Jesus heals impotent man at pool *John 5:1-16*

Peter and John heal man lame from birth *Acts 3:1-11*

Paul heals cripple while preaching *Acts 14:8-10*

See also deformity, healing, lameness

CRITICISM

Sarah causes Hagar to be sent away *Gen 21:9-21*

Moses criticized about lack of food *Exod 16:1-36, Num 11:1-15, 31, 32*

Miriam and Aaron criticize Moses *Num 12:1-16*

Balaam refuses to curse people of God *Num 22:1-46, 23:1-30, 24:1-25*

Joshua determines the fault *Josh 7:1-26, 8:14-21*

Jotham's parable criticizes desire for power *Judg 9:1-15*

Saul declared unfit by Samuel *1 Sam 15:7-26*

Daniel reads the handwriting on the wall *Dan 5:1-31*

Jesus blames cities for disregarding him *Mat 11:20-27*

Jesus criticized for healing on sabbath day *Mat 12:9-13, Mark 3:1-5, Luke 6:6-11*

Jesus criticized for healing *Mat 12:22-30, Mark 3:22-30, Luke 11:14-23*

Jesus' parable of hiring all laborers at same rate *Mat 20:1-16*

Jesus' parable of man without wedding garment *Mat 22:1-14*

Jesus castigates Pharisees and lawyers *Mat 23:1-39, Luke 11:37-54*

Jesus' parable of the barren fig tree *Luke 13:6-9*

Paul describes non-Christians *2 Tim 3:1-17*

See also condemnation, judgment, rebuke

CROSS

Abraham plans to sacrifice his son Isaac *Gen 22:1-19*

Isaiah's prophecy of "man of sorrow" *Isa 53:1-12*

Jesus prophesies his death *Mat 16:21-28, 17:22, 23, 20:17-19, Mark 8:31-38, 9:30-32, 10:32-34, Luke 9:20-27, 43-45, 18:31-34, John 12:20-50*

Peter, unable to face the cross, denies Jesus *Mat 26:57, 58, 69-75, Mark 14:66-72, Luke 22:54-62, John 18:13-18, 25-27*

Crucifixion *Mat 27:32-56, Mark 15:21-41, Luke 23:26-49, John 19:17-30*

Jesus' parable of temple to be raised in three days *John 2:19-22*

Jesus' parable of good shepherd who gives his life for the sheep *John 10:1-18*

Peter accuses high priests of crucifixion *Acts 4:1-23*

See also atonement, Christian, sacrifice, suffering, trials

CROWN

God creates man as his crowning achievement *Gen 1:1-31*

Saul anointed king by Samuel (a mistake) *1 Sam 10:1-8*

David made king of Judah *2 Sam 2:1-4*

David made king of Israel *2 Sam 5:1-5*

Isaiah's vision of Christ as Prince of Peace *Isa 9:2-7*

Jesus as baby received gifts from three kings *Mat 2:1-12*

Pilate asks if he is King of the Jews *Mat 27:1, 2, 11-14, Mark 15:1-5, Luke 23:1-5, John 18:28-38*

Resurrection, the crowning achievement *Mat. 28:1-8, Mark 16:1-8, Luke 24:1-12, John 20:1-10*

Jesus seen ascending to heaven *Mark 16:19, 20, Luke 24:50-53, Acts 1:9-13*

Peter's sermon on resurrection *Acts 2:14-47*

Paul on the prize for a race *1 Cor 9:24-27*

Paul's sermon on resurrection *1 Cor 15:1-58*

Paul on a crown laid up for him *2 Tim 4:1-8*

John's vision of woman crowned *Rev 12:1-17*

See also authority, dominion, king, power, victory

CUP

David's song, "The Lord is my shepherd" *Psal 23:1-6*

Daniel sees Belshazzar and his lords drink out of the vessels stolen from the temple *Dan 5:1-31*

Jesus urges a cup of cold water *Mat 10:42*

Jesus asks if his disciples can drink his cup *Mat 20:20-28, Mark 10:35-45*

Jesus urges scribes and Pharisees to clean whole cup *Mat 23:1-39, Mark 12:38-40, Luke 20:45-47*

Jesus asks that cup pass from him at Gethsemane *Mat 26:36-46, Mark 14:32-42, Luke 22:39-46*

Jesus passes the cup of communion *Mat 26:26-29, Mark 14:22-25, Luke 22:14-30*

Paul's sermon on cup of blessing *1 Cor 10:1-4, 16, 17*

See also atonement, blood, communion, cross, Last Supper, Passover, wine

CURE

See Part II, Elijah, Elisha, and Jesus Christ: Great Works

CUSTOM

Jesus selects Matthew, a customs collector *Mat 9:9-12, Mark 2:13-16, Luke 5:27-32*

Jesus circumcised by custom of law *Luke 2:25-33*

Jesus makes sabbath visit to synagogue *Luke 4:14-17*

See also practice, tradition

D

DAMNATION

See condemnation, judgment, punishment

DANGER

Noah and the flood *Gen 6:6-22*

Jacob fears retribution by Esau *Gen 32:1-32, 33:1-11*

Moses as baby escapes death *Exod 2:1-10*

Moses handles the serpent *Exod 4:1-8*

Pursued by Pharaoh's army with the sea in front *Exod 14:5-31*

David faces Goliath's challenge *1 Sam 17:1-16*

David pursued by the king's men *1 Sam 24:1-22*

Elijah flees for his life *1 King 19:1-8*

Elisha surrounded by Syrian army *2 King 6:8-23*

Hezekiah besieged by Sennacherib *2 King 18:17-37, 19:1-27, 2 Chron 31:20, 21, 32:1-23, Isa 36:1-22, 37:1-38*

Esther sues for her people's life *Esther 3:1-15, 4:1-17, 5:1-14*

David's security in God *Psal 91:1-16, 121:1-8, 139:1-24*

Ezekiel's vision of God's care *Ezek 34:1-31*

Hebrew boys in fiery furnace *Dan 3:1-30*

Daniel in lions' den *Dan 6:1-28*

The flight to Egypt *Mat 2:13-23, Luke 2:39, 40*

Jesus calms wind and sea *Mat 8:23-27, Mark 4:35-41, 6:45-52, Luke 8:22-25, John 6:21*

Jesus passes through the hostile crowd *Luke 4:28-31*
Peter imprisoned, released by angel *Acts 5:17-42, 12:1-17*
Stephen stoned to death *Acts 7: 51-60*
Paul let down over wall in a basket *Acts 9:23-31*
Paul stoned but recovers *Acts 14: 19, 20*
Paul's trials as Christian *Acts 20: 17-38*
Paul's shipwreck *Acts 27:1-44*
Paul's hardships to establish church *2 Cor 11:21-33*
Woman with child faces dragon *Rev 12:1-17*

See also courage, evil, deliverance, preservation, refuge, safety, trials

DANIEL

See Part II, Daniel

DARKNESS

The spirit of God moves in the darkness *Gen 1:1-31*
Isaac's sight dim *Gen 27:11-44*
The pillar of fire by night *Exod 13:20-22, Num 9:15-23*
Gideon attacks Midianites at night *Judg 7:1-25*
David spares the sleeping Saul at night *1 Sam 24:1-24, 26:1-25*
Saul consults familiar spirit at night *1 Sam 28:3-20*
Job's nightmare *Job 4:13-21*
Wise men follow star of Bethlehem *Mat 2:1-12*
Jesus' parable of servants awaiting *Mat 24:42-51*
Jesus' parable of wise and foolish virgins *Mat 25:1-13*
Jesus' birth announced to shepherds *Luke 2:8-20*
Jesus as the light of the world *John 1:1-14, 8:12-32*
Nicodemus visits Jesus at night *John 3:1-21*
Peter released at night by angel *Acts 5:17-42*
Paul escapes over wall at night *Acts 9:23-31*

Paul and Silas sing hymns in prison *Acts 16:19-40*
Paul shipwrecked at night *Acts 27:1-44*

See also blindness, light, night

DAUGHTER

Daughters of Zelophehad sue for inheritance *Num 27:1-11, 36:5-13*
Ruth remains loyal to her mother-in-law *Ruth 1:1-22*
Esther adopted by her uncle, saves him *Esther 2:5-53, 7:1-10*
Zephaniah's vision of salvation to daughter of Zion *Zeph 3:14-17*
Jesus heals Jairus' daughter *Mat 9:18, 19, 23-26, Mark 5:22-24, 35-43, Luke 8:41, 42, 49-56*
Jesus heals woman's daughter *Mat 15:21-28, Mark 7:24-30*
Jesus' parable of wise and foolish virgins *Mat 25:1-13*

See also children, family, parent

DAVID

See Part II, David

DAY

God's creation in six days *Gen 1: 1-31*
Moses follows the pillar of cloud by day *Exod 13:20-22, Num 9: 15-23*
At dawn Elisha finds himself besieged *2 King 6:8-23*
Jesus' parable of temple to be raised in three days *John 2:19-22*
Jesus says Abraham saw his day *John 8:48-59*
Jesus raises Lazarus dead four days *John 11:1-46*
Day of Pentecost *Acts 2:1-13*

See also light, sun, time

DAY OF THE LORD

Isaiah warns of day of the Lord *Isa 2:1-22*
Isaiah on the day the Lord's anger was against Babylon *Isa 13:1-22*
Isaiah on the day of the Lord's vengeance *Isa 34:1-10*

Jeremiah warns of day of the Lord in Egypt *Jer 46:1-28*
Ezekiel reproves lying prophets with coming day of the Lord *Ezek 13:1-23*
Ezekiel warns of day of the Lord in Egypt *Ezek 30:1-26*
Jesus foretells terrible day of the Lord *Mat 24:1-51, Mark 13:1-37*

DEAFNESS

Isaiah's prophecy that deaf will hear *Isa 35:1-10*
Jesus tells why he speaks only in parables *Mat 13:10-17, 34, 35, Mark 4:33, 34*
Jesus heals deaf man *Mark 7:32-37*

See also ear, hearing, listening, obedience

DEATH

Elijah heals widow's son *1 King 17:17-24*
Elisha raises Shunammite's son *2 King 4:8-37*
Jesus' own resurrection *Mat 28:9, 10, Mark 16:9-11, Luke 24:13-49, John 20:11-18*
Jesus' reappearances *Mat 28:16-20, Mark 16:12-18, Luke 24:13-49, John 21:12-25, Acts 1:1-8, 1 Cor 15:5-8*
Jesus raises Jairus' daughter *Mat 9:18, 19, 23-26, Mark 5:22-24, 35-43, Luke 8:41, 42, 49-56*
Jesus raises son of widow of Nain *Luke 7:11-17*
Jesus raises Lazarus four days after death *John 11:1-46*
Jesus on immortality *John 11:21-27*
Peter raises Tabitha *Acts 9:36-43*
Paul stoned but recovers *Acts 14:19, 20*
Paul relates sin to death *Rom 5:1-21*
Paul on the letter versus the spirit *2 Cor 3:4-18*

See also burial, eternity, healing, kill, life

DEBORAH (one of the judges)

See Part II, Deborah

DEBT

Caleb collects his share of promised land *Josh 14:6-15*
Elisha helps widow pay her debts *2 King 4:1-7*
Elisha's servant falsely collects payment *2 King 5:15-27*
Jesus obtains tax money from fish *Mat 17:24-27*
Jesus' parable of forgiven debtor who would not forgive *Mat 18:23-35*
Jesus' parable of farmers who refuse rent *Mat 21:33-46, Mark 12:1-12, Luke 20:9-19*
Jesus' parable of two debtors *Luke 7:36-50*

See also duty, forgiveness, reconciliation

DECAY

Longevity of patriarchs *Gen 5:1-32*
Manna decays next day *Exod 16:1-36, Num 11:1-15, 31-32*
Caleb's strength when old *Josh 14:6-15*
Elisha heals Naaman of leprosy *2 King 5:1-14*
Jeremiah's proverb of good and bad figs *Jer 24:1-10*
Ezekiel's vision of army from dry bones *Ezek 37:1-14*
Nehemiah's news of Jerusalem's misery *Neh 1:1-11*
Daniel's vision of the fall of the kingdom *Dan 2:1-49*
Jesus heals paralysis *Mat 8:5-13, 9:2-8, Mark 2:1-12, Luke 5:17-26, 7:1-10*
Jesus withers fig tree without fruit *Mat 21:18-22, Mark 11:12-14, 20-24*
Paul heals Publius' father of hemorrhage *Acts 28:7-10*

See also age, beauty, corruption, disease, restoration

DECEIT

Eve deceived by serpent *Gen 3:1-5*
Jacob deceives Isaac and obtains blessings *Gen 27:1-44*
Joseph to prison by lie of Potiphar's wife *Gen 39:1-20*

Aaron sets up golden calf while Moses is on mountain *Exod 32: 1-24*

Samson betrayed by Delilah to Philistines *Judg 16:4-30*

Isaiah's threat to hypocrites *Isa 29: 11-24, 30: 1-3, 20, 21*

Jesus' parable of two sons ordered to work *Mat 21:28-32*

Jesus accuses Pharisees and lawyers *Mat 23:1-39, Luke 11:37-54, 12:1-15*

Judas betrays Jesus for price *Mat 26:14-16, Mark 14:10-11, Luke 22: 1-6*

Jesus foretells his betrayal *Mat 26: 20-25, Mark 14:18-21, Luke 22:21, 22, John 13:21-35*

Judas hangs himself *Mat 27:3-10, Acts 1:15-20*

Paul's description of enemies of truth *2 Tim 3:1-17*

See also betrayal, duplicity, error, hypocrisy, lie

DECISIONS

Eve follows the advice of the serpent *Gen 3:1-5*

Abraham decides to look for the promised land *Gen 11:31, 32, 12: 1-9*

Jacob decides to face his brother *Gen 32:1-32*

Moses' reluctance to lead, overcome *Exod 3:9-12*

People go forward through Red Sea *Exod 14:5-31*

Caleb unable to persuade people to enter promised land *Num 13:1-33, 14:1-11, 23-39, Deut 1:19-38*

Rights of women established *Num 27:1-11, 36:5-13*

Moses' address urges choice between good and evil *Deut 30:11-20*

Joshua offers same choice *Josh 24: 1-25*

Gideon demands proof before deciding *Judg 6:19-40*

Ruth stays with Naomi and her religion *Ruth 1:1-22*

Samuel resists people's plea for king *1 Sam 8:1-22*

Samuel anoints Saul to be king *1 Sam 10:1-8*

Samuel repents his decision *1 Sam 15:7-26*

Samuel anoints David king *1 Sam 16:1-13*

Elisha leaves his plow to follow Elijah *1 King 19:19-21*

Esther decides to help her people *Esther 3:1-15, 4:1-17*

Three Jews refuse to worship image *Dan 3:1-30*

Jonah decides eventually to obey God *Jonah 1:1-17, 2:1-10, 3:1-10*

Disciples decide to follow Jesus *Mat 4:17-22, Mark 1:14-20, Luke 5:1-11, John 1:35-42*

Woman with issue of blood decides to touch Jesus' robe and is healed *Mat 9:20-22, Mark 5:25-34, Luke 8:43-48*

Jesus' parable of podigal who returns *Luke 15:11-24*

Peter accepts Gentiles *Acts 10:1-48, 11:1-18*

See also guidance, judgment, mind, obedience

DEDICATION

The chosen people set apart as God's own *Deut 7:6-11*

Joshua sets up twelve stones as memorial *Josh 4:1-24*

David told his son shall build Lord's house *1 Chron 17:1-27*

David receives liberal offering for the temple *1 Chron 29:6-19*

Solomon dedicates temple *1 King 8:22-66, 2 Chron 6:1-42*

Nehemiah reads book of the law on completion of wall *Neh 8:1-12*

David's song, my shepherd *Psal 23: 1-6*

Isaiah called to speak *Isa 6:1-13*

Jesus receives wise men's presents *Mat 2:1-12*

Jesus on "Seek ye first" *Mat 6: 25-34*

Jesus charges disciples to preach and heal *Mat 10:5-42, Mark 6: 7-13, Luke 9:1-6*

Jesus' parable of treasure in a field *Mat 13:44*

Jesus' parable of pearl of great price *Mat 13:45, 46*

Jesus' parable of wise and foolish virgins *Mat 25:1-13*

Jesus approves precious ointment poured on his head *Mat 26:6-13, Mark 14:3-9*

Jesus approves the widow's mite *Mark 12:41-44, Luke 21:1-4*

Jesus anointed by woman, tells story of two debtors *Luke 7: 36-50*

Jesus approves Mary's devotion *Luke 10:38-42*

Jesus' parable of faithful steward *Luke 12:41-48*

Jesus on being born again *John 3:1-21*

Jesus stoned at feast of dedication *John 10:22-42*

Jesus foretells his death and calls for dedication *John 12:20-50*

Jesus washes disciples' feet *John 13:1-20*

Jesus' parable of true vine *John 15:1-17*

Peter and John speak word with boldness *Acts 4:1-23*

Stephen martyred *Acts 6:5-15*

Paul's hardships in establishing the church *2 Cor 11:21-33*

Paul on why we owe all to Christ *Heb 2:1-18*

James on how to bear our cross *Jas 1:1-27*

See also anointing, blood, body, consecration, holiness

DEFEAT

Adam and Eve fall through sin *Gen 3:6-24*

Tower of Babel falls through confusion *Gen 11:1-19*

Army of Egyptians engulfed by Red Sea *Exod 14:5-31*

Moses gets second chance to bring Ten Commandments to Israel *Exod 34:1-8, Deut 10:1-4*

Aaron and Miriam rebel and are quelled *Num 12:1-16*

Joshua fails first attempt to take Ai *Josh 7:1-26, 8:14-21*

Samson fails through sensuality *Judg 16:4-30*

Samuel chooses the wrong man as king *1 Sam 15:7-26*

Saul resorts to magic *1 Sam 28: 3-20*

Saul dies by his own hand *1 Sam 31:1-13*

David's lament, "How are the mighty fallen" *2 Sam 1:17-27*

Elijah discouraged under juniper tree *1 King 19:1-8*

Hezekiah's misplaced trust leads his country into Babylonian captivity *2 King 20:12-21 Isa 39:1-8*

David's song, "Why art thou cast down?" *Psal 42:1-11*

Isaiah's vision of fall of Babylon *Isa 14:4-8, 12-17, 25-27*

Jeremiah encourages captives for eventual release *Jer 29:8-14, 31: 1-14, 31-34*

Daniel interprets handwriting on wall *Dan 5:1-31*

Jesus' parable of wise and foolish virgins *Mat 25:1-13*

Jesus' parable of sheep and goats *Mat 25:31-46*

Peter fails Jesus when he denies him *Mat 26:57, 58, 69-75, Mark 14:66-72, Luke 22:54-62, John 18:13-18, 25-27*

Judas hangs himself *Mat 27:3-10, Acts 1:15-20*

Jesus' parable of rich man with big barns *Luke 12:15-21*

Jesus' parable of unjust steward *Luke 16:1-14*

Jesus' parable of rich man and beggar *Luke 16:19-31*

Paul fails to wipe out Christianity *Acts 8:1-4, 9:1-9, 10-22*

See also discouragement, failure, fallen man, Gethsemane

DEFENSE

Abraham finds the Lord will deliver the city because of righteous men *Gen 18:20-33*

Deborah defeats Sisera, the invader *Judg 4:1-17*

Gideon defends his land against invaders *Judg 7:1-25*

David slays Goliath and repulses Philistines *1 Sam 17:17-37*

Captain of fifty destroyed by fire *2 King 1:3-15*

Hezekiah repulses Sennacherib
*2 King 18:17-37, 19:1-27, 2 Chron
31: 20, 21, 32:1-23, Isa 36:1-26, 37:
1-38*

Jehoshaphat told battle is the Lord's
2 Chron 20:1-32

Nehemiah rebuilds wall of Jerusalem
Neh 4:1-23

Esther defends her uncle and the
Jews *Esther 3:1-15, 4:1-17, 5:
1-14*

David's song of safety *Psal 91:1-16*

David's song of preservation *Psal
121:1-8*

Isaiah hears God's promise in
trouble *Isa 43:1-28, 44:1-24*

Ezekiel's vision of defending army
made from dry bones *Ezek 37:
1-14*

Jesus escapes by passing through
enemies *Luke 4:28-32*

Jesus sees guards fall backwards
when they come to take him *John
18:4-6*

Paul is self-eliminated from perse-
cuting Christians *Acts 9:1-9*

Paul defends himself before King
Agrippa *Acts 26:1-32*

Paul on Christians' armor *Eph 6:
10-17*

See also fortification, preservation,
protection, resistance, security

DEFIANCE

Adam and Eve eat forbidden fruit
Gen 3:1-24

Cain asks, "Am I my brother's
keeper?" *Gen 4:1-16*

David defies Goliath *1 Sam 17:
38-52*

Nathan's parable about the king
2 Sam 12:1-10

Jehoshaphat learns battle is the
Lord's *2 Chron 20:1-32*

Uzziah's heart lifted up to destruction *2 Chron 26:1-23*

Elijah and 450 prophets of Baal
1 King 18:17-40

Three Jews refuse to worship image
Dan 3:1-30

Daniel in lions' den *Dan 6:1-28*

Jonah, sent to Nineveh, flees opposite way *Jonah 1:1-17*

Jesus' parable of husbandmen who
refuse rent *Mat 21:33-46, Mark
12:1-12, Luke 20:9-19*

Jesus defies Pharisees *Mat 23:1-39*

Peter and John speak the word with
boldness *Acts 4:1-23*

See also challenge, disobedience

DEFILE

See corruption, morality, perfection,
purity

DEFINITION

God makes man in his image *Gen
1:26, 27*

Lord God creates man from dust
Gen 2:6-8

Moses defines nature of God *Exod
3:1-18*

Moses defines law *Exod 20:1-19,
Deut 5:1-24*

Elijah defines God *1 King 19:9-13*

Job defines God *Job 38:1-41*

David's song, "What is man?" *Psal
8:1-9*

David on nature of God *Psal 36:1-
12, 139:1-24*

Solomon defines wisdom *Prov 3:
13-26, 4:1-13, 8:1-36*

Solomon defines virtuous woman
Prov 31:1-31

Ecclesiastes on vanity *Eccl 1:1-18,
2:1-26*

Ecclesiastes on time *Eccl 3:15*

Isaiah describes Messiah *Isa 53:
1-12*

Jesus defines neighbor *Luke 10:
25-37*

John Baptist defines Jesus' preaching *John 3:22-36*

Jesus defines God *John 4:1-30*

Jesus on eternal life *Mat 19:16-30,
Mark 10:17-31, Luke 10:25-28, 18:
18-30*

Jesus on prayer *Mat 6:5-15, Mark
11:25, 26, Luke 11:1-4*

Jesus defines Ten Commandments
Mat 22:34-40, Mark 12:28-34

Paul on spirit versus flesh *Rom
8:1-39*

Paul on love *1 Cor 13:1-13*

Paul on salvation by faith *Rom 3:
1-31, Gal 2:14-21*

DEFORMITY

Jacob's thigh out of joint *Gen 32: 1-32*

Jeroboam's withered hand healed *1 King 12:32, 13:1-10*

Jesus heals man's withered hand *Mat 12:9-13, Mark 3:1-5, Luke 6: 6-10*

Jesus heals woman bowed together 18 years *Luke 13:11-17*

See also corruption, cripple, lameness

DELIGHT

Adam in the garden of Eden *Gen 2:9-25*

Solomon visited by Queen of Sheba *1 King 10:1-12*

David's delight in God's law *Psal 1:1-6*

David's songs of rejoicing *Psal 66: 1-20, 100:1-5*

Micah's vision of the mountain of the Lord's house *Mic 4:1-8, 13, Isa 2:1-5*

Jesus' delight at finding lost sheep *Mat 18:12-14, Luke 15:1-7*

Jesus' parable of the Lord who left the talents *Mat 25:14-30, Luke 19: 11-28*

Mary magnifies the Lord on the news about Jesus *Luke 1:26-38*

Jesus receives 70 disciples, sent out to heal *Luke 10:17-24*

Jesus' parable of the father of the prodigal son *Luke 15:11-24*

John's vision of new heaven and earth (the city foursquare) *Rev 21:1-27*

See also happiness, joy, pleasure, satisfaction

DELINQUENCY

Adam and Eve disobey *Gen 3:6-24*

Cain refuses to be his brother's keeper *Gen 4:1-16*

Jacob deceives his father *Gen 27: 1-44*

Miriam and Aaron speak against Moses *Num 12:1-16*

Joshua uncovers Achan's sin at Ai *Josh 7:1-26, 8:14-21*

Samson is betrayed by self-indulgence *Judg 16:4-30*

Saul declared unfit to rule by Samuel *1 Sam 15:7-26*

Saul breaks own law and consults witch *1 Sam 28:3-20*

David kills Uriah for his wife *2 Sam 11:1-27*

Gehazi's greed gets him into trouble *2 King 5:15-27*

Hypocrisy will be punished *Isa 29: 11-24, 30:1-3, 20, 21*

Jonah disobeys, fails to heed directions *Jonah 1:1-17*

Jesus excoriates three cities for disregarding his works *Mat 11:20-30*

Jesus' parable of unmerciful debtor *Mat 18:23-35*

Jesus' parable of two sons ordered to work *Mat 21:28-32*

Jesus' parable of the foolish virgins *Mat 25:1-13*

Jesus' parable of the talents *Mat 25:14-30, Luke 19:11-28*

Judas betrays Jesus *Mat 26:14-16, Mark 14:10, 11, Luke 22:1-6*

Jesus' parable of prodigal son *Luke 15:11-24*

Jesus' parable of rich man and beggar *Luke 16:19-31*

Jesus heals ten lepers *Luke 17:11-19*

Zacchaeus makes up his wrongs *Luke 19:1-10*

Jesus saves woman taken in adultery *John 8:1-11*

Peter goes back to work instead of preaching Christ *John 21:1-11*

See also crime, duty, juvenile, law

DELIVERANCE

Noah builds ark to the saving of his house *Gen 6:5-22, 7:1-24*

Abraham asks God if righteous men can deliver a city *Gen 18:20-33*

Lot escapes Sodom *Gen 19:1, 15-29*

Joseph escapes prison by solving a dream *Gen 41:1-46*

Moses as baby escapes death *Exod 2:1-10*

Israelites escape through Red Sea *Exod 14:5-31*

Moses' song of deliverance *Deut 32:1-47*

Deborah's song of deliverance *Judg 5:1-20*

Gideon's sword delivers from Midianites *Judg 7:1-25*

Elisha besieged by Syrians *2 King 6:8-23*

Hezekiah delivered from invasion of Assyrians *2 King 18:17-37, 19: 1-27, 2 Chron 31:20, 21, 32:1-23, Isa 36:1-22, 37:1-38*

Esther delivers Mordecai and the Jews from Haman *Esther 3:1-15, 6:1-14*

Jeremiah promises deliverance from captivity *Jer 29:8-14*

Three Jews delivered from fiery furnace *Dan 3:1-30*

Daniel delivered from lions' den *Dan 6:1-28*

Jonah delivered from whale *Jonah 2:1-10*

Jesus and family—in flight to Egypt *Mat 2:13-23, Luke 2:39, 40*

Jesus' parable of builder on rock *Mat 7:24-27, Luke 6:48, 49*

Jesus delivers boat from storm *Mat 8:23-27, Mark 4:35-41, Luke 8: 22-25*

Jesus escapes tomb *Mat 28:1-8, Mark 10:1-8, Luke 24:1-13, John 20:1-10*

Jesus escapes death by passing through the crowd *Luke 4:28-31*

Peter escapes prison by angel's help *Acts 5:17-42*

Paul escapes over wall in basket *Acts 9:23-31*

Paul and Silas escape prison *Acts 16:19-40*

Paul delivered from shipwreck *Acts 27:1-44*

See also escape, redemption, restoration, salvation

DELUSION

Man made from dust *Gen 2:6-8*

Moses sees rod become a serpent, and hand, leprous *Exod 4:1-9*

People afraid of giants in land of Canaan *Num 13:1-33, 14:1-11, 23-39, Deut 1:19-38*

Midianites blinded by Gideon's surprise attack *Judg 7:1-25*

Saul's troubled spirits calmed *1 Sam 16:14-23*

The four horsemen *Rev 6:1-17*

The great red dragon *Rev 12:1-17*

See also belief, deceit, dreams, illusion, insanity

DEMOCRACY

Abraham settles strife with his nephew amicably *Gen 13:1-18*

Moses appoints judges to help govern *Exod 18:13-27*

Moses permits Eldad and Medad to prophesy *Num 11:16-30*

Gideon arises from private life to lead his people *Judg 6:19-40*

Gideon refuses to be king *Judg 8: 22, 23*

Samuel resists the people's demand for a king *1 Sam 8:1-22*

Jesus' disciples contend who is greatest *Mat 18:1-11, Mark 9:33-37, Luke 9:46-50, 22:24-30*

Jesus' parable of hiring laborers in vineyard *Mat 20:1-16*

Jesus avoids nepotism of Zebedee's wife *Mat 20:20-28, Mark 10:35-45*

Jesus' parable of good Samaritan *Luke 10:25-37*

Jesus' parable of chief seats at wedding *Luke 14:7-14*

Jesus' parable of those bidden to great supper *Luke 14:15-24*

Jesus washes disciples' feet *John 13:1-20*

Matthias elected to replace Judas *Acts 1:15-26*

Peter allows early Christians to hold things in common *Acts 2:41-47*

Apostles choose seven deacons to administer church *Acts 6:1-4*

Paul on spiritual gifts to all *1 Cor 12:1, 4-31*

James on equality of men *Jas 2:1-13*

See also equality, freedom, independence, tyranny

DEMONSTRATION

Noah's ark demonstrates safety for man *Gen 6:3-22*

Joseph solves problems of Egypt *Gen 41:1-46*

Moses gets proofs by God *Exod 4: 1-9*

Manna and quail in wilderness *Exod 16:1-36, Num 11:1-15, 31, 32*

Jericho falls *Josh 6:1-27*

Gideon receives his answers from God *Judg 6:19-40*

Ruth's loyalty leads to happiness *Ruth 1:1-22, 4:1-22*

David kills Goliath *1 Sam 17:38-52*

Elijah fed by ravens and by a widow *1 King 17:1-16*

Elijah brings fire from heaven *1 King 18:17-40*

Elisha heals Shunammite's son *2 King 4:8-37*

Nehemiah repairs wall of Jerusalem *Neh 4:1-23*

A poor wise man saves his city *Eccl 9:13-18*

Three Jews in fiery furnace *Dan 3:1-30*

Daniel in lions' den *Dan 6:1-28*

Jesus calms storm *Mat 8:23-27, Mark 4:35-41, Luke 8:22-25*

Jesus feeds 5000 *Mat 14:15-21, Mark 6:35-44, Luke 9:12-17, John 6:5-14*

Jesus walks on water *Mat 14:22-33, John 6:15-21*

Jesus transfiguration, talks with Moses and Elijah *Mat 17:1-13, Mark 9:2-13, Luke 9:28-36*

The resurrection *Mat 28:1-8, Mark 16:1-8, Luke 24:1-12, John 20:1-10*

Jesus' ship at destination at once *Mark 6:45-52, John 6:21*

Jesus' escape through enemies *Luke 4:28-31*

Peter's net filled *Luke 5:1-11, John 21:1-11*

See also doubt, evidence, example, proof

DENIAL

Cain asks, "Am I my brother's keeper?" *Gen 4:1-16*

Moses offers thou shalt not's *Exod 20:1-19, Deut 5:1-24*

Balak hires Balaam but he refuses to curse *Num 22:1-41*

Ezekiel denies power of heredity *Ezek 18:1-32*

Daniel and boys refuse to eat king's provision *Dan 1:1-21*

Three Jews refuse to worship image *Dan 3:1-30*

Daniel refuses to appeal to king before prayer *Dan 6:1-28*

Jesus is tempted, denies devil *Mat 4:1-11, Mark 1:12, 13, Luke 4:1-23*

Jesus' control of elements of storm *Mat 8:23-27, Mark 4:35-41, Luke 8:22-25*

Jesus heals Jairus' daughter (not dead, sleeping) *Mat 9:18, 19, 23-26, Mark 5:22-24, 35-43, Luke 8:41, 42, 49-56*

Jesus heals epileptic boy by prayer and fasting *Mat 17:14-21, Mark 9:14-39, Luke 9:37-43*

Jesus' parable of two servants awaiting their lord *Mat 24:42-51*

Jesus' parable of wise and foolish virgins *Mat 25:1-13*

Peter vows never to deny Jesus *Mat 26:31-35, Mark 14:27-31, Luke 22:21-38, John 13:36-38*

Peter denies him *Mat 26:57, 58, 69-75, Mark 14:66-72*

Jesus' parable of man taking long journey *Mark 13:34-37*

Jesus' parable to renounce chief seats *Luke 14:7-14*

Jesus' parable, servant must serve *Luke 17:7-10*

Jesus' parable, Pharisee and publican *Luke 18:9-14*

Paul teaching "think on these things" *Phil 4:1-23*

James' sermon on temptation *Jas 1:1-27*

See also affirmation, fasting, rejection, sacrifice, watch

DEPRESSION

Adam and Eve's fall *Gen 3:6-24*

Jacob flees dismayed *Gen 28:10-22*

People in wilderness remember their times of plenty *Exod 16:1-36, Num 11:1-15, 31, 32*

Moses destroys tablet of Ten Commandments *Exod 32:1-24*

Gideon mourns the rule of the Midianites *Judg 6:19-40*

Ruth and Naomi during hard times *Ruth 1:1-22, 2:1-23*

Elijah in flight *1 King 19:1-8*

Job expresses woe in his trial *Job 3:1-26*

David's song, "Why art thou cast down, O my soul?" *Psal 42:1-11*

Jeremiah encourages people in captivity *Jer 29:8-14*

Jesus heals woman ill twelve years *Mat 9:20-22, Mark 5:25-34, Luke 8:43-48*

Jesus at Gethsemane *Mat 26:30, 36-46, Mark 14:26, 32-42, Luke 22:39-46*

Jesus heals woman bowed together 18 years *Luke 13:11-17*

Jesus' parable of fall of prodigal *Luke 15:11-24*

Paul's thorn in the flesh *2 Cor 12:1-19*

See also defeat, discouragement, doubt, joy

DESCENT

Jacob sees angel descending ladder *Gen 28:10-22*

Peter at the descent of Holy Ghost *Acts 2:1-13*

Peter sees descent of great sheet *Acts 11:1-18*

John's vision of city of God descending *Rev 21:1-27*

See also attack, genealogy, heredity, hill

DESERT

Manna in wilderness *Exod 16:1-36, Num 11:1-15, 31, 32*

Isaiah's prophecy that desert will blossom *Isa 35:1-10*

John Baptist in wilderness *Mat 3:1-12, Mark 1:1-8, Luke 3:1-18*

Jesus tempted in wilderness *Mat 4:1-11, Luke 4:1-13*

Jesus' parable of lost sheep *Mat 18:12-14, Luke 15:1-7*

See also barrenness, fruits, rain, wilderness

DESIGN

God creates perfect universe *Gen 1:1-31*

Noah builds the ark *Gen 6:5-22*

Tower of Babel built to reach heaven *Gen 11:1-9*

God promises Abraham a son and a land *Gen 15:1-21*

Abraham's plan to sacrifice Isaac changed *Gen 22:1-19*

Jacob's duplicity changes plan to bless Esau *Gen 25:24-34*

Moses tells people they are set apart as God's own *Deut 7:6-11*

Isaiah called by God to speak *Isa 6:1-13*

Isaiah foretells coming of Christ *Isa 7:10-16, 9:2-7*

Isaiah foretells his peaceable kingdom *Isa 11:1-12*

Isaiah foretells what Christ is like *Isa 53:1-12*

Jeremiah foretells restoration of Israel *Jer 31:1-14, 31-34*

Ezekiel's vision of holy waters *Ezek 47:1-12*

Daniel predicts king's insanity *Dan 4:28-37*

Jonah cannot change God's plan for him *Jonah 1:1-17, 2:1-10, 3:1-10*

Micah foretells glory of the church *Mic 4:1-8, 13*

Jesus foretells his death and resurrection *Mat 17:22, 23, Mark 9:30-32, Luke 9:43-45*

Jesus' parable of sheep and goats *Mat 25:31-46*

Jesus' parable of rich man and beggar *Luke 16:19-31*

Jesus' parable of temple to be raised in three days *John 2:19-22*

Jesus on being born again *John 3:1-21*

Jesus charges Peter "feed my sheep" *John 21:12-29*

Paul on "Put on the new man" *Col 3:1-17*

John's vision of new heaven and earth *Rev 21:1-27*

See also aims, plan, prophecy, purpose

DESIRE

See covetousness, envy, lust

DESTRUCTION

Only Noah and those in ark escape flood *Gen 7:1-24*

The tower of Babel represents the egotism of man *Gen 11:1-9*

All first sons in Egypt die *Exod 11:4-10, 12:1-14, 21-31*

Jericho's walls crumble *Josh 6: 1-27*

Gideon destroys enemy host *Judg 7:1-25*

David's song, "How are the mighty fallen" *2 Sam 1:17-27*

Elijah destroys 450 prophets of Baal *1 King 18:17-40*

Uzziah's heart lifted up to destruction *2 Chron 26:1-23*

Rebuilding of temple after captivity *Ezra 3:8-13*

Nehemiah receives news of destruction of Jerusalem *Neh 1:1-11*

Nehemiah repairs the wall *Neh 4: 1-23*

Isaiah's vision of fall of Babylon *Isa 14:4-8, 12-17, 25-27*

Jesus' parable of the builders on rock and sand *Mat 7:24-29, Luke 6:48, 49*

Jesus predicts the destruction of the temple and Jerusalem *Mat 24:1-41, Mark 13:1-37, Luke 21: 5-36*

Judas hangs himself *Mat 27:3-10, Acts 1:15-20*

Jesus withers the barren fig tree *Mat 21:18-22, Mark 11:12-14, 20-24, Luke 13:6-9*

Jesus says he will raise temple (body) in three days *John 2: 19-22*

John's vision of war in heaven *Rev 12:1-17*

See also defeat

DEVELOPMENT

God creates perfect universe, step by step *Gen 1:1-31*

Joseph's progress from slavery to governor *Gen 37:1-36, 41:1-46*

Moses from prince to shepherd to leader *Exod 3:1-18, 4:10-17*

Moses delegates his authority to judge *Exod 18:13-27*

Moses' song reviewing God's care *Deut 32:1-47*

Gideon's faith develops *Judg 6: 19-40*

Capsule history of Jews *Neh 8:1-38*

Jeremiah's promise, release from captivity *Jer 31:1-14, 31-34*

Jesus teaches and sends twelve forth *Mat 9:36-38, 10:1-42*

Jesus' parable of unclean spirit *Mat 12:43-45, Luke 11:24-26*

Jesus' parable of sower *Mat 13: 3-23, Mark 4:1-20, Luke 8:4-15*

Jesus' parable of leaven *Mat 13:33, Luke 13:20, 21*

Jesus' parable of talents *Mat 25: 14-30, Luke 19:11-28*

Jesus' parable of seed, blade, ear *Mark 4:26-29*

Jesus heals blind man in two stages *Mark 8:22-26*

Jesus teaches and sends 70 forth *Luke 10:1-16*

Paul on fruits of the spirit *Gal 5: 1-26*

Paul teaching "Put on new man" *Col 3:1-17*

John's vision of new heaven and earth *Rev 21:1-27*

See also evolution, growth, increase, unfoldment

DEVILS

Saul's troubled spirits calmed by music *1 Sam 16:14-23*

Jesus tempted *Mat 4:1-11, Mark 1: 12, 13, Luke 4:1-13*

Jesus heals insanity *Mat 8:28-34, Mark 5:1-20, Luke 8:26-39*

Swine are drowned *Mat 8:30-32*

Jesus instructs his disciples to cast out devils *Mat 9:36-38, 10:5-42, Mark 3:13-21, 6:7-13, Luke 6:13-19, 9:1-6*

Pharisees claim Jesus casts out devils with Beelzebub *Mat 12: 22-30, Mark 3:22-30, Luke 11:14-23*

Jesus heals blind and dumb *Mat 12: 22, 23*

Jesus' parable of seven unclean spirits *Mat 12:43-45, Luke 11: 24-26*

Jesus heals Gentile woman's daughter *Mat 15:21-28, Mark 7:24-30*

Jesus denounces scribes' and Pharisees' father as the devil *Mat 23: 1-39*

Jesus heals man of unclean spirit *Mark 1:21-28, Luke 4:33-37*
Jesus' disciples return *Luke 9: 10,11*
Jesus sends 70 and they return *Luke 10:1-24*
Jesus heals dumb man *Luke 11: 14-23*
Philip casts out unclean spirits *Acts 8:5-8*
Paul heals damsel soothsayer *Acts 16:16-18*
Paul on enemies of the truth *2 Tim 3:1-17*

See also error, evil, disease, healing, hypnotism, temptation

DEVOTION

Cain and Abel worship God differently *Gen 4:1-16*
Enoch walked with God *Gen 5:18, 21-24, Heb 11:5*
Abraham intends to sacrifice his son *Gen 22:1-19*
Ruth remains loyal to her mother-in-law *Ruth 1:1-22*
David and Jonathan as friends *1 Sam 18:1-16*
Solomon dedicates his temple *1 King 8:22-66, 2 Chron 6:1-42*
Elijah finds God in still small voice *1 King 19:9-13*
Elisha stands by Elijah *2 King 2: 1-15*
Esther devotes herself to her people *Esther 3:1-15, 4:1-17*
Job refuses to give up God *Job 1: 13-22, 2:1-10*
Three Jews refuse to worship image *Dan 3:1-30*
Daniel refuses to change his prayers *Dan 6:1-28*
Zechariah's vision of two olive trees *Zech 4:1-14*
Jesus on "Seek ye first" *Mat 6: 25-34*
Jesus heals the centurion's servant *Mat 8:5-13, Luke 7:1-10*
Peter acknowledges Jesus as Christ *Mat 16:13-20, Mark 8:27-30, Luke 9:18-21*
Jesus at Gethsemane *Mat 25:30, 36-46, Mark 14:26, 32-42, Luke 22: 39-46*

Jesus' parable of the good shepherd *John 10:1-18*
Jesus' parable of the true vine *John 15:1-17*
Paul's persecutions *Acts 20:17-38*
Paul's hardships *2 Cor 11:21-33*
James on how to bear our cross *Jas 1:1-27*

See also anointing, consecration, dedication, loyalty, prayer, worship

DIALECTIC

Abraham on deliverance by righteousness *Gen 18:20-33*
Jacob wrestles with angel *Gen 32: 24-32*
Moses tests nature of God *Exod 4:1-9*
Moses talks with God *Exod 19:1-9, 33:7-23, Deut 4:1-15*
Moses urges choice of good or evil *Deut 30:11-20*
Solomon weighs values *1 King 3: 5-15, 2 Chron 1:7-12*
Job's dialogues with friends *Job 4: 1—37:24*
Proverbs on wisdom *Prov 3:13-26, 4:1-13, 8:1-36*
Ecclesiastes on vanity *Eccl 1:1-18, 2:1-26*
Ecclesiastes on time *Eccl 3:1-15*
Jesus instructs disciples *Mat 10:5-42, Mark 6:7-13, Luke 9:1-6, 10, 11*
John Baptist testifies Jesus is Christ *John 1:15-34*
Jesus debates Jews on authority *John 8:37-58*
Pilate asks, "What is truth?" *John 18:37, 38*
Paul reveals the "Unknown" God *Acts 17:15-34*
Paul relates sin with death *Rom 5:12-21*
Paul classifies the virtues *1 Cor 13:1-13*
Paul criticizes anti-Christians *2 Tim 3:1-17*
Paul on true atonement *Heb 10: 1-39*
James on faith without works *Jas 2:14-26*
John analyzes faults of the churches *Rev 1:4-29, 2:1-29, 3:1-22*

See also Christ, recognized; criticism; definition; error; idea; truth

DIET

Adam and Eve eat fruit of tree of knowledge of good and evil *Gen 3:6-24*

Abel offers first fruits of flock to God *Gen 4:1-16*

Jacob buys Esau's birthright for pottage *Gen 25:24-34*

Isaac offered savory meat by two sons *Gen 27:1-44*

Moses feeds Israel with manna *Exod 16:1-36, Num 11:1-15, 31, 32*

Moses orders first fruits for God *Deut 26:1-19*

Ruth gleans in Boaz's field *Ruth 2:1-23*

Elijah fed in a dream *1 King 19:1-8*

Elisha renders poisoned pottage harmless *2 King 4:38-41*

Daniel and pulse *Dan 1:1-21*

Jesus on take no thought what ye shall eat *Mat 6:25-34, Luke 12:22-34*

Jesus' disciples pluck corn on sabbath *Mat 12:1-8, Mark 2:23-28, Luke 6:1-5*

Jesus explains what defiles a man *Mat 15:1-20, Mark 7:1-23*

John Baptist lives on locusts and wild honey *Mark 1:1-8*

Jesus on the bread of life *John 6:26-65*

Jesus' sermon on bread of life causes many to leave *John 6:66-71*

Paul on Spirit vs. flesh *Rom 8:1-39*

John's revelation of angel and little book to be eaten up *Rev 10:1-11*

See also appetite, food, temperance

DIFFICULT

Hagar is turned out to wilderness *Gen 21:9-21*

Jacob wrestles with his fearful thoughts *Gen 32:1-32*

Joseph from slavery is put in prison *Gen 39:1-20*

People have no way out except Red Sea *Exod 14:5-31*

People maintained in wilderness *Exod 16:1-36, Num 11:1-15, 31, 32*

Fiery serpents in the wilderness *Num 21:4-9*

Moses' song of deliverance *Deut 32:1-47*

Ruth and Naomi have hard times *Ruth 2:1-23*

Elijah flees for his life *1 King 19:1-8*

Elisha heals Shunammite's son *2 King 4:8-37*

Zerubbabel rebuilds the temple *Ezra 3:8-13, 4:1-15*

Nehemiah rebuilds the wall *Neh 1:1-11, 2:1-20, 4:1-23, 6:1-19*

Job's trials *Job 1:13-22, 2:1-10, 3:1-26*

David's song, "Why art thou cast down?" *Psal 42:1-11*

Isaiah's vision of the desert in bloom *Isa 35:1-10*

Three Jews in fiery furnace *Dan 3:1-30*

Daniel in lions' den *Dan 6:1-28*

Jonah's difficulties self-imposed *Jonah 1:1-17, 2:1-10, 3:1-10*

Jesus at Gethsemane *Mat 26:30, 36-46, Mark 14:26, 32-42, Luke 22:39-46*

Jesus' crucifixion *Mat 27:32-56, Mark 15:21-41, Luke 23:26-49, John 19:17-30*

Jesus' resurrection *Mat 28:1-8, Mark 16:1-8, Luke 24:1-12, John 20:1-10*

Jesus raises Lazarus four days dead *John 11:1-46*

Paul's hardships establishing the church *2 Cor 11:21-33*

Paul's thorn in the flesh *2 Cor 12:1-19*

James on how to bear our cross *Jas 1:1-27*

See also hardness, science

DIRECTION

God directs man to have dominion *Gen 1:26, 27*

God directs Noah to build the ark of safety *Gen 6:5-22*

Abraham directed to find promised land *Gen 11:31, 32, 12:1-9*

Jacob runs away from home but sees angels *Gen 28:10-22*

Moses' reluctance to lead is overcome *Exod 3:9-12, 4:1-17*

Pillars of cloud and fire *Exod 13: 20-22, Num 9:15-23*

At Red Sea, God commands "Go forward" *Exod 14:5-31*

Moses talks with God and he receives Ten Commandments *Exod 20:1-19, Deut 5:1-24*

Caleb and Joshua urge entrance to promised land *Num 13:1-33, 14: 7-11, 23-39, Deut 1:19-38*

Moses' farewell address, "Choose ye" *Deut 30:11-20*

God tells Gideon the strategy to use *Judg 7:1-25*

Elijah instructed to go to Zarephath *1 King 17:1-15*

Jonah is sent to Nineveh *Jonah 1: 1-17*

Star directs wise men to Bethlehem *Mat 2:1-12*

Joseph and Mary warned to flee *Mat 2:13-43, Luke 2:39, 40*

Jesus instructs twelve disciples and sends them to heal and preach *Mat 9:36-38, 10:1-42, Mark 3:13-21, Luke 9:13-19*

Jesus sends 70 disciples *Luke 10: 1-24*

Jesus' parable of the piece of money *Luke 15:8-10*

Jesus charges Peter, "Feed my sheep" *John 21:12-19*

Saul corrected to Paul *Acts 8:1-4, 9:1-9, 10-22*

See also authority, commandment, control, guidance

DISARMAMENT

Abraham's strife with Lot settled amicably *Gen 13:1-18*

Isaac's strife over wells settled peacefully *Gen 26:12-31*

Esau forgives his brother who expects trouble *Gen 33:1-11*

Elisha pacifies the Syrians by good treatment *2 King 6:8-23*

Hezekiah delivered by epidemic among Assyrians *2 Chron 31:20, 21, 32:1-23, Isa 36:1-22, 37:1-38*

Isaiah's vision of swords into plowshares *Isa 2:1-5, Mic 4:1-8, 13*

Jesus on treatment of enemies *Mat 5:38-48, Luke 6:27-36*

Jesus on Golden Rule for actions *Mat 7:12-14*

Jesus makes Peter put up his sword *Mat 26:51, 52, Luke 22:50, 51*

Jesus causes guards to fall backwards *John 18:4-6*

Paul on charity *1 Cor 13:1-13*

Paul on the Christians' armor *Eph 6:10-17*

See also armor, peace, war, weapons

DISCIPLE

Moses charges Joshua with leadership *Deut 31:7-23, Josh 1:1-9*

Elijah finds Elisha plowing *1 King 19:19-21*

Elisha takes up Elijah's mantle *2 King 2:1-15*

Elisha's disciples build a place to live *2 King 6:1-7*

Elisha feeds his disciples *2 King 4:42-44*

Jesus calls his disciples *Mat 4:17-22, Mark 1:14-20, Luke 5:1-11, John 1:35-40*

Jesus sends twelve forth *Mat 9:36-38, 10:1-42, Mark 3:13-21, 6:7-13, Luke 6:13-19, 9:1-6, 10, 11*

Jesus heals epileptic boy after disciples fail *Mat 17:14-21, Mark 9: 14-29, Luke 9:37-43*

Jesus' parable of laborers in vineyard *Mat 20:1-16*

Jesus' parable of two sons ordered to work *Mat 21:28-32*

Jesus' Last Supper with disciples *Mat 26:26-29, Mark 14:22-25, Luke 22:14-30, 1 Cor 11:23-25*

Jesus has last breakfast with disciples *Mat 28:16-18, John 21:1-14*

Jesus sees two disciples at Emmaus after he is risen *Mark 16:12, 13, Luke 24:13-35*

Mary sits at Jesus' feet *Luke 10: 38-40*

Jesus' parable of watchful servants *Luke 12:35-40*

Jesus' parable of faithful steward *Luke 12:41-48*

Jesus' parable of counting the cost *Luke 14:25-33*

Jesus' parable of servant who serves master *Luke 17:7-10*
Jesus sends 70 forth *Luke 10:1-16*
Jesus washes disciples' feet *John 13:1-20*
Jesus' prayer for disciples *John 17:1-26*
Disciples receive Holy Spirit (Ghost) at Pentecost *Acts 2:1-13*

See also apostle, calling, Christian, follower, master, sonship

DISCIPLINE

Enoch "walked with God" and was translated *Gen 5:18, 21-24, Heb 11:5*
Moses cautions to remember trials *Deut 8:1-20*
Moses urges obedience *Deut 11:1-32*
Moses speaks of false leaders *Deut 13:1-18*
Moses forbids abominations *Deut 18:9-14*
Moses offers people a choice of life or death *Deut 30:11-20*
Samuel tutored by Eli, called by God *1 Sam 3:1-10*
Elisha trained by Elijah *1 King 19:19-21, 2 King 2:1-15*
Hosea's vision of Israel's childhood *Hos 11:1-4*
Jesus' Sermon on the Mount outlines the "discipline" of Christianity *Mat 5:1-32, 6:1-34, 7:1-29*
Jesus teaches the Lord's Prayer *Mat 6:5-15, Mark 11:25, 26, Luke 11:1-4*
Jesus admonishes Peter *Mat 16:21-28, Mark 8:31-38, Luke 9:20-27*
Jesus discusses the healing of hard cases *Mat 17:14-31, Mark 9:2-13, Luke 9:37-43*
Jesus' parable of the prodigal who learns *Luke 15:11-24*
Jesus deserted by some after sermon on bread of life *John 6:66-71*
Jesus' parable of the good shepherd *John 10:1-18*
Jesus asks Peter thrice to "feed my sheep" *John 21:12-19*
Paul's letters to disciples *Col 3:1-17, 1 Tim 5:1-25, 2 Tim 2:1-26, 3:1-17, 4:1-8*

James on faith without works *Jas 2:14-26*
John's vision of the sealed book *Rev 5:1-14*

See also education, obedience, punishment, teaching

DISCORD

Cain strikes Abel for religious motive *Gen 4:1-16*
Abraham's strife with Lot solved *Gen 13:1-18*
Sarah has Hagar sent away *Gen 21:9-21*
Miriam and Aaron speak against Moses *Num 12:1-16*
Three cities excoriated for disregarding Jesus' works *Mat 11:20-30*
Jesus' parable of unmerciful debtor *Mat 18:23-35*
Jesus' parable of laborers for the vineyard *Mat 20:1-16*
Jesus castigates the Pharisees and lawyers *Mat 23:1-39, Luke 11:37-54*
Jesus casts traders out of temple *John 2:13-25*
Paul and Barnabas worshipped as gods *Acts 14:11-18*
Vagabond exorcists imitate Christian healing *Acts 19:11-20*
A silversmith attacks Paul *Acts 19:23-29*
Paul's trials as a Christian *Acts 20:17-38*
Paul seized in Jerusalem *Acts 22:1-30*
Paul describes enemies of the truth *2 Tim 3:1-17*
War in heaven *Rev 12:1-17*

See also argument, disease, war

DISCOURAGEMENT

Jacob wrestles with angel in fear of future *Gen 32:1-32*
Moses afraid to lead children out of Egypt *Exod 3:9-12*
Moses and Israelites pursued to edge of Red Sea *Exod 14:5-31*
Israelites miss the food of Egypt *Exod 16:1-36, Num 11:1-15, 31, 32*

Israelites without water *Exod 17: 1-7, Num 20:1-13*

Moses smashed the first tablet of Commandments *Exod 32:1-24*

Hannah depressed because childless *1 Sam 1:1-28*

Elijah seeks refuge under juniper tree *1 King 19:1-8*

Nehemiah discouraged at plight of Jerusalem *Neh 1:1-11*

Job discouraged by his trials *Job 3:1-26*

David's song of the cast down soul *Psal 42:1-11*

Preacher depressed by vanity of things *Eccl 1:1-18, 2:1-26*

Isaiah comforts the church *Isa 54: 1-6, 11-17*

Ezekiel preaches on heredity *Ezek 18:1-32*

Jesus heals woman who had spent all her living on physicians *Mat 9:20-22, Mark 5:25-34, Luke 8: 43-48*

Jesus has to remind disciples of his great works *Mat 16:5-12, Mark 8:13-21*

Jesus heals epileptic boy whose father is distraught *Mat 17:14-21, Mark 9:14-29, Luke 9:37-43*

Jesus lifts thought of two disciples depressed by his supposed death *Mark 16:12, 13, Luke 24:13-35*

Jesus helps Peter discouraged by poor fishing *Luke 5:1-11*

Jesus heals man waiting at pool of healing waters *John 5:1-16*

Jesus promises Holy Spirit (Ghost) to encourage all *John 14:1-31, 16:1-33*

Paul on trials as a Christian *Acts 20:17-38, 2 Cor 11:21-33*

See also courage, defeat, depression, heart

DISCOVERY

Abraham promised the land *Gen 15:1-21*

Moses finds the burning bush is not consumed *Exod 3:1-18*

To Moses are revealed the Ten Commandments *Exod 20:1-19, Deut 5:1-24*

Caleb and Joshua scout promised land *Num 13:1-33, 14:1-11, 13-29*

Joshua crosses Jordan into promised land *Josh 3:1-17*

Elijah has revelation of still small voice *1 King 19:9-13*

Isaiah's vision of the coming of the Christ *Isa 7:10-16, 9:2-7*

Job discovers the nature of God at last *Job 38:1-41*

Peter acknowledges Jesus as Christ *Mat 16:13-20, Mark 8:27-30, Luke 9:18-21*

Jesus' transfiguration on mount with Moses and Elias *Mat 17:1-13, Mark 9:2-13 Luke 9:28-36*

The risen Jesus recognized by Mary *Mark 16:9-11, John 20:11-18*

Paul arrested by Jesus on road to Damascus *Acts 9:1-9*

John sees a new heaven and new earth *Rev 21:1-27*

See also identity, light, pilgrim, promise, revelation

DISCRIMINATION

New names of Abraham and Sarah *Gen 17:1-9, 15-22*

Lot shelters two angels *Gen 19:1-14*

Hagar is sent away at Sarah's request *Gen 21:9-21*

A proper wife is found for Isaac *Gen 24:1-67*

Isaac plans to bless Esau, not Jacob *Gen 27:1-44*

Jacob given a new name *Gen 32: 1-32, 35:9-15*

Joseph thrown into prison unjustly *Gen 39:1-20*

Persecution of Israelites *Exod 1: 8-14, 5:7-19*

Chosen people set apart as God's own *Deut 7:6-11*

Moses urges judgment *Deut 13:1-18, 18:9-14*

Moses urges choice of life and good against death and evil *Deut 30: 11-20*

Ruth cleaves to Naomi and her religion *Ruth 1:1-22*

Samuel anoints David in place of Saul *1 Sam 16:1-13*

Saul persecutes David *1 Sam 24:1-22, 26:1-25*

Haman persecutes Jews, Esther helps them *Esther 3:1-15, 4:1-17*

David's song, "God is our refuge and strength" *Psal 46:1-11*

Laws made to trap Daniel *Dan 6: 1-28*

Jesus heals Gentile's daughter *Mat 15:21-28, Mark 7:24-30*

Jesus' parable of laborers in vineyard *Mat 20:1-16*

Jesus' parable of prodigal's elder brother *Luke 15:25-32*

Jesus' parable of unjust steward *Luke 16:1-14*

Jesus' parable of rich man and beggar at his gate *Luke 16:19-31*

Jesus' parable of Pharisee and publican *Luke 18:9-14*

See also justice, understanding, wisdom

DISEASE

Moses sees his leprosy transformed *Exod 4:1-9*

Moses heals Miriam's leprosy *Num 12:1-16*

Israelites healed of plague in wilderness *Num 16:3-5, 44-50*

Jeroboam's hand withered and healed *1 King 12:32, 33, 13:1-10*

Elijah heals widow's son *1 King 17:17-24*

Elisha raises Shunammite's son *2 King 4:8-37*

Elisha heals Naaman, the leper *2 King 5:1-14*

Hezekiah's boil healed by Isaiah *2 King 20:1-11, Isa 38:1-22*

Jesus heals man of leprosy *Mat 8: 1-4, Mark 1:40-45, Luke 5:12-16*

Jesus heals centurion's servant of paralysis *Mat 8:5-13, Luke 7:1-10*

Jesus heals paralysis *Mat 9:2-8, Mark 2:1-12, Luke 5:17-26*

Jesus heals issue of blood *Mat 9: 20-22, Mark 5:25-34, Luke 8:43-48*

Jesus heals epileptic boy *Mat 17: 14-21, Mark 9:14-29, Luke 9:37-43*

Jesus raises son of widow of Nain *Luke 7:11-17*

Jesus heals spinal disorder *Luke 13:11-17*

Jesus heals dropsy *Luke 14:1-6*

Jesus heals ten of leprosy *Luke 17:11-19*

Peter heals paralysis *Acts 9:32-35*

Philip heals many *Acts 8:5-8*

Paul heals hemorrhage *Acts 28: 7-10*

See also devils, healing, remedy

DISGRACE

Fall of Adam and Eve *Gen 3:6-24*

Cain branded a murderer *Gen 4: 1-16*

Moses returns to find people worship golden calf *Exod 32:1-24*

Samson falls *Judg 16:4-30*

Samuel declares Saul unfit to be king *1 Sam 15:7-26*

David's moral fall *2 Sam 11:1-27*

Gehazi accepts forbidden reward and is punished *2 King 5:15-27*

Jesus admonishes Peter *Mat 16:21-28, Mark 8:31-38, Luke 9:20-27*

Jesus' parable of the wedding garment *Mat 22:1-14*

Jesus' parable of the talents *Mat 25:14-30, Luke 19:11-28*

Jesus' parable of sheep and goats *Mat 25:31-46*

Peter denies Jesus *Mat 26:57, 58, 69-75, Mark 14:66-72, Luke 22:54-62, John 18:13-18, 25-27*

Jesus saves woman taken in adultery *John 8:1-11*

See also shame

DISHONESTY

The beguiling first lie of the serpent *Gen 3:1-5*

Jacob deceives Isaac *Gen 27:1-44*

Worship of the golden calf *Exod 32:1-24*

Delilah betrays Samson *Judg 16: 4-30*

David takes Bathsheba, wife of Uriah *2 Sam 11:1-27*

Nathan exposes David with a parable *2 Sam 12:1-10*

Isaiah's parable of the wild grapes *Isa 5:1-8*

Jesus' parable of the husbandmen who refuse to pay the rent *Mat 21:33-46, Mark 12:1-12, Luke 20: 9-19*

Judas betrays Jesus *Mat 26:14-16, Mark 14:10, 11, Luke 22:1-6*
Paul's sermon on how Christians should act *Col 3:1-17*

See also corruption, deceit, honesty, lie

DISLOCATION

Jacob's hip is out of joint *Gen 32: 24-32*
Jesus heals woman bowed together *Luke 13:11-17*

See also bones, deformity

DISOBEDIENCE

Adam and Eve fall *Gen 3:6-24*
Miriam and Aaron speak out against Moses *Num 12:1-16*
Saul breaks law, consults familiar spirit *1 Sam 28:3-20*
Gehazi disobeys Elisha's refusal of reward *2 King 5:15-27*
Jonah disobeys God's command to go to Nineveh *Jonah 1:1-17*
Jesus puts some Commandments on a mental basis *Mat 5:21-48*
Jesus' parable of the two sons ordered to work *Mat 21:28-32*
Jesus' parable of husbandmen who refuse to pay rent *Mat 21:33-46, Mark 12:1-12, Luke 20:9-19*
Jesus saves woman who disobeyed Eighth Commandment *John 8:1-11*

See also commandment, denial, law, obedience, rebellion

DISTRESS

Hagar and her son lost in wilderness *Gen 21:9-21*
Jacob wrestles with the fear of facing his brother *Gen 32:1-32*
Israelites persecuted in Egypt *Exod 5:7-19*
Israelites pursued to Red Sea *Exod 14:5-31*
Bites of serpents in wilderness *Num 21:4-9*
David prays for health of his child *2 Sam 12:13-23*
Elijah discouraged *1 King 19:1-8*
The Shunammite's son healed *2 King 4:8-37*

Job's woe *Job 3:1-26*
David's song, "Why art thou cast down?" *Psal 42:1-11*
David's song, "God is our refuge and strength" *Psal 46:1-11*
Jesus heals Peter's mother-in-law *Mat 8:14-17, Mark 1:29-34*
Jesus heals woman's issue of blood *Mat 9:20-22, Mark 5:25-34, Luke 8:43-48*
Jesus heals Syrophenician woman's daughter *Mat 15:21-28, Mark 7: 24-30*
Jesus' parable of the lost sheep *Mat 18:12-14, Luke 15:1-7*
Jesus raises son of widow of Nain *Luke 7:11-17*
Jesus' parable of the good Samaritan *Luke 10:25-37*
Paul shipwrecked *Acts 27:1-44*
Paul's thorn in the flesh *2 Cor 12: 1-19*
James on how to bear our cross *Jas 1:1-27*
John's vision of the dragon attacking the woman *Rev 12:1-27*

See also adversity, affliction, danger, pain

DIVINE

Moses hears voice of God at burning bush *Exod 3:1-18, 4:1-17*
Moses receives Ten Commandments from God *Exod 20:1-19, Deut 5: 1-24*
Joshua meets captain of the host *Josh 5:10-15*
Gideon asks God for proof *Judg 6: 19-40*
Samuel hears God call him *1 Sam 3:1-10*
Elijah supplied with fire and rain *1 King 18:17-40*
Elijah hears still small voice *1 King 19:9-13*
Job hears the voice of thunder *Job 38:1-41*
David's song, "Thou hast been our dwelling place" *Psal 90:1-17*
David's song on the divine presence *Psal 139:1-24*
Isaiah's vision of God's glory *Isa 6:1-13*

Isaiah's prophecy of birth of Messiah *Isa 7:10-16, 9:2-7*
At Jesus' baptism a voice from heaven *Mat 3:13-17, Mark 1:9-11, Luke 3:21, 22*
Jesus acknowledges he is Christ *Mat 16:13-20, Mark 8:27-30, Luke 9:18-21*
Jesus transfigured on mount *Mat 17:1-13, Mark 9:2-13, Luke 9:28-36*
Birth of Jesus announced to Mary *Luke 1:26-38*
Jesus' teaching that he is Christ *John 7:14-40*
Disciples experience divine influx at Pentecost *Acts 2:1-13*
Paul on Christ's resurrection proves our resurrection *1 Cor 15:1-58*
John's sermon on nature of God as Love *1 John 4:1-21*

See also God, holiness, human, man, mind

DIVORCE

Abraham sends Hagar and son away from home *Gen 21:9-21*
Jesus on judge not others *Mat 7:1-5, Luke 6:37-40*
Jesus on Golden Rule *Mat 7:12-14, Luke 6:41, 42*
Jesus on house built on rock *Mat 7:24-29, Luke 6:48, 49*
A house divided *Mat 12:22-37, Mark 3:20-30, Luke 11:14-20*
Jesus on "Who is my mother?" *Mat 12:46-50*
Jesus' parable of lost sheep *Mat 18:12-14, Luke 15:1-7*
Jesus questioned on Moses' bill of divorcement *Mat 19:3-12, Mark 10:2-12*
Jesus on remarriage and resurrection *Mat 22:23-33, Mark 12:18-27, John 20:27-40*
Jesus' parable of good Samaritan *Luke 10:25-37*
Jesus' parable of judge and widow *Luke 18:1-8*
Paul on value of love *1 Cor 13:1-13*
James on how to bear our cross *Jas 1:1-27*

See also marriage, parting, separation

DOCTOR

Asa turns to physicians to heal feet *2 Chron 16:11-14*
Jesus heals woman who had spent all her living on physicians *Mat 9:20-22, Mark 5:25-34, Luke 8:43-48*
At twelve years Jesus talks with rabbis *Luke 2:41-52*
Paul's education as a Pharisee *Acts 8:1-4*

See also healing, medicine, physician, surgery

DOCTRINE

Moses delivers Ten Commandments *Exod 20:1-19, Deut 5:1-24*
Moses outlines the blessings of obedience *Deut 28:1-14*
Isaiah describes the coming Messiah *Isa 2:1-5, 7:10-16, 9:2-7, 11:1-12, 42:1-12, 16-18, 53:1-12, 61:1-11, 62:1-12*
Jesus' parables—all 49 teach (*See* Part II, Jesus Christ: Parables)
Jesus' Sermon on the Mount *Mat 5:1-48, 6:1-34, 7:1-29*
Jesus tells the lineage of the Christ *Mat 22:41-46, Mark 12:35-37, Luke 20:41-44*
Jesus instructing disciples *Mat 28:16-20, Mark 16:15-18*
Jesus on how to preach and heal *Luke 10:1-16*
Jesus on forgiveness and increasing faith *Luke 17:1-6*
Jesus answers rabbis at twelve years old *John 2:41-52*
John Baptist tells how Jesus' doctrine differs *John 3:22-36*
Jesus on the bread of life *John 6:26-65*
Jesus on unity and eternity of Christ *John 8:12-59*
Paul's sermons selected *Rom 5:1-21, 8:1-39, 1 Cor 12:1, 4-31, 13:1-13, 2 Cor 6:-18, Gal 5:1-26, Eph 4:1-32, 6:10-17, Phil 4:1-23, Col 3:1-17, 1 Thess 5:1-28, 2 Tim 2:1-26, Heb 1:1-14, 6:20-40, 7:28, 10:1-39, 11:1-40, 12:1-29*
James' sermons *Jas 1:1-27, 2:1-13, 14-26*

John's sermon on love *1 John 4: 1-21*

See also principle, teaching, tenets

DOMINION

God gives man (not Adam) dominion *Gen 1:26, 27*

Joseph made governor of Egypt *Gen 41:1-46*

Moses gives Israelites manna, quails, water *Exod 16:1-36, 17:1-7*

Joshua sees sun and moon stand still *Josh 10:6-15*

David kills giant *1 Sam 17:17-52*

Jehoshaphat learns that the battle is God's *2 Chron 20:1-32*

Elijah divides water of Jordan *2 King 2:8*

Elisha divides water of Jordan *2 King 2:12-15*

Job hears the infinite speak *Job 38:1-41*

Isaiah declares Messiah will rule as Prince of Peace *Isa 9:2-7*

Jeremiah says captivity will be turned *Jer 29:8-14*

Jesus heals sickness and death (*See* Part II, Jesus Christ: Great Works)

Jesus calms seas *Mat 8:23-27, Mark 4:35-41, Luke 8:22-25*

Jesus' eulogy of John Baptist as strong prophet *Mat 11:7-15, Luke 7:24-30*

Jesus feeds 5000 *Mat 14:15-21, Mark 6:35-44, Luke 9:12-17, John 6:5-14*

Jesus walks on water *Mat 14:22-33, John 6:15-21*

Transfiguration *Mat 17:1-13, Mark 9:2-13, Luke 9:28-36*

Jesus withers fig tree *Mat 21:18-25, Mark 11:12-14, 20-24*

Resurrection *Mat 28:9, 10, Mark 16:9-11, Luke 24:1-13, John 20: 11-31*

Jesus' great works have source in Father *John 5:17-47*

Paul and sailors saved from shipwreck *Acts 27:1-44*

War in heaven *Rev 12:1-17*

New heaven and new earth *Rev 21: 1-27*

See also authority, government, great works, power

DOOR

Jesus' parable of wise and foolish virgins *Mat 25:1-13*

Jesus' parable of unwilling friend *Luke 11:5-13*

Jesus' parable of door shut by the master *Luke 13:22-30*

Jesus on Christ as the door and good shepherd *John 10:1-42*

Jesus' sermon, I am the way *John 14:1-31*

Paul and Silas in prison but earthquake opens doors *Acts 16:19-40*

John's vision of door opened in heaven *Rev 4:1-11*

See also opportunity, way

DOUBT

Abraham and Sarah think they are too old to have a child *Gen 17: 1-9*

Moses uncertain of his abilities *Exod 3:9-12, 4:10-17*

Moses provided food in wilderness when Israelites urge return to Egypt *Exod 16:1-36, Num 11:1-15, 31, 32*

Israelites doubt their ability to enter promised land *Num 13:1-33, 14: 1-11, 23-39*

Gideon's faith develops slowly by testing *Judg 6:19-40*

Asa turns to physicians instead of God *2 Chron 16:11-14*

John Baptist sends to Jesus for proof he is Christ *Mat 11:2-19, Luke 7:18-35*

Pharisees doubt Jesus, demand a sign *Mat 12:38-45, 16:1-4, Mark 8:10-13, Luke 11:16, 29-32*

Peter doubts his ability to walk on water *Mat 14:22-33, John 6:15-21*

Thomas doubts that apostles saw risen Jesus *Mark 16:14, Luke 24: 36-49, John 20:19-23*

Jesus deserted by many after sermon on bread of life *John 6:66-71*

Jesus heals man born blind *John 9:1-41*

See also belief, certainty, faith, fear, truth

DOWNFALL

See destruction

DRAGON

The serpent beguiles Eve with lie
Gen 3:1-5

John's vision of great red dragon
Rev 12:1-17

See also aggression, evil, fear, serpent

DREAMS

Jacob's dream of angels on a ladder
Gen 28:10-22

Joseph's boyhood dreams cause him
trouble *Gen 37:1-36*

Joseph interprets butler's and baker's
dreams *Gen 39:21-23, 40:1-23*

Joseph interprets Pharaoh's dream
of seven years *Gen 41:1-46*

Elijah fed in a dream *1 King 19:
1-8*

Job has a nightmare of fear *Job
4:13-21*

Isaiah is called to prophecy *Isa 6:
1-13*

Jeremiah is called to prophecy *Jer
1:1-10*

Jeremiah warns against false prophets who dream *Jer 23:1-8*

Ezekiel's vision of dry bones *Ezek
37:1-14*

Ezekiel's vision of holy waters
Ezek 47:1-12

Daniel interprets Nebuchadnezzar's
dream *Dan 4:1-27*

Daniel has a vision of meeting
Gabriel *Dan 9:20-23, 10:4-21*

Zechariah's vision of candlestick
Zech 4:1-14

Joseph, husband of Mary, has two
dreams *Mat 1:18-25, 2:13-15, Luke
2:39, 40*

Jesus is transfigured on mountain
*Mat 17:1-13, Mark 9:2-13, Luke 9:
28-36*

Peter's vision of great sheet defends
Gentiles *Acts 11:1-18*

Paul's vision of the Christ causes
blindness *Acts 9:1-9*

John's visions including new heaven
and earth *Rev 21:1-27*

See also hypnotism, mind, revelation, sleep, unreality, vision

DROPSY (Edema)

Jesus heals man instantly *Luke 14.
1-6*

DROUGHT

Hagar and son saved in wilderness
Gen 21:9-21

Isaac's strife over wells *Gen 26:
12-31*

Moses gets water from rock *Exod
17:1-7, Num 20:1-13*

Elijah prays for rain *1 King 18:
41-46*

Elisha supplies water for an army
2 King 3:16-20

David's song, "the fountain of life"
Psal 36:1-12

Isaiah's vision, "the desert will
blossom" *Isa 35:1-10*

John Baptist lives in desert *Mat 3:
1-12, Mark 1:1-8, Luke 3:1-18*

Jesus' discourse with woman at
Jacob's well *John 4:1-42*

See also barrenness, desert, fruits,
rain, wilderness

DUMBNESS

Jesus heals dumb man *Mat 9:32-35*

Jesus heals man blind and dumb
Mat 12:22-30, Luke 11:14-23

Jesus heals a group including dumb
Mat 15:29-31

Jesus heals deaf man with speech
impediment *Mark 7:32-37*

Jesus heals dumb man and is accused
of using Beelzebub *Luke 11:14-26*

See also eloquence, healing, speech

DUPLICITY

Isaac deceived by Jacob for blessing
Gen 27:1-44

Joseph put in prison by lie of
Potiphar's wife *Gen 29:1-20*

Moses opposed by his brother and
sister *Num 12:1-16*

Rahab protects the Israelite spies
Josh 2:1-24

Samson betrayed by Delilah *Judg
16:4-30*

David sends Uriah to his death
2 Sam 11:1-27
Nathan exposes David's duplicity
2 Sam 12:1-10
Gehazi accepts the forbidden reward, result—leprosy *2 King 5: 15-27*
Isaiah warns workers in the dark
Isa 29:11-24, 30:1-3, 20, 21
Jesus' parable of debtor unmerciful to his fellows *Mat 18:23-35*
Jesus' parable of two sons ordered to work *Mat 21:28-32*
Judas gets price for betraying Jesus *Mat 26:14-16, Mark 14:10, 11, Luke 22:1-6, 14-30*

See also betrayal, deceit, hypocrisy, lie

DUST

Lord God makes man from dust
Gen 2:6-8
Lord God orders him to return to dust *Gen 3:6-24*
The walls of Jericho crumble *Josh 6:1-27*
Jeremiah's parable of potter and clay *Jer 18:1-6*
Jesus writes in dust with his finger
John 8:1-11
Jesus makes clay to anoint blind eyes *John 9:1-41*

See also body, earth, materialism, matter, senses

DUTY

Cain asks if he is his brother's keeper *Gen 4:1-16*
Moses accepts the work God gives him *Exod 3:9-12*
Moses urges obedience by chosen people *Deut 4:1-15, 11:1-32*
Elisha takes up the mantle of Elijah
2 King 2:12-15
Nehemiah takes up the task to rebuild the walls *Neh 1:1-11*
Esther undertakes to save her people *Esther 3:1-15, 4:1-17*
David's song of the steps of a good man *Psal 1:1-6*
The poor wise man who saved the city *Eccl 9:13-18*
Daniel and his companions put God

first *Dan 1:1-21, 3:1-30, 6:1-28*
Jonah flees his duty and then does it *Jonah 1:1-17, 2:1-10, 3:1-10*
Malachi urges tithing *Mal 3:10, 4: 1, 2*
Jesus tells disciples they must preach and heal *Mat 10:5-42, 28: 16-20, Mark 6:7-13, 16:15-18, Luke 9:1-6, 10:1-16*
Jesus' parable of two sons ordered to work *Mat 21:28-32*
Jesus on the duty to pay taxes *Mat 22:15-22, Mark 12:13-17, Luke 20: 20-26*
Jesus' parable of the talents *Mat 25:14-30, Luke 19:11-28*
Jesus' parable of faithful steward
Luke 12:41-48
Jesus' parable of dutiful elder brother *Luke 15:25-32*
Jesus tells his parents he must be about his Father's business *John 2:41-52*
Jesus risen, charges Peter to "Feed my sheep" *John 21:12-19*
Paul's sermon on how Christians should act *Col 3:1-17*

See also God, leader, obedience, obligation, parent, service

DWELLING

Adam asked, "Where art thou?"
Gen 3:6-24
Moses and Israelites dwell in wilderness 40 years *Deut 8:1-20, 32:1-47*
David's son to build dwelling for Lord *1 Chron 17:1-27*
Solomon dedicates house of Lord
1 King 8:22-66, 2 Chron 6:1-42
Elisha provided a room by Shunammite *2 King 4:8-37*
David's songs *Psal 90:1-17, 91:1-16, 139:1-24*
Isaiah sees lion and lamb dwell together *Isa 11:1-12*
Isaiah's vision of the quiet habitation *Isa 33:20-24*
Micah's vision of mountain of Lord's house *Mic 4:1-8, 13, Isa 2:1-5*
Jesus' parable of house built on sand and rock *Mat 7:24-27, Luke 6:48, 49*
Jesus tells scribe he has no home
Mat 8:18-22

Jesus asked by two disciples where he dwells *Mat 8:18-20*

Jesus on branches dwelling in vine *John 15:1-17*

Abraham by faith dwelt in tents in land of promise *Heb 11:8, 9*

John's vision of city of God *Rev 21:1-27*

See also abiding, ever-presence, home

E

EAR

Isaiah's vision of Messiah includes ear of deaf to be unstopped *Isa 35:1-10*

Jesus speaks to those who have ears and cannot hear *Mat 13:10-17, 34, 35, Mark 4: 33, 34*

Jesus heals deaf man with speech impediment and in process puts finger in deaf man's ear *Mark 7:32-37*

Jesus restores amputation of Malchus' ear *Luke 22:50, 51*

See also deafness, hearing, listening, senses

EARNESTNESS

Isaac, a serious boy *Gen 22:1-19*

Jacob clings to the angel until his name is changed *Gen 32:24-32*

Moses complains of his speaking ability *Exod 4:10-17*

Moses gives people Ten Commandments *Exod 20:1-19, Deut 5:1-24*

Moses' sermon on choosing good *Deut 30:11-20*

Joshua sets up twelve stones as memorial for deliverance *Josh 4:1-24*

Gideon gradually develops faith in God *Judg 6:19-40*

Ruth remains loyal to her mother-in-law *Ruth 1:1-22*

Solomon in dream requests understanding above all *1 King 3:5-15, 2 Chron 1:7-12*

Elijah finds Elisha plowing *1 King 19:19-21*

Elisha requests double portion of spirit *2 King 2:1-15*

Peter acknowledges Jesus as Christ *Mat 16:13-20, Mark 8:27-30, Luke 9:18-21*

Jesus heals epileptic boy *Mat 17: 14-21, Mark 9:14-29, Luke 9:37-43*

Jesus prays at Gethsemane *Mat 26: 30, 36-46, Mark 14:26, 32-42, Luke 22:39-46*

Jesus heals Bartimaeus *Mark 10: 46-52*

Jesus drives traders from temple *John 2:13-25*

Peter protests he loves Jesus *John 21:12-19*

Peter and John speak word boldly *Acts 4:1-23*

Paul's self-revelings *2 Cor 12:1-19*

See also sincerity

EARTH

God made it and gave man dominion *Gen 1:1-31*

Noah sees flood cover earth *Gen 7:1-24*

Tower of Babel, earth had one language *Gen 11:1-9*

David's song, "full of the goodness of the Lord" *Psal 33:1-22*

David's song, "our dwelling place" *Psal 90:1-17*

Job hears God explain the world *Job 38:1-41*

Preacher on all earthly events within time *Eccl 3:1-15*

Jesus says meek will inherit earth *Mat 5:1-5*

Jesus ascends above earth *Mark 16: 19, 20, Luke 24:50-53, Acts 1:9-13*

John sees new heaven and new earth *Rev 21:1-27*

See also dust, heaven, world

EASTER

Moses and original passover *Exod 11:4-10, 12:1-14, 21-41, Deut 16: 1-22*

Aaron and primitive atonement through scapegoat *Lev. 16:1-28*

Isaiah's vision of the triumphant Messiah *Isa 52:1-15, 60:1-5*

Jesus raises Jairus' daughter *Mat 9:18, 19, 23-26, Mark 5:22-24, 35-43, Luke 8:41, 42, 49-56*

Jesus enters Jerusalem just before Easter *Mat 21:1-11, 14-17, Mark 11:1-11, Luke 19:29-44, John 12: 12-49*

Jesus' parable of the farmers who refused rent *Mat 21:33-46, Mark 12:1-12, Luke 20:9-19*

Signs at crucifixion *Mat 27:50-54, Mark 15:37, 38*

Jesus' body disappears from the tomb *Mat 28:1-8, Mark 16:1-8, Luke 24:1-12, John 20: 1-10*

First appearance to Mary *Mat 28: 9, 10, Mark 16:9-11, Luke 24:13-49, John 20:11-18*

Other appearances *Mat 28:16-20, Mark 16:12-18, Luke 24:13-49, John 20:19-29, 21:1-25, 1 Cor 15: 5-15, Acts 1:1-8*

Jesus raises son of widow of Nain *Luke 7:11-17*

Jesus' parable of temple raised in three days *John 2:19-22*

Jesus teaching that he is Christ *John 7:14-40*

Jesus raises Lazarus after four days *John 11:1-46*

Peter imprisoned again just before Easter *Acts 12:1-17*

Paul on resurrection *1 Cor 15:1-58*

Paul on eternity of Christ *Heb 6: 20, 7:1-28*

John on Love *1 John 4:1-21*

See also lamb, life, passover, resurrection

ECONOMICS

Abraham grows rich, Lot too *Gen 13:1-18*

Isaac's strife over wells *Gen 26: 12-31*

Joseph solves problem of famine *Gen 41:1-46*

Famine in Israel turns them to Egypt *Gen 42:1-8*

Israelites as Egyptian slaves *Exod 5:7-19*

Food scarcity solved in wilderness *Exod 16:1-36, Num 11:1-15, 31, 32*

Water scarcity solved in wilderness *Exod 17:1-7, Num 20:1-13*

Farming community practices in Israel *Ruth 2:1-22*

Solomon builds the temple *1 King 6:1-38, 7:1-51, 2 Chron 3:1-17, 4:1-22, 5:1-14*

Elisha prophesies drop in price of flour *2 King 6:24, 25, 7:1-18*

Hezekiah shows Babylon his treasures *2 King 20:12-21, Isa 39:1-8*

Nehemiah hears of Jerusalem's poverty *Neh 1:1-11*

Malachi urges tithing *Mal 3:10, 4: 1, 2*

Jesus gives Golden Rule for actions *Mat 7:12-14, Luke 6:41, 42*

Jesus' farm parables *Mat 13:3-32, 36-43, Mark 4:1-20, 26-29, 30-32, Luke 8:4-15, 13:18, 19*

Jesus feeds the 5000 *Mat 14:15-21, Mark 6:35-44, Luke 9:12-17, John 6:5-14*

Jesus has Peter obtain tax money from fish *Mat 17:24-27*

Jesus on tribute payable to Caesar *Mat 22:15-22, Mark 12:13-17, Luke 20:20-26*

Jesus' parable of the talents *Mat 25:14-30, Luke 19:11-28*

Jesus explains widow's mite *Mark 12:41-44, Luke 21:1-4*

Peter's net is filled *Luke 5:1-11, John 21:1-11*

Jesus' parable on cost of building a tower *Luke 14:25-33*

Jesus turns water into wine *John 2:1-11*

Jesus casts traders out of temple *John 2:13-25*

Christian communism *Acts 2:41-47*

See also government, politics, wealth

EDEMA (excess fluid in abdomen)

See dropsy

EDEN

Lord God placed man of dust in garden *Gen 2:6-8*

Lord God sends Adam and Eve out of garden *Gen 3:22-24*

Rivers and trees in Eden *Gen 2: 9-17*

See also materialism, paradise, pleasure, spirituality

EDUCATION

Samuel assists Eli in temple *1 Sam 3:1-10*

Elijah takes Elisha for a pupil *1 King 19:19-21*

Ezra reads the book of the law to the people *Neh 8:1-12*

Jesus instructs disciples and sends them *Mat 9:36-38, 10:1-42, Mark 3:13-21, Luke 6:13-19, 9:1-6, 10, 11*

Jesus speaks only in parables *Mat 13: 34, 35, 53, Mark 4:33, 34*

Jesus heals epileptic boy after disciples fail *Mat 17:14-21, Mark 9:14-29, Luke 9:37-43*

Jesus at twelve with rabbis *Luke 2:41-52*

Jesus at Emmaus instructs two disciples about Christ *Luke 24:13-35*

John Baptist tells how Jesus' teaching differs *John 3:22-36*

Jesus washes disciples' feet *John 13:1-20*

Jesus' parable of the true vine *John 15:1-17*

Paul's epistles all teach, especially these *2 Tim 2:1-26, 3:1-17, 4:1-8*

John's letters to seven churches *Rev 1:4-20, 2:1-29, 3:1-22, 4:1-11*

Jesus taught by preaching (*See* Part II, Jesus Christ: Teachings)

See also childlikeness, children, disciple, instruction, teaching

EFFORT

Noah builds his ark of safety *Gen 6:5-22*

Ruth gleans in the field for grain to support her mother-in-law *Ruth 2:1-23*

Solomon builds the temple *1 King 6:1-38, 7:1-51, 2 Chron 3:1-17, 4:1-22, 5:1-14*

Zerubbabel rebuilds the temple *Ezra 3:8-13*

Zerubbabel after pause starts again *Ezra 6:1-3, 7, 8, 14, 15*

Nehemiah rebuilds walls of Jerusalem *Neh 4:1-23*

Jesus on "Seek ye first" *Mat 6:25-34*

Jesus' parable of treasures in field *Mat 13:14*

Jesus' parable of pearl of great price *Mat 13:45, 46*

Jesus heals daughter of persistent woman *Mat 15:21-28, Mark 7:24-30*

Jesus' parable of the talents *Mat 25:14-30, Luke 19:11-28*

Jesus at Gethsemane *Mat 26:30, 36-46, Mark 14:26, 32-42, Luke 22:39-46*

Jesus' parable of the unwilling friend *Luke 11:5-13*

Jesus' parable of the cost of building a tower *Luke 14:25-33*

Jesus' parable of piece of money *Luke 15:8-10*

Jesus' parable of the judge and the widow *Luke 18:1-8*

Seven deacons chosen to administer the church *Acts 6:1-4*

Paul's effort to establish the church *2 Cor 11:21-33*

James on trials *Jas 1:1-27*

James on faith without works *Jas 2:14-26*

See also persistence, power, struggle, trial

EGO

God creates the universe *Gen 1:31, 2:1-5*

Man's egotism at Tower of Babel *Gen 11:1-9*

Moses learns name of God, I Am That I Am *Exod 3:1-18*

Moses learns First Commandment *Exod 20:1-19*

Uzziah's egotism punished *2 Chron 26:1-23*

Job hears God explain Himself *Job 38:1-41*

The vanity of mortal life *Eccl 1:1-18, 2:1-26*

Isaiah sees the body culture of women as vain *Isa 3:16-26*

Jesus' parable of the mote and beam *Mat 7:3-5, Luke 6:37-42*

Jesus heals the Gadarene of insanity *Mat 8:28-34, Mark 5:1-20, Luke 8:26-39*

Jesus on the Son of man is Lord of sabbath *Mat 12:1-8*

Jesus' disciples contend who shall

be greatest *Mat 18:1-11, Mark 9:
33-37, Luke 9:46-50, 22:24-30*

Zebedee's wife tries to advance her
sons *Mat 20:20-28, Mark 10:35-45*

Jesus on the precious ointment used
on him *Mat 26:6-13, Mark 14:3-9*

Jesus' parable of chief seats at wedding *Luke 14:7-14*

Jesus says the source of his great
works is the Father *John 5:17-47*

Jesus on the bread of life *John 6:
26-65*

Jesus on the Christ *John 7:14-40*

See also God, humility, pride, self,
vanity

EGYPT

Joseph sold into slavery *Gen 37:
1-36*

Jacob and children emigrate to
Egypt *Gen 45:25-28, 46:2-7*

Oppression of people *Exod 1:8-14,
5:7-19*

Sorcerers match marvels wth Aaron
Exod 7:1-12

Jesus' family's flight to Egypt *Mat
2:13-23, Luke 2:39, 40*

See also exodus, passover

ELECTION

Jacob deceives his father to obtain
the blessing intended for his
brother *Gen 27:1-44*

Joseph appointed governor by Pharaoh *Gen 41:1-46*

Moses appoints judges to help him
Exod 18:13-27

Moses explains Israelites are chosen
people *Deut 7:6-11*

Moses selects Joshua as his successor *Deut 31:7-23*

Gideon refuses to be king *Judg 8:
22, 23*

Jotham's parable of how to select
ruler *Judg 9:1-15*

Samuel resists demand for a king
1 Sam 8:1-22

Samuel anoints Saul, a mistake
1 Sam 10:1-8

Samuel selects David as king *1 Sam
16:1-13*

Absalom tries to replace his father
as king *2 Sam 15:1-23*

Isaiah's vision of king of kings *Isa
9:2-7*

Daniel appointed by the king to rule
Dan 6:1-28

Jesus calls his disciples *Mat 4:17-
22, Mark 1:14-20, Luke 5:1-11,
John 1:35-42*

Jesus' parable of sheep and goats
Mat 25:31-46

Peter and apostles elect Matthias
Acts 1:15-26

Peter has seven deacons chosen
Acts 6:1-4

James on equality before God *Jas
2:1-13*

See also calling, choice, chosen
people, office

ELEMENTS CONTROLLED

Moses crosses the Red Sea *Exod
14:5-31*

Joshua crosses Jordan *Josh 3:1-17*

Joshua causes sun and moon to stand
still *Josh 10:6-15*

Elijah prays for rain *1 King 18:
41-46*

Elijah crosses Jordan *2 King 2:1-11*

Elisha crosses Jordan *2 King 2:
12-15*

Elisha causes iron to swim *2 King
6:1-7*

Jesus calms wind and seas *Mat 8:
23-27, Mark 4:35-41, Luke 8:22-25*

Jesus walks on water, saves Peter
Mat 14:22-31, John 6:15-21

Jesus withers fig tree *Mat 21:18-
22, Mark 11:12-14, 20-24*

Jesus' crucifixion causes signs *Mat
27:50-54, Mark 15:37, 38*

Jesus calms windstorm and transports ship at once to port *Mark
6:46-51, John 6:21*

Jesus turns water to wine *John 2:
1-11*

Jesus' great works have source in
Father *John 5:17-47*

See also rain, river, sea, storm,
weather, wind

ELEVATION

God gives man dominion *Gen 1:
26, 27*

Enoch walked with God and is translated *Gen 5:18, 21-24, Heb 11:5*

Noah's ark elevated above the flood *Gen 7:1-24*

Tower of Babel *Gen 11:1-9*

Abram walked with God and got new name *Gen 17:1-9, 15-22*

Joseph dreams of sheaves bowing to his sheaf *Gen 37:1-36*

Joseph made governor *Gen 41:1-46*

Moses talks with God on Mt. Sinai *Exod 19:1-9*

The chosen people set apart as God's own *Deut 7:6-11*

Saul anointed king *1 Sam 10:1-8*

Elijah translated to heaven *2 King 2:1-11*

Birth of Messiah prophesied *Isa 7: 1-16, 9:2-7*

Jesus' ascension *Mark 16:19, 20, Luke 24:50, 51, Acts 1:6-12*

Matthias elected to fill Judas' place as apostle *Acts 1:15-26*

See also advancement, exaltation, promote

ELIJAH

See Part II, Elijah

ELISHA

See Part II, Elisha

ELOQUENCE

Moses' speaking ability *Exod 4: 10-17*

Moses, after talks with God, gives Ten Commandments *Exod 19:1-9, 20:1-19, Deut 4:1-15, 5:1-24*

Isaiah called to prophesy *Isa 6:1-13*

Jeremiah called to prophesy *Jer 1:1-10*

Ezekiel called to prophesy *Ezek 2: 1-10*

Jonah converts Nineveh *Jonah 3: 1-10*

Jesus heals dumb man *Mat 9:32-35*

Jesus reproves the Pharisees and scribes *Mat 23:1-39, Mark 12:38-40, Luke 11:37-54, 20:45-47*

Jesus sought by all men to hear him *Mark 1:35-39*

Jesus heals deaf man with speech impediment *Mark 7:32-37*

Zacharias' dumbness released *Luke 1:5-25, 57-80*

Jesus heals dumb man *Luke 11: 14-26*

Jesus' parable of Pharisee and publican *Luke 18:9-14*

Jesus' discourse on bread of life as example of eloquence *John 6: 26-65*

Peter and John speak the word with boldness *Acts 4:1-23*

Paul on "Unknown God" at Athens *Acts 17:15-34*

Paul on charity *1 Cor 13:1-13*

John on God is love *1 John 4:1-21*

See also authority, communication, sincerity, speech, tongue

EMANCIPATION

See freedom, slavery

EMMANUEL (Immanuel)

See Christ, prophecy of

EMOTION

Cain angered, kills Abel *Gen 4:1-16*

Abraham's love for God greater than love for son *Gen 22:1-19*

Jacob afraid of the brother he wronged *Gen 33:1-11*

Joseph hated by brothers *Gen 37: 1-36*

Joseph loved and hated by Potiphar's wife *Gen 39:1-20*

Joseph forgives his brothers *Gen 43:1, 2, 45:1-11, 25, 28*

Moses returns good for evil *Num 12:1-16*

David plays harp to calm Saul *1 Sam 16:14-23*

David has man killed to take his wife *2 Sam 11:1-27*

David grieves for Absalom *2 Sam 18:6-33*

Job's suffering *Job 3:1-26*

David expresses the love between God and man *Psal 23:1-6*

Isaiah describes the pride of women *Isa 3:16-26*

Jesus heals a father's despair *Mat 17:14-21, Mark 9:14-29, Luke 9: 37-43*

Jesus casts out traders *Luke 2: 13-25*

Jesus defines brotherly love *Luke 10:25-37*

Jesus accepts gratitude of tenth leper *Luke 17:11-19*

Mary Magdalene's despair and joy *John 20:11-18*

Paul on degrees of emotion *1 Cor 13:1-13*

Paul reveals his feelings *2 Cor 12: 1-19*

John on love *1 John 4:1-21*

See also anger, fear, hatred, love, organic

EMPLOYMENT

Joseph manages his master's property *Gen 39:1-20*

Jesus heals the centurion's retainer *Mat 8:5-13, Luke 7:1-10*

Jesus' parable of laborers hired for a penny *Mat 20:1-16*

Jesus' parable of two sons ordered to work *Mat 21:28-32*

Jesus' parable of the talents *Mat 25:14-30, Luke 19:11-28*

Jesus' parable of the faithful steward *Luke 12:41-48*

Jesus' parable of the servant *Luke 16:40, 17:7-10*

See also business, calling, occupation, office, place, work

EMPTINESS

See vanity

ENCOURAGEMENT

Moses encouraged by signs from God *Exod 4:1-9*

Moses tells people they are chosen *Deut 7:6-11*

Moses' exhortation to Joshua *Deut 31:7-23, Josh 1:1-9*

Gideon encouraged by signs from God *Judg 6:19-40*

Elijah's discouragement overcome *1 King 19:1-8*

Job's friends fail to comfort him *Job 16:1-22*

David's songs of safety *Psal 91:1-16, 121:1-8, 139:1-24*

Isaiah's reassurance, "Comfort ye!" *Isa 40:1-31*

Jeremiah encourages the captives *Jer 29:8-14, 31:1-14, 31-34*

Zephaniah promises salvation *Zeph 3:14-17*

Jesus encourages his disciples at Last Supper *Mat 26:26-29, Mark 14:22-25, Luke 22:14-30, 1 Cor 11: 23-25*

Jesus heals the depressed invalid *John 15:1-9*

Jesus' parable of the vine and branches *John 15:1-17*

Jesus comforts his disciples *John 16:1-23, 17:1-26*

Jesus risen, follows his disciples to Galilee *John 21:1-19*

Paul's advice to his disciples *2 Tim 2:1-26*

See also comfort, courage, fear

ENDURANCE

God creates the forever universe *Gen 1:1-31*

The patriarchs live to advanced age *Gen 5:1-32*

Moses relieves his burdens by appointing judges *Exod 18:13-27*

Bites of fiery serpents in wilderness healed *Num 21:4-9*

Ruth gleans in field of Boaz *Ruth 2:1-23*

Elijah fed by ravens, fed in a dream *1 King 17:1-7, 19:1-8*

In famine Elisha prophesies incredible plenty *2 King 6:24, 25*

Nehemiah repairs the wall of Jerusalem *Neh 4:1-23*

Job's trials, woe expressed *Job 3: 1-26*

David's song, "The Lord is my shepherd" *Psal 23:1-6*

David's song, "God is our refuge and strength" *Psal 46:1-11*

David's song, God the preserver of man *Psal 121:1-8*

Isaiah's vision of Messiah's suffering *Isa 53:1-12*

Three Jews endure fiery furnace *Dan 3:1-30*

Jesus heals woman who endured issue of blood twelve years *Mat 9: 20-22, Mark 5:25-34, Luke 8:43-48*

Jesus endures the cross *Mat 27:32-56, Mark 15:21-41, Luke 23:26-49, John 19:17-30*

Jesus heals impotent man who suffered 38 years *John 5:1-9*

Stephen is stoned *Acts 7:51-60*

Paul is stoned and recovers *Acts 14:19, 20*

Paul's hardships to establish church *2 Cor 11:21-33*

See also eternity, strength, suffering

ENEMY

Jacob wrestles with adversary before meeting his estranged brother *Gen 32:1-32, 33:1-11*

Joshua encompasses Jericho and it crumbles *Josh 6:1-27*

Deborah defeats invaders *Judg 4:1-17*

Gideon outwits invaders *Judg 7:1-25*

Samson betrayed to enemy *Judg 16:4-30*

David accepts Goliath's challenge *1 Sam 17:17-52*

David spares his enemy, the king *1 Sam 24:1-22, 26:1-25*

Elisha outwits, then forgives, Syrian army *2 King 6:8-23*

Elisha sees invaders destroyed by epidemic *2 King 7:1-18*

Hezekiah sees invaders destroyed by epidemic *2 King 18:17-37, 19:1-27, 2 Chron 31:20-21, 32:1-23, Isa 36:1-22, 37:1-38*

David's songs of security *Psal 23:1-6, 91:1-16, 121:1-8, 139:1-24*

Isaiah's vision of Christ's peaceable kingdom *Isa 11:1-11*

Isaiah's promise of God's help *Isa 43:1-28, 44:1-24*

Ezekiel's vision of safety *Ezek 34:1-31*

Ezekiel's vision of protecting army *Ezek 37:1-14*

Daniel's enemies put him in lion's den *Dan 6:1-28*

Jesus defeats the tempter *Mat 4:1-11, Mark 1:12, 13, Luke 4:1-13*

Jesus on how to treat enemies *Mat 5:38-48, Luke 6:27-36*

Jesus accused of using devil to heal *Mat 12:22-30, Mark 3:22-30, Luke 11:14-23*

Jesus explains why he speaks only in parables *Mat 13:34, 35, Mark 4:33, 34*

Jesus' sermon denounces scribes and Pharisees *Mat 23:1-39*

Judas self-destroyed *Mat 27:3-10, Acts 1:15-20*

Jesus submits to crucifixion *Mat 27:32-56, Mark 15:21-41, Luke 23:6-49, John 19:17-30*

Jesus' enemies seek to destroy him *Mark 11:18, 19*

Jesus delivers himself by passing through enemies *Luke 4:28-32*

Paul, the persecutor, is converted *Acts 8:1-4, 9:1-22*

Paul warned of danger in Jerusalem *Acts 21:10-15*

Paul on the weapons of our warfare *2 Cor 10:3-5*

Paul on enemies of the truth *2 Tim 3:1-17*

See also adversary, devil, hatred

ENERGY

Spiritual creation of universe *Gen 1:1-31, 2:1-5*

Babel tower built without divine help *Gen 11:1-9*

Joseph builds up Potiphar's property *Gen 39:1-5*

Solomon builds temple *1 King 6:1-38, 7:1-51, 2 Chron 3:1-17, 4:1-22, 5:1-14*

Nehemiah repairs wall *Neh 4:1-23*

Jesus' parable of the talents *Mat 25:14-30, Luke 19:11-28*

Jesus prays while disciples sleep *Mat 26:30, 36-46, Mark 14:26, 32-42, Luke 22:35-46*

Jesus parable of faithful steward *Luke 12:41-48*

Jesus' parable on counting the cost *Luke 14:25-33*

Jesus' parable of the servant and master *Luke 17:7-10*

Jesus' parable of judge and widow *Luke 18:1-8*

Jesus says his great works have source in Father *John 5:17-47*

Jesus washes disciples' feet *John 13:1-20*

Jesus causes guards to fall backwards *John 18:4-6*

Paul on his trials as a Christian *Acts 20:17-38*

Paul's hardships *2 Cor 11:21-33*

James' sermon how to bear our cross *Jas 1:1-27*

See also ability, force, power, strength

ENTRANCE

Noah and others enter the ark of safety *Gen 7:1-24*

Caleb and Joshua urge immediate entrance of promised land *Num 13:1-33, 14:1-11, 23-39, Deut 1:19-38*

People cross Jordan and enter promised land *Josh 3:-17*

Jesus enters Jerusalem for last time —to hosannas *Mat 21:1-11, 14-17, Mark 11:-1-11, Luke 19:29-44, John 12:12-19*

The rock rolled away from the entrance to Jesus' tomb *Mat 28:1-8, Mark 16:1-8, Luke 24:1-12, John 20:1-10*

See also door, way

ENVY

Cain kills Abel because Abel's sacrifices had respect *Gen 4:1-16*

Joseph sold into slavery by his brothers *Gen 37:1-36*

Moses rebukes his followers for envying of Eldad and Medad *Num 11:16-30*

Aaron and Miriam wrestle leadership from Moses *Num 12:1-16*

David persecuted by Saul *1 Sam 18:1-16, 24:1-22, 26:1-25*

David obtains Uriah's wife *2 Sam 11:1-27*

Nathan's parable about Uriah's wife *2 Sam 12:1-10*

Daniel's enemies put him in lions' den *Dan 6:1-28*

Jesus accused by Pharisees of healing by the devil *Mat 12:22-30, Mark 3:22-30, Luke 11:14-23*

Disciples contend who shall be greatest *Mat 18:1-11, Mark 9:33-37, Luke 9:46-50*

Jesus' parable of laborers in vineyard *Mat 20:1-16*

Judas betrays Jesus, why? *Mat 26:14:16, Mark 14:10, 11, Luke 22:1-6*

Jesus hears Martha's complaint about her sister *Luke 10:38-42*

Jesus' parable of prodigal son's elder brother *Luke 15:25-32*

Paul attacked by the idol silversmith *Acts 19:23-29*

See also competition, covetousness, excellence, greed, hatred, jealousy

EPIDEMIC

Plague of first-born passes over Israelites *Exod 11:4-10, 12:1-14, 21-31*

Fiery serpents in the wilderness *Num 21:4-9*

David's song of protection from pestilence *Psal 91:1-16*

Jesus heals ten lepers at once *Luke 17:11-19*

See also contagion, disease, fear, infection, plague

EPILEPSY

Jesus cures boy *Mat 17:14-21, Mark 9:14-29, Luke 9:37-43*

EQUALITY

Abraham divides equally with Lot *Gen 13:1-18*

Isaac settles strife over wells *Gen 26:12-31*

Moses exhausts himself dispensing justice *Exod 18:13-27*

Moses permits Eldad and Medad to prophesy *Num 11:16-30*

Moses acknowledges rights of women *Num 27:1-11, 36:5-13*

Gideon refuses to be king *Judg 8:22, 23*

Jotham's parable of the trees *Judg 9:1-15*

Samuel resists people's demand for a king *1 Sam 8:1-22*

Esther obtains equal treatment for persecuted Jews *Esther 5:1-14*

Job asks why the good man should suffer *Job 3:1-26*

Jeremiah promises restoration after captivity *Jer 31:1-14, 31-34*

Ezekiel sees the equity of God's dealing *Ezek 18:1-32*

Jesus eats with publicans and sinners *Mat 9:10-13, Mark 2:13-17, Luke 5:27-32*

Jesus keeps his mother and brothers waiting for him *Mat 12:46-50, Mark 3:31-35, Luke 8:19-21*

Jesus meets equally with Moses and Elijah *Mat 17:1-13, Mark 9:2-13, Luke 9:28-36*

Jesus' disciples contend who shall be greatest *Mat 18:1-11, Mark 9: 33-37, Luke 9:46-50, 22:24-30*

Jesus' parable of unmerciful debtor (forgiven) *Mat 18:23-35*

Jesus' parable of hiring laborers in vineyard *Mat 20:1-16*

Zebedee's wife requests preferential treatment for two sons *Mat 20: 20-28, Mark 10:35-45*

Jesus' parable of the talents *Mat 25:14-30, Luke 19:11-28*

Jesus' parable of chief seats at wedding *Luke 14:7-14*

Jesus' parable of great supper (God no respecter of persons) *Luke 14:15-24*

Jesus' parable of prodigal son's elder brother *Luke 15:25-32*

Jesus washes disciples' feet *John 13:1-20*

Election of Matthias by God's will *Acts 1:15-26*

Peter arranges division of labor *Acts 6:1-4*

Philip offers Christianity to Ethiopian *Acts 8:26-40*

Peter's vision of equality of Gentiles *Acts 11:1-18*

Paul's teaching that circumcised and uncircumcised are equal *Rom 2: 1-29, 3:1-31*

Paul on all talents from God *1 Cor 12:1, 4-31*

James on equality of all men *Jas 2:1-13*

See also democracy, justice, righteousness

EQUALITY, RACIAL

Egyptians oppress Israelites *Exod 1:8-14*

Ruth, the Moabitess, accepted *Ruth 1:1-22, 4:1-22*

Haman persecutes Jews *Esther 3: 1-15, 4: 1-17*

Micah sees all people flow to church *Mic 4:1-8, 13*

Malachi's vision of one father, one creator *Mal 2:10, 15, 17*

Jesus heals Syrophenician's daughter *Mat 15:21-28, Mark 7:24-30*

Jesus on being born again *John 3: 1-21*

Philip converts Ethiopian *Acts 8: 26-40*

Peter's acceptance of Gentiles *Acts 10:1-48, 11:1-18*

Paul on the unknown God *Acts 17: 15-34*

Paul on "there is neither Greek nor Jew" *Col 3:1-17, Gal 3:23-29*

See also brotherhood, equality, race

ERROR

Adam and Eve believe serpent, and fall *Gen 3:1-24*

Jacob deceives his father and flees *Gen 27:1-44*

While Moses is on the mount, Aaron introduces the golden calf *Exod 32:1-24*

Miriam and Aaron speak against Moses *Num 12:1-16*

Moses warns against enticers *Deut 13:1-18*

Moses forbids abominations *Deut 18:9-14*

Joshua uncovers error after failure at Ai *Josh 7:1-26, 8:14-21*

Samson's sensuality destroys him *Judg 16:4-30*

Samuel anoints Saul (a mistake) *1 Sam 10:1-8*

Nathan points out David's error *2 Sam 12:1-10*

Uzziah's pride punished *2 Chron 26:1-23*

Elijah destroys false prophets *1 King 18:17-40*

Hezekiah shows Babylonians his treasure *2 King 20:12-21, Isa 39: 1-8*

David's song, "Create in me a clean heart" *Psal 51:1-19*

The preacher on vanity of human things *Eccl 1:1-18, 2:1-26*

Isaiah's parable of wild grapes *Isa 5:1-8*

Isaiah's vision of fall of Babylon *Isa 14:4-8, 12-17, 25-27*

Jeremiah's sermon of the good and bad figs *Jer 24:1-10*

Jonah disobeys God's call *Jonah 1:1-17*

Jesus' parable of wheat and tares *Mat 13:24-30, 36-43*

Jesus heals boy after disciples failed *Mat 17:14-21, Mark 9:14-29, Luke 9:37-43*

Jesus' sermon denouncing scribes and Pharisees *Mat 23:1-39*

Jesus' parable of the talents *Mat 25:14-30, Luke 19:11-28*

Jesus' parable of sheep and goats *Mat 25:31-46*

Judas betrays Jesus *Mat 26:14-16, Mark 14:10, 11, Luke 22:1-6*

Peter denies he knows Jesus *Mat 26:57, 58, 69-75, Mark 16:66-72, Luke 22:54-62, John 18:13-18, 25-27*

Thomas insists on satisfying his senses *Mark 16:14, Luke 24:36-49, John 20:19-29*

Jesus' parable of rich man and his barns *Luke 12:15-21*

Jesus' parable of prodigal son *Luke 15:11-24*

Jesus' parable of rich man and beggar *Luke 16:19-31*

Peter turns down Simon's offer to buy power of Holy Ghost *Acts 8:14-25*

Paul persecutes Christians, talks with Jesus *Acts 8:1-4, 9:1-9*

Paul's blindness healed and he is converted *Acts 9:10-22*

Exorcists try to imitate Paul's healing *Acts 19:11-20*

Paul on Spirit vs. flesh *Rom 8:1-39*

Paul on enemies of truth *2 Tim 3:1-17*

John's vision of woman with child and dragon *Rev 12:1-17*

See also belief, mistake, morality, mortal, sin

ESCAPE

Isaac not sacrificed by his father *Gen 22:1-19*

Jacob escapes Esau's army *Gen 33:1-11*

Moses as baby escapes death by river *Exod 2:1-10*

Children of Israel pass through Red Sea *Exod 11:4-10, 12:1-14, 21-41, Deut 16:1-22*

Three Hebrew boys survive fiery furnace *Dan 3:1-30*

Daniel survives lion's den *Dan 6:1-28*

Jonah survives storm at sea *Jonah 2:1-10*

Jesus' family's flight to Egypt *Mat 2:13-23, Luke 3:39, 40*

Jesus passes through enemies *Luke 4:28-32*

Jesus avoids stoning *John 10:22-42*

Jesus causes guards to fall backward *John 18:4-6*

Paul escapes ambush, goes over wall *Acts 9:23-31*

Paul and Silas escape prison *Acts 16:19-40*

Paul survives shipwreck *Acts 27:1-44*

See also danger, deliverance, enemy, prison, salvation

ESTHER (Queen of Persia)

See Part II, Esther

ETERNITY

In the beginning God *Gen 1:1-31*

Enoch translated *Gen 5:18, 21-24, Heb 11:5*

Moses learns God's name, "I Am That I Am" *Exod 3:1-18*

David's song, the fountain of life *Psal 36:1-12*

The Preacher's sermon on time *Eccl 3:1-15*

Jesus heals three who were dead *Mat 9:18, 19, 23-26, Mark 5:22-24, 35-43, Luke 7:11-17, 8:41, 42, 49, 50, John 11:1-46*

Jesus on mount speaks with Moses and Elijah *Mat 17:1-13, Mark 9:2-13, Luke 9:28-36*

Jesus instructs rich young ruler *Mat 19:16-30, Mark 10:17-31, Luke 18:18-30*

Jesus' resurrection *Mat 28:1-8, Mark 16:1-8, Luke 24:11, 12, John 20:1-10*

Jesus' parable of the rich man and beggar at his gate *Luke 16:19-31*

John's discourse on the Word of God *John 1:1-14*

Jesus on eternity of Christ *John 8:12-59*

Paul's sermon on resurrection *1 Cor 15:1-58*

Paul on eternity of Christ *Heb 6:20—7:28*

John's vision of new heaven and earth *Rev 21:1-27*

See also age, death, immortality, infinity, life, mortal, time, translation

ETHICS

Jacob and his mother deceive his father *Gen 27:1-44*

Moses receives the Ten Commandments *Exod 20:1-19, Deut 5:1-24*

David's song, "Create in me a clean heart" *Psal 51:1-19*

Isaiah's parable of the wild grapes *Isa 5:1-8*

Jesus' Sermon on the Mount — Beatitudes *Mat 5:1-12, Luke 6:17-26, 36*

Jesus on Mosaic Commandments *Mat 5:21-32, Mark 9:38-51*

Jesus on treatment of enemies *Mat 5:38-48, Luke 6:27-36*

Jesus on Golden Rule *Mat 7:12-14, Luke 6:41, 42*

Why Jesus eats with publicans and sinners *Mat 9:10-13, Mark 2:13-17, Luke 5:27-32*

Jesus accused of using Beelzebub to heal *Mat 12:22-30, Mark 3:22-30, Luke 11:14-23*

Jesus' parable of the unmerciful debtor *Mat 18:23-35*

Paul on love *1 Cor 13:1-13*

Paul's sermon, "think on these things" *Phil 4:1-23*

James on equality of man *Jas 2:1-13*

See also character, morality

EUCHARIST

Jesus' parable of the marriage feast *Mat 22:1-14*

Jesus' Last Supper *Mat 26:26-29, Mark 14:22-25, Luke 22:14-30, 1 Cor 11:23-25*

Jesus' parable of new wine in old bottles *Luke 5:36-39*

Jesus' parable of those bidden to supper *Luke 14:15-24*

Jesus' parable of temple raised in three days *John 2:19-22*

See also communion, Last Supper

EVANGELISM

John the Baptist's ministry *Mat 3:1-12, Mark 1:1-8, Luke 3:1-18*

Jesus charges disciples to preach and heal *Mat 10:5-42, 28:16-20, Mark 6:7-13, 16:15-18, Luke 9:1-6*

Jesus urges disciples to teach all nations *Mat 28:16-20*

Jesus' fame increases *Mark 1:35-39*

Jesus' address from vessel in lake *Mark 4:1-25*

Jesus rejected at Nazareth *Luke 4:14-32*

Jesus as light of the world *John 1:1-14*

Jesus charges Peter, "Feed my sheep" *John 21:12-19*

Peter on meaning of Holy Spirit (Ghost) *Acts 2:14-47*

Peter on healing *Acts 3:12-26*

Peter speaks boldly *Acts 4:24-37*

Philip travels south and converts Ethiopian *Acts 8:26-40*

Paul tells the cost to establish church *Acts 20:17-38*

Paul on the work of an Evangelist *2 Tim 4:1-8*

See also conversion, preaching

EVE

See Part II, Adam and Eve

EVENING

Periods of creation marked by six evenings *Gen 1:1-31*

Jesus at Emmaus is recognized by disciples *Mat 16:12, 13, Luke 24:13-35*

Jesus' parable of laborers in vineyard *Mat 20:1-16*

Jesus at Gethsemane *Mat 25:30, 36-46, Mark 14:26, 32-42, Luke 22:39-46*

Jesus' crucifixion causes early darkness *Mat 27:32-56, Mark 15:21-41, Luke 23:26-49, John 19:17-30*

Jesus' parable of servant who serves his master before he sups *Luke 17:7-10*

Jesus reappears, with Thomas present *John 20:24-29*

See also life, morning, sleep

EVERLASTING

See eternity

EVER-PRESENCE

Lord God asks Adam, "Where art thou?" *Gen 3:6-12*

Jacob dreams of angels and God with him *Gen 28:10-22*

Moses is promised God's presence *Exod 3:9-12*

Song of Moses reviews God's presence *Exod 15:1-19, Deut 32:1-47*

Moses talks with God on Mt. Sinai *Exod 19:1-19, 33:7-23*

Gideon receives signs of God's presence *Judg 6:19-40*

Elijah learns of God as still small voice *1 King 19:9-13*

David's song, "our dwelling place" *Psal 90:1-17*

David's song, "Whither shall I flee from thy presence?" *Psal 139:1-24*

Isaiah's vision, "a quiet habitation" *Isa 33:20-24*

Isaiah's vision of help in trials *Isa 43:1-28, 44:1-24*

Isaiah's vision, "the Lord's hand is not shortened" *Isa 59:1-21*

Ezekiel's vision of God's constant care *Ezek 34:1-31*

Daniel's vision of God's constant care *Dan 9:20-23, 10:4-21*

Jesus on oneness with Father *Mat 6:22-24, John 10:22-42*

Jesus' parable of lost sheep *Mat 18:12-14, Luke 15:1-7*

Jesus' parable of prodigal's elder brother *Luke 15:25-32*

Jesus' parable of good shepherd *John 10:1-18*

See also God, infinite, love

EVIDENCE

Isaac, the child by promise born *Gen 21:1-8*

Moses' rod and leprosy *Exod 4:1-9*

Moses leads through Red Sea *Exod 14:5-31*

Moses obtains water from rock *Exod 17:1-7, Num 20:1-13*

Aaron's rod blossoms *Num 17:1-11*

Gideon convinced by three signs *Judg 6:19-40*

Elijah prays for rain *1 King 18:41-46*

Elisha heals Shunammite's son *2 King 4:8-37*

Elisha prophesies drop in price of flour *2 King 6:24, 25, 7:1-18*

Jesus' healings *(See* Part II, Jesus Christ: Great Works)

John Baptist demands evidence that Jesus is Christ *Mat 11:2-19, Luke 7:18-35*

The Pentecost as proof of Jesus' promised Comforter *Acts 2:1-13*

Philip converts Simon by miracles *Acts 8:9-13*

Paul converted by healing of blindness *Acts 9:10-22*

Paul on Christ's resurrection as proof of ours *1 Cor 15:1-58*

James on faith without works *Jas 2:14-26*

See also proof, testify, witness

EVIL

Adam and Eve listen to the serpent *Gen 3:1-5*

Jacob deceives his father *Gen 27:1-44*

Aaron promotes idolatry of golden calf *Exod 32:1-24*

Saul consults witch of Endor *1 Sam 28:3-20*

David has Uriah destroyed *2 Sam 11:1-27*

Esther and Jews persecuted by Haman *Esther 3:1-15, 4:1-17*

Job suffers reverses *Job 1:13-22, 2:1-10*

Isaiah's parable of the wild grapes *Isa 5:1-8*

Isaiah's vision of hypocrisy punished *Isa 29:11-24, 30:1-3, 20, 21*

Jesus and the swine that drowned *Mat 8:30-34*

Jesus heals paralytic by forgiving his sin *Mat 9:1-8, Mark 2:1-12, Luke 5:17-25*

Jesus eats with publicans and sinners *Mat 9:10-13, Mark 2:13-17, Luke 5:27-32*

Jesus excoriates three cities *Mat 11:20-30, Luke 10:21, 22*

Jesus accused of partnership with devil *Mat 12:22-30, Mark 3:22-30, Luke 11:14-23*

Jesus' parable of unclean spirit *Mat 12:43-45, Luke 11:24-26*

Jesus' parable of wheat and tares *Mat 13:24-30, 36-43*

Jesus' parable of dragnet *Mat 13:47-50*

Jesus' parable of farmers who refuse rent *Mat 21:33-46, Mark 12:1-12, Luke 20:9-19*

Jesus denouncing Pharisees *Mat 23:1-39*

Jesus' parable of sheep and goats *Mat 25:31-46*

Jesus has chief priests against him *Mat 26:1-5, Mark 14:1, 2, John 11:47-54*

Judas betrays him *Mat 26:14-16, Mark 14:10, 11, Luke 22:1-6*

Jesus heals unclean spirit *Mark 1:21-28, Luke 4:33-37*

Jesus on leaven of Pharisees *Luke 12:1-15*

Jesus' parable of barren fig tree *Luke 13:6-9*

Paul on enemies of truth *2 Tim 3:1-17*

John's vision of the dragon *Rev 12:1-17*

See also affliction, crime, corruption, disease, error, serpent, sin

EVIL, SELF-DESTROYED

Jacob deceives Isaac and flees country *Gen 27:1-44*

Samson betrayed by his sensuality *Judg 16:4-30*

Saul sins and falls on his own sword *1 Sam 31:1-13, 1 Chron 10:1-14*

David's child by Uriah's wife dies *2 Sam 12:13-23*

Esther sees Haman hanged on his own gallows *Esther 6:1-14, 7:1-10*

Jesus heals the Gadarene, and swine run into sea *Mat 8:28-34*

Judas betrays Jesus and hangs himself *Mat 27:3-10, Acts 1:15-20*

EVOLUTION

First creation, *Gen 1:1-31, 2:1-5*

Second creation, a different story of the same actions *Gen 2:6-25*

Tower of Babel created by man *Gen 11:1-9*

Isaac born to Abraham and Sarah in their nineties *Gen 21:1-8*

Moses' revelation of I Am That I Am *Exod 3:1-18*

Joshua divides Jordan *Josh 3:1-17*

Samson's birth announced by angel *Judg 13:1-25*

Samuel's miraculous birth *1 Sam 1:1-28*

Elijah divides Jordan *2 King 2:8*

Elisha divides Jordan *2 King 2:12-15*

Elisha foretells birth of Shunammite's son *2 King 4:8-17*

Job hears voice of thunder *Job 38:1-41*

Isaiah prophesies birth of Messiah *Isa 7:10-16, 9:2-7*

Jesus' parable of builders on rock and sand *Mat 7:24-27, Luke 6:48, 49*

Jesus feeds 5000 and 4000 *Mat 14:15-21, 15:32-39, Mark 6:35-44, 8:1-10, Luke 9:12-17, John 6:5-14*

John Baptist's miraculous birth *Luke 1:5-25*

Jesus' miraculous birth *Luke 1:26-38, 2:1-7*

Jesus changes water to wine *John 2:1-11*

Jesus' parable of temple raised in three days *John 2:19-21*

Jesus tells Pharisees difference between him and them *John 8:33-59*

Jesus raises Lazarus four days dead *John 11:1-46*

See also birth, creation, development

EXALTATION

Enoch translated   *Gen 5:18, 21-24, Heb 11:11:5*
Jacob dreams of angels on ladder   *Gen 32:1-32*
Moses talks with God on Mt. Sinai   *Exod 19:1-9, 33:7-23*
Moses needs veil over face   *Exod 34:29-35*
Elijah hears still small voice   *1 King 19:9-13*
Elijah ascends   *2 King 2:1-11*
David's song, "Make a joyful noise"   *Psal 66:1-20, 100:1-5*
Zephaniah's advice to the daughter of Zion   *Zeph 3:14-17*
Isaiah's vision of Lord's house on mountain   *Isa 2:1-5, Mic 4:1-8, 13*
Jesus' transfiguration   *Mat 17:1-13, Mark 9:2-13, Luke 9:28-36*
Jesus at Gethsemane   *Mat 26:30, 36-46, Mark 14:26, 32-42, Luke 22:39-46*
Paul and Silas in prison sing hymns until released by earthquake   *Acts 16:19-40*
Paul's sermon on rejoicing   *Phil 4:1-23*
Paul's teaching to put off old man, put on new   *Col 3:1-17*
John's vision of new heaven and earth   *Rev 21:1-27*

See also inspiration, power, promote, rejoicing, success

EXAMPLE

Man created in God's image and likeness   *Gen 1:26, 27*
Enoch walked with God and was translated   *Gen 5:18, 21-24, Heb 11:5*
Joseph, the ideal problem-solver   *Gen 41:1-46*
Elijah asks for a double measure of Elijah's spirit   *2 King 2:1-11*
David's song, "Mark the perfect man"   *Psal 37:23-40*
Solomon's description of virtuous woman   *Prov 31:1-31*

Isaiah's vision of coming Messiah   *Isa 42:1-12, 16-18, 53:1-12, 61:1-11, 62:1-12*
Jesus' parables:
The unmerciful debtor, a bad example   *Mat 18:23-35*
The talents   *Mat 25:14-30, Luke 19:11-28*
The good Samaritan   *Luke 10:25-37*
The rich man's barns, bad example   *Luke 12:15-21*
The prodigal son, bad example   *Luke 15:11-24*
Rich man and beggar   *Luke 16:19-31*
The good shepherd   *John 10:1-18*
The true vine   *John 15:1-17*
Jesus' healings:
Paralysis   *Mat 9:1-8, Mark 2:1-12, Luke 5:17-26*
Epileptic boy   *Mat 17:14-21, Mark 9:14-29, Luke 9:37-43*
Jesus' instructions to disciples   *Mat 10:5-42, Mark 6:7-13, Luke 9:1-6*
Jesus institutes communion   *Mat 26:26-29, Mark 14:22-25, Luke 22:14-30, 1 Cor 11:23-25*
Jesus' parting advice   *Mat 28:16-20, Mark 16:15-18*
Jesus approves Mary's conduct to Martha   *Luke 10:38-42*
Jesus saves the adulteress from the crowd   *John 8:1-11*
Jesus washes disciples' feet   *John 13:1-20*
Paul imitated by vagabond exorcists   *Acts 19:11-20*
Paul's sermon that Christ's resurrection assures ours   *1 Cor 15:1-58*
Paul's teaching on faithfulness in ministry   *2 Cor 6:1-18*
Paul on cost to him of establishing church   *2 Cor 11:21-33*
Paul on the example of Jesus and himself   *Phil 2:1-15, 3:8-17*
Paul's instruction to strengthen the Christian   *2 Tim 2:1-26*
Paul on the example left by Jesus   *Heb 12:1-29*
James on faith without works   *Jas 2:14-26*

See also imitation, Jesus, teaching

EXCELLENCE

Abraham is blessed by Melchizedek after war with kings *Gen 14:8-20, Heb 6:20, 7:1-28*

Abram receives a new name *Gen 17:1-9, 15-22*

A proper wife is found for Isaac *Gen 24:1-67*

Jacob receives a new name *Gen 32:1-32, 35:9-15*

Joseph appointed governor of Egypt *Gen 41:1-46*

Moses reassured by God of his speaking ability *Exod 4:10-17*

Aaron's rod blossoms *Num 17:1-11*

Jotham's parable of choice among trees to be king *Judg 9:1-15*

David anointed king by Samuel *1 Sam 16:1-13*

Elijah translated, Elisha requests double his spirit *2 King 2:1-15*

David's song, "praise the Lord for his goodness" *Psal 107:1-43*

The nature of a virtuous wife and mother *Prov 31:1-31*

Micah's vision of the church *Isa 2:1-5, Mic 4:1-8, 13*

Isaiah's vision of Messiah *Isa 42:1-12, 16, 18*

Daniel's excellence causes envy *Dan 6:1-28*

Jesus on Beatitudes *Mat 5:1-12*

Jesus on perfecting yourself *Mat 5:48*

Jesus' parable of builders on rock and sand *Mat 7:24-27, Luke 6:48, 49*

Jesus heals epileptic boy after disciples fail *Mat 17:14-21, Mark 9:14-29, Luke 9:37-43*

Jesus' parable of wise and foolish virgins *Mat 25:1-13*

Jesus' parable of the talents *Mat 25:14-30, Luke 19:11-28*

Jesus ascends *Mark 16:19, 20, Luke 24:50, 51, Acts 1:9-12*

Jesus says his works have their source in the Father *John 5:17-47*

Paul's teaching on charity *1 Cor 13:1-13*

See also character, envy, glory, perfection, value

EXILE

Abraham's wandering begins *Gen 11:31, 32, 12:1-9*

Jacob and family leave promised land *Gen 46:2-7*

Joshua re-enters promised land *Josh 3:1-17*

Ruth and Naomi return from Moab *Ruth 1:1-22*

Jehoiachin well-treated in Babylon *2 King 25:27-30*

Haman persecutes Jewish exiles *Esther 3:1-15, 4:1-17*

Captives sing of homeland *Psal 139:1-8*

See also home

EXODUS

Jacob and all children emigrate to Egypt *Gen 46:2-7*

People oppressed *Exod 1:8-14*

Passover and release *Exod 11:4-10, 12:1-14, 21-41, Deut 16:1-22*

Pursuit, Red Sea passed *Exod 14:5-31*

The wilderness experience *Exod 15:22-27, 16:1-36, 17:1-7*

The Ten Commandments *Exod 20:1-19, Deut 5:1-24*

Caleb and Joshua scout promised land *Num 3:1-33, 14:1-11, 23-29, Deut 1:19-38*

Moses charges Joshua with leadership *Deut 31:7-23, Josh 1:1-9*

Moses' song reviewing deliverance *Deut 32:1-47*

People cross over Jordan *Josh 3:1-17*

See also bondage, Egypt, passover

EXPANSION

Abraham's riches grow *Gen 13:1-18*

Joseph prospers in Egypt, gathers family *Gen 46:2-7*

Moses appoints judges to help the people *Exod 18:13-27*

Elijah expands meal and oil for widow to live *1 King 17:1-16*

Elisha enlarges widow's oil *2 King 4:1-7*

Elisha feeds 100 men on a few loaves *2 King 4:42-44*

Ezekiel's vision of holy waters *Ezek 47:1-12*

Jesus' parable of mustard seed *Mat 13:31, 32, Mark 4:30-32, Luke 13:18, 19*

Jesus' parable of leaven *Mat 13:33, Luke 13:20, 21*

Jesus feeds 5000 with few loaves and fishes *Mat 14:15-21, Mark 6:35-44, Luke 9:12-17, John 6:5-14*

Jesus' parable of talents *Mat 25:14-30, Luke 19:11-28*

Jesus' parable, seed, blade, ear *Mark 4:26-29*

Jesus sends out 70 disciples *Luke 10:1-24*

Jesus' parable of barren fig tree *Luke 13:6-9*

Jesus' parable of true vine *John 15:1-17*

Jesus casts net on right side *John 21:1-11*

Peter causes church to grow *Acts 4:24-37*

Paul converts Lydia *Acts 16:7-15*

John's vision of new heaven and earth *Rev 21:1-27*

John's vision of river and tree of life *Rev 22:1-21*

See also evolution, growth, increase, progress, success

EXPECTATION

Noah expects a flood and prepares *Gen 6:5-22*

Isaac expects only good from his father *Gen 22:1-19*

Jacob anticipates revenge by his brother *Gen 32:1-32, 33:1-11*

Moses orders Israelites to go forward *Exod 14:5-31*

Gideon expects victory over Midianites *Judg 7:1-25*

David expects victory over Goliath *1 Sam 17:38-52*

Elijah prays for rain *1 King 18:41-46*

Isaiah prophesies Messiah *Isa 7:10-16, 9:2-7*

Jeremiah expects to turn captivity *Jer 32:2, 6-27, 37-44*

Daniel expects his food to be nutritious *Dan 1:1-21*

Daniel's companions survive the fiery furnace *Dan 3:1-30*

Daniel expects to survive the lion's den *Dan 6:1-28*

Malachi expects blessings from tithing *Mal 3:10, 4:1, 2*

Jesus heals woman who touches hem *Mat 9:20-22, Mark 5:25-34, Luke 8::43-48*

Jesus' parable of two servants awaiting *Mat 24:42-51*

Jesus' parable of wise and foolish virgins *Mat 25:1-13*

Mary expecting the Christ child *Luke 1:39-56*

Simon and Anna waiting at the temple to see the Christ *Luke 2:21-38*

Jesus' parable of judge and widow *Luke 11:1-8*

Jesus' parable of unwilling friend *Luke 11:5-13*

Jesus' parable of unjust steward *Luke 16:1-14*

Jesus heals the man waiting at the pool *John 5:1-16*

Jesus promises the Holy Spirit (Ghost) *John 14:1-31*

See also duty, hope, preparation, promise, prophet, waiting

EXPRESSION

Man made in God's image *Gen 1:26, 27*

Enoch walked with God and was not *Gen 5:18, 21-24, Heb 11:5*

Aaron wears Urim and Thummim of his office *Exod 28:29-36*

Moses' face concealed after talking with God *Exod 34:29-35*

David pacified by Abigail's gentleness *1 Sam 25:2-42*

Elisha heals Shunammite's son *2 King 4:8-37*

David's song, "What is man?" *Psal 8:1-9*

Isaiah's description of Messiah to come *Isa 53:1-12*

Daniel's vision of meeting Gabriel *Dan 9:20-23, 10:4-21*

Jesus on letting your light shine *Mat 5:13-16, Luke 8:16-18*

Jesus on oneness with the Father *Mat 6:22-24, John 10:22-42*

Jesus commended the centurion's faith *Mat 8:5-13, Luke 7:1-10*

Jesus is transfigured on the Mount *Mat 17:1-13, Mark 9:2-13, Luke 9:28-36*

In temple Simon and Anna call Jesus the Christ *Luke 2:21-38*

At twelve years Jesus talks with rabbis *Luke 2:41-52*

Jesus' parable of good Samaritan *Luke 10:25-37*

Jesus as the light of the world *John 1:1-14, 8:12-32*

Jesus says his works have their source in the Father *John 5:17-47*

Jesus' teaching that he is Christ *John 7:14-40*

Jesus' parable of good shepherd *John 10:1-18*

Jesus' parable of the true vine *John 15:1-17*

Paul on charity *1 Cor 13:1-13*

Paul on rejoicing *Phil 4:1-23*

Paul's teaching about putting on the new man *Col 3:1-17*

Paul on character of the Christ *Heb 1:1-14*

See also man, manifestation

EXTERMINATION

See destruction

EYE

Isaac's eye too dim to distinguish which son *Gen 27:1-44*

Moses at advanced age, his eyes not dim *Deut 34:1-11*

Jesus' sermon, "If thine eye be single" *Mat 6:22-24*

Jesus' parable of mote and beam *Mat 7:1-5, Luke 6:37-42*

Jesus anoints eyes of blind man before healing *John 9:1-41*

Paul's eyes blinded by great light *Acts 9:1-22*

See also blindness, light, organic, sight

EZEKIEL

See Part II, Ezekiel

F

FACE

Adam and Eve hide from the Lord God *Gen 3:6-24*

Jacob returns to face his brother *Gen 32:1-32, 33:1-11*

Moses talks with the Lord face to face *Exod 33:7-23*

Veil conceals Moses' face *Exod 34:29-35*

Nathan faces David with a parable of the ewe lamb *2 Sam 12:1-10*

Jehoshaphat goes with God to face enemy *2 Chron 20:1-32*

Isaiah urges, "Arise, shine" *Isa 60:1-5*

Daniel's and boys' faces fatter and fairer than those who eat the king's meat *Dan 1:1-21*

Jesus on washing the face *Mat 6:16-18*

Jesus walks on surface of water *Mat 14:22-33, John 6:15-21*

Jesus transfigured in face and appearance *Mat 17:1-13, Mark 9:2-13, Luke 9:28-36*

See also defiance, expression, purity

FACT

God created man in his image *Gen 1:26, 27*

Enoch walked with God and was not *Gen 5:18, 21-24, Heb 11:5*

Moses leads people through the Red Sea *Exod 14:5-31*

Moses gave people Ten Commandments *Exod 20:1-19, Deut 5:1-24*

David killed Goliath with a sling shot *1 Sam 17:38-52*

Elisha healed Naaman the leper *2 King 5:1-14*

Esther saved her people *Esther 5:1-14, 6.1-14, 7:1-10*

Daniel survives the lions' den *Dan 6:1-28*

Jesus healed the palsied man let down through the tiling *Mat 9:2-8, Mark 2:1-12, Luke 5:17-26*

Jesus healed the withered hand *Mat 12:9-13, Mark 3:1-5, Luke 6:6-11*

Jesus appeared after death *Mat 28: 9, 10, 16-20, Mark 16:9-11, 12-18, Luke 24:13-49, John 20:11-18, 19-29, 21:1-25, 1 Cor 15:5-15, Acts 1: 1-8*

Jesus healed the man born blind *John 9:1-41*

Peter and John healed man lame from birth *Acts 3:1-11*

Paul healed Eutychus of fall *Acts 20:7-12*

Paul established church in Asia Minor *2 Cor 11:21-33*

See also belief, reality, spirituality, substance, truth

FAILURE

Adam and Eve fall *Gen 3:6-24*

Moses destroys first tablet of Ten Commandments *Exod 32:1-24*

David's prayers for Bathsheba's child fail *2 Sam 12:13-23*

Hezekiah fails to maintain security *2 King 20:12-21, Isa 39:1-8*

Asa turns from Lord to physicians *2 Chron 16:11-14*

Uzziah's pride punished by leprosy *2 Chron 26:1-23*

Jonah fails after disobedience *Jonah 1:1-17, 2:1-10*

Jesus' disciples fail to heal epileptic boy *Mat 17:14-21, Mark 9:14-29, Luke 9:37-43*

Jesus' parable of unmerciful debtor *Mat 18:23-35*

Jesus' parable of two sons ordered to work *Mat 21:28-32*

Jesus' parable of wise and foolish virgins *Mat 25:1-13*

Jesus' parable of talents *Mat 25:14-30, Luke 19:11-28*

Jesus' parable of sheep and goats *Mat 25:31-46*

Jesus' crucifixion observed as a failure *Mat 25:41-44, 57-66*

Jesus' parable of barren fig tree *Luke 13:6-9*

Jesus' parable of prodigal son *Luke 15:11-24*

Jesus' parable of unjust steward *Luke 16:1-14*

See also defeat, fallen man, prosperity, success

FAITH

Abraham's faith in God *Gen 22:1-19*

Isaac's faith in his father *Gen 22: 1-19*

Elisha develops faith of Shunammite *2 King 4:8-37*

Job in his suffering still blesses God *Job 2:1-10*

David's song of faith in God *Psal 46:1-11*

Jeremiah prophesies end of captivity *Jer 29:8-14, 31:1-14, 31-34*

Jeremiah demonstrates his confidence *Jer 32:2, 6-27, 37-44*

Daniel's companions in fiery furnace *Dan 3:1-30*

Daniel in lion's den *Dan 6:1-28*

Jesus heals centurion's servant *Mat 8:5-13, Luke 7:1-10*

Jesus heals Jairus' daughter *Mat 9:18, 19, 23-26, Mark 5:22-24, 35-41, Luke 8:41, 42, 49-56*

Jesus' parable of mustard seed *Mat 13:31, 32, Mark 4:30-32, Luke 13: 18, 19*

Jesus heals Gentile woman's daughter *Mat 15:21-28, Mark 7:24-30*

Jesus heals epileptic boy *Mat 17: 14-21, Mark 9:14-29, Luke 9:37-43*

Jesus' parable of faithful steward *Luke 12:41-48*

Jesus' sermon on faith *John 12:44-50, Luke 17:1-6*

Paul on faith *1 Cor 13:1-13, Heb 11:1-40*

Paul on justification *Gal 2:14-21*

Paul on faith and the law *Gal 3:2-29*

Paul on Christian's armor *Eph 6: 10-17*

James on faith without works *Jas 2:14-26*

See also belief, conviction, healing, understanding

FALLEN MAN

Adam created from dust not image *Gen 2:6-8*

Adam and Eve deceived by serpent *Gen 3:1-25*

Cain ruptures brotherhood *Gen 4: 1-16*

Tower of Babel confounds man *Gen 11:1-9*

Jacob deceives his father   *Gen 27: 1-44*

Moses returns to find worship of idols   *Exod 32:1-24*

Samson's sensualism betrays him to to Delilah   *Judg 16:4-30*

Saul consults familiar spirit   *1 Sam 28:3-20*

David arranges death of Uriah to obtain his wife   *2 Sam 11:1-27*

Preacher's sermon on vanity of all human life   *Eccl 1:1-18, 2:1-26*

Isaiah on the pride of women   *Isa 3:16-26*

Isaiah on fall of Babylon   *Isa 14:4-8, 12-17, 25-27*

Nebuchadnezzar's insanity   *Dan 4: 28-37*

Daniel reads handwriting on wall   *Dan 5:1-31*

Jesus denounces three cities   *Mat 11:20-30*

Jesus denounces scribes and Pharisees   *Mat 23:1-39*

Judas sells his Master and hangs himself   *Mat 26:14-16, 27:3-10, Mark 14:10, 11, Luke 22:1-10, Acts 1:15-20*

Peter denies he know Jesus   *Mat 26:57, 58, 69-75, Mark 14:66-72*

Jesus' parable of prodigal son   *Luke 15:11-24*

Jesus saves the adulteress   *John 8: 1-11*

Paul on spirit vs. flesh   *Rom 8:1-39*

See also defeat, failure, sin

FALSEHOOD

See lie, deceit

FAME

Tower of Babel, attempt to make a name   *Gen 11:1-9*

Joseph becomes governor of Egypt   *Gen 41:1-46*

Moses tells Israel they are chosen of God   *Deut 7:6-11*

Gideon refuses to be king   *Judg 8: 22, 23*

Solomon visited by Queen of Sheba   *1 King 10:1-12, 2 Chron 9:1-12*

The Preacher's story of the poor man who saved a city   *Eccl 9: 13-18*

Micah's vision of Lord's house on mountain   *Mic 4:1-8, 13, Isa 2:1-5*

Jesus as babe visited by wise men   *Mat 2:1-12*

Jesus on knowing men by their fruits   *Mat 7:15-20, Luke 6:43-45*

Jesus followed by great multitudes   *Mat 12:14-21, Mark 3:6-12*

Jesus' parable of leaven   *Mat 13:33, Luke 13:20, 21*

Jesus followed to mount by great multitudes   *Mat 15:29-31, Mark 1:35-39*

Jesus' parable of chief seats at wedding   *Luke 14:7-14*

Peter's shadow in the streets heals multitudes   *Acts 5:12-16*

Philip heals and converts many   *Acts 8:5-8*

Paul and Barnabas worshipped as gods   *Acts 14:11-18*

See also excellence, glory

FAMILY

Cain and Abel quarrel   *Gen 4:1-16*

Abraham and Lot, strife settled   *Gen 13:1-18*

Jacob and Esau   *Gen 25:24-34, 27:1-44, 33:1-11*

Joseph and his brethren   *Gen 37: 1-36, 42:1-8, 43:1, 2, 45:1-11*

Jacob prophesies future of twelve sons   *Gen 49:1-28*

Moses, Aaron and Miriam quarrel   *Num 12:1-16*

Zelophehad's daughters sue for inheritance   *Num 27:1-11, 36:5-13*

Ruth and Naomi, loyal kinship   *Ruth 1:1-22, 2:1-23*

Esther saves Mordecai and the Jews   *Esther 2:5-23, 8:1-8*

Solomon's description of a virtuous housewife   *Prov 31:1-31*

Ezekiel's sermon about children's teeth on edge   *Ezek 18:1-32*

Union of two sticks (states)   *Ezek 37:15-28*

Hosea's vision of Israel as God's child   *Hos 11:1-4*

Jesus heals Peter's mother-in-law   *Mat 8:14-17, Mark 1:29-34*

Jesus heals Jairus' daughter   *Mat 9:18, 19, 23-26*

Jesus' mother and brothers wait for him *Mat 12:46-50, Mark 3:31-35, Luke 8:19-21*

Jesus heals epileptic boy *Mat 17:14-21, Mark 9:14-29, Luke 9:37-43*

Jesus requested by Zebedee's wife for two sons *Mat 20:20-28, Mark 10:35-45*

Jesus' parable of two sons ordered to work *Mat 21:28-32*

Jesus at twelve stays behind at Jerusalem *Luke 2:41-52*

Jesus heals son of widow of Nain *Luke 7:11-17*

Jesus hears Martha complain about her sister *Luke 10:38-42*

Jesus' parable of prodigal son and elder brother *Luke 15:11-32*

Jesus heals nobleman's son *John 4:46-54*

Jesus on cross asks John to comfort his mother *John 19:25-27*

Paul's sermon on charity *1 Cor 13:1-13*

Paul on family relationships *Eph 5:22-32, 6:1-10*

Paul's advice to his disciple (son), Timothy *2 Tim 2:1-26*

See also brotherhood, children, father, home, house, mother, parent

FAMINE

Pharaoh dreams of famine to follow *Gen 41:1-46*

Joseph's brethren go to Egypt for food *Gen 42:1-8*

Moses supplies manna in wilderness *Exod 16:1-36, Num 11:1-15, 31, 32*

Naomi and her husband flee to Moab *Ruth 1:1-22*

Elijah fed by ravens and widow of Zarephath *1 King 17:1-16*

Elisha multiplies the widow's pot of oil *2 King 4:1-7*

Elisha prophesies incredible plenty during siege *2 King 6:24, 25, 7:1-18*

Jesus parable of prodigal son during famine *Luke 15:11-24*

Jesus on the bread of life *John 6:26-65*

See also food, hunger, supply

FARMING

Adam ordered to till the soil *Gen 3:6-24*

Cain brings fruit of the ground as an offering *Gen 4:1-16*

Abraham's farm riches grow *Gen 13:1-18*

Gideon threshes wheat when an angel appears *Judg 6:11-40*

Ruth gleans after the reapers *Ruth 2:1-23*

Elijah finds Elisha plowing *1 King 19:19-21*

David's song, "The Lord is my shepherd" *Psal 23:1-6*

Jesus' disciples pluck corn on sabbath *Mat 12:1-8, Mark 2:23-28, Luke 6:1-5*

Jesus' parable of the sower *Mat 13:1-23, Mark 4:1-20, Luke 8:4-15*

Jesus' parable of wheat and tares *Mat 13:24-30, 36-43*

Jesus' parable of mustard seed *Mat 13:31, 32, Mark 4:30-32, Luke 13:18, 19*

Jesus' parable of laborers for the vineyard *Mat 20:1-16*

Jesus' parable of farmers who refuse to pay rent *Mat 21:33-46, Mark 12:1-12, Luke 20:9-19*

Jesus' parable of seed, blade, ear *Mark 4:26-29*

Jesus fills Peter's net *Luke 5:1-11, John 21:1-11*

Jesus' parable of the true vine *John 15:1-17*

See also fruit, harvest, sheep

FASTING

David repents his sins and fasts *2 Sam 12:13-23*

Elijah is fed in a dream *1 King 19:1-10*

Daniel refuses king's meat *Dan 1:1-21*

Jesus fasts 40 days in wilderness *Mat 4:1-11, Mark 1:12, 13, Luke 4:1-13*

Jesus' sermon on fasting in secret *Mat 6:16-18*

Why Jesus' disciples don't fast *Mat 9:14-17, Mark 2:18-22, Luke 5:33-39*

Jesus' breakfast with his disciples
Mat 28:16-18, John 21:1-14

See also abstinence, appetite, denial,
food

FATHER

God creates universe and man *Gen
1:1-31*

Abraham is tempted to sacrifice his
son *Gen 22:1-19*

Jacob prophesies future of his twelve
sons *Gen 49:1-28, Deut 33:1-29*

Jesse's sons surveyed by Samuel
1 Sam 16:1-13

Hosea's vision of Israel as a child
Hos 11:1-4

Angel appears to Joseph, spouse of
Mary *Mat 1:18-25*

Jesus teaches disciples to pray, "Our
Father" *Mat 6:5-15, Mark 11:
25, 26*

Jesus heals Jairus' daughter *Mat
9:18, 19, 23-26, Mark 5:22-24, 35-43,
Luke 8:41, 42, 49-56*

Jesus heals epileptic boy *Mat 17:
14-21, Mark 9:14-29, Luke 9:37-43*

Jesus' parable of two sons ordered
to work *Mat 21:28-32*

Jesus' parable of the marriage feast
Mat 22:1-14

Jesus' parable of talents *Mat 25:14-
30, Luke 19:11-28*

Jesus' parable of prodigal son *Luke
15:11-32*

Jesus on source of his works *John
5:17-47*

Jesus on relation to Father *John
14:1-31*

Paul heals Publius' father *Acts 28:
7-10*

Paul on creator *Rom 1:17-25*

Paul advises his "son" Timothy
2 Tim 2:1-26, 4:1-8

See also children, creation, mother,
parent

FATIGUE

God rested on seventh day and
blessed it *Gen 2:1-5*

Esau exhausted, sells his birthright
Gen 25:24-34

Elijah flees, rests under juniper tree
1 King 19:1-8

Nehemiah has news of Jerusalem
depleted *Neh 1:1-11*

David's song, "Why art thou cast
down?" *Psal 42:1-11*

The energy of a good woman *Prov
31:1-31*

Jesus' disciples sleep at Gethsemane
*Mat 26:36-46, Mark 14:26, 32-
42, Luke 22:39-46*

Jesus heals the woman bowed together 18 years *Luke 13:11-17*

Jesus' sermon on comfort in tribulation *John 16:1-33*

Paul stoned but recovers *Acts 14:
19, 20*

Paul's trials as a Christian *Acts
20:17-38, 2 Cor 11:21-33*

See also energy, power, strength,
weary

FAULT

Eve deceived by serpent *Gen 3:1-5*

Adam's fall *Gen 3:6-24*

Jacob deceives his father *Gen 27:
1-44*

Saul declared unfit to be king
1 Sam 15:7-26

Hezekiah proudly shows his treasures *2 King 20:12-21, Isa 39:1-8*

Uzziah's heart lifted up to destruction *2 Chron 26:1-23*

Job begs to be told what he did
wrong *Job 3:1-26*

David's song, "Why art thou cast
down?" *Psal 42:1-11*

Isaiah's vision, hypocrisy will be
punished *Isa 29:11-24, 30:1-3,
20, 21*

Jeremiah's vision of good and bad
figs *Jer 24:1-10*

Jonah's disobedience is punished
Jonah 1:1-17

Jesus' parable of mote and beam
Mat 7:1-5, Luke 6:37-42

Jesus tells Peter he is an offense
*Mat 16:21-28, Mark 8:31-38, Luke
9:20-27*

Jesus' parable of debtor unmerciful
to fellows *Mat 18:23-35*

Jesus and young man with great
possessions *Mat 19:16-30, Mark
10:17-31, Luke 18:18-30*

Jesus on withered fig tree without
fruit *Mat 21:18-22, Mark 11:12-
14, 20-24*

Jesus' parable of two sons ordered to work *Mat 21:28-32*

Jesus' parable of wedding garment *Mat 22:1-14*

Jesus' parable of man with only one talent *Mat 25:14-30, Luke 19:11-28*

Jesus hears Martha's complaint *Luke 10:38-42*

Jesus castigates Pharisees *Luke 11:37-54*

James on faith without works *Jas 2:14-26*

John lists faults of seven churches *Rev 1:4-20, 2:1-29, 3:1-22*

See also error, failure, mistake, perfection, rebuke, sin

FEAR

Adam hides from the Lord God *Gen 3:6-24*

Jacob fears retaliation by his brother *Gen 33:1-11*

Moses frightened by snake and leprosy *Exod 4:1-9*

Moses urges fearful Israelites through Red Sea *Exod 14:5-31*

Fear delays entry into promised land *Num 13:1-33, 14:1-11, 23-29, Deut 1:19-38*

David — Goliath *1 Sam 17:1-52*

Esther fears for her life and her people's life *Esther 5:1-14*

David's song, "Be still, and know that I am God" *Psal 46:1-11*

David's song, "He that dwelleth in the secret place" *Psal 91:1-16*

David's song, "God, the preserver" *Psal 121:1-8*

Job's nightmare *Job 4:13-21*

Isaiah's vision, comfort ye *Isa 40:1-31*

Isaiah's vision, fear not *Isa 43:1-28, 44:1-24*

Ezekiel's vision of God's care of his flock *Ezek 34:1-31*

Three Jews placed in fiery furnace *Dan 3:1-20*

Daniel in lions' den *Dan 6:1-28*

Jesus saves ship from storm *Mat 8:23-27, Mark 4:35-41, Luke 8:22-25*

Jesus raised Jairus' daughter *Mat 9:18, 19, 23-26*

Peter tries to walk on the sea to Jesus *Mat 14:22-33*

Peter is afraid and denies Jesus *Mat 26:57, 58, 69-75*

Jesus reassures the nobleman and heals son *John 4:46-54*

John's sermon, love overcomes fear *1 John 4:1-21*

See also comfort, courage, danger, heart, love, spirit

FEAST

Passover instituted *Exod 11:4-10, 12:1-14, 21-41, Deut 16:1-22*

Israelites feast on quails *Exod 16:1-36, Num 11:1-5, 31, 32*

Aaron sets aside a jubilee year *Lev 25:9-17*

Moses orders offering of first fruits *Deut 26:1-19*

Elisha prophesies incredible plenty *2 Kings 6:24, 25, 7:1-18*

Belshazzar feasts a thousand lords *Dan 5:1-31*

Jesus at passover time enters Jerusalem *Mat 21:1-11, 14-17, Mark 11:1-11, Luke 19:29-44, John 12:12-19*

Jesus' parable of the king's marriage feast *Mat 22:1-14*

Jesus at Last Supper *Mat 26:26-29, Mark 14:22-25, Luke 22:14-30*

Jesus' last breakfast with disciples *Mat 28:16-18, John 21:-14*

Jesus' parable of those bidden to a great supper *Luk 14:15-24*

Jesus' parable of rich man (who feasted) and beggar at gate *Luke 16:19-31*

Jesus supplies wine at wedding *John 2:1-11*

Peter and disciples at Pentecost *Acts 2:1-13*

Paul and Christians, descent of Holy Spirit (Ghost) *Acts 19:1-10*

See also food, joy, Passover, Pentecost, rest

FELLOWSHIP

Moses explains Israelites as God's chosen people *Deut 7:6-11*

David befriended by Jonathan *1 Sam 18:1-16*

Solomon blesses congregation at dedication *1 King 8:22-66, 2 Chron 6:1-42*

Elisha will not leave Elijah *2 King 2:1-11*

Esther saves her people *Esther 3: 1-15, 4:1-17, 5:1-14*

Job's friends are no help *Job 16: 1-22*

Union of two sticks (states) *Ezek 37:15-28*

Jesus gives Golden Rule for actions *Mat 7:12-14, Luke 6:41, 42*

Jesus makes his disciples equal with his family *Mat 12:46-50, Mark 3: 31-35, Luke 8:19-21*

The disciples sit down to the last supper *Mat 26:26-29, Mark 14:22-25, Luke 22:14-30, 1 Cor 11:23-25*

Jesus' parable of the good Samaritan *Luke 10:25-37*

Jesus washes the disciples' feet *John 13:1-20*

Jesus prays for disciples *John 17: 1-26*

The disciples have breakfast with him *John 21:1-14*

Disciples receive Holy Spirit (Ghost) together *Acts 2:1-13*

Disciples hold all things in common *Acts 4:31-37*

Paul on unity of all *Eph 4:1-32*

John's sermon on love *1 John 4: 1-21*

See also brotherhood, communion, cooperation, equality, friendship, Golden Rule, love

FESTIVAL

See feast

FEVER

Jesus heals Peter's mother-in-law *Mat 8:14-17, Mark 1:29-31*

Jesus heals nobleman's son *John 4:46-54*

Paul heals father of Publius *Acts 28:7-10*

See also fear, fire, heat

FIGHT

See struggle

FIRE

Moses turns aside for the burning bush *Exod 3:1-18*

Moses heals camp of fiery serpents *Num 21:4-9*

Elijah sacrifices with fire *1 King 18: 17-40*

Elijah doesn't find God in the fire *1 King 19:9-13*

Three Hebrew boys protected in fiery furnace *Dan 3:1-30*

Jesus' parable of oil in the virgins' lamps *Mat 25:1-13*

Disciples' hearts burn within *Luke 24:13-35*

Paul bitten by viper out of the fire *Acts 28:1-6*

James tells how to bear the fiery trial *Jas 1:1-27*

Peter describes end of earth by burning *2 Pet 3:10-18*

See also desert, fear, heat, purity

FIRMAMENT

God creates firmament good *Gen 1:1-31*

Noah given rainbow of promise *Gen 9:12-17*

Tower of Babel built to reach heaven *Gen 11:1-9*

Joshua sees sun and moon stand still *Josh 10:6-15*

David's song, "The heavens declare the glory" *Psal 19:1-14*

Jesus' parable of builders on rock or sand *Mat 7:24-27, Luke 6:48, 49*

Jesus calms wind and seas *Mat 8: 23-27, Mark 4:35-41, 6:45-52, Luke 8:22-25*

Jesus foresees signs of Christ's coming *Mat 24:1-41*

Signs at crucifixion *Mat 27:50-53*

Jesus' birth announced by heavenly host *Luke 2:8-20*

Jesus asked for a sign or proof *Luke 12:49-59*

John's vision of a new heaven and earth *Rev 21:1-27*

See also foundation, heaven, support, understanding

FIRST

In the beginning God *Gen 1:1-31*

Cain the first murderer *Gen 4:1-16*

The First Commandment *Exod 20: 1-3*

The First Commandment protects Hebrews in fiery furnace *Dan 3: 1-30*

The First Commandment protects Daniel in lions' den *Dan 6:1-28*

Jesus on seek ye first *Mat 6:25-34*

Jesus' disciples contend who shall be greatest *Mat 18:1-11, Mark 9: 33-37, Luke 9:46-50*

Jesus' parable of the chief seats *Luke 14:7-14*

See also beginning, cause, creator

FIRST-BORN

Esau sells birthright to Jacob *Gen 25:24-34*

Moses declares death of first-born in Egypt *Exod 12:29-31*

Paul on Christ as first-born among men *Col 1:13-19*

See also sons, son of God, son of man

FISH

Creation by God *Gen 1:20-23*

Jonah escapes sea in great fish *Jonah 1:1-17*

Jesus feeds 5000 with a few loaves and fishes *Mat 14:15-21, Mark 6: 35-44, Luke 9:12-17, John 6:5-14*

Jesus sends Peter for tribute money in mouth of fish *Mat 17:24-27*

Jesus provides great draught of fishes — net breaks *Luke 5:1-11*

Peter after resurrection returns to his trade *John 21:1-5*

Jesus obtains great haul of fish; net does not break *John 21:1-11*

Jesus offers disciples bread and fish for breakfast *John 21:1-14*

See also breakfast, Christian

FLESH

Lord God creates man from dust *Gen 2:6-8*

Enoch walked with God and was not *Gen 5:18, 21-24, Heb 11:5*

Joseph overcomes temptations *Gen 39:1-20*

Israelites long for flesh pots of Egypt *Num 11:1-15*

Job smote with sore boils *Job 2: 7-10*

David's song, "Why art thou cast down?" *Psal 42:1-11*

The vanity of human things *Eccl 1:1-18, 2:1-26*

Mortal events all within time *Eccl 3:1-15*

Daniel refuses the king's meat *Dan 1:1-21*

Jesus' sermon, take no thought for material things *Mat 6:25-34*

Jesus heals man of leprosy *Mat 8: 1-4, Mark 1:40-45*

Jesus heals withered hand *Mat 12: 9-13, Mark 3:1-5, Luke 6:6-11*

Jesus is scourged *Mat 27:27-31, Mark 15:16-20, John 19:1-16*

Jesus ascends *Mark 16:19, 20, Luke 24:50-53, Acts 1:9-13*

Jesus' sermon, man must be born again *John 3:1-21*

Jesus' resurrection *John 20:11-18*

Paul on spirit vs. the flesh *Rom 8:1-39*

Paul on putting off old man, putting on new *Col 3:1-17*

See also blood, body, matter, sensuality, spirit

FLOCK

David is away tending the flock *1 Sam 16:1-13*

David's song, "The Lord is my shepherd" *Psal 23:1-6*

Ezekiel's vision of God's care of his flock *Ezek 34:1-31*

Jesus' parable of the good shepherd *John 10:1-18*

Jesus charges Peter "Feed my sheep" *John 21:12-19*

See also Christian, church, sheep

FLOOD

The rivers of Eden *Gen 2:9-17*

Noah builds the ark for safety *Gen 6:5-22*

Noah and all enter the ark and are borne up *Gen 7:1-24*

The raven and the dove go out over the flood *Gen 8:1-22*

The rainbow appears as the flood recedes *Gen 9:12-17*

Moses leads the people through the Red Sea *Exod 14:5-31*

Elijah parts Jordan River with his mantle *2 King 2:8*

Jesus heals woman's issue of blood *Mat 9:20-22, Mark 5:25-34, Luke 8:43-48*

Paul shipwrecked *Acts 27:1-44*

The angel with his foot on the sea *Rev 10:1-11*

The dragon lets out a flood *Rev 12:1-17*

See also ark, rain, sea, ship, water

FLOWER

Man as a flower of the field *Job 14:1-14, Isa 40:6-8, Jas 1:9-11, 1 Pet 1:24, 25*

Isaiah's vision, "the desert will blossom" *Isa 35:1-10*

Jesus on the lilies of the field *Mat 6:25-34*

See also fruit, nature

FOLLOWER

Moses followed out of Egypt *Exod 11:4-10, 12:1-14, 21:41, Deut 16:1-22*

Sons of the prophet observe translation of Elijah; and Elisha takes up mantle *2 King 2:1-15*

Elisha feeds 100 men with 20 loaves *2 King 4:42-44*

Jesus calls his disciples *Mat 4:17-22, Mark 1:14-20, Luke 5:1-11, John 1:35-42*

A scribe offers to follow Jesus *Mat 8:18-22*

Jesus chooses twelve to send out to heal *Mat 9:36-38, 10:1-42, Mark 3:13-21, 6:7-13, Luke 6:13-19, 9:1-6*

Disciples fail to heal epileptic boy *Mat 17:14-21, Mark 9:14-29, Luke 9:37-43*

Jesus sought by all men *Mark 1:35-39*

People follow Jesus like sheep *Mark 6:30-34*

Jesus sends out 70 *Luke 10:1-24*

Jesus urges disciples to the harvest *John 4:31-38*

Jesus washes disciples' feet *John 13:1-20*

Jesus' prayer for his disciples and their disciples *John 17:1-26*

Philip baptizes the Ethiopian *Acts 8:26-40*

See also apostle, Christian, disciple, leader

FOOD

Adam disobeys and is cursed to eat dust *Gen 3:6-24*

Esau sells birthright for potage *Gen 25:24-34*

Joseph's brethren come to Egypt for food *Gen 42:1-8*

Moses feeds Israelites with manna and quail *Exod 16:1-36, Num 11:1-15, 31, 32*

Ruth gleans in the field for food *Ruth 2:1-23*

Elijah fed by ravens *1 King 17:1-16*

Elijah fed in a dream *1 King 19:1-8*

Elisha feeds 100 men with 20 loaves *2 King 4:42-44*

Elisha prophesies drop in price of flour *2 King 6:24, 25, 7:1-18*

Daniel refuses king's meat, eats pulse *Dan 1:1-21*

Jesus feeds 5000 *Mat 14:15-21, Mark 6:35-44, Luke 9:13-17, John 6:5-14*

Jesus' parable of wedding feast *Mat 22:1-14*

Jesus' parable of prodigal son and husks *Luke 15:11-24*

Jesus on bread of life *John 6:26-65*

Jesus has supper with Lazarus whom he raised *John 11:55-57, 12:1, 2, 9-11*

Jesus has breakfast with disciples after resurrection *John 21:1-14*

John's vision of angel with book to be eaten *Rev 10:1-11*

See also bread, diet, feast, life

FORBEARANCE

See forgiveness

FORCE

Lot shelters two angels from the mob *Gen 19:1-14*

David kills Goliath *1 Sam 17:38-52*

Jehoshaphat learns the battle is God's *Chron 20:1-32*

Elijah learns the nature of God *1 King 19:9-13*

Sennacherib invades Israel *2 King 18:17-37, 19:1-27, 2 Chron 31:20, 21, 32:1-23*

David's song on God, the preserver of man *Psal 121:1-8*

Isaiah's prophecy of war no more *Isa 2:1-5, Mic 4:1-8, 13*

Isaiah's vision that the Lord's hand is not shortened *Isa 59:1-21*

Jesus calms wind and seas *Mat 8:23-27, Mark 4:35-41, 6:45-52, Luke 8:22-25, John 6:21*

Jesus speaks in person with Moses and Elijah *Mat 17:1-13, Mark 9:2-13, Luke 9:28-36*

Jesus' parable of husbandmen refusing to pay rent *Mat 21:33-46, Mark 12:1-12, Luke 20:9-19*

Jesus is scourged and mocked *Mat 27:27-31, Mark 15:16-20, John 19:1-16*

Jesus causes guards to fall backwards *John 18:4-6*

See also ability, energy, power

FOREIGNER

Joseph sold into slavery *Gen 37:1-36*

Joseph's brethren come to Egypt for grain *Gen 42:1-8*

Israelites oppressed in Egypt *Exod 1:8-14*

Midianites driven from promised land by Gideon *Judg 7:1-25*

Ruth, a foreigner, comes home with Naomi *Ruth 1:1-22*

Assyrians invade *2 King 18:17-37, 19:1-27, 2 Chron 31:20, 21, 32:1-23*

Babylonians invade *2 King 20:12-21, 25:27-30, Isa 39:1-8*

Jeremiah in prison buys a field in Israel *Jer 32:2, 6-27, 37-44*

Daniel persecuted in foreign land *Dan 6:1-28*

Jesus heals the centurion's servant *Mat 8:5-13, Luke 7:1-10*

Jesus heals foreign woman's daughter *Mat 15:21-28, Mark 7:24-30*

Peter, acceptance in church of the first Gentile *Acts 10:1-48, 11:1-18*

See also Gentile, stranger

FORERUNNER

Abraham blessed by Melchizedek (King of Peace) *Gen 14:8-20, Heb 6:20, 7:1-28*

Jacob's dream of angels on ladder and God's ever-presence *Gen 28:10-22*

Caleb and Joshua scout the land of Canaan and urge entry *Num 13:1-33, 14:1-11, 23-29, Deut 1:19-38*

Early acknowledgement of the rights of women *Num 27:1-11, 36:5-13*

Christ foreshadowed *Deut 18:15-22*

Joshua meets the captain of the host *Josh 5:10-15*

Isaiah on the coming of Christ's kingdom *Isa 2:1-5, Mic 4:1-8, 13*

Isaiah on birth of the Messiah *Isa 7:10-16, 9:2-7*

Isaiah on the office of Christ *Isa 42:1-12, 16, 18, 61:1-11, 62:1-12*

John Baptist heralds Messiah *Mat 3:1-12, Mark 1:1-8, Luke 3:1-18*

Jesus instructs twelve and sends them out to the places where he will come *Mat 9:36-38, 10:1-42, Mark 3:13-21, Luke 9:1-6*

Jesus' parable of husbandmen and son of landlord *Mat 21:33-46, Mark 12:1-12, Luke 20:9-19*

See also angel, herald, messenger, preparation, prophet, signs

FORESIGHT

Abraham goes out to look for a land of promise *Gen 11:31, 32, 12:1-9*

God's promises to Abraham *Gen 15:1-21*

Joseph's boyhood dreams set the pattern of his life *Gen 37:1-36*

Jacob foretells the future of his twelve sons *Gen 49:1-28, Deut 33:1-29*

Caleb and Joshua urge immediate entrance to land of promise but fear delays the people *Num 13:1-33, 14:1-11, 23-29, Deut 1:19-38*

Moses sees chosen people set apart as God's own *Deut 7:6-11*

A prophet is promised *Deut 18:15-22*

Samuel's miraculous birth announced
1 Sam 1:1-28

Samuel anoints Saul (a mistake)
1 Sam 10:1-8

Samuel anoints David as king *1 Sam
16:1-13*

Jehoshaphat promised battle is
God's *2 Chron 20:1-32*

Elisha foretells drop in price of
flour *2 King 6:24, 25, 7:1-18*

Isaiah foretells coming of Christ
Isa 2:1-5, Mic 4:1-8, 13

Isaiah foretells birth of Messiah
Isa 7:10-16, 9:2-7

Isaiah foretells his peaceful kingdom *Isa 11:1-12*

Isaiah foretells the fall of Babylon
Isa 14:4-8, 12-17, 25-27

Isaiah foretells the office of the
Christ *Isa 42:1-12, 16, 18, 61:1-11,
62:1-12*

Jeremiah foretells release from
captivity *Jer 29:8-14, 31:1-14,
31-34*

Ezekiel's vision of holy waters encompassing the universe *Ezek
47:1-12*

Daniel foretells fall of Babylon *Dan
2:1-49*

Daniel foretells insanity of king
Dan 4:1-27

Jonah foretells destruction of
Nineveh *Jonah 3:1-10*

Micah foretells the glory of the
church *Mic 4:1-8, 13, Isa 2:1-5*

Zephaniah foretells salvation of
Zion *Zeph 3:14-17*

The wise men visit "King of the
Jews" *Mat 2:1-12*

Jesus' family flees to Egypt *Mat
2:13-23, Luke 2:39, 40*

Jesus foretells his own death and
resurrection *Mat 16:21-28, 17:22,
23, 20:17-19, Mark 8:31-38, 9:30-32,
10:32-34, Luke 9:20-27, 43-45, 18:
31-34, 19:47, 48, John 12:20-50*

Jesus foretells destruction of temple
and Jerusalem *Mat 24:1-41, Mark
13:1-37, Luke 21:5-36*

Jesus foretells his second coming
Mat 24:1-41

Jesus foretells his betrayal *Mat 26:
20-25, Mark 14:18-21, Luke 22:21,
22, John 13:21-35*

Jesus' parable of temple to be raised
in three days *John 2:19-22*

Jesus foretells the coming of the
Holy Spirit (Ghost) *John 14:1-31*

See also forerunner, future, prophet,
seer

FOREVER
See eternity

FORGETFULNESS
Cain forgets brotherhood of man
Gen 4:1-16

Joseph forgotten by chief butler
Gen 40:1-23

Moses finds Israelites worshipping
calf *Exod 32:1-24*

Moses gives Ten Commandments
Exod 20:1-19, Deut 5:1-24

Caleb claims his reward *Josh 14:
6-15*

David shows kindness to his
friend's son *2 Sam 9:1-13*

Nathan reminds David of his sin
2 Sam 12:1-10

Nehemiah reviews history of God's
guidance *Neh 9:1-38*

Jesus' parable of debtor unmerciful
to fellows *Mat 18:23-35*

Jesus' parable of rich man and beggar *Luke 16:19-31*

Jesus reminds disciples of former
healings *Luke 22:35-38*

Paul advises his disciple, Timothy
2 Tim 2:1-26

See also duty, memorial, remembrance

FORGIVENESS
Jacob forgiven by Esau *Gen 33:
1-11*

Joseph forgives his brethren *Gen
45:1-11*

Moses forgives rebellion of Miriam
Num 12:1-16

David forgives Abigail's husband
1 Sam 25:2-42

Elisha releases his besiegers *2 King
6:8-23*

Jonah forgiven when he goes to
Nineveh *Jonah 3:1-10*

Jesus' parable of debtor unmerciful to fellows *Mat 18:23-35*

Jesus forgives mockers at crucifixion *Luke 23:34*

Jesus' parable of two debtors forgiven *Luke 7:36-50*

Jesus urges his disciples to forgive *Luke 17:1-6*

Jesus' parable of judge and widow *Luke 18:1-8*

Jesus' parable of Pharisee and publican *Luke 18:9-14*

Peter retaliates against Malchus, Jesus heals him *Luke 22:50, 51*

Stephen forgives those who stone him *Acts 7:51-69*

Paul healed by Ananias *Acts 9: 10-22*

Paul on charity *1 Cor 13:1-13*

John on love *1 John 4:1-21*

See also debt, pardon, punishment, resentment

FORM

Earth without form, and void *Gen 1:1-10*

God made man in his image *Gen 1:26, 27*

Lord God formed man of dust *Gen 2:6-8*

Noah builds ark *Gen 6:5-22*

Moses sees God at burning bush *Exod 3:1-18*

Moses' rod becomes a serpent *Exod 4:1-9, 7:1-12*

Pillar of cloud and fire guides *Exod 13:20-22, Num 9:15-23*

Aaron's rod blossoms *Num 17:1-11*

Joshua sets up memorial of twelve stones *Josh 4:1-24*

Jesus restores withered hand *Mat 12:9-13, Mark 3:1-5, Luke 6:6-11*

Jesus restores body *Mat 28:1-8, Mark 16:1-8, Luke 24:1-12, John 20:1-10*

Jesus appears in another form to two disciples *Mark 16:12, 13, Luke 24:13-35*

Christ Jesus appears in human form *Luke 2:1-7*

Jesus heals woman bowed together *Luke 13:11-17*

Jesus says man must be born again *John 3:1-21*

Paul on Christ Jesus in form of a servant *Phil 2:6, 7*

Paul urges to put on the new man *Col 3:1-17*

Paul warns of the form of godliness *2 Tim 3:1-7*

See also body, custom, image

FORTIFICATION

Jacob wrestles with angel to prepare to meet his brother *Gen 32:1-32*

Joseph prepares Egypt against famine *Gen 41:1-46*

Nehemiah repairs the wall of Jerusalem *Neh 4:1-23*

David's song on God, our refuge and strength *Psal 46:1-11*

David's song on the secret place of the most High *Psal 91:1-16*

A poor wise man saves a city *Eccl 9:13-18*

Jesus' parable of builders on rock and sand *Mat 7:24-27, Luke 6: 48, 49*

Jesus prepares at Gethsemane *Mat 26:30, 36-46, Mark 14:26, 36-42, Luke 22:39-46*

Jesus prays for his disciples *John 17:1-26*

Paul on the Christian's armor *Eph 6:10-17*

Paul's advice *2 Tim 2:1-26, 3:1-17, 4:1-8*

James on how to bear our cross *Jas 1:1-27*

See also defense, morality, resistance, strength

FORTUNE

Moses as baby is discovered by princess *Exod 2:1-10*

Naomi's relatives die *Ruth 1:1-22*

Ruth selects the field of Boaz *Ruth 2:1-23*

People and Mordecai persecuted by rulers *Esther 3:1-15, 4:1-17*

Job's fortunes change *Job 1:13-22, 2:1-10*

David's song, "the happiness of the godly" *Psal 1:1-6*

David's song, "What is man?" *Psal 8:1-9*

Mortal life is vain *Eccl 1:1-18, 2: 1-26*

Mortal events all within time *Eccl 3:1-15*

Ezekiel's vision of the children's teeth on edge *Ezek 18:1-32*

Jesus calms the wind and seas *Mat 8:23-27, Mark 4:35-41, 6:45-52, Luke 8:22-25, John 6:21*

Jesus' parable of the prodigal's progress *Luke 15:11-24*

Jesus heals the man born blind *John 9:1-41*

Paul heals Eutychus of fall from window *Acts 20:7-12*

Paul escapes shipwreck *Acts 27: 1-44*

See also accident, chance, happiness, wealth

FORSAKE

Noah builds the ark *Gen 6:5-22*

Abraham sends Hagar and her son into the wilderness *Gen 21:9-21*

Joseph is left in pit and sold into slavery *Gen 37:1-36*

Jacob and his children leave promised land for Egypt *Gen 45:25-28, 46:2-7*

People forsake God for idols and sensuality *Exod 32:1-24*

Moses warns against idolatry, necromancy *Deut 13:1-18*

Moses offers choice for good or evil *Deut 30:11-20*

Ruth leaves her native land, is loyal to her mother-in-law *Ruth 1:1-22*

Saul turns from God to consult familiar spirit *1 Sam 28:3-20*

Rehoboam departs from old counsellors of his father *1 King 12:1-18, 2 Chron 10:1-15*

Asa forsakes God for physicians, dies *2 Chron 16:11-14*

Elisha leaves plowing to follow Elijah *1 King 19:19-21*

Jonah forsakes his duty to preach *Jonah 1:1-17*

Disciples forsake their nets to follow Jesus *Mat 4:17-22, Mark 1: 14-20, Luke 5:1-11, John 1:35-40*

Jesus' crucifixion *Mat 27:37-56, Mark 15:21-41, Luke 23:20-49, John 19:17-30*

Jesus' parable of the prodigal son *Luke 15:11-24*

Jesus saves adulteress and tells her to sin no more *John 8:1-11*

Conversion of Paul *Acts 8:1-4, 9: 1-22*

See also repentance

FOUNDATION

Moses gives basis of all law *Exod 20:1-19, Deut 5:1-24*

Solomon builds the temple *1 King 6:1-38, 7:1-51, 2 Chron 3:1-17, 4: 1-22, 5:1-14*

Elijah lays the base of prophecy *1 King 19:9-13*

David's song, "our dwelling place" *Psal 90:1-17*

Jesus founds gospels on Beatitudes *Mat 5:1-12, Luke 6:17-26, 36*

Jesus teaches the Lord's Prayer *Mat 6:5-15, Mark 11:25, 26, Luke 11:1-4*

Jesus' parable of builders on rock and sand *Mat 7:24-27, Luke 6: 48, 49*

Jesus teaches healing *Mat 9:36-38, 10:1-42, Mark 3:13-21, 6:7-13, Luke 9:1-6, 10:1-24*

Jesus talks with Moses (law) and Elijah (prophecy) *Mat 17:1-13, Mark 9:2-13, Luke 9:28-36*

Jesus' resurrection establishes church *Mat 28:1-8, Mark 16:1-8, Luke 24: 1-12, John 20:1-10*

Jesus' final instructions *Mat 28:16-20, Mark 16:15-18*

Jesus heals the woman bowed together *Luke 13:11-17*

Paul establishes church *2 Cor 11: 21-33*

See also church, cornerstone, origin, platform, purity

FOUNTAIN

Moses obtains water from rock *Exod 17:1-7, Num 20:1-13*

David's song on the fountain of life *Psal 36:1-12*

Ezekiel's vision of the holy waters flowing outward *Ezek 47:1-12*

Zechariah's vision of two olive trees as source of oil *Zech 4:1-14*

See also origin, source

FRAUD

See deceit, duplicity, hypocrisy, lie

FREEDOM

Joseph sold into slavery in Egypt
Gen 37:1-36
Israelites in Egypt oppressed *Exod
1:8-14*
Israelites' release from bondage
*Exod 11:4-10, 12:1-14, 30, 31, Deut
16:1-22*
Gideon expels the oppressive Mid-
ianites *Judg 7:1-25*
A poor wise man saves the city *Eccl
9:13-18*
Jeremiah's vision of turning the
captivity *Jer 29:8-14*
Jeremiah's promise of restoration
Jer 31:1-14, 31-34
Jeremiah in prison buys a field in
Israel *Jer 32:6-27, 37-44*
Jesus frees men from sin, disease
and death (*See* Part II, Jesus
Christ: Great Works)
John Baptist in prison sends mes-
sengers to Jesus *Mat 11:2-19,
Luke 7:18-35*
Peter and John released by church
council *Acts 4:1-37*
Peter imprisoned again *Acts 5:
17-42*
Peter imprisoned by Herod *Acts
12:1-17*
Paul and Silas released from prison
by earthquake *Acts 16:19-40*

See also democracy, liberty, slavery,
tyranny

FRESHNESS

See refreshment

FRIENDSHIP

Ruth and Naomi *Ruth 1:1-22*
David and Jonathan *1 Sam 18:1-16*
David spares Saul *1 Sam 24:1-22,
26:1-25*
Job's friends no comfort *Job 16:
1-22*
Solomon and Queen of Sheba *1 King
10:1-12, 2 Chron 9:1-12*

Jezebel swears enmity to Elijah
1 King 17:1-16
Elija and Elisha *2 King 2:1-15*
Jesus as the friend of publicans and
sinners *Mat 9:10-13, Mark 2:13-
17, Luke 5:27-32*
Jesus' disciples as close to him as
his family *Mat 12:46-50, Mark 3:
31-35, Luke 8:19-21*
Rulers conspire against Jesus *Mat
26:1-5, Mark 14:1, 2*
Chief priests seek to destroy Jesus
Mark 11:18, 19
Mary and Elizabeth as friends *Luke
1:39-56*
Jesus' parable of the good Samaritan *Luke 10:25-37*
Jesus' parable of the unwilling
friend *Luke 11:5-13*
Paul's love for his disciple, Timothy
2 Tim 2:1-26

See also brotherhood, enemy, fellowship, Golden Rule

FRUITS

God's command "Be fruitful, and
multiply" *Gen 1:1-31*
Eve and Adam try the fruit of the
tree of the knowledge of good and
evil *Gen 3:1-5*
Abel offers first fruits *Gen 4:1-16*
Abraham's riches grow *Gen 13:1-18*
Aaron's rod blossoms *Num 17:1-11*
Moses urges offering first fruits
Deut 26:1-19
Jotham's parable of the trees *Judg
9:1-15*
Isaiah's parable of the wild grapes
Isa 5:1-8
Jeremiah's story of the good and bad
figs *Jer 24:1-10*
Ezekiel's vision of fathers eating
sour grapes *Ezek 18:1-32*
Song, "the winter is past" *Song Sol
2:1-17*
Jesus says to know men by their
fruits *Mat 7:15-20, Luke 6:43-45*
Jesus withers the fig tree *Mat 21:
18-22, Mark 11:12-14, 20-24*
Jesus' parable of the fig tree leaf-
ing *Mat 24:32, 33, Mark 13:28, 29*
Jesus' parable of seed, blade, ear,
full corn *Mark 4:26-29*
Jesus' parable of man who built
larger barns *Luke 12:15-21*

Jesus' parable of barren fig tree
Luke 13:6-9

Jesus turns water to wine *John 2: 1-11*

Jesus points out that the harvest is now *John 4:31-38*

Jesus' parable of the vine and branches *John 15:1-17*

Paul's sermon on fruits of spirit *Gal 5:1-26*

See also barrenness, farming, harvest, multiply, seed, success, tree

FRUSTRATION

See defeat

FULFILLMENT

Abraham and Sarah have promised son at advanced age *Gen 21:1-8*

Joseph's boyhood dreams fulfilled *Gen 37:5-10, 42:1-8*

Joseph interprets dreams of baker, and butler *Gen 39:21, 23, 40:1-23*

Joshua crosses Jordan into promised land *Josh 3:1-17*

Samson born to Manoah's wife *Judg 13:1-25*

Samuel born to Hannah *1 Sam 1: 1-28*

David crowned *1 Sam 16:1-13, 2 Sam 2:1-4, 5:1-5*

Elijah prays for rain *1 King 18: 41-46*

Shunammite tells Elisha all is well *2 King 4:8-37*

Elisha tells his disciples poison in potage is harmless *2 King 4: 38-41*

Elisha prophesies drop in price of flour *2 King 6:24, 25, 7:1-16*

Nathan reveals to David that his son will build a house for God *1 Chron 17:1-27*

Jahaziel says "the battle is God's" *2 Chron 20:1-32*

Jesus fulfills prophesies of Messiah by the land of Zabulon and Nephthalim *Mat 4:12-16*

     by healing people *Mat 15:29-31, 19:1, 2*

     by suffering crucifixion *Mat 27: 32-56, Mark 15:21-41, Luke 23: 26-49, John 19:17-30*

     by overcoming death *Mat 28:9, 10, Mark 16:9-11, Luke 24:13-49, John 20:11-18*

     by ascension *Mark 16:19, 20, Luke 24:50, 51, Acts 1:6-12*

     by birth in line of David at Bethlehem *Luke 2:1-7*

Disciples receive promised Holy Spirit (Ghost) *Acts 2:1-13*

Paul on love, the fulfilling of law *Rom 13:7-14*

Paul on Christ's resurrection proves our resurrection *1 Cor 15:1-58*

Paul on eternity of Christ *Heb 6: 20, 7:1-28*

See also birth, dreams, manifestation, perfection, prayer, promise, prophecy, success

FUNCTIONAL

Jesus heals Peter's wife's mother of fever *Mat 8:14-17, Mark 1: 29-34*

Jesus heals paralysis *Mat 9:2-8, Mark 2:1-12, Luke 5:17-26*

Jesus heals nobleman's son's fever *John 4:46-54*

Jesus heals lame man *John 5:1-16*

Peter heals lame *Acts 3:1-11*

Peter heals paralysis *Acts 9:32-35*

Paul heals lame *Acts 14:8-10*

See also activity, office, organic

FUTURE

God's promises to Abraham *Gen 15: 1-21*

God's promises to Isaac *Gen 26:1-5*

Joseph's dreams of God's plan for him *Gen 37:1-36*

Joseph predicts future of fellow prisoners *Gen 39:21-23, 40:1-23*

Joseph predicts future of Egypt's famine *Gen 41:1-46*

Jacob foresees future of his twelve sons *Gen 49:1-28, Deut 33:1-29*

Elisha foretells a drop in the price of flour *2 King 6:24, 25, 7:1-18*

Isaiah on the coming of the Messiah *Isa 7:10-16, 9:2-7*

Jeremiah foretells the restoration of Israel *Jer 31:1-14, 31-34*

Daniel reads the handwriting on the wall *Dan 5:1-31*

Jesus' parable of the leaven foretells spread of Christ *Mat 13:
33, Luke: 13:20, 21*
Jesus promises to come again *Mat
24:1-41*
Jesus promises the Holy Ghost
John 14:1-31
John's vision of new heaven and
earth *Rev 21:1-27*

See also eternity, prophet, seer, time

G

GAIN

Abraham's riches grow *Gen 13:1-18*
Joseph rises from slave in prison to
governor of Egypt *Gen 41:1-46*
Solomon brings people to summit of
prosperity *1 King 10:1-12,
2 Chron 9:1-12*
Isaiah's vision, "the desert will blos-
som *Isa 35:1-10*
Malachi urges tithing *Mal 3:10, 4:
1, 2*
Jesus' parable of the sower *Mat 13:
3-23, Mark 4:1-20, Luke 8:4-15*
Jesus' parable of treasure in field
Mat 13:44
Jesus' parable of pearl of great
price *Mat 13:45, 46*
Jesus' parable of householder's
treasures *Mat 13:51, 52*
Jesus feeds 5000 *Mat 14:15-21,
Mark 6:35-44, Luke 9:12-17, John
6:5-14*
Peter gets tribute money from fish
Mat 17:24-27
Jesus casts traders out of temple
*Mat 21:12, 13, Mark 11:15-17, Luke
19:45, 46, John 2:13-25*
Jesus' parable of the talents *Mat
25:14-30, Luke 19:11-28*
Jesus' parable of the ear and full
corn *Mark 4:26-29*
Peter's net filled *Luke 5:1-11, John
21:1-11*
Jesus' parable of rich man and
bigger barns *Luke 12:15-22*
Signs and wonders cause church
growth *Acts 4:24-37*
Paul's sermon on abundance *2 Cor
8:11-15, 9:6-15*
Paul on faith as substance *Heb
11:1-40*

James on works and faith *Jas 2:
14-26*

See also increase, loss, profit, wealth

GAMBLING

Soldiers cast lots at foot of cross
Mat 27:35, Mark 15:24
Disciples cast lots to elect Matthias
Acts 1:15-26

See also chance, fortune, money

GARDEN

Description of Garden of Eden *Gen
2:9-17*
Banishment from garden *Gen 3:
6-24*
David's song, "the desert will blos-
som" *Isa 35:1-10*
Jesus' parable of laborers in the
vineyard *Mat 20:1-16*
Jesus in Gethsemane *Mat 26:30,
36-46, Mark 14:26, 32-42, Luke 22:
39-46*
Jesus' parable of the true vine *John
15:1-17*
Jesus mistaken for the gardener
John 20:11-18
Paul's sermon on fruits of the spirit
Gal 5:1-26
John's vision of the river and the
tree of life *Rev 22:1-21*

See also consciousness, Eden, fruits

GARMENT

Leaves for first garments *Gen 3:
6-24*
Joseph's coat of many colors *Gen
37:1-36*
Aaron's robe with Urim and Thum-
mim *Exod 28:29-36*
Gehazi accepts garments Elisha
rejects *2 King 5:15-27*
Elijah and Elisha use mantle to cross
Jordan *2 King 2:1-15*
Isaiah on the pride of women's
clothes *Isa 3:16-26*
Jesus heals the insane Gadarene and
clothes him *Mat 8:28-34, Mark
5:1-20, Luke 8:26-39*
Jesus' garments shine at transfigu-
ration *Mat 17-1-13, Mark 9:2-13,
Luke 9:28-36*

Jesus' parable of the wedding garment *Mat 22:1-14*

Jesus clothed in purple and mocked *Mat 27:27-31, Mark 15:16-20, John 19:1-16*

See also armor, clothing, dedication, protection

GATE

Nehemiah repairs wall and then puts up door at gates of Jerusalem *Neh 4:1-23*

David's song of king of glory entering *Psal 24:1-10*

Jesus enters Jerusalem for last time *Mat 21:1-11, 14-17, Mark 11: 1-11, Luke 19: 29-44, John 12:12-19*

Jesus heals dead man at gates of Nain *Luke 7:11-17*

While Jews watch gates, Paul is let down over wall in a basket *Acts 9:23-31*

See also door, mind, justice

GENEALOGY

God creates man in his image *Gen 1:26, 27*

Early man lives to advanced age *Gen 5:1-32*

Jacob prophesies the future of his sons *Gen 49:1-28, 33:1-29*

Ruth and Boaz as the forebearers of line of David *Ruth 2:1-22, 4: 1-22*

Jesus' genealogy *Mat 1:1-17, Luke 3:23-38*

Jesus' discourse about Abraham and the eternity of Christ *John 8: 12-59*

The story of Melchizedek *Heb 6: 20, 7:1-28*

See also father, heredity, parent

GENEROSITY

Abraham allows Lot to have his choice of land *Gen 13:1-18*

Isaac's herdmen's strife over wells *Gen 26:12-31*

Ruth receives help from Boaz *Ruth 2:1-23*

David spares Saul in cave and in Ziph *1 Sam 24:1-22, 26:1-25*

David shows kindness to Saul's son *2 Sam 9:1-13*

David receives liberal offerings for temple *1 Chron 29:6-19*

Elisha multiplies the widow's pot of oil *2 King 4:1-7*

Jehoiachin receives allowance for life *2 King 25:27-30*

Proverb on virtuous woman *Prov 31:1-31*

Isaiah's "Comfort ye" *Isa 40:1-31*

Malachi urges tithing *Mal 3:10, 4: 1-2*

Jesus on benevolence in secret *Mat 6:1-4*

Jesus' parable of debtor unmerciful to fellows *Mat 18:23-35*

Jesus sees widow cast in her mite *Mark 12:41-44, Luke 21:1-4*

Jesus' parable of two debtors forgiven *Luke 7:36-50*

Jesus' parable of good Samaritan *Luke 10:25-37*

Jesus' parable of prodigal's elder brother *Luke 15:25-32*

Jesus' parable of rich man and beggar *Luke 16:19-31*

Jesus visits Zacchaeus *Luke 19: 1-10*

Jesus' parable of good shepherd *John 10:1-18*

Peter raises Tabitha *Acts 9:36-43*

Paul on charity *1 Cor 13:1-13*

Paul on giving and receiving *2 Cor 8:11-15, 9:6-15*

See also abundance, benevolence, kindness, love

GENESIS

See creation, creator, dust, image, likeness

GENIUS

Joseph, a problem-solving genius *Gen 41:1-46*

Moses, a leader, judge, legislator *Exod 18: 13-27, 20: 1-19, Deut 5: 1-24*

David, warrior, king, psalmist *1 Sam 16:14-23, 17:38-52, 2 Sam 2:1-4, 5: 1-5*

Solomon, judge and builder *1 King 3:5-15, 6:1-38*

Elijah, the seer *2 King 2:1-11*
Elisha, the demonstrator of the science of religion *2 King 4:8-37*
Job, the philosopher of God's nature *Job 38:1-41*
Isaiah, the prophet of the Messiah *Isa 6:1-13, 7:10-16, 9:2-7*
Jesus, the preacher *Mat 5:1-12, Luke 6:17-26, 36*
Jesus, the seer *Mat 6:5-14, Mark 11:25, 26, Luke 11:1-4*
Jesus, the perfect man and Saviour *Mat 27:32-56, Mat 28:1-8*
Paul promoter of Christianity *Acts 17:15-34, Rom 5:1-21, 8:1-39, 1 Cor 15:1-58, Col 3:1-17*
John, the Revelator *Rev 21:1-27, 22:1-21*

See also character, mind, problem-solving, talent

GENTILE

Abraham receives new name and is circumcised *Gen 17:1-9, 15-22*
Moses sets chosen people apart as God's own *Deut 7:6-11*
David kills Goliath, the uncircumcised Philistine *1 Sam 17:38-52*
Roman centurion's servant healed by Jesus *Mat 8:5-13, Luke 7:1-10*
Jesus calls himself the light of the world *John 8:12-32*
Peter accepts conversion of Cornelius, a Roman *Acts 10:1-48*
Peter's vision of great sheet *Acts 11:1-18*
Philip converts an Ethiopian *Acts 8:26-40*

See also Christian, circumcision, foreigner, nation, race

GENTLENESS

Abraham in strife with Lot gives way, is rewarded *Gen 13:1-18*
Moses heals Miriam after her rebellion against him *Num 12:-16*
Ruth follows her mother-in-law when Orpah returns *Ruth 1:1-22*
David pacified by Abigail's gentleness *1 Sam 25:2-42*
David's song, "The Lord is my shepherd" *Psal 23:1-6*

Ezekiel's vision of God as shepherd of flock *Ezek 34:1-31*
Hosea's vision of God's forgiveness and care *Hos 11:1-4*
Zephaniah's vision of Zion as daughter of God *Zeph 3:14-17*
Jesus gives qualities that make a Christian *Mat 5:1-12, Luke 6:17-26, 36*
Jesus' golden rule of action *Mat 7:12-14, Luke 6:41, 44*
Jesus sets little child in midst *Mat 18:1-22, Mark 9:33-50, Luke 9:46-50*
Jesus' parable of the lost sheep *Mat 18:12-14, Luke 15:1-7*
Mary's visit with Elizabeth *Luke 1:39-56*
Jesus anointed by a woman *Luke 7:36-50*
Jesus' parable of the good Samaritan *Luke 10:25-37*
Jesus' parable of the prodigal son's father *Luke 15:11-32*
Jesus on offense *Luke 17:1-6*
Jesus' parable of the vine and branches *John 15:1-17*
Jesus' parable of the good shepherd *John 10:1-18*
Jesus washes disciples' feet *John 13:1-20*
Jesus on humility *John 13:12-20*
Jesus on cross arranges for care of his mother *John 19:25-27*
Ananias heals Saul *Acts 9:10-22*
Paul's sermon on the example left by Jesus *Heb 12:1-29*

See also childlikeness, compassion, goodness, humility, kindness

GETHSEMANE

Isaiah's prophecy of the man of sorrows *Isa 53:1-12*
Zechariah's vision of two olive trees *Zech 4:1-14*
Jesus in the garden of the oil press *Mat 25:30, 36-46, Mark 14:26, 32-42, Luke 22:39-46*
Paul on the example left by Jesus *Heb 12:1-29*

See also defeat, suffering, trials

GHOST (Holy)

See Holy Spirit (Ghost)

GIDEON (one of the Judges)

See Part II, Gideon

GIVING

Abram and Sarai are given new names *Gen 17:1-9, 13-22*
Moses gives Ten Commandments *Exod 20:1-19, Deut 5:1-24*
David receives liberal offering to build temple *1 Chron 29:6-19*
Solomon dedicates temple to the Lord *1 King 8:22-66, 2 Chron 6: 1-42*
Elijah first receives cake from the widow *1 King 17:1-16*
Zechariah's vision of candlestick fed by two olive trees *Zech 4: 1-14*
Malachi urges all the tithes into the storehouse *Mal 3:10*
Jesus receives gifts of wise men *Mat 2:1-12*
Pharisees require a sign of Jesus *Mat 12:38-45, 16:1-4, Mark 8:10-13, Luke 11:16, 29-32*
Jesus approves widow's mite *Mark 12:41-44, Luke 21:1-4*
Jesus on laying down life for his sheep *John 10:1-38*
Peter can't give alms to cripple but heals him *Acts 3:1-11*
John's vision of angel giving the little book *Rev 10:1-11*
Paul on giving and receiving *2 Cor 8:11-15, 9:6-15*

See also Christmas, dedication, denial, generosity

GLADNESS

Abraham surveys with satisfaction land left him *Gen 13:1-18*
Abraham and Sarah promised a son *Gen 15:1-21*
Aaron proclaims jubilee year *Lev 25:9-19*
Moses' song of deliverance *Deut 32:1-47*
Samuel's miraculous birth *1 Sam 1: 1-28*

David's song, "Rejoice in the Lord" *Psal 33:1-22*
David's song, "Make a joyful noise" *Psal 66:1-20, 100:1-5*
Jesus heals woman and she tells about it *Mat 9:20-22, Mark 5:25-34, Luke 8:43-48*
Jesus' parable of rejoicing over lost sheep *Mat 18:12-14, Luke 15:1-7*
Jesus' entry into Jerusalem with hosannas *Mat 21:1-11, 14-17, Mark 11:1-11, Luke 19:29-44, John 12:12-19*
Jesus seen by Mary Magdalene *Mark 16:9-11, John 20:11-18*
Jesus' birth announced with joy to the world *Luke 2:8-20*
Jesus' parable of prodigal returned *Luke 15:11-24*
Jesus heals ten lepers, one returns thanks *Luke 17:11-19*

See also gratitude, grief, joy, satisfaction

GLORY

Noah sees the rainbow as a token of God's covenant *Gen 9:12-17*
Moses' shining face concealed by veil *Exod 34:29-35*
Moses' song of mercy and deliverance *Deut 32:1-47*
Joshua sets up twelve stones as memorial *Josh 4:1-24*
Elisha takes up mantle of Elijah *2 King 2:12-15*
David's song, "the beauty of the Lord our God be upon us" *Psal 90:1-17*
David's song, "Let the redeemed of the Lord say so" *Psal 107:1-43*
Isaiah's vision of God's glory *Isa 6:1-13*
Isaiah's vision "Arise, shine" *Isa 60:1-5*
Ezekiel's vision of the holy waters *Ezek 47:1-12*
Jesus, a baby visited by three kings *Mat 2:1-12*
Jesus' baptism by John Baptist *Mat 3:13-17, Mark 1:9-11, Luke 3:21, 22*
Jesus' transfiguration on the mount *Mat 17:1-13, Mark 9:2-13, Luke 9: 28-36*

Jesus' entry into Jerusalem riding on an ass *Mat 21:1-11, 14-17, Mark 11:1-11, Luke 19:29-44, John 12:12-19*

Jesus' head anointed with precious oil *Mat 26:6-13, Mark 14:3-9*

Jesus' resurrection *Mat 28:1-8, Mark 16:1-8, Luke 24:1-12, John 20:1-10*

Jesus' ascension *Mark 16:19, 20, Luke 24:50, 51, Acts 1:6-12*

Jesus' birth announced by angels *Luke 2:8-20*

Jesus says he is light of the world *John 1:1-14, 8:12-32*

Jesus explains kingdom of God and his second coming *John 17:20-37*

Stephen's appearance when being stoned *Acts 7:59, 60*

Paul stricken by light *Acts 9:1-9*

John's vision of new heaven and new earth *Rev 21:1-21*

See also beauty, light, perfection, praise, radiance

GO FORWARD

Noah, the raven and the dove, as signs to go forth *Gen 8:-1-22*

Jacob in fear goes forward to meet his estranged brother *Gen 33:1-11*

Moses at Red Sea with the Egyptians following *Exod 14:5-31*

Joshua goes forward through midst of Jordan *Josh 3:1-17*

Jehoshaphat's cry, "the battle is not yours but God's" *2 Chron 20:1-32*

Elijah goes forward towards his translation *2 King 2:1-11*

Elisha takes up his mantle *2 King 2:12-15*

David runs to meet the challenge of Goliath *1 Sam 17:38-52*

Zerubbabel despite adversaries starts rebuilding *Ezra 4:1-5*

Nehemiah takes up repair of the wall *Neh 4:1-23*

Jeremiah in prison buys a field in Israel *Jer 32:2, 6-27, 37-44*

Three Hebrews enter the fiery furnace *Dan 3:1-30*

Daniel enters the lions' den *Dan 6:1-28*

Jonah goes in opposite way, then follows God's way *Jonah 1:1-17, 2:1-10, 3:1-10*

Jesus and Peter walk on sea *Mat 14:22-33, John 6:15-21*

Jesus foretells his own death and admonishes Peter for advising him to avoid it *Mat 16:21-28, Mark 8:31-38, Luke 9:20-27*

Jesus at Gethsemane accepts his passion as inevitable *Mat 25:30, 36-46, Mark 14:26, 32-42, Luke 22:39-46*

Jesus instructs 70 to go preach and heal *Luke 10:1-16*

Jesus urges Peter to feed his sheep instead of returning to his trade of fishing *John 20:12-19*

See also growth, improvement, opportunity, progress, promote

GOD

God (Elohim) creates the spiritual universe *Gen 1:1-31, 2:1-3*

Lord God (Jehovah) creates material universe *Gen 2:6-25*

To Moses is revealed the nature of God as I Am *Exod 3:1-18*

God writes basis of all law (Ten Commandments) *Exod 20:1-19, Deut 5:1-24*

David promises to build a temple for God *2 Sam 7:1-29*

Elijah and the still small voice *1 King 19:9-13*

Job hears voice of thunder describe God's nature *Job 38:1-41*

David's song, "The Lord is my shepherd" *Psal 23:1-6*

David's song, soul and its expressions *Psal 84:1-12*

David's song, God, our dwelling place *Psal 90:1-17*

David's song, God, our protector *Psal 91:1-16*

David's song, God, the preserver of man *Psal 121:1-8*

David's song on God's ever-presence *Psal 139:1-24*

Isaiah praises God for his benefits *Isa 25:1, 4, 6-10*

Isaiah's vision of God as creator and saviour *Isa 45:1-13, 18-25*

Jeremiah's vision of the potter and his clay *Jer 18:1-6*

Ezekiel's vision of equity of God's dealings *Ezek 18:1-32*

Ezekiel's vision of God's care of his flock *Ezek 34:1-31*

Hosea's vision of God's care of Israel *Hos 11:1-4*

Jesus announced as beloved son *Mat 3:13-17, Mark 1:9-11, Luke 3:21, 22*

Jesus' parable of the marriage feast *Mat 22:1-14*

Jesus' coming, immaculate birth announced to Mary *Luke 1:26-38*

Jesus' parable on those bidden to great supper *Luke 14:15-24*

Jesus' parable of the father of prodigal son and elder brother *Luke 15:11-32*

Jesus' sermon on his great works have source in the Father *John 5:17-47*

Jesus speaks of his oneness with Father *John 10:30-39*

John's sermon, God is Love *1 John 4:1-21*

See also father, life, love, maker, mind, mother, saviour, soul, spirit, truth

GODS

Moses finds people worshipping golden calf *Exod 32:1-24*

Moses gives people First, Second, and Seventh Commandments *Exod 20:1-19*

Idol, Dagon, falls and breaks before ark of the Lord *1 Sam 5:1-5*

Elijah defeats 450 prophets of Baal *1 King 18:17-40*

Daniel interprets king's dream of great image *Dan 2:1-49*

Three Jews refuse to worship king's image *Dan 3:1-30*

Paul attacked by the idol silversmith *Acts 19:23-29*

See also adultery, idolatry, image, superstition

GOLDEN RULE

Cain ruptures brotherhood of man *Gen 4:1-15*

Abraham ceases strife with his nephew *Gen 13:1-18*

Jacob deceives his brother and father *Gen 25:24-34, 27:1-44*

Ruth refuses to desert her mother-in-law *Ruth 1:1-22*

David spares Saul who is hunting him *1 Sam 24:1-22*

Jesus gives the Golden Rule for actions *Mat 7:12-14, Luke 6:41, 42*

Jesus on humility and handling of aggressions *Mat 18:1-22, Mark 9:33-50, 10:13-16*

Jesus' parable of debtor unmerciful to fellows *Mat 18:23-35*

Jesus' parable of good Samaritan *Luke 10:25-37*

Jesus' parable of rich man and beggar *Luke 16:19-31*

Peter arranges division of labor in the church *Acts 6:1-4*

Tabitha's good work rewarded *Acts 9:36-43*

Paul on charity *1 Cor 15:1-58*

James on equality of man *Jas 2:1-13*

John on love *1 John 4:1-21*

See also brotherhood, fellowship, friendship, love, neighbor

GOODNESS

God creates good universe *Gen 1:1-31, 2:1-5*

Noah's goodness promised safety *Gen 6:1-22*

Abraham asks how many good men it takes to save a city *Gen 18:20-33*

Jacob starts out life with duplicity *Gen 27:1-44*

Joseph overcomes the temptations of his owner's wife *Gen 39:1-20*

Moses' face illumined by speaking with God *Exod 33:7-23*

Moses lists God's promises to the obedient *Deut 4:1-15, 11:1-32*

Ruth's reward for her goodness *Ruth 2:1-22, 3:1-23*

Samuel selects David to anoint *1 Sam 16:1-13*

Solomon's request for proper values *1 King 3:5-15, 2 Chron 1:7:12*

Jehoshaphat's good reign *2 Chron 17:1-13, 19:4-11*

Job's goodness is tested *Job 1:13-22*

David's song, "the earth is full of the goodness of the Lord" *Psal 33:1-22*

David's song, "praise the Lord for his goodness" *Psal 107:1-43*

Solomon lists the qualities of the virtuous woman *Prov 31:1-31*

Jeremiah's vision of good and bad figs *Jer 24:1-10*

Ezekiel's vision of the holy waters *Ezek 47:1-12*

Zechariah's vision of good supplied by two olive trees *Zech 4:1-14*

Isaiah's vision of new Jerusalem *Isa 65:17-25*

Jesus on giving in secret *Mat 6:1-4*

Jesus on oneness with Father *Mat 6:22-24*

Jesus' parable of unclean spirit *Mat 12:43-45, Luke 11:24-26*

Jesus' parable of wheat and tares *Mat 13:24-30, 36-43*

Jesus' parable of the dragnet *Mat 13:47-50*

Jesus distinguishes between the goodness of Martha and Mary *Luke 10:38-42*

Jesus' parable of good shepherd *John 10:1-18*

Paul's sermon to think on good things *Phil 4:1-23*

See also benevolence, character, evil, excellence, God, holiness, purity, righteousness, value

Saul's malice towards David *1 Sam 16:14-23*

David shows kindness to Jonathan's son *2 Sam 9:1-13*

Solomon's wisdom acknowledged by Sheba *1 King 10:1-12, 2 Chron 9:1-12*

Jehoiachin well-treated by captors *2 King 25:27-30*

King Cyrus helps rebuild temple *Ezra 1:1-11*

Artaxerxes' letter to Ezra *Ezra 7:11-26*

Isaiah's vision of Christ's peaceable kingdom *Isa 11:1-12*

Zephaniah's promise of salvation to Zion *Zeph 3:14-17*

Jesus' parable of the lost sheep *Mat 18:12-14, Luke 15:1-7*

At Jesus' birth angels proclaim good will to man *Luke 2:1-20*

Jesus says he is light of world *John 8:12-23*

Gamaliel intercedes with council *Acts 5:17-42*

Philip baptizes the Ethiopian *Acts 8:26-40*

Peter accepts conversion of a Gentile *Acts 10:1-48*

Peter's vision of great sheet *Acts 11:1-18*

James on equality of man *Jas 2:1-13*

John on love *1 John 4:1-21*

See also benevolence, compassion, goodness, grace, love

GOOD WILL

God urges man to to be fruitful and multiply *Gen 1:1-31*

Noah gets God's covenant to be fruitful *Gen 9:1-17*

Abraham receives God's promises *Gen 15:1-21*

Isaac receives God's promises *Gen 26:1-5*

Moses is promised God's presence *Exod 3:9-12*

Moses talks with God face to face *Exod 33:7-23*

Moses says Israelites are God's chosen *Deut 7:6-11*

Gideon sees signs of God's good will *Judg 6:19-40*

GOSPEL

Abraham blessed by forerunner of Christ *Gen 14:8-20, Heb 6:20, 7:1-28*

Isaiah prophesies birth of Messiah *Isa 7:10-16, 9:2-7*

Isaiah describes office of Christ *Isa 42:1-12, 16, 18*

Isaiah tells what Christ is like *Isa 53:1-12*

Isaiah outlines the promises of Christ *Isa 55:1-13*

Isaiah on office of Christ *Isa 61:1-11, 62:1-12*

Jesus' Sermon on the Mount *Mat 5:1-48, 6:1-34, 7:1-29*

Jesus on gospel revealed to babes *Mat 11:25-30, Luke 10:21, 22*

Jesus' parable of sower *Mat 13:3-23, Mark 4:1-20, Luke 8:4-15*

Jesus' parable of leaven *Mat 13:20, 21, 33*

Jesus heals multitudes *Mat 15:29-31*

Jesus' parable of seed, blade, ear *Mark 4:26-29*

Jesus' parable of new wine in old bottles *Luke 5:36-39*

Jesus' parable of temple to be raised in three days *John 2:19-22*

Jesus' parable of good shepherd *John 10:1-18*

Jesus' parable of true vine *John 15:1-17*

Paul on life story of Jesus *Acts 13:16-52*

See also Bible, Christ, news, publish, revelation, salvation, testament

GOVERNMENT

Joseph appointed governor of Egypt by Pharaoh *Gen 41:1-46*

Moses sees people oppressed by Egypt *Exod 1:8-14*

Moses appoints judges to help him *Exod 18:13-27*

Ten Commandments are basis of all law *Exod 20:1-19, Deut 5:1-24*

Gideon refuses to be king *Judg 8:22, 23*

Jotham's parable of trees and bramble *Judg 9:1-15*

Samuel resists people's demand for a king *1 Sam 8:1-22*

Samuel anoints Saul *1 Sam 10:1-8*

Samuel declares Saul unfit to govern *1 Sam 15:7-26*

David made king of Judah and Israel *2 Sam 2:1-4, 5:1-5*

Solomon as king asks an understanding heart *1 King 3:5-15, 2 Chron 1:7-12*

Rehoboam consults with friends rather than his father's old advisers *1 King 12:1-18, 2 Chron 10:1-19*

The promised government by Messiah *Isa 2:1-5, 9:2-7, Mic 4:1-8, 13*

Isaiah's vision of the peaceable kingdom *Isa 11:1-12*

Jeremiah's vision of the potter and the clay *Jer 18:1-6*

Daniel prophesies fall of Babylonian government *Dan 4:1-27*

Jesus' family's flight to Egypt to escape death *Mat 2:13-23, Luke 2:39, 40*

Jesus pays his tax money *Mat 17:24-27*

Jesus concerning paying tribute to Caesar *Mat 22:15-22, Mark 12:13-17, Luke 20:20-26*

Rulers conspire against Jesus *Mat 26:1-5, Mark 11:18, 19, 14:1, 2*

Chief priest urges council to put Jesus to death *John 11:47-54*

Matthias elected bishop *Acts 1:15-26*

John's revelation of new heaven and earth *Rev 21:1-27*

See also authority, church, democracy, dominion, king, law, power, reign, rule

GRACE

Abram and Sarai receive new names *Gen 17:1-9, 15-22*

Moses' face shone from talking with God *Exad 34:29-35*

Aaron's rod blossoms *Num 17:1-11*

Samuel selects David as king *1 Sam 16:1-13*

David plays harp to soothe Saul *1 Sam 16:14-23*

David's song, "Mark the perfect man" *Psal 37:23-40*

David's song, "truth in the inward parts" *Psal 51:1-19*

David's song, the beauty of the Lord upon us *Psal 90:1-17*

Solomon's proverb on the nature of a good woman *Prov 31:1-31*

Isaiah shows that body culture is in vain *Isa 3:16-26*

Isaiah is called to prophesy *Isa 6:1-13*

Zephaniah promises salvation to Zion *Zeph 3:14-17*

Jesus lists qualities that make a Christian *Mat 5:1-12, Luke 6:17-26*

Jesus blesses loaves and fishes, feeds 5000 *Mat 14:15-21, Mark 6:35-49, Luke 9:12-17, John 6:5-14*

Jesus transfigured on mount *Mat 17:1-13, Mark 9:2-13, Luke 9:28-36*

Jesus' understanding astonishes rabbis *Luke 2:41-52*

Jesus as light of the world *John 1:1-14, 8:12-32*

Descent of Holy Ghost promotes understanding *Acts 2:1-13*

Paul on source of spiritual gifts *1 Cor 12:1, 4-31*

Paul on charity, rates grace with it *1 Cor 13:1-13*

Paul on his hardships *2 Cor 11:21-33*

Paul on the effects of grace *Eph 2:1-22*

Paul on example left by Jesus *Heb 12:1-17*

See also attraction, beauty, good will, kindness, mercy, pardon, thanksgiving, understanding

GRATITUDE

Abel's offerings contrast with Cain's *Gen 4:1-16*

Song of Moses' gratitude for deliverance *Exod 15:1-19, Deut 32:1-47*

Aaron declares jubilee year in thanks *Lev 25:9-17*

Joshua sets up a memorial for deliverance *Josh 4:1-27*

Deborah rejoices in God's victory *Judg 5:1-20*

David repays his friend through the son *2 Sam 9:1-13*

Solomon dedicates the temple he built *1 King 8:22-66, 2 Chron 6:1-42*

Solomon's wisdom acknowledged by Queen of Sheba *1 King 10:1-12, 2 Chron 9:1-12*

Nehemiah gives capsule history of Jews *Neh 9:1-38*

Some psalms of gratitude *Psal 19:1-14, 66:1-20, 91:1-16, 100:1-5, 107:1-43, 121:1-8*

A poor wise man saves a city, but is forgotten *Eccl 9:13-18*

Isaiah praises God for his benefits *Isa 25:1, 4, 6-10*

Jesus' parable of the unmerciful debtor *Mat 18:23-35*

A grateful woman pours precious ointment on Jesus' head *Mat 26:6-13, Mark 14:3-9*

Mary magnifies the Lord *Luke 1:46-55*

Jesus' parable of two debtors forgiven *Luke 7:36-50*

Jesus' parable of barren fig tree *Luke 13:6-9*

Jesus' parable of prodigal son's ungrateful brother *Luke 15:25-32*

Jesus heals ten lepers, only one returns *Luke 17:11-19*

Jesus acknowledges source of his great works *John 5:17-47*

Jesus expresses thanks to God before he raises Lazarus *John 11:1-46*

Paul on why we owe Christ obedience *Heb 2:1-18*

See also acknowledge, grace, praise, thanksgiving

GREATNESS

Joseph not recognized by brothers *Gen 42:1-8*

Nature of God revealed to Moses *Exod 3:1-18*

Passage of Red Sea *Exod 14:5-31*

Moses' song of mercy and deliverance *Deut 32:1-47*

Deborah's song of victory *Judg 5:1-20*

Jehoshaphat learns battle is God's *2 Chron 20:1-32*

Job learns God's nature from voice of thunder *Job 38:1—41:34*

David's song, "The heavens declare the glory" *Psal 19:1-14*

David's song, "The earth is the Lord's" *Psal 24:1-10*

David's song, "Bless the Lord, O my soul" *Psal 103:1-22*

David's song, "Whither shall I go?" *Psal 139:1-24*

The greatness of the church *Isa 2:1-5, Mic 4:1-8, 13*

Isaiah's vision of God's glory *Isa 6:1-13*

Three kings visit babe Jesus *Mat 2:1-12*

Jesus' parable of the mustard seed *Mat 13:31, 32, Mark 4:30-32, Luke 13:18, 19*

Jesus' parable of the leaven *Mat 13:33, Luke 13:20, 21*

Jesus feeds 5000 *Mat 14:15-21, Mark 6:35-44, Luke 9:12-17, John 6:5-14*

Jesus walks on water *Mat 14:22-33, John 6:15-21*

Jesus talks with Moses and Elijah *Mat 17:11-13, Mark 9:2-13, Luke 9:28-36*

Jesus' resurrection *Mat 28:1-8, Mark 16:1-8, Luke 24:1-12, John 20:1-10*

Jesus calms storm *Mark 6:45-52, John 6:21*

Peter's great haul of fishes *Luke 5:1-11, John 21:1-11*

Jesus tells the source of his great works *John 5:17-47*

John's vision of God's throne *Rev 4:1-11*

The new heaven and earth *Rev 21:1-27*

See also great works, importance, power

GREAT WORKS (other than healings)

Moses and the passover *Exod 11:4-10, 12:1-14, 21-41, Deut 16:1-22*

Moses guided by pillars *Exod 13:20-22, Num 9:15-23*

Moses passes through Red Sea *Exod 14:5-31*

Moses makes waters sweet *Exod 15:22-27*

Moses feeds people with manna and quails *Exod 16:1-36, Num 11:1-15, 31, 32*

Joshua crosses Jordan *Josh 3:1-17*

Walls of Jericho crumble *Josh 6:1-27*

Gideon defeats host with 300 men *Judg 7:1-25*

David defeats Goliath *1 Sam 17:38-52*

Elijah causes fire *1 King 18:17-40*

Elijah causes rain *1 King 18:41-46*

Elijah crosses Jordan *2 King 2:8*

Elijah is translated *2 King 2:1-11*

Elisha crosses Jordan *2 King 2:12-15*

Elisha, poison water nullified *2 King 2:16-22*

Elisha replenishes widow's pot of oil *2 King 4:1-7*

Elisha, poison pottage made harmless *2 King 4:38-41*

Elisha, 100 men fed with 20 loaves *2 King 4:42-44*

Elisha causes axe head to swim *2 King 6:1-7*

Elisha causes blindness of Syrian army *2 King 6:8-23*

Three Jews survive fiery furnace *Dan 3:1-30*

Daniel survives lions' den *Dan 6:1-28*

Jonah rescued from sea by big fish *Jonah 2:1-10*

Jesus (*See* Part II, Jesus Christ: Great Works)

Jesus excoriates three cities for disregarding his mighty works *Mat 11:20-30, Luke 10:21, 22*

Jesus orders 70 disciples to preach and heal *Luke 10:1-16*

Jesus tells source of his great works *John 5:17-47*

Paul and Silas released from prison by earthquake *Acts 16:19-40*

Paul's hardships to establish church *2 Cor 11:21-33*

James on faith without works *Jas 2:14-26*

See also dominion

GREED

Abraham's strife with Lot solved *Gen 13:1-18*

Israelites' desire for flesh to eat *Exod 16:1-36, Num 11:1-15, 31, 32*

David takes Uriah's wife *2 Sam 11:1-27*

Nathan's parable of the ewe lamb *2 Sam 12:1-10*

David's and Bathsheba's child dies *2 Sam 12:13-23*

Solomon settles a dispute between two mothers *1 King 3:16-28*

Elisha's servant punished *2 King 5:15-27*

Ahab takes Naboth's vineyard *1 King 21:1-27*

Mortal life vain *Eccl 1:1-18, 2:1-26*

Jesus on thought-taking *Mat 6:25-34, Luke 12:22-34*

Zebedee's wife tries to set preference for her sons *Mat 20:20-28, Mark 10:35-45*

Jesus casts traders from temple *Mat 21:12, 13, Mark 11:15-17, Luke 19:45, 46, John 2:13-25*

Jesus' parable of rich man, bigger barns *Luke 12:15-21*

Zacchaeus promises to restore all he extorted *Luke 19:1-10*

See also appetite, covetousness, generosity, wealth

GRIEF

Cain expresses no grief at death of Abel *Gen 4:1-16*

David weeps for Saul and Jonathan *2 Sam 1:17-27*

Shunammite does not mourn her dead son *2 King 4:8-37*

Nehemiah's sorrow at condition of Jerusalem *Neh 1:1-11*

Job mourns the loss of his children *Job 1:13-22*

David's song, "the fountain of life" *Psal 36:1-12*

David's song, "Why art thou cast down?" *Psal 42:1-11*

David's song, "Make a joyful noise" *Psal 66:1-20, 100:1-5*

Isaiah's reassurance, "Comfort ye" *Isa 40:1-31*

Isaiah's promises of help in trials *Isa 43:1-28, 44:1-24*

Isaiah comforts the church *Isa 54:1-6, 11-17*

Isaiah's vision, "the Lord's hand is not shortened" *Isa 59:1-21*

Ezekiel's vision of equity of God's dealing *Ezek 18:1-32*

Ezekiel's vision of God's care over his flock *Ezek 34:1-31*

Zephaniah's vision of salvation promised *Zeph 3:14-17*

Jesus raises Jairus' daughter *Mat 9:18, 19, 23-26, Mark 5:22-24, 35-43, Luke 8:41, 42, 49-56*

Jesus promises rest to heavy laden *Mat 11:28-30*

Peter's grief when he denies Jesus *Mat 26:57, 58, 69-75, Mark 14:66-72, 22:54-62, Luke 18:13-18, 25-27*

Jesus at twelve is lost by parents *Luke 2:41-52*

Jesus raises son of widow of Nain *Luke 7:11-17*

Jesus urges faith in Christ *John 12:44-50*

Jesus' promise of comfort in tribulation *John 16:1-33*

Mary mourning in the garden finds Jesus risen *John 20:11-18*

Paul's sermon on resurrection *1 Cor 15:1-58*

Paul's urgings "think on these things" *Phil 4:1-23*

James on how to bear our cross *Jas 1:1-27*

John's sermon, God is Love *1 John 4:1-21*

John's vision of river and tree of life *Rev 22:1-21*

See also comfort, complaint, joy, mourning, pain, sorrow

GROUP HEALING

"All manner of sickness" *Mat 4:23-25, Luke 4:40-44*

"Healed many" *Mat 12:14-21, Mark 3:6-12, 6:53-56*

By the touch of the hem of his garment *Mat 14:14, 34-46*

"Great multitudes healed" *Mat 19:1, 2*

"All who touched him" *Luke 6:17-19*

Peter's shadow in the streets *Acts 5:12-16*

Stephen's miracles *Acts 6:5-15*

GROWTH

The Tower of Babel collapses *Gen 11:1-9*

Abraham's riches grow *Gen 13:1-18*

Isaiah's vision of growth in the desert *Isa 35:1-10*

Daniel grows well on pulse *Dan 1:1-21*

Jesus' parable of mustard seed *Mat 13:31, 32, Mark 4:30-32, Luke 13:18, 19*

Jesus' parable of the leaven *Mat 13:33, Luke 13:20, 21*

Jesus' parable of talents *Mat 25:14-30, Luke 19:11-28*

Jesus' parable of seed, blade, ear *Mark 4:26-29*

Jesus' parable of the rich man with bigger barns *Luke 12:15-21*

Jesus' parable of the faithful steward *Luke 12:41-48*

Jesus' parable of counting the cost *Luke 14:25-33*

Jesus says his great works have their source in the Father *John 5:17-47*

Jesus' parable of true vine and branches *John 15:1-17*

Peter shows Christianity is infectious *Acts 4:24-37*

Growth of Christians requires division of labor *Acts 6:1-4*

Philip increases conversions *Acts 8:9-13, 26-40*

Paul's church building *Acts 11: 19-26*

Cost to Paul of establishing the church *2 Cor 11:21-33*

James on faith without works *Jas 2:14-26*

John's letters to seven churches *Rev 1:4-20, 2:1-29, 3:1-22*

See also evolution, improvement, organic, progress, profit, strength

GUARD

Cherubim guard Eden from material man *Gen 3:6-24*

Jacob promised God's continuous presence *Gen 28:10-22*

Elisha besieged by Syrians, sees angel army *2 King 6:8-23*

David's song, "the secret place" *Psal 91:1-16*

David's song, on safety of the godly *Psal 121:1-8*

David's song, "Whither shall I go?" *Psal 139:1-24*

Ezekiel's vision of God watching over us *Ezek 34:1-31*

Jesus' parable of the man taking a long journey *Mat 13:34-37*

Jesus' parable of servants awaiting *Mat 24:42-51*

Guards at Jesus' tomb paid to give false report *Mat 28:11-15*

Jesus' parable of watchful servants *Luke 12:35-40*

Jesus' parable of the faithful steward *Luke 12:41-48*

Peter released from prison by angel *Acts 5:17-42*

Paul and Silas convert the keeper of the prison *Acts 16:19-40*

See also angel, danger, defense, protection, watch

GUIDANCE

Noah gets signs to go forth, raven and dove *Gen 8:1-22*

Abraham gets God's word to leave his home city for the promised land *Gen 11:31, 32, 12:1-9*

The pillars of cloud and fire lead Israelites *Exod 13:20-22, Num 9: 15-23*

Gideon's faith developed by three signs *Judg 6:19-40*

Solomon asks for understanding heart to guide him as king *1 King 3:5-15, 2 Chron 1:7-12*

Rehoboam consults the wrong people *1 King 12:1-18, 2 Chron 10: 1-19*

Elisha, besieged by Syrians, guides them into the midst of their enemies *2 King 6:8-23*

Daniel reads handwriting on wall to king *Dan 5:1-31*

Hosea's vision of God as father of his child *Hos 11:1-4*

An angel advises Joseph about Jesus' birth *Mat 1:18-25*

Jesus' parable of lost sheep *Mat 18:12-14, Luke 15:1-7*

Judas guides soldiers to Jesus in Gethsemane *Mat 26:47-56, Mark 14:43-54, Luke 22:47-53, John 18: 1-12*

Jesus' promise to send Holy Ghost to guide his disciples *John 14: 1-31*

Peter hails arrival of Holy Ghost *Acts 2:1-13*

Paul advises his disciple *2 Tim 2: 1-26, 4:1-8*

Paul outlines the example left by Jesus *Heb 12:1-29*

See also advice, instruction, leader, signs, teaching, way

GUILT

Adam and Eve hide from the Lord God *Gen 3:6-24*

Cain kills his brother *Gen 4:1-16*

Jacob wrestles with his fear of his brother *Gen 32:1-32*

Saul consults familiar spirit *1 Sam 28:3-20*

Saul destroys himself *1 Sam 31: 1-13, 1 Chron 10:1-14*

David has man killed for his wife *2 Sam 11:1-27*

Nathan reveals David's moral fall *2 Sam 12:1-10*

Uzziah's heart lifted up to destruction *2 Chron 26:1-23*

Gehazi's greed punished by leprosy *2 King 5:15-27*

Hezekiah's unwise trust in Babylonians *2 King 20:12-21, Isa 39: 1-8*

Haman hanged on the gallows he built *Esther 6:1-14, 7:1-10*

David's song, "create in me a clean heart" *Psal 51:1-19*

Isaiah's vision of the fall of Babylon *Isa 14:4-8, 12-17, 25-27*

Jesus on what defiles a man *Mat 15:1-20, Mark 7:1-23*

Jesus' parable of unmerciful debtor *Mat 18:23-35*

Jesus' parable of the wedding garment *Mat 22:1-14*

Jesus' parable of the talents *Mat 25:14-30, Luke 19:11-28*

Peter denies Jesus when arrested *Mat 26:57, 58, 69-75, Mark 14: 66-72, Luke 22:54-62, John 18:13-18, 25-27*

Judas hangs himself *Mat 27:3-10, Acts 1:15-20*

Jesus' parable of barren fig tree *Luke 13:6-9*

Jesus' parable of the prodigal son *Luke 15:11-24*

Jesus saves woman taken in adultery *John 8:1-11*

See also condemnation, law, remorse, sin, wicked

H

HABIT

See custom, practice

HALT

See cripple, lameness, paralysis

HAND

Moses puts hand in his bosom twice *Exod 4:1-9*

Moses' hands upheld during battle *Exod 17:8-16*

Jeroboam's hand is withered and then healed *1 King 12:32, 33, 13: 1-10*

Nehemiah arms builders of wall with sword in one hand *Neh 4: 1-23*

Isaiah's vision of justice, "the Lord's hand is not shortened" *Isa 59: 1-21*

Jeremiah's vision of the potter and the clay *Jer 18:1-6*

Daniel reads the handwriting on the wall *Dan 5:1-31*

Hosea's vision of God's care of his child *Hos 11:1-4*

Jesus heals woman who touched hem of his garment *Mat 9:20-22, Mark 5:25-34, Luke 8:43-48*

Jesus heals withered hand on sabbath *Mat 12:9-13, Mark 3:1-5, Luke 6:6-11*

Jesus' parable of laborers in the vineyard *Mat 20:1-16*

Zebedee's wife requests right and left-hand seats for her sons *Mat 20:20-28, Mark 10:35-45*

Jesus' parable of sheep and goats on right hand and left *Mat 25: 31-46*

Pilate washes his hands before the multitude *Mat 27:24-26*

John's vision of angel with book in hand *Rev 10:1-11*

See also ability, authority, power, work

HAPPINESS

Abraham and Sara happy at the prospect of a son *Gen 15:1-21*

Joseph reveals himself to his brothers *Gen 43:1, 2, 45:1-11*

Song of Moses after deliverance *Exod 15:1-19, Deut 32:1-47*

Saul elated by his appointment as king *1 Sam 10:9-27*

David plays harp to calm Saul's spirits *1 Sam 16:14-23*

David's song of thanksgiving to God *2 Sam 22:1-51, 1 Chron 16:17-36*

Solomon dedicates temple *1 King 8:22-66, 2 Chron 6:1-42*

People glad to hear book of the law read *Neh 8:1-12*

David's song of delight in God's law *Psal 1:1-6*

David's song, "Why art thou cast down?" *Psal 42:1-11*

David's song, rejoice *Psal 66:1-20, 100:1-5*

Happy nature of a good woman *Prov 21:1-31*

Isaiah on the inspiration to be Christlike *Isa 60:1-5*

Isaiah on the blessed state of new Jerusalem *Isa 65:17-25*

Jeremiah's new covenant—Israel restored *Jer 31:1-14, 31-34*

Ezekiel's vision of God watching over us *Ezek 34:1-31*

Zephaniah's promise of salvation to Zion *Zeph 3:14-17*

Jesus' parable, the pearl of great price *Mat 13:45, 46*

Jesus' parable, of householder's treasures *Mat 13:51, 52*

Jesus' parable of lost sheep *Mat 18:12-14, Luke 15:1-7*

The rich young ruler sorrowfully leaves Jesus *Mat 19:16-30, Mark 10:17-31, Luke 18:18-30*

Jesus enters Jerusalem to hosannas *Mat 21:1-11, 14:17, Mark 11:1-11, Luke 19:29-44, John 12:12-19*

Angels at Jesus' birth *Luke 2:8-20*

Twelve disciples return to Jesus with joy *Luke 9:10, 11*

Seventy disciples return to Jesus with success *Luke 10:17-24*

The father's happiness at return of the prodigal *Luke 15:11-24*

Apostles report with joy seeing the risen Jesus *Luke 24:36-49, John 20:19-23*

Jesus Christ, the light of the world *John 1:1-14*

Jesus' parable of the good shepherd *John 10:1-18*

Jesus' parable of true vine and branches *John 15:1-17*

Mary Magdalene's joy at seeing Jesus arisen *John 20:11-18*

Apostles receive Holy Ghost *Acts 2:1-13*

Lame man leaping, walking and praising God *Acts 3:1-11*

Paul on rejoicing *Phil 4:1-23*

John's vision of new heaven and earth—no weeping *Rev 21:1-27*

See also blessing, contentment, friendship, healing, heaven, joy, wealth

HARDNESS

Abraham sends Hagar and son away into desert *Gen 21:9-21*

Joseph sold into slavery in Egypt *Gen 37:1-37*

Moses reluctant to lead people out of Egypt *Exod 3:9-12*

Israelites blocked by Red Sea *Exod 14:5-31*

Moses and people wander in wilderness *Exod 16:1-36, Num 11:1-15, 31, 32*

Moses cautions them to remember their trials *Deut 8:1-20*

Gideon defeats host with 300 men *Judg 7:-25*

David accepts Goliath's challenge *1 Sam 17:17-37*

Elijah's discouragement overcome *1 King 19:1-9*

Elisha asks a hard thing of Elijah *2 King 2:1-11*

Elisha prophesies incredible plenty *2 King 6:24, 25, 7:1-18*

Nehemiah sees obstacles to be overcome *Neh 2:1-20*

Job asks why the good man should suffer *Job 3:1-26*

David's song, "Why art thou cast down?" *Psal 42:1-11*

David's song, "Be still, and know that I am God" *Psal 46:1-11*

David's song, "He that dwelleth in the secret place" *Psal 91:1-16*

Isaiah reassures those in difficulty *Isa 40:1-31*

Isaiah urges "Look unto the rock" *Isa 51:1-12*

Jeremiah on "nothing too hard for Thee" *Jer 32:2, 6-27, 37-44*

Three Jews placed in fiery furnace *Dan 3:1-30*

Daniel in lions' den *Dan 6:1-28*

Jonah in great fish *Jonah 2:1-10*

Jesus heals woman sick twelve years *Mat 9:20-22, Mark 5:25-34, Luke 8:43-48*

Jesus feeds 5000 with a few loaves and fishes *Mat 14:15-21, Mark 6: 35-44, Luke 9:12-17, John 6:5-14*

Jesus heals epileptic boy after disciples had failed *Mat 17:14-21, Mark 9:14-29, Luke 9:37-43*

Jesus' parable of lost sheep *Mat 18:12-14, Luke 15:1-7*

Risen Jesus, victor after seeming failure *Mat 28:1-8, Mark 16:1-8, Luke 24:1-12, John 20:1-10*

Jesus' parable of unwilling friend *Luke 11:5-13*

Jesus heals woman bowed together 18 years *Luke 13:11-17*

Jesus' parable of prodigal *Luke 15: 11:24*

Jesus' parable of judge and widow *Luke 18:1-8*

Jesus' parable of temple to be raised in three days *John 2:19-22*

Jesus heals man impotent for 38 years *John 5:1-16*

Jesus says source of his great works is the Father *John 5:17-47*

Jesus raises Lazarus dead four days *John 11:1-46*

Jesus comforts disciples against tribulation *John 16:1-33*

Jesus locates fish for disciples who had caught nothing all night *John 21:1-11*

Paul recounts his hardships to establish church *2 Cor 11:21-33*

James on how to bear our cross *Jas 1:1-27*

John's vision of the difficult birth of spiritual truth *Rev 12:1-17*

See also difficult, misfortune, obstacle, persecution, perseverance, rock, stone, trials

HARMONY

Abraham's strife with Lot settled *Gen 13:1-18*

Isaac settles strife with herdsmen *Gen 26:12-31*

In Jacob's home discord among twelve sons *Gen 37:1-36*

Ruth returns home with her mother-in-law *Ruth 1:1-22*

David plays harp for Saul *1 Sam 16:14-23*

Jonathan befriends David, Saul envies him *1 Sam 18:1-16*

David pacified by Abigail's gentleness *1 Sam 25:2-42*

Elijah and Elisha journey together *2 King 2:1-15*

Elisha forgives Syrians and peace is restored *2 King 6:8-23*

Nehemiah gets wall-builders to work in harmony *Neh 4:1-23*

Isaiah's vision of peaceable kingdom *Isa 11:1-12*

Isaiah's vision of blessed state of new Jerusalem *Isa 65:17-25*

Mary's visit to Elizabeth *Luke 1: 39-56* ..

Angels announce Jesus' birth to shepherds *Luke 2:8-20*

Apostles work by division of labor in the church *Acts 6:1-4*

Paul's sermon on the harmony of the talents *1 Cor 12:1, 4-31*

Paul's sermon on the unity of all *Eph 4:1-32*

John on love *1 John 4:1-21*

See also agreement, friendship, heaven, music, oneness, peace, unity

HARVEST

God creates grass, herb, fruit complete with seed within itself *Gen 1:11-13*

Abraham's abundance—obeys command to be fruitful and multiply *Gen 13:1-18*

Joseph impounds crops against famine *Gen 41:47-57*

Moses urges offering first fruits to God *Deut 26:1-19*

Ruth gleans in the field of Boaz *Ruth 2:1-23*

Elijah prays for rain *1 King 18: 41-46*

Elijah calls Elisha from his plowing *1 King 19:19-21*

Isaiah's parable of the wild grapes *Isa 5:1-8*

Isaiah's vision of the desert blossoming *Isa 35:1-10*

Jesus on knowing men by their fruits *Mat 7:15-20, Luke 6:43-45*

Jesus' prayer that Lord of harvest send more laborers *Mat 9:36-38*

Jesus' disciples pluck corn on sabbath *Mat 12:1-8, Mark 2:23-28, Luke 6:1-5*

Jesus' parable of sower who went forth *Mat 13:3-23, Mark 5:1-20, Luke 8:4-15*

Jesus' parable of wheat and tares *Mat 13:24-30, 36-43*

Jesus' parable of mustard seed *Mat 13:31, 32, Mark 4:30-32, Luke 13: 18, 19*

Jesus feeds 5000 with only few loaves and fishes *Mat 14:15-21, Mark 6:35-44, Luke 9:12-17*

Jesus' parable of hiring laborers for vineyard *Mat 20:1-16*

Jesus' parable of the talents *Mat 25:14-30, Luke 19:11-28*

Jesus' parable of rich man and bigger barns *Luke 12:15-21*

Jesus' parable of barren fig tree *Luke 13:6-9*

Jesus tells disciples fields are white to harvest *John 4:31-38*

Jesus' parable of the true vine and branches *John 15:1-17*

Jesus produces great haul of fish for Peter *John 21:1-11*

John's vision of tree of life and twelve fruits *Rev 22:1-21*

See also farming, fruits, gain, labor, ministry, profit, reaping, seed, sowing

HATRED

Cain hates Abel because of God's preference for him *Gen 4:1-16*

Joseph's brothers hate him because their father prefers him *Gen 37: 1-36*

Saul hates David for his success *1 Sam 18:1-16*

David spares Saul when he sleeps *1 Sam 24:1-22*

Jesus on treatment of enemies *Mat 5:38-48, Luke 6:27-36*

Jesus casts traders out of temple *Mat 21:12, 13, Mark 11:15-17, Luke 19:45, 46, John 2:13-25*

Jesus denounces scribes and Pharisees *Mat 23:1-39*

Rulers conspire against Jesus *Mat 26:1-5, Mark 14:1, 2*

Jesus scourged and mocked *Mat 27:27-31, Mark 15:16-20, John 19: 1-16*

Stephen, the first martyr, is stoned but forgives *Acts 7:51-60*

Saul (Paul) makes havoc of the church *Acts 8:1-4, 9:1-3*

Paul on charity *1 Cor 13:1-13*

Paul on the Christian's armor *Eph 6:10-17*

Paul's description of anti-Christians *2 Tim 3:1-17*

John's vision of the great red dragon *Rev 12:1-17*

See also adversary, enemy, resentment, war

HEAD

Jacob foretells future of his children *Gen 49:1-28, Deut 33:1-29*

Moses selected to lead people *Exod 3:9-12*

Moses' hands upheld during battle *Exod 17:8-16*

Aaron's rod blossoms demonstrating his leadership *Num 17:1-11*

Moses appoints Joshua to lead people *Deut 31:7-23, Josh 1:1-9*

David's song, "Who is this king of glory?" *Psal 24:1-10*

David's song, "the fountain of life" *Psal 36:1-12*

Daniel appointed president *Dan 6: 1-28*

Jotham's parable of trees who select a ruler *Judg 9:1-15*

The baby Jesus worshipped by kings *Mat 2:1-12*

Jesus instructs his disciples to heal *Mat 9:36-38, 10:1-42, Mark 3:13-21, Luke 9:1-6, 10, 11, Luke 10:1-24*

Jesus' parable of chief seats at wedding *Luke 14:7-14*

Jesus as light of the world *John 1:1-14, 8:12-32*

Christ as the door and good shepherd *John 10:1-38*

Jesus' parable of the true vine *John 15:1-17*

Paul on example left by Jesus *Heb 12:1-29*

See also authority, intelligence, leader, master, rule, source, understanding

HEALING

Moses healed of leprosy *Exod 4: 1-9*

Moses heals his sister of leprosy *Num 12:1-16*

Moses heals people of plague in camp *Num 16:35, 44-50*

Moses heals bites of fiery serpents *Num 21:4-9*

Jeroboam's hand withered and healed *1 King 12:32, 33, 13:1-10*

Elijah raises widow's dead son *1 King 17:17-24*

Elisha raises Shunammite's dead son *2 King 4:8-37*

Elisha nullifies poisoned pottage *2 King 4:38-41*

Elisha heals Naaman of leprosy *2 King 5:1-14*

Isaiah heals king's boil *2 King 20: 1-11, Isa 38:1-22*

Jesus' healings (*See* Part II, Jesus Christ: Great Works)

Peter and John heal lame man *Acts 3:1-4*

Peter's shadow in streets heals sick *Acts 5:12-16*

Peter heals Aeneas of palsy *Acts 9:32-35*

Peter raises Tabitha from death *Acts 9:36-43*

Philip heals many diseases *Acts 8: 5-8*

Paul healed of blindness *Acts 9: 10-22*

Paul heals lame man *Acts 14:8-10*

Paul heals Eutychus of fatal fall *Acts 20:7-12*

Paul heals himself of poisonous viper bite *Acts 28:1-6*

Paul heals Publius' father of hemorrhage and fever *Acts 28:7-10*

See also disease, faith, methods in healing, physician, practice, prayer

HEARING

Moses hears the voice from the burning bush *Exod 3:1-18*

Samuel is called by the Lord *1 Sam 3:1-10, 19-21*

Elijah hears the still small voice *1 King 19:9-13*

Job hears the voice of thunder *Job 38:1-41*

Jesus hears voice from heaven when baptized *Mat 3:13-17*

Jesus refuses to listen to Satan *Mat 4:1-11, Luke 4:1-13*

Jesus tells why he speaks in parables *Mat 13:34, 35, Luke 4:33, 34*

Jesus refuses to listen to Peter *Mat 16:21-28, Mark 8:31-38, Luke 9: 20-27*

Jesus heals deaf man with speech impediment *Mark 7:32-37*

Jesus' parable of unwilling friend *Luke 11:5-13*

Jesus' parable of judge and persistent widow *Luke 18:1-8*

Jesus heals Malchus' ear (cut off) *Luke 22:50, 51*

Paul's companion hears voice but sees no one *Acts 9:1-9*

See also deafness, ear, listening, obedience

HEART

Samson betrayed by Delilah to Philistines *Judg 16:4-30*

Solomon asks God for an understanding heart *1 King 3:5-15, 2 Chron 1:7-12*

Uzziah's heart lifted up to destruction *2 Chron 26:1-23*

David's song the fountain of life *Psal 36:1-12*

David's song, "Why art thou cast down?" *Psal 42:1-11*

David's song, "Create in me a clean heart" *Psal 51:1-19*

Jeremiah's vision of the new covenant—God's law in their hearts *Jer 31:31-34*

Jesus on source of true treasure *Mat 6:19-21*

Jesus says what defiles a man comes out of his heart *Mat 15:1-20, Mark 7:1-23*

Paul says Agabus' warnings break his heart *Acts 21:8-15*

See also affection, conscience, courage, organic, soul, strength

HEAT

Moses sees the bush burn but it is not consumed *Exod 3:1-18*

Moses heals bites of fiery serpents *Num 21:4-9*

Elijah calls down fire from heaven (450 prophets of Baal unsuccessful) *1 King 18:17-40*

Elijah does not find God in the fire *1 King 19:9-13*

David's song, the Lord is a sun and shield *Psal 84:1-12*

Three Jews in fiery furnace *Dan 3:1-30*

Jesus heals Peter's mother-in-law of fever *Mat 8:14-17, Mark 1:29-34*

Jesus heals nobleman's son of fever *John 4:46-54*

Paul heals Publius' father of fever *Acts 28:7-10*

Peter describes end of world when elements will melt with fervent heat *2 Pet 3:10-14*

See also desert, fear, fever, fire, temperature

HEATHEN

Aaron matches marvels with sorcerers *Exod 7:1-12*

Isaiah's vision of fall of Babylon *Isa 14:4-8, 12-17, 25-27*

Wise men visit the King of the Jews *Mat 2:1-12*

Jesus heals Syrophenician's daughter *Mat 15:21-28, Mark 7:24-30*

Peter accepts a Gentile in the church *Acts 10:1-48, 11:1-18*

See also Gentile, idolatry, nation

HEAVEN

Enoch translated *Gen 5:18, 21-24, Heb 11:5*

Noah sees the rainbow as a token of the covenant *Gen 9:12-17*

Jacob sees angels on ladder *Gen 28:10-22*

Elijah taken to heaven in whirlwind *2 King 2:1-11*

Job's trials planned in heaven *Job 1:1-12*

David's song, "consider thy heavens" *Psal 8:1-9*

Isaiah's vision of blessed state of new Jerusalem *Isa 65:17-25*

Micah's vision of the mountain of the Lord's house *Mic 4:1-8, 13*

Jesus likens the kingdom of heaven to:

a man that sowed good seed *Mat 13:3-23, Mark 4:1-20, Luke 8:4-15*

a grain of mustard seed *Mat 13:31, 32, Mark 4:30-32, Luke 13:18, 19*

leaven in three measures of meal *Mat 13:33, Luke 13:20, 21*

treasure buried in a field *Mat 13:44*

the pearl of great price *Mat 13:45, 46*

a dragnet *Mat 13:47-50*

a householder with treasure *Mat 13:51, 52*

Zebedee's wife asks precedence for her sons *Mat 20:20-28, Mark 10:35-45*

Jesus' parable of the marriage feast *Mat 22:1-14*

Jesus on remarriage and heaven *Mat 22:23-33, Mark 12:18-27, Luke 20:27-40*

Jesus' parable of wise and foolish virgins *Mat 25:1-13*

Jesus' parable of sheep and goats *Mat 25:31-46*

Jesus ascends *Mark 16: 19, 20, Luke 24:50, 51, Acts 1:9-12*

Jesus tells 70 disciples their names are written in heaven *Luke 10:17-24*

Jesus' parable of rich man and beggar *Luke 16:19-31*

Jesus says kingdom of heaven is within *Luke 17:20-37*

Jesus tells Nicodemus he must be born again *John 3:1-21*

Paul on Christ's resurrection proves our resurrection *1 Cor 15:1-58*

John's vision of new heaven and earth *Rev 21:1-27*

See also earth, happiness, harmony, hell, kingdom of heaven, paradise

HEIGHT

See exaltation, heaven, mountain

HEIR

See heredity, inherit, possess

HELL

Adam's and Eve's fall and punishment *Gen 3:6-24*

Cain's sin and punishment *Gen 4:1-16*

Jacob wrestles with an angel *Gen 32:1-32*

David's and Bathsheba's child of sin dies *2 Sam 12:13-23*

Job's trials *Job 1:13-22, 2:1-10*

Job's nightmare of fear *Job 4:13-21*

David's song, "Why art thou cast down?" *Psal 42:1-11*

Peter in distress after denial of Jesus *Mat 26:57, 58, 69-75, Mark 14:66-72, Luke 22:54-62, John 18:13-18, 25-27*

Judas hangs himself *Mat 27:3-10, Acts 1:15-20*

Jesus' parable on the troubles of the prodigal *Luke 15:11-24*

Jesus' parable of rich man in hell *Luke 16:19-31*

See also death, error, judgment, punishment

HELP

Abraham saves Lot in war of kings *Gen 14:8-20*

Lot shelters two angels from the mob *Gen 19:1-14*

Joseph helps his brothers with food *Gen 42:1-8*

Moses' hands upheld during battle *Exod 17:8-16*

Moses appoints judges to help him *Exod 18:13-27*

Rahab helps the spies in Jericho *Josh 2:1-24*

Joshua meets the captain of the host *Josh 5:10-15*

Deborah's song, "The stars in their courses fought against Sisera" *Judg 5:1-20*

Jehoshaphat is assured the battle is God's *2 Chron 20:1-32*

Esther helps her people escape persecution *Esther 5:1-14*

Job's friends no help in trouble *Job 16:1-22*

David's song of God, "A very present help in trouble" *Psal 46:1-11*

David's song of God as the preserver of man *Psal 121:1-8*

Isaiah's reassurance, "Comfort ye" *Isa 40:1-31*

Ezekiel's vision of help from dry bones *Ezek 37:1-14*

Zechariah's vision of two olive trees and candllestick *Zech 4:1-14*

Jesus' healings and great works *(See Part II, Jesus Christ: Great Works)*

Jesus' sermon on benevolence in secret *Mat 6:1-4*

Elizabeth helps Mary during her pregnancy *Luke 1:39-56*

Jesus' parable of good Samaritan *Luke 10:25-37*

Jesus rescues woman taken in adultery *John 8:1-11*

Gamaliel helps Christians *Acts 5:17-42*

See also heal, improvement, neighbor, strength, supply, support

HEMORRHAGE

Woman's issue of blood for twelve years, healed *Mat 9:20-22, Mark 5:25-34, Luke 8:43-48*

Publius' father on Melita healed *Acts 28:7-10*

See also blood

HERALD

Caleb and Joshua report on promised land *Num 13:1-33, 14:1-11, 23-39, Deut 1:19-38*

Elisha foretells incredible plenty *2 King 6:24, 25, 7:1-18*

Messengers inform Job of disasters *Job 1:13-22, 2:1-10*

David's song, "the heavens declare the glory" *Psal 19:1-14*

Isaiah announces coming of Messiah *Isa 7:10-16, 9:2-7*

Jonah preaches to Nineveh *Jonah 3:1-10*

John the Baptist as forerunner *Mat 3:1-12, Mark 1:1-8, Luke 3:1-18*

Mary Magdalene runs to tell disciples that Jesus is risen *Mat 28:1-8, Mark 16:9-11, Luke 24:1-12, John 20:1, 2*

Angels announce Jesus' birth *Luke 2:8-20*

See also angel, messenger, preparation, prophet, signs

HEREDITY

God creates man in His image *Gen 1:26, 27*

Cain, son of Adam, commits murder *Gen 4:1-16*

Jacob prophesies the future of his twelve sons (characterizes each) *Gen 49:1-28*

Isaiah urges us to look to our source *Isa 51:1-12*

Ezekiel's vision, children's teeth not set on edge by father's sins *Ezek 18:1-32*

Hosea's vision of God's care of his child *Hos 11:1-4*

Jesus asks, Who are my mother and brethren? *Mat 12:46-50*

Jesus' divine origin announced *Luke 1:26-38*

Jesus on the source of his great works as in the Father *John 5: 17-47*

Jesus heals man blind from birth *John 9:1-41*

Jesus on his oneness with the Father *John 10:10-39*

Peter and John heal man lame from birth *Acts 3:1-11*

Paul on Adam vs. Christ *Rom 5: 1-21*

Paul on spiritual gifts *1 Cor 12: 1, 4-31*

Paul on God as the source *Eph 4: 1-32*

Paul about putting on the new man *Col 3:1-17*

See also children, evolution, inherit, parent

HEZEKIAH (one of the kings)

See Part II, Hezekiah

HILL

Moses on hill observes battle *Exod 17:8-16*

Elijah ordered upon the mount *1 King 19:9-13*

David's song, "I will lift up mine eyes unto the hills" *Psal 121:1-8*

Jesus taken to top of pinacle by Satan *Mat 4:1-11, Luke 4:1-13*

Jesus' Sermon on the Mount *Mat 5:1-12*

Jesus' parable of rich man and beggar *Luke 16:19-31*

See also elevation, mountain, obstacle

HISTORY

Moses' song reviews events *Deut 32:1-47*

Nehemiah gives capsule history of Jews *Neh 9:1-38*

Stephen reviews history of Jewish persecutions of the prophets *Acts 7:1-53*

Paul's defense before King Agrippa *26:1-32*

Paul's story of establishing church *2 Cor 11:21-33*

Paul's story of Melchizedek *Heb 6:20, 7:1-28*

See also politics, nation

HOLINESS

Enoch walked with God *Gen 5:18, 21-24, Heb 11:5*

Noah walked with God *Gen 6:5-22*

Moses stands on holy ground *Exod 3:1-18*

Moses gives command to remember sabbath *Exod 20:8-11*

Aaron consecrated with Urim and Thummim *Exod 28:29-36*

Moses covers his face with veil *Exod 34:29-35*

Aaron's rod blossoms *Num 17:1-11*

Moses warns against unholiness *Deut 13:1-18, 18:9-14*

Samuel called by God *1 Sam 3:1-10*

Elijah taken to heaven by whirlwind *2 King 2:1-11*

David's song on "Mark the perfect man" *Psal 37:23-40*

David's song, "Create in me a clean heart" *Psal 51:1-19*

Isaiah's vision of God, "Holy, holy, holy" *Isa 6:1-13*

Ezekiel's vision of holy waters *Ezek 47:1-12*

Daniel's meeting with angel Gabriel *Dan 9:20-23, 10:4-21*

At Jesus' baptism, a voice from heaven   *Mat 3:13-27, Mark 1:9-11, Luke 3:21, 22*

Jesus explains he is Lord of the sabbath   *Mat 12:1-8, Mark 2:23-28, Luke 6:1-5*

Jesus' transfigured, talks with Moses and Elijah   *Mat 17:1-13, Mark 9:2-23, Luke 9:28-36*

Jesus ascended   *Mark 16:19, 20, Luke 24:50, 51, Acts 1:6-12*

Jesus tells disciples their names are written in heaven   *Luke 10:17-24*

Jesus promises the Holy Ghost *John 14:1-31*

Disciples receive Holy Ghost   *Acts 2:1-13*

Peter turns people from his own holiness to God   *Acts 3:12-26*

Paul's teaching to come out and be separate   *2 Cor 6:1-18*

Paul's teaching to put off the old man, put on the new   *Col 3:1-17*

Paul on atonement   *Heb 10:1-39*

John's vision of new heaven and new earth   *Rev 21:1-27*

See also consecration, God, purity, righteousness, saint, sin

HOLY SPIRIT (Ghost)

Isaiah's reassurance, "Comfort ye" *Isa 40:1-31*

Jesus promises Holy Ghost to disciples   *John 14:1-31*

At Pentecost descent of promised Holy Ghost   *Acts 2:1-13*

Simon offers to buy power of the Holy Ghost   *Acts 8:14-25*

Paul preaches Holy Ghost to Ephesians   *Acts 19:1-10*

See also comforter, communion, Pentecost, spirit, trinity

HOME

Abraham searches and finds the promised land   *Gen 11:31, 32, 12: 1-9, 13: 1-18*

Abraham turns Hagar and Ishmael out   *Gen 21:9-21*

Joshua crosses Jordan and re-enters promised land   *Josh 3:1-17*

Ruth returns with Naomi to her native land   *Ruth 1:1-22*

David promises to build a house for God   *2 Sam 7:1-29*

David receives liberal offerings to build   *1 Chron 29:6-19*

Solomon builds temple   *1 King 6:1-38, 7:1-51, 2 Chron 3:1-17, 4:1-22, 5:1-14*

Solomon dedicates temple to God *1 King 8:22-66, 2 Chron 6:1-42*

Elisha welcomed at home of Shunammite   *2 King 4:8-17*

Shunammite returns to claim her home   *2 King 8:1-6*

Returned captives start to rebuild temple   *Ezra 3:8-13*

Captives' song of their homeland *Psal 137:1-9*

Isaiah's vision of a quiet habitation *Isa 33:20-24*

Jeremiah's prophecy that captivity will be turned   *Jer 29:8-14*

Micah's vision of mountain of Lord's house   *Mic 4:1-8, 13, Isa 2:1-5*

Jesus' parable of builders on rock and sand   *Mat 7:24-27, Luke 6: 48, 49*

Jesus describes his lack of home *Mat 8:18-22*

Jesus' parable of householder's treasures   *Mat 13:51, 52*

Jesus' parable of the prodigal son's return   *Luke 15:11-24*

Jesus' parable of elder son who remained at home   *Luke 15:25-32*

Jesus heals nobleman's son before he returns home   *John 4:46-54*

Jesus' parable of the true vine to abide in   *John 15:1-17*

Peter goes home to his old job, fishing   *John 21:1-8*

John's vision of new heaven and new earth   *Rev 21:1-27*

See also abide, building, dwelling, family, heart, heaven, house

HONESTY

Jacob misrepresents himself   *Gen 27:1-44*

Moses gives Eighth Commandment "Thou shalt not steal"   *Exod 20:15*

Balaam cannot reverse God's blessing   *Num 22:1-41, 23:1-30, 24:1-25*

Jesus' parable of man set upon by thieves *Luke 10:25-37*

Jesus' visit causes Zacchaeus to restore all that he extorted *Luke 19:1-10*

Jesus catches woman of Samaria in lie *John 4:1-30*

Jesus names the devil as the father of lies *John 8:33-59*

Jesus as door of sheep prevents robbers *John 10:1-17*

Paul on enemies of truth *2 Tim 3:1-17*

Paul's preaching that only true sacrifice remits sin *Heb 10:1-39*

See also justice, sincerity, truth, upright

HONOR

Joseph's dreams of honors to come *Gen 37:1-36*

Moses' first five Commandments honor God *Exod 20:1-12, Deut 5:1-16*

Aaron wears Urim and Thummim of his office *Exod 28:29-36*

Aaron consecrated by Moses *Lev 8:1-13*

Aaron's rod blossoms *Num 17:1-11*

Gideon refuses honor of being king *Judg 8:22, 23*

Parable of trees choosing a king *Judg 9:1-15*

Samuel anoints David *1 Sam 16: 1-13*

David made king of Israel and Judah *2 Sam 2:1-4, 5:1-5*

Solomon honored by visit of Queen of Sheba *1 King 10:1-12, 2 Chron 9:1-12*

David's song, "The Lord is my shepherd" *Psal 23:1-6*

David's song, "Bless the Lord, O my soul" *Psal 103:1-22*

David's song, "Praise the Lord for his goodness" *Psal 107:1-43*

Wise men present "King of the Jews" with gifts *Mat 2:1-12*

Jesus teaches the Lord's Prayer *Mat 6:5-15, Mark 11:25, 26, Luke 11:1-4*

Jesus says a prophet is without honor at home *Mat 13:53-58, Mark*

6:1-6, Luke 4:22-24, John 4:43-45

Jesus enters Jerusalem to acclaim of crowds *Mat 21:1-11, 14-17, Mark 11:1-11, Luke 19:29-44, John 12:12-19*

Precious ointment on Jesus' head *Mat 26:6-13, Mark 14:3-9*

All men seek Jesus, increasing his fame *Mark 1:35-39*

Jesus' parable of chief seats at the wedding *Luke 14:7-14*

John's vision of God's throne *Rev 4:1-11*

See also excellence, glory, morality, righteousness

HOPE

Noah and family enter ark to avoid flood *Gen 7:1-24*

Abraham and Sarah promised a son *Gen 15:1-21*

Deborah, the hope of Israel, to defeat Sisera *Judg 4:1-17*

Elijah gives widow hope to live *1 King 17:1-16*

Isaiah inspires Hezekiah to resist Assyrians *2 King 18:17-37, 19:1-27, Isa 36:1-22, 37:1-38, 2 Chron 32:1-23*

David's song of hope in God *Psal 42:1-11*

David's song of security in God *Psal 91:1-16*

Isaiah's vision "unto us a child is born" *Isa 7:10-16, 9:2-7*

Isaiah's vision of Christ's peaceable kingdom *Isa 11:1-12*

Isaiah's vision of reassurance *Isa 40:1-31*

Isaiah's vision "look to the rock" *Isa 51:1-12*

Jeremiah's vision of captivity turned *Jer 29:8-14, 31:1-14, 31-34*

Ezekiel's vision of help even from dry bones *Ezek 37:1-14*

Jonah prays when all hope is gone *Jonah 1:1-17, 2:1-10*

Jesus and the lost sheep *Mat 18: 12-14, Luke 15:1-7*

Jesus' parable of the door shut by the master *Luke 13:22-30*

The Holy Ghost will come to replace the loss of Jesus *John 14:1-31*

The storm at sea when all hope was gone *Acts 27:1-44*

Paul's sermon on hope, faith, charity *1 Cor 13:1-13*

See also fear, reliance, trust, waiting

HOSEA

See Part II, Hosea

HOSPITALITY

Lot shelters two angels from the mob *Gen 19:1-4*

Abraham entertains angels *Gen 18:1-18*

Esau gives Jacob friendly reception *Gen 33:1-11*

Rahab conceals spies *Josh 2:1-24*

Queen of Sheba visits Solomon *1 King 10:1-12, 2 Chron 9:1-12*

The Shunammite builds a room for Elisha *2 King 4:8-17*

Wise men visit "King of the Jews" *Mat 2:1-12*

Jesus' mother and brothers wait for him *Mat 12:46-50, Mark 3:31-35, Luke 8:19-21*

Jesus anointed at supper *Mat 26:6-13, Mark 14:3-9*

Mary's visit to Elizabeth *Luke 1:39-56*

Jesus dines with a Pharisee *Luke 7:36-50*

Jesus' parable of good Samaritan *Luke 10:25-37*

Martha complains about her sister *Luke 10:38-42*

Jesus' parable of unwilling friend *Luke 11:5-13*

Jesus' parable of chief seats at wedding *Luke 14:7-14*

Jesus' parable of those bidden to great supper *Luke 14:15-24*

Jesus' parable of prodigal and elder brother *Luke 15:11-32*

Jesus visits Zacchaeus *Luke 19:1-10*

At supper Jesus' feet anointed *John 12:3-8*

Ananias heals Paul, a stranger and enemy *Acts 9:10-22*

Paul received by barbarous people after shipwreck *Acts 27:1-44*

Paul on charity *1 Cor 13:1-13*

See also friendship, kindness, love, stranger

HOUSE

Lot shelters two angels from the mob *Gen 19:1-14*

Joseph makes the house of Potiphar prosper *Gen 39:1-16*

Angel passes over each Israelite's house *Exod 11:4-10*

Rahab hides the spies in her house *Josh 2:1-24*

David promises to build a house for the Lord *2 Sam 7:1-29*

Nathan reveals to David that his son will do it *1 Chron 17:1-27*

David receives liberal offerings for the temple *1 Chron 29:6-19*

Solomon builds the temple *1 King 6:1-38, 7:1-51, 2 Chron 3:1-17, 4:1-22, 5:1-14*

Solomon dedicates temple *1 King 8:22-66, 2 Chron. 6:1-42*

Shunammite makes place for Elisha in her house *2 King 4:8-17*

Hezekiah shows Babylonians all his treasure *2 King 20:12-21, Isa. 39:1-8*

Rebuilding of temple starts *Ezra 3:8-13*

David's song on our dwelling place *Psal 90:1-17*

David's song on security and protection *Psal 91:1-16*

Micah's vision of the mountain of the Lord's house *Isa 2:1-5, Mic 4:1-8, 13*

Isaiah's vision of the quiet habitation *Isa 33:20-24*

Ezekiel's vision of holy waters issued from under the threshold of the house *Ezek 47:1-12*

Jesus' parable of house built on rock or sand *Mat 7:24-27, Luke 6:48, 49*

Jesus foretells destruction of the temple *Mat 24:1-41, Mark 13:1-37, Luke 21:5-36*

Jesus arranges Last Supper in an upper room *Mat 26:17-19, Mark 14:12-16, Luke 22:7-13*

Jesus heals man with palsy, let down through roof *Mark 2:1-12, Luke 5:17-26*

Jesus' parable of the watchful servants *Luke 12: 35-40*

Jesus' parable of the door of the house shut *Luke 13: 22-30*

Jesus' parable of counting the cost of building *Luke 14: 25-33*

Jesus' parable of prodigal son who returned *Luke 15: 11-24*

Jesus' parable of the rich man with a beggar at gate *Luke 16: 19-31*

Jesus has dinner at house of Zacchaeus *Luke 19: 1-10*

Jesus risen, seen by disciples, doors closed *Luke 24: 36-49, John 20: 19-23*

Jesus casts traders out of temple *John 2:13-25*

Jesus' parable of temple to be raised in three days *John 2: 19-22*

Paul heals Eutychus after fall from third story window *Acts 20: 7-12*

See also building, church, consciousness, dwelling, home, protection, shelter, temple

HOW TO HEAL

Ezekiel preaches again false shepherds *Ezek 34:1-31*

Jesus astonished at centurion's understanding of healing *Mat 8:5-13, Luke 7:1-10*

Jesus teaches disciples to heal *Mat 10: 5-42, Mark 3: 13-21, 6: 7-13, Luke 3:13-21, 9:1-6*

Jesus explains binding the strong man *Mat 12:22-30, Mark 3:22-30, Luke 11: 14-23*

Jesus heals Canaanite's daughter (persistence) *Mat 15:21-28, Mark 7: 24-30*

Jesus heals epileptic boy (prayer and fasting) *Mat 17:14-21, Mark 9: 14-29, Luke 9: 37-43*

Jesus heals Jairus' daughter (not dead but sleeping) *Luke 8: 41, 42, 49-56*

Jesus heals woman with infirmity 18 years (breaks Satan's bond) *Luke 13: 11-17*

Jesus heals ten lepers *Luke 17:11-19*

Jesus on source of his works *John 14: 1-30*

Peter's sermon, how healings occurred *Acts 3: 12-26*

HUMAN

Jacob wants Esau's blessing, obtains it by duplicity *Gen 27: 1-44*

Moses' self-doubt holds him back *Exod 3:9-12*

Israelites in wilderness regret leaving Egyptian bondage *Exod 16: 1-36, Num 11: 1-15, 31, 32*

Israelites, after all God's miracles, turn to idolatry *Exod 32: 1-24*

Miriam and Aaron object to Moses' leadership *Num 12: 1-16*

Fear delays entry into promised land *Num 13: 1-33, 14: 1-11, 23-29, Deut 1: 19-38*

Gideon demands proofs of God before he undertakes battle *Judg 6: 19-40*

Samuel declares Saul unfit to be king *1 Sam 15: 7-26*

David forsakes his standards for a woman *2 Sam 11: 1-27*

Hezekiah puts unwise trust in others *2 King 20: 12-21, Isa. 39: 1-8*

Job asks why the good man should suffer *Job 3:1-26*

David's song about marking the perfect man *Psal 37: 23-40*

The nature of a good woman *Prov 31: 1-31*

The vanity of all mortal things *Eccl 1: 1-18, 2: 1-26*

Mortal events all within time *Eccl 3: 1-15*

The pride of women *Isa 3: 16-26*

Isaiah's parable of the wild grapes *Isa 5: 1-8*

Ezekiel denies human heredity *Ezek 18:1-32*

Jonah's disobedience finally turned *Jonah 1: 1-17, 2: 1-10, 3: 1-10*

Peter fails in attempt to walk on sea *Mat 14: 22-33, John 6: 15-21*

Jesus has to remind disciples of his great works *Mat 16: 5-12, Mark 8: 13-21*

Jesus' parable of unmerciful debtor *Mat 18: 23-35*

Peter after vowing loyalty denies he knows Jesus *Mat 26: 57, 58, 69-75,*

Mark 14: 66-72, Luke 22: 54-62, John 18: 13-18, 25-27
Jesus hears Martha's complaint about her sister *Luke 10: 38-42*
Jesus' parable of man with bigger barns *Luke 12: 15-21*
Jesus' parable of chief seats at the feast *Luke 14: 7-14*
Nine lepers fail to express gratitude *Luke 17: 11-19*
The human Jesus vs. the divine Christ *John 7: 14-40*
Jesus comforts his disciples *John 16: 1-33*
Peter inquires about John's future *John 21: 20-24*
Simon offers to buy Christian power *Acts 8: 14-25*
Ananias objects to healing Paul *Acts 9: 10-22*
After healing miracles people try to worship Paul *Acts 14: 11-18*
Paul on his hardships *2 Cor 11: 21-33*
Paul's sermon on self-revealings *2 Cor 12: 1-19*
James on how to bear our cross *Jas 1: 1-27*
John's letters to the seven churches *Rev. 1: 4-20, 2: 1-29, 3: 1-22*

See also animal, divine, family, man, mind, mortal

HUMILITY

Abraham lets Lot have his choice of land *Gen 13: 1-18*
Moses deprecates his speaking ability *Exod 4:10-17*
Moses indicates he has no monopoly of prophecy *Num 11: 16-30*
Solomon asks for an understanding heart *1 King 3: 5-15, 2 Chron 1: 7-12*
Naaman healed by his humility *2 King 5:1-14*
Uzziah's heart lifted up to destruction *2 Chron 26: 1-23*
David's song, "The Lord is my shepherd" *Psal 23: 1-6*
Vanity of mortal life *Eccl 1: 1-18, 2: 1-26*
Isaiah's vision of the pride of women *Isa 3:16-26*

Jesus has himself baptized by John *Mat 3: 13-17, Mark 1: 9-11, Luke 3: 21-22*
Jesus heals daughter of Gentile woman *Mat 15: 21-28, Mark 7: 24-30*
Disciples contend who shall be greatest *Mat 18: 1-11, Mark 9: 33-37, Luke 9: 46-50, 22: 24-30*
Jesus blesses little children *Mat 18: 1-22, 19: 13-15, Mark 9: 33-50, 10: 13-16, Luke 18: 15-17*
Jesus' parable of chief seats at wedding *Luke 14: 7-14*
Jesus' parable of Pharisee and publican *Luke 18: 9-14*
Jesus tells source of his great works *John 5: 17-47*
Jesus washes disciples' feet *John 13: 1-20*
Disciples taught about humility *John 13: 12-20*
Peter explains his ability to heal *Acts 3: 12-26*
Paul's sermon on self-revealings *2 Cor 12:1-19*
Paul on example of Christ's humility *Phil 2:1-15*
James' sermon, how to bear our cross *Jas 1: 1-27*

See also ego, gentleness, meekness, pride, spirit, vanity

HUNGER

Jacob buys Esau's birthright for pottage *Gen 25: 24-34*
Joseph's brethren come to Egypt for food *Gen 42: 1-8*
Moses supplies manna and quails in wilderness *Exod 16: 1-36, Num 11: 1-15, 31 32*
Ruth gleans after the reapers for food *Ruth 2: 1-23*
Elijah fed by ravens; by widow *1 King 17:1-16*
Elijah fed in a dream *1 King 19: 1-8*
Elisha feeds 100 men with 20 rolls *2 King 4: 42-44*
Elisha prophesies incredible plenty in famine *2 King 6: 24, 25, 7:1-18*
David angered by refusal to give his men food *1 Sam 25:2-42*

David's song, "The Lord is my shepherd" *Psal 23:1-6*

The virtuous woman cares for her family *Prov 31:1-31*

Isaiah's vision of the desert blossoming *Isa 35:1-10*

Daniel lives on pulse *Dan 1:1-21*

Hunger after righteousness *Mat 5:6*

Jesus' disciples pluck corn on sabbath *Mat 12:1-8, Mark 2:23-28, Luke 6:1-5*

Jesus feeds the 5000 with few loaves and fishes *Mat 14:15-21, Mark 6:35-44, Luke 9:12-17, John 6:5-14*

Jesus feeds the 4000 *Mat 15:32-39, Mark 8:1-10*

Jesus withers the fig tree without fruit *Mat 21:18-22, Mark 11:12-14, 20-24*

Jesus' parable of the prodigal son famished *Luke 15:11-24*

Jesus on the bread of life *John 6:26-65*

Jesus feeds his disciples who had fished all night *John 21:1-11*

John's vision of the little book to be eaten *Rev 10:1-11*

See also bread, famine, food, manna

HURT

Jacob's hip out of joint while he wrestles *Gen 32:24-32*

Poisonous pottage rendered harmless *2 King 4:38-41*

Asa diseased in his feet *2 Chron 16:11-14*

Jesus heals Peter's wife's mother *Mat 8:14-17, Mark 1:29-34*

Jesus is scourged and mocked *Mat 27:27-31, Mark 15:16-20, John 19:1-16*

Jesus' parable of the good Samaritan *Luke 10:25-37*

Jesus' parable of rich man and beggar *Luke 16:19-31*

Paul's hardships to establish church *2 Cor 11:21-33*

James on how to bear our cross *Jas 1:1-27*

See also injury, pain, suffering

HUSBAND

Ruth's and Naomi's husbands die *Ruth 1:1-22*

David angered by Abigail's husband, but pacified by Abigail *1 Sam 25:2-42*

David has Bethsheba's husband killed to put her in his harem *2 Sam 11:1-27*

Jesus on divorce *Mat 19:3-12, Mark 10:2-12*

Jesus on remarriage and resurrection *Mat 22:23-33, Mark 12:18-27, Luke 20:27-40*

Jesus tells woman she has had five husbands *John 4:7-19*

Paul on husbands and wives *Eph 5:22-33*

John's vision of new Jerusalem adorned for husband *Rev 21:1-27*

See also bridegroom, family, father, home, house

HUSBANDMEN

Adam consigned to till the ground *Gen 3:6-24*

Abraham and Lot grow rich *Gen 13:1-18*

Ruth gleans in the field of Boaz *Ruth 2:1-23*

Elijah finds Elisha plowing *1 King 19:19-21*

David's song, "The Lord is my shepherd" *Psal 23:1-6*

Isaiah's vision of the desert in blossom *Isa 35:1-10*

Jesus' parable of sower *Mat 13:3-23, Mark 4:1-20, Luke 8:4-15*

Jesus' parable of wheat and tares *Mat 13:24-30, 36-43*

Jesus' parable of mustard seed *Mat 13:31, 32, Mark 4:30-32, Luke 13:18, 19*

Jesus' parable of laborers in vineyard *Mat 20:1-16*

Jesus' parable of husbandmen who refuse rent *Mat 21:33-46, Mark 12:1-12, Luke 20:9-19*

Jesus' parable of seed, blade, ear *Mark 4:26-29*

Jesus' parable of rich man and barns *Luke 12:15-21*

Jesus on reaping, for the harvest is now   *John 4:31-38*
Jesus on vine and branches   *John 15:1-27*

See also farming, harvest, seed

HYMN

Moses' song of deliverance   *Exod 15:1-19, Deut 32:1-47*
Song of Deborah's victory   *Judg 5: 1-20*
David's song, "How are the mighty fallen"   *2 Sam 1:17-27*
David's psalm of thanksgiving   *2 Sam 22:1-51, 1 Chron 16:17-36*
David's song, "The happiness of the godly"   *Psal 1:1-6*
David's song, "The heavens declare the glory"   *Psal 19:1-14*
David's song, "Rejoice in the Lord"   *Psal 33:1-22*
David's song, "God is our refuge and strength"   *Psal 46:1-11*
David's song, "My soul longeth for the courts"   *Psal 84:1-12*
David's song, "Whither ... from Thy spirit"   *Psal 139:1-24*
Jesus enters Jerusalem to hosannas   *Mat 21:1-11, 14-17, Mark 11:1-11, Luke 19:29-44, John 12:12-19*
Jesus and disciples sing a hymn after Last Supper   *Mat 26:26-30, Mark 14:22-26*
Angels' song at birth of Jesus   *Luke 2:8-20*
Paul and Silas sing hymns in prison   *Acts 16:19-40*

See also harmony, praise, psalm, worship

HYPOTHESIS

Alternate explanations of creation of man   *Gen 1:26, 27, 2:6-8*
Tower of Babel can reach heaven   *Gen 11:1-9*
Abraham: conception possible in old age   *Gen 21:1-8*
Joseph: food problems can be solved   *Gen 41:1-46*
Moses: God is source of law   *Exod 20:1-19, Deut 5:1-24*

Caleb: immediate entrance to promised land   *Num 13:1-33, 14:1-11, 23-39, Deut 1:19-38*
Ruth: loyalty succeeds   *Ruth 1: 1-22*
Solomon: understanding heart is highest value   *1 King 3:5-15, 2 Chron 1:7-12*
Elijah: God is in a still small voice   *1 King 19:9-13*
David: security is in God   *Psal 91: 1-16*
Solomon: wisdom is the principal thing   *Prov 3:13-26, 4:1-13*
Isaiah: the Messiah will come   *Isa 7:10-16, 9:2-7*
Jesus: I and my Father are one   *Mat 6:22-24, John 10:22-42*
Jesus: source of great works is the Father   *John 5:17-47*
Paul: justification is by faith   *Rom 3:1-31, Gal 2:14-21*
Paul: Jesus' resurrection proves ours   *1 Cor 15:1-58*

See also argument, principle, theory

HYPNOTISM

Adam put to sleep for creation of woman   *Gen 2:21-25*
Potiphar's wife unsuccessful in seducing Joseph   *Gen 39:1-20*
Egyptian sorcerers' contest with Aaron   *Exod 7:1-12*
Balak unable to get Balaam to curse Israel   *Num 22:1-41, 23:1-30, 24:1-25*
Moses warns against necromancy   *Deut 13:1-18*
Moses denounces abominations   *Deut 18: 9-14*
Samson betrayed by Delilah   *Judg 16:4-30*
Saul consults with familiar spirit   *1 Sam 28:3-20*
Jesus accused of healing by Beelzebub   *Mat 12:22-30, Mark 3:22-30, Luke 11:14-23*
Paul heals the damsel soothsayer   *Acts 16:16-18*
Paul's healings imitated by vagabond exorcists   *Acts 19:11-20*
Paul's teaching to come out sepa-

rate from among them, and be ye
2 Cor 6:1-18

See also delusion, illusion, magnetism, mesmerism, necromancy, sleep, suggestion

HYPOCRISY

David sends Uriah to his death
2 Sam 11:1-27
Isaiah sees hypocrisy punished *Isa
29:11-24, 30:1-3, 20, 21*
Jesus calls Pharisees hypocrites *Mat
23:1-39, Luke 11:37-54*
Judas after plotting against him has supper with Jesus and disciples *Mat 26:14-16, 20-29, Mark 19:10, 11, 22-25*
Jesus' parable of Pharisee and publican *Luke 18:9-14*
Paul on enemies of the truth *2 Tim 3:1-17*

See also deceit, duplicity, lie, treachery

I

I AM

In the beginning God *Gen 1:1*
Enoch extends his existence by walking with God *Gen 5:18, 21-24*
Moses learns nature of God I Am That I Am *Exod 3:1-18*
Elijah communicates with God on mount *1 King 19:9-13*
Job hears the infinite speak to man *Job 38:1-41*
David's song on the fountain of life *Psal 36:1-12*
David's song, "Be still, and know that I am God" *Psal 46:1-11*
David's song on ever-presence *Psal 139:1-24*
Jesus teaches disciples to pray "Our Father" *Mat 6:5-15, Mark 11:25, 26, Luke 11:1-4*
Jesus' oneness with the Father *John 10:22-42*
Jesus tells young man how to inherit eternal life *Mat 19:16-30, Mark 10:17-21, Luke 18:18-30*

Paul on the Unknown God *Acts 17:15-34*

See also ego, God, life

IDEA

Man created in the image of God *Gen 1:26, 27*
Abraham entertains angels *Gen 18:1-18*
Joseph's ideas solve Pharaoh's dream *Gen 41:1-46*
Moses gets idea to lead Israelites out of Egypt *Exod 3:1-18*
Idea to go forward through Red Sea *Exod 14:5-31*
Jethro's idea to delegate authority *Exod 18:13-27*
Moses receives idea of Commandments *Exod 20:1-19*
Gideon's strategy defeats host *Judg 7:1-25*
David conceives a house for God *2 Sam 7:1-29*
Cyrus proclaims rebuilding of the temple *Ezra 1:1-11*
Nehemiah begins to rebuild the wall *Neh 2:1-20*
David's song, "Be still, and know" *Psal 46:1-11*
Poor wise man's idea saves city *Eccl 9:13-18*
Daniel enlightened to solve king's dream *Dan 2:1-49*
Jesus' oneness with the Father *John 10:22-42*
Jesus' parable of the talents *Mat 25:14-30, Luke 19:11-28*
Jesus escapes his enemies *Luke 4:28-31*
Jesus' parable of unwilling friend *Luke 11:5-13*
Jesus' parable of counting the cost *Luke 14:25-33*
Jesus tells source of great works *John 5:17-47*
Jesus admits he is the Christ *John 7:14-40*
The unity and eternity of Christ *John 8:12-59*
Christ as the door and good shepherd *John 10:1-38*
Jesus promises the Holy Ghost *John 14:1-31*
Paul on resurrection *1 Cor 15:1-58*

Paul's teaching to put on the new man *Col 3:1-17*

Paul's sermon on character of the Christ *Heb 1:1-14*

Peter on Christ the ideal *1 Pet 2:1-25*

See also image, likeness, mind, reason, reflection

IDEAL

See perfection

IDENTITY

God creates man as his image and likeness *Gen 1:26, 27*

Adam created from dust by Lord God *Gen 2:6-8*

Enoch translated because he walked with God *Gen 5:18, 21-24*

Abram and Sarai given new names *Gen 17:1-9, 15-22*

Jacob receives a new name *Gen 32:24-32*

Joseph identifies himself to brethren *Gen 43:1, 2, 45:1-11*

Moses identifies God as I Am *Exod 3:1-18*

Samuel anoints David among his brothers *1 Sam 16:1-13*

Elijah identifies God as a still small voice *1 King 19:9-13*

Elisha inseparable from Elijah *2 King 2:1-15*

David's song about the perfect man *Psal 37:23-40*

David's song, "Let the redeemed of the Lord say so" *Psal 107:1-43*

David's song of ever-presence *Psal 139:1-24*

Jeremiah's vision of potter and clay *Jer 18:1-6*

Wise men identify Jesus as King of the Jews *Mat 2:1-12*

Jesus' oneness with the Father *John 10:22-42*

John Baptist, in doubt, sends to Jesus for proof he is Christ *Mat 11:2-19, Luke 7:18-35*

Jesus' parable, the pearl of great price *Mat 13: 45, 46*

Peter identifies Jesus as the Christ *Mat 16:13-20, Mark 8:27-30, Luke 9:18-21*

Jesus identifies himself with Moses and Elijah *Mat 17:1-13, Mark 9:2-13, Luke 9:28-36*

Jesus identifies scribes and Pharisees *Mat 23:1-39, Mark 12:38-40, Luke 20:45-47, John 8:33-59*

Jesus called Christ by Simon and Anna *Luke 2:21-38*

Jesus' parable of prodigal son reunited with his father *Luke 15:11-24*

Jesus says he is light of the world *John 1:1-14, 8:12-32*

John Baptist testifies that Jesus is Christ *John 1:15-34*

Jesus identifies himself as Christ *John 7:14-40*

Jesus' sermon on unity and eternity of Christ *John 8:12-59*

Saul takes new name of Paul *Acts 8:1 to 9:22*

Paul's sermon on Adam vs. Christ *Rom 5:1-21*

Paul's teaching to put on the new man *Col 3:1-17*

Paul identifies the enemies of the truth *2 Tim 3:1-17*

Paul outlines the character of Christ *Heb 1:1-14*

John identifies God as Love *1 John 4:1-21*

See also image, individuality, likeness, oneness, name, personality, unity

IDOLATRY

Israelites worship the golden calf *Exod 32:1-24*

Moses gives Second Commandment *Exod 20:1-6*

Moses warns against idols, etc. *Deut 13:1-18, 18:9-14*

Moses lists the blessings of obedience *Deut 28:1-14*

Idol Dagon falls and breaks before the ark of the Lord *Isa 5:1-5*

Saul consults witch at Endor *1 Sam 28:3-20*

Elijah destroys 450 prophets of Baal *1 King 18:17-40*

In Josiah's good reign, idolatry destroyed *2 King 23:1-22, 2 Chron 34:1-8, 29-33*

Isaiah's parable of the wild grapes
Isa 5:1-8

Jeremiah's parable of good and bad
figs *Jer 24:1-10*

Daniel interprets dream of great
image *Dan 2:1-49*

Three Jews refuse to worship image
Dan 3:1-30

Daniel refuses to pray to king ahead
of God *Dan 6:1-28*

Jesus heals Syrophenician woman's
daughter *Mat 15:21-28, Mark 7:24-30*

Paul and Barnabas worshipped as
gods *Acts 14:8-18*

Paul's sermon at Athens to the Unknown God *Acts 17:15-24*

Paul attacked by idol silversmith
Acts 19:23-29

Paul on come out ... be ye separate
2 Cor 6:1-18

See also adultery, compromise, gods,
image, superstition, worship

IGNORANCE

Esau gives up his birthright for pottage *Gen 25:24-34*

Jotham's parable of the trees *Judg
9:1-15*

Hezekiah shows ambassadors all his
treasure *2 King 20:12-21, Isa 39:1-8*

Ezra reads book of the law to the
people *Neh 8:1-12*

The poor wise man is ignored *Eccl
9:13-18*

John sends to Jesus for information
Mat 11:2-19, Luke 7:18-35

Jesus tells why he speaks in parables
Mat 13:34, 35, Mark 4:33, 34

Jesus a prophet without honor in
his own country *Mat 13:53-58,
Mark 6:1-6, Luke 4:22-24, John
4:43-45*

Disciples reminded by Jesus of his
great works *Mat 16:5-12, Mark
8:13-21*

Jesus helps father's unbelief and
heals son *Mat 17:14-21, Mark 9:14-25, Luke 9:37-43*

Zebedee's wife wants preference for
her sons *Mat 20:20-28, Mark 10:35-45*

Jesus reproves scribes and Pharisees
*Mat 23:1-39, Mark 12:38-40, Luke
20:45-49, John 8:33-59*

Jesus at twelve years answers rabbis'
questions *Luke 2:41-52*

Jesus' parable of the prodigal son's
elder brother *Luke 15:25-32*

Jesus' parable of Pharisee and publican *Luke 18:9-14*

Saul persecutes, then is converted
Acts 8:1-4, 9:1-9

Simon offers to buy power of Holy
Ghost *Acts 8:14-40*

Philip enlightens the Ethiopian
Acts 8:26-40

Paul enlightens Ephesians on Holy
Ghost *Acts 19:1-10*

Exorcists find spiritual healing can't
be imitated *Acts 19:11-20*

John's vision of sealed book and
key *Rev 5:1-14*

See also education, intelligence,
knowledge, unknown, wisdom

ILLUSION

A mist precedes creation of Adam
Gen 2:6-8

Tower of Babel builds to heaven
Gen 11:1-9

Jeroboam's hand withered, then
healed *1 King 12:32, 33, 13:1-10*

Elijah fed in a dream *1 King 19:1-8*

Hezekiah believes he is safe *2 King
20:12-21, Isa 39:1-8*

Isaiah's vision of pride of women
Isa 3:16-26

Daniel interprets king's dreams *Dan
2:1-49, 4:1-27*

Insanity of Nebuchadnezzar predicted *Dan 4:28-37*

Daniel reads the handwriting on the
wall *Dan 5:1-31*

Herod thinks Jesus is John Baptist
whom he beheaded *Mat 14:1-13,
Mark 6:14-29, Luke 9:7-9*

Jesus tells scribes what really defiles *Mat 15:1-20, Mark 7:1-23*

See also belief, deceit, delusion,
dream, insanity, reality, unreality

IMAGE

God makes man in His image *Gen
1:26, 27*

Enoch walks with God and is translated *Gen 5:18, 24-27, Heb 11:5*

Moses finds worship of golden calf *Exod 32:1-24*

Moses makes a serpent of brass *Num 21:4-9*

Idol Dagon falls and breaks before the ark of the Lord *1 Sam 5:1-5*

David's song, "He spake and it was done" *Psal 33:1-22*

David's song, "Mark the perfect man" *Psal 37:23-40*

David's song on soul *Psal 84:1-12*

Jeremiah's parable of potter and clay *Jer 18:1-6*

Ezekiel's distinctions between father and children *Ezek 18:1-32*

Daniel interprets dream of great image *Dan 2:1-49*

His companions refuse to worship image *Dan 3:1-30*

The qualities that make a Christian *Mat 5:1-12, Luke 6:17-26, 36*

Jesus is transfigured on the mount *Mat 17:1-13, Mark 9:2-13, Luke 9:28-36*

Jesus approves little children *Mat 19:13-15, Mark 10:13-16, Luke 18:15-17*

Jesus says he is the light of the world *John 1:1-14, 8:12-32*

Jesus' great works have their source in the Father *John 5:17-47*

Jesus is the Christ *John 7:14-40*

Paul on character of Christ *Heb 1:1-14*

See also expression, idea, idolatry, imitation, likeness, manifestation, reflection

IMAGINATION

Joseph solves the problem of Egyptian famine *Gen 41:1-46*

Jacob prophesies the future of his twelve sons *Gen 49:1-28, Deut 33:1-29*

Moses delivers the basis of all law *Exod 20:1-19, Deut 5:1-24*

Gideon defeats a host by strategy *Judg 7:1-25*

Samuel selects David *1 Sam 16:1-13*

David eliminates Goliath by new weapon *1 Sam 17:38-52*

Solomon discovers the real mother *1 King 3:16-28*

Elijah finds the nature of God *1 King 19:9-13*

Elisha puts his finger on Naaman's real need *2 King 5:1-14*

Elisha saves himself and stops the war by new strategy *2 King 6:8-23*

Nehemiah foils a conspiracy *Neh 6:1-19*

Esther gives banquet to save her people *Esther 5:1-14*

A poor wise man saves his city *Eccl 9:3-18*

Isaiah describes what the Messiah will be like *Isa 53:1-12, 61:1-11, 63:1-12*

Ezekiel's vision of holy waters of truth flowing outward *Ezek 47:1-12*

Daniel interprets dreams and signs *Dan 2:1-49, 4:1-27, 5:1-31*

Jesus shows John proof he is Christ *Mat 11:2-19, Luke 7:18-35*

Jesus selects his successor *Mat 16:13-20, Mark 8:27-30, Luke 9:18-21*

Jesus' parable in answer to "Who is my neighbor?" *Luke 10:25-37*

Jesus' parable of prodigal son and elder brother *Luke 15:11-32*

Jesus visits Zacchaeus with surprising results *Luke 19:1-10*

Jesus promises the Holy Ghost *John 14:1-31*

Paul on the unknown God *Acts 17:15-34*

Paul on spiritual warfare *2 Cor 10:3-5*

Paul on the Christians' armor *Eph 6:10-17*

John's vision of new heaven and earth *Rev 21:1-27*

See also creation, idea, mind

IMITATION

Lord God imitates creation of man in God's likeness *Gen 1:26, 27, 2:6-8*

Jacob disguises himself as Esau *Gen 27:1-44*

Egyptian sorcerers watch Aaron's marvel *Exod 7:1-12*

Eldad and Medad prophesy like Moses *Num 11:16-30*

Elisha reproduces the works of Elijah *2 King 2:1-15*

Jeremiah's parable of potter and his clay *Jer 18:1-6*

Jesus' parable of wheat imitated by tares *Mat 13:24-30, 36-43*

Peter tries to walk on water to Jesus *Mat 14:22-33, John 6:15-21*

Disciples give poor imitation of Jesus' healing *Mat 17:14-21, Mark 9:14-29, Luke 9:37-43*

Disciples asked to be as little children *Mat 19:13-15, Mark 10:13-16, Luke 18:15-17*

Young man asked to follow Christ *Mat 19:16-30, Mark 10:17-31, Luke 18:18-30*

Jesus urges disciples to have communion *Mat 26:26-29, Mark 14: 22-25, Luke 22:14-30*

Disciples asked to imitate widow and mite *Mark 12:41-44, Luke 21: 1-4*

Jesus instructs in his way of healing *Luke 10:1-26*

Jesus' great works have source in Father *John 5:17-47*

Jesus is the Christ *John 7:14-40*

Eternity of Christ *John 8:12-59*

Jesus promises substitute for his personal presence—the Comforter *John 14:1-31*

Vagabond exorcists imitate Paul's healing *Acts 19:11-20*

Christ's resurrection proves ours *1 Cor 15:1-58*

Paul's sermon, "come out . . . and be ye separate" *2 Cor 6:1-18*

Paul on pressing toward the high calling of God in Christ Jesus *Phil 3:8-17*

Paul's advice to disciple *2 Tim 4: 1-8*

Paul on what Christ is *Heb 1:1-14*

See also Christ, example, follower, image, likeness

IMMACULATE

God creates man in His likeness *Gen 1:26, 27*

God creates a universe that is all good *Gen 1:1-31*

Enoch "walked with God" and was translated *Gen 5:18, 21-24, Heb 11:5*

Noah sees the rainbow after the flood *Gen 9:12-17*

Jacob purified by wrestling with angel *Gen 32:24-32*

Joseph resists Potiphar's wife *Gen 39:1-20*

Moses' face concealed by veil *Exod 34:29-35*

David's song, mark the perfect man *Psal 37:23-40*

Moses sees chosen people set apart as God's own *Deut 7:6-11*

Jesus tempted in wilderness *Mat 4:1-11, Mark 1:12, 13, Luke 4: 1-13*

Jesus eats with publicans and sinners *Mat 9:10-13, Mark 2:13-17, Luke 5:27-32*

Jesus' parable of pearl of great price *Mat 13:45, 46*

Jesus explains what defiles a man *Mat 15:1-20, Mark 7:1-23*

Jesus' ascension *Mark 6:19, 20, Luke 24:50, 53, Acts 1:6-12*

Jesus' birth announced to Mary *Luke 1:26-38*

Jesus' parable of new wine in new bottles *Luke 5:36-39*

Jesus Christ as the light of the world *John 1:1-14, 8:12-32*

Jesus is the Christ *John 7:14-40*

Jesus saves woman taken in adultery *John 8:1-11*

Paul's sermon on Adam vs. Christ *Rom 5:1-21*

Paul's sermon on Spirit vs. flesh *Rom 8:1-39*

Paul's sermon on Christians' armor *Eph 6:10-17*

See also cleaning, perfection, purity, sin

IMMANUEL (Emmanuel)

See Christ, prophecy of

IMMEDIATE

God creates universe in seven days *Gen 1:1-31, 2:1-6*

Disciples leave their nets and follow Jesus *Mat 4:17-22, Mark 1:14-20, Luke 9:1-11, John 1:35-42*

Jesus transports ship to destination at once *Mark 6:45-52, John 6:21*

All healings of Jesus immediate without convalescent period (*See* Part II, Jesus Christ: Great Works)

See also time

IMMORTALITY

Enoch translated *Gen 5:18, 21-24, Heb 11:5*

Elijah taken to heaven in whirlwind *2 King 2:1-11*

David's song, the fountain of life *Psal 36:1-12*

David's song, "Whither shall I flee" *Psal 139:1-24*

Vanity of human things *Eccl 1:1-18, 2:1-26*

Mortal events all within time *Eccl 3:1-15*

Isaiah's vision look unto the rock *Isa 51:1-12*

Ezekiel's vision of resurrection of dry bones *Ezek 37:1-14*

Jesus raises Jairus' daughter *Mat 9:18, 19, 23-26, Mark 5:22-24, 35-43, Luke 8:41, 42, 49-56*

Jesus' parable of wheat and tares *Mat 13:24-30, 36-43*

Jesus' parable of mustard seed *Mat 13:31, 32, Mark 4:30-32, Luke 13:18-19*

Jesus' parable of leaven *Mat 13:33, Luke 13:20, 21*

Jesus' parable of treasure in field *Mat 13:44*

Jesus' parable of pearl of great price *Mat 13:45, 46*

Jesus' parable of householder's treasures *Mat 13:51, 52*

Peter acknowledges Jesus as Christ *Mat 16:13-20, Mark 8:27-30, Luke 9:18-21*

Jesus foretells his resurrection *Mat 17:22, 23, Mark 9:30-32, Luke 9:43-45*

Jesus' parable of laborers for a penny *Mat 20:1-16*

Again Jesus foretells his resurrection *Mat 20:17-19, Mark 10:32-34, Luke 18:31, 34, Luke 19:47, 48*

Zebedee's wife requests immortal place for her sons *Mat 20:20-28, Mark 10:35-45*

Jesus' parable of marriage feast and wedding garment *Mat 22:1-14*

Jesus' parable of servants awaiting Lord *Mat 24:42-51*

Jesus' parable of virgins *Mat 25:1-13*

Jesus' parable of the talents *Mat 25:14-30, Luke 19:11-28*

Jesus' parable of sheep and goats *Mat 25:31-46*

Jesus is risen *Mat 28:1-8, Mark 16:1-8, Luke 24:1-12, John 20:1-10*

Jesus ascends *Mark 16:19, 20, Luke 24:50, 51, Acts 1:6-12*

Jesus raises son of widow of Nain *Luke 7:11-17*

Jesus' parable of rich man and bigger barns *Luke 12:15-21*

Jesus' parable of rich man and beggar *Luke 16:19-31*

Jesus' teaching that he is Christ *John 7:14-40*

Jesus on eternity of Christ *John 8:12-59*

Jesus raises Lazarus after four days *John 11:1-46*

Thomas confirms the risen Jesus *John 20:24-29*

Paul on resurrection *1 Cor 15:1-58*

Paul on eternity of Christ *Heb 6:20—7:28*

John's vision of new heaven and earth *Rev 21:1-27*

See also age, ascension, death, divine, Easter, eternity, human, mortal, resurrection

IMPETUOUS

Cain kills Abel *Gen. 4:1-16*

Esau sells his birthright for food *Gen 25:24-34*

Moses breaks tablet of Ten Commandments *Exod 32:1-24*

Miriam and Aaron speak against Moses *Num 12:1-16*

David has Uriah killed to marry his wife *2 Sam 11:1-27*

Hezekiah shows all his treasures to enemy *2 King 20:12-21, Isa 39:1-8*

Jesus admonishes Peter *Mat 16:21-28, Mark 8:31-38, Luke 9:20-27*

Jesus casts out traders from temple
Mat 21:12, 13, John 2:13-25

Peter and John speak the word with
boldness *Acts 4:1-23*

Philip baptizes the Ethiopian *Acts
8:26-40*

Paul casts devil out of soothsayer
Acts 16:16-18

See also activity

IMPORTANCE

God creates spiritual universe *Gen
1:1-31*

Moses at burning bush *Exod 3:1-18*

Moses leads people through Red Sea
Exod 14:5-31

Moses gives Ten Commandments
Exod 20:1-19, Deut 5:1-24

David kills Goliath with slingshot
1 Sam 17:38-52

Elijah communicates with God
1 King 19:9-13

Isaiah prophesies birth of Messiah
Isa 7:10-16, 9:2-7

Jesus' Sermon on the Mount *Mat
5:1-12, Luke 6:17-26, 36*

Jesus teaches the Lord's Prayer
*Mat 6:5-15, Mark 11:25, 26, Luke
11:1-4*

Jesus' resurrection *Mat 28:1-8, Mark
16: 1-8, Luke 24:1-12, John 20:1-10*

Paul's conversion *Acts 8:1-4, 9:1-22*

See also greatness, great works,
value

IMPROVEMENT

Abraham's riches grow *Gen 13:1-18*

New names given to Abram and
Sarai *Gen 17:1-9, 15-22*

Jacob receives a new name and
nature *Gen 32:24-32*

Moses told source of eloquence
Exod 4:10-17

Moses learns to delegate authority
Exod 18:13-27

Aaron's rod blossoms *Num 17:1-11*

Some rights of women acknowledged
Num 27:1-11, Num 36:5-13

Moses sets chosen people apart *Deut
7:6-11*

Moses' song of gratitude for deliverance *Deut 32:1-32*

Joshua's exhortation to more obedience *Josh 23:1-10*

Ruth's success on return to Israel
Ruth 2:1-22

Samuel finds Saul unfit and turns
to David *1 Sam 15:7-26*

David's song, "How are the mighty
fallen!" *2 Sam 1:17-27*

Elisha renders poisonous pottage
harmless *2 King 4:38-41*

David's song, "Create in me a clean
heart" *Psal 51:1-19*

Isaiah foretells Christ's coming *Isa
7:10-16, 9:2-7*

Isaiah foretells Christ's peaceable
kingdom *Isa 11:1-12, 35:1-10*

Jeremiah's prophecy of restoration
Jer 31:1-14, 31-34

Jonah repents and reforms *Jonah
2:1-10*

Micah's prophecy of glory of the
church *Mic 4:1-8, 13, Isa 2:1-5*

Jesus tells qualities that improve
Mat 5:1-12, Luke 6:17-26, 36

Jesus' parable of builders on rock
and sand *Mat 7:24-27, Luke 6:
48, 49*

Jesus' parable of unclean spirit
which returns *Mat 12:43-45, Luke
11:24-26*

Jesus' parable of leaven *Mat 13:33,
Luke 13:20, 21*

Jesus' parable of mustard seed *Mat
13:31, 32, Mark 4:30-32, Luke 13:
18, 19*

Jesus' parable of the talents *Mat
25:14-30, Luke 19:11-28*

Jesus' parable of seed, blade, ear
Mark 4:26-29

Jesus healing: blind man improved,
then healed *Mark 8:22-26*

Jesus' parable of rich man and bigger barns *Luke 12:15-21*

Jesus' parable of rich man and beggar *Luke 16:19-31*

Zacchaeus becomes a changed man
Luke 19:1-10

Jesus' healing: son began to amend
in the seventh hour *John 4:46-54*

Jesus promises Holy Ghost when he
leaves *John 14:1-31*

Peter aids church growth *Acts 4:
24-37*

Saul improves and gets a new name
—Paul *Acts 8:1-4, 9:1-22*

Paul on Adam and Christ   *Rom 5: 1-21*

Paul on "come out...be ye separate"   *2 Cor 6:1-18*

Paul's teaching on thinking on good things   *Phil 4:1-32*

Paul's teaching to put on new man   *Col 3:1-17*

Paul's advice to his disciple   *2 Tim 2:1-26*

See also education, evolution, growth, increase, progress, purity

IMPULSE

Esau gives up his birthright for pottage   *Gen 25:24-34*

Achan admits he stole spoils   *Josh 7:1-26*

David offers to fight Goliath   *1 Sam 17:17-37*

David orders Uriah killed to take his wife   *2 Sam 11:1-27*

Elisha leaves off plowing to follow Elijah   *1 King 19:19-21*

Hezekiah unwisely shows Babylonians all his treasures   *2 King 20:12-21, Isa 39:1-8*

Jonah disobeys   *Jonah 1:1-17*

Peter leaves nets to follow Jesus   *Mat 4:17-22, Mark 1:14-20, Luke 5:1-11, John 1:35-42*

Jesus' hem touched by sick woman   *Mat 9:20-22, Mark 5:25-34, Luke 8:43-48*

Peter tries walking on water to Jesus   *Mat 14:22-33*

Peter acknowledges Jesus as Christ   *Mat 16:13-20, Mark 8:27-30, Luke 9:18-21*

Peter cuts off Malchus' ear   *Luke 22:50, 51*

Peter refuses to allow Jesus to wash his feet   *John 13:1-20*

Peter returns to his work as fisherman   *John 21:1-11*

Ethiopian asks to be baptized   *Acts 8:26-40*

Paul gets letters to persecute Christians   *Acts 9:1-9*

See also force, mind, spirit

INCARNATION

Annunciation to Mary   *Mat 1:19-25, Luke 1:30-33, 1 Tim 3:16*

The Word was made flesh   *John 1:1-14*

Paul on Jesus Christ made in the likeness of men   *Phil 2:1-15*

See also son of God, son of man

INCOME

Abraham's riches grow   *Gen 13:1-18*

Isaac's riches grow   *Gen 26:12-31*

Joseph solves problem of feast and famine   *Gen 41:1-46*

Moses lists blessings of obedience   *Deut 28:1-14*

Ruth gleans after reapers   *Ruth 2:1-23*

David gets liberal offerings for temple   *1 Chron 29:6-19*

Solomon gets material to build temple   *1 King 6:1-38, 7:1-51, 2 Chron 3:1-17, 4:1-22, 5:1-14*

Elijah finds widow without income   *1 King 17:1-16*

Elisha and widow's pot of oil   *2 King 4:1-7*

Jehoiachin well-treated as captive   *2 King 25:27-30*

David's song, the earth is full of the goodness of the Lord   *Psal 33:1-22*

David's song, "be still, and know"   *Psal 46:1-11*

Isaiah's vision of desert blossoming   *Isa 35:1-10*

Zechariah's vision of candlestick and two olive trees   *Zech 4:1-14*

Malachi urges tithing   *Mal 3:10, 4:1, 2*

Jesus' parable of sower and seed   *Mat 13:3-25, Mark 4:1-20, Luke 8:4-15*

Jesus obtains tribute money from fish   *Mat 17:24-27*

Jesus' parable of unmerciful debtor   *Mat 18:23-35*

Jesus' parable of laborers in vineyard   *Mat 20:1-16*

Jesus' parable of husbandmen who refuse to pay rent   *Mat 21:33-46, Mark 12:1-12, Luke 20:9-19*

Jesus on tribute to Caesar   *Mat 22:15-22, Mark 12:13-17, Luke 20:20-26*

Jesus' parable of the talents   *Mat 25:14-30, Luke 19:11-28*

Jesus' parable of seed, blade, ear
Mark 4:26-29
Jesus and the widow's mite *Mark 12:41-44, Luke 21:1-4*
Jesus tells his disciples laborer is worthy of his hire *Luke 10:1-16*
Jesus casts traders out of temple *John 2:13-25*
Paul on supply for all *2 Cor 8:11-15, 9:6-15*

See also business, harvest, profit, supply, wages

INCREASE

God commands his spiritual creation to be fruitful and multiply *Gen 1:1-31*
Abraham's riches grow *Gen 13:1-18*
God promises Abraham his seed shall be many as the stars *Gen 15:1-21*
The blessings of obedience *Deut 28:1-14*
David receives liberal offerings to build temple *1 Chron 29:6-19*
Elijah multiplies the widow's food *1 King 17:1-16*
Elisha and widow's pot of oil *2 King 4:1-7*
Job gets all he had and more, restored *Job 42:1-34*
David's song, "praise the Lord for his goodness" *Psal 107:1-43*
Isaiah's vision of desert that bloomed *Isa 35:1-10*
Isaiah's vision of glory of church *Isa 2:1-5, Mic 4:1-8, 13*
Isaiah's vision of blessed state of new Jerusalem *Isa 65:17-25*
Zechariah's vision of olive trees pouring forth oil *Zech 4:1-14*
Jesus explains necessity of good fruits *Mat 7:15-20, Luke 6:43-45*
Jesus' parable of sower *Mat 13:3-23, Mark 4:1-20, Luke 8:4-13*
Jesus' parable of mustard seed *Mat 13:31, 32, Mark 4:30-32, Luke 13:18, 19*
Jesus feeds 5000 *Mat 14:15-21, Mark 6:37-44, Luke 9:12-17, John 6:5-14*
Jesus feeds 4000 *Mat 15:32-39, Mark 8:1-10*
Jesus withers fig tree without fruit

Mat 21:18-22, Mark 11:12-14, 20-24
Jesus' parable of the talents *Mat 25:14-30, Luke 19:11-28*
Jesus' parable of seed, blade, ear *Mark 4:26-29*
Peter's net filled *Luke 5:1-11*
Jesus' parable of rich man and bigger barns *Luke 12:15-21*
Jesus' parable of barren fig tree *Luke 13:6-9*
Jesus' discourse on increase of faith *Luke 17:1-6*
Peter's net filled again *John 21:1-11*
Peter sees church grow *Acts 4:24-37*
Peter sees need for division of labor *Acts 6:1-4*

See also expansion, family, improvement, power, profit, supply

INDEPENDENCE

Cain asks if he is his brother's keeper *Gen 4:1-16*
Moses sees oppression of Israelites *Exod 1:8-14*
Moses releases them from bondage *Exod 1:4-10, 12:1-14, 21-41, Deut 16:1-22*
Song of Moses for deliverance *Exod 15:1-19, Deut 32:1-47*
Deborah frees her country from invaders *Judg 4:1-17*
Gideon frees his country from enemy host *Judg 7:1-25*
Samson betrayed and sustained *Judg 16:4-30*
David made king of Judah and Israel *2 Sam 2:1-4, 5:1-5*
Israel enters period of captivity under Babylon *2 King 25:1-30*
David's song on God, the preserver of man *Psal 121:1-8*
Jeremiah's prophecy that captivity will be turned *Jer 29:8-14*
Jeremiah promises restoration of Israel *Jer 31:1-14, 31-34*
Ezekiel sees children independent of father *Ezek 18:1-32*
Jesus ready for independence at twelve years *John 2:41-52*
Jesus says the truth makes free *John 8:12-32*

See also democracy, freedom, liberty, slavery, tyranny

INDIGNATION

Lord God asks Adam, "Where art thou?" *Gen 3: 6-24*

Lord God asks Cain, "What hast thou done?" *Gen 4:1-16*

Lord God warns Noah of the flood *Gen 6: 5-22*

Abraham makes peace with Lot *Gen 13: 1-18*

Sarah causes Hagar and her son to be cast out *Gen 21: 9-21*

Joseph forgives his brethren *Gen 43: 1, 2, 45: 1-11*

Moses breaks tablet of Ten Commandments *Exod 32: 1-24*

Moses forgives prophecies of Eldad and Medad *Num 11: 16-30*

Naaman indignant at Elisha's prescription *2 King 5: 1-14*

Asa angry with seer for pointing out his errors *2 Chron 16: 7-14*

Nehemiah resents conspiracy to stop building *Neh 8: 1-12*

Job tells his friends they are miserable comforters *Job 16: 1-22*

Elihu's wrath kindled against Job and friends *Job 32: 1-22*

Isaiah's warning that hypocrisy will be punished *Isa 29: 11-24, 30: 1-3, 20, 21*

Jesus reproves three cities for disregarding his works *Mat. 11: 20-30*

Jesus' parable of unmerciful debtor *Mat 18: 23-35*

Jesus' parable of husbandmen who refuse to pay rent *Mat 21: 33-46, Mark 12: 1-12, Luke 20: 9-19*

Jesus' parable of the wedding garment *Mat. 22: 1-14*

Jesus reproves scribes and Pharisees *Mat 23: 1-39, Mark 12: 38-40, Luke 20: 45-47, John 8: 33-59*

Jesus' parable of the talents *Mat 25: 14-30, Luke 19: 11-28*

Jesus' parable of sheep and goats *Mat 25: 31-46*

Jesus casts traders out of temple *John 2: 13-25*

Stephen forgives his slayers *Acts 7: 51-60*

Peter reproves Simon for offer to buy Holy Ghost *Acts 8: 14-25*

See also anger, forgiveness, harmony, wrath

INDIVIDUALITY

God creates man as His image *Gen 1: 26-27*

Lord God creates man from dust *Gen 2: 6-8*

Abraham blessed by Melchizedek *Gen 14: 8-20, Heb 6: 20, 7: 1-28*

Abram and Sarai receive new names *Gen 17:1-9, 15-22*

Jacob receives new name *Gen 32: 24-32*

Revelation of nature of God, to Moses *Exod 3: 1-18*

The chosen people set apart as God's own *Deut 7: 6-11*

The Lord calls Samuel *1 Sam 3: 1-10, 19-21*

Samuel selects David among Jesse's sons *1 Sam 16: 1-13*

Esther's true beauty recognized *Esther 2: 5-23*

The nature of a good woman *Prov 31: 1-31*

Isaiah is called by God to speak *Isa 6: 1-13*

Isaiah outlines the office of the Christ *Isa 42:1-12, 16, 18*

Isaiah describes the Messiah *Isa 53: 1-12*

Isaiah describes works of Christ *Isa 61: 1-11, 62: 1-12*

Ezekiel says children not responsible for parents' character *Ezek 18: 1-32*

Jesus' oneness with Father *John 10: 22-42*

Jesus' parable of wheat and tares *Mat 13: 24-30, 36-43*

Jesus' parable of pearl of great price *Mat 13: 45, 46*

Peter acknowledges Jesus as Christ *Mat 16: 13-20, Mark 8: 27-30, Luke 9: 18-21*

Jesus meets with Moses and Elijah *Mat 17: 1-13, Mark 9: 2-13, Luke 9: 28-36*

Jesus' parable of two sons ordered to work *Mat 21: 28-32*

Jesus' parable of wise and foolish virgins *Mat 25: 1-13*

Jesus' parable of the talents *Mat 25:14-30, Luke 19:11-28*

Jesus' unique origin *Luke 1: 26-38*

At twelve years Jesus equals the rabbis *Luke 2:41-52*

Jesus' parable of rich man and beggar *Luke 16: 19-31*

Jesus as the light of the world *John 1: 1-14, 8: 12-32*

Jesus' parable of true vine *John 15: 1-17*

Jesus' parable of the good shepherd *John 10: 1-18*

Paul's sermon on Adam vs. Christ *Rom 5: 1-21*

See also identity, oneness, personality

INDUCTION

From material evidence writer concludes man was made from dust *Gen 2: 6-8*

From sinful world Noah anticipates flood *Gen 7: 1-24*

From dream evidence Joseph prepares for famine *Gen 41: 1-46*

To relieve pressure on Moses, Jethro suggests appointing judges *Exod 18: 13-27*

From signs Gideon has faith in God *Judg 6: 1-40*

From Saul's action Samuel declares him unfit to rule *1 Sam 15:7-26*

To convince Job God lists particulars of his government *Job 38: 1-41*

From world condition Preacher concludes all is vanity *Eccl 1: 1-18, 2: 1-26*

Pharisees demand evidence that Jesus is Christ *Mat 16: 1-4, Mark 8: 10-13*

The resurrection proves immortality *Mat 28: 1-8, Mark 16: 1-8, Luke 24: 1-12, John 20: 1-10*

Paul: Jesus' resurrection proves ours *1 Cor 15: 1-58*

See also particular, reason, thinking

INFECTION

Solomon's prayer at dedication *1 King 8:22-66, 2 Chron 6:1-42*

Leper touched and healed by Jesus *Mat 8: 1-4, Mark 1: 40-45, Luke 5: 12-16*

Ten lepers healed at once *Luke 17: 11-19*

INFIDELITY

Adam and Eve taste the knowledge of good and evil *Gen 3: 1-24*

In Moses' absence people worship golden calf *Exod 32: 1-24*

Miriam and Aaron speak against Moses *Num 12: 1-16*

Saul consults familiar spirit *1 Sam 28: 3-20*

David takes another man's wife *2 Sam 11:1-27*

Gehazi does not obey Elisha *2 King 5: 15-27*

Asa's death due to infidelity *2 Chron 16:11-14*

David's song, "Create in me a clean heart" *Psal 51: 1-19*

Isaiah's parable of the wild grapes *Isa 5: 1-8*

Isaiah's vision of fall of Babylon *Isa 14: 4-8, 12-17, 25-27*

Jonah's actions punished *Jonah 1: 1-17, 2: 1-10*

Jesus' parable of lost sheep *Mat 18: 12-14, Luke 15: 1-7*

Jesus reproves scribes and Pharisees *Mat 23: 1-39*

Jesus' parable of sheep and goats *Mat 25: 31-46*

Judas betrays the Master *Mat 26: 14-16, Mark 14: 10, 11, Luke 22: 1-6*

Peter denies Jesus *Mat 26: 57, 58, 69-75, Mark 14: 66-72, Luke 22: 54-62, John 18: 13-18, 25-27*

See also adultery, belief, devotion, faith, idolatry

INFINITY

God creates the entire universe and finds it good *Gen 1: 1-31*

Enoch walks with God and is translated *Gen 5: 18, 21-24, Heb 11: 5*

Jacob is promised God's ever-presence *Gen 28: 10-22*

Moses at bush sees God as I Am That I Am *Exod 3: 1-18*

Moses receives God's eternal laws *Exod 20: 1-19, Deut 5: 1-24*

Elijah sees God's nature in still small voice *1 King 19: 9-13*

Elijah translated *2 King 2: 1-11*

Job hears the voice of the infinite *Job 38: 1-41*

David's song of God's ever-presence *Psal 139: 1-24*

Importance of knowledge of the infinite *Prov 3:13-26, 4:1-13, 8: 1-36*

Mortal events all limited within time *Eccl 3: 1-15*

Isaiah's vision of justice from the infinite *Isa 59: 1-21*

Ezekiel's vision of Truth encompassing the universe *Ezek 47:1-12*

The infinite nature of the Christ *Mat 22: 41-46, Mark 12: 35-37, Luke 20: 41-44*

Jesus is the Christ *John 7:14-40*

The unity and eternity of the Christ *John 8: 12-59*

Oneness with the Father *John 10: 22-42*

Symbols of infinity; river and tree of life *Rev 22: 1-21*

See also allness, eternity, God, omniaction, omnipotence, omnipresence, omniscience, perfection

INFLUENCE

Serpent persuades Eve to eat fruit *Gen 3: 1-5*

Potiphar's wife fails to seduce Joseph *Gen 39:1-20*

Moses urges obedience *Deut 4: 1-15, 11: 1-32*

Moses warns against enticers *Deut 13: 1-18*

Moses charges Joshua with leadership *Deut 31: 7-23, Josh 1: 1-9*

Delilah influences Samson to his destruction *Judg 16: 4-30*

Naomi influences Ruth to her good *Ruth 1: 1-22, 2: 1-23*

David pacified by Abigail's gentleness *1 Sam 25: 2-42*

Nathan's parable makes David repent *2 Sam 12: 1-10*

Rehoboam consults first old men, then his friends *1 King 12: 1-18, 2 Chron 10: 1-19*

Elijah finds Elisha plowing *1 King 19: 19-21*

Elisha asks for a double portion of Elijah's spirit *2 King 2: 1-11*

David's charge to Solomon *1 Chron 22: 6-19, 23: 1, 28: 2-10, 20*

Job's friends try to get him to repent *Job 2: 11-13, 4: 1-21*

David's song, "Consider thy heavens" *Psal 8: 1-9*

David's song, of God's law converting the soul *Psal 19: 1-14*

The happy value of wisdom *Prov 3: 13-26, 4: 1-13, 8: 1-36*

Jesus calls his disciples *Mat 4: 17-22, Mark 1: 14-20, Luke 5: 1-11, John 1: 35-42, 2: 35-51*

Jesus charges disciples to preach and heal *Mat 10: 5-42, Mark 16: 15-18, Mat 28: 16-20, Mark 6: 7-13, Luke 9: 1-6, 10: 1-16*

Jesus' parable of the leaven *Mat 13: 33, Luke 13: 20, 21*

Why Jesus uses only parables *Mat 13: 34, 35, Mark 4: 33, 34*

Jesus on what defiles a man *Mat 15: 1-20, Mark 7: 1-23*

Jesus on humility *Mat 18: 1-22, Mark 9: 33-50, 10: 13-16, John 13: 12-20*

Judas betrays Jesus for money *Mat 26: 14-16, Mark 14: 10, 11, Luke 22: 1-6*

Jesus sought by all men *Mark 1: 35-39*

Jesus' parable of the unwilling friend *Luke 11: 5-13*

Jesus on forgiveness *Luke 17: 1-6*

Jesus' parable of the judge and the widow *Luke 18: 1-8*

Jesus' parable of Pharisee and publican *Luke 18: 9-14*

Peter sees signs and wonders in growth of church *Acts 4: 24-37*

Philip converts many *Acts 8: 9-13*

Peter permits conversion of Gentiles *Acts 11: 1-18*

Paul converts Lydia *Acts 16: 7-15*

See also astrology, authority, control, evil, goodness, heaven, power

INHERIT

Man the image and likeness of his Maker *Gen 1: 26, 27*

God promises Canaan to Abraham *Gen 15: 1-21*

Jacob buys Esau's birthright for pottage *Gen 25: 24-34*

Moses inherits life of noble Egyptian *Exod 2: 1-10*

Daughters of Zelophehad sue for inheritance *Num 27: 1-11, 36: 5-13*

Joshua takes over from Moses *Josh 1: 1-9*

Caleb gets his share of Canaan at last *Josh 14: 6-15*

David's charge to Solomon, his son *1 Chron 22: 6-19, 23: 1, 28: 2-16*

Elisha asks for a double portion of Elijah's spirit *2 King 2: 1-15*

Ezekiel's vision of fathers and children *Ezek 18: 1-32*

The rich young ruler wants to inherit eternal life *Mat 19: 16-30, Mark 10: 17-31, Luke 18: 18-30*

Nature of Jesus' origin made known to Mary *Luke 1: 26-38*

A lawyer asks how he can inherit eternal life *Luke 10: 25-29*

Jesus asked to settle an inheritance *Luke 12: 13, 14*

Jesus' parable of prodigal son *Luke 15: 11-24*

Jesus heals man born blind *John 9: 1-41*

Paul on talents all coming from God *1 Cor. 12: 1, 4-31*

See also birth, heredity, possess, rights

INJURY

Jacob's thigh out of joint wrestling *Gen 32: 24-32*

Bites of fiery serpents healed *Num 21: 4-9*

Samson blinded by Philistines *Judg 16: 4-30*

David has chance to injure Saul *1 Sam 24:1-22*

David has second chance, but doesn't use it *1 Sam 26: 1-25*

Jeroboam's hand withered and healed *1 King 12: 32, 33, 13: 1-10*

Uzziah self-punished *2 Chron 26: 1-23*

Isaiah foretells suffering of Christ *Isa 42: 1-12, 16, 18*

Jesus is scourged *Mat 27: 27-31, Mark 15: 16-20, John 19: 1-16*

Jesus is crucified *Mat 27: 32-56, Mark 15: 21-41, Luke 23: 26-49, John 19: 17-30*

Paul's sermon on his hardships *2 Cor 11:21-33*

Paul's thorn in the flesh *2 Cor 12: 1-19*

James' sermon on how to bear our cross *Jas 1:1-27*

Paul heals Eutychus after accident *Acts 20: 7-12*

See also accident, affliction, hurt, loss, pain, suffering

INNOCENCE

God's original pure creations *Gen 1: 26, 27*

Adam made from dust, his fall and punishment *Gen 2: 6-8, 3: 6-24*

Enoch walked with God and was translated *Gen 5: 18, 21-24, Heb 11: 5*

Abram and Sarai renamed for walking with God *Gen 17: 1-9, 15-22*

Isaac's innocence rewarded *Gen 22: 1-19*

Joseph's boyhood dreams result in slavery *Gen 37: 1-36*

Joseph's chastity results in prison *Gen 39: 1-20*

Job hold his integrity despite trials *Job 1: 1-22, 2: 1-10*

David's song, "Blessed is the man" *Psal 1: 1-6*

Isaiah's vision of Christ's peaceable kingdom *Isa 11: 1-12*

Children innocent of father's sins *Ezek 18 :1-32*

Daniel pleads innocent to rebellion towards king *Dan 6:1-28*

Birth of Jesus *Mat 2: 1-12, Luke 2: 1-7*

Jesus says gospel revealed unto babes *Mat 11: 25-27, Luke 10: 21, 22*

Jesus tells what defiles a man *Mat 15: 1-20, Mark 7: 1-23*

Jesus foretells his betrayal *Mat 26: 20-25, Mark 14: 18-21, Luke 22: 21, 22, John 13: 21-35*

Jesus' parable of sheep and goats *Mat 25: 31-46*

Jesus heals Malchus after Peter's rash attack *Luke 22:50, 51*

See also childlikeness, guilt, lamb, purity, sheep, sin

INSANITY

Daniel foretells king's insanity *Dan 4:1-27*
Nebuchadnezzar's insanity healed *Dan 4:28-37*
Jesus heals divers diseases, torments and the lunatic *Mat 4:23-25, Luke 4:40-44*
Jesus heals the insane Gadarene *Mat 8:28-34, Mark 5:1-20, Luke 8:26-39*
Jesus accused of casting out devils by Beelzebub *Mat 12:22-30, Mark 3:22-30, Luke 11:14-23*
Jesus heals Syrophenician woman's daughter *Mat 15:21-28, Mark 7: 24-30*
Jesus heals lunatic boy *Mat 17:14-21, Mark 9:14-29, Luke 9:37-43*

See also mind, reason

INSIGHT

Daniel interprets dream *Dan 2:1-49*
Daniel reads writing on wall *Dan 5:1-31*
Moses gives people choice between good and evil *Deut 30:11-20*
Joshua uncovers sin in a man *Josh 7:1-26, 8:14-21*
Nathan exposes David's sin to him *2 Sam 12:1-10*
Nathan reveals to David that his son will build the temple *1 Chron 17:1-27*
Elijah and Elisha know that Elijah is about to be translated *2 King 2:1-11*
Elisha knows words king speaks in his bedchamber *2 King 6:8-23*
Elisha prophesies drop in price of flour *2 King 6:24, 25, 7:1-18*
Jeremiah in prison buys a field in Israel to show his confidence that captivity will be turned *Jer 32: 2, 6-27, 37-44*
Jesus heals palsied man by telling him his sins are forgiven *Mat 9: 2-8, Mark 2:1-12, Luke 5:17-26*
Jesus astonishes woman by telling

her facts of her past life *John 4:1-30*
Paul's self-revealings *2 Cor 12:1-19*

See also intuition, prophecy, revelation, truth, understanding

INSISTENCE

Jacob persists wrestling with angel *Gen 32:24-32*
Elisha insists on following Elijah *2 King 2:1-15*
The Shunammite affirms all is well *2 King 4:8-37*
His friends insist Job has sinned *Job 2:11-13, 4:1-12, 8:1-22*
Palsied man's friends let him down through the roof *Mat 9:2-8, Mark 2:1-12, Luke 5:17-26*
Syrophenician woman follows Jesus until he heals her daughter *Mat 15:21-28, Mark 7:24-30*
Bartimaeus gets Jesus' attention *Mark 10:46-52*
Jesus' parable of the unwilling friend *Luke 11:5-13*
Jesus' parable of the judge and the widow *Luke 18:1-8*

See also perseverance, persistence

INSPIRATION

God communicates his covenant to Noah *Gen 9:1-17*
God's promises to Abraham *Gen 13:1-18*
Abraham blessed by Melchizedek *Gen 14:8-20, Heb 6:20, 7:1-28*
Joseph interprets Pharaoh's dream *Gen 41:1-46*
Jacob foretells future of his twelve sons *Gen 49:1-28, Deut 33:1-29*
Moses learns source of eloquence *Exod 4:10-17*
God tells Moses to go forward through the Red Sea *Exod 14: 5-31*
Moses receives Ten Comandments *Exod 20:1-19, Deut 5:1-24*
Eldad and Medad prophesy in camp *Num 11:16-30*
God tells Gideon how to defeat host, with 300 men *Judg 7:1-25*

Samuel selects David for anointing
1 Sam 16:1-13

David refuses Saul's armor and uses
sling *1 Sam 17:17-52*

God shows Elijah his nature as still
small voice *1 King 19:9-13*

Elisha and widow's pot of oil
2 King 4:1-7

Ezra reads book of the law to inspire
people *Neh 8:1-12*

David's song, "Be still and know"
Psal 46:1-11

The happy value of wisdom *Prov
3:13-26, 4:1-13, 8:1-36*

Isaiah' inspiration to be Christlike
Isa 60:1-5

Ezekiel's vision of holy waters
Ezek 47:1-12

Daniel discerns the meaning of
king's dream *Dan 2:1-49*

Daniel reads handwriting on wall
Dan 5:1-31

Zechariah's vision of two olive trees
Zech 4:1-14

Jesus teaches twelve and sends them
to heal and preach *Mat 9:36-38,
10:1-42, Mark 3:13-21, 6:7-19, Luke
9:1-16*

Mary's response to immaculate conception *Luke 1:46-55*

Jesus' parable of new wine in old
bottles *Luke 5:36-39*

Jesus teaches 70 and sends them
forth *Luke 10:1-24*

Risen Jesus makes hearts of disciples burn within *Luke 24:13-35*

Jesus changes water into wine *John
2:1-11*

Jesus tells source of his great works
John 5:17-47

Descent of Holy Ghost *Acts 2:1-13*

Peter and John speak with boldness
Acts 4:1-23

Key found to open sealed book *Rev
5:1-14*

See also breath, creation, light, soul,
spirit, truth, wine, zealous

INSTRUCTION

Moses urges obedience to God *Deut
11:1-32*

Moses warns against idolatry, necromancy *Deut 13:1-18*

Moses forbids abominations *Deut
18:9-14*

Moses urges offering first fruits
Deut 26:1-19

Moses warns the people they must
choose *Deut 30:11-20*

Moses charges Joshua with leadership *Deut 31:7-23, Josh 1:1-9*

Naomi tells Ruth how to act with
Boaz *Ruth 3:1-18*

Rehoboam consults with old men,
then his friends *1 King 12:1-18,
2 Chron 10:1-19*

Elisha asks for a double portion of
Elijah's spirit *2 King 2:1-15*

Elisha instructs widow about her
pot of oil *2 King 4:1-7*

David's charge to Solomon *1 Chron
22:6-19, 23:1, 28:2-10, 20*

Ezra reads from book of the law
Neh 8:1-12

His friends advise Job *Job 2:11-13,
4:1-12, 8:1-22*

Value of wisdom to man *Prov 3:
13-26, 4:1-13, 8:1-36*

The vanity of mortal life *Eccl 1:
1-18, 2:1-26*

Hosea's vision, "When Israel was a
child" *Hos 11:1-4*

Jesus teaches twelve disciples to
preach and heal *Mat 10:1-42, Mark
6:7-13, Luke 9:1-6, 10, 11*

Jesus explains the parable of the
sower *Mat 13:3-23, Mark 4:1-20,
Luke 8:4-15*

Jesus explains why he instructs by
parables *Mat 13:10-13, Mark 4:
33, 34*

Jesus explains why his disciples
failed to heal a case *Mat 17:14-
21, Mark 9:14-29, Luke 9:37-43*

At twelve years Jesus exchanges
questions and answers with the
rabbis *Luke 2:41-52*

Jesus instructs 70 disciples *Luke
10:1-24*

Jesus charges Peter to feed his
sheep *John 21:12-19*

Forty-nine parables of Jesus (See
Part II, Jesus Christ: Parables)

Fifty-two teachings of Jesus (See
Part II, Jesus Christ: Teachings)

Peter's sermons *Acts 2:14-47, 3:12-
26, 4:1-23, 1 Pet 2:1-25*

Paul's sermons *Acts 13:16-52, 17:15-34, 19:1-10, 22:1-30*

Paul's epistles *Rom 5:1-21, 8:1-39, 1*

Paul's epistles *Rom 5:1-21, 8:1-39, 1 Cor 12:1-31, 13:1-13, 15:1-58, 2 Cor 6:1-18, 8:21-25, 9:6-15, Gal 5:1-26, Eph 6:10-17, Phil 4:1-23, Col 3:1-12, 1 Thess 5:1-28, 2 Tim 2:1-26, 3:1-17, 4:1-8, Heb 1:1-14, 2:1-18, 7:1-28, 10:1-39*

James' epistles *Jas 1:1-27, 2:1-13*

John's epistle *1 John 4:1-21*

See also advice, disciple, discipline, education, study, teaching

INSTRUMENT

Joseph says God sent him before his brethren to preserve life *Gen 43:1, 2, 45:1-11*

David plays harp to calm Saul's trouble *1 Sam 16:14-23*

Esther, although queen in a foreign land, saves her people *Esther 5:1-14*

David's song, "Rejoice in the Lord" *Psal 33:1-22*

David's song, "Make a joyful noise" *Psal 66:1-20, 100:1-5*

Zechariah's vision of the two anointed ones that supply the golden oil *Zech 4:1-14*

The ministry of John Baptist to prepare the way *Mat 3:1-12, Mark 1:1-8, Luke 3:1-18*

Jesus on Christ as the door and good shepherd *John 10:1-30*

God tells Ananias to heal Paul, a chosen vessel for Him *Acts 9:10-22*

See also harmony, music, work

INTEGRITY

Enoch walked with God *Gen 5:18, 21-24, Heb 11:5*

Noah alone found righteous *Gen 6:5-22*

Abraham asks how many righteous men to save a city *Gen 18:20-33*

Joseph cannot be tempted *Gen 39:1-20*

Gideon refuses to be king *Judg 8:22, 23*

Nathan reveals David's lapse of integrity *2 Sam 12:1-10*

Nehemiah avoids conspiracy to halt building *Neh 6:1-19*

Job's integrity unmarred *Job 1:1-22, 2:1-10*

David's song, "Mark the perfect man" *Psal 37:23-40*

Three Hebrew boys refuse to worship image *Dan 3:1-30*

Daniel worships as usual *Dan 6:1-28*

Daniel's vision of meeting Gabriel *Dan 9:20-23, 10:4-21*

Jesus on what defiles a man *Mat 15:1-20, Mark 7:1-23*

Jesus' sermon on unity and eternity of Christ *John 8:12-59*

Jesus' sermon on Christ as door and good shepherd *John 10:1-30*

Paul's sermon on the Christians' armor *Eph 6:10-17*

Someone is found to open the sealed book *Rev 5:1-14*

See also character, conscience, honesty, morality, purity, righteousness

INTELLIGENCE

Joseph, the problem-solver in Egypt *Gen 39:1-6*

Joseph foresees famine and prepares for it *Gen 41:1-46*

Gideon takes enemy host by surprise *Judg 7:1-25*

David refuses armor and solves problem with his sling *1 Sam 17:17-52*

Nehemiah foils conspiracy against him *Neh 6:1-19*

Esther foils Haman's plot against her people *Esther 5:1-14, 6:1-14, 7:1-10*

Job demands to know why the good suffer *Job 3:1-26*

Why man needs wisdom *Prov 3:13-26, 4:1-13, 8:1-36*

Mortal life recognized as vain *Eccl 1:1-18, 2:1-26*

Daniel interprets king's dream *Dan 2:1-49*

Jesus' parable of builders upon rock and upon sand *Mat 7:24-27, Luke 6:48, 49*

Jesus heals the Gadarene of insanity *Mat 8:28-34, Mark 5:1-20, Luke 8:26-39*

Jesus' parable of the talents *Mat 25:14-30, Luke 19:11-28*

Jesus reads the mind of the Samaritan woman *John 4:1-30*

Jesus saves the woman taken in adultery *John 8:1-11*

See also mind, omniscience, problem-solving, reason, understanding, wisdom

INTERCESSION

Angel prevents sacrifice of Isaac by Abraham *Gen 22:1-19*

A proper wife is found for Isaac *Gen 24:1-67*

Balak hires Balaam to curse Israel *Num 22:1-41, 23:1-30, 24:1-25*

David pacified by Abigail's gentleness *1 Sam 25:2-42*

Esther sues for life of her people *Esther 5:1-14*

Isaiah's vision of coming Messiah *Isa 7:10-16, 9:2-7*

Jesus crucified *Mat 27:32-56, Mark 15:21-41, Luke 23:26-49, John 19:17-30*

Jesus Christ as light of the world *John 1:1-14, 8:12-32*

Jesus declares, "I am the bread of life" *John 6:26-65*

Jesus on Christ as door and shepherd *John 10:1-30*

Jesus' prayer for disciples *John 17:1-26*

Paul's sermon, Jesus' resurrection proves ours *1 Cor 15:1-58*

John's vision of the Lamb able to open the sealed book *Rev 5:1-14*

See also advocate, atonement, Christ, Jesus, mediator, reconciliation

INTOLERANCE

Cain murders Abel for a religious motive *Gen 4:1-16*

Saul can't abide David *1 Sam 18:1-16, 24:1-22, 26:1-25*

Jesus' parable of mote and beam *Mat 7:1-5, Luke 6:37-42*

Jesus' healing on sabbath day opposed *Mat 12:9-13, Mark 3:1-5, Luke 6:6-11*

Jesus accused of healing by Beelzebub *Mat 12:22-30, Mark 3:22-30, Luke 11:14-23*

Jesus' parable of unmerciful debtor *Mat 18:23-35*

Jesus' parable of husbandmen who refuse to pay rent *Mat 21:33-46, Mark 12:1-12, Luke 20:9-19*

Jesus reproves Pharisees *Mat 23:1-39, Mark 12:38-40, Luke 20:43-47, John 8:33-39*

Jesus' parable of good Samaritan *Luke 10:25-37*

Jesus' parable of barren fig tree *Luke 13:6-9*

Peter and John tried for preaching *Acts 4:1-23*

Paul's treatment of Christians *Acts 9:1, 2*

Paul describes enemies of the truth *2 Tim 3:1-17*

See also Pharisee, prejudice, worship

INTUITION

Abraham entertains angels *Gen 18:1-18*

Abraham stopped from sacrifice of his son *Gen 22:1-19*

Joseph interprets dreams *Gen 39:21, 23, 40:1-23, 41:1-46*

Balaam refuses to curse Israel *Num 22:1-41, 23:1-30, 24:1-25*

Ruth returns with Naomi and becomes ancestor of David *Ruth 1:1-22, 4:1-22*

Samuel and the importance of listening *1 Sam 3:1-10, 19-21*

Solomon selects proper values *1 King 3:5-15, 2 Chron 1:7-12*

Solomon displays wisdom in human relations *1 King 3:16-28*

Elisha senses trouble with the Shunammite *2 King 4:8-37*

Elisha refuses to see Naaman but heals him *2 King 5:1-14*

Elisha foretells the actions of the Syrians *2 King 6:8-23*

Nehemiah senses the nature of conspiracy *Nah 6:1-19*

David's song, "Be still, and know that I am God" *Psal 46:1-11*

The value of spiritual wisdom *Prov 3:13-26, 4:1-13, 8:1-36*

The vanity of mortal life *Eccl 1: 1-18, 2:1-26*

The poor wise man who saved a city *Eccl 9:13-18*

Isaiah's vision of God's glory *Isa 6:1-13*

Isaiah's prophecy of Messiah to come *Isa 7:10-16, 9:2-7*

Jeremiah says captivity will be turned *Jer 29:8-14*

Daniel interprets king's dream *Dan 2:1-49*

Jesus selects his disciples swiftly *Mat 4:17-22, 9:9, Mark 1:14-20, Luke 5:1-11, John 1:35-42*

Jesus tells why he speaks in parables *Mat 13:10-17, 34, 35, Mark 4: 10-12, 33, 34*

John Baptist testifies that Jesus is the Christ *John 1:15-34*

Jesus rightly judges the morality of the woman of Samaria *John 4:1-30, 39-42*

Jesus' parable of true vine *John 15:1-17*

Peter confirms his Master's intuition *Acts 3:1-26*

See also angel, insight, inspiration, knowledge, listening, spirit, woman

INVASION

Isaac handles strife over wells *Gen 26:12-31*

Joshua invades promised land at Jericho *Josh 3:1-17, 6:1-27*

Deborah repels Sisera *Judg 4:1-17*

Gideon expels Midianites *Judg 7: 1-25*

Elisha's vision of army of angels and his treatment of Syrian host *2 King 6:8-23*

Israel turns back the Syrians *2 King 6:24, 25, 7:1-18*

Hezekiah repels Sennacherib, the Assyrian *2 King 18:17-37, 19: 1-27, 2 Chron 31:20, 21, 32:1-23, Isa 36:1-22, 37:1-38*

Hezekiah and Jerusalem fall to Babylonian invaders *2 King 20: 12-21, Isa 39:1-8*

Jehoshaphat repels coalition *2 Chron 20:1-32*

David's song of security *Psal 91: 1-16, 121:1-8*

A poor wise man saves his city from a great king *Eccl 9:13-18*

Isaiah's promise in trials, "fear not" *Isa 43:1-12*

Ezekiel's vision of army from dry bones *Ezek 37:1-14*

Paul's description of enemies of truth *2 Tim 3:1-17*

See also aggression, attack

IRRITATION

Hagar sent away because of Sarah *Gen 21:9-21*

Saul annoyed by David's success *1 Sam 18:1-16*

David aroused by Nabal's surliness *1 Sam 25:2-42*

David's song, "Fret not thyself" *Psal 37:23-40*

Jesus excoriates three cities for disregarding his works *Mat 11:20-30*

Jesus admonishes Peter *Mat 16:21-28, Mark 8:31-38, Luke 9:20-27*

Disciples fail to heal epileptic boy *Mat 17:14-21, Mark 9:14-29, Luke 9:37-43*

Jesus casts out traders *Mat 21:12, 13, Mark 11:15-17, Luke 19:45, 46, John 2:13-25*

Jesus denounces scribes as hypocrites *Mat 23:1-39*

Jesus' parents rebuke him at twelve years of age *Luke 2:41-52*

Jesus' parable of unwilling friend *Luke 11:5-13*

Jesus' parable of prodigal's elder brother *Luke 15:25-32*

Jesus' parable of judge and widow *Luke 18:1-8*

See also anger, resentment

ISAAC (son of Abraham)

See Part II, Isaac

ISAIAH

See Part II, Isaiah

J

JACOB (son of Isaac)

See Part II, Jacob

JAMES

See Part II, James

JEALOUSY

Cain jealous of Abel's offering *Gen 4:1-16*

Joseph's brethren resent his father's love *Gen 37:1-36*

Miriam and Aaron speak against Moses *Num 12:1-16*

Moses describes God as jealous, Second Commandment *Exod 20: 1-4*

Saul envies David's success *1 Sam 18:1-16*

Saul pursues David *1 Sam 24:1-22, 26:1-25*

Elijah explains he was jealous for the Lord *1 King 19:9-13*

Ezekiel's vision of God's care of his flock *Ezek 34:1-31*

Pharisees accuse Jesus of healing by Beelzebub *Mat 12:22-30, Mark 3: 22-30, Luke 11:14-23*

Jesus' disciples contend who shall be greatest *Mat 18:1-11, Mark 9: 33-37, Luke 9:46-50, John 22:24-30*

Martha complains to Jesus about her sister *Luke 10:38-42*

Jesus' parable of prodigal's elder brother *Luke 15:25-32*

An idol silversmith contends with Paul *Acts 19:23-29*

John's vision of the dragon and the woman with child *Rev 12:1-17*

See also competition, covetousness, envy, fear, zealous

JEHOIACHIN (last of kings)

See Part II, Jehoiachin

JEHOSHAPHAT (one of the kings)

See Part II, Jehoshaphat

JEREMIAH

See Part II, Jeremiah

JEROBOAM (one of the kings)

See Part II, Jeroboam

JERUSALEM

King of Salem blesses Abraham *Gen 14:8-20, Heb 6:20, 7:1-28*

David made king of Judah *2 Sam 2:1-4*

Sennacherib invades city, repelled *2 King 18:17-37, 19:1-27, 2 Chron 31:20, 21, 32:1-23, Isa 36:1-22, 37: 1-38*

City falls to Babylon, people taken captive *2 King 25:8-12, 27-30*

Zerubbabel starts to rebuild temple *Ezra 3:8-13*

Nehemiah repairs wall *Neh 4:1-23*

Isaiah's vision of Jerusalem redeemed *Isa 52:1-15*

Isaiah on the blessed state of New Jerusalem *Isa 65:17-25*

Zephaniah's salvation promised to daughter of Zion *Zeph 3:14-17*

Jesus enters Jerusalem *Mat 21:1-11, 14-17, Mark 11:1-11, Luke 19: 29-44, John 12:12-19*

Jesus foretells destruction of Jerusalem *Mat 24:1-41, Mark 13:1-37, Luke 21:5-36*

Paul warned not to go to Jerusalem *Acts 21:8-15*

The city foursquare *Rev 21:1-27*

See also city, heaven, Zion

JESUS, JESUS CHRIST

See Part II, Jesus Christ: Parables, Great Works, Teachings

See also Christ, lamb, master, mediator, Messiah, Saviour, son, word

JOB

See Part II, Job

JOHN, THE APOSTLE (son of Zebedee)

See Part II, John the Apostle

JONAH

See Part II, Jonah

JORDAN

Lot chooses the plain of Jordan, but Abraham gets Canaan *Gen 13:1-18*

Joshua crosses Jordan into promised land *Josh 1:10-18, 3:1-17*

Elijah divides waters of Jordan *2 King 2:1-11*

Elisha divides waters on return *2 King 2:12-15*

Elisha prescribes dip in Jordan to Naaman *2 King 5:1-14*

Elisha makes axe head swim in Jordan *2 King 6:1-7*

Jesus baptized in Jordan *Mat 3:13-17, Mark 1:9-11, Luke 3:21, 22*

John's vision of river of life *Rev 22:1-21*

See also river

JOSEPH (son of Jacob)

See Part II, Joseph

JOSHUA (son of Nun)

See Part II, Joshua

JOSIAH (one of kings)

See Part II, Josiah

JOY

Abraham and Sarah joyful at the promise of a son *Gen 15:1-21*

Jacob and Esau meet in harmony *Gen 33:1-11*

Joseph's joy when he revealed himself *Gen 43:1, 2, 45:1-11*

The jubilee year *Gen 45:1-11, Lev 25:9-17*

Moses' song of deliverance *Deut 32:1-47*

Deborah's song of rejoicing *Judg 5:1-20*

David dances before the ark *2 Sam 6:12-23, 1 Chron 15:25-29*

David's song, "Make a joyful noise" *Psal 66:1-20, 100:1-5*

Jesus' parable of lost sheep *Mat 18:12-14, Luke 15:1-7*

Jesus welcomed with hosannas *Mat 21:1-16*

Jesus' parable of the talents *Mat 25:14-30, Luke 19:11-28*

Angels announce the birth of Jesus *Luke 2:8-20*

Jesus' 70 disciples return and report *Luke 10:17-24*

Jesus' parable of the piece of money *Luke 15:8-10*

Jesus' parable of the prodigal son *Luke 15:11-24*

Paul on rejoicing *Phil 4:1-23*

John's vision of joy felt when sealed book is opened *Rev 5:1-14*

See also delight, exaltation, gladness, happiness, rejoicing, sorrow, success

JUDGMENT

Judges delegated to help Moses *Exod 18:13-27*

Daughters of Zelophehad sue for inheritance *Num 27:1-11, 36:5-13*

Joshua uncovers Achan's sin *Josh 7:1-26, 8:14-21*

Samuel judges Saul unfit to rule *1 Sam 15:7-26*

Solomon requests understanding to judge *1 King 3:5-15, 2 Chron 1:7-12*

Solomon's wisdom as judge *1 King 3:16-28*

David's song, "The law of the Lord is perfect" *Psal 19:1-14*

Ezekiel's vision of the equity of God's dealing *Ezek 18:1-32*

Jesus' parable of mote and beam — "Judge not" *Mat 7:1-5, Luke 6:37-42*

Jesus denounces scribes and Pharisees *Mat 23:1-39*

Jesus' parable of sheep and goats *Mat 25:11-46*

Jesus condemned by priests and council *Mat 26:59-68, Mark 14:55-65, Luke 22:63-71, John 18:19-24*

Pilate examines Jesus *Mat 27:1, 2, 11-14, Mark 15:1-5, Luke 23:1-5, John 18:28-38*

Jesus on judge not others *Luke 6:37-40*

Jesus' parable of judge and widow *Luke 18:1-8*

Jesus saves woman taken in adultery *John 8:1-11*

Paul on the law and judgment *Rom 2:1-29*

Paul on the day when every man's work shall be revealed *1 Cor 3: 10-15*

James on equality of men *Jas 2:1-13*

John on faults of seven churches *Rev 1:4-29, 2:1-29, 3:1-22*

See also condemnation, day of the Lord, decisions, hell, law, morality, wisdom

JUSTICE

Adam and Eve punished *Gen 3:6-24*

Cain punished for Abel's death *Gen 4:1-16*

Moses appoints judges for the people *Exod 18:13-27*

Daughters of Zelophehad and rights of inheritance *Num 27:1-11, 36: 5-13*

David's lust for Bathsheba—their child dies *2 Sam 11:1-29, 12:13-23*

Solomon's wisdom proves which is the real mother *1 King 3:16-28*

Shunammite woman returns to claim property *2 King 8:1-6*

Uzziah's pride punished by leprosy *2 Chron 26:1-23*

Haman hanged on his own gallows *Esther 6:1-14, 7:1-10*

Job demands to know why the good suffer *Job 3:1-26*

God replies to Job (the infinite speaks to man) *Job 38:1-41*

David's song, "The law of the Lord is perfect" *Psal 19:1-14*

Isaiah's vision of divine justice *Isa 59:1-21*

Jeremiah on reward and punishment *Jer 24:1-10*

Ezekiel on equity of God's dealing on heredity *Ezek 18:1-32*

Amos calls for social justice *Amos 5:4-15*

Jonah's repentance accomplished *Jonah 1:1-17, 2:1-10, 3:1-10*

Malachi promises rewards for tithing *Mal 3:10, 4:1, 2*

Jesus' parable of laborers in vineyard *Mat 20:1-16*

Jesus' trial before Pilate *Mat 27: 1, 2, 11-24, Mark 15:1-5, Luke 23: 1-5, John 18:28-38*

Jesus' parable of elder brother who complains *Luke 15:25-32*

God is no respecter of persons *Jas 2:1-13*

See also day of the Lord, equality, honesty, law, punishment, reward, rights, vengeance

JUSTIFICATION

David pleads for mercy instead of justice *Psal 143:1-12*

Paul on justification by faith *Rom 3:1-31, Gal 2:14-21*

Paul on reconciliation by Christ *Rom 5:1-21*

Paul on justification not by the law *Gal 3:2-29*

Paul explains not through works, but by grace are ye saved *Eph 2:1-22*

James on faith and works *Jas 2: 13-26*

See also judgment, justice, mercy, reconciliation

JUVENILE

Cain murders Abel *Gen 4:1-16*

Jacob deceives his father to get blessing *Gen 27:1-44*

Joseph put in a pit by his brothers *Gen 37:1-36*

Samuel is called by the Lord *1 Sam 3:1-10*

Samuel selects David from sons of Jesse *1 Sam 16:1-13*

David kills Goliath with sling shot *1 Sam 17:38-52*

Jonathan befriends David *1 Sam 18:1-16*

Absalom rebels against his father *2 Sam 15:1-23, 18:6-33*

Daniel refuses king's meat and eats pulse *Dan 1:1-21*

Jesus heals Syrophenician's daughter *Mat 15:24-28, Mark 7:24-30*

Jesus heals epileptic boy *Mat 17: 14-21, Mark 9:14-29, Luke 9:37-43*

Jesus blesses little children *Mat 19:13-15, Mark 10:13-16, Luke 18: 15-17*

The rich young ruler who wanted eternal life *Mat 19:16-30, Mark 10:17-31, Luke 18:18-30*

Jesus' parable of two sons ordered to work *Mat 21:28-32*

Jesus' parable of wise and foolish virgins *Mat 25:1-13*

Jesus at twelve years talks with rabbis *Luke 2:41-52*

Jesus' parable of the prodigal son *Luke 15:11-24*

Jesus' parable of the elder brother *Luke 15:25-32*

Jesus heals nobleman's son *John 4:46-54*

Paul heals Eutychus of fall from window *Acts 20:7-12*

See also children, delinquency

K

KEEPER

Cain asks, "Am I my brother's keeper?" *Gen 4:1-16*

Jacob promised God's ever-presence *Gen 28:10-22*

God sets apart the chosen people as his own *Deut 7:6-11*

"The Lord is thy keeper" *Psal 121: 1-8*

Ezekiel's vision of God's care over his flock *Ezek 34:1-31*

Hosea's vision of God's care of his child *Hos 11:1-4*

Jesus' parable of the lost sheep *Mat 18:12-14, Luke 15:1-7*

Jesus' parable of the good shepherd *John 10:1-18*

Peter is led out of prison past the keepers *Acts 12:1-17*

Paul and Silas convert keeper of prison *Acts 16:19-40*

See also care, guard, sheep, watch

KEY

God's spiritual creation as the key to Scriptures *Gen 1:26, 27*

Elisha asks for a double portion of

Elijah's spirit and receives his mantle *2 King 2:1-15*

Jesus explains ease of healing both sin and sickness *Mat 9:2-8, Mark 2:1-12, Luke 5:17-26*

Pharisees demand a sign of Jesus *Mat 12:39-45, Luke 11:16, 29-32*

Jesus explains his parable of the sower *Mat 13:3-23, Mark 4:1-20, Luke 8:4-15*

Jesus explains his parable of wheat and tares *Mat 13:24-30, 36-43*

Jesus explains why he speaks in parables *Mat 13:10-17, 34, 35, Mark 4:10-12, 33, 34*

Peter acknowledges Jesus as Christ and receives keys to kingdom *Mat 16:13-20, Mark 8:27-30, Luke 9: 18-21*

Jesus explains why disciples failed to heal epileptic boy *Mat 17:14-21, Mark 9:14-29, Luke 9:37-43*

Jesus tells young ruler key to eternal life *Mat 19:16-30, Mark 10: 17-31, Luke 18:18-30*

The Lamb has key to open the sealed book *Rev 5:1-14*

The angel with the little book *Rev 10:1-11*

See also authority, seal, secret

KILL

Cain murders Abel *Gen 4:1-16*

Sacrifice of scapegoat by Aaron *Lev 16:1-28*

Joshua uncovers sin and executes Achan *Josh 7:1-26, 8:14-21*

Samson's betrayal and death *Judg 16:4-30*

David kills Goliath with single shot from sling *1 Sam 17:38-52*

Saul kills himself *1 Sam 31:1-13, 1 Chron 10:1-24*

David has Uriah killed to possess his wife *2 Sam 1:1-27*

Nathan's parable of this action by David *2 Sam 12:1-10*

Elijah and 450 prophets of Baal *1 King 18:17-40*

Haman hanged on his own gallows *Esther 6:1-14, 7:1-10*

Jesus crucified *Mat 27:32-56, Mark 15:21-41, Luke 23:26-49, John 19: 17-30*

Stephen stoned as martyr *Acts 7: 51-60*

Paul stoned but resurrected *Acts 14:19, 20*

See also cross, death, life, stone

KINDNESS

Abraham gives Lot first choice of land *Gen 13:1-18*

Joseph helps his brothers who come to Egypt for food *Gen 42:1-8*

Ruth and Naomi help each other *Ruth 1:1-22, 2:1-23*

Jonathan befriends David *1 Sam 18:1-16*

David shows kindness to Jonathan's son *2 Sam 9:1-13*

Shunammite makes room in her house for Elisha *2 King 4:8-37*

Jesus on benevolence in secret *Mat 6:1-4*

Jesus on Golden Rule *Mat 7:12-14, Luke 6:41, 42*

Jesus heals the kindly centurion's servant *Mat 8:5-13, Luke 7:1-10*

Elizabeth shows kindness to Mary *Luke 1:39-56*

Jesus' parable of good Samaritan *Luke 10:25-37*

Jesus' parable of good shepherd *John 10:1-18*

Jesus washes disciples' feet *John 13:1-20*

Jesus on comfort in tribulations *John 16:1-33*

Peter raises Tabitha, the woman of good deeds *Acts 9:36-43*

John's sermon, God is Love *1 John 4:1-21*

See also affection, compassion, friendship, gentleness, goodness, grace, mercy

KING

Abraham and the war of kings *Gen 14:8-20, Heb 6:20, 7:1-28*

Gideon refuses to be king *Judg 8:22, 23*

Parable of trees by Gideon's son, Jothan *Judg 9:1-15*

Samuel resists people's demand for a king *1 Sam 8:1-22*

Samuel anoints Saul, first king *1 Sam 10:1-8*

David, king of Judah, then Israel *2 Sam 2:1-4, 5:1-5*

Solomon visited by Queen of Sheba *1 King 10:1-12, 2 Chron 9:1-12*

Isaiah heals sick king of boil *2 King 20:1-11, Isa 38:1-22*

Wise men visit King of the Jews *Mat 2:1-12*

Jesus on the son of man as Lord of the sabbath *Mat 12:1-8, Mark 2:23-28, Luke 6:1-5*

Jesus' parable of the king's wedding feast *Mat 22:1-14*

Jesus parable of sheep and goats *Mat 25:31-46*

Pilate asks Jesus, Art thou a king? *John 18:28-38*

Jesus as king of kings *Rev 19:11-21*

See also authority, Christ, crown, heredity, Melchizedek, rule

KINGDOM OF HEAVEN
(kingdom of God)

Abraham seeks the promised land *Gen 11:31 32, 12-19*

Elijah translated *2 King 2:1-11*

Isaiah's vision of the Messiah's peaceful kingdom *Isa 11:1-12*

Jesus on true treasures *Mat 6:19-21*

Jesus' parable of wheat and tares *Mat 13:24-30, 36-43*

Jesus' parable of mustard seed *Mat 13:31, 32, Mark 4:30-32, Luke 13: 18, 19*

Jesus' parable of leaven *Mat 13:33, Luke 13:20, 21*

Jesus' parable of treasure *Mat 13:44*

Jesus' parable of pearl of great price *Mat 13:45, 46*

Jesus' parable of dragnet *Mat 13: 47-50*

Jesus' parable of householder *Mat 13:51, 52*

Jesus' parable of the marriage feast *Mat 22:1-14*

Jesus' parable of seed, blade, ear *Mark 4:26-29*

Jesus ascends *Mark 16:19, 20, Luke 24:50-53, Acts 1:9-13*

Jesus' parable of those bidden to supper *Luke 14:15-24*

Paul on Jesus' resurrection proves ours *1 Cor 15:1-58*

John's vision of new heaven *Rev 21:1-27*

See also heaven, king

KINSMAN

Abraham rescues his nephew *Gen 14:8-20, Heb 6:20, 7:1-28*

Daughters of Zelophehad sue for inheritance *Num 27:1-11*

Naomi and Boaz *Ruth 2:1-22*

Mordecai adopts his niece *Eseher 2:5-23*

Jesus heals Peter's wife's mother *Mat 8:14-17, Mark 1:29-34*

Jesus baptized by cousin, John *Mat 3:13-17, Mark 1:9-11, Luke 3:21, 22*

See also blood, brotherhood, family, marriage

KNOWING

God creates spiritual universe by "let there be" *Gen 1:1-31*

Enoch "walked wth God" and was translated *Gen 5:18, 21-24, Heb 11:5*

Moses transforms rod and leprosy mentally *Exod 4:1-9*

Jericho crumbles without physical contact *Josh 6:1-29*

Elijah raises widow's son *1 King 17:17-24*

Elijah prays for rain *1 King 18:41-46*

Elijah sees nature of God *1 King 19:9-13*

Jesus is transfigured, talks with Moses and Elias *Mat 17:1-13, Mark 9:2-13, Luke 9:28-36*

Jews delivered from fiery furnace *Dan 3:1-30*

Daniel delivered from lions' den *Dan 6:1-28*

Jesus heals centurion's servant who is absent *Mat 8:5-13, Luke 7:1-10*

Jesus heals woman's daughter who is absent *Mat 15:21-28, Mark 7:24-30*

Jesus' parable of wise and foolish virgins *Mat 25:1-13*

Jesus' resurrection *Mat 28:1-8, Mark 16:1-8, Luke 24:1-12, John 20:1-10*

Jesus heals nobleman's son who is absent *John 4:46-54*

See also prayer, understanding, wisdom

KNOWLEDGE

God sees universe He created; it is good *Gen 1:1-31*

Adam and Eve eat fruit of tree of knowledge of good and evil *Gen 3:6-24*

People build tower of Babel *Gen 11:1-9*

Aaron's rod swallows up rods of Egyptian sorcerers *Exod 7:1-12*

Solomon's dream shows a sense of values *1 King 3:5-15, 2 Chron 1:7-12*

Solomon's wisdom acknowledged *1 King 10:1-12, 2 Chron 9:1-12*

Elisha prophesies drop in price of flour *2 King 6:24, 25, 7:1-18*

Book of the law is read to the people *Neh 8:1-12*

The excellency of wisdom *Prov 3:13-26, 4:1-13, 8:1-36*

The vanity of human things *Eccl 1:1-18, 2:1-26*

All mortal events within the framework of time *Eccl 3:1-15*

Daniel interprets the king's dream *Dan 2:1-49*

Why Jesus speaks only in parables *Mat 13:10-17, 34, 35, Mark 9:10-12, 33, 34*

Jesus' parable of wise and foolish virgins *Mat 25:1-13*

At twelve Jesus astonishes the rabbis *Luke 2:41-52*

Philip explains scripture to Ethiopian *Acts 8:26-40*

The sealed book is opened *Rev 5:1-14*

The angel with a book *Rev 10:1-11*

See also ignorance, intelligence, omniscience, science, senses, understanding, wisdom, world

L

LABOR

Noah builds the ark   *Gen 6:5-22*
The people build the tower of Babel
   Gen 11:1-9
Children of Israel enslaved   *Exod
   1:8-14*
Children of Israel make bricks with-
   out straw   *Exod 5:7-19*
Ruth gleans in fields after reapers
   Ruth 2:1-23
Solomon builds temple   *1 King 6:
   1-38, 7:1-51, 2 Chron 3:1-17, 4:1-
   22, 5:1-4*
Elijah finds Elisha plowing   *1 King
   19:19-21*
Zerubbabel starts rebuilding temple
   Ezra 3:8-13
Nehemiah rebuilds wall of Jerusalem
   Neh 4:1-23
The work of a virtuous woman
   Prov 31:1-31
Jesus' parable of houses built on
   rock and sand   *Mat 7:24-27, Luke
   6:48, 49*
Jesus' parable of laborers in the
   vineyard   *Mat 20:1-16*
Jesus' parable of two sons ordered
   to work   *Mat 21:28-32*
Jesus fills Peter's net after fruit-
   less fishing   *Luke 5:1-11*
Jesus outlines the work of a dis-
   ciple   *Luke 10:1-16*
Jesus' parable of rich man and big-
   ger barns   *Luke 12:15-21*
Jesus' parable of faithful steward
   Luke 12:41-48
Jesus' parable of counting the cost
   of building   *Luke 14:25-33*
Jesus' parable of the servant who
   serves before he eats   *Luke 17:
   7-10*
Jesus washes his disciples' feet
   John 13:1-20
Peter's net filled again after fish-
   ing all night   *John 21:1-11*
Seven deacons chosen to divide
   labor in church   *Acts 6:1-4*
Tabitha's good works   *Acts 9:36-43*
Paul lists his labors to establish
   church   *2 Cor 11:21-33*

James tells how to bear our cross
   Jas 1:1-27

See also activity, building, business,
employment, fatigue, wealth, work

LACK

Hagar and her son perishing in the
   wilderness   *Gen 21:9-21*
Esau sells birthright for pottage
   Gen 25:24-34
Joseph's brethren come to Egypt
   for food   *Gen 42:1-8*
Moses obtains manna and quail
   Exod 16:1-36, Num 11:1-15, 31, 32
Elijah fed by ravens, then by widow
   1 King 17:1-16
Elisha and widow's pot of oil
   2 King 4:1-7
Elisha feeds 100 men with a few
   loaves   *2 King 4:42-44*
Elisha prophesies end of famine
   2 King 6:24, 25, 7:1-18
David's song, "I shall not want"
   Psal 23:1-6
David's song "the fountain of life"
   Psal 36:1-12
Isaiah sees the desert in blossom
   Isa 35:1-10
Ezekiel's vision of God's care   *Ezek
   34:1-31*
Zechariah's vision of candlestick
   fed by two olive trees   *Zech 4:1-14*
Malachi urges tithing, a cure for
   lack   *Mal 3:10, 4:1, 2*
Jesus feeds 5000   *Mat 14:15-21, Mark
   6:35-44, Luke 9:12-17, John 6:5-14*
Jesus feeds 4000   *Mat 15:32-39
   Mark 8:1-10*
Jesus gets tribute money from fish
   Mat 17:24-27
Jesus withers the fig tree without
   fruit   *Mat 21:18-22, Mark 11:12-14,
   20-24*
Jesus approves the widow who casts
   in her mite   *Mark 12:41-44, Luke
   21:1-4*
Peter's net filled twice   *Luke 5:1-11,
   John 21:1-11*
Jesus' parable of prodigal son turn-
   ing back to his father   *Luke 15:
   11-24*
Jesus questions disciples about lack
   Luke 22:35-38

Jesus turns water to wine *John 2:1-11*

Jesus on the bread of life *John 6:26-65*

See also abundance, need, poverty, supply

LAMB

Moses instructs ritual of Passover lamb *Exod 12:1-14, 21-41*

Nathan's parable of the one ewe lamb *2 Sam 12:1-10*

David's song, "The Lord is my shepherd" *Psal 23:1-6*

Isaiah's description of the Messiah *Isa 53:1-12*

Ezekiel sees God's care over his flock *Ezek 34:1-31*

Jesus' parable of the lost sheep *Mat 18:12-14, Luke 15:1-7*

Jesus crucified *Mat 27:32-56, Mark 15:21-41, Luke 23:26-49, John 19: 17-30*

Jesus' parable of the good shepherd *John 10:1-18*

Jesus on Christ, the door of the sheepfold *John 10:1-30*

The Lamb found able to open the sealed book *Rev 5:1-14*

See also atonement, Easter, gentleness, Jesus, Passover, sacrifice, sheep

LAMENESS

David shows kindness to lame son of Jonathan *2 Sam 9:1-13*

Asa, diseased in his feet; physicians unable to help him *2 Chron 16: 11-14*

Group healings of lameness by Jesus *Mat 4:23-25, Mark 15:29-31, Luke 4:40-44*

Impotent man at pool healed by Jesus *John 5:1-16*

Peter and John heal lame man at temple *Acts 3:1-26*

Philip heals the lame *Acts 8:5-8*

Paul heals lame man at Lystra *Acts 14:8-10*

See also bones, cripple, paralysis

LAMENTATION

See grief, mourning, sorrow

LAND

God creates it *Gen 1:9-13*

Land appears to Noah after flood *Gen 9:1-17*

Abraham searches for promised land *Gen 11:31, 32, 12:1-9*

Abraham and Lot divide the land *Gen 13:1-18*

Joshua leads people across Jordan into promised land *Josh 3:1-17*

Isaiah's vision of the desert in blossom *Isa 35:1-10*

Jesus' parable of builders on rock or sand *Mat 7:24-27, Luke 6:48, 49*

Jesus' parable of the sower *Mat 13: 3-23, Mark 4:1-20, Luke 8:4-15*

Jesus' parable of treasure buried in field *Mat 13:44*

Jesus' parable of laborers in vineyard *Mat 20:1-16*

John's vision of angel with one foot on land *Rev 10:1-11*

See also earth, property

LANGUAGE

The motive for building the tower of Babel confounds the one language *Gen 11:1-9*

Moses complains of his speaking ability *Exod 4:10-17*

Moses talks with God on the mount *Exod 19:1-9, 33:7-23, Deut 4:10-13*

Elijah hears God as a still small voice *1 King 19:9-13*

Job hears the voice of the infinite speak *Job 38:1-41*

Jesus asks whether it is easier to say "Thy sins be forgiven thee" or to say "Arise and walk" *Mat 9: 2-8, Mark 2:1-12, Luke 5:17-26*

Jesus tells why he speaks only in parables *Mat 13:10-17, 34, 35, Mark 4:10-12, 33, 34*

John the Baptist tells how his preaching differs from Jesus' *John 3:22-36*

Pentecost, the opposite of the tower of Babel *Acts 2:1-13*

Philip explains the meaning of Isaiah to the Ethiopian *Acts 8: 26-40*

See also confusion, expression, Pentecost, speech, tongue, word

LAST SUPPER

Moses institutes the Passover supper *Exod 12:1-14, 21-41*
Jesus sends disciples to prepare supper *Mat 26:17-19, Mark 14: 12-16, Luke 22:7-13*
Jesus announces at supper that he will be betrayed *Mat 26:20-25, Mark 14:17-21, Luke 22:21, 22, John 13:21-35*
When eating Jesus gives them bread and wine *Mat 26:26-29, Mark 14: 22-25, Luke 22:14-30*
Then Peter vows never to deny Jesus *Mat 26:31-35, Mark 14:27-31, Luke 22:31-34, John 13:36-38*
Jesus has last spiritual breakfast with disciples *Mat 28:16-18, John 21:1-14*
Jesus reminds them of miracles of supply *Luke 22:35-38*
Jesus speaks on the bread of life *John 6:26-65*
After eating, Jesus washes disciples' feet *John 13:1-20*
Paul on Last Supper *1 Cor 11:23-29*
Paul on the true sacrifice that remits sin *Heb 10:1-39*

See also atonement, bread, communion, wine

LAYING ON OF HANDS

Isaac blesses the second son *Gen 27:1-44*
Aaron and sons consecrated *Lev 8:1-13*
Samuel anoints Saul (a mistake) *1 Sam 10:1-8*
Samuel selects David *1 Sam 16:1-13*
Jesus puts hand on leper and heals him *Mat 8:1-4, Mark 1:29-34*
Jesus blesses little children *Mat 19: 13-15, Mark 10:13-16, Luke 18: 15-17*
Jesus puts finger in deaf ears and heals *Mark 7:32-37*

Jesus puts hand on bier and raises dead *Luke 7:11-17*
Jesus lays hand on woman bowed together *Luke 13:11-17*
Jesus touches Malchus' severed ear *Luke 22:50, 51*
Jesus anoints eyes of blind *John 9:1-41*
Peter grasps hand of lame man *Acts 3:1-11*
Simon offers Peter money for the power to lay on hands *Acts 8:14-25*
Peter raises Tabitha from death, then gives her his hand (to help her up) *Acts 9:36-43*

See also authority, benediction, consecration, dedication, devotion, power

LAW

Jehovah forbids the tree of knowledge of good and evil *Gen 3:1-5*
Moses appoints judges to give justice to the people *Exod 18:13-27*
Moses receives Ten Commandments *Exod 20:1-19, Deut 5:1-24*
God's warnings against enticers, necromancy *Deut 13:1-18*
Abominations forbidden *Deut 18: 9-14*
The blessings of obedience *Deut 28:1-14*
Moses offers choice of life or death *Deut 30:11-20*
Book of the law read to the people *Neh 8:1-12*
David's song, "The law of the Lord is perfect" *Psal 19:1-14*
Daniel trapped by law of Medes and Persians *Dan 6:1-28*
Jesus puts Mosaic commands on mental basis *Mat 5:21-32, 9:38-50*
Expansion of Third Commandment *Mat 5:33-37*
Jesus' Golden Rule for actions *Mat 7:12-14, Luke 6:41, 42*
Jesus on breaking the sabbath *Mat 12:1-8*
A young ruler asks how he can inherit eternal life *Mat 19:16-30, Mark 10:17-21, Luke 18:18-30*
Jesus is asked which is the great commandment *Mat 22:34-40, Mark 12:28-34*

A lawyer asks how he can inherit eternal life   *Luke 10:25-29*

Jesus' parable of the judge and the widow   *Luke 18:1-8*

Peter and John tried before the council   *Acts 4:1-23*

Paul on judgment and law   *Rom 2:1-29*

See also authority, book, commandment, covenant

LEADER

Moses' reluctance to lead overcome   *Exod 3:9-12*

The pillar of cloud by day, fire by night   *Exod 13:20-22, Num 9:15-23*

Moses' hands upheld during battle   *Exod 17:8-16*

Veil conceals Moses' face   *Exod 34:29-35*

A prophet (Messiah) is promised   *Deut 18:15-22*

Moses transfers leadership to Joshua   *Deut 31:7-23, Josh 1:1-9*

Deborah takes over leadership   *Judg 4:1-17*

Samuel resists people's demand for a king   *1 Sam 8:1-22*

Samuel anoints Saul as king   *1 Sam 10:1-27*

Saul unfit to be king, Samuel anoints David   *1 Sam 16:1-13*

David accepts Goliath's challenge   *1 Sam 17:17-37*

Solomon's request for understanding   *1 King 3:5-13, 2 Chron 1:7-12*

David's song, "The Lord is my shepherd"   *Psal 23:1-6*

A poor wise man saves the city   *Eccl 9:13-18*

Birth of Messiah promised   *Isa 7:10-16, 9:2-7*

Description of Messiah   *Isa 53:1-12*

Zechariah's vision of two olive trees   *Zech 4:1-14*

Jesus followed by great multitudes   *Mat 12:14-21, Mark 3:6-11*

Jesus says a prophet is without honor in his own country   *Mat 13:53-58, Mark 6:1-6, Luke 4:22-24, John 4:43-45*

Jesus approves Peter's acknowledgment   *Mat 16:13-20, Mark 8:27-30, Luke 9:18-21*

Jesus talks with Moses and Elijah   *Mat 17:1-13, Mark 9:2-13, Luke 9:28-36*

The disciples contend who shall be greatest   *Mat 18:1-11, Mark 9:33-37, Luke 9:46-50*

All men seek Jesus, increasing his fame   *Mark 1:35-39*

People follow Jesus like sheep   *Mark 6:30-34*

After sermon on bread of life many followers leave Jesus   *John 6:66-71*

Jesus is the Christ   *John 7:14-40*

Jesus says he is the light of the world   *John 8:12-32*

Jesus' parable of the good shepherd   *John 10:1-18*

Jesus promises the Holy Ghost   *John 14:1-31*

Jesus' parable of the true vine   *John 15:1-17*

Jesus urges Peter, "Feed my sheep"   *John 20:12-19*

Disciples elect a bishop   *Acts 1:15-26*

The cost to Paul to establish church   *2 Cor 11:21-33*

Paul on why we are obedient to the Christ   *Heb 2:1-18*

John's vision of woman and dragon   *Rev 12:1-17*

See also authority, guidance, sheep

LEAGUE

Asa's league with Syrians against Israel   *1 King 15:9-24, 2 Chron 14:1-7*

Jesus denounces the scribes and Pharisees   *Mat 23:1-39*

The rulers conspire against Jesus   *Mat 26:1-5, Mark 14:1, 2*

The earth helps the woman against the dragon   *Rev 12:1-17*

See also agreement, association, cooperation, covenant, nation

LEAVEN

The serpent speaks the leaven of evil to Eve   *Gen 3:1-5*

Elijah tells widow to bake him a cake first   *1 King 17:8-16*

Jesus' parable of the leaven *Mat 13:33, Luke 13:20, 21*

Jesus urges to beware of leaven of Pharisees and Sadducees *Mat 16: 1-12, Mark 8:14, 15*

Jesus' fame increasing; all men seek him *Mark 1:35-39*

Jesus on the bread of life *John 6: 26-65*

Peter's signs and wonders cause church growth *Acts 4:24-37*

Gamaliel urges council to let Christianity alone *Acts 5:29-42*

Paul on a little leaven *1 Cor 5:1-13*

Paul's teaching, "put on the new man" *Col 3:1-17*

See also bread, corruption, influence, transformation, truth

LEGACY

See heredity, property

LEPROSY (skin disease)

Moses' leprosy healed *Exod 4:1-9*

Miriam healed by Moses *Num 12: 1-16*

Naaman healed by Elisha *2 King 5:1-14*

Jesus heals a leper *Mat 8:1-4, Mark 1:40-45*

Ten men healed *Luke 17:11-19*

See also purity, self-righteousness, sin

LIBERTY

Moses releases Israelites from bondage *Exod 11:4-10, 12:1-14, 29-41, Deut 16:1-22*

Moses' song of deliverance *Deut 32:1-47*

Gideon frees his people *Judg 6:10-40, 7:1-25*

Gideon refuses to be king *Judg 8: 22, 23*

Samuel resists demand for a king *1 Sam 8:1-22*

David's song, "how are the mighty fallen!" *2 Sam 1:17-27*

Elisha besieged by Syrians *2 King 6:8-23*

Hezekiah sees divine deliverance *2 King 18:17-37, 19:1-27, 2 Chron 31:20, 21, 32:1-23, Isa 36:1-22, 37: 1-38*

Nehemiah rebuilds walls of Jerusalem *Neh 4:1-23*

Mordecai and Jews released by Esther *Esther 8:1-8*

All is restored to Job *Job 42:1-11*

Restoration of Israel promised *Jer 31:1-14, 31-34*

Three Jews released from fiery furnace *Dan 3:1-30*

Daniel lifted out of lions' den *Dan 6:1-28*

Jonah's repentance brings liberty *Jonah 3:1-10*

Jesus' charge to preach and heal *Mat 10:5-42, Mark 6:7-13, Luke 9: 1-6, 10:1-16*

Jesus teaches effective prayer *Mat 17:14-21, Mark 11:22-26, Luke 11: 1-13*

Jesus saves woman taken in adultery *John 8:1-11*

Jesus says he is light of world and truth will make free *John 8: 12-32*

Peter and John freed from prison *Acts 4:24-37*

Peter released from prison by angel *Acts 5:17-42, 12:1-17*

Paul delivered from Jews *Acts 9: 23-31*

Paul and Silas freed by earthquake *Acts 16:19-40*

See also deliverance, democracy, freedom, independence, politics, slavery

LIE

Serpent deceives Eve in first lie *Gen 3:1-5*

Jacob deceives his father Isaac *Gen 27:1-44*

Potiphar's wife lies to put Joseph in prison *Gen 39:1-20*

Jesus denounces scribes and Pharisees as hypocrites *Mat 23:1-39*

Judas kisses Jesus to betray him *Mat 26:47-56, Mark 14:43-54, Luke 22:47-53, John 18:1-12*

Jesus says father of Pharisees is a liar *John 8:33-59*

Paul describes non-Christians as enemies of the truth *2 Tim 3:1-17*

Serpent in Genesis becomes dragon in Apocalypse   *Rev 12:1-17*

See also deceit, devils, duplicity, morality, truth

LIFE

God creates man in His image   *Gen 1:26, 27*

Lord God creates man "a living soul" from dust   *Gen 2:6-8*

Moses offers choice: life and good vs. death and evil   *Deut 30:11-20*

Instances of miraculous birth:
Isaac   *Gen 15:1-21, 21:1-8*
Samson   *Judg 13:1-25*
Samuel   *1 Sam 1:1-28*
Shunammite's son   *2 King 4:8-37*
Jesus   *Luke 1:26-38*

Instances of translation over death:
Enoch   *Gen 5:18, 21-24, Heb 11:5*
Elijah   *2 King 2:1-11*
Jesus   *Mark 6:19, 20, Luke 24:50-53, Acts 1:6-12*

David's song, "The fountain of life"   *Psal 36:1-12*

David's song on the safety of the godly   *Psal 91:1-16*

Jeremiah's vision of the potter and his clay   *Jer 18:1-6*

Instances of resurrection:
Army from dry bones   *Ezek 37:1-14*
Jairus' daughter   *Mat 9:18, 19, 23-26, Mark 5:22-24, 35-43, Luke 8: 41, 42, 49-56*
Jesus raises himself   *Mat 28:1-8, Mark 16:1-8, Luke 24:1-12, John 20:1-10*
Son of widow of Nain   *Luke 7:11-17*
Lazarus after four days   *John 11:1-46*
Tabitha by Peter   *Acts 9:36-43*
Paul after stoning   *Acts 14:19, 20*
Eutychus   *Acts 20:7-12*

Jesus foretells his own death and resurrection   *Mat 17:22, 23, 20:17-19, Mark 9:30-32, 10:32-34, Luke 9:43-45, 18:31-34, 19:47, 48*

A young ruler asks about eternal life   *Mat 19:16-30, Mark 10:17-31, Luke 18:18-30*

A lawyer asks about eternal life   *Luke 10:25-28*

Jesus' parable of the rich man and his barns   *Luke 12:15-21*

Jesus' parable of rich man and the beggar   *Luke 16:19-31*

Jesus on taking no thought for material life   *Luke 12:22-34*

Jesus' sermon "I am the bread of life   *John 6:26-65*

Jesus on oneness with the Father   *John 10:22-42*

Paul on creator   *Rom 1:17-25*

Paul on the spirit as life   *Rom 8:1-39*

Paul on Christ's resurrection proves ours   *1 Cor 15:1-58*

Paul on the letter versus the spirit   *2 Cor 3:4-18*

John's vision of Jesus dead but alive forevermore   *Rev 1:12-18*

John's vision of river and tree of life   *Rev 22:1-21*

See also blood, bread, breath, Easter, growth, I Am, manna, mortal, organic, soul, translation

LIGHT

God creates light   *Gen 1:1-5*

Joseph enlightens meaning of dreams   *Gen 39:21-23, 40:1-23, 41:1-46*

Moses at burning bush   *Exod 3:1-18*

Moses guided by pillar of fire   *Exod 13:20-22, Num 9:15-23*

Joshua sees sun and moon stand still   *Josh 10:6-15*

Gideon breaks pitchers and shows lighted lamps   *Judg 7:1-25*

David's song, "The Lord is my light"   *Psal 27:1-4*

Isaiah's "Arise, shine"   *Isa 60:1-5*

Daniel interprets king's dream   *Dan 2:1-49*

Zechariah's vision of candlestick   *Zech 4:1-14*

Jesus on letting your light shine   *Mat 5:13-16, Luke 8:16-18*

Jesus' parable of ten virgins   *Mat 25:1-13*

Signs at crucifixion   *Mat 27:50-53*

Jesus Christ as the light of the world   *John 1:1-14, 8:12-32*

Paul blinded by great light   *Acts 9:1-9, 22:1-30, 26:1-32*

The children of light *Eph 5:8-14*
See also darkness, vision

LIKENESS

God makes man in his likeness *Gen 1:26, 27*
Jacob sees his brother's face as face of God *Gen 33:1-11*
God talks with Moses face to face *Exod 33:7-23*
Veil conceals Moses' face *Exod 34: 29-35*
Isaiah's vision, "Arise, shine" *Isa 60:1-5*
Daniel's meeting with Gabriel *Dan 9:20-23, 10:4-21*
Peter acknowledges Jesus as Christ *Mat 16:13-20, Mark 8:27-30, Luke 9:18-21*
Jesus sees something in Zacchaeus *Luke 19:1-10*
Two disciples at Emmaus fail to recognize Jesus after resurrection *Luke 24:13-35*
Jesus' discourse to Nicodemus on man must be born again *John 3:1-21*
Jesus' teaching that he is Christ *John 7:14-40*
Jesus raises Lazarus after four days *John 11:1-46*
Paul on Jesus, the example *Heb 12:1-29*

See also image, reflection

LISTENING

Eve listens to the serpent not God *Gen 3:1-5*
Noah listens to God and is safe *Gen 6:5-22*
Abraham called by God to promised land *Gen 11:31, 32, 12:1-9*
Abraham listens to angel as he prepares to sacrifice his son *Gen 22:1-19*
God overcomes Moses' reluctance to lead *Exod 3:9-12*
God talks with Moses face to face *Exod 33:7-23*
Moses urges obedience to God *Deut 4:1-15, 11:1-32*
Joshua urges obedience to God *Josh 23:1-16*

Listening to David's harp calms Saul *1 Sam 16:14-23*
Elijah on mount listens for God's voice *1 King 19:9-13*
Naaman refuses to listen to Elisha at first *2 King 5:1-14*
Nehemiah refuses to listen to his enemies *Neh 6:1-19*
The infinite speaks to Job *Job 38:1-41*
David's song, "Be still, and know" *Psal 46:1-11*
Isaiah's vision of a voice behind thee *Isa 29:11-24, 30:1-3, 20, 21*
Why Jesus speaks only in parables *Mat 13:10-17, 34, 35, Mark 4:10-12, 33, 34*
Jesus on a prophet without honor *Mat 13:53-58, Mark 6:1-6, Luke 4:22-24, John 4:43-45*
Jesus' parable of two sons ordered to work *Mat 21:28-32*
Jesus heals deaf man with speech impediment *Mark 7:32-37*
At twelve years rabbis listen to Jesus *Luke 2:41-52*
Jesus' parable of unwilling friend *Luke 11:5-13*
Jesus' parable of those bidden to great supper *Luke 14:15-24*
Jesus' parable of the judge and the widow *Luke 18:1-8*
Jesus' parable of good shepherd and sheep who know his voice *John 10:1-18*
John's vision of what the Spirit saith to the churches *Rev 1:4-20, 2:1-25, 3:1-22*

See also deafness, ear, hearing, obedience

LOCK

Adam and Eve shut out of Eden *Gen 3:6-24*
Jesus' parable of servants awaiting Lord *Mat 24:42-51*
Jesus' parable of wise and foolish virgins *Mat 25:1-13*
Jesus' parable of the door shut by the master *Luke 13:22-30*
Paul and Silas locked in inner prison *Acts 16:19-40*
John's vision of the Lamb able to unlock the book *Rev 5:1-14*

See also door, key, seal, secret

LOGIC

God finished the universe and called it good *Gen 1:31, 2:1-5*

Adam from dust, Eve from rib, Cain from womb *Gen 2:6-8, 21-25, 4: 1, 2*

Abraham is 99 but God promises him a son *Gen 15:1-21*

Moses, burdened by judging, delegates authority *Exod 18:13-27*

Moses tells people they must choose life or death, good or evil *Deut 30:11-20, Josh 24:1-25*

Failing to take city, Joshua searches for sin in ranks *Josh 7:1-26, 8: 14-21*

Gideon's faith is built by signs from God *Judg 6:19-40*

David tries Saul's armor but returns to his sling *1 Sam 17:17-37*

Shunammite insists "it is well" until her son is healed *2 King 4:8-37*

Naaman says the rivers of his own land can wash him clean *2 King 5:1-14*

The study of wisdom *Prov 3:13-26, 4:1-13, 8:1-36*

Mortal events all within time *Eccl 3:1-15*

Sins of the fathers are not visited on their children *Ezek 18:1-32*

Daniel persuades his tutor to let him eat pure food *Dan 1:1-21*

Three Jews that are faithful rely on God to save them even from fiery furnace *Dan 3:1-30*

Daniel too is faithful and is saved from lions *Dan 5:1-31*

Story of Jonah's disobedience and reform *Jonah 1:1-17, 2:1-10, 3: 1-10*

Malachi promises rewards for tithing *Mal 3:10, 4:1, 2*

Jesus' parable of builder on rock and sand *Mat 7:24-27, Luke 6: 48, 49*

Jesus explains why he eats with sinners *Mat 9:10-13, Mark 2:13-17, Luke 5:27-32*

Jesus is accused of casting out devils by Beelzebub *Mat 12:22-30, Mark 3:22-30, Luke 11:14-23*

He explains why he speaks only in parables *Mat 13:10-17, 34, 35, Mark 4:10-12, 33, 34*

Jesus' parable of the wheat and tares *Mat 13:24-30, 36-43*

Jesus' parable of pearl of great price *Mat 13:45-46*

Jesus asks Peter why he doubted *Mat 14:22-33, John 6:15-21*

Jesus convinced by Syrophenician woman *Mat 15:21-28, Mark 7: 24-30*

Jesus' parable of unmerciful debtor *Mat 18:23-25*

He explains eternal life to lawyer and young ruler *Mat 19:16-30, Mark 10:17-31, Luke 10:2-28, 18: 18-30*

Jesus' parable of laborers in vineyard *Mat 20:1-16*

Jesus asks whether sin is easier to heal than sickness *Mark 2:1-12, Luke 5:17-26*

Jesus' parable of seed, blade, ear *Mark 4:26-29*

At twelve years Jesus is listened to by rabbis *Luke 2:41-52*

Jesus' parable on new wine in old bottles *Luke 5:36-39*

Jesus' parable on the mote and the beam *Luke 6:37-42*

Jesus' parable of two debtors *Luke 7:36-50*

Jesus explains why a house divided can't stand *Luke 11:14-36*

Jesus explains why he heals on the sabbath *Luke 13:11-17*

Jesus' parable of chief seats at wedding *Luke 14:7-14*

Jesus' parable of prodigal who decided to return *Luke 15:11-24*

Jesus' parable of elder brother who was resentful *Luke 15:25-32*

He saves woman taken in adultery *John 8:1-11*

Church growth through signs and wonders *Acts 4:24-37, 8:14-25, 16: 7-15*

James on faith without works *Jas 2:14-26*

John's sermon on relation of love to fear *1 John 4:1-21*

See also argument, consistency, intelligence, mind, principle, reason, word

LOGOS

In the beginning was the Word, the Creator *Gen 1:1, John 1:1-14*

Tower of Babel (egotism leads to confusion) *Gen 11:1-9*

The Word of God in the form of "thou shalt not" *Exod 20:1-19, Deut 5:1-24*

Elijah's key to prophecy—the still small voice *1 King 19:9-13*

David's song, "He spake, and it was done" *Psal 33:1-22*

Isaiah's vision of Messiah as Maker and Saviour *Isa 45:1-13, 18-21*

Jesus explains why his disciples don't fast *Mat 9:14-17, Mark 2: 18-22, Luke 5:33-39*

Jesus offers John healing as proof of Christ *Mat 11:2-19, Luke 7: 18-35*

Jesus Christ as the light of the world *John 1:14, 8:12-32*

John the Baptist tells how Jesus' preaching differs *John 3:22-36*

Jesus' teaching that he is Christ *John 7:14-40*

A key found to open the sealed book *Rev 5:1-14*

The angel with the little book *Rev 10:1-11*

See also Bible, Christ, logic, messenger, principle, thinking, word

LONELINESS

Abraham turns out Hagar and their son into wilderness *Gen 21:9-21*

Jacob fleeing from home gets God's promise of ever-presence *Gen 28: 10-22*

Elijah flees under the juniper bush *1 King 19:1-8*

David's song, "Why art thou cast down, O my soul?" *Psal 42:1-11*

The captives in a foreign land by the river *Psal 137:1-9*

David's song, "Whither shall I go from thy spirit?" *Psal 139:1-24*

A poor wise man saved the city *Eccl 9:13-18*

Jesus at Gethsemane faces his trial alone *Mat 25:30, 36-46, Mark 14: 26, 32-42, Luke 22:39-46*

Paul's self-revealing *2 Cor 12:1-19*

See also depression, family, retirement

LONGEVITY

The patriarchs live to advanced age *Gen 5:1-32*

Moses' faculties keen when elderly *Deut 34:1-11*

Jesus heals centurion's old servant *Mat 8:5-13, Luke 7:1-10*

Jesus talks with Moses and Elias *Mat 17:1-13, Mark 9:2-13, Luke 9: 28-36*

See also age, life, time

LONG-SUFFERING

See forgiveness

LORD

Lord God creates man from dust *Gen 2:6-8*

Revelation of God at burning bush *Exod 3:1-18*

Revelation of God to Elijah *1 King 19:9-13*

David's song, "The Lord is my shepherd" *Psal 23:1-6*

Birth of our Lord promised *Isa 7: 10-16, 9:2-7*

Isaiah's vision of Maker and Saviour *Isa 45:1-13, 18-21*

Jesus calms wind and seas *Mat 8: 23-27, Mark 4:35-41, 6:45-52, Luke 8:22-25, John 6:21*

Jesus on son of man as Lord of sabbath *Mat 12:1-8*

Jesus feeds 5000 *Mat 14:15-21, Mark 6:35-44, Luke 9:12-17, John 6:5-14*

Jesus walks on water *Mat 14:22-33, John 6:15-21*

Jesus talks with Moses and Elias *Mat 17:1-13, Mark 9:2-13, Luke 9:28-36*

Jesus' parable of laborers in vineyard *Mat 20:1-16*

Jesus' parable of servants awaiting lord *Mat 24:42-51*

Jesus' resurrection *Mat 28:1-8, Mark 16:1-8, Luke 24:1-12, John 20:1-10*

Jesus' ascension *Mark 16:19, 20, Luke 24:50-53, Acts 1:6-12*

Jesus passes through enemies *Luke 4:28-31*

Jesus fills Peter's net *Luke 5:1-11*

Jesus' teaching that he is Christ *John 7:14-40*

Jesus heals man born blind *John 9:1-41*

Jesus raises Lazarus *John 11:1-46*

Paul's vision of Jesus *Acts 9:1-9*

Paul on absence from the body and presence with the Lord *2 Cor 4:14-18, 5:1-21*

See also, God, Jesus, master, prayer

LOSS

Joseph separated from family—a slave in Egypt *Gen 37:1-36*

David's and Bathsheba's child dies *2 Sam 12:13-23*

Elisha loses Elijah *2 King 2:1-11*

Hezekiah loses kingdom by unwise trust *2 King 20:12-21, Isa 39:1-8*

Job loses everything he possesses *Job 1:13-22, 2:1-10*

David's song, "Make a joyful noise" *Psal 66:1-20, 100:1-5*

Mortal life vain *Eccl 1:1-18, 2:1-26*

Changing times and season *Eccl 3:1-15*

Isaiah's "Comfort ye" *Isa 40:1-31*

Isaiah's promise of help in trials *Isa 43:1-28, 44:1-24*

Jeremiah's promise of release from captivity *Jer 29:8-14, 31:1-14, 31-34*

Zephaniah's promise of comfort *Zeph 3:14-17*

Jesus' parable of lost sheep *Mat 18:12-14, Luke 15:1-7*

Jesus on the subject of divorce *Mat 19:3-12, Mark 10:2-12*

Jesus on remarriage and resurrection *Mat 22:23-33, Mark 12:18-27, Luke 20:27-40*

Risen Jesus appears to Mary *Mat 28:9, 10, Mark 16:9-11, Luke 24:13-49, John 20:11-18*

Jesus restores her son to the widow of Nain *Luke 7:11-17*

Jesus' parable of lost piece of money *Luke 15:810*

Jesus promises Holy Ghost to compensate for his loss *John 14:1-31*

Jesus' sermon on comfort in tribulation *John 16:1-33*

Jesus' prayer for his disciples *John 17:1-26*

Jesus gives John care of his mother *John 19:25-27*

Paul's sermon on spirit vs. flesh *Rom 8:1-39*

Paul's sermon that Christ's resurrection proves ours *1 Cor 15:1-58*

See also divorce, gain, injury, mourning, parting, possess, profit, separation

LOVE

Abraham chooses between love for God and love for his son *Gen 22:1-19*

Ruth shows her love for her mother-in-law *Ruth 1:1-22*

Jonathan proves his love for David *1 Sam 18:1-16*

David's song, "The Lord is my shepherd" *Psal 23:1-6*

David's song, "He that dwelleth" *Psal 91:1-16*

Ezekiel's view of God's care for us *Ezek 34:1-31*

Hosea's vision of God and child *Hos 11:1-4*

Zephaniah's vision of God and child *Zeph 3:14-17*

Jesus on treatment of enemies *Mat 5:38-48, Luke 6:27-36*

Jesus on benevolence in secret *Mat 6:1-4*

He teaches his disciples to pray *Mat 6:5-15, Mark 11:25, 26, Luke 11:1-4*

Jesus on Golden Rule *Mat 7:12-14, Luke 6:41, 42*

Jesus' compassion on the multitudes *Mat 12:14-21, Mark 3:6-12*

Jesus on "Who is my mother? and who are my brethren?" *Mat 12:46-50*

Jesus' parable of lost sheep *Mat 18:12-14, Luke 15:1-7*

Jesus' love for little children *Mat 19:13-15, Mark 10:13-16, Luke 18:15-17*

Jesus crucified for love of mankind *Mat 27:32-56, Mark 15:21-41, Luke 23:26-49, John 19:17-30*

The people follow Jesus like sheep *Mark 6:30-34*

Jesus' parable of two debtors *Luke 7:36-50*

Jesus' parable of good Samaritan *Luke 10:25-37*

Jesus' parable of the father of the prodigal *Luke 15:11-24*

Jesus' parable of the father of the elder brother *Luke 15:25-32*

Jesus' parable of good shepherd *John 10:1-18*

Mary shows her love for Jesus *John 12:3-8*

Jesus washes his disciples' feet *John 13:1-20*

Jesus' parable of the true vine *John 15:1-17*

Jesus gives John care of his mother *John 19:25-27*

Paul on the fulfilling of the law *Rom 13:7-14*

Paul on love as the highest value *1 Cor 13:1-13*

John's sermon, "God is love" *1 John 4:1-21*

See also affection, brotherhood, care, charity, compassion, enemy, fellowship, God, heart, neighbor

LOYALTY

Abraham so faithful to God he is willing to sacrifice his son *Gen 22:1-19*

Joseph so loyal to his master and God that he refused Potiphar's wife *Gen 39:1-20*

Caleb collects the reward of the faithful *Josh 14:6-15*

Gideon refuses to be king because God rules his people *Judg 8:22, 23*

Ruth refuses to leave Naomi *Ruth 1:1-22*

David spares Saul, his king, twice *1 Sam 24:1-22, 26:1-25*

David loyal to Saul even after death *2 Sam 1:17-27*

David loyal to his dead friend, Jonathan *2 Sam 9:1-13*

Esther loyal to her people *Esther 5:1-14*

Job remains faithful despite trials *Job 2:1-10, 3:1-26*

David's song about delight in God's law *Psal 1:1-6*

Isaiah's promise, "O Lord, thou art my God" *Isa 25:1, 4, 6-10*

Daniel balances loyalty to God with loyalty to the king *Dan 6:1-28*

Zechariah's vision of two olive trees that supply oil to the candlestick *Zech 4:1-14*

The wise men seek the King of the Jews *Mat 2:1-12*

The temptations of Jesus *Mat 4:1-11, Mark 1:12, 13, Luke 4:1-13*

Jesus' parable of two sons *Mat 21:28-32*

Jesus' parable of servants awaiting the Lord *Mat 24:42-51*

Jesus' parable of the talents *Mat 25:14-30, Luke 19:11-28*

Peter vows never to deny Jesus *Mat 26:31-35, Mark 14:27-31, Luke 22:31-34, John 13:36-38*

Peter denies him *Mat 26:57, 58, 69-75, Mark 14:66-72, Luke 22:54-62, John 18:13-18, 25-27*

Jesus says that no one looking back is fit for the kingdom *Luke 9:57-62*

Jesus' parable of watchful servants *Luke 12:35-40*

Jesus' parable of faithful steward *Luke 12:41-48*

Jesus' parable of the servant before he sups *Luke 17:7-10*

Jesus on faith in Christ *John 12:44-50*

Jesus on vine and branches *John 15:1-27*

Jesus charges Peter, "Feed my sheep" *John 21:12-19*

Peter and John speak the word with boldness *Acts 4:1-23*

Paul on why we owe obedience to Christ *Heb 2:1-18*

Paul on faith, the substance of religion *Heb 11:1-40*

Paul on the example left by Jesus *Heb 12:1-29*

James on how to bear our cross *Jas 1:1-27*

See also devotion, faith, love, service

LUST

Potiphar's wife pursues Joseph *Gen 39:1-20*

People demand meat in wilderness *Exod 16:1-36, Num 11:1-15, 31, 32*

People follow golden calf *Exod 32:1-24*

Samson betrayed by Delilah *Judg 16:4-30*

David takes Uriah's wife *2 Sam 11:1-27*

Nathan exposes the sin of David *2 Sam 12:1-10*

David's song, "Create in me a clean heart" *Psal 51:1-19*

Jesus puts Commandments on mental basis *Mat 5:21-37, Mark 9:38-50*

Jesus saves the adultress *John 8:1-11*

John's vision of great red dragon *Rev 12:1-17*

See also adultery, appetite, senses, sensuality

M

MAGIC

Egyptian sorcerers try to match wonders of Aaron *Exod 7:1-12*

The golden calf *Exod 32:1-24*

Balaam refuses to curse Israelites *Num 22:1-41, 23:1-30, 24:1-25*

God warns against necromancy *Deut 13:1-18*

Abomination forbidden *Deut 18:9-14*

Saul consults a familiar spirit *1 Sam 28:3-20*

Isaiah's vision of the fall of Babylon *Isa 14:4-8, 12-17, 25-27*

Jesus accused of casting out devils by Beelzebub *Mat 12:22-30, Mark 3:22-30, Luke 11:14-23*

Peter's shadow heals the sick in the streets *Acts 5:12-16*

Paul and Barnabas worshipped as gods *Acts 14:11-18*

Paul casts devil out of damsel soothsayer *Acts 16:16-18*

Vagabond exorcists imitate Paul's healings *Acts 19:11-20*

See also hypnotism, magnetism, necromancy, science

MAGNETISM

Lord God creates animals out of the ground *Gen 2:18-20*

Serpent beguiles Eve with a lie *Gen 3:1-5*

Joseph resists Potiphar's wife *Gen 39:1-20*

Israelites drawn to golden calf *Exod 32:1-24*

Samuel drawn to Saul—finds him unfit *1 Sam 10:1-8, 15:7-26*

Saul turns to mesmerism *1 Sam 28:3-20*

Attraction for Bathsheba causes David's downfall *2 Sam 11:1-27*

Isaiah's vision of the attractiveness of Christ *Isa 55:1-13*

Micah's vision of the glory of church *Mic 4:1-8, 13, Isa 2:1-5*

The disciples follow immediately when Jesus calls *Mat 4:17-22, Mark 1:14-20, Luke 5:1-11, John 1:35-42*

A scribe volunteers to follow him *Mat 8:18-22*

Jesus' parable of unclean spirit returning *Mat 12:43-45, Luke 11:24-26*

Little children approach him *Mat 19:13-15, Mark 10:13-16, Luke 18:15-17*

All men seek Jesus; his fame increases *Mark 1:35-39*

People follow him like sheep *Mark 6:30-34*

At twelve years Jesus attracts the rabbis *Luke 2:41-52*

Jesus' parable of prodigal drawn away by sin *Luke 15:11-24*

John describes Jesus as the light of the world *John 1:1-14, 8:12-32*

Nicodemus visits Jesus at night *John 3:1-21*

See also affection, animal, attraction, hypnotism, mesmerism

MAGNIFY

People build tower of Babel to glorify themselves *Gen 11:1-9*

Song of Moses for deliverance *Exod 15:1-19, Deut 32:1-47*

Song of Deborah rejoicing in God's victory   *Judg 5:1-20*

David's song, "how are the mighty fallen!"   *2 Sam 1:17-27*

David's song of thanksgiving   *2 Sam 22:1-51, 1 Chron 16:17-36*

Solomon's dedication of the temple   *1 King 8:22-66, 2 Chron 6:1-42*

Prophet says the battle is the Lord's   *2 Chron 20:1-32*

Nehemiah admits guidance by God   *Neh 9:1-38*

David's song, "The law of the Lord is perfect"   *Psal 19:1-14*

David's song, "He spake, and it was done"   *Psal 33:1-22*

David's song, "Make a joyful noise"   *Psal 66:1-20, 100:1-5*

David's song, "Praise the Lord for his goodness"   *Psal 107:1-43*

David's song, "Whither ... from thy spirit"   *Psal 139:1-24*

Isaiah's vision of God's glory   *Isa 6:1-13*

Isaiah praises God for his benefits   *Isa 25:1, 4, 6-10*

Isaiah calls, "Awake," for Jerusalem is redeemed   *Isa 52:1-15*

Jesus ascends   *Mark 16:19, 20, Luke 24:50-53, Acts 1:9-13*

Mary magnifies the Lord   *Luke 1:39-56*

Angels announce Jesus' birth to shepherds   *Luke 2:8-20*

Paul's sermon on the unity of all— God, the source   *Eph 4:1-32*

See also exaltation, glory, increase, majesty, praise

MAIMED

Jeroboam's hand withered and healed   *1 King 12:32, 33, 13:1-10*

Jesus heals withered hand   *Mat 12:9-13, Mark 3:1-5, Luke 6:6-11*

Jesus heals group including maimed   *Mat 15:29-31*

Jesus heals impotent man   *John 5:1-16*

Peter heals man lame from birth   *Acts 3:1-11*

Philip heals many   *Acts 8:5-8*

Paul heals lame man   *Acts 14:8-10*

See also cripple, deformity, lameness

MAJESTY

Moses directed to remove shoes on holy ground   *Exod 3:1-18*

Moses receives command to go forward through the Red Sea   *Exod 14:5-31*

Moses communicates with God on mount   *Exod 19:1-9, Deut 4:1-15*

God, the basis of all law   *Exod 20:1-19, Deut 5:1-24*

Moses listens to God's voice face to face   *Exod 33:7-23*

Jehoshaphat finds that the battle is God's   *2 Chron 20:1-32*

Job hears the voice of God   *Job 38:1-41*

David's song, "consider thy heavens"   *Psal 8:1-9*

David's song, "The law of the Lord is perfect"   *Psal 19:1-14*

Isaiah's vision of God's glory   *Isa 6:1-13*

Angels announce Jesus' birth   *Luke 2:8-20*

The new heaven and earth of the spiritual universe   *Rev 21:1-27*

The river and tree of life   *Rev 22:1-21*

See also authority, crown, glory, king, magnify, queen

MAKER

God creates man in his likeness   *Gen 1:26, 27*

Lord God creates Adam and Eve   *Gen 2:6-8, 21-25*

God promises Abraham will be father of many nations   *Gen 15:1-21*

God's promise renewed to Isaac   *Gen 26:1-5*

Moses meets I Am That I Am   *Exod 3:1-18*

Solomon builds temple   *1 King 6:1-38, 7:1-51, 2 Chron 3:1-17, 4:1-22, 5:1-14*

The infinite speaks to Job   *Job 38:1-41*

David's song, "What is man?"   *Psal 8:1-9*

David's song, "the fountain of life"   *Psal 36:1-12*

Isaiah's vision of Creator and Saviour   *Isa 43:1-13, 18-21*

Jeremiah's parable of the potter and the clay *Jer 18:1-6*

Samuel's miraculous birth *1 Sam 1:1-28*

At baptism Jesus recognized as Son of God *Mat 3:13-17, Mark 1:9-11, Luke 3:21, 22*

The Christ, whose son is he? *Mat 22:41-46, Mark 12:35-37, Luke 20:41-44*

Jesus' ascension *Mark 16:19, 20, Luke 24:50-53, Acts 1:9-13*

Immaculate birth of Jesus *Luke 1:26-38*

Jesus tells Nicodemus he must be born again *John 3:1-21*

Jesus on his great works that have their source in the Father *John 5:17-47*

Jesus heals the man born blind *John 9:1-41*

John's vision of nature of creator *1 John 4:1-21*

See also creator, father, God, mother, parent

MALACHI (messenger)

See Part II, Malachi

MALPRACTICE

Aaron's rod swallows those of the sorcerers *Exod 7:1-12*

Miriam and Aaron speak against Moses *Num 12:1-16*

Balak hires Balaam to curse Israel *Num 22:1-41, 23:1-30, 24:1-25*

God warns against enticers and necromancy *Deut 13:1-18*

Mesmerism denounced *Deut 18:9-14*

Elijah destroys 450 prophets of Baal *1 King 18:17-40*

Conspiracy against Nehemiah *Neh 6:1-19*

Haman persecutes the Jews *Esther 3:1-15, 4:1-17*

David's song of safety and security *Psal 91:1-16*

Isaiah's vision of the fall of Babylon *Isa 14:4-8, 12-17, 25-27*

Isaiah's vision that hypocrisy will be punished *Isa 29:11-24, 30:1-3, 20, 21*

Ezekiel on sins of the fathers *Ezek 18:1-32*

Jesus heals woman who spent all her living on physicians *Mat 9:20-22, Mark 5:25-30, Luke 8:43-48*

Jesus accused of healing by Beelzebub *Mat 12:22-30, Mark 3:22-30, Luke 11:14-23*

Jesus on what defiles a man *Mat 15:1-20, Mark 7:1-23*

Jesus on leaven of Pharisees *Luke 12:1-15*

Paul heals damsel soothsayer *Acts 16:16-18*

Vagabond exorcists imitate Paul *Acts 19:11-20*

Paul on his trials as Christian *Acts 20:17-38*

Instances of malpractice within the churches *Rev 1:4-20, 2:1-29, 3:1-22*

See also hypnotism, magnetism, medicine, mesmerism, physician, treatment

MAN

God creates man in his image and likeness *Gen 1:26, 27*

Lord God creates man from dust *Gen 2:6-8*

Enoch walks with God and is translated *Gen 5:18, 21-24, Heb 11:5*

Abram and Sarai are given new natures *Gen 17:1-8, 15-22*

Jacob also receives a new name *Gen 32:24-32*

Moses's face covered with veil after talking with God *Exod 34:29-35*

The chosen people are set apart as God's own *Deut 7:6-11*

Caleb, a faithful man, receives reward *Josh 14:6-15*

Solomon requests understanding as man's most important quality *1 King 3:5-15, 2 Chron 1:7-12*

Job asks why the good man suffers *Job 3:1-26*

David's song on the happiness of the godly *Psal 1:1-6*

David's song, "Mark the perfect man" *Psal 37:23-40*

David's song, "Be still, and know" *Psal 46:1-11*

David's song on soul *Psal 84:1-12*

David's song on man's safety *Psal 91:1-16*

David's song, "God, the preserver of man" *Psal 121:1-8*

The nature of a good woman *Prov 31:1-31*

Isaiah's prophecy of the perfect man *Isa 7:10-16, 9:2-7*

The peaceable kingdom of the Messiah *Isa 11:1-12*

Isaiah's descriptions of the perfect Christ *Isa 42:1-12, 16, 18, 53:1-12, 61:1-11, 62:1-12*

Gabriel tells Daniel of God's care for him *Dan 9:20-23, 10:4-21*

Jesus explains his oneness with the Father *John 10:22-42*

Jesus on judging man by his fruits *Mat 7:15-20, Luke 6:43-45*

Jesus calls himself the Son of Man *Mat 12:1-8*

Jesus' parable of sower (receptivity to the gospel) *Mat 13:3-23, Mark 4:1-20, Luke 8:4-15*

Jesus' parable of the leaven *Mat 13:33, Luke 13:20, 21*

Jesus' parable of the pearl of great price *Mat 13:45, 46*

Jesus tells what defiles a man *Mat 15:1-20, Mark 7:1-23*

Jesus and man's dominion over time *Mat 17:1-13, Mark 9:2-13, Luke 9: 28-36*

Jesus' parable of faithful steward *Luke 12:41-48*

Jesus' parable of watchful servants *Luke 12:35-40*

Jesus' parable of prodigal son *Luke 15:11-24*

Jesus' parable of the temple to be raised in three days *John 2:19-22*

Jesus' parable of Jesus' love for all men *John 10:1-18*

Paul contrasts Adam and Christ *Rom 5:1-21*

Paul on inward versus outward man *2 Cor 4:14—5:21*

Paul's teaching to put on the new man *Col 3:1-17*

Paul on the character of the Christ *Heb 1:1-14*

Paul on example left by Jesus *Heb 12:1-29*

James on the equality of man *Jas 2:1-13*

See also consciousness, dust, expression, human, idea, image, likeness, manifestation, mortal, reflection, woman

MANIFESTATION

God manifests himself by creating his image, man and the universe *Gen 1:1-31*

Lord God makes man from dust *Gen 2:6-8*

Enoch walks with God and manifests His nature *Gen 5:18, 21-24, Heb 11:5*

Real nature of Abram symbolized by new name *Gen 17:1-9, 15-22*

Real nature of Jacob begins to appear *Gen 32:24-32*

Jacob shows the characters of his sons *Gen 49:1-28, Deut 33:1-29*

God reveals himself to Moses at bush *Exod 3:1-18*

Guidance of God by pillars of cloud and fire *Exod 13:20-22, Num 9: 15-23*

God's care manifest in supply of manna, etc. *Exod 16:1-36, 17:1-7, Num 11:1-15, 31, 32, 20:1-13*

The Lord talks with Moses face to face *Exod 33:7-23*

Aaron's rod illustrates spirituality *Num 17:1-11*

Gideon's faith developed by three signs from God *Judg 6:19-40*

God calls Samuel *1 Sam 3:1-10*

David anointed by Samuel *1 Sam 16:1-13*

Elijah calls down the fire of God *1 King 18:17-40*

Nature of God revealed to Elijah *1 King 19:9-13*

God's voice speaks to Job *Job 38: 1-41*

David's song, "the earth is full of the goodness of the Lord" *Psal 33:1-22*

David's song on God's expressions *Psal 84:1-12*

David's song, "the beauty of the Lord upon us" *Psal 90:1-17*

Isaiah's vision of God's glory *Isa 6:1-13*

Isaiah's vision of supply and healing promised by Messiah *Isa 35: 1-10*

Jesus says to know men by their fruits *Mat 7:21-23, Luke 6:43-45*

Jesus offers healing as the proof of Christ *Mat 11:2-19, Luke 7:18-35*

Pharisees request a sign of Jesus
Mat 12:38-45, Luke 11:16, 29-32

Jesus' parable of leaven   *Mat 13:33,
Luke 13:20, 21*

Jesus shows dominion by walking
on water   *Mat 14:22-33, John 6:
15-21*

Precious ointment poured on Jesus'
head   *Mat 26:6-13, Mark 14:3-9*

Jesus' parable of seed, blade, ear
Mark 4:26-29

People follow Jesus like sheep
Mark 6:30-34

Jesus' parable of what love means
Luke 10:25-37

Jesus' parable of necessity of fruits
Luke 13:6-9

Jesus Christ is the light of the
world   *John 1:1-14, 8:12-32*

Jesus' teaching that he is Christ
John 7:14-40

Jesus' parable of the good shepherd
John 11:1-18

Peter on healing   *Acts 3:12-26*

James on works needed to prove
faith   *Jas 2:14-26*

John on "God is Love"   *1 John 4:1-21*

See also consciousness, discovery,
evidence, expression, idea, image,
likeness, reflection, revelation

MANNA

Lord tells Moses he will rain bread
from heaven   *Exod 16:1-36, Num
11:1-15, 31, 32*

Moses cautions people to remember
trials   *Deut 8:1-20*

Moses urges offering of first fruits
to God   *Deut 26:1-19*

Moses lists the blessings of obedience   *Deut 28:1-14*

Moses' song of mercy and deliverance   *Deut 32:1-47*

Elijah fed by ravens   *1 King 17:1-16*

Elijah fed in a dream   *1 King 19:1-8*

Elisha feeds 100 men on a few loaves
2 King 4:42-44

Elisha prophesies famine will end
2 King 6:24, 25, 7:1-18

Nehemiah reviews God's help of
Israel   *Neh 9:1-38*

David's song, "The Lord is my shepherd"   *Psal 23:1-6*

Isaiah's vision of the desert bloom-
ing   *Isa 35:1-10*

Daniel eats pulse instead of king's
meat   *Dan 1:1-28*

Jesus' teaching on take no thought
for material things   *Mat 6:25-34,
Luke 12:22-34*

Jesus feeds 5000   *Mat 14:15-21,
Mark 6:35-44, Luke 9:12-17, John
6:5-14*

Disciples reminded by Jesus of his
great works   *Mat 16:5-12, Mark
8:10-21*

Jesus gets tribute money from fish
Mat 17:24-27

Jesus' parable of marriage feast
Mat 22:1-14

Jesus' Last Supper   *Mat 26:26-29,
Mark 14:22-25, Luke 22:14-30*

Jesus' last breakfast with disciples
Mat 28:16-18, John 21:1-14

Peter's net filled by Jesus   *Luke
5:1-11, John 21:1-11*

Jesus' parable of the great supper
Luke 14:15-24

Jesus on the bread of life   *John 6:
26-65*

After this sermon many disciples
leave him   *John 6:66-71*

Descent of the Holy Ghost   *Acts
2:1-13*

The city of God descends out of
heaven   *Rev 21:1-21*

See also bread, food, giving, heaven,
hunger, life, supply, word

MANY

Abraham promised progeny like the
stars   *Gen 15:1-6*

Multitudes in valley of decision
Joel 3:14

Great multitudes follow him, many
healed *Mat 12:14-21, 19:1, 2, Mark
3:6-12*

Jesus feeds 5000   *Mat 14:15,21,
Mark 6:35-44, Luke 9:12-17, John
6:5-14*

Peter adds many to church   *Acts
4:24-37*

See also abundance, multiply

MARRIAGE

Abraham heals Abimelech and his
wife of barrenness   *Gen 20:1-7, 17*

Hagar and their son turned out by
Abraham   *Gen 21:9-21*

Abraham selects a wife for Isaac *Gen 24:1-67*

Joseph refuses Potiphar's wife *Gen 39:1-20*

In order to add Bathsheba to his wives, David has Uriah killed *2 Sam 11:1-27*

Esther is preferred by king and made queen *Esther 2:5-23*

Job's wife urges him to curse God *Job 2:1-10*

The virtuous wife *Prov 31:1-31*

Christ and church compared to bride and bridegroom *Isa 61:1-11*

An angel prevents Joseph from putting Mary away *Mat 1:18-25*

Jesus' parable of the marriage feast *Mat 22:1-14*

Jesus on remarriage and resurrection *Mat 22:23-33, Mark 12: 18-27, Luke 20:27-40*

Jesus' parable of wise and foolish virgins *Mat 25:1-13*

At Cana wedding Jesus turns water into wine *John 2:1-11*

Jesus saves woman taken in adultery *John 8:1-11*

Paul on family relations *Eph 5: 22-33*

John's vision of marriage of the Lamb *Rev 19:7-9*

See also bride, bridegroom, children, Christ, church, family, husband, wedding, wife

MARTYR

Gideon refuses to be king *Judg 8: 22, 23*

Job asks why the good should suffer *Job 3:1-26*

David's song, "Why art thou cast down?" *Psal 42:1-11*

David's song, "God is our refuge and strength" *Psal 46:1-11*

Isaiah's vision of the sufferings of Christ *Isa 42:1-12, 16, 18*

Jesus foretells his own death *Mat 16:21-28, 17:22, 23, Mark 8:31-38, 9:30-32, Luke 9:20-27, 43-45*

Jesus' parable of the husbandmen who killed the lord's son *Mat 21: 33-46, Mark 12:1-12, Luke 20:9-19*

Rulers conspire against Jesus *Mat 26:1-5, Mark 14:1, 2*

Jesus crucified *Mat 27:32-56, Mark 15:21-41, Luke 23:26-49, John 19: 17-30*

Jesus sets his face toward Jerusalem and death *Luke 9:51-56, John 7:1-13*

Martha complains to Jesus about her sister *Luke 10:38-42*

Jesus' parable of the faithful steward *Luke 12:41-48*

Jesus' parable of counting the cost *Luke 14:25-33*

Jesus says he is light of world and truth sets free *John 8:12-32*

Stephen's trial *Acts 6:5-15*

Stephen stoned *Acts 7:51-60*

Paul stoned to death but recovers *Acts 14:-19, 20*

Paul's hardships to establish church *2 Cor 11:21-33*

Paul tells why we are obedient to Christ *Heb 2:1-18*

James' sermon on how to bear our cross *Jas 1:1-27*

See also death, faith, pain, persecution, principle, profession, sacrifice, witness

MASTER

Joseph in slavery is faithful in his master's service *Gen 39:1-20*

Elisha cleaves to Elijah and inherits his mantle *2 King 2:1-15*

Isaiah's vision of Christ's peaceable kingdom *Isa 11:1-12*

Jeremiah's parable of the potter and his clay *Jer 18:1-6*

Jesus' dominion over elements *Mat 8:23-27, 14:22-33, 17:1-13, Mark 4: 35-41, 6:45-52, 9:2-13, Luke 8:22-25, John 6:15-21*

Jesus tells why his disciples don't fast *Mat 9:14-17, Mark 2:18-22, Luke 5: 33-39*

John the Baptist sends to Jesus for proof he is Christ *Mat 11: 2-19, Luke 7: 18-35*

Jesus says son of man is Lord of the Sabbath *Mat 12: 1-8*

Peter acknowledges Jesus as Christ *Mat 16: 13-20, Mark 8: 27-30, Luke 9: 18-21*

Jesus heals a case that disciples failed on *Mat 17: 14-21, Mark 9: 14-29, Luke 9: 37-43*

Jesus' parable of unmerciful debtor *Mat 18: 23-35*

Jesus' parable of servants awaiting the lord *Mat 24: 42-51*

Jesus' resurrection over death *Mat 28: 1-8, Mark 16: 1-8, Luke 24: 1-12, John 20: 1-10*

At twelve years rabbis listen to him *Luke 2: 41-52*

Jesus gives disciples instructions *Luke 10: 1-16*

Jesus' parable of door shut by the master *Luke 13: 22-30*

Jesus' parable of serving the master before you sup *Luke 17: 7-10*

Jesus as the light of the world *John 1: 1-14, 8: 12-32*

John the Baptist tells how Jesus' preaching differs *John 3:22-36*

Jesus tells the source of his great works *John 5: 17-47*

Jesus' teaching that he is Christ *John 7: 14-40*

Jesus on faith in Christ *John 12: 44-50*

Jesus washes disciples' feet *John 13: 1-20*

The Master prays for his disciples *John 17: 1-26*

Peter heals in the name of Jesus Christ *Acts 3: 1-11, 9: 32-35*

Paul's teaching that Christ's resurrection proves ours *1 Cor 15: 1-58*

Paul's advice to his disciples *1 Thess 5: 1-28, 2 Tim 2: 1-26, 4: 1-8*

Paul on why we owe obedience to Christ *Heb 2: 1-18*

Paul on the example left by Jesus *Heb 12: 1-29*

See also art, Christ, dominion, Jesus, leader, lord, Messiah, skill, teaching

MATERIALISM

Lord God makes man from dust, woman from rib *Gen 2: 6-8, 21-25*

Cain worships God with less spiritual fruits *Gen 4: 1-16*

Abraham has two sons *Gen 16: 1-16, 21: 1-8*

Esau sells his birthright for pottage *Gen 25: 24-36*

People released from bondage of Egypt *Exod 11: 4-10, 12: 1-14, 21-41, Deut 16: 1-22*

People worship golden calf *Exod 32: 1-24*

David's song, "the fountain of life" *Psal 36: 1-12*

Isaiah's vision that body culture is in vain *Isa 3: 16-26*

Isaiah's vision of the fall of Babylon *Isa 14: 4-8, 12-17, 25-27*

Isaiah's vision that workers in the dark will be punished *Isa 29: 11-24, 30: 1-3, 20, 21*

Jesus on taking no thought for material things *Mat 6: 25-34, Luke 12: 22-34*

Judas settles price to betray Jesus *Mat 26: 14-16, Mark 14: 10, 11, Luke 22: 1-6*

Jesus on bread of life *John 6: 26-65*

Thomas demands to see the body after resurrection *John 20:19-29*

Paul on Spirit vs. flesh *Rom 8: 1-39*

Paul's teaching to put off the old man *Col 3: 1-17*

John's vision of old heaven and earth passed away *Rev 21: 1-27*

See also belief, matter, mind, mortal, substance

MATTER

Man made from dust, woman from rib *Gen 2: 6-8, 21-25*

Moses sees bush burning but not consumed *Exod 3: 1-18*

The golden calf as a tangible god *Exod 32: 1-24*

Gideon asks for three material signs *Judg 6: 19-40*

Goliath's material strength frightens army *1 Sam 17: 1-16*

Elisha causes axe head to float *2 King 6:1-7*

Isaiah's parable of wild grapes *Isa 5: 1-8*

Isaiah's prophecy of fall of Babylon *Isa 14: 4-8, 12-17, 25-27*

Jeremiah's vision of potter and his clay *Jer 18: 1-6*

Daniel interprets dream of great image *Dan 2: 1-49*

Jesus on where treasure is *Mat 6: 19-21*

Jesus' teaching on taking no thought

for material things *Mat 6 : 25-34,
Luke 12 : 22-34*

Jesus restores withered hand *Mat
12 : 9-13, Mark 3 : 1-5, Luke 6 : 6-11*

Jesus' parable of wheat and tares
Mat 13 : 24-30, 36-43

Jesus' parable of the dragnet *Mat
13 : 47-50*

Jesus feeds 5000 *Mat 14:15-21,
Mark 6 : 35-44, Luke 9 : 12-17, John
6 : 5-14*

Jesus walks on water *Mark 6 : 45-52,
John 6 : 21*

Jesus' parable of rich man and bigger
barns *Luke 12 : 15-21*

Paul on Spirit vs. flesh *Rom 8 : 1-
39*

Paul on faith as substance *Heb
11 : 1-40*

See also belief, materialism, mind,
mortal, physiology, space, spirit,
substance

MATURITY

Abram and Sarai receive new names
Gen 17 : 1-9, 15-22

Jacob outgrows his duplicity and
gets a new name *Gen 32 : 1-32*

Joseph reveals himself to the brethren he has been separated from
Gen 43 : 1, 2, 45 : 1-11

Jacob prophesies how his sons will
turn out *Gen 49 : 1-28, Deut 33:
1-29*

Moses charges Joshua with leadership *Deut 31 : 7-23, Josh 1 : 1-9*

Caleb's maturity and reward *Josh
14 : 6-15*

Samuel finds his first choice unfit
and has to select a new king
1 Sam 15 :7-26, 16 :1-13

David refuses Saul's armor and uses
tried weapons *1 Sam 17 : 17-52*

Solomon requests from God mature
values *1 King 3 : 5-15, 2 Chron
1 : 7-12*

Isaiah's vision of Messiah's coming
means war no more *Isa 2 : 1-5,
Mic 4 : 1-8, 13*

Daniel's meeting with the angel Gabriel *Dan 9 : 20-23, 10 : 4-21*

Jonah learns to obey God *Jonah
1 : 1-17, 2 : 1-10, 3 : 1-10*

Jesus' mission to Christianize the
law *Mat 5 : 17-20*

Jesus expands the meaning of Commandments *Mat 5 : 21-37, Mark 9 :
38-50*

Jesus tells why his disciples don't
fast *Mat 9 : 14-17, Mark 2 : 18-22,
Luke 5 : 33-39*

Jesus on what defiles *Mat 15 : 1-20,
Mark 7 : 1-23*

Jesus shows Christianity communicating with law and prophets *Mat
17 :1-13, Mark 9 :2-13, Luke 9 :28-
36*

Jesus tells disciples how to heal a
difficult case *Mat 17 : 14-21, Mark
9 : 14-29, Luke 9 : 37-43*

Two men ask about eternal life *Mat
19 : 16-30, Luke 10 : 25-28, 18 : 18-30*

Jesus partially heals blind man, com-
pletes healing in second treatment
Mark 8 : 22-26

At twelve years Jesus astounds the
rabbis *Luke 2 :41-52*

Jesus raises young man, young girl,
Lazarus, and then he himself is
raised *Luke 7 :11-17, 8 :41, 42,
49-56, John 11 :1-46, 20 :1-10*

No one looking back is fit for the
kingdom *Luke 9 : 57-62*

Jesus replies to Martha's complaint
about her sister *Luke 10 : 38-42*

Jesus' parable of prodigal son *Luke
15 : 11-24*

Jesus' parable of rich man and
beggar *Luke 16 :19-31*

Jesus' teaching that man must be
born again *John 3 : 1-21*

Jesus' teaching that God is Spirit
and must be worshipped spiritually *John 4 : 1-30, 39-42*

After Jesus' sermon on bread of
life many disciples leave him *John
6 : 66-71*

Jesus adds to Peter's growth *John
21 : 12-19*

Paul's change in character *Acts 8 :
1-4, 9 : 1-31*

Peter accepts conversion of Gentiles
Acts 10 : 1-48, 11 : 1-18

Paul on the growth from child to
man *1 Cor. 13 : 9-13*

Paul's self-revealings *2 Cor 12 : 1-19*

Paul's teaching to put off old man,
put on new *Col 3 : 1-17*

James on how to bear our cross *Jas
1 : 1-27*

John's vision of new Jerusalem *Rev 21: 1-27*

John's vision of river and tree of life *Rev. 22: 1-21*

See also age, growth, mind, perfection, spirituality

MECHANICS

Noah builds the ark *Gen 6: 5-22*

People passed through Red Sea *Exod 14: 5-31*

Walls of Jericho fall *Josh 6: 1-20*

Gideon and fleece *Judg 6: 36-40*

David's effective weapon *1 Sam 17: 38-52*

Solomon builds temple *1 King 5: 1-18, 6: 1-38, 7: 1-51, 2 Chron 3: 1-17, 4: 1-22, 5: 1-14*

Nehemiah rebuilds wall of Jerusalem *Neh. 4: 1-23*

Jesus' parable of builders on rock and sand *Mat 7: 24-27, Luke 6: 48, 49*

Jesus walks on water *Mat 14: 22-33, John 6: 15-21*

Jesus restores body to action *John 20: 19-29*

See also body, building, force, physics, principle

MEDIATOR

After war of kings Abraham is blessed by Melchizedek *Gen 14: 8-20, Heb. 6: 20, 7: 1-28*

Aaron sacrifices for the sins of the people *Lev 16: 1-28*

Elisha prays to heal the Shunammites' son *2 King 4: 8-37*

Elisha prays to open his servant's eyes *2 King 6: 8-23*

Esther rescues her people from persecution *Esther 5: 1-14*

Job prays for his friends *Job 42: 1-17*

Isaiah foretells the sacrifice of the Messiah *Isa 53: 1-12*

Jesus accused of intercession with Beelzebub *Mat 12: 22-30, Mark 3: 22-30, Luke 11: 14-23*

Pharisees demand Jesus show his connection with God by a sign *Mat 12: 38-45, 16: 1-4, Mark 8: 10-13, Luke 11: 16, 29-32*

Jesus' parable of the lost sheep *Mat 18: 12-14, Luke 15: 1-7*

Jesus saves the woman taken in adultery *John 8: 1-11*

Jesus' parable of the good shepherd *John 10: 1-18*

Jesus thanks God for hearing his prayer to heal Lazarus *John 11: 1-46*

Peter's teaching that God heals through Christ *Acts 3: 12-26*

Paul's teaching that Christ's resurrection proves ours *1 Cor 15: 1-58*

Paul on why we owe obedience to Christ *Heb 2: 1-18*

Paul's teaching that only true sacrifice remits sin *Heb 10: 1-39*

Paul on example left by Jesus *Heb 12: 1-29*

John's teaching that we have an advocate *1 John 2: 1-8*

Paul's letter to Timothy preaching on the one mediator *1 Tim 2: 1-15*

See also advocate, atonement, Christ, intercession, Jesus, reconciliation

MEDICINE

Moses sets up pole to cure snake bite *Num 21:4-9*

The children of Israel are oppressed in Egypt *Exod 1:8-14*

Solomon urges turning to the temple in time of any trouble *1 King 8:22-66, 2 Chron 6:1-42*

Asa's foot disease fatal because he turned to physicians not God *2 Chron 16:11-14*

Elisha nullifies poisoned pottage with meal *2 King 4:38-41*

Elisha heals Naaman's leprosy by baths *2 King 5:1-14*

The balm of Gilead *Jer 8:22*

Jesus on cross given vinegar and gall *Mat 27:32-34*

Good Samaritan binds up wounds pouring in wine and oil *Luke 10: 25-37*

Rich man in hell asks for water for relief *Luke 16:19-31*

Jesus anoints eyes of the blind man with clay and tells him to wash in the pool *John 9:1-41*

John's vision of tree of life whose

leaves were for the healing of the nations *Rev 22:1-21*

See also disease, healing, physician, prevention, remedy

MEDITATION

Joseph has boyhood dreams *Gen 37:5-10*
Daniel asks time to solve the king's dream *Dan 2:16-45*
David's songs on meditation *Psal 1:1-6, 19:1-14, 119:1-176*
Jesus' temptations *Mat 4:1-11, Luke 4:1-13*
Jesus' parable of the wise fool *Luke 12:15-21*
Paul's self-revealings *2 Cor 12:1-19*
John's vision of a new heaven and earth *Rev 21:1-27*
John's vision of the river and tree of life *Rev 22:1-21*

See also devotion, heart, mind, prayer, study, watch

MEEKNESS

Enoch walked with God *Gen 5:18, 21-24, Heb 11:5*
Abraham gives Lot his choice of land *Gen 13:1-18*
Isaac trusts his father not to harm him *Gen 22:1-19*
Moses does not resent Eldad and Medad as prophets *Num 11:16-30*
Moses does not resent rebellion of Miriam but heals her *Num 12: 1-16*
Naaman resents order to bathe but reconsiders *2 King 5:1-14*
David's song, "The Lord is my shepherd" *Psal 23:1-6*
Ezekiel's vision of God as shepherd of flock *Ezek 34:1-31*
Jesus accepts baptism by John the Baptist *Mat 3:13-17, Mark 1:9-11, Luke 3:21, 22*
Jesus' teaching "Blessed are the meek" *Mat 5:1-12, Luke 6:17-26*
Jesus points to his unity with Father *John 10:22-42*
Woman healed who touched hem of Jesus' garment *Mat 9:20-22, Mark 5:25-34, Luke 8:43-48*

Jesus accepts God's will at Gethsemane *Mat 26:30, 36-46, Mark 14: 26, 32-42, Luke 22:39-46*
Jesus heals Syrophenician's daughter *Mat 15:21-28, Mark 7:24-30*
Jesus' parable of the unmerciful debtor *Mat 18:23-35*
Jesus uses little children as an example *Mat 19:13-15, Mark 10:13-16, Luke 18:15-17*
Jesus, the baby, laid in a cow's manger *Luke 2:1-7*
Jesus' parable of chief seats *Luke 14:7-14*
Jesus says source of great works is Father *John 5:17-47*
Jesus' parable of good shepherd *John 10:1-18*
Jesus on humility *John 13:12-20*
Ananias heals Paul despite misgivings *Acts 9:10-22*
Paul's sermon that talents all come from God *1 Cor 12:1, 4-31*

See also dominion, gentleness, humility, innocence, patience, peace, sheep

MELCHIZEDEK

Abraham blessed by this prototype of the spiritual priest-king *Gen 14:18-20, Heb 6:20, 7:1-28*
The king is called priest after this order *Psal 110:1-7*
The coming of the Messiah *Isa 9: 2-7*
The Messiah's peaceable kingdom *Isa 11:1-12*
Paul's description of Savior's priesthood *Heb 4:14 to 5:8*

See also Christ, king, Messiah, peace, priest

MEMBERSHIP

The children of Israel are oppressed in Egypt *Exod 1:8-14*
Rahab recognizes that children of God must win *Josh 2:1-24*
Gideon eliminates men of army to picked 300 *Judg 7:1-25*
Mordecai persecuted by Haman *Esther 3:1-15*
The promise of restoration to Israel *Jer 31:1-14, 31-34*

Jesus calls his disciples *Mat 4:17-22, Mark 1:14-20, Luke 5:1-11, John 1:35-42*

Jesus heals all manner of sickness *Mat 4:23-25, Luke 4:40-44*

He sends disciples to preach and heal *Mat 9:36-38, Mark 3:12-21. Luke 9:1-6*

Parable of lost sheep *Mat 18:12-14, Luke 15:1-7*

Parable of laborers in vineyard *Mat 20:1-16*

Jesus establishes communion for his followers *Mat 26:26-29, Mark 14:22-25, Luke 22:14-30, 1 Cor 11:23-25*

Jesus answers question, "Who is my neighbor?" *Luke 10:25-37*

Jesus on unity and eternity of Christ *John 8:12-59*

Jesus' love for us *John 10:1-18*

Jesus' prayer for his disciples and their disciples *John 17:1-26*

The apostles elect Matthias in place of Judas *Acts 1:15-26*

Peter's successful healings cause church growth *Acts 4:24-37*

Philip baptizes an African *Acts 8:26-40*

Peter accepts Gentiles into fellowship of church *Acts 11:1-18*

Paul on the unity of members *Eph 4:1-32*

Paul's points for guidance of church members *1 Thess 5:1-28*

Paul's advice to strengthen church members *2 Tim 2:1-26*

Paul's precepts to disciples *2 Tim 4:1-8*

Paul gives example left disciples by Jesus *Heb 12:1-29*

Peter on the ideal church member *1 Pet 2:1-25*

John's letters to church members *Rev 1:4-20, 2:1-29, 3:1-22*

See also association, body, church, communion, fellowship

MEMORIAL

God's covenant with Noah "Be fruitful, and multiply" *Gen 9:1-17*

Abraham gets news of the promised land *Gen 15:1-21*

God's promise renewed to Isaac *Gen 26:1-5*

The song of Moses *Exod 15:1-19, Deut 32:1-47*

Joshua sets up twelve stones in memory of Jordan crossing *Josh 4:1-24*

The song of Deborah's victory *Judg 5:1-20*

Dedication of Solomon's temple *1 King 8:22-66, 2 Chron 6:1-42*

David's song of rejoicing *Psal 66:1-20, 100:1-5*

Peter offers to build memorials for Elijah, Moses and Jesus *Mat 17:1-13, Mark 9:2-13, Luke 9:28-36*

Jesus asks that communion be a memorial to him *Mat 26:26-29, Mark 14:22-25, Luke 22:14-30, 1 Cor 11:23-25*

The crucifixion makes the cross a memorial of Christ *Mat 27:32-56, Mark 15:21-41, Luke 23:26-49, John 19:17-30*

See also remembrance

MEMORY

See duty, forgetfulness, remembrance

MENTAL DERANGEMENT

Nebuchadnezzar goes mad and is healed *Dan 4:28-37*

Jesus heals the Gadarene (one or two insane men) *Mat 8:28-34, Mark 5:1-20, Luke 8:26-39*

Woman's daughter healed of devil by Jesus *Mat 15:21-28, Mark 7:24-30*

Unclean spirit comes out of man in temple *Mark 1:2-28, Luke 4:33-37*

Philip casts out unclean spirit *Acts 8:5-8*

Damsel soothsayer healed by Paul *Acts 16:16-18*

See also insanity

MERCY

Lot shelters two angels from mob *Gen 19:1-14*

Joseph provides food for his brethren *Gen 42:1-9*

David shows kindness to his friend's son *2 Sam 9:1-13*

Elisha feeds and releases the Syrians *2 King 6:8-23*

The compassion of the coming Messiah *Isa 42:1-12, 16, 18*

Christ's compassionate works *Isa 61:1-11, 62:1-12*

God's covenant to restore the captivity of Israel *Jer 31:1-14, 31-34*

Hosea's vision of God's care *Hos 11:1-4*

Zephaniah's vision of salvation to Zion *Zeph 3:14-17*

Jesus on Beatitudes includes mercy *Mat 5:1-12, Luke 6:17-26*

Jesus heals centurion's servant of palsy *Mat 8:5-13, Luke 7:1-10*

Jesus heals Jairus' daughter of death *Mat 9:18, 19, 23-26, Mark 5:22-24, 35-43, Luke 8:41, 43, 49-56*

Jesus' parable of the lost sheep *Mat 18:12-14, Luke 15:1-7*

Jesus' parable of the unmerciful debtor *Mat 18:23-35*

Jesus' parable of the good Samaritan *Luke 10:25-37*

Jesus heals lame man at pool *John 5:1-16*

Jesus' parable of the good shepherd *John 10:1-18*

See also charity, compassion, grace, justice, pity, punishment

MESMERISM

The second account of creation begins with a mist *Gen 2:6-8*

Aaron contests with Egyptian sorcerers *Exod 7:1-12*

Goliath's challenge immobilizes Israelites *1 Sam 17:1-16*

Saul consults familiar spirit *1 Sam 28:3-20*

David's morals fall seeing Bathsheba *2 Sam 11:1-27*

Jesus' parable of unclean spirit which returns with seven others *Mat 12:43-45, Luke 11:24-26*

After vowing never, Peter denies the Master *Mat 26:57, 58, 69-75, Mark 14: 66-72, Luke 22:54-62, John 18:13-18, 25-27*

Jesus' parable of the prodigal's elder brother *Luke 15:25-32*

Paul heals damsel soothsayer *Acts 16:16-18*

Paul on sinning against his own will *Rom 7:14-25*

Paul lists the enemies of the truth *2 Tim 3:1-17*

See also hypnotism, illusion, magnetism, sleep

MESSENGER

Abraham blessed by Melchizedek, forerunner of Messiah *Gen 14: 8-20, Heb 6:20, 7:1-28*

Moses returns from Sinai with Ten Commandments *Exod 19:1-9, 20: 1-19, Deut 4:1-15, 5:1-24*

Caleb and Joshua scout the land of promise *Num 13:1-33, 14:1-11, 23-29, Deut 1:19-38*

Joshua meets the captain of the host before Jericho *Josh 5:10-15*

Forty years later Caleb's and Joshua's message is justified *Josh 14:6-15*

Angel announces birth of Samson *Judg 13:1-25*

Elijah tells men that God is a still small voice *1 King 19:9-13*

Elihu tells Job to consider him in God's place *Job 33:1-6*

The calling of Isaiah to prophesy *Isa 6:1-13*

Isaiah's message of reassurance, "Comfort ye" *Isa 40:1-31*

Jeremiah's prophecy that captivity will be turned in 70 years *Jer 29:8-14*

Ezekiel tells of God's care for us *Ezek 34:1-31*

Daniel's vision of Gabriel *Dan 9: 20-23, 10:4-21*

Micah's message of the glory of church *Mic 4:1-8, 13, Isa 2:1-5*

Zephaniah's message of salvation *Zeph 3:14-17*

Malachi urges tithing *Mal 3:10, 4: 1, 2*

John the Baptist prepares way of the Lord *Mat 3:1-12, Mark 1:1-8, Luke 3:1-18*

Jesus' parable of the sower *Mat 13: 3-23, Mark 4:1-20, Luke 8:4-15*

Jesus says a prophet is without honor in his own country *Mat 13: 53-58, Mark 6:1-6, Luke 4:22-24, John 4:43-45*

Jesus Christ as the light of the world *John 1:1-14, 8:12-32*

See also angel, communication, disciple, herald, ministry, prophet

MESSIAH

Abraham blessed by Melchizedek (priest-king) *Gen 14:8-20, Heb 6:20, 7:1-28*
God promises a prophet will arise like unto Moses *Deut 18:15-22*
Isaiah on birth of Messiah *Isa 7:10-16, 9:2-7*
Isaiah on effect of Christ's kingdom *Isa 11:1-12*
Isaiah of office of the Christ *Isa 42:1-12, 16, 18*
Isaiah on Christ as Creator and Saviour *Isa 45:1-13, 18-21*
Isaiah on description of Messiah *Isa 53:1-12*
Isaiah on promises of Christ *Isa 55:1-13*
Isaiah on inspiration to be Christlike *Isa 60:1-5*
Isaiah on description of his compassionate works *Isa 61:1-11, 62:1-12*
Jesus' parable of the sower *Mat 13:3-23, Mark 4:1-20, Luke 8:4-15*
Peter acknowledges Jesus as Christ *Mat 16:13-20, Mark 8:27-30, Luke 9:18-21*
Jesus' parable of lost sheep *Mat 18:12-14, Luke 15:1-7*
Jesus' parable of husbandmen refusing rent *Mat 21:33-46, Mark 12:1-12, Luke 20:9-19*
Jesus' parable of marriage feast *Mat 22:1-14*
Jesus on signs of second coming *Mat 24:1-41*
Jesus' parable of servants awaiting their lord *Mat 24:42-51*
Jesus' parable of sheep and goats *Mat 25:31-46*
Proof of the Messiah: the resurrection *Mat 28:1-8, Mark 16:1-8, Luke 24:1-12, John 20:1-10*
Jesus ascends *Mark 16:19, 20, Luke 24:50-53, Acts 1:9-13*
The birth of Jesus *Luke 2:1-7*
John the Baptist sends to Jesus for proof he is Messiah *Luke 7:18-35, Mat 11:2-19*

Jesus' parable of door shut by the master *Luke 13:22-30*
Jesus' teaching that he is Christ *John 7:14-40*
Jesus on unity and eternity of Christ *John 8:12-59*
Jesus' parable of good shepherd *John 10:1-18*
Jesus' parable of true vine *John 15:1-17*
Jesus' 52 healings and great works (See Part II, Jesus Christ: Great Works)
Paul on Jesus as Messiah *Acts 13:16-52*
Paul on Adam vs. Christ *Rom 5:1-21*
Paul on character of Christ *Heb 1:1-14*
Paul on why we owe Christ obedience *Heb 2:1-18*
Paul on example left by Jesus *Heb 12:1-29*
John's vision of King of Kings *Rev 19:11-16*

See also anointing, Christ, deliverance, Jesus, Lord, master, Saviour

METABOLISM

See body, chemistry

METAPHYSICS

God creates only his likeness *Gen 1:26, 27*
Man of dust could not be created by Spirit *Gen 2:6-8*
Enoch passed over death by "walking with God" *Gen 5:18, 21-24, Heb 11:5*
Moses examines God's nature at the bush *Exod 3:1-18*
Moses communicates directly with God *Exod 19:1-9, 20:1-19, 33:7-23, Deut 4:1-15, 5:1-24*
Elijah raises dead *1 King 17:17-24*
Elijah prays for rain *1 King 18:41-46*
Elijah probes the nature of God *1 King 19:9-13*
Elijah works out his translation over death *2 King 2:1-11*
God's law sets aside physical law *2 King 6:1-7*

The infinite speaks to Job *Job 38: 1-41*

David's song on the nature of man *Psal 8:1-9*

David's song on the basis of life *Psal 36:1-12*

David's song on ever-presence *Psal 139:1-24*

Proverbs on the value of wisdom *Prov 3:13-26*

All mortal events within time *Eccl 3:1-15*

Isaiah prophesies birth of Messiah *Isa 7:10-16, 9:2-7*

Jesus lists Christian qualities *Mat 5:1-12, Luke 6:17-26*

Jesus instructs disciples in healing arts *Mat 9:36-38, 10:1-42, Mark 3:13-21, Luke 9:1-6*

Jesus' parable on pearl of great price *Mat 13:45, 46*

Jesus heals where disciples fail *Mat 17:14-21, Mark 9:14-29, Luke 9: 37-43*

Jesus tells which is the great commandment *Mat 22:34-40, Mark 12:28-34*

At twelve years Jesus answers rabbis' questions *Luke 2:41-52*

Jesus tells Nicodemus man must be born again *John 3:1-21*

Jesus tells woman God is Spirit *John 4:1-30, 39-42*

Jesus' discourse on bread of life *John 6:26-65*

Jesus on the unity and eternity of Christ *John 8:12-59*

Jesus promises Holy Ghost *John 14:1-31*

Peter on healing *Acts 3:12-26*

Paul on Spirit vs. flesh *Rom 8:1-39*

Paul on love *1 Cor 13:1-13*

Paul's teaching that Jesus' resurrection proves ours *1 Cor 15:1-58*

Paul on Melchizedek *Heb 6:20, 7: 1-28*

John's teaching on God is Love *1 John 4:1-21*

John's vision of new heaven and earth *Rev 21:1-27*

See also cause, life, nature, wisdom

METEOROLOGY

Joshua sees sun and moon stand still *Josh 10:6-15*

Elijah controls rainfall *1 King 17: 1-4, 18:41-46*

David's song, "The heavens declare the glory of God" *Psal 19:1-14*

Jesus calms wind and sea *Mat 8:23-27, Mark 4:35-41, 6:45-52, Luke 8: 22-25, John 6:21*

Atmospheric events at the crucifixion *Mat 27:45-56*

Paul shipwrecked on voyage to Rome *Acts 27:1-44*

See also atmosphere, weather, wind

METHODS IN HEALING

Moses is shown that leprosy and fear are illusions *Exod 4:1-9*

The Shunammite refuses to accept death *2 King 4:8-27*

Jesus casts devils out of Gadarene *Mat 8:28-34, Mark 5:1-20, Luke 8:26-39*

Jesus charges his apostles to heal *Mat 10:5-42, Mark 6:7-13, Luke 9: 1-6*

Pharisees say Jesus heals by Beelzebub *Mat 12:22-30, Mark 3:22-30, Luke 11:14-20*

Jesus explains need of prayer and fasting *Mat 17:14-21, Mark 9:14-29, Luke 9:37-43*

Jesus shows relation of sin to sickness *Mark 2:1-12, Luke 5:17-26*

Jesus instructs his disciples in healing *Luke 10:1-16*

Jesus explains that his great works have their source in the Father *John 5:17-47*

Jesus expresses gratitude before raising Lazarus *John 11:1-46*

Peter and John heal lame man by referring to Christ *Acts 3:1-26*

See also healing

MICAH

See Part II, Micah

MIGHT

God creates the universe *Gen 1:1-31*

Enoch walked with God and overcame death *Gen 5:18, 21-24, Heb 11:5*

Noah saves himself from flood by God's direction *Gen 6:5-22, 7:1-24*

People pass through Red Sea *Exod 14:5-31*

Walls of Jericho crumble before attack *Josh 6:1-27*

David overcomes the giant, Goliath *1 Sam 17:38-52*

Jehoshaphat proves "battle is not yours, but God's" *2 Chron 20:1-32*

Elijah and the fire of God *1 King 18:17-40*

David's song, "The earth is the Lord's" *Psal 24:1-10*

David's song, "God is our refuge and strength" *Psal 46:1-11*

David's song, "the secret place" *Psal 91:1-16*

Daniel's companions in fiery furnace *Dan 3:1-30*

Daniel in lions' den *Dan 6:1-28*

Jesus controls the elements *Mat 8:23-27, 14:22-33, Mark 4:35-41, 6:45-52, Luke 8:22-25, John 6:15-21*

Jesus' resurrection *Mat 28:1-8, Mark 16:1-8, Luke 24:1-12, John 20:1-10*

Jesus fills Peter's net *Luke 5:1-11*

Jesus' parable of temple to be raised in three days *John 2:19-22*

Jesus says the source of his great works is the Father *John 5:17-47*

Lazarus raised after four days *John 11:1-46*

Jesus promises the Holy Ghost *John 14:1-31*

Paul and Silas released by earthquake *Acts 16:19-40*

James says works needed to prove faith *Jas 2:14-26*

See also omnipotence, power, strength

MIND (divine)

Man created in image of God *Gen 1:26, 27*

Joseph turns to God to interpret Pharaoh's dream *Gen 41:1-46*

Moses is promised directions by God *Exod 3:9-12*

Moses learns the source of eloquence *Exod 4:10-17*

Moses receives the basis of all law from God *Exod 19:1-9, 20:1-19, Deut 4:1-15, 5:1-24*

Gideon turns to divine mind for guidance *Judg 7:1-25*

God directs Samuel in the selection of a king *1 Sam 15:7-26, 16:1-13*

Solomon asks God for understanding *1 King 3:5-15, 2 Chron 1:7-12*

Man directed to search for wisdom *Prov 3:13-26, 4:1-13, 8:1-36*

Daniel prays, then solves king's problem *Dan 2:1-49*

Jesus heals insanity *Mat 8:28-34, Mark 5:1-20, Luke 8:26-39*

Jesus heals woman's daughter *Mat 15:21-28, Mark 7:24-30*

Jesus heals mental derangement *Mark 1:21-28, Luke 4:33-37*

At twelve years Jesus' wisdom astonishes the rabbis *Luke 2:41-52*

John's vision of the light of the world *John 1:1-14*

Paul on material versus spiritual thinking *Rom 8:1-39*

Paul on transforming the mind *Rom 12:1-3*

Paul on the mind of Christ *1 Cor 2:1-16, Phil 2:1-15*

Paul's teaching to put off old man, put on new *Col 3:1-17*

See also God, intelligence, life, love, principle, reason, truth, soul, spirit

MIND (human)

Man of dust becomes a living soul *Gen 2:6-8*

Serpent tells beguiling lie about good and evil *Gen 3:1-5*

Cain shows the mentality that results in murder *Gen 4:1-16*

Rebekah and Jacob show duplicity of thinking *Gen 27:1-44*

Joseph demonstrates his ability as a problem-solver *Gen 41:1-46*

Solomon illustrates wisdom in human relations *1 King 3:16-28*

Gehazi shows selfishness of human thought *2 King 5:15-27*

Job, naturally, asks why the good should suffer *Job 3:1-16*

David's song, "Be still, and know" *Psal 46:1-11*

Isaiah exposes the thoughts of vain women *Isa 3:16-26*

Isaiah says human fears are groundless *Isa 43:1-28, 44:1-24*

Isaiah's human plea for justice *Isa 59:1-21*

Jonah's attempts to flee from God's direction *Jonah 1:1-17, 2:1-10, 3:1-10*

Jesus' parable of the mote and the beam *Mat 7:3-5, Luke 6:37-42*

Jesus heals Gadarene of insanity *Mat 8:28-34, Mark 5:1-20, Luke 8:26-39*

Jesus tells why he speaks in parables *Mat 13:10-17, 34, 35, Mark 4:10-12, 33, 34*

Jesus on what defiles a man *Mat 15:1-20, Mark 7:1-23*

Jesus heals daughter of Syrophenician *Mat 15:21-28, Mark 7:24-30*

Peter vows never to deny Jesus and then does *Mat 26:31-35, 57, 69-75, Mark 14:27-31, 66-72, Luke 22:31-34, 54-62, John 13:36-38, 18:13-18, 25-27*

Jesus heals man in temple *Mark 1:21-28, Luke 4:33-37*

Jesus on the leaven of the Pharisees *Luke 12:1-15*

Paul on the carnal mind as enmity against God *Rom 8:1-39*

Paul on being of one mind with Christ *Phil 2:1-15*

See also body, consciousness, heart, human, intelligence, psychiatry, psychology, Mind (divine)

MINISTRY

Abraham blessed by Melchizedek after war of kings *Gen 14:8-20, Heb 6:20, 7:1-28*

Aaron and sons anointed for priesthood *Lev 8:1-13*

Eldad and Medad prophesy in the camp *Num 11:16-30*

Samuel called by the Lord to serve *1 Sam 3:1-10*

David's song, "Create in me a clean heart" *Psal 51:1-19*

David's song, "Whither shall I go from thy spirit?" *Psal 139:1-24*

Isaiah called to speak God's word *Isa 6:1-13*

Isaiah outlines the office of the Christ *Isa 42:1-12, 16, 18*

Zechariah's vision of two olive trees *Zech 4:1-14*

Ministry of John the Baptist *Mat 3:1-12, Mark 1:1-8, Luke 3:1-18*

Jesus heals groups of people *Mat 4:23-25, 12:14-21, 14:14, 34-36, 15:29-31, 19:1, 2, Luke 4:40-44, 6:17-19, Mark 3:6-12, 6:53-56*

Jesus sends twelve to heal and preach *Mat 9:36-38, 10:1-42, Mark 3:13-21, 6:7-13, Luke 6:13-19, 9:1-6*

Jesus instructs and sends 70 disciples —they return *Luke 10:1-24*

Jesus' parable of good Samaritan *Luke 10:25-37*

Jesus' parable of the faithful steward *Luke 12:41-48*

Jesus' parable of servant before he sups *Luke 17:7-10*

John's vision of Jesus Christ as the light of the world *John 1:1-14, 8:12-32*

John the Baptist tells how Jesus' preaching differs *John 3:22-36*

Jesus' parable of good shepherd *John 10:1-18*

Jesus washes his disciples' feet *John 13:1-20*

Jesus' parable of the true vine *John 15:1-17*

Philip explains Isaiah to the Ethiopian *Acts 8:26-40*

Peter accepts conversion of Gentiles *Acts 11:1-48*

Paul on the cost of establishing church *2 Cor 11:21-33*

Paul gives point for guidance of disciples *1 Thess. 5:1-28*

Paul gives advice to his disciple *2 Tim 2:1-26*

Paul gives more precepts to his disciple *2 Tim 4:1-8*

James on how to bear our cross *Jas 1:1-27*

James on faith without works *Jas 2:14-26*

See also disciple, harvest, office, preaching, priest, profession, service

MIRACLE

All great works of Jesus (*See* Part II, Jesus Christ: Great Works)

See also dominion, healing, power, signs, wonder

MISERY

Hagar is turned out into the wilderness *Gen 21:9-21*

Israelites oppressed in Egypt *Exod 1:8-14*
Elijah discouraged *1 King 19:1-8*
The Shunammite is greatly troubled, but does not admit it *2 King 4:8-37*
Jerusalem's misery during captivity *Neh 1:1-11*
Job's trials and woe *Job 2:1-10, 3:1-26*
David's song, "Why art thou cast down?" *Psal 42:1-11*
The misery of captivity *Psal 137:1-9*
Isaiah comforts the church in its sorrow *Isa 54:1-6, 11-17*
Isaiah offers reassurance to afflicted *Isa 40:1-31*
Jeremiah promises that captivity will be restored *Jer 29:8-14*
Jonah, in a precarious position, prays *Jonah 2:1-10*
Jesus cures the epileptic boy *Mat 17:14-21, Mark 9:14-29, Luke 9:37-43*
Jesus restores her son to the widow of Nain *Luke 7:11-17*
Jesus' parable of the rich man in hell *Luke 16:19-31*
Jesus heals the impotent man at the pool *John 5:1-16*
Paul's hardships to establish church *2 Cor 11:21-33*

See also affliction, comfort, distress, happiness, pain, sorrow

MISFORTUNE

Abraham puts Hagar and their son out *Gen 21:9-21*
Joseph unjustly sold into slavery and put into prison *Gen 37:1-36, 39:1-20*
Sensuality betrays Samson *Judg 16:4-30*
Ruth and Naomi lose everything *Ruth 1:1-22, 2:1-23*
Samuel discovers he made a mistake *1 Sam 15:7-26*
David finds he has earned Saul's hatred *1 Sam 18:1-16*
Elijah flees to the wilderness *1 King 19:1-8*
The Shunammite is given a son and he is taken away, then restored *2 King 4:8-37*

Hezekiah loses his throne by trusting unwisely *2 King 20:12-21, Isa 39:1-8*
Mordecai and Jews persecuted by Haman *Esther 3:1-15, 4:1-17*
Job suffers great losses without cause *Job 2:1-10, 3:1-26*
David's song, "Why art thou cast down?" *Psal 42:1-11*
David's song, "Make a joyful noise" *Psal 66:1-20, 100:1-5*
The vanity of human things *Eccl 1:1-18, 2:1-26*
Isaiah's parable of the wild grapes *Isa 5:1-8*
Jeremiah's parable of good and bad figs *Jer 24:1-10*
Sins of fathers visited on children *Ezek 18:1-32*
Daniel put in lions' den without cause *6:1-28*
Jonah in trouble *Jonah 1:1-17, 2:1-10*
Jesus heals a leper *Mat 8:1-4, Mark 1:40-45, Luke 5:12-16*
Jesus' parable of traveler helped by good Samaritan *Luke 10:25-37*
Jesus heals the man born blind *John 9:1-41*
Peter and John heal man lame from birth *Acts 3:1-11*
Paul heals young man fallen from window *Acts 20:7-12*
Paul's sermon on his trials as a Christian *Acts 20:17-38*
Paul saved from shipwreck *Acts 27:1-44*
James on how to bear our cross *Jas 1:1-27*

See also accident, adversity, hardness, prosperity, success

MISSION

Abraham called by God to search for promised land *Gen 11:31, 32, 12:1-9*
Joseph's dream of sheaves foretells his future purpose *Gen 37-1-36*
Moses called to deliver people from Egypt *Exod 3:9-12, 4:10-17*
Moses introduces law to the people *Exod 18:13-27, 20:1-19*
Aaron starts the priesthood *Lev 8:1-13*

Song of Moses reviews mission accomplished *Deut 32:1-47*

Joshua given command *Josh 1:1-9*

The Lord calls Samuel to serve in his temple *1 Sam 3:1-10*

David anointed king of Judah and Israel *2 Sam 2:1-4, 5:1-5*

Solomon builds the temple *1 King 6:1-38, 7:1-51, 2 Chron 3:1-17, 4: 1-22, 5:1-14*

Zerubbabel called to rebuild the temple *Ezra 1:1-11, 3:8-13*

Nehemiah sent to rebuild the walls of Jerusalem *Neh 4:1-23*

Isaiah called to prophesy *Isa 6:1-13*

Jonah sent to preach to Nineveh, disobeys at first *Jonah 1:1-17, 2: 1-10, 3:1-10*

Micah's vision of the glory of the church *Mic 4:1-8, 13, Isa 2:1-5*

Jesus' parable of the sower *Mat 13: 3-23, Mark 4:1-20, Luke 8:4-15*

Jesus sends twelve disciples to heal and preach *Mat 9:36-38, 10:1-42, Mark 3:13-21, 6:7-13, Luke 6:13-19, 9:1-6, 10, 11*

Jesus sends 70 disciples more *Luke 10:1-24*

Jesus, the light of the world *John 1:1-14*

Jesus charges Peter to feed his sheep *John 21:10-19*

See also calling, church, disciple, gospel, Jesus, messenger, ministry

MISTAKE

Eve and Adam believe serpent's lie *Gen 3:1-5*

Isaac blesses Jacob, thinking it is Esau *Gen 27:1-44*

People fail to take advice of Caleb and Joshua *Num 13:1-33, 14:1-11, 23-39, Deut 1:19-38*

Samuel anoints Saul king *1 Sam 10: 1-8, 15:7-26*

Hezekiah shows his enemy all his treasures *2 King 20:12-21, Isa 39:1-8*

The excellency of wisdom *Prov 3: 13-26, 4:1-13, 8:1-36*

Jesus' parable of rich man and bigger barns *Luke 12:15-21*

Jesus' parable of rich man and beggar *Luke 16:19-21*

Jesus' parable of prayer of the Pharisee *Luke 18:9-14*

Saul persecutes Christians at first *Acts 8:1-4*

People worship Paul and Barnabas as gods *Acts 14:11-18*

See also error, repentance, sin, wisdom

MODERATION

Manna and quails, gathered in excess, spoil *Exod 16:1-36, Num 11:1-15, 31, 32*

After destroying first tablets Moses is given new chance *Exod 34:1-8, Deut 10:1-4*

Gideon refuses crown because God governs *Judg 8:22, 23*

David spares Saul instead of taking revenge *1 Sam 24:1-22, 26:1-25*

Elijah asks the widow to make his portion first *1 King 17:1-16*

David's song, "Create in me a clean heart" *Psal 51:1-19*

David's song, "the beauty of the Lord our God be upon us" *Psal 90:1-17*

The happy value of wisdom *Prov 3:13-26, 4:1-13, 8:1-36*

The practical wife and mother *Prov 31:1-31*

Jeremiah's vision of the potter and clay *Jer 18-1-6*

Daniel refuses the king's portion of food *Dan 1:1-21*

Jesus makes concession by accepting baptism *Mat 3:13-17, Mark 1:9-11, Luke 3:21, 22*

Jesus overcomes temptation *Mat 4: 1-11, Mark 1:12, 13, Luke 4:1-13*

Jesus on treatment of enemies *Mat 5:38-48, 18:15-22, Luke 6:27-36*

Jesus' parable of the mote and the beam *Mat 7:1-5, Luke 6:37-42*

Jesus eats with publicans and sinners *Mat 9:10-13, Mark 2:13-17, Luke 5:27-32*

Why Jesus' disciples don't fast *Mat 9:14-17, Mark 2:18-22, Luke 5:33-39*

Jesus' parable of the wheat and the tares *Mat 13:24-30, 36-43*

Rich young ruler balks at selling all he has *Mat 19:16-30, Mark 10: 17-31, Luke 18:18-30*

Precious ointment on Jesus' head
   Mat 26:6-13, Mark 14:3-9
Jesus approves the widow's mite
   Mark 12:41-44, Luke 21:1-4
Martha complains to Jesus about
   her sister *Luke 10:38-42*
Jesus' parable of rich man and big-
   ger barns *Luke 12:15-21*
Jesus' parable of the chief seats at
   the feast *Luke 14:7-14*
Jesus on humility *John 13:12-20*
Paul on faith, hope and charity
   1 Cor 13:1-13
Paul's description of enemies of the
   truth *2 Tim 3:1-17*

See also abstinence, appetite, control, food, temperance

MONARCHY

See king

MONEY

Aaron collects jewelry and metal to
   mold golden calf *Exod 32:1-24*
David receives liberal offerings to
   build temple *1 Chron 29:6-19*
Elisha prophesies drop in price of
   flour *2 King 6:24, 25, 7:1-18*
Hezekiah shows his treasures un-
   wisely *2 King 20:12-21, Isa 39:
   1-8*
Jehoiachin assigned continual al-
   lowance for life *2 King 25:27-30*
Jesus sends disciples forth with
   money *Mat 10:5-42, Mark 6:7-13,
   Luke 9:1-6*
Jesus' parable of treasure in field
   Mat 13:44
Jesus' parable of pearl of great price
   Mat 13:45, 46
Jesus' parable of householder's treas-
   ures *Mat 13:51, 52*
Jesus sends Peter for tribute money
   in mouth of fish *Mat 17:24-27*
Jesus' parable of the laborers in vine-
   yard *Mat 20:1-16*
Jesus' parable of men who refused
   rent *Mat 21:33-46, Mark 12:1-12,
   Luke 20:9-19*
Jesus' parable of the talents *Mat
   25:14-30, Luke 19:11-28*
Judas settles price for betrayal at
   30 pieces of silver *Mat 26:14-16,
   Mark 14:10, 11, Luke 22:1-6*

Jesus approves the widow's mite
   Mark 12:41-44, Luke 21:1-4
Jesus' parable of lost coin *Luke
   15:8-10*
Zaccheus volunteers to return all
   money extorted *Luke 19:1-10*

See also riches, supply, treasure,
wealth

MONOTHEISM

God creates complete universe in his
   image *Gen 1:1-31*
To Moses is revealed the nature of
   God *Exod 3:1-18*
Moses receives First Commandment
   Exod 20:1-3
Golden calf worship breaks mono-
   theism *Exod 32:1-24*
The watchword of Israel *Deut 6:
   4-6*
God's warning against enticers to
   idolatry *Deut 13:1-18*
Moses offers people their choice
   Deut 30:11-20
Contest of Elijah with 450 prophets
   of Baal *1 King 18:17-40*
The infinite speaks to Job *Job 38:
   1-41*
David's song of infinite's ever-pres-
   ence *Psal 139:1-24*
Three Jews refuse to worship an-
   other god *Dan 3:1-30*
Daniel refuses to worship another
   god first *Dan 6:1-28*
Jesus accused of healing by Beelze-
   bub *Mat 12:22-30, Mark 3:22-30,
   Luke 11:14-23*
Jesus proves unity of gospel with
   law and prophets *Mat 17:1-13,
   Mark 9:2-13, Luke 9:28-36*
Jesus tells how to inherit eternal
   life *Mat 19:16-30, Mark 10:17-31,
   Luke 10:25-28, John 18:18-30*
Jesus telescopes Ten Command-
   ments into two *Mat 22:34-40,
   Mark 12:28-34*
Jesus urges no thought for material
   life *Mat 6:25-34, Luke 12:22-34*
Jesus tells the source of his great
   works *John 5:17-47*
Paul's teaching that all talents come
   from God *1 Cor 12:1, 4-31*
Paul's teaching to come out and be
   separate *2 Cor 6:1-18*

Paul's sermon on God, the unity of all *Eph 4: 1-32*

See also God, gods, oneness, unity

MORALITY

Enoch translated because he walked with God *Gen 5: 18, 21-24, Heb 11: 5*

Noah and the righteous promised safety *Gen 6: 5-22*

Joseph overcomes temptation *Gen 39: 1-20*

Moses says choice must be made between good and evil *Deut 30: 11-20, Josh 24: 1-25*

Joshua uncovers sin *Josh 7: 1-26, 8: 14-21*

David's morals fall after triumphs *2 Sam 11: 1-27*

Nathan's courage to uncover the king's fault *2 Sam 12: 1-10*

Uzziah's pride punished by leprosy *2 Chron 26: 1-23*

Job raises the question, why should the good suffer? *Job 3: 1-26*

Job receives his answer from the voice of thunder *Job 38: 1-41*

David's song, "The law of the Lord is perfect" *Psal 33: 1-22*

David's song, "Create in me a clean heart" *Psal 51: 1-19*

Isaiah's vision of war no more *Isa 2: 1-5, 11: 1-12, Mic 4: 1-8, 13*

Isaiah's vision of fall of evil *Isa 14: 4-8, 12-17, 25-27, 29: 11-24, 30: 1-3, 20, 21*

Isaiah's plea for justice *Isa 59: 1-21*

Ezekiel on visiting the iniquities of the fathers on the children *Ezek 18: 1-32*

Jesus put some commands on mental basis *Mat 5: 21-37, Mark 9: 38-50*

Jesus' parable of the unmerciful debtor *Mat 18: 23-25*

Jesus casts traders out of temple *Mat 21: 12, 13, Mark 11: 15-17, Luke 19: 45, 46, John 2: 13-25*

Jesus' parable of the farmers refusing to pay rent *Mat 21: 33-46, Mark 12: 1-12, Luke 20: 9-19*

Jesus' parable of the sheep and goats *Mat 25: 31-46*

Judas settles price to betray Jesus *Mat 26: 14-16, Mark 14: 10, 11, Luke 22: 1-6*

Pilate washes his hands of the decision to crucify *Mat 27: 24-26*

Jesus on the leaven of the Pharisees *Luke 12: 1-15*

Jesus' parable of the faithful steward *Luke 12: 41-48*

Jesus' parable of the prodigal son *Luke 15: 11-24*

Jesus' parable of the unjust steward *Luke 16: 1-14*

Jesus tells impotent man to sin no more *John 5: 1-16*

Jesus tells adultress he saved, to sin no more *John 8: 1-11*

Paul on judgment and law *Rom 2: 1-26*

Paul on Spirit vs. flesh *Rom 8: 1-39*

Paul on how Christians act when tempted *Eph 6: 10-17*

John's list of faults of churches *Rev 1: 4-29, 2: 1-29, 3: 1-22*

See also character, integrity, justice, principle, purity, science

MORNING

Days of creation divided into seven evenings and mornings *Gen 1: 1-31*

Jacob wrestles until break of day and receives new name *Gen 32: 24-32*

Jesus is risen early on resurrection morning *Mat 28: 9, 10, Mark 16: 9-11, Luke 24: 13-49, John 20: 11-18*

Jesus is seen after resurrection and has breakfast with eleven disciples *Mat 28: 16-18, John 21: 1-14*

See also awakening, breakfast, evening

MORTAL

Mortal man made from dust *Gen 2: 6-8*

Lord God remands his man to return to dust *Gen 3: 17-19*

David's song on nature of man and the universe *Psal 8: 1-9*

David's song on "the fountain of life" *Psal 36: 1-12*

David's song on "the secret place of the most High" *Psal 91: 1-16*

David sings that men's days are as grass *Psal 103: 15-22*

David's song on God, the preserver of man *Psal 121: 1-8*

The preacher on the vanity of human things *Eccl 1: 1-18, 2: 1-26*

The preacher on mortal events within the frame work of time *Eccl 3: 1-15*

Isaiah on all flesh is grass *Isa 40: 6-11, 1 Pet 1:24*

Isaiah's vision of the Messiah that will redeem the mortal *Isa 61: 1-11*

A young man asks Jesus about eternal life *Mat 19: 16-30, Mark 10: 17-32, Luke 18: 18-32*

Jesus' body buried *Mat 25: 57-66, Mark 15: 42-57, Luke 23: 50-56, John 19: 31-42*

Jesus raises widow's son from death *Luke 7: 11-17*

Jesus raises Jairus' daughter from death *Luke 8: 41, 42, 49-56, Mark 5: 22-24, 35-43*

A lawyer asks Jesus about eternal life *Luke 10: 25-28*

Jesus' parable of rich man and bigger barns *Luke 12: 15-21*

Jesus' teaching on no thought for material things *Luke 12: 22-34, Mat 6: 25-34*

Jesus' parable of rich man and beggar *Luke 16: 19-31*

Jesus raised from death *Luke 24: 1-49*

Jesus' teaching that God is Spirit and must be worshipped in spirit *John 4: 1-30*

Jesus raises Lazarus four days dead *John 11: 1-46*

Paul and Barnabas worshipped as gods *Acts 14: 11-18*

Paul on Adam vs. Christ *Rom 5: 1-21*

Paul on Spirit vs. flesh *Rom 8: 1-39*

Paul on Christ's resurrection proves ours *1 Cor 15: 1-58*

See also death, eternity, human, immortality, life

MOSES

See Part II, Moses

MOTHER

Eve becomes mother of Cain and Abel *Gen 4: 1, 2*

Hagar becomes mother of Ishmael *Gen 16: 3, 15, 16*

Sarah becomes mother of Isaac *Gen 21: 1-8*

Rebekah helps Jacob deceive his father *Gen 27: 1-44*

Moses' mother preserves him as a baby *Exod 2: 1-10*

Angel announces Samson's birth to his mother *Judg 13: 1-25*

Samuel's miraculous birth (childlessness healed) *1 Sam 1: 1-28*

Solomon's decision: the true mother of the baby *1 King 3: 16-28*

Elijah heals the widow's son *1 King 18: 17-40*

Elisha heals Shunammite's son *2 King 4:8-37*

The nature of a good wife and mother *Prov 31: 1-31*

Isaiah on a mother's comfort *Isa 66: 12, 13*

Jesus heals Peter's mother-in-law *Mat 8: 14-17, Mark 1: 29-34*

Jesus on "Who is my mother?" *Mat 12: 40-50*

Jesus' mother waits for him outside *Mat 12: 46-50, Mark 3: 31-35, Luke 8: 19-21*

Zebedee's wife pushes her sons forward *Mat 20: 20-28, Mark 10: 35-45*

Birth of Jesus announced to Mary *Luke 1: 26-38*

Mary finds Jesus, lost in Jerusalem *Luke 2: 41-52*

Jesus restores dead man to his mother *Luke 7: 11-17*

Jesus gives John the care of his mother *John 19: 25-29*

John's vision of woman with child *Rev 12: 1-17*

See also children, family, father, parent

MOTIVE

Cain kills his brother for a religious motive *Gen 4: 1-16*

Abraham sets out to prove his faith by sacrifice of his son *Gen 22: 1-19*

Jacob's desire for blessing moves him to deceit *Gen 27: 1-44*

Moses' farewell address, "Choose ye" *Deut 30: 11-20*

Ruth follows Naomi from her homeland to Israel *Ruth 1: 1-22*

David moved by lust gets rid of Uriah *2 Sam 11: 1-27*

Solomon prays for understanding *1 King 3: 5-15, 2 Chron 1: 7-12*

Elisha explains his reason for following Elijah *2 King 2: 1-15*

Hezekiah shows men of Babylon his treasures *2 King 23: 12-22, 39:1-8*

Why Esther, the Queen, risks helping her people *Esther 5: 1-14*

Jeremiah buys a field in Jerusalem to show confidence *Jer 32: 2, 6-27, 37-44*

Daniel's purity makes him refuse king's meat *Dan 1: 1-21*

Three Jews refuse to worship image *Dan 3: 1-30*

Daniel refuses to put God second *Dan 6: 1-28*

Jonah moves contrary to God's direction *Jonah 1: 1-17, 2: 1-10, 3: 1-10*

Jesus puts law on mental basis *Mat 5: 21-48, Mark 9: 38-50, Luke 6: 27-36*

Jesus changes the reasons for giving *Mat 6: 1-4*

Jesus gives Golden Rule for actions *Mat 7: 12-14, Luke 6: 41, 42*

Jesus on what defiles a man *Mat 15: 1-20, Mark 7: 1-23*

Jesus' parable of the lost sheep *Mat 18: 12-14, Luke 15: 1-7*

Jesus' parable of unmerciful debtor *Mat 18: 23-25*

Jesus' purpose in life revealed at Gethsemane *Mat 30, 36-46, Mark 14: 26, 32-42, Luke 22: 39-46*

Jesus approves widow's action giving mite *Mark 12: 41-44, Luke 21: 1-4*

Jesus' parable of good Samaritan *Luke 10: 25-37*

Jesus' parable of rich man and bigger barns *Luke 12: 15-21*

Jesus' parable of prodigal *Luke 15: 11-24*

Jesus' parable of elder brother *Luke 15: 25-32*

Jesus' parable of the good shepherd *John 10: 1-18*

Jesus washes disciples' feet *John 13: 1-20*

Pentecost gives disciples new impetus *Acts 2: 1-13*

Paul persecutes Christians *Acts 8: 1-4*

Ananias heals Paul *Acts 9: 10-22*

Paul on charity *2 Cor 13: 1-13*

Paul's teaching to think on good things *Phil 4: 1-23*

Paul explains why to obey Christ *Heb 2: 1-18*

John's sermon, "God is Love" *1 John 4: 1-21*

See also aims, idea, influence, plan, purpose, reason, will

MOUNTAIN

Moses finds the burning bush on Mt. Horeb *Exod 3: 1-12*

Moses talks with God on Mt. Sinai *Exod 19: 1-9, Deut 4: 1-15*

Moses comes back down with Ten Commandments *Exod 20: 1-19, Deut 5: 1-24*

Moses goes back up for second tablets *Exod 33: 7-23, 34: 1-8*

David's song, "I will lift up mine eyes unto the hills" *Psal 121: 1-8*

Micah's vision of the glory of the church on top of the mountains *Mic 4: 1-8, 11, Isa 2: 1-5*

Jesus, transfigured, talks with Moses and Elijah on the mountain *Mat 17: 1-13, Mark 9: 2-13, Luke 9: 28-36*

See also ascension, exaltation, hill, obstacle

MOURNING

David's song, "How are the mighty fallen!" *2 Sam 1:17-27*

The child of David and Bathsheba dies *2 Sam 12: 13-23*

Nehemiah is informed of Jerusalem's misery *Neh 1: 1-11*

Job's troubles and woe *Job 2: 1-10, 3: 1-26*

David's song, "the fountain of life" *Psal 36: 1-12*

A psalm, "By the rivers of Babylon . . . we wept" *Psal 137: 1-9*

The vanity of mortal life *Eccl 1: 1-18, 2: 1-26*

All mortal events within a time framework *Eccl 3: 1-15*

Isaiah's vision of comfort *Isa 40: 1-31*

Isaiah's plea for justice *Isa 59:1-21*

Jeremiah's promise of restoration *Jer 31: 1-14, 31-34*

"Blessed are they that mourn" (Jesus' teaching) *Mat 5:1-12, Luke 6: 17-26*

Jesus invites heavy laden to come to him *Mat 11: 28-30*

Jesus' parable of wheat and tares *Mat 13: 24-30, 36-43*

Jesus' parable of dragnet *Mat 13: 47-50*

Jesus' parable of laborers in vineyard *Mat 20: 1-16*

Jesus greets sorrowing Mary after crucifixion—her joy returns *Mark 16: 9-11, John 20: 11-18*

Jesus stops widow's mourning by raising her son *Luke 7: 11-17*

Jesus' parable of faithful steward *Luke 12: 41-48*

Jesus' parable of judge and widow *Luke 18: 1-8*

Jesus' parable of the temple to be raised in three days *John 2: 19-22*

Jesus says he is the light of the world and makes free those that mourn *John 8: 12-32*

Jesus' parable of good shepherd *John 10: 1-18*

Jesus comforts Martha, "I am the resurrection, and the life" *John 11: 21-27*

Jesus' parable of true vine *John 15: 1:-17*

Jesus comforts those in tribulation *John 16: 1-33*

Peter raises Tabitha who is being mourned *Acts 9: 36-43*

Paul on immortality *Rom 8: 6-14, 35-39*

Paul explains that Christ's resurrection proves ours *1 Cor 15: 1-58*

Paul on faith, the substance of religion *Heb 11: 1-40*

James' sermon on how to bear our cross *Jas 1: 1-27*

John's sermon, "God is Love" *1 John 4:1-21*

John's vision of new heaven and earth—no weeping *Rev 21: 1-27*

John's vision of the river of life *Rev 22: 1-21*

See also death, grief, immortality, joy, loss, parting, separation, sorrow

MULTIPLY

God's blessing to his creation, "Be fruitful, and multiply" *Gen 1: 22-28*

Abraham's riches grow *Gen 13: 1-18*

The blessings of obedience—a sure reward *Deut 28: 1-14*

Elijah's work supplies widow with food *1 King 17: 1-16*

Elisha multiplies the pot of oil *2 King 4:1-7*

David's song, "The earth is the Lord's, and the fulness thereof" *Psal 24: 1-10*

David's song, "the fountain of life" *Psal 36: 1-12*

Isaiah's vision of the desert that blossomed *Isa 35: 1-10*

Jesus on seek ye first *Mat 6: 25-34, Luke 12: 22-34*

Jesus on knowing men by their fruits *Mat 7: 15-20, Luke 6: 43-45*

Jesus' parable of the sower *Mat 13: 3-23, Mark 4: 1-20, Luke 8: 4-15*

Jesus' parable of mustard seed *Mat 13: 31, 32, Mark 4: 30-32, Luke 13: 18, 19*

Jesus feeds 5000 with a few loaves and fishes *Mat 14: 15-21, Mark 6: 35-44, Luke 9: 12-17, John 6: 5-14*

Jesus feeds 4000 men and families *Mat 15: 32-39, Mark 8: 1-10*

Jesus reminds disciples of his great works *Mat 16: 5-12, Mark 8: 13-21*

Jesus withers fig tree without fruit *Mat 21: 18-22, Mark 11: 12-14, 21-24*

Jesus' parable of the talents *Mat 25: 14-30, Luke 19: 11-28*

All men seek Jesus increasing his fame *Mark 1: 35-39*

Jesus' parable of seed, blade, ear *Mark 4: 26-29*

Jesus' parable of rich man and bigger barns *Luke 12:15-21*

Jesus' parable of the true vine *John 15:1-17*

Peter adds many to church *Acts 4:24-37*

Peter heals multitudes *Acts 5:12-16*

Paul on talents coming from God *1 Cor 12:1, 4-31*

Paul on abundance *2 Cor 8:11-15, 9: 6-15*

Paul on fruits of the Spirit *Gal 5:1-26*

James on faith without works *Jas 2:14-26*

See also barrenness, fruits, increase, supply

MURDER

See kill

MUSIC

Moses' song of mercy and deliverance *Exod 15:1-19, Deut 32:1-47*

Deborah's song of God's victory *Judg 5:1-20*

David dances before the ark *1 Sam 6:12-23, 1 Chron 15:25-29*

David plays harp to calm Saul *1 Sam 16:14-23*

Singing in streets on return from slaughter of the Philistines *1 Sam 18:6-9*

David's lament, "How are the mighty fallen!" *2 Sam 1:17-27*

David's song of thanksgiving *2 Sam 22:1-51, 1 Chron 16:17-36*

Book of 150 psalms *Psal 1:1—150:6*

Music as signal for idol worship *Dan 3:1-30*

Hosannas as Jesus enters Jerusalem *Mat 21:1-11, 14-17, Mark 11: 1-11, Luke 19:29-44, John 12:12-19*

The disciples sing a hymn before going with Jesus to Gethsemane *Mat 26:30, 36-46, Mark 14:26, 32-42, Luke 22:39-46*

Prodigal's elder brother hears music and dancing *Luke 15:25-32*

Paul and Silas sing hymns in prison *Acts 16:19-40*

See also harmony, hymn, instrument, praise, psalm

MYSTERY

Moses sees rod transformed to serpent, Aaron too *Exod 4:1-9, 7: 1-12*

Moses' face concealed by veil *Exod 34:29-35*

Moses does not object to Eldad's and Medad's prophesying *Num 11:16-30*

Gideon's faith built by signs and wonders *Judg 6:19-40*

God communicates his nature to Elijah *1 King 19:9-13*

Elisha asks for a double portion of Elijah's spirit *2 King 2:1-15*

Job asks why the good should suffer *Job 3:1-26*

David's song, "What is man?" *Psal 8:1-9*

The coming of the Messiah *Isa 7: 10-16, 9:2-7*

The office of the Messiah *Isa 42: 1-12, 16, 18*

Daniel's insight interprets the king's dream *Dan 2:1-49, 4:1-27, 5:1-31*

Zechariah's vision of two candlesticks *Zech 4:1-14*

Jesus' parable of the leaven hidden *Mat 13:33, Luke 13:20, 21*

Why Jesus speaks in parables *Mat 13:10-17, 34, 35, Mark 4:10-12, 33, 34*

The Eucharist is instituted *Mat 26: 26-29, Mark 14:22-25, Luke 22:14-30, 1 Cor 11:23-25*

Angel announces immaculate birth to Mary *Luke 1:26-38*

Jesus on the bread of life *John 6: 26-65*

Jesus' teaching that he is Christ *John 7:14-40*

Jesus promises coming of Holy Ghost *John 14:1-31*

Simon offers to buy secret of Holy Ghost *Acts 8:14-25*

Paul and Barnabas are worshipped as gods due to success in healing *Acts 14:11-18*

Paul called a god because viper sting did not kill him *Acts 28:1-6*

Paul explains Melchizedek *Heb 6: 20, 7:1-28*

John's vision of the key found to open the sealed book *Rev 5:1-14*

John's vision of the woman with child *Rev 12:1-17*

See also Eucharist, sacrament, secret, wonder

N

NAME

Adam gives names to every living creature *Gen 2:9-25*

Abram and Sarai given new names by "walking with God" *Gen 17: 1-9, 15-22*

Jacob wrestles with angel and is called Israel *Gen 32:24-32*

Peter (Simon) acknowledges Jesus as Christ and receives a new name himself *Mat 16:13-20, Mark 8:27-30, Luke 9:18-21*

Saul is converted and takes name of Paul *Acts 8:1-4, 9:1-22*

Paul's teaching to put on the new man *Col 3:1-27*

King of kings *Rev 19:11-21*

See also baptism, character, family, individuality, nature, origin, spirituality

NATION

God promises Abraham He will make of him a great nation *Gen 12:1-9*

Jacob prophesies the future of his children *Gen 49:1-28, Deut 33:1-29*

Oppression of Israelites by Egyptians *Exod 1:8-14*

The song of Moses reviews escape from Egypt *Exod 15:1-19, Deut 32:1-47*

The chosen people set apart as God's own *Deut 7:6-11*

Children of Israel cross Jordan and enter promised land *Josh 3:1-17*

David made king of Judah, then Israel *2 Sam 2:1-4, 5:1-5*

Solomon dedicates temple and blesses people *1 King 8:22-66, 2 Chron 6:1-42*

Jeremiah promises the restoration from captivity *Jer 29:8-14, 31:1-14, 31-34*

Hosea's vision of Israel as a child in God's care *Hos 11:1-4*

Jesus heals servant of centurion who helped the nation *Mat 8: 5-13, Luke 7:1-10*

Jesus shows the union of the gospel with the law and the prophets *Mat 17:1-13, Mark 9:2-13, Luke 9:28-36*

The nations of the saved shall walk in the city foursquare *Rev 21: 16-27*

See also Gentile, language, patriotism, people, religion, world

NATURE

Rivers and trees in Eden *Gen 2: 9-17*

Animals created out of the ground *Gen 2:18-20*

The flood and Noah's ark *Gen 7: 1-24*

The raven and the dove on the ark *Gen 8:1-22*

The rainbow *Gen 9:12-17*

Manna and quails in the wilderness *Exod 16:1-36, Num 11:1-15, 31, 32*

Water from the rock *Exod 17:1-7, Num 20:1-13*

Elijah fed by ravens *1 King 7:1-16*

Elijah prays for rain *1 King 18: 41-46*

Elijah communes with God on the mount *1 King 19:9-13*

Job hears voice of thunder explain wonders of nature *Job 38:1-41*

David's song on the nature of God's universe and man *Psal 8:1-9*

Isaiah's vision of the desert blossoming *Isa 35:1-10*

Jesus' parables of agriculture:

the sower *Mat 13:3-23, Mark 4: 1-20, Luke 8:4-15*

the wheat and tares *Mat 13:24-30, 36-43*

the mustard seed *Mat 13:31, 32, Mark 4: 30-32, Luke 13:18, 19*

seed, blade, ear *Mark 4:26-29*

the barren fruit tree *Luke 13:6-9*

the true vine *John 15:1-17*

Jesus calms wind and sea *Mat 8: 23-27, Mark 4:35-41, Luke 8:22-25*

Jesus walks on water *Mat 14:22-33, John 6:15-21*

Jesus calms windstorm *Mark 6:45-52, John 6:21*

The net of Peter, the fisherman, is filled *Luke 5:1-11, John 21:1-11*

Paul is shipwrecked on an island *Acts 27:1-44*

See also character, earth, ego, name, primitive, principle, universe

NECROMANCY

Lord God breathes life into man made from dust *Gen 2:6-8*

Sorcerers of Egypt unable to match Aaron *Exod 7:1-12*

Balaam refuses to curse Israelites *Num 22:1-41, 23:1-30, 24:1-25*

Moses warns against enticers, necromancers *Deut 13:1-18*

Moses forbids abominations *Deut 18:9-14*

Isaiah foretells fall of Babylon *Isa 14:4-8, 12-17, 25-27*

Isaiah foretells that workers in dark will be punished *Isa 29-11-24, 30: 1-3, 20, 21*

Daniel excels the astrologers *Dan 2:1-49*

Wise men follow star to King of the Jews *Mat 2:1-12*

Jesus accused of healing by Beelzebub *Mat 12:22-30, Mark 3:22-30, Luke 11:14-23*

Paul heals the damsel soothsayer *Acts 16:16-18*

Paul on wrestling with powers of darkness *Eph 6:10-17*

Paul describes enemies of truth *2 Tim 3:1-17*

See also hypnotism, idolatry, magic, magnetism, mesmerism

NEED, NECESSITY

Hagar and son athirst in wilderness *Gen 21:9-21*

Esau sells his birthright for pottage *Gen 25:24-34*

Joseph's brethren come to Egypt for food *Gen 42:1-8*

Manna in the wilderness; quails *Exod 16:1-36, Num 11:1-15, 31, 32*

Water in the desert *Exod 17:1-7, Num 20:1-13*

Ruth gleans corn in the field *Ruth 2:1-23*

Elijah supplies food to the widow *1 King 17:1-16*

Elijah prays for rain *1 King 18: 41-46*

Elisha fills widow's pot of oil *2 King 4:1-7*

Elisha feeds 100 men with 20 rolls of bread *2 King 4:42-44*

Elisha prophesies incredible plenty *2 King 6:24, 25, 7:1-18*

Nehemiah learns of Jerusalem's misery *Neh 1:1-11*

David's song, "The Lord is my shepherd" *Psal 23:1-6*

David's song, "Let the redeemed of the Lord say so" *Psal 107:1-43*

Isaiah's vision of the desert blossoming *Isa 35:1-10*

Jesus teaches the Lord's Prayer *Mat 6:5-15, Mark 11:25, 26, Luke 11:1-4*

Jesus' teaching, take no thought *Mat 6:25-34, Luke 12:22-24*

Jesus' disciples pluck corn on sabbath *Mat 12:1-8, Mark 2:23-28, Luke 6:1-5*

Jesus feeds 5000 *Mat 14:15-21, Mark 6:35-44, Luke 9:12-17, John 6:5-14*

Jesus fills Peter's net *Luke 5:1-11, John 21:1-11*

Jesus' parable of the unwilling friend *Luke 11:5-13*

Jesus' parable of the barren fig tree *Luke 13:6-9*

Paul on source of abundance *2 Cor 8:11-15, 9:6-15*

See also lack, supply

NEGATIVE, NEGATION

Joseph resists advances of Potiphar's wife *Gen 39:1-20*

Ten Commandments of Moses *Exod 20:1-19, Deut 5:1-24*

Balaam refuses to curse Israel *Num 22:1-41, 23:1-30, 24:1-25*

Moses' warnings against enticers to idolatry *Deut 13:1-18*

Moses forbids abominations *Deut 18:9-14*

Elisha refuses reward of clothing from Naaman; Gehazi accepts *2 King 5:15-27*

David's song, "Fret not thyself because of evildoers" *Psal 37:23-40*

Isaiah's vision of fall of Babylon *Isa 14:4-8, 12-17, 25-27*

Isaiah's advice, "Fear not" *Isa 43:1-28, 44:1-24*

Daniel refuses King's meat *Dan 1:1-21*

Three Jews refuse to worship image *Dan 3:1-30*

Daniel refuses to give up prayers *Dan 6:1-28*
Jesus on Moses' Commandments *Mat 5:21-48, Mark 9:38-50, Luke 6:27-36*
Jesus' teaching on take no thought *Mat 6:25-34, Luke 12:22-34*
Jesus' teaching to judge not *Mat 7:1-5, Luke 6:37-40*
Jesus explains that Jairus' daughter is not dead and raises her *Mat 9:18, 19, 23-26, Mark 5:22-24, 35-43, Luke 8:40, 41, 49-56*
Peter denies Jesus *Mat 26:57, 58, 69-75, Mark 14:66-72, Luke 22:54-62 John 18:13-18, 25-27*
Jesus' teaching, do not offend but forgive *Luke 17:1-6*
Jesus casts out traders from temple *John 2:13-25*
Paul's teaching to put off the old man *Col 3:1-17*

See also affirmation, denial

NEGRO

Moses married an Ethiopian woman *Num 12:1-16*
Philip baptizes Ethiopian envoy *Acts 8:26-40*

See also Africa

NEHEMIAH

See Part II, Nehemiah

NEIGHBOR

Abraham's nearness causes conflict with Lot *Gen 13:1-18*
David lusts for his neighbor's wife *2 Sam 11:1-27*
Nathan's parable exposes David's moral fall *2 Sam 12:1-10*
Job's friends call on him in trouble— lend no comfort *Job 16:1-22*
Jesus asks, Who is my mother? and ... brethren? *Mat 12:46-50*
Jesus says a prophet is without honor in his own country *Mat 13:53-58, Mark 6:1-6, Luke 4:22-24*
Jesus' parable of unmerciful debtor *Mat 18:23-25*
Zebedee's wife asks favors for her sons *Mat 20:20-28, Mark 10:35-45*

Mary's visit to Elizabeth *Luke 1:39-56*
Jesus' parable of good Samaritan *Luke 10:25-37*
Jesus' parable of rich man and beggar *Luke 16:19-31*
Jesus' parable of Pharisee and publican *Luke 18:9-14*
Peter opens Christianity to the Gentiles *Acts 11:1-18*
Paul on charity *1 Cor 13:1-13*
Paul on unity *Eph 4:1-23*
James preaches on equality of man *Jas 2:1-13*
John on God is love *1 John 4:1-21*

See also brotherhood, fellowship, friendship, kindness, love

NERVES

Lord God breathes life into man of dust *Gen 2:6-8*
David's song, "What is man?" *Psal 8:1-9*
David's song, "Why art thou cast down?" *Psal 42:1-11*
Herod thinks Jesus is John the Baptist whom he has beheaded *Mat 14:1-13, Mark 6:14-29, Luke 9:7-9*

See also body, intelligence, life, mind, senses

NEUTRALITY

Serpent offers the "improvement" of knowing good and evil *Gen 3:1-5*
Moses insists people must choose between good and evil *Deut 30:11-20*
Joshua poses same choice before them *Josh 24:1-25*
Elijah, "How long halt ye between two opinions?" *1 King 18:17-40*
Shunammite refuses to accept negative news about her son *2 King 4:8-37*
Mordecai persuades Esther not to remain neutral *Esther 3:1-15, 4:1-17*
Jesus says he who is not with me is against me *Mat 12:28-30*
Jesus' parable of the unclean spirit that returned with seven others *Mat 12:43-45, Luke 11:24-26*

Jesus' parable of the talents *Mat 25:14-30, Luke 19:11-28*

Jesus' parable of sheep and goats *Mat 25:31-46*

Pilate washes his hands of responsibility *Mat 27:15-26, Mark 15: 6-15, Luke 23: 13-25, John 18:39, 40*

Persistence wins blind Bartimaeus his sight *Mark 10:46-52*

Jesus' parable of unjust steward *Luke 16:1-14*

Jesus' parable of rich man and beggar *Luke 16:19-31*

Jesus' parable of judge and widow *Luke 18:1-8*

Paul's sermon at Athens on Unknown God *Acts 17:15-34*

James on faith without works *Jas 2:14-26*

John's letter to church of Laodiceans who are neither hot nor cold *Rev 3:14-22*

See also body, evil, goodness, mind, negative, war

NEW

New spiritual natures for Abram and Sarai *Gen 17:1-9, 15-20*

Jacob receives new nature and name *Gen 32:24-36*

Moses gets a new revelation of God as I Am *Exod 3:1-18*

Moses delivers a new concept of law *Exod 20:1-19, Deut 5:1-24*

Moses institutes judges for the law *Exod 18:13-27*

The priesthood is instituted with Aaron *Lev 8:1-13*

The beginning of legal rights for women *Num 27:1-11, 36:5-13*

Samuel anoints the first king, Saul *1 Sam 10:1-8*

Solomon builds the first temple *1 King 6:1-38, 7:1-51, 2 Chron 3:1-17, 4:1-22, 5:1-14*

Isaiah's prophecy of the Messiah *Isa 7:10-16, 9:2-7*

Jesus puts Mosaic commands on mental basis *Mat 5:21-48, Luke 6:27-36*

Jesus institutes first communion *Mat 26:26-29, Mark 14:22-25, Luke 22:14-30*

Jesus is risen *Mat 28:1-8, Mark 16: 1-8, Luke 24:1-12, John 20:1-10*

Jesus' parable of seed, blade, ear *Mark 4:26-29*

Angels announce glad tidings *Luke 2:8-20*

Jesus' parable of new wine in old bottles *Luke 5:36-39*

Jesus heals man born blind (never done before) *John 9:1-41*

Jesus heals man dead four days (never done before) *John 11:1-46*

Jesus promises to send the Holy Ghost *John 14:1-31*

Peter accepts the Gentiles *Acts 11: 1-18*

See also birth, gospel, life, man, name, publish, renewal, tongue

NEWS

Moses learns that he is to lead his people out of Egypt *Exod 3:9-12*

Moses hears that Eldad and Medad prophesy in the camp *Num 11: 16-30*

Caleb and Joshua scout the land of promise *Num 13:1-33, 14:1-11, 23-39, Deut 1:19-38*

Moses informs Israelites that they are God's chosen people *Deut 7: 6-11*

Rahab shelters two spies in Jericho *Josh 2:1-24*

Nehemiah hears of Jerusalem's misery *Neh 2:1-20*

Job hears of the disasters from messengers *Job 1:13-22*

Jesus enters Jerusalem to hosannas *Mat 21:1-11, 14-17, Mark 11: 1-11, Luke 19:29-44, John 12:12-19*

Jesus sends disciples to preach the word *Mat 28:16-20, Mark 16:15-18*

Jesus' fame spreads *Mark 1:35-39*

Jesus' coming birth announced to Mary *Luke 1:26-38*

Jesus' birth announced to shepherds *Luke 2:8-20*

Jesus' parable wherein the elder brother hears of prodigal's return *Luke 15:25-32*

Multitudes. follow Jesus, Zacchaeus climbs tree *Luke 19:1-10*

See also annunciation, gospel, messenger, publish

NEW TESTAMENT

Jesus' parable of sower *Mat 13:3-23, Mark 4:1-20, Luke 8:4-15*

Jesus establishes the sacrament of communion at the Last Supper *Mat 26:26-29, Mark 14:22-25, Luke 22:14-30, 1 Cor 11:23-25*

Jesus' last instruction to go to all the world *Mat 28:16-20, Mark 16:15-18*

Jesus' parable of seed, blade, ear *Mark 4:26-29*

Jesus' parable of new wine in old bottles *Luke 5:31-39*

Jesus' parable of rich man and beggar *Luke 16:19-31*

Jesus promises to send the Holy Ghost *John 14:1-31*

Peter and apostles at Pentecost *Acts 2:1-13*

John's vision of the sealed book *Rev 5:1-14*

John's vision of the angel with a book *Rev 10:1-11*

See also covenant, gospel, Jesus, testament, word

NIGHT

God divided the light from darkness —first day *Gen 1:1-5*

Jacob wrestles with angel until day breaks *Gen 32:24-32*

The pillar of fire by night *Exod 13:20-22, Num 9:15-23*

Gideon defeats enemy host by surprise at night *Judg 7:1-25*

Samuel is called by God at night *1 Sam 3:1-10*

Job's nightmare *Job 4:13-21*

David's song, "The heavens declare the glory of God" *Psal 19:1-14*

Daniel interprets king's dream in a night vision *Dan 2:1-49*

Daniel spends a night in the lions' den *Dan 6:1-28*

Daniel's vision of meeting Gabriel *Dan 9:20-23, 10:4-21*

Wise men visit Jesus *Mat 2:1-12*

Jesus' teaching on letting your light shine *Mat 5:13-16, Luke 8:16-18*

Jesus heals two blind men *Mat 9:27-31*

Jesus heals blind and dumb *Mat 12:22-30, Luke 11:14-23*

Jesus heals blind Bartimaeus *Mat 20:29-34, Mark 10:46-52*

Jesus' parable of servants awaiting their lord *Mat 24:42-51*

Jesus' parable of wise and foolish virgins *Mat 25:1-13*

Jesus prays at Gethsemane *Mat 26:30, 36-46, Mark 14:26, 32-42, Luke 22:39-46*

Jesus heals blind man in two treatments *Mark 8:22-26*

Birth of Jesus *Luke 2:1-20*

Jesus' parable of the unwilling friend *Luke 11:5-13*

Jesus' parable of serving the master before supper *Luke 17:7-10*

Jesus heals blind beggar *Luke 18:35-43*

Nicodemus visits Jesus at night *John 3:1-21*

Jesus heals man born blind *John 9:1-41*

Peter released from prison by angel at night *Acts 5:17-42, 12:1-17*

Paul healed of blindness by Ananias *Acts 9:10-22*

Paul let down over wall in basket *Acts 9:23-31*

Paul, imprisoned at night, sings hymns *Acts 16:19-40*

Eutychus falls from window at night *Acts 20:7-12*

See also adversity, affliction, darkness, day, death, watch

NOAH

See Part II, Noah

NOTHINGNESS

God makes man from dust *Gen 2:6-8*

God's warning against idolatry, necromancy, abominations *Deut 13:1-18, 18:9-14*

Shunammite insists all is well with her dead son *2 King 4:8-47*

David's song, "Fret not thyself because of evildoers" *Psal 37:23-40*

Vanity of human things *Eccl 1:1-18, 2:1-26*

Body culture is in vain *Isa 3:16-26*

Isaiah's parable, can evil be the fruit of good? *Isa 5:1-8*

Isaiah's vision of fall of Babylon *Isa 14:4-8, 12-17, 25-27*

Jesus on true treasures *Mat 6:19-21*

The fever of Peter's wife's mother disappears *Mat 8:14-17, Mark 1: 29-34*

In Jesus' ascension the body disappears *Mark 16:19, 20, Luke 24:50-53, Acts 1:6-12*

Jesus' parable of the rich fool and his barns *Luke 12:15-21*

Jesus' parable of prodigal who discovers unreal values *Luke 15: 11-24*

John's vision of war that cast out old serpent *Rev 12:1-17*

See also destruction, idolatry

O

OBEDIENCE

Adam and Eve disobey *Gen 3:1-6*

Abraham obeys God, Isaac obeys his father *Gen 22:1-19*

Moses exhorts to obedience *Deut 6:1-25, 11:1-32, 18:9-14*

The blessings of obedience *Deut 28:1-14*

Joshua exhorts to obedience *Josh 23:1-16*

Saul disobeys his own rules and sees a witch *1 Sam 28:3-20*

Job's integrity tested *Job 1:1-22*

David's song on delight in God's law *Psal 1:1-6*

Daniel obeys God before king *Dan 1:1-21, 6:1-28*

Jonah disobeys and then obeys *Jonah 1:1-17, 2:1-10, 3:1-10*

Rewards promised for tithing *Mal 3:10, 4:1, 2*

Jesus puts Commandments on mental basis *Mat 5:17-48*

Jesus' parable of two sons ordered to work *Mat 21:28-32*

Jesus' parable of servants awaiting lord *Mat 24:42-51*

Jesus' parable of sheep and goats *Mat 25:31-46*

Jesus' parable of the watchful servants *Luke 12:35-40*

Jesus' parable of the faithful steward *Luke 12:41-48*

Paul's teaching to come out and be separate *2 Cor 6:1-18*

Paul's sermon on example left by Jesus *Heb 12:1-29*

See also authority, commandment, law, master, principle, servant

OBLIGATION

Cain learns that man is his brother's keeper *Gen 4:1-16*

Moses receives the Ten Commandments *Exod 20:1-19, Deut 5:1-24*

Moses exhorts to obey *Deut 6:1-25, 18:9-14, 26:1-19, 28:1-14*

Joshua exhorts to obey *Josh 23:1-16*

Mordecai persuades Esther to help the people *Esther 3:1-15, 4:1-17*

David's song, "Bless the Lord, O my soul" *Psal 103:1-22*

David's song, "Let the redeemed of the Lord say so" *Psal 107:1-43*

Three Jews fulfill their duty to God before king *Dan 3:1-30*

Daniel worships God first *Dan 6: 1-28*

Jesus on mental nature of commandments *Mat 5:21-32, Mark 9: 38-50*

Jesus' teaching to seek God first *Mat 6:25-34, Luke 12:22-34*

Jesus on judging others *Mat 7:1-5, Luke 6:37-40*

Jesus on Golden Rule *Mat 7:12-14, Luke 6:41, 42*

Jesus heals centurion's servant *Mat 8:5-13, Luke 7:1-10*

Jesus tells why his disciples do not fast *Mat 9:14-27, Mark 2:18-22, Luke 5:33-39*

Jesus speaks of his family obligations *Mat 12:46-50, John 19: 25-27*

Jesus' parable of two sons ordered to work *Mat 21:28-32*

Jesus' parable of husbandmen who refuse to pay rent *Mat 21:33-46, Mark 12:1-12, Luke 20:9-19*

Jesus' parable of servants awaiting their lord *Mat 24:42-51*

Jesus' parable of the talents *Mat 25:14-30, Luke 19:11-28*

Jesus gives final instructions to disciples *Mark 16:15-18*

Jesus approved the widow's mite *Mark 12:41-44, Luke 21:1-4*

Jesus' parable of good Samaritan *Luke 10:25-37*

Jesus' parable of watchful servants *Luke 12:35-40*

Jesus' parable of faithful steward *Luke 12:41-48*

Jesus' parable of unjust steward *Luke 16:1-14*

Jesus' parable of servant's duty before he sups *Luke 17:7-10*

Jesus heals ten lepers and remarks on gratitude *Luke 17:11-19*

Jesus calls for a confession of faith from Martha *John 12:20-27*

Jesus' parable of the true vine *John 15:1-17*

Jesus gives final instructions to Peter *John 21:12-19*

Peter and John must speak the word with boldness *Acts 4:1-23*

Paul's teaching to come out and be separate *2 Cor 6:1-18*

Paul on the Christian's armor *Eph 6:10-17*

Paul's teaching to put on the new man *Col 3:1-17*

Paul on Christian precepts *1 Thess 5:1-28*

Paul's charge to the faithful *2 Tim 4:1-8*

Paul preaches obedience to Christ *Heb 2:1-18*

Paul's teaching that only true sacrifice remits sin *Heb 10:1-39*

Paul on the example left by Jesus *12:1-29*

James on how to bear our cross *Jas 1:1-27*

James states importance of works *Jas 2:14-26*

John's revelation on reading the scripture *Rev 10:1-11*

See also contract, covenant, debt, duty, law, promise, responsibility

OBSTACLE

Hagar in the wilderness *Gen 21:9-21*

Esau stands in the way of Jacob's return home *Gen 32:1-32, 33:1-11*

Moses' speaking ability solved *Exod 4:10-17*

Moses gets release from bondage *Exod 11:4-10, 12:1-14, 21-41, Deut 16:1-22*

Red Sea blocks escape of Jews *Exod 14:5-31*

Caleb and Joshua advise immediate entrance of promised land, others fearful *Num 13:1-33, 14:1-11, 23-29, Deut 1:19-38*

Balak hires Balaam to curse Israel *Num 22:1-41, 23:1-30, 24:1-25*

Jordan crossed *Josh 3:1-17*

Goliath blocks the Hebrew army *1 Sam 17:1-16*

Adversaries block Zerubbabel's rebuilding of temple *Ezra 4:1-5*

Conspiracy to halt rebuilding of wall fails *Neh 6:1-19*

Jesus' control over time *Mat 7:1-18, Mark 9:2-13, Luke 9:28-36*

Jesus' parable, the wheat and tares *Mat 13:24-30, 36-43*

Jesus has no money *Mat 17:24-27*

Blind Bartimaeus told to be quiet *Mat 20:29-34, Mark 10:46-52*

Jesus in tomb had to free his limbs and remove the stone *Mat 28:1-8, Mark 16:1-8, Luke 24:1-22, John 20:1-10*

Jesus heals palsied man whose friends let him down through roof *Mark 2:1-12, Luke 8:17-26*

Jesus heals impotent man at pool *John 5:1-16*

See also difficult, hardness, mountain, opposition, progress

OCCUPATION

Esau, a hunter *Gen 25:24-34*

Moses as a shepherd *Exod 3:1-18*

Moses appoints judges to help the people *Exod 18:13-27*

Aaron and sons anointed as priests *Lev 8:1-13*

Moses charges Joshua with leadership *Deut 31:7-23, Josh 1:1-9*

Gideon refuses to be king of the people *Judg 8:22, 23*

Boaz, the farmer *Ruth 2:1-23*

Solomon prays for qualities needed by a king *1 King 3:5-15, 2 Chron 1:7-12*

To Elijah, a prophet, is revealed the nature of God *1 King 19:9-13*

Isaiah foretells the coming of a Messiah *Isa 7:10-16, 9:2-7*

Isaiah describes the office of Christ *Isa 42:1-12, 16, 18, 53:1-12*

Jesus heals centurion's servant *Mat 8:5-13, Luke 7:1-10*

Jesus teaches his disciples to be healers and preachers *Mat 10:5-42, Mark 6:7, 8, Luke 9:1-6*

Jesus' parable of the sower *Mat 13:3-23, Mark 4:1-20, Luke 8:4-15*

Jesus' parable of laborers in vineyard *Mat 20:1-16*

Jesus casts traders out of temple *Mat 21:12, 13, John 2:13-25*

Jesus' parable of husbandmen and rent *Mat 21:33-46, Mark 12:1-12, Luke 20:9-19*

Peter's effectiveness as a fisherman *Luke 5:1-11*

Jesus' parable of the rich man and bigger barns *Luke 12:15-21*

Jesus' parable of the faithful steward *Luke 12:41-48*

Jesus' parable of the Pharisee and publican *Luke 18:9-14*

Nicodemus, a ruler of the Jews, visits Jesus *John 3:1-21*

Jesus compares disciples to harvest workers *John 4:31-38*

Jesus' parable of the good shepherd *John 10:1-18*

An idol silversmith contends with Paul *Acts 19:23-29*

See also business, calling, employment, work

OFFENSE

Adam and Eve offend God *Gen 3:6-24*

Cain ruptures brotherhood of man *Gen 4:1-16*

Tower of Babel *Gen 11:1-9*

Abraham settles strife with Lot *Gen 13:1-18*

Hagar offends Sarah and is turned out *Gen 21:1-21*

Jacob offends his brother *Gen 27:1-44*

Moses is offended by idolatry *Exod 32:1-24*

Jesus whips traders from temple *Mat 21:12, 13, John 2:13-25*

Jesus admonishes Peter *Mat 16:21-28, Mark 8:31-38, Luke 9:20-27*

Jesus' parable of husbandmen and rent *Mat 21:33-46, Mark 12:1-12, Luke 20:9-19*

Jesus' parable of marriage feast *Mat 22:1-14*

Jesus' parable of sheep and goats *Mat 25:31-46*

Jesus on giving offense *Luke 17:1-6*

Some of disciples are offended and leave Jesus *John 6:64-71*

The disciples ask Jesus why a man was born blind *John 9:1-41*

See also aggression, anger, law, pain, sin

OFFERING

Cain and Abel make different offerings *Gen 4:1-16*

Abraham is tempted to sacrifice his son *Gen 22:1-19*

Aaron's atonement through scapegoat *Lev 16:1-28*

Moses urges offering first fruits *Deut 26:1-19*

David's songs offer praise *Psal 66:1-20, 100:1-5, 103:1-22, 107:1-43*

Malachi urges tithing *Mal 3:10, 4:1, 2*

Jesus tells Peter to get tribute money from fish *Mat 17:24-27*

Jesus foretells his sacrifice and resurrection *Mat 20:17-19, Mark 20:32-34, Luke 18:31-34, 19:47, 48*

Jesus discusses precious ointment used on him *Mat 26:6-13, Mark 14:3-9*

Jesus comments on the widow's mite *Mark 12:41-44, Luke 21:1-4*

Jesus finds only one of ten lepers offers thanks for healing *Luke 17:11-19*

Jesus foretells his life sacrifices and calls for a confession of faith *John 12:20-27*

Simon offers money to buy power of the Holy Ghost *Acts 8:14-25*

See also atonement, blood, devotion, fruits, giving, gratitude, sacrifice, worship

OFFICE

Joseph appointed governor by Pharaoh *Gen 41:1-46*

Judges appointed to help Moses *Exod 18:13-27*

Aaron and sons anointed priests *Lev 8:1-13*

Gideon refuses to be king *Judg 8:22, 23*

Samuel resists peoples' demand for a king *1 Sam 8:1-22*

Samuel anoints Saul king *1 Sam 10:1-8*

Saul declared unfit to be king *1 Sam 15:7-26*

David made king of Judah and Israel *2 Sam 2:1-4, 5:1-5*

Elisha takes up mantle of Elijah *2 King 2:12-15*

Isaiah outlines the office of Christ *Isa 42:1-12, 16, 18, 53:1-12, 61:1-11, 62:1-12*

John the Baptist sends to Jesus for proof he is Christ *Mat 11:2-19, Luke 7:18-35*

Disciples instructed in office of communion *Mat 26:26-29, Luke 14:22-25, 22:14-30, 1 Cor 11:23-25*

Disciples' office to preach and heal *Mat 28:16-20, Mark 16:15-18, Luke 10:1-16*

Jesus' teaching that he is Christ *John 7:14-40*

Paul's points for guidance of the ministry *1 Thess 5:1-28*

Paul's advice to a disciple *2 Tim 2:1-26*

Paul's charge to the faithful *2 Tim 4:1-8*

See also authority, communion, duty, function, place, profession, service

OFFSPRING

Perfect God creates man in his image and likeness *Gen 1:26-27*

Lord God creates man from dust *Gen 2:6-8*

At 99 Abraham promised a son *Gen 15:1-21*

Jacob prophesies future of his twelve sons *Gen 49:1-28, Deut 33:1-29*

Samuel reviews offspring of Jesse, selects David to anoint *1 Sam 16:1-13*

David finds offspring of Jonathan to help *2 Sam 9:1-13*

David's and Bathsheba's child dies *2 Sam 12:13-23*

Solomon judges which woman is the mother *1 King 3:16-28*

Isaiah's vision of Messiah springing from Jesse (father of David) *Isa 11:1-12*

Ezekiel's question on the equity of God's punishing children for sins of fathers *Ezek 18:1-12*

John's vision of dragon ready to eat the child *Rev 12:1-17*

See also children, family, fruits

OIL

Aaron anointed priest *Lev 8:1-13*

Elijah and the widow's cruse of oil *1 King 17:1-16*

Elisha and the widow's pot of oil *2 King 4:1-7*

Zechariah's vision of two olive trees *Zech 4:1-14*

Jesus' parable of wise virgins who took oil for their lamps *Mat 25:1-13*

Precious ointment poured on Jesus' head by a woman *Mat 26:6-13, Mark 14:3-9*

Jesus' parable of good Samaritan that poured oil and wine into wounds *Luke 10:25-37*

Jesus Christ as the light of the world *John 1:1-14, 8:12-20*

Jesus' feet anointed by Mary *John 12:3-8*

See also anointing, consecration, dedication, devotion, ointment

OINTMENT

Aaron and sons anointed as priests *Lev 8:1-13*

Samuel anoints Saul king *1 Sam 10:1-8*

Samuel anoints David king *1 Sam 16:1-13*

Jesus anoints eyes of blind with spit before healing *Mat 8:22-26*

Jesus' head anointed with precious ointment *Mat 26:6-13, Mark 14:3-9*

Jesus anoints eyes of blind with clay before healing *John 9:1-41*

Jesus' feet anointed by Mary, Martha's sister *John 12:3-8*

See also anointing, consecration, dedication, devotion, oil

OLD

The patriarchs lived to advanced age *Gen 5:1-32*

At 99 God promises Abraham a son *Gen 15:1-21*

Old Jacob prophesies the future of his twelve sons *Gen 49:1-28*

Caleb has good faculties when old *Josh 14:6-15*

Rehoboam consults old men, then his friends *1 King 12:1-18, 2 Chron 10:1-19*

Elijah prepares for translation *2 King 2:1-11*

David's song, "the fountain of life" *Psal 36:1-12*

David's song, "My soul longeth ... for the courts of the Lord" *Psal 84:1-12*

Mortal events all within time framework *Eccl 3:1-15*

Old Daniel's vision of meeting Gabriel *Dan 9:20-22, 10:4-21*

Jesus heals centurion's old servant *Mat 8:5-13, Luke 7:1-10*

Jesus heals Peter's mother-in-law *Mat 8:14-17, Mark 1:29-34*

Paul heals Publius' father *Acts 28:7-10*

Paul's teaching to put off the old man *Col 3:1-17*

See also life, longevity, man, new, testament, time, year

OLD TESTAMENT

God's covenant repeated to Noah *Gen 9:1-17*

God calls Abraham *Gen 11:31, 32, 12:1-9*

God reveals himself to Moses *Exod 3:1-18*

God gives Moses the Ten Commandments *Exod 20:1-19, Deut 5:1-24*

People set apart as God's own *Deut 7:6-11*

God reveals himself to Elijah *1 King 19:9-13*

Book of the law read to the people *Neh 8:1-12*

Isaiah foresees birth of Messiah *Isa 7:10-16, 9:2-7*

Jesus visits Zabulon to fulfill prophecy *Mat 4:12-16*

Jesus puts Moses' Commandments on a mental basis *Mat 5:21-48, Mark 9:38-50*

Jesus says Son of man is Lord of the sabbath *Mat 12:1-8*

Jesus heals withered hand and discusses work on the sabbath *Mat 12:9-13, Mark 3:1-5, Luke 6:6-11*

Jesus at transfiguration shows unity of the gospel with the law (Moses) and the prophets (Elias) *Mat 17:1-13, Mark 9:2-13, Luke 9:28-36*

See also covenant, law, New Testament, promise, prophet

OLIGARCHY

Rehoboam asks his friends advice on how to govern *1 King 10:1-12, 12:1-18*

Chief priests challenge Jesus' authority *Mat 21:23-27, Mark 11:27-33, Luke 20:1-8*

Judas betrays Jesus to priests *Mat 26:14-16, Mark 14:10, 11, Luke 22:1-6*

Priests and council condemn Jesus *Mat 26:59-68, Mark 14:55-65, Luke 22:63-71, John 18:19-24*

Priests pay guards to give false report *Mat 28:11-15*

Council urged to put Jesus to death *John 11:47-54*

Peter and John tried before council *Acts 4:1-23*

See also aristocracy, corruption, government, power, nation

OMNI-ACTION

God creates entire universe *Gen 1:1-31*

Moses sees God as, I Am That I Am *Exod 3:1-18*

Job hears infinite speak to man *Job 38:1-41*

David's song, "The heavens declare the glory" *Psal 19:1-14*

David's song, "The earth is the Lord's" *Psal 24:1-10*

David's song, "He spake, and it was done" *Psal 33:1-22*

David's song, "the fountain of life" *Psal 36:1-12*

David's song, "God is our refuge and strength" *Psal 46:1-11*

David's song, "Whither shall I flee from thy presence" *Psal 139:1-24*

Ezekiel's vision of the holy waters encompassing the universe *Ezek 47:1-12*

Micah's vision of the glory of church *Mic 4:1-8, 13, Isa 2:1-5*

Paul on all talents from God *1 Cor 12:1-31*

Paul on unity of all *Eph 4:1-32*

See also activity, God, mind, spirit

OMNIPOTENCE

God creates universe and man *Gen 1:1-31, 2:1-5*

Flood destroys all living *Gen 7:1-24*

Moses sees rod and leprosy transformed *Exod 4:1-9*

Aaron's rod swallows Egyptian sorcerer's rods *Exod 7:1-12*

Red Sea parted *Exod 14:5-31*

David's song, "How are the mighty fallen!" *2 Sam 1:17-27*

Jordan parted *Josh 3:1-17, 2 King 2:8, 12-15*

Sun and moon stand still *Josh 10:6-15*

Elijah prays for fire *1 King 18:17-40*

Elijah prays for rain *1 King 18:1-46*

Elisha causes iron to swim *2 King 6:1-7*

Job hears the infinite speak *Job 38:1-41*

David's song, "The heavens declare" *Psal 19:1-14*

David's song, "The earth is the Lord's" *Psal 24:1-10*

David's song, "For he spake, and it was done" *Psal 33:1-22*

Isaiah's vision of the fall of the mighty *Isa 14:4-8, 12-17, 25-27*

Isaiah's vision, "the Lord's hand is not shortened" *Isa 59:1-21*

Jeremiah on the potter and the clay *Jer 18:1-6*

Three Jews escape the fiery furnace *Dan 3:1-30*

Daniel escapes the lions' den *Dan 6:1-28*

Jonah escapes the fish's belly *Jonah 2:1-10*

Jesus calms wind and seas *Mat 8:23-27, Mark 4:35-41, Luke 8:22-25*

Jesus and Peter walk on waters *Mat 14:22-33, John 6:15-21*

Jesus ascends *Mark 16:19, 20, Luke 24:50-53, Acts 1:9-13*

Jesus controls time *Mat 17:1-13, Mark 9:2-13, Luke 9:28-36*

Jesus rends tomb *Mat 28:1-8, Mark 16:1-8, Luke 24:1-12, John 20:1-10*

Jesus calms windstorm *Mark 6:45-52, John 6:21*

Jesus supplies a great haul of fish *Luke 5:1-11, John 21:1-11*

Jesus says his great works have source in the Father *John 5:17-47*

James' sermon on faith without works *Jas 2:24-26*

See also authority, God, omni-action, possibility, power, strength

OMNIPRESENCE

See ever-presence

OMNISCIENCE

Joseph interprets dreams *Gen 39:21-23, 40:1-23, 41:1-46*

Jacob prophesies the nature of each tribe *Gen 49:1-28, Deut 33:1-29*

Samuel selects the true king among seven sons *1 Sam 1:1-13*

Solomon's request for understanding to govern *1 King 3:5-15, 2 Chron 1:7-12*

Solomon's wisdom in finding the true mother of the baby *1 King 3:16-28*

Elisha prophesies drop in price of flour *2 King 6:24, 25, 7:1-18*

Nehemiah sees through conspiracy *Neh 6:1-19*

David's song on the nature of man and the universe *Psal 8:1-9*

David's song on secret place of the most High *Psal 91:1-16*

The excellency of wisdom *Prov 3:13-26, 4:1-13, 8:1-36*

Isaiah prophesies birth of Messiah *Isa 7:10-16, 9:2-7*

Isaiah describes the coming Messiah *Isa 42:1-12, 16, 18, 53:1-12, 61:1-11, 62:1-12*

Jeremiah says captivity will end in 70 years *Jer 29:8-14*

Daniel interprets king's dream in a night vision *Dan 2:1-49*

Daniel reads the handwriting on the wall *Dan 5: 1-31*

Jesus tells Peter where he can find tribute money *Mat 17: 24-27*

Jesus analyzes the thought of scribes and Pharisees *Mat 23:1-39, Mark 12: 38-40, Luke 11: 37-54, 20: 45-47, John 8: 33-59*

Jesus heals woman who touched hem of his garment *Mark 5: 25-34, Luke 8: 43-48*

Jesus at twelve years holds attention of rabbis *Luke 2:41-52*

Jesus recognizes the possibilities in Zacchaeus *Luke 19: 1-10*

See also intelligence, knowledge, mind, wisdom

ONENESS

Man created as very image and likeness of God *Gen 1: 26, 27*

Man challenges God's supremacy at Babel *Gen 11: 1-9*

God talks with Moses face to face *Exod 33: 7-23*

Primitive atonement through the scapegoat *Lev 16: 1-28*

Ruth will not leave her mother-in-law *Ruth 1: 1-22*

Soul of Jonathan knit with David *1 Sam 18: 1-16*

Elisha refuses to leave Elijah *2 King 2:1-11*

David's song, "The Lord is my shepherd" *Psal 23: 1-6*

David's song, "Whither shall I flee" *Psal 139: 1-24*

Isaiah's vision, "Fear not . . . I will be with thee" *Isa 43: 1-28, 44: 1-24*

Union of two sticks (states) *Ezek 37: 15-28*

Jesus on oneness with Father *John 10: 22-42*

Peter vows never to deny Jesus *Mat 26: 31-35, Mark 14: 27-31, Luke 22: 31-34, John 13: 36-38*

Peter denies him *Mat 26:57, 58, 69-75, Mark 14: 66-72, Luke 22: 54-62, John 18: 13-18, 25-27*

Jesus' parable of prodigal's elder brother *Luke 15: 25-32*

Jesus on his great works have source in Father *John 5: 17-47*

Jesus on unity of the Christ *John 8: 12-59*

Jesus' prayer for disciples to be one *John 17: 1-26*

Descent of promised Holy Ghost *Acts 2: 1-13*

Paul on unity of all *Eph 4: 1-32*

John's sermon on God is Love *1 John 4:1-21*

See also atonement, harmony, identity, love, monotheism, principle, unity

OPEN

Serpent pretends to open Eve's eyes *Gen 3: 1-5*

Peter gets tribute money from fish's mouth *Mat 17: 24-27*

Jesus' tomb is opened *Mat 28: 1-8, Mark 16: 1-8, Luke 24: 1-12, John 20: 1-10*

Jesus opens ears of deaf man *Mark 7: 32-37*

Jesus opens eyes of man born blind *John 9: 1-41*

Peter in prison, doors opened by angel *Acts 5: 17-42, 12: 1-17*

Earthquake opens prison doors for Paul and Silas *Acts 16: 19-40*

Eutychus falls from open window *Acts 20: 7-12*

Lamb has key to open sealed book *Rev 5: 1-14*

See also book, expansion, eye, revelation, uncover

OPINION

Samuel resists people's demand for a king *1 Sam 8: 1-22*

Ruler of synagogue thinks Jesus should not heal on the sabbath *Luke 13: 11-17*

Herod thinks Jesus is John the Baptist *Mat 14: 1-13, Mark 6: 14-29, Luke 9: 7-9*

Jesus asks disciples what people say about him *Mat 16: 13-20, Mark 8: 27-30, Luke 9: 18-21*

Public opinion favorable to Jesus *Mark 1: 35-39*

Martha complains about her sister's actions *John 10: 38-42*

Paul and Barnabas worshipped as gods *Acts 14: 11-18*

See also belief, conviction, idea, judgment

OPPORTUNITY

Slavery is an opportunity for Joseph *Gen 39: 1-6*

Prison, an opportunity for Joseph *Gen 39: 21-23, 40: 1-23*

Joseph solves Pharaoh's problems *Gen 41: 1-46*

Moses gets second chance on Ten Commandments *Exod 34:1-8, Deut 10: 1-4*

Saul the king declared unfit by Samuel *1 Sam 15: 7-26*

David spares Saul in cave *1 Sam 24: 1-22, 26: 1-25*

Elisha refuses to be deterred from growth *2 King 2: 1-15*

Zerubbabel starts rebuilding the temple *Ezra 3: 8-13*

Nehemiah repairs Jerusalem's walls *Neh 4: 1-23*

Ezekiel's vision, "if the wicked will turn from all his sins" *Ezek 18: 1-32*

Jonah given second chance to go to Nineveh *Jonah 1: 1-17, 2: 1-10, 3: 1-10*

Jesus' parable of all bidden to marriage feast *Mat 22: 1-14*

Jesus' parable of wise and foolish virgins *Mat 24: 1-13*

Jesus' parable of sheep and goats *Mat 25: 31-46*

Jesus' parable of all bidden to great supper *Luke 14: 15-24*

Jesus' teaching that man must be born again *John 3: 1-21*

Jesus gives Peter a second opportunity to be his disciple *John 21: 12-19*

Paul's teaching to put on the new man *Col 3: 1-17*

Paul's sermon on atonement *Heb 10: 1-39*

John's letters to seven churches *Rev 1: 4-20, 2: 1-29, 3: 1-22*

See also chance, place, time

OPPOSITION

Abraham blessed after war with kings *Gen 14: 8-20, Heb. 6: 20, 7: 1-28*

Lot shelters two angels from mob *Gen 19: 1-14*

Isaac's herdmen strive over wells *Gen 26: 12-31*

Miriam and Aaron speak against Moses *Num 12: 1-16*

Balak hires Balaam to curse Israelites *Num 22:1-41, 23:1-30, 24:1-25*

Moses offers people choice of good or evil *Deut 30: 11-30*

Joshua offers people choice of good or evil *Josh 24: 1-25*

Deborah opposes Sisera *Judg 4:1-17*

Gideon defeats Midianites *Judg 7: 1-25*

Gideon refuses to be king *Judg 8: 22, 23*

Samuel resists people's demand for a king *1 Sam 8: 1-22*

Nathan calls David to account *2 Sam 12:1-10*

Jahaziel says the battle is not your's, but God's *2 Chron 20: 1-32*

Elijah defeats 450 prophets of Baal *1 King 18: 17-40*

Conspirators fail to halt Nehemiah *Neh 6: 1-19*

Esther helps Mordecai and her people in persecution *Esther 3: 1-15, 4: 1-17*

Isaiah's vision of no more war *Isa 2: 1-5, Mic 4: 1-8, 13*

From dry bones God can supply a protective army *Ezek 37: 1-14*

Jonah refuses to obey God and is punished *Jonah 1:1-17*

Jesus is tempted but without sin *Mat 4: 1-11, Luke 4: 1-13*

Jesus calms wind and sea *Mat 8: 23-27, Mark 4: 35-41, 6: 45-52, Luke 8: 22-25, John 6: 21*

Jesus accused of casting out devils by Beelzebub *Mat 12: 22-30, Mark 3: 22-30, Luke 11: 14-23*

Jesus' parable of two sons ordered to work *Mat 21: 28-32*

Jesus reproves Pharisees *Mat 23: 1-39, Mark 12: 38-40, Luke 11: 37-54, 20: 45-47, John 8: 33-59*

Jesus' parable of Pharisee versus publican *Luke 18: 9-14*

Jesus casts traders out of temple *John 2: 13-25*

Gamaliel advises Jews not to oppose Christians *Acts 5: 17-42*

Paul lists his trials as a Christian *Acts 20: 17-38, 2 Cor 11: 21-33*

Paul's sermon on Adam vs. Christ *Rom 5: 1-21*

Paul's teaching on Spirit vs. flesh *Rom 8: 1-39*

Paul on Christians' armor *Eph 6: 10-17*

Paul's exhorts to put on the new man *Col 3: 1-17*

Paul's sermon on enemies of the truth *2 Tim 3: 1-17*

James preaches on temptation and trials *Jas 1: 1-27*

John's vision of the four horsemen *Rev 6: 1-17*

John's vision of the war between the dragon and the woman with child *Rev 12: 1-17*

See also affirmation, argument, blood, denial, energy, enemy, force, obstacle, resistance

OPPRESSION

Joseph sold into slavery in Egypt *Gen 37: 1-36*

Israelites in Egypt oppressed *Exod 1: 8-14*

Israelites in Egypt—bricks without straw *Exod 5: 7-19*

Gideon oppressed by Midianites *Judg 6: 19-40*

The challenge of Goliath *1 Sam 17: 1-16*

Elijah flees for his life *1 King 19: 1-8*

The Syrians oppress the Israelites *2 King 6: 8-23*

Sennacherib of Assyria invades Israel *2 King 18:17-37, 19:1-27, 2 Chron 31:20, 21, 32:1-23, Isa 36: 1-23, 37: 1-38*

Nehemiah hears of misery of Jerusalem *Neh 1: 1-11, 2: 1-20*

The Israelites in Persia are persecuted *Esther 3: 1-15, 4: 1-17*

Job asks why the good should suffer *Job 3: 1-26*

David's song, "The Lord is my shepherd" *Psal 23: 1-6*

David's song, "The secret place of the most High" *Psal 91: 1-16*

Isaiah's vision that God eliminates the mighty *Isa 14: 4-8, 12-17, 25-27*

Isaiah's vision that hypocrisy will be punished *Isa 29: 11-24, 30:1-3, 20, 21*

Jeremiah foretells release from captivity *Jer 29: 8-14*

Jeremiah promises new covenant with God *Jer 31: 1-14, 31-34*

Jesus heals woman sick for twelve years *Mat 9:20-22, Mark 5:25-34, Luke 8:43-48*

Jesus' parable of unclean spirit that returns *Mat 12: 43-45, Luke 11: 24-26*

Jesus' parable of the unmerciful debtor *Mat 18: 23-35*

Rulers conspire against Jesus *Mat 26: 1-5, Mark 14: 1, 2*

The priests and council condemn him *Mat 26: 59-68, Mark 14: 55-65, Luke 22: 63-71, John 18: 19-24*

Jesus heals man impotent for 38 years *John 5: 1-16*

Jesus says he is light of the world and that the truth will free *John 8: 12-32*

Jesus comforts disciples against tribulations *John 16: 1-33*

Peter imprisoned *Acts 5: 17-42, 12: 1-17*

Stephen tried and stoned to death *Acts 6: 5-15, 7: 51-60*

Saul (Paul) makes havoc of the church *Acts 8: 1-4*

Paul delivered from Jews *Acts 9: 23-31*

Paul's sermon on trials as a Christian *Acts 20: 17-38*

Paul states cost of establishing church *2 Cor 11: 21-33*

Paul on the Christians' armor *Eph 6: 10-17*

Paul on enemies of the truth *2 Tim 3: 1-17*

Paul preaches on example left by Jesus *Heb 12: 1-29*

James on how to bear our cross *Jas 1: 1-27*

John's vision of four horsemen let loose *Rev 6: 1-17*

John's vision of dragon oppressing woman with child *Rev 12: 1-27*

See also bondage, burden, depression, encouragement, force, independence, slavery

OPTIMISM

Enoch expects immortality, walks with God *Gen 5: 18, 21-24, Heb 11: 5*

Noah when promised safety, builds the ark *Gen 6: 5-22*

Abraham answers God's call to look for promised land *Gen 11: 31, 32, 12: 1-9*

Jacob conquers his fear of his brother and is reconciled *Gen 32: 1-32, 33: 1-11*

Joseph succeeds while in slavery *Gen 39: 1-5*

Joseph succeeds while in prison *Gen 40: 1-23, 41: 1-46*

Moses' reluctance to deliver Israelites overcome *Exod 3: 9-12*

Caleb and Joshua urge immediate entry to promised land *Num 13: 1-33, 14: 1-11, 23-29, Deut 1: 19-38*

God's promise of goodness rewarded *Lev 26: 1-20*

A Messiah is promised the Israelites *Deut 18: 15-22*

Moses' song of deliverance *Deut 32: 1-47*

David's son shall build a temple *1 Chron 17:11-27*

Jahaziel prophesies that the battle is God's *2 Chron 20: 1-32*

Elijah prays for fire *1 King 18: 17-40*

Elijah prays for rain *1 King 18: 41-46*

Elijah expects translation *2 King 2: 1-11*

Nehemiah surveys the misery of Jerusalem before rebuilding wall *Neh 2: 1-20*

Job after trials continues his hope in God *Job 1: 13-22, 2: 1-10*

David's song about the happiness of the godly *Psal 1: 1-6*

David's song, "God is our refuge and strength" *Psal 46: 1-11*

David's song, "My soul longeth" *Psal 84: 1-12*

David's song on safety of the godly *Psal 121: 1-8*

Isaiah foretells war no more *Isa 2: 1-5, Mic 4: 1-8, 13*

Isaiah foretells the Messiah *Isa 7: 10-16, 9: 2-7*

Jeremiah foretells release of captives *Jer 29: 8-14, 31: 1-14, 31-34*

Ezekiel's vision of God's care *Ezek 34: 1-31*

Ezekiel's vision of truth encompassing the universe *Ezek 47:1-12*

Jesus' parable of lost sheep *Mat 18: 12-14, Luke 15: 1-7*

Jesus' parable of lost piece of money *Luke 15: 8-10*

Jesus' parable of judge and widow *Luke 18: 1-8*

Jesus heals man waiting at pool *John 5: 1-16*

Jesus promises the Comforter in his place *John 14: 1-31*

Peter finds the commitment to Christ infectious *Acts 4:24-37*

Paul's teaching that Christ's resurrection proves ours *1 Cor 15: 1-58*

Paul's sermon to think on good things *Phil 4: 1-23*

Paul encourages his disciples *2 Tim 2:1-26*

John's vision of the new heaven and earth *Rev 21: 1-27, 22: 1-21*

See also comfort, faith, goodness, healing, hope, reality, thinking, trust

ORBIT

Man begins to revolve in a material orbit separate from Spirit, God *Gen 2: 6-8*

Sun and moon stand still at Ajalon *Josh 10: 6-15*

The stars in their courses fought against Sisera *Judg 5: 1-20*

Star of Bethlehem leads wise men *Mat 2: 1-12*

Jesus Christ as the light of the world *John 1: 1-14, 8: 12-32*

See also revolution

ORDER

Orderly creation by days *Gen 1: 1-31*

Joseph meets problem of famine in orderly way *Gen 41: 1-46*

Moses appoints judges to help *Exod 18: 13-27*

Nehemiah arms builders of the wall *Neh 4: 1-23*

Job hears the infinite describe accomplishments *Job 38: 1-41*

David's song, "The heavens declare the glory" *Psal 19: 1-14*

David's song, "My soul longeth" *Psal 84: 1-12*

Jesus initiates his disciples in healing and preaching *Mat 9: 36-38, 10: 1-42, Mark 3: 13-21, 6: 7-13, Luke 9: 1-6*

Jesus' parable of wheat and tares *Mat 13:24-30, 36-43*

Jesus' parable of two sons ordered to work *Mat 21:28-32*

Jesus' parable of seed, blade, ear, corn *Mark 4:26-29*

Jesus' parable on new wine in old bottles *Luke 5:36-39*

Jesus' parable of rich man and bigger barns *Luke 12:15-21*

Jesus' parable of chief seats at wedding *Luke 14:7-14*

Jesus teaches 70 disciples and sends them out *Luke 10:1-16, 17-24*

Orderly succession of apostles *Acts 1:15-26*

Paul advises a disciple *2 Tim 2:1-26, 4:1-8*

See also brotherhood, commandment, law, logic, methods, ministry, peace, priest, principle, rule, system

ORDAIN

Abraham blessed by Melchizedek *Gen 14:8-20, Heb 6:20, 7:1-28*

Aaron ordained as priest *Lev 8:1-13*

David ordained king of Judah and Israel *2 Sam 2:1-4, 5:1-5*

Elisha inherits the mantle of Elijah *2 King 2:12-15*

Isaiah's vision of what the Lord said to his anointed *Isa 45:1-13, 18-21*

Jonah, commissioned by God, disobeys *Jonah 1:1-17, 2:1-10, 3:1-10*

Jesus baptized at beginning of his ministry *Mat 3:13-17, Mark 1:9-11, Luke 3:21, 22*

Jesus calls his disciples *Mat 4:17-22, 9:9, Mark 1:14-20, Luke 5:1-11, John 1:35-42*

Jesus sends disciples to heal and preach *Mat 9:36-38, 10:1-42, Mark 3:13-21, Luke 9:1-6*

Jesus approves Peter's acknowledgement that he is Christ *Mat 16:13-20, Mark 8:27-30, Luke 9:18-21*

Jesus fills Peter's net and tells him he is a fisher of men *Luke 5:1-11*

Jesus' parable of the faithful steward *Luke 12:41-48*

Jesus charges Peter "Feed my sheep" three times *John 21:12-19*

Ananias told Paul is a "chosen vessel" *Acts 9:10-22*

Paul's advice to a disciple *2 Tim 2:1-26*

James on works needed to prove faith *Jas 2:14-26*

See also appointing, calling, commandment, election, office

ORGANIC

Lord God breathes life into the man of dust *Gen 2:6-8*

Uzziah's heart lifted up to destruction *2 Chron 26:1-23*

David's song, "Create in me a clean heart" *Psal 51:1-19*

Jesus heals two blind men *Mat 9: 27-31*

Jesus heals dumb man *Mat 9:32-35*

Jesus heals sight and speech *Mat 12:22-30, Luke 11:14-23*

Jesus heals sight *Mat 20:29-34, Mark 10:46-52, Luke 18:35-43*

Jesus heals deaf man *Mark 7:32-37*

Jesus heals blind man in two treatments *Mark 8:22-26*

Jesus heals Malchus' ear *Luke 22: 50, 51*

Jesus heals man born blind *John 9:1-41*

Ananias heals Paul of blindness *Acts 9:10-22*

See also affliction, animal, growth, healing, heart, life, mind, plant, senses, unity

ORIGIN

God creates man his spiritual likeness *Gen 1:26, 27*

Lord God creates Adam from dust *Gen 2:6-8*

Lord God makes woman from a rib *Gen 2:21-25*

Cain conceived in Eve's womb *Gen 3:1*

Abraham the father of Israelites, is called *Gen 11:31, 32, 12:1-9*

Isaac's miraculous birth *Gen 21:1-8*

Samson's miraculous birth *Judg 13:1-25*

Samuel's miraculous birth *1 Sam 1:1-28*

Elisha prophesies Shunammite's son's birth *2 King 4:8-37*

David's song, "What is man?" *Psal 8:1-9*

David's song, "For he spake, and it was done" *Psal 33:1-22*

David's song, "the fountain of life" *Psal 36:1-12*

Jeremiah's vision of the potter and his clay *Jer 18:1-6*

Ezekiel's parable on hereditary traits *Ezek 18:1-32*

Jesus' immaculate birth announced to Mary *Luke 1:26-38*

Jesus says man must be born again *John 3:1-21*

Paul on all talents come from God *1 Cor 12:1, 4-31*

Paul points to God as the source *Eph 4:1-32*

See also beginning, cause, creation, foundation, fountain, life, parent

P

PAIN

Cain's punishment more than he can bear *Gen 4:1-16*

Jacob's hip out of joint *Gen 32:24-32*

Israelites bitten by fiery serpents *Num 21:4-9*

David's pain at death of Bathsheba's child *2 Sam 12:13-23*

In trouble Shunammite replies "It is well" *2 King 4:8-37*

Job's troubles increase *Job 2:1-10*

David's song, "Why art thou cast down, O my soul?" *Psal 42:1-17*

David's song, "Bless the Lord, O my soul" *Psal 103:1-22*

David's song, "praise the Lord for his goodness" *Psal 107:1-43*

Jesus heals centurion's servant *Mat 8:5-13, Luke 7:1-10*

Jesus heals Peter's wife's mother *Mat 8:14-17, Mark 1:29-34*

Jesus heals epileptic boy *Mat 17:14-21, Mark 9:14-29, Luke 9:37-43*

Jesus prays at Gethsemane *Mat 26:30, 36-46, Mark 14:26, 32-42, Luke 22:39-46*

Judas hangs himself *Mat 27:3-10*

Jesus scourged and mocked *Mat 27:27-31, Mark 15:16-20, John 19:1-16*

Jesus' crucifixion *Mat 27:32-56, Mark 15:21-41, Luke 23:26-49, John 19:17-30*

Jesus heals son of widow of Nain *Luke 7:11-17*

Stephen stoned *Acts 7:51-60*

Paul stoned *Acts 14:19, 20*

Paul's trials as a Christian *Acts 20:17-38, 2 Cor 11:21-33*

John's vision of new heaven and earth with no more pain *Rev 21:1-27*

See also affliction, birth, comfort, disease, distress, escape, grief, hell, hurt, injury, pleasure, punishment, suffering, torment, wound

PALM TREE

Deborah dispensed judgment under palm tree *Judg 4:1-5*

Jesus welcomed with palms *Mat 21:1-11, 14-17, Mark 11:1-11, Luke 19:29-44, John 12:12-19*

John's vision of multitude with palms before the Lamb *Rev 7:9-17*

See also fruits, peace, tree, victory

PALSY

See paralysis

PARABLE

Adam and Eve in Eden *Gen 2:6-25, 3:1-24*
Balaam's parable to Balak *Num 23: 1-30, 24:1-25*
Parable of the trees by Gideon's son Jotham *Judg 9:1-15*
Nathan's parable of the one ewe lamb *2 Sam 12:1-10*
Isaiah's parable of the wild grapes *Isa 5:1-8*
Jeremiah's parable of the potter and his clay *Jer 18:1-6*
Jeremiah's parable of the good and bad figs *Jer 24:1-10*
Zechariah's parable of the two olive trees *Zech 4:1-14*
Forty-seven parables of Jesus *(See Part II, Jesus Christ: Parables)*
Jesus explains why he speaks in parables *Mat 13:10-17, 34, 35, Mark 4:10-12, 33, 34*
Visions of John:
  A door opened in heaven *Rev 4: 1-11*
  The sealed book *Rev 5:1-14*
  The four horsemen *Rev 6:1-17*
  The angel with a book *Rev 10: 1-11*
  The woman with child and the dragon *Rev 12:1-17*
  The new heaven and the new earth *Rev 21:1-27*
  The river of life and tree of life *Rev 22:1-21*

See also example, Jesus, morality, spirituality, symbols, truth

PARADISE

Garden of Eden story *Gen 2:6-25*
David's song, "Make a joyful noise" *Psal 66:1-20, 100:1-5*
David's song, "Our dwelling place" *Psal 90:1-17*
David's song, "the secret place" *Psal 91:1-16*
Isaiah's vision of Christ's kingdom *Isa 2:1-5, Mic 4:1-8, 13*
Isaiah's vision of his peaceable kingdom *Isa 11:1-12*
Isaiah's vision of the desert blossoming *Isa 35:1-10*
Ezekiel's vision of truth flowing outward, encompassing the universe *Ezek 47:1-12*

Jesus tells thief on next cross he will be with him in paradise *Luke 23:39-43*
The new heaven and new earth *Rev 21:1-27*

See also death, Eden, garden, happiness, heaven, materialism, pleasure, spirituality

PARALYSIS (palsy)

Jesus and centurion's servant *Mat 8:5-13, Luke 7:1-10*
Jesus heals man let down through roof *Mat 9:1-8, Mark 2:1-12, Luke 5:17-26*
Peter heals Aeneas *Acts 9:32-35*
Philip heals paralysis *Acts 8:5-8*
See also healing

PARDON

Esau pardons Jacob *Gen 33:1-11*
Joseph reveals himself to his brethren *Gen 43:1, 2, 45:1-11*
Moses pardons and heals Miriam *Num 12:1-16*
Jeremiah foretells restoration of Israel *Jer 29:8-14, 31:1-14, 31-34*
Jonah repents and starts again *Jonah 2:1-10*
Jesus' parable of lost sheep *Mat 18:12-14, Luke 15:1-7*
Jesus' parable of unmerciful debtor *Mat 18:23-35*
Jesus heals paralysis in connection with forgiving sin *Mark 2:1-12, Luke 5:17-26*
Jesus' parable of two debtors forgiven *Luke 7:36-50*
Jesus' parable of prodigal son *Luke 15:11-24*
Stephen forgives his slayers *Acts 7:51-60*
Paul's teaching to put on the new man *Col 3:1-17*
Paul's teaching that true sacrifice remits sin *Heb 10:1-39*

See also atonement, forgiveness, reconciliation, reformation, reunion, sin

PARENT

God creates man in his image *Gen 1:26, 27*

Lord God creates man from dust
Gen 2:6-8

At 99 God promises Abraham a son
Gen 15:1-21

Abraham tempted to sacrifice Isaac
Gen 22:1-19

Jacob deceives his father *Gen 27:1-44*

Jecob foretells future of his twelve
sons *Gen 49:1-28, Deut 33:1-29*

Ruth will not be separated from her
mother-in-law *Ruth 1:1-22*

Nathan reveals to David that his
son will build the Lord's house
1 Chron 17:1-27

Mordecai's niece, Esther, is made
queen *Esther 2:5-23*

Job loses seven sons and three
daughters *Job 1:13-22*

David's song, "The earth is the
Lord's" *Psal 24:1-10*

David's song, "The fountain of life"
Psal 36:1-12

A woman's care of her family *Prov 31:1-31*

Jeremiah's vision of the potter and
his clay *Jer 18:1-6*

Ezekiel on heredity *Ezek 18:1-32*

Hosea's vision of God's care of his
child *Hos 11:1-4*

God's promise of salvation to the
daughter of Zion *Zeph 3:14-17*

Jesus heals Peter's wife's mother
Mat 8:14-17, Mark 1:29-34

Jesus heals Jairus' daughter *Mat
9:18, 19, 23-26, Mark 5:22-24, 35-43,
Luke 8:41, 42, 49-56*

Jesus' teaching on "Who is my
mother?" *Mat 12:46-50*

Jesus heals woman's daughter *Mat
15:21-28, Mark 7:24-30*

Jesus heals epileptic boy *Mat 17:14-21, Mark 9:14-29, Luke 9:37-43*

Zebedee's wife tries to advance her
sons *Mat 20:20-28, Mark 10:35-45*

Jesus' parable of two sons ordered
to work *Mat 21:28-32*

Jesus' parable of marriage feast of
king's son *Mat 22:1-24*

Jesus' origin announced to his
mother *Luke 1:26-38*

Jesus' parents lose him in Jerusalem
Luke 2:41-52

Jesus heals son of widow of Nain
Luke 7:11-17

Jesus' parable of the prodigal and
his brother *Luke 15:11-32*

Jesus heals the nobleman's son
John 4:46-54

Jesus contrasts his parentage with
that of Jews who oppose him
John 8:37-57

Paul heals Publius' father *Acts 28:7-10*

Paul on the relations of parents
and children *Eph 6:1-4*

John's vision of the woman with
child *Rev 12:1-17*

See also birth, cause, children,
creator, father, heredity, mother,
source

PARTICULAR

Enoch translated because he walked
with God *Gen 5:18, 21-24*

Animals enter ark in pairs *Gen 7:1-24*

Abraham: how many righteous men
needed to save city? *Gen 18:20-33*

Moses lists idolatries to be avoided
Deut 18:9-14

Moses lists blessings of obedience
Deut 28:1-14

Caleb's share of Canaan *Josh 14:6-15*

Elisha selects the gift of greatest
value *2 King 2:1-15*

Jesus' parable of pearl of great
price *Mat 13:45, 46*

Jesus heals ten lepers—one returns
Luke 17:11-19

Jesus selects and heals one of many
at pool of Bethesda *John 5:1-16*

God selects a chosen vessel *Acts
9:10-22*

Paul on Jesus as Messiah *Acts
13:16-52*

Paul on diversities from same spirit
1 Cor 12:1-31

Paul on fruits of the Spirit *Gal
5:1-26*

Paul on things to think on *Phil
4:1-23*

See also individuality, many, separation

PARTING

Abraham casts Hagar and her son
out to the wilderness *Gen 21:9-21*

Waters of Red Sea parted *Exod 14:5-31*

Elisha refused to be separated from Elijah *2 King 2:1-15*

Job loses his sons and daughters *Job 1:13-22*

David's song, "The Lord is my shepherd" *Psal 23:1-6*

David's song, "Why art thou cast down?" *Psal 42:1-11*

David's song, "Our dwelling place" *Psal 90:1-17*

David's song, "Whither shall I flee from thy spirit?" *Psal 139:1-24*

Isaiah offers comfort *Isa 40:1-31*

Jesus restores Jairus' daughter *Mat 9:18, 19, 23-26, Mark 5:22-24, 35-43, Luke 8:41, 42, 49-56*

Jesus' parable of lost sheep *Mat 18:12-14, Luke 15:1-7*

Jesus has Last Supper with his disciples *Mat 26:26-29, Mark 14:22-25, Luke 22:14-30, 1 Cor 11:23-25*

Jesus ascends and leaves disciples *Mark 16:19, 20, Luke 24:50-53, Acts 1:6-12*

Jesus restores widow of Nain's son *Luke 7:11-17*

Jesus' parable of rich man and bigger barns *Luke 12:15-21*

Jesus' parable of prodigal and brother *Luke 15:11-32*

Jesus restores Lazarus *John 11:1-46*

Paul's teaching that Jesus' resurrection proves ours *1 Cor 5:1-58*

Paul's teaching to come out and be separate *2 Cor 6:1-18*

John's vision of new Jerusalem with no parting *Rev 21:1-27, 22:1-21*

See also death, divorce, joy, loss, separation, sorrow

PARTNER

Lord God creates a helper for Adam *Gen 2:20-25*

Abraham's possessions grow—they conflict with Lot's, so they agree to separate *Gen 13:1-18*

Aaron as Moses' mouthpiece *Exod 4:10-17*

Ruth stays with Naomi *Ruth 1:1-22, 2:1-23*

Jonathan and David become friends *1 Sam 18:1-16*

Elisha will not be separated from Elijah *2 King 2:1-8*

Hezekiah, the king, and Isaiah, the prophet, work together *2 King 20:1-11, 2 Chron 32:1-23, Isa 36:1-22, 37:1-38, 38:1-22*

Esther helps Mordecai, her uncle and foster father *Esther 3:1-15, 4:1-17*

The virtues of a good woman as life partner *Prov 31:1-31*

Jesus' sermon, "Who is my mother? ...brethren?" *Mat 12:46-50*

Peter's partners help him haul in the full net *Luke 5:1-11*

Peter and John heal lame man *Acts 3:1-11*

Peter and John tried before council *Acts 4:1-23*

Seven deacons chosen to divide labor *Acts 6:1-4*

Paul and Barnabas help establish church *Acts 14:11-18*

Paul and Silas travel together *Acts 16:19-40*

Paul on diversity of talents *1 Cor 12:1, 4-31, Eph 4:1-32*

Paul on sharing abundance *2 Cor 8:11-15, 9:6-15*

See also alliance, business, cooperation, fellowship

PASSOVER

The first passover and release from bondage *Exod 11:4-10, 12:1-4, 29-41, Deut 16:1-22*

Aaron's atonement for people through scapegoat *Lev 16:1-28*

David's song, "Create in me a clean heart" *Psal 51:1-19*

Isaiah's prophecy of the office of the Christ *Isa 42:1-12, 16, 18, 53:1-12, 58:1-14, 61:1-11, 62:1-12*

Jesus foretells his betrayal and sacrifice *Mat 17:22, 23, 26:20-25, Mark 9:30-32, 14:18-21, Luke 22:21, 22, John 13:21-35*

Jesus' parable of lost sheep *Mat 18:12-14, Luke 15:1-7*

Jesus' parable of sheep and goats *Mat 25:31-46*

His apostles prepare the passover

meal and eat it *Mat 26:17-29, Mark 14:12-25, Luke 22:7-30*
Jesus' crucifixion *Mat 27:32-56, Mark 15:21-41, Luke 23:26-49, John 19:17-30*
Jesus' resurrection *Mat 28:1-8, Mark 16:1-8, Luke 24:1-12, John 20:1-10*
Jesus' parable of prodigal son *Luke 15:11-24*
Jesus turns water to wine *John 2: 1-11*
Jesus' parable of the true vine *John 15:1-17*
Paul on atonement *Heb 10:1-39*

See also atonement, bread, cross, Easter, exodus, lamb, resurrection, wine

PASTOR

Moses asks God how to explain Him to the people *Exod 3:1-18*
Moses complains of his speaking ability *Exod 4:10-17*
Moses brings Ten Commandments to Israel *Exod 20:1-19, Deut 5: 1-24*
Moses gives his congregation a choice *Deut 30:11-20*
David's song of thanksgiving to God *2 Sam 22:1-51, 1 Chron 16:17-36*
Solomon dedicates temple *1 King 8:22-26, 2 Chron 6:1-42*
Elijah's trial by fire *1 King 18: 17-40*
David's song, "The Lord is my shepherd" *Psal 23:1-6*
Isaiah's vision of Christ's peaceable kingdom *Isa 11:1-12*
Zechariah's vision of candlestick fed by two olive trees *Zech 4:1-14*
Jesus sends forth his disciples *Mat 10:5-42, Mark 6:7-13, Luke 9:1-6, 10:1-24*
Jesus' parable of the sower *Mat 13: 3-23, Mark 4:1-20, Luke 8:4-15*
Jesus' parable of the leaven *Mat 13:33, Luke 13:20, 21*
Jesus' parable of the lost sheep *Mat 18:12-14, Luke 15:1-17*
Jesus tells Peter he will be fisher of men *Luke 5:1-11*
Jesus' parable of the true vine *John 15:1-17*

Jesus' parable of the good shepherd *John 10:1-18*
Jesus washes his disciples' feet *John 13:1-20*
Jesus charges Peter "Feed my sheep" *John 21:12-19*
Paul on ministry *2 Cor 6:1-18, 1 Thess 5:1-28, 2 Tim 2:1-26, 3:1-17, 4:1-8*
John's letters to seven churches *Rev 1:4-20, 2:1-29, 3:1-22*

See also church, ministry, priest, prophet, sheep

PATH

Jacob promised God's presence wherever he goes *Gen 28:10-22*
People ordered forward through the Red Sea *Exod 14:5-31*
People refuse Caleb's urging to enter promised land *Num 13:1-33, 14:1-11, 23-39, Deut 1:19-38*
David's song, "The Lord is my shepherd" *Psal 23:1-6*
Wise men led by star to Bethlehem *Mat 2:1-12*
Jesus' family flee to Egypt and return *Mat 2:13-23, Luke 2:39, 40*
Jesus foretells his own death and resurrection *Mat 17:22, 23, Mark 9:30-32, Luke 9:43-45, 51-56, John 7:1-13*
Jesus' parable of the lost sheep *Mat 18:12-14, Luke 15:1-7*
Paul's sermon on example left by Jesus *Heb 12:1-29*

See also guidance, pilgrim, way

PATIENCE

David spares Saul at Engedi *1 Sam 24:1-22*
David spares Saul at Ziph *1 Sam 26:1-25*
Job blesses God after his trials *Job 2:1-10*
Jesus' parable of wheat and tares *Mat 13:23-30, 36-43*
Jesus at Gethsemane *Mat 26:30, 36-46, Mark 14:26, 32-42, Luke 22: 39-46*
Jesus scourged and mocked *Mat 27:27-31, Mark 15:16-20, John 19: 1-16*

Jesus heals the man at the pool 38 years *John 5:1-16*

James teaches how to bear our cross *Jas 1:1-27*

See also faith, meekness, waiting

PATIENT

Moses heals his sister of leprosy *Num 12:1-16*

Elijah heals the widow's son *1 King 17:17-24*

Elisha heals Naaman of leprosy *2 King 5:1-14*

Isaiah heals the king's sickness *2 King 20:1-11, Isa 38:1-22*

Jesus heals the withered hand *Mat 12:9-13, Mark 3:1-5, Luke 6:6-11*

Jesus heals a case the disciples failed to cure *Mat 17:14-21, Mark 9:14-29, Luke 9:37-43*

Jesus heals the nobleman's son *John 4:46-54*

Jesus raises Lazarus after four days *John 11:1-46*

Peter raises Tabitha *Acts 9:36-43*

Paul heals Eutychus of a fall *Acts 20:7-12*

See also healing, pain, physician, practice, trials

PATRIOTISM

Gideon leaves farm to free his country *Judg 6:7-40, 7:1-25*

Gideon refuses to be king *Judg 8:22, 23*

Zerubbabel returns to rebuild the temple *Ezra 1:1-11, 3:8-12*

Nehemiah returns to rebuild walls of Jerusalem *Neh 1:1-11, 2:1-20, 4:1-23*

Esther acts to protect her people *Esther 5:1-14*

A poor wise man saves a city *Eccl 9:13-18*

Jeremiah foretells the end of captivity *Jer 29:8-14, 31:1-14, 31-34*

Jeremiah acts in prison to buy a field in Israel *Jer 32:2, 6-27, 37-44*

Jesus on paying tribute to Caesar *Mat 22:15-22, Mark 12:13-17, Luke 20:20-26*

Peter accepts Cornelius, a Roman, as a Christian *Acts 10:1-48*

Peter's vision of the great sheet *Acts 11:1-18*

Philip teaches and baptizes an Ethiopian *Acts 8:26-40*

Paul's preaching on the oneness of all *Eph 4:1-32*

James on equality of man *Jas 2:1-13*

See also freedom, independence, nation

PAUL (Saul of Tarsus)

See Part II, Paul

PAYMENT

See debt, satisfaction

PEACE

Abraham ends the war of kings and is blessed *Gen 14:8-20, Heb 6:20, 7:1-28*

David's song, "our dwelling place" *Psal 90:1-17*

Isaiah's vision of war no more *Isa 2:1-5, Mic 4:1-8, 13*

Isaiah's vision of Messiah's peaceable kingdom *Isa 11:1-12*

Jesus calms wind and seas *Mat 8:23-27, Mark 4:35-41, 6:45-52, Luke 8:22-25, John 6:21*

Jesus' parable on counting the cost of war *Luke 14:25-33*

John on God as love *1 John 4:1-21*

John's vision of the new heaven and earth *Rev 21:1-27*

See also disarmament, harmony, war

PEACEMAKER

Abraham settles the strife with Lot *Gen 13:1-18*

David pacified by Abigail's gentleness *1 Sam 25:2-42*

Isaiah's vision of war no more *Isa 2:1-5, Mic 4:1-8, 13*

Isaiah's vision of the peaceable kingdom *Isa 11:1-12*

Jesus on blessed qualities of a Christian *Mat 5:1-12, Luke 6:17-26, 36*

Angels announce "peace on earth" *Luke 2:8-20*

Jesus restores Malchus' ear, cut off by Peter *Luke 22:50, 51*

Melchizedek, King of Peace, as a forerunner of Christ *Heb 6:20, 7:1-28*

See also disarmament, harmony, reconciliation, war

PENTECOST

Jesus promises to send the Holy Spirit *John 14:1-31*

Disciples witness descent of Holy Spirit *Acts 2:1-13*

Paul preaches Holy Spirit at Ephesus *Acts 19:1-10*

See also comforter, communion, Holy Ghost, science, truth

PEOPLE

God promises Abraham to be father of many *Gen 15:1-21*

Jacob foretells the nature of his twelve sons *Gen 49:1-28, Deut 33: 1-29*

Moses' song of deliverance of Israelites *Deut 32:1-32*

Esther sues for her people's life *Esther 5:1-14*

Jeremiah foretells the people's release from captivity *Jer 29:8-14, 31:1-14, 31-34*

Ezekiel tells of God's care of his flock *Ezek 34:1-31*

Jesus at first refuses to heal the Syrophenician *Mat 15:21-28, Mark 7:24-30*

Peter's vision of great sheet supports conversion of Gentiles *Acts 11:1-18*

See also human, nation, race

PERFECTION

Man made in the image and likeness of God *Gen 1:26, 27*

Enoch walks with God *Gen 5:18, 21-24, Heb 11:5*

The Lord talks with Moses face to face *Exod 33:7-23*

David's song of the good man *Psal 1:1-6*

David's song, "The law of the Lord is perfect" *Psal 19:1-14*

David's song, "Mark the perfect man" *Psal 37:23-40*

Jesus' beatitudes from Sermon on Mount *Mat 5:1-12, Luke 6:17-26*

Jesus' summary "be ye therefore perfect" *Mat 5:38-48*

Jesus' parable of the mote and the beam *Mat 7:1-5, Luke 6:37-42*

Peter acknowledges Jesus as Christ *Mat 16:13-20, Mark 8:27-30, Luke 9:18-21*

Jesus' transfiguration (control over time) *Mat 17:1-13, Mark 9:2-13, Luke 9:28-36*

Jesus' ascension *Mark 16:19, 20, Luke 24:50-53, Acts 1:6-12*

Peter's sermon on Christ, the chief cornerstone *1 Pet 2:1-25*

See also excellence, goodness, greatness, supremacy, whole

PERFORMANCE

God creates universe in seven days *Gen 1:1-31*

Noah builds the ark *Gen 6:5-22*

Joseph becomes governor of Egypt *Gen 41:1-46*

Song of Moses reviews deliverance of Jews *Exod 15:1-19, Deut 32: 1-47*

Moses delivers Ten Commandments *Exod 20:1-19, Deut 5:1-24*

People cross over Jordan into promised land *Josh 3:1-17*

Jericho falls *Josh 6:1-27*

Gideon defeats enemy host with 300 men *Judg 7:1-25*

David made king of Judah and Israel *2 Sam 2:1-4, 5:1-5*

Solomon builds the temple and dedicates it *1 King 8:22-66, 2 Chron 6:1-42*

Nehemiah rebuilds the wall of Jerusalem *Neh 4:1-23*

A poor wise man saved a city *Eccl 9:13-18*

Paul's discussion on the cost of establishing the church *2 Cor 11:21-33*

Jesus' great works: water into wine, healings, calming the storm, walking on water, transfiguration, ascension, etc. (*See* Part II, Jesus Christ: Great Works)

See also achievement, fulfillment, great works, success, work

PERSECUTION

Israelites oppressed by Egyptians *Exod 1:8-14*

Bricks must be made without straw *Exod 5:7-19*

Saul attempts to destroy David *1 Sam 18:1-16, 24:1-22, 26:1-25*

Haman persecutes the Jews but is hanged *Esther 3:1-15, 7:1-10*

Jeremiah reports the captivity in Babylon *Jer 29:8-14, 31:1-14, 31-34*

Their political enemies cause Jews to be put in fiery furnace *Dan 3:1-30*

His political enemies cause Daniel to be put in lions' den *Dan 6:1-28*

Jesus' parable of the unmerciful debtor *Mat 18:23-35*

The rulers conspire against Jesus *Mat 26:1-5, Mark 14:1, 2*

Stephen's trial and persecution *Acts 6:5-15*

Stephen's stoning *Acts 7:51-60*

Paul's hardships *2 Cor 11:21-33*

James on how to bear our cross *Jas 1:1-27*

See also affliction, Christian, hardness, martyr, oppression, tyranny

PERSEVERANCE

Jacob refuses to let go of the angel until he is blessed *Gen 32:24-32*

Joseph rises out of the threat of death and slavery in Egypt *Gen 37:1-36*

Caleb is out-voted but stays until he is rewarded *Josh 14:6-15*

David continues to offer Saul good for evil *1 Sam 18:1-16, 24:1-22, 26:1-25*

Elijah, despite discouragement, continues until translated *1 King 19:1-8, 2 King 2:1-11*

Nehemiah, victor over conspirators, builds the wall *Neh 4:1-23, 6:1-19*

Job refuses to blame God and finally hears God speak *Job 2:1-10, 38:1-41*

David's song of delight in God's law *Psal 1:1-6*

David's song of hope *Psal 37:23-40, 42:1-11*

Jeremiah's promise of restoration *Jer 31:1-14, 31-34*

Jesus on treatment of enemies *Mat 5:38-48, Luke 6:27-36*

Jesus' parable of servants awaiting their lord *Mat 24:42-51*

Jesus heals blind man after second treatment *Mark 8:22-26*

Jesus' parable of man on long journey *Mark 13:34-37*

Jesus' parable of the unwilling friend *Luke 11:5-13*

Jesus' parable of the watchful servants *Luke 12:35-40*

Jesus' parable of the faithful steward *Luke 12:41-48*

Jesus' parable of the door shut by the master *Luke 13:22-30*

Jesus' parable of the servant before he sups *Luke 17:7-10*

Jesus' parable of the judge and widow *Luke 18:1-8*

Peter and John, tried before council, persist in preaching *Acts 4:24-37*

Paul's hardships prove his perseverance *2 Cor 11:21-33*

See also persistence, resolution, steadfastness, watch

PERSISTENCE

Jacob continues to wrestle with angel until his name is changed *Gen 32:24-32*

Ruth remains with her mother-in-law *Ruth 1:1-22, 2:1-23*

Samuel yields to people's persistence for a king *1 Sam 10:1-8*

Saul pursues David *1 Sam 24:1-22, 26:1-25*

The Shunammite insists, "It is well" *2 King 4:8-37*

Zerubbabel overcomes obstacles rebuilding temple *Ezra 3:8-13, 4:1-15*

Nehemiah persists in rebuilding the wall *Neh 4:1-23, 6:1-19*

Job never loses his faith in God *Job 1:13-22, 2:1-10*

Ezekiel's question whether parents' traits persist in children *Ezek 18:1-32*

Jews continue to refuse to worship image *Dan 3:1-30*
Daniel persists in praying as usual *Dan 6:1-28*
Jonah finds he cannot avoid doing God's bidding *Jonah 1:1-17, 2:1-10, 3:1-10*
Jesus heals blind man on second try *Mark 8:22-26*
Jesus sets his face toward Jerusalem and death *Luke 9:51-56, John 7:1-13*
Jesus' parable of the unwilling friend *Luke 11:5-13*
Jesus' parable of judge and widow *Luke 18:1-8*
Jesus persists telling Peter, "Feed my sheep" *John 21:12-19*
Peter and John persist in preaching *Acts 4:1-23*
Paul establishes the church *2 Cor 11:21-33*

See also effort, perseverance, steadfastness

PERSONALITY

Abram receives a new name and nature *Gen 17:1-9, 13-22*
Jacob changes from duplicity to spirituality *Gen 27:1-44, 32:24-32*
Ruth proves her nature by staying with Naomi *Ruth 1:1-22*
How Samuel selected David to be king *1 Sam 16:1-13*
Esther learns courage *Esther 5:1-14*
David's song, "What is man?" *Psal 8:1-9*
The ideal of a good wife and mother *Prov 31:1-31*
Women learn body culture is in vain *Isa 3:16-26*
Isaiah foretells the nature of Christ *Isa 7:10-16, 9:2-7, 42:1-12, 16, 18, 53:1-22, 61:1-11, 62:1-12*
Jonah as a study in personality *Jonah 1:1-17, 2:1-10, 3:1-10, 4:1-11*
Peter as a study in personality *Mat 16:13-20, 26:31-35, 57, 58, 69-75, 28:16-18, Mark 8:27-30, 14:27-31, 66-72, Luke 5:1-11, 9:18-21, 22:31-34, 54-62, John 13:1-20, 36-38, 13-18, 25-27, 21:1-24, Acts 3:1-11, 4:1-23*

Paul's self-revealing *2 Cor 12:1-19*

See also body, character, identity, individuality, soul

PERSUASION

The serpent persuades Eve and Adam *Gen 3:1-5*
Potiphar's wife unable to persuade Joseph *Gen 39:1-20*
Moses exhorts Israel to follow God *Deut 30:11-20*
Joshua exhorts to obedience *Josh 23:1-16*
David pacified by Abigail's gentleness *1 Sam 25:2-42*
David's song, "God is our refuge and strength" *Psal 46:1-11*
Malachi urges the people to tithe *Mal 3:10, 4:1, 2*
Jesus persuades his followers with 47 Parables *(See* Part II, Jesus Christ: Parables)
Jesus convinces his followers with healings and great works *(See* Part II, Jesus Christ: Great Works)
Jesus exhorts his followers with 52 discourses *(See* Part II, Jesus Christ: Teachings)
Jesus charges Peter to feed his sheep *John 21:12-19*

See also argument, belief, conviction, demonstration, influence, preaching, proof, reason

PESTILENCE

The plague in the wilderness *Num 16:3-5, 44-50*
The fiery serpent bites in the wilderness *Num 21:4-9*
Epidemic among Assyrians saves Israel *2 King 18:17-37, 19:1-27, 2 Chron 31:20, 21, 32:1-23, Isa 36:1-26, 37:1-38*
David's song of deliverance from pestilence *Psal 91:1-16*

See also contagion, epidemic, infection, plague

PETER (Simon Barjona)

See Part II, Peter

See also personality

PHARISEE

Pharisees accuse Jesus of using Beelzebub in healing *Mat 12: 22-30, Mark 3: 22-30, Luke 11: 14-23*

Pharisees request a sign of Jesus *Mat 12: 38-45, 16: 1-4, Mark 8: 10-13, Luke 11: 16, 29-32*

Jesus reproves Pharisees and they try to stone him *Mat 23:1-39, Mark 12: 38-40, Luke 11: 37-54, 20: 45-47*

Jesus while dining with Simon the Pharisee is anointed *Luke 7:36-50*

Jesus on leaven of the Pharisees *Luke 12: 1-15*

Jesus' parable of Pharisee and publican *Luke 18: 9-14*

Paul and Pharisee persecute Christians *Acts 8: 1-4, 9: 1-9*

See also hypocrisy, intolerance, ritual, self-righteousness, tradition

PHILIP (the Evangelist)

See Part II, Philip

PHILOSOPHY

Joseph calmly overcomes his problems *Gen 37: 1-36, 39: 21, 23, 40: 1-23, 41: 1-46*

Moses urges people to choose between good and evil *Deut 30: 1-20*

Moses instructs his successor *Deut 31: 7-23, Josh 1: 1-9*

Joshua urges choice of good or evil *Josh 24: 1-25*

David's song, "how are the mighty fallen!" *2 Sam 1: 17-27*

Nehemiah refuses to interrupt his work on wall *Neh 6: 1-19*

Job argues with his friends the nature of God *Job 2: 11-13, 4: 1-21, 6: 1-30*

The infinite speaks to man *Job 38: 1-41*

David's song on happiness of the godly *Psal 1: 1-6*

David's song on "what is man. . . ?" *Psal 8: 1-9*

David's song, "the fountain of life" *Psal 36: 1-12*

David's song, "Fret not thyself because of evildoers" *Psal 37: 23-40*

Proverbs on wisdom *Prov 3: 13-26, 4: 1-13, 8: 1-36*

The vanity of human things *Eccl 1: 1-18, 2: 1-26*

Mortal events all within time *Eccl 3: 1-15*

Wisdom is better than strength *Eccl 9: 13-18*

Body culture in vain *Isa 3: 16-26*

Truth flows encompassing universe *Ezek 47: 1-12*

Jesus' healings illustrate his philosophy:
  Woman's issue of blood *Mat 9: 20-22, Mark 5:25-34, Luke 8:43-48*
  Peter tries to walk on water *Mat 14:22-23, John 6:15-21*
  Epileptic boy *Mat 17: 14-21, Mark 9:14-29, Luke 9:37-43*
  Blind beggar, Bartimaeus *Mat 20: 29-34, Mark 10:46-52*

Forty-seven parables of Jesus as key points in Christian philosophy *(See* Part II, Jesus Christ: Parables)

Fifty-two teachings of Jesus explain Christian philosophy *(See* Part II, Jesus Christ: Teachings)

Peter's teachings develop Christian ideals *Acts 2: 14-47, 11: 1-18, 1 Pet 2:1-25*

Paul's letters on Christian precepts *Col 3: 1-17, 1 Thess 5: 1-28, 2 Tim 2: 1-26, 3: 1-17, 4: 1-8, Heb 1: 1-14, 2: 1-18, 10: 1-39, 12: 1-29*

John's letters to seven churches in Asia *Rev 1: 4-20, 2: 1-29, 3: 1-22*

John's revelations give key points *Rev 4:1-11, 5:1-14, 6:1-17, 10: 1-11, 12: 1-17, 21: 1-27, 22: 1-21*

See also ethics, knowledge, logic, metaphysics, morality, principle, reality, wisdom

PHYSICIAN

Abraham cures Abimelech and wife of barrenness *Gen 20: 1-7, 17*

Moses heals his sister of leprosy *Num 12: 1-16*

Elijah raises widow's son *1 King 17: 17-24*

Elisha raises Shunammite's son *2 King 4:8-37*

Elisha heals Naaman of leprosy *2 King 5:1-14*

Isaiah heals the king *2 King 20:1-11, Isa 38: 1-22*

Jesus' healings (*See* Part II, Jesus Christ: Great Works)

Jesus heals woman who had spent all her money on physicians *Mat 9: 20-22, Mark 5: 25-34, Luke 8: 43-48*

Jesus on the Father as the source of his great works *John 5: 17-47*

Peter and John heal the lame man *Acts 3: 1-26*

Peter heals Aeneas of paralysis *Acts 9: 32-35*

Peter raises Tabitha *Acts 9: 36-43*

Philip heals many *Acts 8: 5-8*

Ananias heals Paul of blindness *Acts 9: 10-22*

Paul heals cripple at Lystra *Acts 14: 8-10*

Paul raises Eutychus *Acts 20: 7-12*

Paul heals Publius' father *Acts 28: 7-10*

See also doctor, healing, medicine, practice

PHYSICS

Lord God creates material universe *Gen 2:6—3:24*

Noah protected from the flood *Gen 7: 1-24*

Babel, a material tower, built to heaven *Gen 11: 1-9*

Moses sees bush burn but not consumed *Exod 3: 1-18*

Israel passes through Red Sea *Exod 14: 5-31*

Moses draws water from rock *Exod 17: 1-7, Num 20: 1-13*

Aaron's rod blossoms *Num 17: 1-11*

Israel crosses over Jordan *Josh 3: 1-17*

Jericho's walls crumble *Josh 6: 1-27*

Sun and moon stand still at Ajalon *Josh 10: 6-15*

Gideon's three signs *Judg 6: 19-40*

Jeroboam's hand withered and healed *1 King 12: 32, 33, 13: 1-10*

Elijah prays for rain *1 King 18: 42-46*

Elijah crosses Jordan, Elisha crosses back *2 King 2: 1-15*

Elisha causes iron to swim *2 King 6: 1-7*

David's song, "The heavens declare the glory" *Psal 19: 1-14*

David's song, "The earth is the Lord's" *Psal 24: 1-10*

Isaiah's vision of the desert in blossom *Isa 35: 1-10*

Ezekiel's vision of dry bones raised *Ezek 37: 1-14*

Daniel's friends in fiery furnace *Dan 3: 1-30*

Jonah in the big fish *Jonah 2: 1-10*

Jesus calms wind and sea *Mat 8: 23-27, Mark 4: 35-41, Luke 8: 22-25*

Jesus raises dead *Mat 9: 18, 19, 23-26, Mark 5: 22-24, 35-43, Luke 7: 11-17, 8:41, 42, 49-56, John 11:1-46*

Jesus heals withered hand *Mat 12: 9-13, Mark 3: 1-5, Luke 6: 6-11*

Jesus walks on water *Mat 14: 22-33, John 6: 15-21*

Jesus seen talking with Moses and Elijah *Mat 17: 1-13, Mark 9: 2-13, Luke 9: 28-36*

Jesus' own resurrection *Mat 28: 1-8, Mark 6: 1-8, Luke 24: 1-12, John 20: 1-20*

Jesus' ascension *Mark 16: 19, 20, Luke 24: 50-53, Acts 1: 6-12*

Jesus' immaculate birth *Luke 1: 26-38*

Jesus changes water into wine *John 2: 1-11*

Jesus promises to raise "temple in three days" *John 2: 19-22*

Paul on spirit vs. the flesh *Rom 8: 1-39*

See also heat, light, matter, nature, sound

PHYSIOLOGY

Lord God makes man from dust *Gen 2: 6-8*

Patriarchs live to advanced age *Gen 5: 1-32*

Abraham at 99 begets a son *Gen 21: 1-8*

Elijah fed in a dream *1 King 19: 1-8*

Elisha annuls poison in pottage *2 King 4:38-41*

David's song, "What is man?" *Psal 8: 1-9*

David's song, "Why art thou cast down, O my soul?" *Psal 42:1-11*

Ezekiel on heredity *Ezek 18:1-32*

Ezekiel's vision of army from dry bones *Ezek 37: 15-28*

Daniel and three friends live well on pulse *Dan 1: 1-21*

Three Jews survive the fiery furnace *Dan 3: 1-30*

Jesus heals Peter's mother-in-law instantly *Mat 8: 14-17, Mark 1: 29-34*

Jesus is seen talking with Moses and Elijah *Mat 17: 1-13, Mark 9: 2-13, Luke 9: 28-36*

Jesus' resurrection *Mat 28: 1-8, Mark 16: 1-8, Luke 24: 1-12, John 20: 1-10*

Jesus' parable of "temple" raised in three days *John 2: 19-22*

Jesus on man must be born again *John 3: 1-21*

Jesus (absent from patient) reduces fever *John 4: 46-54*

Paul's blindness and healing *Acts 9: 1-22*

Paul on Spirit vs. flesh *Rom 8:1-39*

Paul on putting on the new man *Col 3: 1-17*

Jesus' many healings (*See* Part II, Jesus Christ: Great Works)

See also body, chemistry, life, organic, physics

PILGRIM

God calls Abraham to search for promised land *Gen 11: 31, 32, 12: 1-9*

Jacob flees from home but receives God's promise *Gen 28:10-22*

Jacob returns to Canaan in fear *Gen 32: 1-32*

Joseph is sold into slavery in Egypt *Gen 37:1-36*

Israelites emigrate to Egypt *Gen 45: 25-28, 46: 2-7*

Naomi emigrates from Israel and returns *Ruth 1: 1-22, 2: 1-23*

David's song, "The Lord is my shepherd" *Psal 23:1-6*

David's song, "our dwelling place" *Psal 90: 1-17*

David's song, "the secret place of the most High" *Psal 91: 1-16*

David's song, "Whither . . . from thy spirit" *Psal 139: 1-24*

Jeremiah's promise that captivity will be turned *Jer 29: 8-14, 31: 1-14, 31-34*

Jesus says he is homeless *Mat 8: 18-20, Luke 9: 57, 58*

Paul's hardships to establish church *2 Cor 11: 21-33*

See also Christian, discovery, sacredness, separation, travel

PIONEER

Abraham leaves home for the promised land *Gen 11: 31, 32, 12:1-9*

Israelites pass through Red Sea to wilderness *Exod 14: 5-31*

Moses brings new laws to the people *Exod 20: 1-19, Deut 5: 1-24*

Caleb and Joshua scout the promised land *Num 13: 1-33, 14: 1-11, 23-39, Deut 1: 19-38*

Zerubbabel returns to rebuild the temple *Ezra 3: 8-13*

Nehemiah returns to rebuild wall of Jerusalem *Neh 1:1-11, 2:1-20, 4: 1-23*

David's song, "Whither shall I go from thy spirit?" *Psal 139: 1-24*

Jesus' parable of the leaven *Mat 13: 33, Luke 13: 20, 21*

Peter acknowledges Jesus as the Christ *Mat 16: 13-20, Mark 8: 27-30, Luke 9: 18-21*

Jesus' resurrection *Mat 28: 1-8, Mark 16: 1-8, Luke 24: 1-12, John 20: 1-10*

Jesus as the light of the world *John 1: 1-14, 8: 12-32*

Jesus' doctrine, God is Spirit and must be worshipped spiritually *John 4: 1-30, 39-42*

Peter and John speak the word with boldness *Acts 4: 1-23*

Signs and wonders in the early church *Acts 4: 24-37*

Philip heals and converts many *Acts 8: 5-13*

Paul establishes a church at Antioch *Acts 11: 19-26*

Paul's hardships as pioneer *2 Cor 11: 21-33*

The example left by Jesus *Heb 12: 1-29*

James on faith without works *Jas 2: 14-26*

John's letters to the early churches *Rev 1: 4-20, 2: 1-29, 3: 1-22*

See also discovery, guidance, path, preparation, wilderness

PITY

David shows kindness to son of his friend *2 Sam 9: 1-13*

David prays for his own sick child *2 Sam 12: 13-23*

Solomon's judging finds the right mother *1 King 3: 16-28*

Elisha supplies an income for the widow to live on *2 King 4: 1-7*

Elisha raises the Shunammite's son *2 King 4: 8-37*

Nehemiah surveys Jerusalem's misery *Neh 1: 1-11, 2: 1-20*

Job asks why the good man should suffer *Job 3: 1-26*

David's song, "Why art thou cast down?" *Psal 42: 1-11*

Captives' song, "By the rivers of Babylon" *Psal 137: 1-9*

Isaiah's promise of God's help *Isa 43: 1-28, 44: 1-24*

Ezekiel's vision of God's care over his flock *Ezek 34: 1-31*

Hosea's vision of God's care over his child *Hos 11: 1-4*

Zephaniah's promise of salvation *Zeph 3: 14-17*

Jesus heals the multitude *Mat 4: 23-25, 12: 14-21, 14: 14, 15: 29-31, 19: 1, 2, Mark 3: 6-12, 6: 53-56, Luke 4: 40-44, 6: 53-56*

Jesus blesses little children *Mat 19: 13-15, Mark 10: 13-16, Luke 18: 15-17*

Jesus is crucified *Mat 27: 32-56, Mark 15: 21-41, Luke 23: 26-49, John 19: 17-30*

Jesus' parable of good Samaritan *Luke 10: 25-37*

Jesus' parable of the father of the prodigal son *Luke 15: 11-32*

Jesus' parable of good shepherd *John 10: 1-18*

Paul on charity *1 Cor 13: 1-13*

John's sermon on Love *1 John 4: 1-21*

John's vision of the sealed book *Rev 5: 1-14*

See also comforter, compassion, mercy

PLACE

Jacob steals Esau's blessing *Gen 27: 1-44*

Joseph prospers as Egyptian slave *Gen 37: 1-6*

Joseph prospers in prison *Gen 39: 21-23, 40: 1-23*

Joseph prospers as governor *Gen 41: 1-46*

Moses reluctant to take his place as leader *Exod 3: 9-12*

Moses consecrates Aaron as priest *Lev 8: 1-13*

Moses charges Joshua with leadership *Deut 31: 7-23, Josh 1: 1-9*

Gideon requires three signs of God *Judg 6: 19-40*

Jotham's parable of the trees *Judg 9: 1-15*

Samuel selects David based on inner man *1 Sam 16: 14-23*

Elisha takes up mantle of Elijah *2 King 2: 12-15*

David's song, "The heavens declare the glory" *Psal 19: 1-14*

David's song, "the secret place" *Psal 91: 1-16*

David's song, "whither shall I go?" *Psal 139: 1-24*

Jeremiah foretells end of captivity *Jer 29: 8-14, 31: 1-14, 31-34*

Enemies plot to take Daniel's place *Dan 6: 1-28*

Jonah resists his right place *Jonah 1: 1-17, 2: 1-10, 3: 1-10*

John the Baptist sends to Jesus for proof of Christ *Mat 11: 2-19, Luke 7: 18-35*

Jesus' parable of wheat and tares *Mat 13: 24-31, 36-43*

Peter says Jesus is the Christ *Mat 16: 13-20, Mark 8: 27-30, Luke 9: 18-21*

Disciples contend who shall be greatest *Mat 18: 1-11, Mark 9: 33-37, Luke 9: 46-50*

Jesus' parable of laborers in vineyard *Mat 20: 1-16*

Zebedee's wife asks preference for her sons *Mat 20: 20-28, Mark 10: 35-45*

Jesus' parable of door shut by master *Luke 13: 22-30*

Jesus' parable of chief seats at feast *Luke 14:7-14*

Jesus' parable of those bidden to great supper *Luke 14:15-24*

Jesus as the light of the world *John 1: 1-14, 8: 12-32*

Election of Matthias to replace Judas *Acts 1: 15-26*

See also business, employment, guidance, office, position, supply, work

PLAGUE

Israelites are passed over when firstborn Egyptians die *Exod 11: 4-10, 12: 1-14, 21-41, Deut 16: 1-22*

Children of Israel healed by Moses *Num 16:3-5, 44-50*

Plague of fiery serpents *Num 21: 4-9*

Jesus heals ten men at once, of leprosy *Luke 17: 11-29*

Angel with seven vials full of seven last plagues *Rev. 21: 9*

See also contagion, infection, pestilence, poison

PLAN

God creates the perfect universe *Gen 1:1-31*

Noah builds an ark for safety from flood *Gen 6:5-22*

Tower of Babel built to reach heaven *Gen 11:1-9*

God tells Moses his plan to free people *Exod 3:1-18*

Joshua tells plan to take Jericho *Josh 6:1-27*

Gideon tells his plan to defeat host *Judg 7:1-25*

Esther's plan to release her people *Esther 5:1-14*

Jonah at first refuses God's plan for him *Jonah 1:1-17, 2:1-10, 3: 1-10*

Jesus' parable of builders on rock and sand *Mat 7:24-27, Luke 6: 48, 49*

Judas conspires with rulers to betray Jesus *Mat 26:1-5, 14-16, Mark 14:1, 2, 10, 11, Luke 22:1-6*

Jesus' parable of rich man and bigger barns *Luke 12:15-21*

Jesus' parable on counting the cost of building *Luke 14:25-33*

See also aims, ambition, purpose

PLANT

God creates plants in the earth *Gen 1:11-13*

Lord God creates plants out of the ground *Gen 2:8, 9*

Cain offers fruit of ground *Gen 4: 1-16*

Moses at the burning bush *Exod 3:1-18*

Manna as source of food *Exod 16: 1-36, Num 11:1-15, 31, 32*

Aaron's rod blossoms and bears almonds *Num 17:1-11*

Moses on importance of offering first fruits *Deut 26:1-19*

Jotham's parable of the trees *Judg 9:1-13*

Elijah discouraged under juniper tree *1 King 19:1-8*

Isaiah's vision of desert blossoming *Isa 35:1-10*

Zechariah's vision of two olive trees feeding candlestick *Zech 4:1-14*

Jesus' sermon, urging to know men by their fruits *Mat 7:15-20, Luke 6:43-45*

Jesus' parable of the sower *Mat 13:3-23, Mark 4:1-20, Luke 8:4-15*

Jesus' parable of the wheat and tares *Mat 13:24-30, 36-43*

Jesus enters city on path of palms *Mat 21:1-11, 14-17, Mark 11:1-11, Luke 19:29-44, John 12:12-19*

Jesus withers the fig tree *Mat 21: 18-22, Mark 11:12-14, 20-24*

Jesus' parable of the fig tree leafing *Mat 24:32, 33, Mark 13:28, 29*

Jesus' parable of the seed, blade, ear, full corn *Mark 4:26-29*

Jesus' parable of the barren fig tree *Luke 13:6-9*

Jesus' parable of the abiding vine *John 15:1-17*

John's vision of tree of life *Rev 22:1-21*

See also creation, harvest, seed, tree

PLATFORM

Moses lays out the Ten Commandments *Exod 20:1-19, Deut 5:1-24*
Solomon dedicates the temple *1 King 8:22-66, 2 Chron 6:1-42*
Isaiah's prophecies of the coming Messiah *Isa 7:10-16, 9:2-7, 42:1-12, 16, 18, 53:1-22, 55:1-13, 61:1-11, 62: 1-12*
Jesus' Sermon on the Mount *Mat 5:1-48, 6:1-34*
Jesus Christ as the light of the world *John 1:1-14, 8:12-32*
Peter on the meaning of Christianity *Acts 2:14-47*
Peter defends conversion of Gentiles *Acts 11:1-18*
Peter's sermon on Christ, the cornerstone *1 Pet 2:1-25*
Paul on love as the highest value *1 Cor 13:1-13*
James preaches on necessity of works *Jas 2:14-26*
John's statement of being *1 John 3:1-3*
John's sermon, God is Love *1 John 4:1-21*

See also design, foundation, plan, principle

PLEASURE

God sees all he made and finds it good *Gen 1:31*
Eve finds forbidden fruit pleasant *Gen 3:1-5*
Delilah betrays Samson *Judg 16:4-30*
David's song, "Rejoice in the Lord" *Psal 33:1-22*
David's song, "Make a joyful noise" *Psal 66:1-20, 100:1-5*
Isaiah on the pride of women *Isa 3:16-26*
Ezekiel's vision of God's pleasure in his people *Ezek 34:1-31*
The temptations of Jesus *Mat 4:1-11, Mark 1:12, 13, Luke 4:1-13*
Why his disciples do not fast *Mat 9:14-17, Mark 2:18-22, Luke 5:33-39*
Jesus' parable of the sower *Mat 13:3-23, Mark 4:1-20, Luke 8:4-15*

Rich young ruler asks how to inherit eternal life *Mat 19:16-30, Mark 10:17-31, Luke 18:18-30*
Jesus' parable of two sons ordered to work *Mat 21:28-32*
Jesus' parable of prodigal son *Luke 15:11-24*
Jesus' parable of rich man and beggar *Luke 16:19-31*
Paul on rejoicing *Phil 4:1-23*

See also contentment, delight, happiness, joy, pain, senses, will

PLENTY

God creates adequate universe *Gen 1:1-31*
Abraham's riches grow *Gen 13:1-18*
Joseph reads Pharaoh's dream *Gen 41:1-46*
Joseph's brothers come to Egypt for food *Gen 42:1-8*
Manna and quails in wilderness *Exod 16:1-36, Num 11:1-15, 31, 32*
Moses lists blessings of obedience *Deut 28:1-14*
David receives liberal offerings for temple *1 Chron 29:6-19*
Solomon's prosperity acknowledged by Queen of Sheba *1 King 10:1-12*
Elijah fed in a dream *1 King 19:1-8*
Elisha enables widow to make a living *2 King 4:1-7*
Elisha feeds 100 men with a few loaves *2 King 4:42-44*
Elisha predicts plenty in midst of a famine *2 King 6:24, 25, 7:1-18*
David's song, "The Lord is my shepherd" *Psal 23:1-6*
David's song, "praise the Lord for his goodness" *Psal 107:1-43*
Isaiah's vision of desert blossoming *Isa 35:1-10*
Ezekiel's vision of God's care *Ezek 34:1-31*
Jesus feeds thousands and their families *Mat 14:15-21, 15:32-39, Mark 6:35-44, 8:1-10, Luke 9:12-17, John 6:5-14*
Jesus obtains tribute money from fish *Mat 17:24-27*
Jesus' parable of prodigal's elder brother *Luke 15:25-32*
Jesus turns water into wine *John 2:1-11*

Jesus' parable of the true vine *John 15:1-17*

Jesus fills Peter's net *John 21:1-11, Luke 5:1-11*

Paul on abundance *2 Cor 8:11-15, 9:6-15*

See also abundance, supply

PLOT

Jacob and Rebekah plan to deceive Isaac *Gen 27:1-44*

Joseph's brother sells him into slavery *Gen 37:1-36*

Miriam and Aaron plot against Moses *Num 12:1-16*

Balak hires Balaam to curse Israel *Num 22:1-41, 23:1-30, 24:1-25*

David plans Uriah's death *2 Sam 11:1-27*

Nathan uncovers David's sin *2 Sam 12:1-10*

Ahab takes Naboth's vineyard *1 King 21:1-27*

Elisha besieged by Syrians *2 King 6:8-23*

Nehemiah avoids the conspiracy to stop his work *Neh 6:1-19*

Haman hanged on his own gallows *Esther 6:1-14, 7:1-10*

David's song, "Fret not thyself because of evildoers" *Psal 37:23-40*

David's song, "the secret place of the most High" *Psal 91:1-16*

Isaiah's vision of workers in the dark *Isa 29:11-24, 30:1-3, 20, 21*

Chaldeans accuse Jews, resulting in their being cast into fiery furnace *Dan 3:1-30*

Daniel's political enemies plot against him *Dan 6:1-28*

Jesus' parents flee with him to Egypt *Mat 2:13-23, Luke 2:39, 40*

Jesus foretells his betrayal and resurrection *Mat 16:21-28, 17:22, 23, 20:17-19, 26:20-25, 47-56, Mark 8: 31-38, 9:30-32, 10:32-34, 14:18-21, 43-54, Luke 9:20-27, 43-45, 18:31-34, 19:47, 48, 22:21, 22, 47-53, John 12:20-50, 13:21-35, 18:1-12*

Jesus' parable of husbandmen who plot death of the son *Mat 21:33-46, Mark 12:1-12, Luke 20:9-19*

Rulers conspire against Jesus *Mat 26:1-5, Mark 14:1, 2*

Judas settles the price of betrayal *Mat 26:14-16, Mark 14:10, 11, Luke 22:1-16*

Elders pay soldiers to say Jesus' body was taken away *Mat 28: 11-15*

Chief priests seek to destroy Jesus *Mark 11:18, 19*

Jesus delivers himself by passing through enemies *Luke 4:28-31*

See also betrayal, conspiracy, death, plan

POETRY

See psalm, songs

POISON

Serpent deceives Eve with lie *Gen 3:1-5*

Bites of fiery serpent healed *Num 21:4-9*

Moses' rod becomes serpent and he flees *Exod 4:1-9*

Elisha heals waters of city *2 King 2:16-22*

Poisoned pottage rendered harmless *2 King 4:38-41*

Jesus preaches men need suffer no hurt from a deadly drink *Mark 16:14-18*

Paul recovers from viper's bite *Acts 28:1-6*

See also blood, death, lie

POLITICS

Despotic actions of the Pharaohs *Exod 1:8-14*

Moses delegates authority to judges *Exod 18:13-27*

Moses lays down the law *Exod 20: 1-19, Deut 5:1-24*

Gideon refuses to be king *Judg 8: 22, 23*

Jotham's parable of the trees *Judg 9:1-15*

Samuel resists the demand for a king *1 Sam 8:1-22*

Samuel relents and makes Saul king *1 Sam 10:1-8*

Saul declared unfit by Samuel *1 Sam 15:7-26*

Rehoboam consults old advisors,

then his friends *1 King 12:1-18, 2 Chron 10:1-19*
The coming of Christ's kingdom *Isa 2:1-5, 11:1-12, 65:17-25, Mic 4: 1-8, 13*
Jeremiah foretells captivity will be over *Jer 29:8-14, 31:1-14, 31-34*
The presidents effect Daniel's placement in lions' den *Dan 6:1-28*
Chaldeans succeed in placing three Jews in fiery furnace *Dan 3:1-30*
Jesus' parables about kingdom of God:
Sower *Mat 13:3-23, Mark 4:1-20, Luke 8:4-15*
Wheat and tares *Mat 13:24-30, 36-43*
Leaven *Mat 13:33, Luke 13:20, 21*
Treasure buried *Mat 13:44*
Pearl of price *Mat 13:45, 46*
Dragnet *Mat 13:47-50*
Householder's treasure *Mat 13: 51, 52*
Seed, blade, ear *Mark 4:26-29*
Mustard seed *Mark 4:30-32, Luke 13:18, 19*
Matthias elected to replace Judas *Acts 1:15-26*
See also economics, government, history, law, leader, nation

POOR

Ruth gleans after the reapers *Ruth 2:1-23*
Elijah helps widow who feeds him *1 King 17:1-16*
Elisha helps widow earn living *2 King 4:1-7*
Job's woe expressed *Job 3:1-26*
A poor wise man saved a city *Eccl 9:13-18*
Jesus watches widow contribute her mite *Mark 12:41-44, Luke 21:1-4*
Jesus' parable of rich man and beggar *Luke 16:19-31*
Paul on abundance *2 Cor 8:11-15, 9:6-15*
See also abundance, affliction, barrenness, lack, pity, poverty, receptivity, wealth

POPULARITY

Gideon refuses to be king *Judg 8: 22, 23*

David returns from killing Goliath *1 Sam 18:1-16*
David made king of Judah *2 Sam 2:1-4*
David made king of Israel *2 Sam 5:1-5*
Josiah's good reign *2 King 23:1-22, 2 Chron 34:1-8, 29-33*
Great multitudes follow Jesus *Mat 12:14-21, Mark 3:6-12*
Jesus, a prophet without honor in his own country *Mat 13:53-58, Mark 6:1-6, Luke 4:22-24, John 4:43-45*
Multitudes come to Jesus on mountain *Mat 15:29-31*
Great multitudes healed by Jesus *Mat 19:1, 2*
Jesus enters Jerusalem to applause *Mat 21:1-11, 14-17, Mark 11:1-11, Luke 19:29-44, John 12:12-19*
Precious ointment poured on his head *Mat 26:6-13, Mark 14:3-9*
All men seek him; his fame increases *Mark 1:35-39*
Jesus says he is the light of the world *John 1:1-14, 8:12-32*
Paul and Barnabas worshipped as gods *Acts 14:11-18*
See also democracy, fame, friendship, people

POSITION

Joseph, sold into slavery, does well *Gen 39:1-6*
Joseph works his way out of prison to be governor *Gen 41:1-46*
Moses' reluctance to lead overcome *Exod 3:9-12*
Judges appointed to help Moses *Exod 18:13-27*
Aaron and sons anointed as priests *Lev 8:1-13*
Rights of women acknowledged *Num 27:1-11, 36:5-13*
Chosen people set apart as God's own *Deut 7:6-11*
Joshua given the command *Josh 1:1-9*
Gideon refuses to be king *Judg 8:22, 23*
Jotham's parable of the trees *Judg 9:1-15*
Ruth's right place, with her mother-in-law *Ruth 1:1-22*

Samuel anoints Saul as king *1 Sam 10:1-8*

Saul declared unfit *1 Sam 15:7-26*

David anointed *1 Sam 16:1-13*

Solomon's position acknowledged by Queen of Sheba *1 King 10:1-12, 2 Chron 9:1-12*

Isaiah's vision of the place of the Christ *Isa 7:10-16, 9:2-7*

Daniel's friends temporarily displaced *Dan 3:1-30*

Daniel is temporarily displaced *Dan 6:1-28*

John sends to Jesus for proof of Christ *Mat 11:2-19, Luke 7:18-35*

Peter acknowledges Jesus as Christ *Mat 16:13-20, Mark 8:27-30, Luke 9:18-21*

Jesus' parable of chief seats at the wedding *Luke 14:7-14*

Jesus' teaching that he is Christ *John 7:14-40*

See also business, employment, place, supply

POSSESS

Adam and Eve take and eat the forbidden fruit *Gen 3:6-24*

Abraham's growth in riches causes conflict with Lot *Gen 13:1-18*

Daughters of Zelophehad sue to inherit father's property *Num 27:1-11, 36:5-13*

First fruits of possessions to God *Deut 26:1-19*

Jericho possessed by Israelites *Josh 6:1-27*

David arranges Uriah's death to possess his wife *2 Sam 11:1-27*

Importance of having wisdom *Prov 3:13-26, 4:1-13, 8:1-36*

Vanity of all human things *Eccl 1:1-18, 2:1-26*

Malachi urges tithing of possessions *Mal 3:10, 4:1, 2*

Jesus on true treasures *Mat 6:19-21*

Jesus' teaching, seek ye first *Mat 6:25-34, Luke 12:22-34*

Jesus heals mental derangement of Legion *Mat 8:28-34, Mark 5:1-20, Luke 8:26-39*

Jesus permits devils to enter swine *Mat 8:30-32*

Jesus heals a daughter of a devil *Mat 15:21-28, Mark 7:24-30*

Jesus heals epileptic boy *Mat 17:14-21, Mark 9:14-29, Luke 9:37-43*

Jesus heals mental derangement of man in temple *Mark 1:21-28, Luke 4:33-37*

Jesus' parable of the rich man and bigger barns *Luke 12:15-21*

Jesus' parable of the rich man and beggar *Luke 16:19-31*

Philip heals unclean spirits *Acts 8:5-8*

Paul casts devil out of soothsayer *Acts 16:16-18*

See also body, control, devil, dominion, heredity, inherit, knowledge, property, wealth

POSSIBILITY

God creates the perfect universe *Gen 1:1-31*

Noah shows protection from nature possible *Gen 7:1-24*

Children possible at advanced age *Gen 15:1-21*

Joseph proves that treachery, slavery, temptation, prison can be overcome *Gen 37:1-36, 39:1-20, 21-23, 40:1-23, 41:1-46*

Moses proves God can deliver *Deut 32:1-47*

God shows Gideon his ability *Judg 6:19-40, 7:1-25*

David and Goliath *1 Sam 17:38-52*

Elijah shows Elisha translation is possible *2 King 2:1-11*

Elisha raises the dead *2 King 4:8-37*

Jehoshaphat shows the battle is God's *2 Chron 20:1-32*

Jeremiah, in prison, buys a field in Israel *Jer 32:2, 6-27, 37-44*

David's song, "God is our refuge and strength" *Psal 46:1-11*

David's song, "the secret place of the most High" *Psal 91:1-16*

Three Jews saved from fiery furnace *Dan 3:1-30*

Daniel saved from lions' den *Dan 6:1-28*

Jesus controls wind and sea *Mat 8:23-27, Mark 9:35-41, Luke 8:22-25*

Jesus multiplies loaves and fishes *Mat 14:15-21, Mark 6:35-44, Luke 9:12-17, John 6:5-14*

Jesus walks on water *Mat 14:22-33, John 6:15-21*

Jesus controls time and talks with Moses *Mat 17:1-13, Mark 9:2-13, Luke 9:28-36*

The resurrection of Jesus *Mat 28:1-8, Mark 16:1-8, Luke 24:1-12, John 20:1-10*

The ascension of Jesus *Mark 16:19, 20, Luke 24:50-53, Acts 1:6-12*

Jesus heals man born blind *John 9:1-41*

Jesus raises Lazarus dead four days *John 11:1-46*

See also ability, omnipotence, power, strength

POVERTY

Ruth gleans in fields after reapers *Ruth 2:1-23*

Elijah supplies widow with food *1 King 17:1-16*

David's song, "The Lord is my shepherd" *Psal 23:1-6*

Jesus' Sermon on the Mount, "Blessed are the poor" *Mat 5:1-12, Luke 6:17-26, 36*

Jesus observes widow cast in her mite *Mark 12:41-44, Luke 21:1-4*

Jesus' parable of rich man and bigger barns *Luke 12:15-21*

Jesus' parable of rich man and beggar at gate *Luke 16:19-31*

Jesus' sermon, "I am the bread of life" *John 6:26-65*

See also abundance, lack, need, poor, supply, wealth

POWER

God creates the perfect universe and man *Gen 1:1-31*

Red Sea passed through *Exod 14:5-31*

Moses' song of deliverance *Exod 15:1-19, Deut 32:1-47*

Jordan crossed dry-shod *Josh 3:1-17*

Jericho crumbles *Josh 6:1-27*

Sun and moon stand still at Ajalon *Josh 10:6-15*

Gideon and 300 men defeat a host *Judg 7:1-25*

David and Goliath *1 Sam 17:38-52*

Elijah and 450 prophets of Baal *1 King 18:17-40*

Elijah and the nature of God *1 King 19:9-13*

Elisha raises Shunammite's son *2 King 4:8-37*

Hezekiah delivered from Assyrians *2 Chron 32:1-23, Isa 36:1-22, 37:1-38*

David's song, "The heavens declare the glory" *Psal 19:1-14*

David song, "the fountain of life" *Psal 36:1-12*

David's song, "God is our refuge and strength" *Psal 46:1-11*

David's song, "the secret place" *Psal 91:1-16*

David's song, "Bless the Lord, O my soul" *Psal 103:1-22*

David's song, God, the preserver of man *Psal 121:1-8*

Safe out of the fiery furnace *Dan 3:1-30*

Jonah and the whale *Jonah 2:1-10*

Jesus controls wind and sea *Mat 8:23-27, Mark 4:35-41, Luke 8:22-25*

Jesus raises dead *Mat 9:18, 19, 23-26, Luke 7:11-17, John 11:1-46*

Jesus controls time—talks with Moses *Mat 17:1-13, Mark 9:2-13, Luke 9:28-36*

Jesus' ascension *Mark 16:19, 20, Luke 24:50-53, Acts 1:6-12*

Jesus on source of his great works *John 5:17-47*

Paul on example left by Jesus *Heb 12:1-29*

James on faith without works *Jas 2:14-26*

See also ability, authority, dominion, force, king, majesty, might, omnipotence

PRACTICE

Abraham's faith is proved by willingness to sacrifice Isaac *Gen 22:1-19*

Moses heals his sister of leprosy *Num 12:1-16*

Moses urges obedience to God *Deut 11:1-32*

Moses lists blessings of discipline *Deut 28:1-14*

David refuses armor and chooses his slingshot *1 Sam 17:17-37*

Elijah raises widow's son *1 King 17:17-24*

Elisha raises Shunammite's son *2 King 4:8-37*

Elisha heals Naaman of leprosy *2 King 5:1-14*

Daniel refuses to change his prayers *Dan 6:1-28*

Jesus' parables:

the man taking a long journey *Luke 13:34-37*

the treasure in a field *Mat 13:44*

the pearl of great price *Mat 13:45, 46*

the householder's treasures *Mat 13:51, 52*

the two sons ordered to work *Mat 21:28-32*

the wise and foolish virgins *Mat 25:1-13*

the talents *Mat 25:14-30, Luke 19:11-28*

the sheep and the goats *Mat 25:31-46*

the unwilling friend *Luke 11:5-13*

the watchful servants *Luke 12:35-40*

the faithful steward *Luke 12:41-48*

the door shut by the Master *Luke 13:22-30*

the unjust steward *Luke 16:1-14*

the rich man and the beggar *Luke 16:19-31*

the judge and the widow *Luke 18:1-8*

the true vine *John 15:1-17*

Jesus' 52 healings and great works (*See* Part II, Jesus Christ: Great Works)

Jesus' teachings (*See* Part II, Jesus Christ: Teachings)

Peter and John heal lame man and explain how *Acts 3:1-26*

Paul heals lame man and explains how *Acts 14:8-18*

See also action, discipline, healing, medicine, patient, perfection, preaching, principle, profession

PRAISE

Noah saved because righteous *Gen 6:5-22*

Abraham blessed by Melchizedek *Gen 14:8-20, Heb 6:20, 7:1-28*

Moses' song of deliverance *Exod 15:1-19, Deut 32:1-47*

Joshua sets up memorial for God's help *Josh 4:1-24*

David's psalm of thanksgiving *2 Sam 22:1-51, 1 Chron 16:17-36*

Solomon's dedication of temple *1 King 8:22-66, 2 Chron 6:1-42*

Praise of Solomon by Queen of Sheba *1 King 10:1-12, 2 Chron 9:1-12*

David's songs of praise *Psal 19:1-14, 23:1-6, 24:1-10, 33:1-22, 36:5-10, 46:1-11, 51:1-19, 66:1-20, 84:1-12, 90:1-17, 91:1-16, 100:1-5, 103:1-22, 107:1-43, 121:1-8*

In praise of wisdom *Prov 3:13-26, 4:1-13, 8:1-36*

Isaiah's vision of God's glory *Isa 6:1-13*

Daniel approved by Gabriel *Dan 9:20-23, 10:4-21*

Jesus praises Peter for saying he is Christ *Mat 16:13-20, Mark 8:27-30, Luke 9:18-21*

Lame man healed (leaps and praises God) *Acts 3:1-11*

See also condemnation, glory, gratitude, honor, magnify, prayer, psalm, thanksgiving, worship

PRAYER

Hagar and Ishmael pray for water in the wilderness *Gen 21:9-21*

Jacob sees angel thoughts ascending and descending *Gen 28:10-22*

Moses at Red Sea turns to God for next step *Exod 14:5-31*

Moses gets beginning of the law, "Thou shalt not" *Exod 20:1-19, Deut 5:1-24*

Solomon asks for understanding *1 King 3:5-15, 2 Chron 1:7-12*

Elijah prays for rain *1 King 18:41-46*

Elijah says the Lord is in a still small voice *1 King 19:9-13*

Job prays for understanding *Job 3:1-26*

David's song, "Create in me a clean heart" *Psal 51:1-19*

Daniel's three friends escape fiery furnace *Dan 3:1-30*

Daniel prays daily to God *Dan 6: 1-28*

Jonah's prayer in belly of whale *Jonah 2:1-10*

The Lord's Prayer *Mat 6:9-13, Mark 11:25, 26, Luke 11:1-4*

Jesus' prayer of true petition *Mat 7:6-11*

Jesus heals epileptic boy after disciples fail *Mat 17:14-21, Mark 9: 14-29, Luke 9:37-43*

Jesus in garden of Gethsemane *Mat 26:30, 36-46, Mark 14:26, 32-42, Luke 22:39-46*

Jesus continues all night in prayer *Luke 6:12*

Jesus' parable of the unwilling friend *Luke 11:5-13*

Jesus' parable of judge and widow *Luke 18:1-8*

Jesus' parable of Pharisee and publican *Luke 18:9-14*

Jesus prays before raising Lazarus *John 11:1-46*

Jesus' prayer for his disciples and their disciples *John 17:1-26*

Paul and Silas released from prison by earthquake *Acts 16:19-40*

See also affirmation, authority, communication, denial, healing, meditation, praise

PREACHING

Moses lays down the basis of all law *Exod 20:1-19, Deut 5:1-24*

Moses gives the watchword of Israel *Deut 6:4-6*

Moses cautions to remember trials *Deut 8:1-20*

Moses on obedience *Deut 11:1-32*

Moses warns against idolatry, necromancy *Deut 13:1-18*

Moses on forbidden abominations *Deut 18:9-14*

Moses on a prophet promised *Deut 18:15-22*

Moses preaches on first fruits *Deut 26:1-19*

Moses on blessings of obedience *Deut 28:1-14*

Moses on proper choices *Deut 30: 11-20*

Joshua exhorts to obedience *Josh 23:1-16*

Solomon on dedication of temple *2 King 8:22-66, 2 Chron 6:1-42*

Nehemiah has book of the law read to the people *Neh 8:1-12*

David's song, "What is man?" *Psal 8:1-9*

Proverbs on the value of wisdom *Prov 3:13-26, 4:1-13, 8:1-36*

The vanity of mortal life *Eccl 1: 1-18, 2:1-26*

Mortal events all within time framework *Eccl 3:1-15*

Isaiah's warning that hypocrisy will be punished *Isa 29:11-24, 30:1-3, 20, 21*

Isaiah's reassurance to Israel, "Comfort ye" *Isa 40:1-31*

Isaiah's sermon on help in trials *Isa 43:1-28, 44:1-24*

Isaiah's sermon on office of the Christ *Isa 61:1-11, 62:1-12*

Jeremiah's prophecy of release from captivity *Jer 29:8-14, 31:1-14, 31-34*

Ezekiel on equity of God's dealing *Ezek 18:1-32*

Ezekiel on God's care of his flock *Ezek 34:1-31*

Hosea on God's care of his child *Hos 11:1-4*

Micah on the glory of the church *Mic 4:1-8, 13, Isa 2:1-5*

Zephaniah on salvation promised *Zeph 3:14-17*

Malachi urges tithing *Mal 3:10, 4: 1, 2*

Jesus chooses twelve and sends them to heal and preach *Mat 9:36-38, 10:1-42, Mark 3:13-21, Luke 9:1-6*

Jesus tells why he speaks only in parables *Mat 13:10-17, 34, 35, Mark 4:10-12, 33, 34*

Jesus discourses on remarriage and resurrection *Mat 22:23-33, Mark 12:18-27, Luke 20:27-40*

Jesus followed by the people *Mark 1:35-39, 6:30-34*

Jesus, at twelve, questions and answers rabbis *Luke 2:41-52*

Jesus preaches at Nazareth and is rejected by his acquaintances *Luke 4:14-32*

Jesus sends out 70 more disciples *Luke 10:1-24*

Jesus on Christ as the light of the world *John 1:1-14, 8:12-32*

John the Baptist tells how Jesus' preaching differs from his own *John 3:22-36*

After Jesus' sermon on bread of life many disciples leave him *John 6:66-71*

Jesus charges Peter, "Feed my sheep" *John 21:12-19*

Peter on the meaning of Christianity *Acts 2:14-47*

Peter on healing through Christ *Acts 3:12-26*

Stephen on persecution of the prophets *Acts 7:1-53*

Paul on Christ and Jesus as the Messiah *Acts 13:16-52*

Paul on his trials as a Christian *Acts 20:17-38*

Paul on his own healing *Acts 26: 1-32*

Paul on Adam versus Christ *Rom 5:1-21*

Paul on Spirit versus flesh *Rom 8:1-39*

Peter on Christ, the chief cornerstone *1 Pet 3:1-25*

John's sermon, "God is Love" *1 John 4:1-21*

John's letters to seven churches *Rev 1:4-20, 2:1-29, 3:1-22*

Jesus' lesson in each of 47 parables (*See* Part II, Jesus Christ: Parables)

Jesus' sermons and discourses (*See* Part II, Jesus Christ: Teachings)

Paul on manner of preaching *1 Cor 1:17-31, 2:1-16, 3:18-23*

Paul on spiritual gifts *1 Cor 12: 1-31*

Paul on charity *1 Cor 13:1-13*

Paul on resurrection *1 Cor 15:1-58*

Paul on the outward and inward man *2 Cor 4:14-18, 5:1-21*

Paul on giving and receiving *2 Cor 8:11-15, 9:6-15*

See also gospel, ministry, persuasion, practice, prophet, sermon, teaching, word

PREDESTINATION

See election, plan, purpose

PREJUDICE

Cain murders Abel *Gen 4:1-16*

Joseph sold into slavery by his brothers *Gen 37:1-36*

Egyptians oppress Israelites *Exod 1:8-14, 5:7-19*

God's chosen people *Deut 7:6-11*

Haman persecutes the Jews *Esther 3:1-15, 4:1-17*

Isaiah's vision of the peaceable kingdom *Isa 11:1-12*

Jesus' parable of mote and beam *Mat 7:1-5, Luke 6:37-42*

Jesus touches the leper and heals him *Mat 8:1-4, Mark 1:40-45, Luke 5:12-16*

Jesus heals the Gentile's servant *Mat 8:5-13, Luke 7:1-10*

Jesus accused by Pharisees of healing by Beelzebub *Mat 12:22-30, Mark 3:22-30, Luke 11:14-23, 37-54*

Jesus heals daughter of Syrophenician woman *Mat 15:21-28, Mark 7:24-30*

Jesus' parable of unmerciful debtor *Mat 18:23-35*

Jesus reproves scribes and Pharisees *Mat 23:1-39, Mark 12:38-40, Luke 20:45-47, John 8:33-59*

Rulers conspire against him *Mat 26-1-5, Mark 14:1, 2*

Jesus' parable of good Samaritan *Luke 10:25-37*

Jesus' parable of Pharisee and publican *Luke 18:9-14*

Caiaphas urges council to put Jesus to death *John 11:47-54*

Paul's prejudice against Christians *Acts 8:1-4, 9:1-4*

Philip baptizes the Ethiopian *Acts 8:26-40*

Peter's struggles with accepting the Gentiles *Acts 10:1-48, 11:1-18*

Paul on the cost of establishing the church *2 Cor 11:21-33*

James on equality of man *Jas 2: 1-13*

John's sermon, "God is Love" *1 John 4:1-21*

See also condemnation, discrimination, ignorance, judgment, reason

PREPARATION

Enoch prepared for translation by walking with God *Gen 5:18, 21-24, Heb 11:5*

Noah prepares for flood *Gen 6:5-22*

David collects offering to build temple *1 Chron 29:6-19*

Isaiah foretells Christ's kingdom *Isa 2:1-5, Mic 4:1-8, 13*

Isaiah foretells birth of Messiah *Isa 7:10-16, 9:2-7*

John the Baptist prepares for coming of Messiah *Mat 3:1-12, Mark 1:1-8, Luke 3:1-18*

Jesus prepares for resurrection with three raisings from death *Mat 9:18, 19, 23-26, Mark 5:22-24, 35-43, Luke 7:11-17, 8:41, 42, 49-56, John 11:1-46*

Jesus charges his disciples to preach and heal *Mat 10:5-42, Mark 6:7-13, Luke 9:4-6*

Jesus tells the signs of Christ's coming *Mat 24:1-41*

Jesus' parable of wise and foolish virgins *Mat 25:1-13*

Jesus' parable of the talents *Mat 25:14-30, Luke 19:11-28*

Jesus prepares disciples for his coming resurrection *Mat 26:31-56*

Jesus tells disciples time to reap is now *Luke 10:1-16, John 4:31-38*

Jesus' parable of unjust steward *Luke 16:1-14*

Jesus' parable of rich man and beggar *Luke 16:19-31*

Jesus promises the Holy Ghost *John 14:1-31*

Jesus offers disciples co nfort against tribulations *John 16:1-33*

Paul prepares his disciples *1 Thess 5:1-28, 2 Tim 2:1-26, 3:1-17, 4:1-8, Heb 12:1-29*

See also messenger, prophet, readiness, ripeness, study

PRESENCE

See ever-presence

PRESENT

Shunammite states, "It is well!" and her son is raised *2 King 4:8-37*

David's song, "The Lord is my shepherd", shows confidence in God's grace now *Psal 23:1-6*

All mortal events within time framework *Eccl 3:1-15*

The present generation cannot be chained to their parents' mistakes *Ezek 18:1-32*

Jesus heals instantly the woman with issue of blood twelve years *Mat 9:20-22, Mark 5:25-34, Luke 8:43-48*

Jesus talks with Moses and Elias *Mat 17:1-13, Mark 9:2-13, Luke 9:28-36*

Jesus' ship at destination at once *Mark 6:45-52, John 6:21*

Jesus' parable of new wine in old bottles *Luke 5:36-39*

Jesus heals woman bowed together 18 years *Luke 13:11-17*

Jesus' parable of prodigal's elder brother *Luke 15:25-32*

Jesus' parable of servant's duties before he sups *Luke 17:7-10*

Jesus heals instantly the man impotent for 38 years *John 5:1-16*

See also eternity, ever-presence, immediate, time

PRESERVATION

See defense, deliverance, guard, salvation

PREVENTION

Noah builds an ark to save from the flood *Gen 6:5-22*

Tower of Babel prevented from reaching heaven *Gen 11:1-9*

Abraham stopped from sacrifice of Isaac *Gen 22:1-19*

Jacob wrestles with the angel to avoid Esau's anger *Gen 32:1-32*

Joseph's genius foresees and offsets famine *Gen 41:1-46, 42:1-8*

Moses delivers laws to prevent sin *Exod 20:1-19, Deut 5:1-24*

Aaron atones through scapegoat to prevent God's anger *Lev 16:1-28*

Balak prevented from cursing Israelites *Num 22:1-41, 23:1-30, 24:1-25*

David's retaliation prevented by Abigail *1 Sam 25:2-42*

Elisha proves poison harmless *2 King 4:38-41*

Epidemic prevents Assyrians invading Israel *2 Chron 31: 20, 21, 32: 1-23, Isa 36:1-22, 37:1-38*

Enemies block work of rebuilding temple *Ezra 4:1-15, 6:1-3, 7, 8, 14, 15*

Nehemiah foils conspiracy *Neh 6: 1-19*

Esther prevents extermination of her people *Esther 5:1-14, 6:1-14, 7:1-10*

Jesus' parables:

the unclean spirit *Mat 12:43-45, Luke 11:24-26*

servant waiting *Mat 24:42-51*

wise and foolish virgins *Mat 25: 1-13*

the talents *Mat 25:14-30, Luke 19:11-18*

the watchful servants *Luke 12: 35-40*

the faithful steward *Luke 12:41-48*

the prodigal's elder brother *Luke 15:25-32*

the unjust steward *Luke 16:1-14*

rich man and beggar *Luke 16:19-31*

servant who must serve *Luke 17: 7-10*

Jesus' family retires to Egypt *Mat 2: 13-23, Luke 2: 29, 40*

Jesus' sermon, Christ is the door *John 10:1-30*

Jesus' prayer for disciples and their disciples *John 17: 1-26*

Paul's advice to his disciples *1 Thess 5:1-28, 2 Tim 2:1-26, 3: 1-17, 4:1-8*

John's letter to seven churches *Rev 1: 4-20, 2: 1-29, 3: 1-22*

See also disease, medicine, opposition, preparation, protection, readiness

PRIDE

Tower of Babel built by man to reach heaven *Gen 11:1-9*

Caleb reviews his good life with pride *Josh 14: 6-15*

Saul corrupted by the pride of kingship *1 Sam 15:7-26*

Uzziah's heart is lifted up to destruction *2 Chron 26:1-23*

Naaman's first reaction to Elisha's prescription *2 King 5:15-27*

Hezekiah shows Babylonian ambassadors all his treasures *2 King 20:12-21, Isa 39:1-8*

David's song, "Create in me a clean heart" *Psal 51:1-19*

Isaiah on the pride of women *Isa 3:16-26*

Isaiah on the fall of Babylon *Isa 14: 4-8, 12-17, 25-27*

Jesus' parable of the mote and the beam *Mat 7: 1-5, Luke 6: 37-42*

Jesus' parable of the chief seats at the wedding *Luke 14:7-14*

Jesus' parable of the Pharisee and publican *Luke 18: 9-14*

Disciples debate who shall be greatest *Luke 22: 24-30*

See also ego, humility, meekness, self, vanity, worth

PRIEST

Abraham blessed by Melchizedek *Gen 14: 8-20, Heb 6: 20, 7: 1-28*

Moses anoints Aaron and sons for priesthood *Lev 8: 1-13*

Priests enter Jordan before people cross *Josh 3: 1-17*

Samuel anoints Saul as first king *1 Sam 10: 1-8*

Solomon dedicates the temple *1 King 8:22-66, 2 Chron 6:1-42*

Elijah out-performs 450 prophets of Baal *1 King 18: 17-40*

Book of the law read to people *Neh 8:1-12*

Isaiah foretells that hypocrisy will be punished *Isa 29: 11-24, 30: 1-3, 20, 21*

Ezekiel warns shepherds who feed only themselves, not the flocks *Ezek 34: 1-31*

Jesus is baptized by John *Mat 3: 13-27, Mark 1: 9-11, Luke 3: 21, 22*

Jesus' parable of mustard seed *Mat 13: 31, 32, Mark 4: 30-32, Luke 13: 18, 19*

Jesus' parable of leaven *Mat 13: 33, Luke 13: 20, 21*

Pharisees demand a sign of Jesus

Mat 12: 38-45, 16: 1-4, Mark 8: 10-13, Luke 11: 16, 29-32

Jesus' parable of treasure in a field *Mat 13: 44*

Chief priests query Jesus on his authority *Mat 21: 23-27, Mark 11: 27-33, Luke 20: 1-8*

The priests and council condemn Jesus *Mat 26: 59-68, Mark 14: 55-65, Luke 22: 63-71, John 18: 19-24*

Jesus' parable of seed, blade, ear, full corn *Mark 4: 26-29*

At twelve years Jesus talks with rabbis *Luke 2:41-52*

Jesus dines with a Pharisee *Luke 7: 36-50*

Jesus' parable of good Samaritan (priest passed by) *Luke 10:25-37*

Jesus' parable of Pharisee and publican *Luke 18: 9-14*

John the Baptist tells how his preaching differs from Jesus *John 3: 22-36*

Paul's training as Pharisee makes him a persecutor of the Christians *Acts 8: 1-14, 9: 1-4*

Simon offers to buy the power of laying on of hands *Acts 8: 14-25*

Paul describes the enemies of the truth *2 Tim 3: 1-17*

James' sermon on how to bear our cross *Jas 1: 1-27*

See also baptism, Eucharist, marriage, ministry, pastor, prophet, sheep

PRIMITIVE

Patriarchs lived to advanced age *Gen 5: 1-32*

The ark as a prototype of ships *Gen 6:5-22*

Abraham plans to sacrifice his son *Gen 22:1-19*

Ten Commandments as basis of all law *Exod 20:1-19, Deut 5:1-24*

Gideon asks for signs to prove God *Judg 6:19-40*

Jesus outlines qualities that make a Christian *Mat 5:1-12, Luke 6: 17-26, 36*

Jesus teaches disciples the Lord's Prayer *Mat 6:5-15, Mark 11:25, 26, Luke 11:1-4*

Jesus raises Jairus' daughter *Mat 9:18, 19, 23-27, Mark 5:22-24, 35-43, Luke 8:41, 42, 49-56*

Jesus casts out unclean spirit *Mark 1:21-28, Luke 4:33-37*

Jesus heals paralytic let down from roof *Mark 2:1-12, Luke 5:17-26*

Peter and John cause signs and wonders in early church *Acts 4: 24-37*

Paul on example left by Jesus *Heb 12:1-29*

John's letters to early churches *Rev 1:4-20, 2:1-29, 3:1-22*

See also Christian, church, nature, origin

PRINCIPLE

God creates spiritual universe *Gen 1:1-31*

Lord God creates man from dust *Gen 2:6-8*

Moses has revelation of God as I Am *Exod 3:1-18*

Moses brings down Ten Commandments *Exod 20:1-19, Deut 5:1-24*

Moses warns people to make a principle-based choice *Deut 30:11-20*

Elijah reveals God as still small voice *1 King 19:9-13*

Voice of thunder speaks to Job *Job 38:1-41*

David's song, "the fountain of life" *Psal 36:1-12*

Jesus' parable of the leaven *Mat 13:33, Luke 13:20, 21*

Jesus' parable of the laborers in the vineyards *Mat 20:1-6*

Jesus on God as a Spirit and to be worshipped spiritually *John 4:1-30, 39-42*

Jesus on great works having their source in Father *John 5:17-47*

After Jesus' sermon, "I am bread of life", many disciples leave him *John 6:66-71*

Paul on Christ's resurrection proves ours *1 Cor 15:1-58*

Paul on God as the source *Eph 4: 1-32*

James on God, no respecter of persons *Jas 2:1-13*

See also cause, doctrine, God, law, platform, rule, substance, truth

PRISON

Joseph unjustly imprisoned *Gen 39:21-23, 40:1-23, 41:1-46*

Israelites in bondage *Exod 1:8-14*

Samson, betrayed, is put in chains *Judg 16:4-30*

Jehoiachin well treated in captivity *2 King 25:27-30*

Jeremiah predicts release from captivity *Jer 29:8-14, 31:1-14, 31-34*

Daniel put in lions' den *Dan 6:1-28*

Jesus' parable of the dragnet *Mat 13:47-50*

Jesus' parable of the lost sheep *Mat 18:12-14, Luke 15:1-7*

Jesus betrayed and made prisoner *Mat 26:47-56, Mark 14:43-54, Luke 22:47-53, John 18:1-12*

Jesus scourged and mocked *Mat 27:27-31, Mark 15:16-20, John 19:1-16*

Jesus entombed *Mat 27:57-66, Mark 15:42-47, Luke 23:50-56, John 19:31-42*

Peter and John on trial before council *Acts 4:1-23*

Peter imprisoned, released by angel *Acts 5:17-42*

Peter imprisoned again, released by angel *Acts 12:1-17*

Paul and Silas released by earthquake *Acts 16:19-40*

Paul seized in Jerusalem *Acts 22:1-30*

Paul defends himself before Agrippa *Acts 26:1-32*

Paul sent to Rome in chains *Acts 27:1-44*

Paul describes himself as prisoner of the Lord *Eph 3:1, 4:1, 2 Tim 1:8*

See also bondage, captivity, chains, freedom, justice, law, liberty

PROBATION

Noah preserved and man makes a fresh start *Gen 9:12-17*

Moses given new chance after destroying Ten Commandments *Exod 34:1-8, Deut 10:1-4*

Caleb and Joshua offer promised land, but people stay in wilderness for 40 years *Num 13:1-33, 14:1-11, 23-29, Deut 1:19-38*

The trials of Job *Job 1:13-22, 2:1-10, 3:1-26*

David's song, "Create in me a clean heart" *Psal 51:1-19*

Vanity of human things *Eccl 1:1-18, 2:1-26*

Jeremiah predicts release from captivity *Jer 29:8-14, 31:1-4, 31-34*

Jonah finally obeys *Jonah 1:1-17, 2:1-10, 3:1-10*

Jesus' parable of the lost sheep *Mat 18:12-14, Luke 15:1-7*

Jesus' parable of wise and foolish virgins *Mat 25:1-13*

Jesus' parable of the talents *Mat 25:14-30, Luke 19:11-28*

Peter denies the Master *Mat 26:57, 58, 69-75, Mark 14:66-72, Luke 22:54-62, John 18:13-18, 25-27*

For events between resurrection and ascension (probation period after death) *Mat 28:1-20, Mark 16:1-20, Luke 24:1-53, John 20:1-29, 21:1-24*

Jesus' parable of the faithful steward *Luke 12:41-48*

Jesus' parable of the unjust steward *Luke 16:1-14*

Jesus' parable of rich man and beggar *Luke 16:19-31*

Jesus heals man at pool, but says, "sin no more" *John 5:1-16*

Jesus saves adultress but says, "sin no more" *John 8:1-11*

Jesus on Christ as the door *John 10:1-30*

Jesus urges Peter "Feed my sheep" *John 21:12-19*

Paul on putting on the new man *Col 3:1-17*

See also death, proof, punishment, **trials**

PROBLEM-SOLVING

Joseph succeeds in slavery *Gen 39:1-6, 21-23, 40:1-23*

Joseph interprets Pharaoh's dream *Gen 41:1-46*

Moses overcomes the obstacle of the Red Sea *Exod 14:5-31*

Moses appoints judges to help him *Exod 18:13-27*

Joshua takes the city of Ai on second attempt *Josh 7:1-26, 8:14-21*

Gideon defeats host with only 300 men *Judg 7:1-25*

David refuses armor, uses sling *1 Sam 17:38-52*

Abigail wards off danger to her husband *1 Sam 25:2-42*

Solomon decides which is the right mother *1 King 3:16-28*

Rehoboam consults his father's advisers, then his own friends *1 King 12:1-18, 2 Chron 10:1-19*

Esther, victor over persecutor of her people *Esther 5:1-14, 6:1-14, 7:1-10*

David's song, "The Lord is my shepherd" *Psal 23:1-6*

A poor wise man saved a city *Eccl 9:13-18*

Jesus calms wind and seas *Mat 8:23-27, Mark 4:35-41*

Jesus feeds 5000 *Mat 14:15-21, Mark 6:35-44, Luke 9:12-17, John 6:5-14*

Jesus' resurrection *Mat 28:1-8, Mark 16:1-8, Luke 24:1-12, John 20:1-10*

Jesus saves woman taken in adultery *John 8:1-11*

See also business, difficulty, success

PROFESSION

Moses instructed on what to say about God *Gen 3:1-18*

Aaron and sons anointed as priests *Lev 8:1-13*

Solomon dedicates temple he built to God *1 King 8:22-66, 2 Chron 6:1-42*

Isaiah called to be a prophet *Isa 6:1-13*

Isaiah describes the office of Christ *Isa 61:1-11, 62:1-12*

Zechariah's vision of two olive trees *Zech 4:1-14*

Jesus heals man of leprosy *Mat 8:1-4, Mark 1:40-45, Luke 5:12-16*

Jesus instructs disciples and sends them out *Mat 9:36-38, 10:1-42, 6:5-15, Mark 3:13-21, 6:7-13, 11:25, 26, Luke 9:1-6, 10:1-16, 11:1-4*

Jesus heals man of withered hand *Mat 12:9-13,, Mark 3:1-5, Luke 6:6-11*

Jesus accused of healing by Beelzebub *Mat 12:22-30, Mark 3:22-30, Luke 11:14-23*

Jesus' parable of treasure buried in field *Mat 13:44*

Jesus' parable of pearl of great price *Mat 13:45, 46*

Peter acknowledges Jesus as Christ *Mat 16:13-20, Mark 8:27-30, Luke 9:18-21*

Jesus' parable of two sons ordered to work *Mat 21:28-32*

Jesus' parable of sheep and goats *Mat 25:31-46*

Jesus asked a technical question by a lawyer *Luke 10:25-28*

Jesus rebuked for practicing healing on sabbath *Luke 13:11-17*

John the Baptist testifies that Jesus is Christ *John 1:15-34*

Jesus heals nobleman's son of fever *John 4:46-54*

Jesus foretells his death and calls for confession of faith *John 12:20-50*

Thomas convinced *John 20:24-29*

Paul on establishing churches *2 Cor 11:21-33*

See also acknowledge, business, calling, confession, faith, medicine, ministry, office, work

PROFIT

Abraham's riches grow *Gen 13:1-18*

Joseph's management prospers *Gen 39:1-6*

Elisha profits by association with Elijah *2 King 2:1-15*

Gehazi accepts reward refused by Elisha *2 King 5:15-27*

David's song, "The Lord is my shepherd" *Psal 23:1-6*

David's song, "Bless the Lord, O my soul" *Psal 103:1-22*

The need for wisdom *Prov 3:13-20, 4:1-13, 8:1-36*

Isaiah's vision of desert blossoming *Isa 35:1-10*

Isaiah's vision of new Jerusalem *Isa 65:17-25*

Jeremiah's vision of good and bad figs *Jer 24:1-10*

Jesus on house on rock compared to house on sand *Mat 7:24-29, Luke 6:48, 49*

Jesus' parable of the sower *Mat 13:3-23, Mark 4:1-20, Luke 8:4-15*

Jesus' parable of mustard seed *Mat*

13:31, 32, Mark 4:30-32, Luke 13: 18, 19

Tribute money from fish *Mat 17: 24-27*

Jesus' parable of laborers in vineyards *Mat 20:1-16*

Jesus withers fig tree *Mat 21:18-22, Mark 11:12-14, 20-24*

Jesus' parable of the talents *Mat 25: 14-30, Luke 19:11-28*

Jesus' parable of seed, blade, ear, full corn *Mark 4:26-29*

Peter's net filled *Luke 5:1-11, John 21:1-11*

Disciples report success with Jesus' teachings *Luke 10:17-24*

Jesus' parable of rich man and bigger barns *Luke 12:15-21*

Jesus' parable of barren fig tree *Luke 13:6-9*

Paul's success affects business of the idol maker *Acts 19:23-29*

Paul on abundance *2 Cor 8:11-15, 9:6-15*

James on faith without works *Jas 2:14-26*

See also business, growth, harvest, increase, progress

PROGRESS

Enoch translated over death *Gen 5:18, 21-24, Heb 11:5*

Abraham's riches grow *Gen 13:1-18*

Abram and Sarai receive new names *Gen 17:1-9, 15-22*

Lot escapes from Sodom—his wife does not *Gen 19:1, 15-19*

Jacob loses duplicity and receives new name *Gen 32:24-32*

Joseph works himself up from slavery *Gen 39:1-6, 21-23, 40:1-23, 41: 1-46*

Moses reviews progress of Israelites *Deut 32:1-47*

Ruth, the Moabitess, is faithful and becomes grandmother of David *Ruth 1:1-22, 2:1-23, 4:1-22*

Captivity ends and temple is rebuilt *Ezra 3:8-13*

Nehemiah repairs the walls of Jerusalem *Neh 4:1-23*

David's song, "Bless the Lord, O my soul" *Psal 103:1-22*

Isaiah predicts coming of Messiah *Isa 7:10-16, 9:2-7*

Isaiah predicts Christ's peaceable kingdom *Isa 11:1-12*

Isaiah predicts the desert will blossom *Isa 35:1-10*

Isaiah predicts comfort to Israel *Isa 40:1-31*

Jeremiah promises release from captivity *Jer 29:8-14, 31:1-14, 31-34*

Jonah turns from disobedience to preaching *Jonah 1:1-17, 2:1-10, 3:1-10*

Jesus heals woman who had issue of blood twelve years *Mat 9:20-22, Mark 5:25-34, Luke 8:43-48*

Jesus' parables on growth of the church *Mat 13:31-33, Mark 4:30-32, Luke 12:20, 21, 13:18, 19*

Jesus' parables on preparation for spiritual future *Mat 25:1-30, Luke 16:1-14, 19-31, 19:11-28*

From crucifixion to resurrection to ascension *Mark 15:21-41, Luke 24: 1-12, Acts 1:6-12*

Jesus' parables on persistence in prayer *Luke 11:5-13, 18:1-8*

Jesus heals woman bowed together 18 years *Luke 13:11-17*

Jesus cures lame man 38 years at the healing pool *John 5:1-16*

Jesus on the Comforter as promised *John 14:1-31*

Jesus on greater works than his *John 14:10-12*

Peter and apostles at Pentecost (Holy Spirit) *Acts 2:1-13*

Peter accepts Gentiles in church *Acts 10:1-48, 11:1-18*

Paul and Barnabas establish church *Acts 11:19-26*

Paul on how he was converted *Acts 26:1-32*

Paul on putting on the new man *Col 3:1-17*

John's vision of new heaven and new earth *Rev 21:1-27*

John's vision of river and tree of life *Rev 22:1-21*

See also advancement, development, evolution, growth, improvement, increase, promote, unfoldment

PROMISE

God promises the man in his image (not Adam) dominion *Gen 1:1-31*

God's covenant with Noah "Be fruitful and multiply" *Gen 9:1-17*

Abraham is promised a land and a son *Gen 15:1-21*

Isaac received renewed promise *Gen 26:1-5*

Jacob is promised God's presence *Gen 28:10-22*

Moses is promised God's presence *Exod 3:9-12*

Aaron recounts God's promises to the faithful *Lev 26:1-20*

God sets apart Israelites as chosen people *Deut 7:6-11*

Moses predicts a prophet *Deut 18: 15-22*

Moses lists the blessings of obedience *Deut 28:1-14*

Gideon receives three signs from God *Judg 6:19-40*

Solomon promised his heart's desire *1 King 3:5-15, 2 Chron 1:7-12*

Elisha asks for double Elijah's spirit *2 King 2:1-15*

Isaiah hears God promise help in trials *Isa 43:1-28, 44:1-24*

Isaiah predicts coming of Messiah *Isa 7:10-16, 9:2-7*

Isaiah lists the promises of Christ *Isa 55:1-13*

Isaiah foretells God's promises to the penitent *Isa 58:1-14*

Jeremiah predicts end of captivity *Jer 29:8-14, 31:1-14, 31-34*

Ezekiel's vision of God's care over his flock *Ezek 34:1-31*

Micah predicts glory of the church *Mic 4:1-8, 13, Isa 2:1-5*

Zephaniah promises salvation *Zeph 3:14-17*

Malachi promises rewards for tithing *Mal 3:10, 4:1, 2*

Jesus promises to make disciples fishers of men *Mat 4:17-22, Mark 1:14-20, Luke 5:1-11, John 1:35-42*

Jesus promises all these other things shall be added *Mat 6:25-34*

Jesus' parable of mustard seed *Mat 13:31, 32, Mark 4:30-32, Luke 13: 18, 19*

Jesus' parable of the leaven *Mat 13: 33, Luke 13:20, 21*

Jesus' parable of the lost sheep *Mat 18:12-14, Luke 15:1-7*

Jesus' parable of seed, blade, ear, full corn *Mark 4:26-29*

Jesus assures Peter his net will be filled *Luke 5:1-11, John 21:1-11*

Jesus' parable of the unwilling friend *Luke 11:5-13*

Jesus parable of the judge and widow *Luke 18:1-8*

Jesus tells nobleman his son lives *John 4:46-54*

Jesus' parable of the good shepherd *John 10:1-18*

Jesus promises the Holy Ghost will follow *John 14:1-31*

Jesus promises greater works than his *John 14:10-12*

Jesus' parable of the true vine *John 15: 1-17*

John's vision of new heaven and earth *Rev 21:1-27*

John's vision of river and tree of life *Rev 22:1-21*

See also assurance, blessing, covenant, land

PROMOTE

Enoch translated because he walked with God *Gen 5:18, 21-24, Heb 11:5*

Joseph made governor of Egypt *Gen 41:1-46*

Moses appoints judges to help him *Exod 18:13-27*

Moses anoints Aaron and sons as priests *Lev 8:1-13*

Aaron lists God's promises to the faithful *Lev 26:1-20*

Moses charges Joshua to succeed him *Deut 31:7-23, Josh 1:1-9*

Gideon refuses to be king *Judg 8:22, 23*

Jotham's parable of the trees *Judg 9:1-15*

Samuel anoints Saul as king *1 Sam 10:1-8*

David made king *2 Sam 2:1-4, 5:1-5*

David's charge to Solomon who is succeeding him *1 Chron 22:6-19, 23:1, 28:2-10, 20*

Elisha takes up the mantle of Elijah *2 King 2:12-15*

The value of wisdom *Prov 3:13-26, 4:1-13, 8:1-36*

Jesus on letting your light shine *Mat 5:13-16, Luke 8:16-18*

Peter advances when he calls Jesus "Christ" *Mat 16:13-20, Mark 8: 27-30, Luke 9:18-21*

Zebedee's wife pushes forward her sons *Mat 20:20-28, Mark 10:35-45*

Jesus' parable of wise and foolish virgins *Mat 25:1-13*

Jesus' parable of the talents *Mat 25:14-30, Luke 19:11-28*

Jesus' ascension *Mark 16:19, 20, Luke 24:50-53, Acts 1:6-12*

Jesus' parable of chief seats at the wedding *Luke 14:7-14*

Disciples argue who shall be greatest *Luke 22:24-30*

Election of Matthias *Acts 1:15-26*

James on being no respecter of persons *Jas 2:1-13*

See also advancement, exaltation, growth, help, prosperity

PROOF

Moses' rod and leprosy transformed *Exod 4:1-9*

Gideon receives three signs from God *Judg 6:19-40*

Hebrews unharmed by fiery furnace *Dan 3:1-30*

Daniel preserved in lions' den *Dan 6:1-28*

John the Baptist sends to Jesus for proof of Christ *Mat 11:2-19, Luke 7:18-35*

Jesus' resurrection *Mat 28:1-8, Mark 16:1-8, Luke 24:1-12, John 20:1-10*

Seventy disciples return to report their success *Luke 10:17-24*

Jesus heals nobleman's son while absent *John 4:46-54*

Jesus heals man born blind *John 9:1-41*

Jesus has supper with Lazarus whom he raised from dead *John 11:55-57, 12:1, 2, 9-11*

Thomas convinced of resurrection *John 20:24-29*

Peter and John heal man lame from birth *Acts 3:1-26, 4:1-23*

Paul converted by his healing of blindness *Acts 9:10-22*

See also conviction, demonstration, **evidence, healing, testify, truth, witness**

PROPERTY

Abraham divides the land with Lot *Gen 13:1-18*

Esau gives his birthright for pottage *Gen 25:24-34*

Daughters of Zelophehad sue for their inheritance *Num 27:1-11, 36:5-13*

Caleb claims his share of Canaan *Josh 14:6-15*

Nathan's parable of the ewe lamb *2 Sam 12:1-10*

King Ahab takes Naboth's vineyard *1 King 21:1-27*

Shunammite returns to claim her property *2 King 8:1-6*

Hezekiah shows off his treasure *2 King 20:12-21, Isa 39:1-8*

Job loses all his possessions *Job 1:13-22, 2:1-10*

David's song, "The earth is the Lord's" *Psal 24:1-10*

Jeremiah buys a field while still in prison *Jer 32:2, 6-27, 37-44*

Jesus' parable of treasure buried *Mat 13:44*

Jesus' parable of pearl of great price *Mat 13:45, 46*

Jesus' parable of householder's treasure *Mat 13:51, 52*

Jesus' parable of rich man and bigger barns *Luke 12:15-21*

Jesus' parable of the lost coin *Luke 15:8-10*

See also land, possession, wealth

PROPHET, PROPHECY

Eldad and Medad prophesy without hindrance *Num 11:16-30*

Moses promises a prophet *Deut 18:15-22*

After anointing, Saul prophesies *1 Sam 10:9-27*

Jahaziel says, the battle is not yours but God's *2 Chron 20:1-32*

Elijah outdoes the 450 prophets of Baal *1 King 18:17-40*

Elijah predicts rain *1 King 18:41-46*

Elisha predicts drop in price of flour *2 King 6:24, 25, 7:1-18*

Isaiah predicts coming of Messiah *Isa 2:1-5, 7:10-16, 9:2-7, 42:1-12, 16, 18, 53:1-12, 55:1-13, Mic 4:1-8, 13*

Jeremiah predicts release from captivity *Jer 29:8-14, 31:1-14, 31-34*

Daniel interprets king's dream *Dan 2:1-49, 4:1-27*

Daniel reads handwriting on wall *Dan 5:1-31*

Jesus says a prophet is without honor in own country *Mat 13:53-58, Mark 6:1-6, Luke 4:22-24, John 4:43-45*

Jesus foretells his own death and resurrection *Mat 16:21-28, 17:22, 23, 20:17-19, Mark 8:31-38, 9:30-32, 10:32-34, Luke 8:31-34, 9:20-27, 43-45, John 12:20-50, 18:31-34, 19:47, 48*

Jesus foretells destruction of temple and Jerusalem *Mat 24:1-4, Mark 13:1-37, Luke 21:5-36*

Jesus foretells his betrayal *Mat 26:20-25, Mark 14:18-21, Luke 22:21, 22, John 13:21-25*

Jesus' parable of temple raised in three days *John 2:19-22*

Jesus on the bread of life *John 6:26-65*

Jesus on himself as Christ *John 7:14-40*

Jesus on the Holy Spirit *John 14:1-31*

At Pentecost disciples speak with new tongues *Acts 2:1-13*

Paul heals the damsel soothsayer *Acts 16:16-18*

John's vision of new heaven and new earth *Rev 21:1-27, 22:1-21*

See also foresight, future, messenger, priest, revelation, seer, spirituality

PROSPERITY

Abraham's riches grow, Lot's too *Gen 13:1-18*

Jacob and Esau both have plenty *Gen 33:1-11*

Joseph's brethren come to him in Egypt for food *Gen 42:1-8*

Jacob and sons prosper in Egypt *Gen 45:25-28, 46:2-7*

Moses lists the blessings of obedience *Deut 28:1-14*

David's song of thanksgiving *2 Sam 22:1-51, 1 Chron 16:17-36*

Queen of Sheba acknowledges Solomon's greatness *1 King 10:1-12, 2 Chron 9:1-12*

David's songs of well-being *Psal 33:1-22, 66:1-20, 100:1-6, 103:1-22, 107:1-43*

Isaiah's vision of desert blossoming *Isa 35:1-10*

Isaiah's vision of blessed state of Jerusalem *Isa 65:17-25*

Micah's vision of glory of the church *Mic 4:1-8, 13, Isa 2:1-5*

Malachi urges tithing *Mal 3:10, 4:1, 2*

Jesus' parable of the talents *Mat 25:14-30, Luke 19:11-28*

Seventy disciples return to report success *Luke 10:17-24*

Jesus' parable of rich man and bigger barns *Luke 12:15-21*

Jesus' parable of rich man and beggar *Luke 16:19-31*

The early church grows *Acts 4:24-37*

See also failure, progress, success, supply, thanksgiving

PROTECTION

Noah builds ark to protect from natural events *Gen 6:5-22*

Moses at birth escapes by the river *Exod 2:1-10*

Moses urges obedience for protection *Deut 11:1-32*

Chosen people set apart as God's own *Deut 7:6-11*

Rahab protects the spies in Jericho *Josh 2:1-24*

Jonathan protects David from jealousy of Saul *1 Sam 18:1-16*

Asa supported by allies in war *1 King 15:9-24, 2 Chron 14:1-7*

Elisha protected from besieging army *2 King 6:8-23*

Hezekiah protected from invaders by epidemic *2 Chron 31:20, 21, 32:1-23, Isa 36:1-22, 37:1-38*

Nehemiah protected from conspiracy *Neh 6:1-19*

Esther protects her people from persecution *Esther 5:1-14*

David's songs of protection *Psal 1:1-6, 23:1-6, 36:1-12, 37:23-40, 46:1-11, 91:1-16, 121:1-8*

A poor wise man saved a city *Eccl 9:13-18*

Christ's peaceable kingdom to come *Isa 11:1-12*

Isaiah predicts God's help in trials *Isa 43:1-28, 44:1-24*

Isaiah predicts redemption is of God *Isa 51:1-12*

Ezekiel's vision of God's care of his flock *Ezek 34:1-31*

Ezekiel's vision of help from nowhere *Ezek 37:1-14*

Protection from the fiery furnace *Dan 3:1-30*

Daniel protected in lions' den *Dan 6:1-28*

Hosea's vision of God's care of his child *Hos 11:1-4*

Jonah protected from sea and great fish *Jonah 1:1-17, 2:1-10*

Jesus' parents flee to Egypt *Mat 2:13-23, Luke 2:39, 40*

Jesus' parable of returning evil spirit *Mat 12:43-45, Luke 11:24-26*

Jesus' parable of lost sheep *Mat 18:12-14, Luke 15:1-7*

Jesus delivers himself by passing through enemies *Luke 4:28-31*

Jesus' parable of prodigal's elder brother *Luke 15:25-32*

Jesus' parable of good shepherd *John 10:1-18*

Paul's teaching to come out and be separate *2 Cor 6:1-18*

Paul on the Christian's armor *Eph 6:10-17*

See also attack, defense, guard, prevention, safety, security, watch

PRUDENCE

Noah builds ark *Gen 6:5-22*

Abraham's riches grow *Gen 13:1-18*

Joseph's prudence in prosperity saves Egypt *Gen 41:30-41*

Moses delegates authority to judges *Exod 18:13-27*

Hezekiah unwisely shows Babylonians his treasures *2 King 20: 12-21, Isa 39:1-8*

Nehemiah's prudence foils conspiracy *Neh 6:1-19*

Flight to Egypt *Mat 2:13-23, Luke 2:39, 40*

Jesus' parable of builders on rock or sand *Mat 7:24-27, Luke 6: 48, 49*

Jesus gives reasons why wedding guests regret *Mat 22:1-14*

Jesus' parable of wise and foolish virgins *Mat 25:1-13*

Jesus says no looking back *Luke 9:57-62*

Jesus' parable of counting the cost first *Luke 14:25-33*

Jesus' parable of man taking big journey *Mark 13:34-37*

Thomas refuses to believe Jesus is risen *John 20:19-29*

Ananias resists healing the blind Paul *Acts 9:10-22*

Paul on source of supply *2 Cor 8: 11-15*

Paul on the armor of divinity *Eph 6:10-17*

See also business, discipline, economics, foresight, morality, reason, wisdom

PSALM

Moses' song of gratitude for deliverance *Exod 15:1-19*

Moses' song of God's care of Israel *Deut 32:1-47*

Deborah's song of rejoicing in God's victory *Judg 5:1-20*

David plays harp to calm Saul *1 Sam 16:14-23*

David's song, "how are the mighty fallen!" *2 Sam 1:17-27*

David's song of thanksgiving *2 Sam 22:1-51, 1 Chron 16:17-36*

Jehoshaphat's army preceded by singers *2 Chron 20:1-32*

Selections from Book of Psalms:

"Happiness of the godly" *Psal 1:1-6*

"What is man?" *Psal 8:1-9*

"The heavens declare the glory" *Psal 19:1-4*

"The Lord is my shepherd" *Psal 23:1-6*

"The earth is the Lord's" *Psal 24: 1-6*

"Rejoice in the Lord" *Psal 33:1-22*

"The fountain of life" *Psal 36: 1-12*

"Fret not thyself because of evildoers" *Psal 37:23-40*

"Why art thou cast down?" *Psal 42:1-11*

"God is our refuge and strength"
    Psal 46:1-11
"Create in me a clean heart"   *Psal 51:1-9*
"Make a joyful noise"   *Psal 66: 1-20, 100:1-5*
"My soul longeth... for the courts of the Lord"   *Psal 84:1-12*
"Our dwelling place"   *Psal 90:1-17*
"The secret place of the most High"   *Psal 91:1-16*
"Bless the Lord, O my soul"   *Psal 103:1-22*
"Praise the Lord for his goodness"   *Psal 107:1-43*
"Safety of the godly"   *Psal 121: 1-8*
"Whither shall I go from thy spirit?"   *Psal 139:1-24*
Jesus enters Jerusalem to hosannas   *Mat 21:1-11, 14-17, Mark 11: 1-11, Luke 19:29-44, John 12: 12-19*
Disciples sing a hymn after Last Supper   *Mat 26:30*
Angels sign at Saviour's birth   *Luke 2:8-20*
Paul and Silas sing hymns in prison   *Acts 16:19-40*

See also music, praise, song, worship

PSYCHIATRY

Rivalry between mothers of Ishmael and Isaac   *Gen 21:1-21*
Abraham torn between love of God and love of son   *Gen 22:1-19*
Isaac's favoritism causes duplicity by Jacob   *Gen 27:1-44*
Jacob faces his fears and receives new nature   *Gen 32:1-32*
Power corrupts Saul as king   *1 Sam 15:7-26, 16:14-23*
Saul consults familiar spirit at Endor   *1 Sam 28:3-20*
David's song, "What is man?"   *Psal 8:1-9*
David's song, "Why art thou cast down?"   *Psal 42:1-11*
David's song, "Bless the Lord, O my soul"   *Psal 103:1-22*
Ezekiel's vision of the sins of the fathers on the children   *Ezek 18: 1-32*
Daniel predicts insanity of king and his recovery   *Dan 4:1-37*

Jonah refuses to face his duty, at first   *Jonah 1:1-17, 2:1-10, 3:1-10*
Jesus tempted   *Mat 4:1-11, Mark 1: 12, 13, Luke 4:1-13*
Jesus on qualities that make a Christian   *Mat 5:1-12, Luke 6:17-26, 36*
Jesus on the Golden Rule for actions   *Mat 7:12-14, Luke 6:41, 42*
Jesus' parable of builders on rock and sand   *Mat 7:24-27, Luke 6: 48, 49*
Jesus heals insane Gadarene   *Mat 8:28-34, Mark 5:1-20, Luke 8:26-39*
Jesus heals Syrophenician's daughter   *Mat 15:21-28, Mark 7:24-30*
Jesus' parable of the lost sheep   *Mat 18:12-14, Luke 15:1-7*
Jesus' parable of the debtor unmerciful to his fellows   *Mat 18: 23-35*
Jesus casts out unclean spirit in man   *Mark 1:21-28, Luke 4:33-37*
Jesus' parable of two debtors forgiven   *Luke 7:36-50*
Jesus as the light of the world   *John 1:1-14, 8:12-32*
Jesus on man must be born again   *John 3:1-21*
The conversion of Paul   *Acts 8:1-4, 9:1-31*
Paul casts out devil in damsel soothsayer   *Acts 16:16-18*
Vagabond exorcists discomforted   *Acts 19:11-20*
Paul on love   *1 Cor 13:1-13*
Paul's self-revealings   *2 Cor 12:1-19*
Paul's sermon, "think on these things"   *Phil 4:1-23*
Paul's sermon, "put on the new man"   *Col 3:1-17*
John's sermon, "God is love"   *1 John 4:1-21*
John's vision of new heaven and earth   *Rev 21:1-27*

See also human, medicine, mind, nerves, soul

PSYCHOLOGY

Balak hires Balaam to curse Israel   *Num 22:1-41, 23:1-30, 24:1-25*
The theory of God's chosen people sets Israelites apart   *Deut 7:6-11*
Gideon's plan of battle causes panic in enemy   *Judg 7:1-25*

David's success causes Saul's jealousy *1 Sam 18:1-16*

Elisha sends Syrian army home—result: permanent peace *2 King 6:8-23*

Hezekiah shows treasure and arouses cupidity *2 King 20:12-21, Isa 39: 1-8*

Nehemiah foils conspiracy *Neh 6: 1-19*

David's song, "Fret not thyself" *Psal 37:23-40*

David's song, "Make a joyful noise" *Psal 66:1-20, 100:1-5*

Ezekiel's vision of children's teeth on edge *Ezek 18:1-32*

Jesus' parable of mote and beam *Mat 7:1-5, Luke 6:37-42*

Jesus says prophet without honor in own country *Mat 13:53-58, Mark 6:1-6, Luke 4:22-24, John 4:43-45*

Disciples contend who is greatest *Mat 18:1-11, Mark 9:33-37, Luke 9:46-50, 22:24-30*

Jesus' parable of unmerciful debtor *Mat 18:23-35*

Jesus' parable of laborers in vineyard *Mat 20:1-16*

Judas' motives in betrayal *Mat 26: 14-16, Mark 14:10, 11, Luke 22:1-6*

Jesus' parable of two debtors forgiven *Luke 7:36-50*

Martha complains about her sister *Luke 10:38-42*

Jesus' parable of counting the cost *Luke 14:25-33*

Jesus' parable of prodigal's elder brother *Luke 15:25-32*

Jesus parable of Pharisee and publican *Luke 18:9-14*

Jesus on man must be born again *John 3:1-21*

Jesus on God as Spirit and to be worshipped in spirit *John 4:1-30, 39-42*

Jesus saves woman from adultery *John 8:1-11*

Jesus charges Peter to feed his sheep *John 21:12-19*

Peter and John tried before the council *Acts 4:1-23*

Paul on love *1 Cor 13:1-13*

Paul on the Christian's armor *Eph 6:10:17*

Paul on atonement *Heb 10:1-39*

John on God is love *1 John 4:1-21*

John's vision of woman and dragon *Rev 12:1-17*

See also consciousness, intelligence, mind, organic, psychiatry, senses, soul

PUBLISH

Moses brings down Ten Commandments from Mt. Sinai *Exod 19: 1-9, 20:1-19, Deut 4:1-15, 5:1-24*

Eldad and Medad prophesy as well as Moses *Num 11:16-30*

David announces his son will build temple *1 Chron 17:1-27*

Solomon dedicates temple *1 King 8:22-66, 2 Chron 6:1-42*

Cyrus proclaims rebuilding of temple *Ezra 1:1-11*

Book of the law is read by the people *Neh 8:1-12*

Isaiah proclaims coming of Messiah *Isa 7:10-16, 9:2-7*

Jeremiah preaches restoration *Jer 29:8-14, 31:1-14, 31-34*

Daniel reads handwriting on wall *Dan 5:1-31*

John the Baptist, the voice in the wilderness *Mat 3:1-12, Mark 1:1-8, Luke 3:1-18*

Jesus heals Gadarene of insanity *Mat 8:28-34, Mark 5:1-20, Luke 8:26-39*

Jesus' parable of the leaven *Mat 13:33, Luke 13:20, 21*

Jesus enters Jerusalem for last time *Mat 21:1-11, 14-17, Mark 11:1-11, Luke 19:29-44, John 12:12-19*

His fame increasing, all men seek Jesus *Mark 1:35-39, 45*

Jesus heals deaf man and he speaks *Mark 7:32-37*

Angels announce Jesus' birth *Luke 2:8-20*

Peter and John cannot be prevented from speaking the gospel *Acts 4: 1-23*

Paul's sermon on the Unknown God *Acts 17:15-34*

A key found to open sealed book *Rev 5:1-14*

The effects of reading scripture *Rev 10:1-11*

See also annunciation, gospel, news, preaching

PUNISHMENT

Adam and Eve disobey *Gen 3:6-24*

Cain cast out for murder *Gen 4:1-16*

Miriam rebellious, becomes leper, healed *Num 12:1-16*

David's immorality followed by death of his child *2 Sam 12:13-23*

Asa's foot disease fatal *2 Chron 16: 11-14*

Uzziah's pride causes leprosy *2 Chron 26:1-23*

Gehazi's greed causes leprosy *2 King 5:15-27*

Hezekiah's unwise trust causes defeat *2 King 20:12-21, Isa 39:1-8*

Haman hanged on gallows he built for Mordecai *Esther 6:1-14, 7: 1-10*

Job asks why good man should suffer *Job 3:1-26*

Isaiah's vision of how God eliminates the proud and mighty *Isa 14:4-8, 12-17, 25-27*

Isaiah predicts punishment of workers in dark *Isa 29:11-24, 30:1-3, 20, 21*

Isaiah's plea for justice *Isa 59:1-21*

Jeremiah on reward and punishment *Jer 24:1-10*

Ezekiel on the injustice of punishing children for father's sins *Ezek 18:1-32*

Jonah punished until he obeys *Jonah 1:1-17, 2:1-10, 3:1-10*

Jesus' parable of unmerciful debtor *Mat 18:23-35*

Jesus' parable of farmers and rent *Mat 21:33-46, Mark 12:1-12, Luke 20:9-19*

Jesus' parable of marriage garment lacking *Mat 22:1-14*

Jesus' parable of the talents *Mat 25:14-30, Luke 19:11-28*

Jesus' parable of sheep and goats *Mat 25:31-46*

Judas self-punished *Mat 27:3-10, Acts 1:15-20*

Jesus' parable of prodigal son *Luke 15:11-24*

Jesus' parable of rich man and beggar *Luke 16:19-31*

Jesus heals man and says, "sin no more, lest a worse ... thing come unto thee" *John 5:1-16*

Jesus saves adultress from punishment *John 8:1-11*

See also atonement, crime, discipline, pain, probation, reformation, sin

PURITY

Man created as God's own image *Gen 1:26, 27*

Enoch translated because he "walked with God" *Gen 5:18, 21-24, Heb 11:5*

Abram and Sarai given new names for walking with God *Gen 17:1-9, 15-22*

Moses talks with God face to face *Exod 33:7-23, 34:29-35*

Sin uncovered in camp after failure to take the city of Ai *Josh 7: 1-26, 8:14-21*

Elisha prescribes washing seven times in Jordan *2 King 5:1-14*

David's song, "the happiness of the godly" *Psal 1:1-6*

David's song, "What is man?" *Psal 8:1-9*

David's song, "Create in me a clean heart" *Psal 51:1-19*

Daniel refuses to eat king's provisions *Dan 1:1-21*

Temptation of Jesus *Mat 4:1-11, Mark 1:12, 13, Luke 4:1-13*

Jesus on qualities that make a Christian *Mat 5:1-12, Luke 6:17-26*

Jesus on oneness with Father *Mat 6:22-24, John 10:22-42*

Jesus heals lepers *Mat 8:1-4, Mark 1:40-45, Luke 17:11-19*

Jesus eats with publicans and sinners *Mat 9:10-13, Mark 2:13-17, Luke 5:27-32*

Jesus accused of casting out devils by Beelzebub *Mat 12:22-30, Mark 3:22-30, Luke 11:14-23*

Jesus on defilement *Mat 15:1-20, Mark 7:1-23*

Jesus approves childlike thought *Mat 19:13-15, Mark 10:13-16, Luke 18:15-17*

Jesus casts out traders from temple *Mat 21:12, 13, Mark 11:15-17, Luke 19:45, 46, John 2:13-25*

Coming birth of Jesus announced to Mary *Luke 1:26-38*

Jesus' parable of abiding in true vine *John 15:1-17*

Peter accepts Gentiles previously forbidden *Acts 10:1-48, 11:1-18*
Paul on Spirit vs. flesh *Rom 8:1-39*
Paul's teaching to come out and be separate *2 Cor 6:1-18*
John's vision of Lamb pure enough to open sealed book *Rev 5:1-14*

See also adultery, baptism, chastity, cornerstone, dedication

PURPOSE

God's purpose for man: "Be fruitful, and multiply" *Gen 9:1-17*
Moses fulfills God's plan to lead out of Egypt *Exod 3:9-12*
Moses gives Ten Commandments for guidance *Exod 19:1-9, 20:1-19, Deut 5:1-24*
Israelites re-enter promised land through Jordan *Josh 3:1-17*
David promises to build a temple *2 Sam 7:1-29*
Solomon dedicates temple to God *1 King 8:22-66, 2 Chron 6:1-42*
Ahab takes Naboth's vineyard *1 King 21:1-27*
David receives liberal offerings *1 Chron 29:6-19*
Cyrus proclaims the rebuilding of the temple *Ezra 1:1-11*
Nehemiah decides to rebuild the walls *Neh 4:1-23*
Job's aim to find nature of God *Job 3:1-26, 38:1-41*
David's song on aim of godly—delight in God's law *Psal 1:1-6*
David's song on "What is man?" *Psal 8:1-9*
The study of wisdom *Prov 3:13-26, 4:1-13, 8:1-36*
Isaiah's vision of war no more *Isa 2:1-5*
Isaiah's vision of Messiah's peaceable kingdom *Isa 11:1-12*
Isaiah's vision of Messiah—office of the Christ *Isa 42:1-12, 16, 18*
Ezekiel's vision of God's care of his flock *Ezek 34:1-31*
God's plan for Jonah *Jonah 1:1-17, 2:1-10, 3:1-10*
Micah's vision of glory of church *Mic 4:1-8, 13*
Jesus on letting your light shine *Mat 5:13-16, Luke 8:16-18*

Jesus on seek ye first *Mat 6:25-34, Luke 12:22-34*
Jesus' parable of builders on rock or sand *Mat 7:24-27, Luke 6:48, 49*
Jesus explains why he eats with sinners *Mat 9:10-13, Mark 2:13-17, Luke 5:27-32*
Jesus sends disciples to heal and preach *Mat 9:36-38, 10:1-42, Mark 3:13-21, Luke 9:1-6*
Jesus on preaching and healing *Mat 10:5-42, Mark 6:7-13, Luke 9:1-6, 10:1-16*
Jesus explains why he speaks in parables *Mat 13:10-17, 34, 35, Mark 4:10-12, 33, 34*
Jesus' parable of the lost sheep *Mat 18:12-14, Luke 15:1-7*
Jesus shows the purpose of the crucifixion to be the resurrection *Mat 26:20-25, 28:1-8, Mark 16:1-8, Luke 24:1-12, John 20:1-10*
Jesus institutes Eucharist as reminder *Mat 26:26-29, Mark 14:22-25, Luke 22:14-30, 1 Cor 11:23-25*
Jesus' parable of rich man and bigger barns *Luke 12:15-21*
Jesus' parable of rich man and beggar at gate *Luke 16:19-31*
Jesus Christ as the light of the world *John 1:1-14, 8:12-32*
Jesus on man must be born again *John 3:1-21*
Jesus on the bread of life *John 6:26-65*
Paul on the cost of establishing church *2 Cor 11:21-33*
John's vision of spiritual universe *Rev 21:1-27*

See also aims, ambition, guidance, motive, plan, resolution, will

Q

QUALITY

God calls his creation very good *Gen 1:29-31*
Lord God drives out the man he made *Gen 3:22-24*
Enoch translated; he "walked with God" *Gen 5:18, 21-24*
Abraham asks how many righteous men will save city *Gen 18:20-33*

Aaron's rod alone blossoms *Num 17:1-11*

Gideon defeats host with only 300 men *Judg 7:1-25*

Jotham's parable of the trees *Judg 9:1-15*

Samuel anoints David, for Saul is unfit *1 Sam 16:1-13*

Elijah excells 450 prophets of Baal *1 King 18:17-40*

Jeremiah on the good and bad figs *Jer 24:1-10*

Jesus' parable of pearl of great price *Mat 13:45, 46*

Jesus denounces the religion of the scribes and Pharisees *Mat 23:1-38*

Jesus' parable of new wine in old bottles *Luke 5:36-39*

Paul on the values of faith, hope and charity *1 Cor 13:1-13*

Paul on being separate *2 Cor 6:1-18*

Paul on spiritual qualities that protect *Eph 6:10-17*

See also aristocracy, character, excellence, supremacy

QUANTITY

Abraham promised seed like the stars *Gen 15:1-6*

Manna in desert where food is scarce *Exod 16:1-36, Num 11:1-15, 31, 32*

Gideon defeats host with 300 men *Judg 7:1-25*

Elisha feeds 100 men with 20 barley loaves *2 King 4:42-44*

One poor wise man saves city from invading host *Eccl 9:13-18*

God raises an army from dry bones *Ezek 37:1-28*

Jesus followed by multitudes, heals many *Mat 12:14-21, Mark 3:6-12*

The sower receives varying yield *Mat 13:33, Mark 4:1-20, Luke 8:4-15*

Jesus feeds 5000 *Mat 14:15-21, Mark 6:35-44, Luke 9:12-17, John 6:5-14*

Hiring laborers in vineyard *Mat 20:1-16*

Jesus' parable of talents *Mat 25:14-30, Luke 19:11-28*

Jesus heals ten men of leprosy *Luke 17:11-19*

Peter adds many to the church *Acts 4:24-37*

See also many, number

QUEEN

Deborah, a judge, leads in battle against Sisera *Judg 4:1-17*

Song of Deborah's rejoicing *Judg 5:1-20*

Solomon visited by Queen of Sheba *1 King 10:1-12*

Elisha flees anger of Queen Jezebel *1 King 19:1-8*

Esther, Jewess, made Queen of Persia *Esther 2:5-23*

Esther helps her people who are persecuted *Esther 3:1-15, 4:1-17, 5:1-14, 6:1-14, 7:1-10*

The virtuous woman *Prov 31:1-31*

The woman clothed with sun, and moon under feet *Rev 12:1-17*

See also authority, crown, heredity, mother, rule, woman

QUIET

Jehoshaphat's good reign *2 Chron 17:1-13, 19:4-11*

Elijah and the still small voice *1 King 19:9-13*

Josiah's good reign *2 King 23:1-22, 2 Chron 34:1-8, 29-33*

David's song, the happiness of the godly *Psal 1:1-6*

David's song, "our dwelling place" *Psal 90:1-17*

Isaiah's vision of war no more *Isa 2:1-5, Mic 4:1-8, 13*

Isaiah's vision of Christ's peaceable kingdom *Isa 11:1-10*

Isaiah's vision of a quiet habitation *Isa 33:20-24*

Isaiah's vision of reward of the good *Isa 65:17-25*

Jesus calms wind and seas *Mat 8:23-27, Mark 4:35-41, Luke 8:22-25*

Jesus calms wind *Mark 6:45-52, John 6:21*

Jesus spends all night in prayer *Luke 6:12*

See also peacemaker, security

QUICK

See death, justification, life, sin

R

RACE

God sets his chosen people apart *Deut 7:6-11*

Egyptians oppress Israelites *Exod 1:8-14, 5:7-19*

Esther saves her people *Esther 3: 1-15, 4:1-17, 5:1-14, 6:1-14, 7:1-10*

Jesus heals the Gentile's servant *Mat 8:5-13, Luke 7:1-10*

Jesus sends his twelve disciples only to lost sheep of house of Israel *Mat 10:5-12, Mark 6:7-13, Luke 9:1-6*

Jesus heals the Syrophenician's daughter *Mat 15:21-28, Mark 7: 24-30*

Jesus' parable of good Samaritan *Luke 10:25-37*

Jesus discusses differences in worship *John 4:1-30*

Peter accepts conversion of Gentiles *Acts 10:1-48, 11:1-18*

Philip baptizes the Ethiopian *Acts 8:26-40*

Paul preaches to the Greeks *Acts 17:15-34*

Paul is cared for by the barbarous people of Melita *Acts 27:1-44*

Paul heals the father of Publius (the head man) *Acts 28:7-10*

Paul on the prize for a race *1 Cor 9:24-27*

Paul on the unity of all *Eph 4:1-32*

See also equality, family, human, man, nation, people

RADIANCE

Noah sees rainbow as a token of God's covenant *Gen 9:12-17*

Abraham entertains angels *Gen 18: 1-18*

Moses' face concealed by veil after talk with God *Exod 34:29-35*

Samuel anoints David, his selection based on inner man *1 Sam 16:1-13*

Elijah is translated *2 King 2:1-15*

David's song, "The heavens declare the glory" *Psal 19:1-14*

David's song, "Who is this King of glory?" *Psal 24:1-10*

David's song, "The beauty of the Lord our God be upon us" *Psal 90:1-17*

Isaiah's vision of God's glory *Isa 6:1-13*

Isaiah's vision of Christlikeness "Arise, shine" *Isa 61:1-5*

Daniel's meeting with the angel Gabriel *Dan 9:20-23, 10:4-21*

Jesus' baptism by John *Mat 3:13-17, Mark 1:9-11, Luke 3:21, 22*

Jesus on letting your light shine *Mat 5:13-16, Luke 8:16-18*

Jesus' transfiguration *Mat 17:1-13, Mark 9:2-13, Luke 9:28-36*

Jesus' parable of the missing wedding garment *Mat 22:1-14*

Precious ointment poured on his head by woman *Mat 26:6-13, Mark 14:3-9*

Jesus' resurrection *Mat 28:1-8, Mark 16:1-8, Luke 24:1-12, John 20:1-10*

Two disciples meet him after resurrection *Mark 16:12, 13, Luke 24: 13-35*

Jesus' ascension *Mark 16:19, 20, Luke 24:50-53, Acts 1:6-12*

Angels announce the birth of Jesus *Luke 2:8-20*

John sees Jesus Christ as the light of the world *John 1:1-14, 8:12-32*

Paul blinded by light from heaven *Acts 9:1-9*

John's teaching "God is Love" *1 John 4:1-21*

John's vision of woman clothed with the sun *Rev 12:1-17*

John's vision of the light of the city foursquare *Rev. 21:1-27*

See also angel, glory, happiness, joy, light, love

RAIN

Noah sees the flood of rain *Gen 7:1-24*

God rains bread from heaven *Exod 16:1-36, Num 11:1-15, 31, 32*

Elijah prays for rain *1 King 18: 41-46*

Isaiah's vision of desert blossoming *Isa 35:1-10*

Jesus' parable of house built on rock or sand *Mat 7:24-27, Luke 6:48, 49*

Paul's party in shipwreck protected from rain *Acts 28:1-6*

See also desert, flood, rainbow, refreshment, renewal, restoration, water

RAINBOW

Noah sees the token of the covenant with God *Gen 9:12-17*

Jacob dreams of angels ascending and descending *Gen 28:10-22*

God makes sun and moon stand still at Ajalon *Josh 10:6-15*

Jesus tells the signs of Christ's coming *Mat 24:1-41, John 8:12-32*

Jesus Christ as the light of the world *John 1:1-14, 8:12-32*

John's vision of angel with book, rainbow overhead *Rev 10:1-11*

See also covenant, rain, renewal, signs

READER

Moses delivers Ten Commandments *Exod 20:1-19, Deut 5:1-24*

Aaron and sons anointed to conduct services *Lev 8:1-13*

Aaron's rod blossoms *Num 17:1-11*

Moses offers people choice of good or evil *Deut 30:11-20*

David's charge to Solomon to complete work *1 Chron 22:6-19, 23:1*

Artaxerxes' letter to Ezra read to people *Ezra 7:11-26*

Book of law read to people *Neh 8:1-12*

David's song of security near God *Psal 91:1-16*

Isaiah's vision of the prophet called to speak *Isa 6:1-13*

Isaiah reassured of God's help in trials *Isa 43:1-28, 44:1-24*

Isaiah's inspiration to be Christlike *Isa 60:1-5*

Daniel's meeting with Gabriel *Dan 9:20-23, 10:4-21*

Zechariah's vision of candlestick fed by two olive trees *Zech 4:1-14*

Ministry of John the Baptist *Mat 3:1-12, Mark 1:1-8, Luke 3:1-18*

Jesus' parable of the sower and receptivity *Mat 13:3-23, Mark 4:1-20, Luke 8:4-15*

Jesus' parable of leaven *Mat 13:33, Luke 13:20, 21*

Jesus' parable of householder's treasures *Mat 13:51, 52*

Jesus sought by all men; his fame increases *Mark 1:35-39, 45*

Jesus' parable of the faithful steward *Luke 12:41-48*

Jesus' parable of the true vine *John 15:1-17*

Paul on qualities that protect *Eph 6:10-17*

John's vision of the sealed book *Rev 5:1-14*

Angel with book *Rev 10:1-11*

See also Bible, church, disciple, ministry, sermon, preaching, pastor

READINESS

Enoch is translated; "he walked with God" *Gen 5:18, 21-24, Heb 11:5*

Noah builds the ark against the flood *Gen 6:5-22*

Moses complains of his speaking ability *Exod 4:10-17*

Caleb urges entrance into promised land *Num 13:1-33, 14:1-11, 23-29, Deut 1:19-38*

David accepts Goliath's challenge *1 Sam 17:17-52*

Elijah translated *2 King 2:1-11*

Elisha takes up the mantle *2 King 2:12-15*

Nehemiah finds people ready to rebuild wall *Neh 4:1-23*

David's song, "Whither shall I go from thy spirit" *Psal 139:1-24*

Isaiah called to speak *Isa 6:1-13*

Jonah at last prepared to preach to Nineveh *Jonah 3:1-10*

Jesus' parable of the sower *Mat 13:3-23, Mark 4:1-20, Luke 8:4-15*

Jesus' parable of wheat and tares *Mat 13:24-30, 36-43*

Jesus' parable of pearl of great price *Mat 13:45, 46*

Jesus saves Peter who tries to walk on water *Mat 14:22-33, John 6:15-21*

Peter acknowledges Jesus as Christ *Mat 16:13-20, Mark 8:27-30, Luke 9:18-21*

Jesus' parable of the marriage feast *Mat 22:1-14*

Jesus' parable of servants awaiting lord *Mat 24:42-51*

Jesus' parable of wise and foolish virgins *Mat 25:1-13*

Jesus parable of seed, blade, ear, full corn *Mark 4:26-29*

Mary ready for birth of Jesus *Luke 1:26-38*

Jesus preaches at Nazareth and is rejected by them *Luke 4:14-32*

Jesus' parable of unwilling friend *Luke 11:5-13*

Jesus' parable of the rich man who built bigger barns *Luke 12:15-21*

Jesus' parable of the watchful servants *Luke 12:35-40*

Jesus' parable of door shut by master *Luke 13:22-30*

Jesus' parable of cost of following Christ *Luke 14:25-33*

Jesus' parable of the unjust steward *Luke 16:1-14*

Jesus says he is not ready to turn water into wine *John 2:1-11*

Jesus' teaching, to reap for the harvest is now *John 4:31-38*

After resurrection the unready Peter returns to his trade *John 21:1-14*

Philip talks with Ethiopian and baptizes him *Acts 8:26-40*

Paul healed, preaches Christ *Acts 9:10-22*

Peter accepts Gentiles' conversion *Acts 11:1-18*

Paul's teaching that "now is the accepted time" *2 Cor 6:1-18*

See also preparation, ripeness, watch, willing

REALITY

God creates the perfect universe and man *Gen 1:1-31*

Lord God creates material universe *Gen 2:6-25, 3:1-24*

Patriarchs lived to advanced age *Gen 5:1-32*

Moses at bush sees God revealed *Exod 3:1-18*

Moses at bush has proofs involving his rod and leprosy *Exod 4:1-9*

Manna and quails in wilderness *Exod 16:1-36, Num 11:1-15, 31, 32*

Water in the desert *Exod 17:1-7, Num 20:1-13*

God gives Gideon certainty in three signs *Judg 6:19-40*

Solomon realizes David's dream of a house of God *1 King 6:1-36, 7:1-51, 2 Chron 3:1-17, 4:1-22, 5:1-14*

Solomon's reputation acknowledged by Queen of Sheba *1 King 10:1-12*

Elijah fed in a dream *1 King 19:1-8*

The vanity of mortal life *Eccl 1:1-18, 2:1-26*

Mortal events all within time framework *Eccl 3:1-15*

Ezekiel's vision of God's care of his flock *Ezek 34:1-31*

Jesus' parable of builders on rock or sand *Mat 7:24-27, Luke 6:48, 49*

Jesus' control of the elements *Mat 8:23-27, Mark 4:35-41, Luke 8:22-25*

Jesus' parable of the sheep and goats *Mat 25:31-46*

Jesus' resurrection *Mat 28:1-8, Mark 16:1-8, Luke 24:1-12, John 20:1-10*

Eleven apostles see Jesus risen at Galilee *Mat 28:16-18, John 21:1-14*

Jesus' parable of rich man and bigger barns *Luke 12:15-21*

Jesus' parable of counting the cost *Luke 14:25-33*

Jesus on God as Spirit *John 4:1-30*

Jesus heals man born blind *John 9:1-41*

Thomas acknowledges that Jesus has really risen *John 20:24-29*

Paul on Christ's resurrection proves ours *1 Cor 15:1-58*

Paul on source of supply for all *2 Cor 8:11-15, 9:6-15*

John's sermon, "God is love" *I John 4:1-21*

See also life, spirituality, substance, truth, unreality

REAPING

Moses lists the blessings of obedience *Deut 28:1-14*

Ruth gleans in the field of Boaz *Ruth 2:1-23*

Uzziah's pride culminates in disease *2 Chron 26:1-23*

Gehazi's greed punished *2 King 5:15-27*

Haman hanged on his own gallows *Esther 6:1-14, 7:1-10*

Jesus on knowing men by their fruits *Mat 7:15-20, Luke 6:43-45*

Jesus' parable of the wheat and the tares *Mat 13:24-30, 36-43*

Jesus' parable of the dragnet *Mat 13:47-50*

Peter obtains money from a fish *Mat 17:24-27*

Jesus' parable of laborers in the vineyard *Mat 20:1-16*

Jesus' parable of the talents *Mat 25:14-30, Luke 19:11-28*

Peter's net filled *Luke 5:1-11, John 21:1-11*

Seventy disciples report success *Luke 10:17-24*

Jesus on reaping because the harvest is now *John 4:31-38*

See also farming, fruits, harvest, labor, reward, sowing, vine, work

REASON

Abraham reasons with God on righteousness *Gen 18:20-33*

Joseph solves problem of Pharaoh's dream *Gen 41:1-46*

Moses at bush comprehends nature of God *Exod 3:1-18*

Moses' father-in-law solves problem of judging *Exod 18:13-27*

Moses' sermon on rational choice *Deut 30:11-20, Josh 24:1-25*

Gideon reasons from signs to solution *Judg 6:19-40, 7:1-25*

David tries Saul's armor but refuses it *1 Sam 17:17-37*

Solomon selects the greatest gift *1 King 3:5-15, 2 Chron 1:7-12*

Solomon judges rightly *1 King 3:16-28*

Rehoboam reasons wrongly *1 King 12:1-18, 2 Chron 10:1-19*

Elijah's thoughts about the nature of God *1 King 19:9-13*

Elisha sends Syrians home unharmed and war ceases *2 King 6:8-23*

Job reasons with friends on nature of things *Job 4:1—37:24*

David's song, "What is man?" *Psal 8:1-9*

David's song, "the fountain of life" *Psal 36:1-12*

Vanity of human life *Eccl 1:1-18, 2:1-26*

Mortal events all within time framework *Eccl 3:1-15*

Jeremiah in prison of Babylon buys field in Israel *Jer 32:2, 6:27, 37-44*

Jews explain why they will not worship an image *Dan 3:1-30*

Jonah finally sees the light *Jonah 1:1-17, 2:1-10, 3:1-10*

Jesus' temptations *Mat 4:1-11, Mark 1:12, 13, Luke 4:1-13*

Jesus tells why he eats with sinners *Mat 9:10-13, Mark 2:13-17, Luke 5:27-32*

Jesus tells why his disciples do not fast *Mat 9:14-27, Mark 2:18-22, Luke 5:33-39*

John the Baptist sends to Jesus for proof of Christ *Mat 11:2-19, Luke 7:18-35*

Jesus tells why he speaks only in parables *Mat 13:10-17, 34, 35, Mark 4:10-12, 33, 34*

Jesus' parable of unmerciful debtor *Mat 18:23-35*

Jesus' parable of laborers in vineyard *Mat 20:1-16*

Jesus replies to chief priests on his authority *Mat 21:23-27, Mark 11:27-33, Luke 20:1-8*

Jesus discusses paying tribute to Caesar *Mat 22:15-22, Mark 10:13-17, Luke 20:20-26*

Jesus telescopes Ten Commandments into two *Mat 22:34-40, Mark 12:28-34*

Jesus' parable of talents *Mat 25:14-30, Luke 19:11-28*

Jesus comments on Judas' objection to use of precious ointment *Mat 26:6-13, Mark 14:2-9*

Jesus comments on widow's mite *Mark 12:41-44, Luke 21:1-4*

Jesus' parable of two debtors forgiven *Luke 7:36-50*

Jesus answers Martha's complaint *Luke 10:38-42*

Jesus' parable of counting the cost *Luke 14:25-33*

Jesus' parable of prodigal son and his brother *Luke 15:11-32*

Jesus Christ as the light of the world *John 1:1-14, 8:12-32*

Jesus' teaching that man must be born again *John 3:1-21*

Jesus on God as Spirit *John 3:22-36*

Jesus heals nobleman's son at seventh hour *John 4:46-54*

Jesus debates at festival *John 7: 14-53*

Jesus saves adultress from stoning *John 8:1-11*

Jesus heals man born blind *John 9:1-41*

Thomas doubts but is finally convinced *John 20:19-29*

Jesus convinces Peter of his duty *John 21:12-19*

Paul is convinced he should reverse himself *Acts 9:10-22, 20:17-38*

Peter comes to accept conversion of Gentiles *Acts 10:1-48, 11:1-18*

See also intelligence, light, mind, motive, principle, revelation, understanding

REBELLION

Adam's and Eve's fall and punishment *Gen 3:1-24*

Moses leads Israel out of bondage *Exod 15:1-19*

Aaron sets up golden calf worship *Exod 32:1-24*

Aaron and Miriam speak against Moses *Num 12:1-16*

Absalom rebels against David (his father, the king) *2 Sam 15:1-23*

Jonah refuses God's command to preach to Nineveh *Jonah 1:1-17*

Jesus' parable of unclean spirit and seven others *Mat 12:43-45, Luke 11:24-26*

Jesus' parable of husbandmen who refuse to pay rent *Mat 21:33-46, Mark 12:1-12, Luke 20:9-19*

Judas settles price to betray Jesus *Mat 26:14-16, Mark 14:10, 11, Luke 22:1-6*

Peter and John speak the word with boldness *Acts 4:1-37*

See also authority, government, resistance, revolution

REBUKE

Adam and Eve rebuked *Gen 3:6-24*

Cain rebuked for murder *Gen 4:1-16*

Balak rebuked by Balaam (hired to curse Israel) *Num 22:1-41, 23:1-30, 24:1-25*

Nathan's parable rebukes David's sin *2 Sam 12:1-10*

Isaiah rebukes pride of women *Isa 3:16-26*

Isaiah promises the fall of mighty Babylon *Isa 14:4-8, 12-17, 25-27*

Isaiah promises hypocrisy will be punished *Isa 29:11-24, 30:1-3, 20, 21*

Daniel reads handwriting on wall *Dan 5:1-31*

Jesus' parables:

mote and beam *Mat 7:1-5, Luke 6:37-42*

unmerciful debtor *Mat 18:23-35*

two sons ordered to work *Mat 21:28-32*

sheep and goats *Mat 25:31-46*

good Samaritan *Luke 10:25-37*

rich fool and bigger barns *Luke 12:15-21*

barren fig tree *Luke 13:6-9*

chief seats at wedding *Luke 14:7-14*

prodigal son and brother *Luke 15:11-32*

Pharisee and publican *Luke 18:9-14*

Jesus orders devils into swine *Mat 8:30-32*

Jesus excoriates three cities for disregarding him *Mat 11:20-24*

Jesus admonishes Peter *Mat 16:21-28, Mark 8:31-38, Luke 9:20-27*

Jesus casts traders out *Mat 21:12, 13, Mark 11:15-17, Luke 19:45, 46, John 2:13-25*

Jesus withers fig tree without fruit *Mat 21:18-22, Mark 11:12-14, 20-24*

Jesus reproves Pharisees *Mat 23:1-39, Luke 11:37-54, John 8:33-59*

Jesus casts out unclean spirit *Mark 1:21-28, Luke 4:33-37*

Paul's charge to the faithful *2 Tim 4:1-8*

Peter rebukes Simon who offers to buy power *Acts 8:14-25*

See also condemnation, punishment

RECEPTIVITY

Abraham entertains angels *Gen 18:1-18*

Lot shelters two angels from a mob *Gen 19:1-14*

Jacob dreams of angels on a ladder *Gen 28:10-22*

Jacob holds on to angel to receive his blessings *Gen 32:24-32*

Samuel called by the Lord *1 Sam 3:1-10*

Elijah finds God in still small voice *1 King 19:9-13*

Elisha stays with Elijah to receive double his spirit *2 King 2:1-15*

Nehemiah finds the people of a mind to work *Neh 4:1-23*

Ezra reads Book of the law to the people *Neh 8:1-12*

David's song, "The Lord is my shepherd" *Psal 23:1-6*

Isaiah ready for his call to speak *Isa 6:1-13*

Jonah not at first receptive to God's word *Jonah 1:1-17, 2:1-10, 3:1-10*

Beatitudes in Sermon on the Mount *Mat 5:1-12, Luke 6:17-26, 36*

Jesus heals woman who touches hem of garment *Mat 9:20-22, Mark 5:25-34, Luke 8:43-48*

Three cities excoriated for disregarding his works *Mat 11:20-24*

Jesus' parable of the sower *Mat 13:3-23, Mark 4:1-20, Luke 8:4-15*

Jesus' parable of the pearl of great price *Mat 13:45, 46*

Jesus' parable of the servants awaiting their lord *Mat 24:42-51*

Jesus' parable of the talents *Mat 25:14-30, Luke 19:11-28*

Jesus' parable of the Pharisee and publican *Luke 18:9-14*

Jesus heals Syrophenician's daughter *Mat 15:21-28, Mark 7:24-30*

Peter acknowledges Jesus as Christ *Mat 16:13-20, Mark 8:27-30, Luke 9:18-21*

Jesus heals blind Bartimaeus *Mark 10:46-52*

Mary magnifies the Lord *Luke 1:39-56*

Seventy disciples are instructed by Jesus and prove they understand *Luke 10:1-24*

Descent of Holy Ghost *Acts 2:1-13*

Signs and wonders cause church growth *Acts 4:24-37*

Paul preaches successfully to Ephesians *Acts 19:1-10*

Paul on giving and receiving *2 Cor 8:11-15, 9:6-15*

See also angel, communication, doubt, mind, poor, senses

RECONCILIATION

Abraham and Lot agree to separate *Gen 13:1-18*

Jacob and Esau are united again *Gen 33:1-11*

Joseph forgives his brothers *Gen 43:1, 2, 45:1-11*

Jacob and his other children join his son Joseph in Egypt *Gen 45:25-28, 46:2-7*

Miriam speaks against Moses but later is healed by him *Num 12:1-16*

Jesus on treatment of enemies *Mat 5:24, 38-48, Luke 6:27-36*

Jesus on oneness with the Father *John 10:22-42*

Jesus' parable of the lost sheep *Mat 18:12-14, Luke 15:1-7*

Jesus' parable of prodigal son and his brother *Luke 15:11-32*

Paul on remitting sin *Heb 10:1-39*

Paul on reconciliation *2 Cor 5:1-21*

See also atonement, debt, friendship, harmony, mediator, oneness, reformation, reunion

REDEMPTION

Abraham and the righteous man *Gen 18:20-33*

Aaron to redeem sin by sacrifice *Lev 16:1-28*

The chosen people set apart as God's own *Deut 7:6-11*

David's song, "Why art thou cast down?" *Psal 42:1-11*

David's song, "Create in me a clean heart" *Psal 51:1-19*

Isaiah's vision of redemption by Christ *Isa 42:1-12, 16, 18*

Isaiah's vision, "look unto the rock" *Isa 51:1-12*

Isaiah's vision, "Awake, awake" *Isa 52:1-15*

Jeremiah's vision of captivity turned *Jer 29:8-14*

Jeremiah's vision of restoration promised *Jer 31:1-14, 31-34*

Zephaniah's vision of salvation promised *Zeph 3:14-17*

Peter acknowledges Jesus as Christ *Mat 16:13-20, Mark 8:27-30, Luke 9:18-21*

Jesus' parable of the lost sheep *Mat 18:12-14, Luke 15:1-7*

Jesus' crucifixion *Mat 27:13-56, Mark 15:21-41, Luke 23:26-49, John 19:17-30*

Jesus' resurrection *Mat 28:1-8, Mark 16:1-8, Luke 24:1-12, John 20:1-10*

Jesus' parable of the piece of money *Luke 15:8-10*

Jesus' parable of the prodigal son *Luke 15:11-24*

Paul's teaching that Christ's resurrection proves ours *1 Cor 15:1-58*

Paul's teaching that only true sacrifice remits sin *Heb 10:1-39*

James on faith without works *Jas 2:14-26*

See also atonement, Christ, conversion, deliverance, freedom, rescue, restoration, salvation, sin

REFLECTION

God creates perfect universe and man in his image *Gen 1:1-31*

Enoch "walked with God" and is translated *Gen 5:18, 21-24, Heb 11:5*

Noah sees the rainbow as a token of the covenant *Gen 9:12-17*

Moses face to face with I Am That I Am *Exod 3:1-18, 33:7-23*

Aaron receives Urim and Thummim *Exod 28:29-36*

Samuel selects David on basis of inner man *1 Sam 16:1-13*

Elijah translated *2 King 2:1-11*

David's song, "the happiness of the godly" *Psal 1:1-6*

David's song, "What is man?" *Psal 8:1-9*

David's song, "Mark the perfect man" *Psal 37:23-40*

Isaiah's description of the Messiah *Isa 53:1-12*

Jesus' teaching "let your light shine" *Mat 5:13-16, Luke 8:16-18*

Jesus on oneness with the Father *John 10:22-42*

Jesus' transfiguration *Mat 17:1-13, Mark 9:2-13, Luke 9:28-36*

Jesus' resurrection *Mat 28:1-8, Mark 16:1-8, Luke 24:1-12, John 20:1-10*

Jesus' ascension *Mark 16:19, 20, Luke 24:50-53, Acts 1:6-12*

Descent of Holy Ghost *Acts 2:1-13*

Paul's teaching to put on the new man *Col 3:1-17*

Paul on the character of Christ *Heb 1:1-14*

See also consciousness, expression, idea, image, likeness, manifestation

REFORMATION

Lot escapes Sodom, wife looks back *Gen 19:1, 15-29*

Jacob changes his character and receives new name *Gen 32:24-32*

Naaman pockets his pride and is healed *2 King 5:1-14*

David's song, "Create in me a clean heart" *Psal 51:1-19*

Preacher at last sees vanity of mortal life *Eccl 1:1-18, 2:1-26*

Jonah repents and does God's bidding *Jonah 1:1-17, 2:1-10, 3:1-10*

Jesus on qualities that make a Christian *Mat 5:1-12, Luke 6:17-26*

Jesus' teaching to take no thought but seek first the kingdom *Mat 6:25-34, Luke 12:22-34*

Judas repents and hangs himself *Mat 27:3-10, Acts 1:15-20*

Jesus risen is seen by Mary Magdalene out of whom he cast seven devils *Mark 16:9-11, John 20:11-18*

Jesus' parable of new wine in old bottles *Luke 5:36-39*

Jesus' parable of prodigal son *Luke 15:11-24*

Zacchaeus reformed when Jesus visits his house *Luke 19:1-10*

Jesus' teaching that man must be born again *John 3:1-21*

Jesus' teaching to worship God in spirit *John 4:1-30, 39-42*

Peter who denied Jesus, accepts charge, "Feed my sheep" *John 21:12-19*

Saul, the persecutor of Christians, becomes Paul, the Christian *Acts 9:1-41, Acts 20:17-38, 22:1-30, 26:1-32*

Paul's sermon, "come out ... and be ye separate" *2 Cor 6:1-18*

Paul's sermon "put on the new man" *Col 3:1-17*

See also atonement, character, error, pardon, punishment, reconciliation, repentance

REFRESHMENT

Hagar and her son find water in desert *Gen 21:9-21*

Elijah rests under juniper tree *1 King 19:1-10*

David's song, "The Lord is my shepherd" *Psal 23:1-6*

David's song, "the fountain of life" *Psal 36:1-12*

David's song, "The Lord is our refuge" *Psal 46:1-11*

Isaiah's vision of desert blossoming *Isa 35:1-10*

Jesus turns to God at Gethsemane *Mat 26:30, 36-46, Mark 14:32-42, Luke 22:39-46*

Jesus' teaching that man must be born again *John 3:1-21*

At Jacob's well Jesus asks Samaritan woman for a drink *John 4:1-42*

Jesus says his great works have their source in the Father *John 5:17-47*

Jesus promises to send the Comforter *John 14:1-31*

Jesus' parable of the true vine *John 15:1-17*

Pentecost—descent of Comforter *Acts 2:1-13*

Paul's hardships counted by him as nothing *2 Cor 11:21-33*

Paul on putting off old man, putting on new *Col 3:1-17*

See also rain, restoration

REFUGE

Noah builds the ark *Gen 6:5-22*

People cross Jordan into land of promise *Josh 3:1-17*

The Shunammite builds a refuge for Elisha *2 King 4:8-37*

Elisha defended by chariots of fire *2 King 6:8-23*

David's song, "The Lord is my shepherd" *Psal 23:1-6*

David's song, "God is our refuge and strength" *Psal 46:1-11*

David's song, "secret place of the most High" *Psal 91:1-16*

Isaiah's vision of Christ's peaceable kingdom *Isa 1:1-12*

God's care of his flock *Ezek 34:1-31*

Jesus' family flees to Egypt *Mat 2:13-23, Luke 2:39, 40*

Jesus' parable of the lost sheep *Mat 18:12-14, Luke 15:1-7*

Jesus suffers children to come to him *Mat 19:13-15, Mark 10:13-16, Luke 18:15-17*

Jesus turns to God at Gethsemane *Mat 26:30, 36-46, Mark 14:26, 32-42, Luke 22:39-46*

Jesus' parable of the good shepherd *John 10:1-18*

Jesus' parable of the true vine *John 15:1-17*

See also danger, God, protection, safety, shelter

REFUTATION

See argument, reason

REGENERATION

Jacob receives a new name, Israel *Gen 32:24-32*

The chosen people set apart as God's own *Deut 7:6-11*

Walls of Jerusalem rebuilt *Neh 4:1-23*

Temple of Jerusalem rebuilt *Ezra 6:1-3, 7, 8, 14, 15*

David's song, "the fountain of life" *Psal 36:1-12*

David's song, "hope thou in God" *Psal 42:1-11*

David's song, "create in me a clean heart" *Psal 51:1-19*

David's song of the Lord who heals and redeems *Psal 103:1-22*

Isaiah's vision of the desert blossoming *Isa 35:1-10*

Jeremiah promises the return from captivity *Jer 29:8-14, 31:1-14, 31-34*

Ezekiel's vision of the resurrection of dry bones *Ezek 37:1-14*

Jonah escapes fish and does God's will *Jonah 2:1-10, 3:1-10*

Jesus on becoming a little child *Mat 18:1-22, Mark 9:33-50, 10:13-16*

Jesus' parable of the lost sheep *Mat 18:12-14, Luke 15:1-7*

Mary Magdalene sees the risen Jesus *Mark 16:9-11, John 20:11-18*

Jesus' parable of new wine in old bottles *Luke 5:36-39*

Jesus' parable of prodigal son *Luke 15:11-24*

Jesus' teaching that man must be born again *John 3:1-21*

Paul converted to Christianity *Acts 9:1-31*

Paul's sermon, "Put on the new man" *Col 3:1-17*

See also awakening, baptism, birth, life, redemption, reformation, restoration, spirit

REGRET

Lord God regrets his creation and tells Noah he will start again *Gen 6:5-22*

Lot's wife regrets leaving Sodom and Gomorrah *Gen 19:1, 15-29*

Jacob regrets his duplicity, fears his brother *Gen 32:1-32*

Joseph's brethren regret their treatment of him *Gen 42:1-8*

People regret leaving comforts of Egypt *Num 11:1-15*

Samuel regrets making Saul king *1 Sam 15:7-26*

David repents killing of Uriah *2 Sam 12:1-10*

Peter weeps over his denial of Jesus *Mat 26:57, 58, 69-75, Mark 14:66-72, Luke 22:54-62, John 18:13-18, 25-27*

Judas hangs himself *Mat 27:3-10, Acts 1:15-20*

Jesus' parable of rich man and beggar *Luke 16:19-31*

Paul converted from persecution of Christians *Acts 9:10-22*

Paul's self-revealings *2 Cor 12:1-19*

Paul's sermon that true sacrifice remits sin *Heb 10:1-39*

See also mistake, remorse, repentance, self-condemnation

REHOBOAM

See Part II, Rehoboam

REIGN

Gideon refuses to be king because God rules *Judg 8:22, 23*

Jotham's parable of the trees *Judg 9:1-15*

Samuel resists the people's demand for a king *1 Sam 8:1-22*

Samuel later anoints Saul to be king *1 Sam 10:1-8*

Still later Samuel anoints David *1 Sam 16:1-13*

David made king of Judah *2 Sam 2:1-4*

David made king of Israel *2 Sam 5:1-5*

Solomon turns to God for wisdom in ruling *1 King 3:5-15, 2 Chron 1:7-12*

Solomon visited by Queen of Sheba *1 King 10:1-12, 2 Chron 9:1-12*

Rehoboam consults his friends *1 King 12:1-18, 2 Chron 10:1-19*

Jehoshaphat's good reign *2 Chron 17:1-13, 19:4-11*

Hezekiah leads his people against invaders *2 Chron 31:20, 21, 32:1-23, Isa 36:1-22, 37:1-38*

Josiah's good reign *2 King 23:1-22, 2 Chron 34:1-8, 29-33*

Isaiah foretells the coming of Christ's kingdom *Isa 2:1-5*

Isaiah foretells Christ's peaceable kingdom *Isa 11:1-12, Mic 4:1-8, 13*

Jesus' parable of the king and his wedding feast *Mat 22:1-14*

The Christ as the son of David *Mat 22:41-46, Mark 12:35-37, Luke 20:41-44*

Jesus foretells his second coming *Mat 24:1-41*

Jesus questioned by Pilate whether he is king *Mat 27:1, 2, 11-14, Mark 15:1-5, Luke 23:1-5, John 18:28-38*

Jesus crowned with thorns *Mat 27:27-31, Mark 15:16-20, John 19:1-16*

Pilate posts sign at cross, "The King of the Jews" *Mat 27:32-56, Mark 15:21-41, Luke 23:26-49, John 19:17-30*

John's vision of king of kings *Rev 19:11-16*

See also authority, dominion, government, king, power, rule

REJECTION

God casts out Adam and Eve from Eden *Gen 3:6-24*

God casts out Cain *Gen 4:1-16*

Abraham dismisses Hagar and Ishmael *Gen 21:9-21*

Joseph rejects adultery of Potiphar's wife *Gen 39:1-20*

Moses warns against idolatry and necromancy *Deut 13:1-18*

Gideon refuses to be king *Judg 8:22, 23*

Samuel refuses to appoint a king *1 Sam 8:1-22*

Samuel rejects Saul as king *1 Sam 15:7-26*

Shunammite rejects evidence of her son's death *2 King 4:8-37*

Naaman rejects prescription of Elisha *2 King 5:1-14*

Jesus repels Satan *Mat 4:1-11, Luke 4:1-13*

Jesus' teaching "Seek ye first" *Mat 6:25-34, Luke 12:22-34*

Jesus heals Jairus' daughter (puts mourners out) *Mat 9:18, 19, 23-26, Mark 5:22-24, 35-43, Luke 8:41, 42, 49-56*

Jesus excoriates three cities for disregarding him *Mat 11:20-24*

Jesus' parable of the sower *Mat 13:3-23, Mark 4:1-20, Luke 8:4-15*

Jesus' parable of the wheat and tares *Mat 13:24-30, 36-43*

Jesus' story of prophets rejected by own country *Mat 13:53-58, Mark 6:1-6, Luke 4:22-24, John 4:43-45*

Woman answers Jesus' objections and her daughter is healed *Mat 15:21-28, Mark 7:24-30*

Jesus' parable of husbandmen who refuse to pay rent *Mat 21:33-46, Mark 12:1-12, Luke 20:9-19*

Jesus' parable of marriage guest without wedding garment *Mat 22:1-14*

Jesus castigates Pharisees and lawyers *Mat 23:1-39, Luke 11:37-54*

Jesus' parable of wise and foolish virgins *Mat 25:1-13*

Jesus at Gethsemane *Mat 26:30, 36-46, Mark 14:26, 32-42, Luke 22:39-46*

Peter vows never to deny Jesus but does *Mat 26:31-35, 57, 58, 69-75, Mark 14:27-31, 66-72, Luke 22:31-34, 54-62, John 13:36-38, 18:13-18, 25-27*

Crowd offered Jesus or Barabbas *Mat 27:15-26, Mark 15:6-15, Luke 23:13-25, John 18:39, 40*

Jesus' parable of fig tree *Luke 13:6-9*

Thomas refuses to believe resurrection *Luke 24:36-40, John 20:19-23*

After teaching on bread of life many disciples leave Jesus *John 6:66-71*

Peter puts out mourners and raises Tabitha *Acts 9:36-43*

See also denial, receptivity

REJOICING

Abraham and Sarah rejoice at God's promises *Gen 15:1-21*

The jubilee year *Lev 25:9-19*

Moses' song of deliverance *Deut 32:1-47*

Deborah's song of deliverance *Judg 5:1-20*

David's song of delight in God's law *Psal 1:1-6*

David's song of creation *Psal 33:1-22*

David's song "Make a joyful noise" *Psal 66:1-20, 100:1-5*

Jesus' parable of lost sheep *Mat 18:12-14, Luke 15:1-7*

Jesus' parable of the marriage feast *Mat 22:1-14*

Angels at birth of Jesus *Luke 2:1-20*

Seventy disciples report their healings *Luke 10:17-24*

Jesus' parable of prodigal son's return *Luke 15:11-24*

Paul on rejoicing *Phil 4:1-23*

See also gladness, happiness, heart, joy, praise

RELAPSE

See reversal

RELATION

Cain and Abel rupture brotherhood *Gen 4:1-16*

Abraham and Lot separate after strife *Gen 13:4-18*

Abraham tempted to sacrifice his son *Gen 22:1-19*

Jacob promised God's ever-presence *Gen 28:10-22*

Moses through contact with God gives Ten Commandments *Exod 20:1-19, Deut 5:1-24*

Israelites set apart as God's own *Deut 7:6-11*

Ruth makes relations with Naomi permanent *Ruth 1:1-22*

Jonathan befriends David *1 Sam 18:1-16*

Solomon detemines true mother of a child *1 King 3:16-28*

Elisha is established as Elijah's successor *2 King 2:1-15*

David's song on relation of happiness to godliness *Psal 1:1-6*

David's song on relation of man and God *Psal 23:1-16*

Jeremiah's vision of potter and clay *Jer 18:1-6*

Ezekiel's vision of heredity *Ezek 18:1-32*

Jesus' parable of mote and beam *Mat 7:1-5, Luke 6:37-42*

Jesus' parable on neighbors *Luke 10:25-37*

Jesus' parable of prodigal's elder brother *Luke 15:25-32*

Disciples discuss who shall be greatest *Luke 22:24-30*

John the Baptist tells how Jesus' preaching differs *John 3:22-36*

Jesus' parable of the true vine *John 15:1-17*

Paul on the Unknown God *Acts 17:15-34*

Paul on relation of sin and death *Rom 5:1-21*

Paul on Spirit and flesh *Rom 8:1-39*

Paul on Jesus' resurrection and ours *1 Cor 15:1-58*

See also family, human, kinsman, universe

RELIANCE

Moses is promised God's presence *Exod 3:9-12*

Moses relies on God for eloquence *Exod 4:10-17*

God's promises to faithful *Lev 26:1-20*

Samuel resists demand to replace God as king *1 Sam 8:1-22*

David refuses Saul's armor *1 Sam 17:17-37*

Rehoboam relies on friends instead of counselors *1 King 12:1-18, 2 Chron 10:1-19*

Prophet proclaims battle is not yours but God's *2 Chron 20:1-32*

David's song, God, the preserver of men *Psal 121:1-8*

Centurion relies on Jesus' authority to heal *Mat 8:5-13, Luke 7:1-10*

Jesus relies on prayer and fasting to heal *Mat 17:14-21, Mark 9:14-29, Luke 9:37-43*

Peter's net is filled *Luke 5:1-11, John 21:1-11*

Seventy disciples report success *Luke 10:17-24*

See also confidence, faith, hope, promise, trust

RELIGION

Enoch walked with God *Gen 5:18, 21-24, Heb 11:5*

Moses receives Ten Commandments *Exod 20:1-19, Deut 5:1-24*

Aaron consecrated for priesthood *Lev 8:1-13*

Aaron sacrifices for atonement *Lev 16:1-28*

Chosen people set apart as God's own *Deut 7:6-11*

Moses' farewell address on moral choices *Deut 30:11-20*

David promises to build a house for God *2 Sam 7:1-29*

David accepts offerings to build the temple *1 Chron 29:6-19*

Solomon dedicates the temple *1 King 8:22-66, 2 Chron 6:1-42*

Elijah discovers the still small voice *1 King 19:9-13*

David's song, "The Lord is my shepherd" *Psal 23:1-6*

David's song, "the secret place of the most High" *Psal 91:1-16*

Isaiah prophesies the Christ *Isa 7: 10-16, 9:2-7*

Micah on the glory of the church *Isa 2:1-5, Mic 4:1-8, 13*

Jesus teaches his disciples the Lord's Prayer *Mat 6:5-15, Mark 11:25, 26, Luke 11:1-4*

Jesus compliments centurion's faith and heals servant *Mat 8:5-13, Luke 7:1-10*

Jesus' parable of the mustard seed *Mat 13:31, 32, Mark 4:30-32, Luke 13:18, 19*

Jesus at first refuses to help Syrophenician, then heals her daughter *Mat 15:21-28, Mark 7:24-30*

Jesus' parable of sheep and goats *Mat 25:31-46*

Jesus' parable of seed, blade, ear, full corn *Mark 4:26-29*

Jesus' parable of the faithful steward *Luke 12:41-48*

Jesus' parable of Pharisee and publican *Luke 18:9-14*

Source of Jesus' works is in the Father *John 5:17-47*

Peter on the meaning of Christianity *Acts 2:14-47*

See also belief, Christ, church, devotion, God, worship, zeal

REMEDY

Moses sees leprosy transformed at once *Exod 4:1-9*

Moses heals poison of serpents by looking at image *Num 21:4-9*

Jeroboam's hand is withered and healed *1 King 12:32, 33, 13:1-10*

Asa's foot disease fatal because he did not turn to God *2 Chron 16:11-14*

Elisha nullifies poisoned water *2 King 2:16-22*

Elisha nullifies poison in pottage *2 King 4:38-41*

Elisha prescribes bitter remedy for Naaman *2 King 5:1-14*

Woman touched hem of Jesus' garment *Mat 9:20-22, Mark 5:25-34, Luke 8:43-48*

Jesus accused of using Beelzebub to heal *Mat 12:22-30, Mark 3:22-30, Luke 11:14-23*

Jesus' secret of healing difficult cases *Mat 17:14-21, Mark 9:14-29, Luke 9:37-43*

Jesus on the source of his great works *John 5:17-47*

Peter explains how he healed lame man *Acts 3:12-26*

John's revelation of tree of life as a remedy for ills of man *Rev 22: 1-21*

See also disease, healing, medicine

REMEMBRANCE

Joseph helps King's baker who later forgets him *Gen 39:21, 23, 40:1-23*

Song of Moses reviews deliverance by God *Exod 15:1-19, Deut 32: 1-47*

Moses gives Fourth Commandment on sabbath *Exod 20:1-19, Deut 5: 1-24*

Joshua sets up memorial of twelve stones *Josh 4:1-24*

Jesus' discourse on "Who is my mother... my brethren?" *Mat 12: 46-50*

Jesus reminds disciples of his great works *Mat 16:5-12, Mark 8:13-21*

Jesus' parable of need for faithful service *Luke 12:41-48*

Jesus thanked by one of ten lepers he heals *Luke 17:11-19*

Jesus gives John the care of his mother *John 19:25-27*

Paul recalls his healing and conversion *Acts 22:1-30, 26:1-32*

See also forgetfulness, memory, mind

REMORSE

Adam and Eve hide *Gen 3:6-24*

Saul destroys himself *1 Sam 31:1-13, 1 Chron 10:1-14*

David repents at story of ewe lamb *2 Sam 12:1-10*

David's child dies *2 Sam 12:13-23*

Peter denies he knows Jesus *Mat 26:57, 58, 69-75, Mark 14:66-72, Luke 22:54-62, John 18:13-18, 25-27*

Judas hangs himself *Mat 27:3-10, Acts 1:15-20*

Jesus' parable of prodigal son *Luke 15:11-24*

Jesus' parable of rich man and beggar at gate *Luke 16:19-31*

See also confession, conscience, guilt, pain, repentance, sin

RENEWAL

Noah sees the rainbow *Gen 9:12-17*
Abram and Sarai receive new names *Gen 17:1-9, 15-22*
Moses goes to mount for second tablet *Exod 34:1-8*
Elijah starts again after discouragement *1 King 19:1-8*
Nehemiah rebuilds wall of Jerusalem *Neh 1:1-11, 4:1-23, 6:1-19*
Job is restored *Job 42:1-17*
David's song, "the fountain of life" *Psal 36:1-12*
David's song, "Create in me a clean heart" *Psal 51:1-19*
Isaiah's vision of the desert blossoming *Isa 35:1-10*
Jeremiah's vision of Jerusalem restored *Jer 29:8-14, 31:1-14, 31-34*
Jesus' parable of the lost sheep *Mat 18:12-14, Luke 15:1-7*
Jesus foretells his return *Mat 24:1-41*
Jesus' resurrection *Mat 28:1-8, Mark 16:1-8, Luke 24:1-12, John 20:1-10*
Jesus' parable of new wine in old bottles *Luke 5:36-39*
Jesus raises son of widow of Nain *Luke 7:11-17*
Jesus' parable of the lost coin *Luke 15:8-10*
Jesus saves adultress for a new start *John 8:1-11*
John's vision of new heaven and earth *Rev 21:1-27*

See also birth, life, perfection, rain, rainbow, regeneration, restoration, spirituality

RENUNCIATION

Abraham sends Hagar and her son away *Gen 21:9-21*
Esau gives up birthright for pottage *Gen 25:24-34*
Balaam hired to curse Israel *Num 22:1-41, 23:1-30, 24:1-25*
Moses warns against idolatry *Deut 13:1-18*
Moses warns against abominations *Deut 18:9-14*

Gideon refuses to be king *Judg 8:22, 23*
Ruth renounces her people and religion *Ruth 1:1-22*
Samuel declares Saul unfit to be king *1 Sam 15:7-26*
Elisha leaves his plowing to follow Elijah *1 King 19:19-21*
Mortal life declared vain *Eccl 1:1, 18, 2:1-26*
Isaiah questions, can evil be the fruit of good? *Isa 5:1-8*
Isaiah's vision of God eliminating the proud and mighty *Isa 14:4-8, 12-17, 25-27*
Jesus tempted but renounces the devil *Mat 4:1-11, Mark 1:12, 13, Luke 4:1-13*
Peter, Andrew, James and John leave their nets *Mat 4:17-22, Mark 1:14-20, Luke 5:1-11, John 1:35-42*
Jesus' teaching, "Take no thought for your life" *Mat 6:25-34, Luke 12:22-34*
Jesus rejects Peter *Mat 16:21-28, Mark 8:31-38, Luke 9:20-27*
Jesus' parable of wedding guest without wedding garment *Mat 22:1-14*
Paul on spirit versus the flesh *Rom 8:1-39*
Paul's teaching to put off the old man *Col 3:1-17*

See also denial, materialism, old, rejection, repentance

REPAIR

Moses returns for the second tablet of stone *Exod 34:1-8, Deut 10:1-4*
Cyrus proclaims the rebuilding of the temple *Ezra 1:1-11*
Rebuilding of temple starts *Ezra 3:8-13*
Rebuilding of temple starts again *Ezra 6:1-3, 7, 8, 14, 15*
Rebuilding of the wall of Jerusalem *Neh 4:1-23*
With the help of Esther, Mordecai is promoted and the Jews released *Esther 8:1-8*
Full restoration made to Job *Job 42:1-17*
David's song, "Bless the Lord, O my soul" *Psal 103:1-22*

Jeremiah promises captivity will be turned *Jer 29:8-14*

Jeremiah promises a new covenant with God *Jer 31:1-14, 31-34*

God supplies an army from dry bones *Ezek 37:1-14*

Jesus heals withered hand *Mat 12: 9-13, Mark 3:1-5, Luke 6:6-11*

Jesus makes water wine when supply is gone *John 2:1-11*

Jesus' parable of temple to be raised in three days *John 2:19-22*

See also decay, healing, injury, renewal, restoration, wound

REPEL

Joseph repels Potiphar's wife *Gen 39:1-20*

Deborah repels Sisera's attack *Judg 4:1-17*

Gideon repulses Amalekites *Judg 7:1-25*

David repels Goliath *1 Sam 17:1-52*

David and Abigail *1 Sam 25:2-42*

Asa repels invaders *1 King 15:9-24, 2 Chron 14:1-7*

Jehoshaphat sends back invaders *2 Chron 20:1-32*

Elisha besieged by Syrians *2 King 6:8-23*

Hezekiah and Sennacherib *2 King 18:17-37, 19:1-27, 2 Chron 31:20, 21, 32:1-23, Isa 36:1-22, 37:1-38*

God supplies an army from dry bones *Ezek 37:1-14*

Jesus' temptations *Mat 4:1-11, Luke 4:1-13*

Jesus at first refuses to help woman, then later heals her daughter *Mat 15:21-28, Mark 7:24-30*

Jesus admonishes Peter *Mat 16:21-28, Mark 8:31-38, Luke 9:18-21*

Jesus repels Pharisees and lawyers *Mat 23:1-39, Luke 20:45-47, John 8:33-59*

After sermon on bread of life many disciples leave Jesus *John 6:66-71*

Paul's hardships in establishing church *2 Cor 11:21-33*

Paul describes non-Christians *2 Tim 3:1-17*

The woman with child and the dragon *Rev 12:1-17*

See also attraction, enemy, invasion, revolution

REPENTANCE

Jacob reforms his duplicity *Gen 32:24-32*

Moses returns to mount for second tablet *Exod 34:1-8*

Aaron atones through scapegoat *Lev 16:1-28*

David repents Uriah's death *2 Sam 12:1-10*

Jonah repents and turns back to Nineveh *Jonah 2:1-10, 3:1-10*

John the Baptist's ministry *Mat 3:1-12, Mark 1:1-8, Luke 3:1-18*

Jesus' parable of lost sheep *Mat 18:12-14, Luke 15:1-7*

Peter denies Jesus *Mat 26:57, 58, 69-75, Mark 14:66-72, Luke 22:54-62, John 18:13-18, 25-27*

Judas hangs himself *Mat 27:3-10, Acts 1:15-20*

Jesus' parable of lost coin *Luke 15:8-10*

Jesus' parable of prodigal son *Luke 15:11-24*

Jesus visits Zacchaeus *Luke 19:1-10*

Paul's jailor repents and is converted *Acts 16:19-40*

See also atonement, change, conversion, heart, reformation, regret, remorse

REPULSE

See repel

REPUTATION

Balaam unable to curse whom God had blessed *Num 22:1-41, 23:1-30, 24:1-25*

Saul declared unfit by Samuel *1 Sam 15:7-26*

Solomon's reputation acknowledged by Queen of Sheba *1 King 10:1-12, 2 Chron 9:1-12*

Elisha as prophet tells what his enemy conceals *2 King 6:8-18*

The virtuous woman's nature *Prov 31:1-31*

Description of coming Messiah *Isa 53:1-12, 61:1-11, 62:1-12*

Jesus accused of casting out devils by Beelzebub *Mat 12:22-30, Mark 3:22-30, Luke 11:14-23*

Jesus says a prophet is without honor in his own country *Mat 13:53-58, Mark 6:1-6, Luke 4:22-24, John 4:43-45*

Jesus on what defiles a man *Mat 15:1-20, Mark 7:1-23*

Peter acknowledges Jesus as Christ *Mat 16:13-20, Mark 8:27-30, Luke 9:18-21*

Jesus sought by all men *Mark 1:35-39, 45*

John testifies that Jesus is the Christ *John 1:15-34*

See also character, fame, honor, name, senses

RESCUE

Abraham rescues Lot from the kings *Gen 14:8-20*

Hagar sent into desert but saved *Gen 21:9-21*

Isaac rescued from being sacrificed *Gen 22:1-19*

Moses rescues Israelites from Egyptian's army *Exod 14:5-31*

Deborah rescues her people from Sisera *Judg 4:1-17*

Elisha besieged by Syrians *2 King 6:8-23*

Esther saves her people from Haman *Esther 5:1-14, 6:1-14, 7:1-10*

David's song, "Bless the Lord, O my soul" *Psal 103:1-22*

David's song, "God, the preserver of man" *Psal 121:1-8*

A poor wise man saves his city *Eccl 9:13-18*

Isaiah's vision of Creator and Saviour *Isa 45:1-13, 18-21*

Jesus' family's flight to Egypt *Mat 2:13-23*

Jesus calms wind and seas *Mat 8:23-27, Mark 4:35-41, 6:45-52, Luke 8:22-25, John 6:21*

Jesus' parable about the lost sheep *Mat 18:12-14, Luke 15:1-7*

Jesus' parable of sheep and goats *Mat 25:31-46*

Jesus delivers himself from crowd *Luke 4:28-31*

Jesus' parable of good Samaritan *Luke 10:25-37*

Jesus' parable of judge and widow *Luke 18:1-8*

Jesus saves the woman taken in adultery *John 8:1-11*

Peter escapes prison *Acts 5:17-42, 12:1-17*

Paul escapes over wall in a basket *Acts 9:23-31*

Paul escapes prison *Acts 16:19-40*

Paul escapes shipwreck *Acts 27:1-44*

John's vision of woman and dragon *Rev 12: 1-17*

See also danger, deliverance, freedom, redemption, save

RESEARCH

See search

RESENTMENT

Cain resents approval of Abel *Gen 4:1-16*

Esau threatens revenge for duplicity *Gen 27:1-44*

Esau unexpectedly forgives Jacob *Gen 33:1-11*

Joseph punished by Potiphar's wife *Gen 39:1-20*

Moses does not retaliate against Miriam *Num 12:1-16*

Saul envies David's success *1 Sam 18:1-16*

David pacified by Abigail's gentleness *1 Sam 25:2-42*

Elisha releases besiegers in his power *2 King 6:8-23*

David's song, "Fret not thyself because of evildoers" *Psal 37:23-40*

Envious intrigue puts three Jews in fiery furnace *Dan 3:1-30*

Envious intrigue puts Daniel in lions' den *Dan 6:1-28*

Jesus on treatment of enemies *Mat 5:38-48, Luke 6:27-36*

Jesus on judging others *Mat 7:1-5, Luke 6:37-40*

Jesus' parable of laborers in vineyard *Mat 20:1-16*

Jesus is scourged and mocked *Mat 27:27-31, Mark 15:16-20, John 19:1-16*

Jesus castigates Pharisees and lawyers *Luke 11:37-54*

Jesus' parable of prodigal's elder brother *Luke 15:25-32*

Jesus casts traders out of temple *John 2:13-25*

John's sermon, "God is love" *1 John 4:1-21*

See also anger, envy, hatred, pain, revenge, senses

RESISTANCE

Isaac submits to sacrifice *Gen 22: 1-19*

Deborah defeats invaders *Judg 4: 1-17*

Gideon defeats invaders *Judg 7:1-25*

Samuel resists people's demand for a king *1 Sam 8:1-22*

Asa resists invaders *1 King 15:9-24, 2 Chron 14:1-7*

Isaiah and Hezekiah resist invaders *2 King 18:17-37, 19:1-27, 2 Chron 31:20, 21, 32:1-23, Isa 36:1-22, 37: 1-38*

Jehoshaphat resists invaders *2 Chron 20:1-32*

Esther resists persecution of her people *Esther 3:1-15, 4:1-17*

Ezekiel's vision of an army from dry bones *Ezek 37:1-14*

Jesus teaches disciples how to bind the strong man *Mat 12:22-30, Mark 3:22-30*

Jesus denounces scribes and Pharisees *Mat 23:1-39, John 8:33-59*

Peter and John insist on preaching *Acts 4:24-37*

Paul on Spirit vs. flesh *Rom 8:1-39*

Paul's teaching to put off old man, put on new *Col 3:1-17*

See also disease, opposition, prevention, rebellion, revolution

RESOLUTION

Abraham begins his search for promised land *Gen 11:31, 32, 12:1-9*

Joseph solves Egyptian king's problem *Gen 41:1-46*

Moses' reluctance to lead overcome by God *Exod 3:9-12*

Moses' decision supported by two miracles *Exod 4:1-9*

Caleb's advice to enter promised land refused *Num 13:1-33, 14:1-11, 23-39, Deut 1:19-38*

Moses urges firm choice *Deut 30: 11-20*

Joshua repeats the demand of Moses to choose *Josh 24:1-25*

Ruth remains loyal to Naomi and her God *Ruth 1:1-22*

David refuses Saul's armor and depends on God *1 Sam 17:17-37*

David promises to build a house for God *2 Sam 7:1-29*

Elisha decides to follow Elijah *1 King 19:19-21*

David's charge to Solomon *1 Chron 22:6-19, 23:1, 28:2-10, 20*

Jehoshaphat and people resist invasion *2 Chron 20:1-32*

Zerubbabel proclaims rebuilding of temple *Ezra 1:1-11*

Nehemiah resolves to repair the wall *Neh 4:1-23*

Esther decides to risk all to protect her people *Esther 5:1-14*

Job remains loyal despite troubles *Job 1:13-22, 2:1-10*

David's song, "The Lord is my shepherd" *Psal 23:1-6*

Jeremiah in prison buys a field in Israel *Jer 32:2, 6-27, 37-44*

David and Hebrew boys refuse king's portion and eat pulse *Dan 1:1-21*

Hebrews refuse to worship image *Dan 3:1-30*

Daniel refuses to stop praying to God *Dan 6:1-28*

Malachi urges tithing *Mal 3:10, 4: 1, 2*

Disciples follow Jesus immediately *Mat 4:17-22, 9:9, Mark 1:14-20, Luke 5:1-11, John 1:35-42*

Jesus on seeking God first *Mat 6: 25-34, Luke 12:22-34*

Jesus admonishes Peter *Mat 16: 22-28, Mark 8:31-38, Luke 9:20-27*

Jesus tells how harder cases are healed *Mat 17:14-21, Mark 9:14-29, Luke 9:37-43*

Jesus heals persistent Bartimaeus *Mat 20:29-34, Mark 10:46-52*

Jesus enters Jerusalem for last time to face enemies *Mat 21:1-11, 14-17, Mark 11:1-11, Luke 19:29-44, John 12:12-19*

Peter vows never to deny Jesus *Mat 26: 31-35, Mark 14: 27-31, Luke 22: 31-34, John 13: 36-38*

Jesus' instruction to preach and heal *Luke 10: 1-16, Mark 16: 15-18*

Jesus' parable of faithful steward *Luke 12: 41-48*

Jesus' parable of door shut by Master *Luke 13: 22-30*

Jesus charges Peter, "Feed my sheep" *John 21: 12-19*

Peter and John speak the word with boldness *Acts 4: 1-23*

Paul's teaching to think on good things *Phil 4: 1-23*

Paul's teaching to put on new man *Col 3: 1-17*

John's advice to seven churches *Rev 1: 4-20, 2: 1-29, 3: 1-22*

See also loyalty, perseverance, purpose, steadfastness

RESPONSIBILITY

God creates man in his image, with dominion *Gen 1: 26, 27*

Cain asks, "Am I my brother's keeper?" *Gen 4: 1-16*

Abraham is willing to sacrifice his son *Gen 22: 1-19*

Abraham entrusts his servant to find a wife for Isaac *Gen 24: 1-67*

Joseph entrusted with preserving all Egypt *Gen 41: 1-46*

Moses accepts duty to release his people from Egypt *Exod 3: 1-18*

Aaron lists God's promises to faithful *Lev 26: 1-20*

Moses sets chosen people apart as God's own *Deut 7: 6-11*

Moses insists on their choice of good or evil *Deut 30: 11-20*

Joshua offers same choice *Josh 24: 1-25*

Saul declared unfit to be king *1 Sam 15: 7-26*

Jehoshaphat learns that the battle is God's *2 Chron 20: 1-32*

David's song, "God is our refuge" *Psal 46:1-11*

David's song, "Let the redeemed of the Lord say so" *Psal 107: 1-43*

Ezekiel's vision of God's care for his flock *Ezek 34: 1-31*

Hosea's vision of God's care for his child *Hos 11: 1-4*

Zechariah's vision of good supplied by two anointed *Zech 4: 1-14*

Malachi urges tithing *Mal 3: 10, 4: 1, 2*

Jesus on seeking God first *Mat 6: 25-34*

Jesus' parable of mote and beam *Mat 7: 1-5, Luke 6: 37-42*

Jesus sends disciples to heal and preach *Mat 9: 36-38, 10: 1-42, Mark 3: 13-21, Luke 9: 1-6*

Jesus on "Who is my mother? . . . my brethren?" *Mat 12:46-50*

Jesus' parable of unmerciful debtor *Mat 18: 23-35*

Jesus' parable of two sons ordered to work *Mat 21:28-32*

Jesus' teaching to disciples on their duties *Mat 28: 16-20, Mark 16: 15-18*

Jesus sends 70 to heal and preach *Luke 10: 1-24*

Jesus' parable of good Samaritan *Luke 10: 25-37*

Jesus' parable of rich man and bigger barns *Luke 12: 15-21*

Jesus' parable of watchful servants *Luke 12: 35-40*

Jesus' parable of barren fig tree *Luke 13: 6-9*

Jesus' parable of servant who serves before he sups *Luke 17: 7-10*

Jesus on his great works having source in the Father *John 5:17-47*

Jesus charges Peter, "Feed my sheep" *John 21:12-19*

Peter and John speak word with boldness *Acts 4: 1-23*

Paul on charity *1 Cor 13: 1-13*

Paul on faithfulness in ministry *2 Cor 6:1-18*

Paul's teaching about thinking on good things *Phil 4: 1-23*

Paul's sermon "put on the new man" *Col 3: 1-17*

Paul's advice to disciple *2 Tim 3: 1-17*

See also authority, cause, duty, morality, trust

REST

God rested on seventh day of creation *Gen 2: 1-4*

Elijah rests under juniper tree *1 King 19:1-8*

Shunammite builds a room for Elisha to rest in *2 King 4: 8-16*

Isaiah's vision of a quiet habitation *Isa 33: 20-24*

Ezekiel's vision of God's care while his flock rests *Ezek 34: 1-31*

Angels minister to Jesus after temptation *Mat 4: 1-11, Luke 4: 1-13*

Jesus calms storm *Mat 8:23-27, Mark 4:35-41, 6:45-52, Luke 8:22-25, John 6: 21*

Jesus heals insane Gadarene who then sits quietly at his feet *Mat 8: 28-34, Mark 5: 1-20, Luke 8: 26-39*

At Gethsemane Jesus refreshes himself with prayer but his disciples keep falling asleep *Mat 26: 30, 36-46, Mark 14: 26, 32-42, Luke 22: 39-46*

See also death, peace, sabbath, sleep

RESTORATION

Noah after the flood receives the covenant *Gen 9: 1-17*

Zelophehad's daughters are restored their inheritance *Num 27: 1-11, 36: 5-13*

Moses reviews restoration of Israel to freedom after slavery in Egypt *Deut 32: 1-47*

Joshua leads over Jordan to promised land *Josh 3: 1-17*

Jeroboam's hand withered and healed *1 King 12: 32, 33, 13: 1-10*

Elijah restores widow's son *1 King 17: 17-24*

Job's possessions restored *Job 42: 1-17*

David's song, "Bless the Lord, O my soul" *Psal 103: 1-22*

Jeremiah foretells release from Babylon captivity *Jer 29: 8-14, 31: 1-14, 31-34*

Jesus' parable of lost sheep *Mat 18: 12-14, Luke 15: 1-7*

Jesus' body is restored *Mat 28:1-10, Mark 16:1-11, Luke 24:1-12, John 20:1-18*

Jesus restores son to widow of Nain *Luke 7: 11-17*

Jesus parable of prodigal son *Luke 15: 11-24*

Jesus' resurrection proves ours *1 Cor 15:1-58*

See also decay, healing, loss, new, regeneration, renewal, repair

RESULT

God finds his creation good *Gen 1: 26, 27, 31*

Man created from dust proves sinful *Gen 2: 6-8, 3: 6-24*

Jacob wrestles with angel and Esau forgives him *Gen 32: 1-32, 33: 1-11*

Moses provides manna and quail *Exod 16: 1-36, Num 11: 1-15, 31, 32*

Moses provides water from a rock *Exod 17: 1-7, Num 20: 1-13*

Gideon defeats enemy host with 300 men *Judg 7: 1-25*

David relies on proven things instead of Saul's armor for success *1 Sam 17: 17-52*

Solomon offers to divide the baby *1 King 3: 16-28*

Asa's foot disease fatal because he did not turn to God *2 Chron 16: 11-14*

David's song, "The Lord is my shepherd" *Psal 23: 1-6*

Ezekiel's vision of claim of heredity *Ezek 18: 1-32*

Malachi urges tithing *Mal 3: 10, 4: 1, 2*

Jesus' teaching to seek God first *Mat 6: 25-34, Luke 12: 22-34*

Jesus' parable of building upon rock and sand *Mat 7: 24-27, Luke 6: 48, 49*

Charge to disciples to preach and heal *Mat 10: 5-42, 28: 16-20, Mark 6: 7-13, 16: 15-18, Luke 9: 1-6*

Jesus' parable of the unwilling friend *Luke 11: 5-13*

Jesus' parable of rich man and bigger barns *Luke 12: 15-21*

Jesus' parable of the judge and widow *Luke 18: 1-8*

Seventy disciples return and report success *Luke 10:1-24*

Peter's shadow heals sick *Acts 5: 12-16*

Paul starts a church at Antioch *Acts 11: 19-26*

Paul preaches and then demonstrates by healing Eutychus *Acts 20: 7-12*

James on being doers not hearers only *Jas 1: 1-27*

See also cause, fruits, harvest, healing, reaping

RESURRECTION

Elijah raises widow's son *1 King 17: 17-24*

Elisha raises Shunammite's son *2 King 4:8-37*

Ezekiel's vision of the resurrection of dry bones *Ezek 37: 1-14*

Jesus raises Jairus' daughter *Mat 9: 18, 19, 23-26, Mark 5: 22-24, 35-43, Luke 8: 41, 42, 49-56*

Jesus foretells his death and resurrection *Mat 16: 21-28, 17: 22, 23, 20: 17-19, Mark 8: 31-38, 9: 30-32, 10: 32-34, Luke 9: 20-27, 43-45, 18: 31-34, 19: 47, 48, John 12: 20-30*

Jesus communicates with Moses and Elijah *Mat 17:1-13, Mark 9:2-13, Luke 9: 28-36*

Jesus himself is resurrected *Mat 28: 1-8, Mark 16: 1-8, Luke 24: 1-12, John 20: 1-10*

Jesus raises son of widow of Nain *Luke 7: 11-17*

Jesus' parable of temple to be raised in three days *John 2: 19-22*

Jesus raises Lazarus four days after death *John 11: 1-46*

Lazarus observed by the curious at supper *John 1: 55-57, 12: 1, 2, 9-11*

Thomas confirms resurrection of Jesus' body *John 20:24-29*

Peter on resurrection *Acts 2: 14-47*

Paul's teaching that Christ's resurrection proves ours *1 Cor 15:1-58*

See also body, death, life, Easter, flesh, immortality

RETALIATION

Sarah causes Hagar to be cast out *Gen 21: 1-8*

Jacob expects his brother to retaliate *Gen 32: 1-32, 33: 1-11*

His brethren expect Joseph to retaliate *Gen 43: 1, 2, 45: 1-11, 25-28*

Moses does not retaliate but heals his sister *Num 12: 1-16*

Eye for eye, tooth for tooth and its opposite *Exod 21: 23-25, Mat 5: 38*

David is prevented from retaliation by Abigail *1 Sam 25: 2-42*

Peter retaliates with sword, Jesus heals cut ear *Luke 22: 50, 51*

Ananias heals Saul, the persecutor of Christians *Acts 9: 10-22*

Idol silversmith contends with Paul *Acts 19: 23-29*

See also hatred, injury

RETIREMENT

Jacob prophesies the future of his twelve sons *Gen 49:1-28, Deut 33: 1-29*

Moses' farewell address *Deut 30: 11-20*

Elijah considers giving up *1 King 19: 1-8*

See also age

RETREAT

See retirement, struggle

REUNION

Lot escapes Sodom and rejoins Abraham *Gen 19: 1, 15-29*

Jacob returns and meets his brother *Gen 32: 1-32, 33: 1-11*

Joseph united to his brethren again *Gen 43: 1, 2, 45: 1-11, 25-28*

Jacob and his children join Joseph in Egypt *Gen 45: 25-28, 46: 2-7*

People cross Jordan to re-enter promised land *Josh 3: 1-17*

Jeremiah promises restoration of Israel *Jer 29: 8-14, 31: 1-14, 31-34*

Jesus returns Jairus' daughter to her parents *Mat 9: 18, 19, 23-26, Mark 5: 22-24, 35-43, Luke 8: 41, 42, 49-56*

Widow of Nain receives her raised son *Luke 7: 11-17*

Jesus' parable of prodigal son *Luke 15: 11-24*

Risen Jesus joins disciples in Galilee
John 21: 1-14

See also atonement, pardon, reconciliation, reformation

REVELATION

Abraham called by God to find the
promised land *Gen 11: 31, 32, 12:
1-9*
Jacob's dream of angels on ladder
Gen 28: 10-22
The solution to famine revealed to
Joseph *Gen 41: 1-46*
Moses sees God's nature at burning
bush *Exod 3: 1-18*
The nature of fear and sickness is
revealed to Moses *Exod 4: 1-9*
The nature of law is revealed to
Moses *Exod 20: 1-19, Deut 5: 1-
24*
God reveals himself to Samuel *1 Sam
3:1-10*
God talks with Solomon in a dream
1 King 3: 5-15, 2 Chron 1: 7-12
Nature of God revealed to Elijah on
mount *1 King 19: 9-13*
Job hears the voice of thunder *Job
38: 1-41*
Isaiah foretells the coming of Mes-
siah *Isa 7: 10-16, 9: 2-7*
Isaiah sees God's nature as creator
and saviour *Isa 45: 1-13, 18-25*
Ezekiel sees equity of God's dealing
Ezek 18: 1-32
Daniel reads handwriting on wall
Dan 5: 1-31
Jesus heals unclean spirit of man
who recognized the Christ *Mark
1: 21-28, Luke 4: 33-37*
Coming birth of Messiah announced
to Mary *Luke 1: 26-38*
Peter convinced by first revelation
of Jesus' power *Luke 5: 1-11*
Jesus as the light of the world *John
1: 1-14, 8: 12-32*
Jesus says knowing the truth will
free *John 8: 12-32*
Jesus describes the unity and eter-
nity of Christ *John 8: 12-59*
Jesus promises to send Holy Ghost
John 14: 1-31
Paul's vision of Jesus *Acts 9: 1-9*
Paul reveals his inner self *2 Cor
12: 1-19*

John's revelation of new heaven and
earth, also the tree of life *Rev
21: 1-27, 22: 1-21*

See also discovery, God, light,
prophet, reason

REVENGE

See retaliation

REVERENCE

See fear, worship

REVERSAL

After complete creation, Lord God
begins again by making man from
dust *Gen 2: 6-8*
Because Joseph resists his master's
wife he is thrown into prison *Gen
39: 1-20*
Caleb and Joshua urge entry into
promised land but people wait 40
years *Num 13: 1-33, 14: 1-11, 23-
39, Deut 1: 19-38*
Balak hires Balaam to curse Israel
but he blesses them *Num 22:1-41,
23: 1-30, 24: 1-25*
Daughters of Zelophehad sue for
their lost inheritance *Num 27: 1-
11, 36: 5-13*
Joshua fails to take city of Ai—sin
uncovered *Josh 7: 1-26, 8: 14-21*
David's moral fall after victory
2 Sam 11:1-27
Asa dies after turning from God to
physicians *2 Chron 16: 11-14*
Elisha besieged by army, ends war
2 King 6:8-23
Job's good fortune reversed *Job 1:
13-22, 2:1-10*
David's song, "Fret not because of
evildoers" *Psal 37:23-40*
David's song, "Why art thou cast
down, O my soul?" *Psal 42:1-11*
Daniel does good work but is thrown
in lions' den *Dan 6:1-28*
Jesus heals boy where disciples fail
*Mat 17:14-21, Mark 9:14-29, Luke
9:37-43*
Jesus' parable of unmerciful debtor
Mat 18:23-35
Jesus overcomes the crucifixion,
reversed by resurrection *Mat 28:
1-8, Mark 16:1-8, Luke 24:1-12,
John 20:1-10*

Jesus threatened but escapes *Luke 4:28-31*

Jesus' parable of unwilling friend *Luke 11:5-13*

Jesus' parable of the unjust steward *Luke 16:1-14*

Jesus' parable of rich man and beggar *Luke 16:19-31*

Jesus' parable of judge and widow *Luke 18:1-8*

Saul persecutes Christians until converted *Acts 9:1-9*

See also change, failure, magnetism, repel

REVIVAL

See awakening, renewal

REVOLUTION

Moses leads people to freedom *Exod 11:4-10, 12:1-14, 21-41, Deut 16:1-22*

Sun and moon stand still in their orbits *Josh 10:6-15*

Gideon revolts against Midianites *Judg 6:19-40, 7:1-25*

Jeremiah foretells release from captivity *Jer 29:8-14, 31:1-14, 31-34*

Sermon on Mount preaches new concepts:
on treatment of enemies *Mat 5:38-48, Luke 6:27-36*
on charity in secret *Mat 6:1-4*
on material things *Mat 6:25-34, Luke 12:22-34*
on the Golden Rule *Mat 7:12-14, Luke 6:41, 42*

Jesus heals without medicine *Mat 8:14-17, Mark 1:29-34*

Jesus walks on water *Mat 14:22-33, John 6:15-21*

Jesus eliminates time and talks with Moses and Elias *Mat 17:1-13, Mark 9:2-13, Luke 9:28-36*

Jesus castigates the ruling class *Mat 23:1-39, Luke 11:37-54, John 8:33-59*

Rulers are successful in crucifying Jesus but resurrection causes revolt to flame again *Mat 27:32-56, 28:1-8, 16-18, Acts 4:24-37*

Jesus' parable of new wine in old bottles *Luke 5:36-39*

Jesus raises the dead *Luke 7:11-17*

Jesus instructs his followers *Luke 10:1-24*

Rulers plan to stop the revolution *John 11:47-54*

Peter and John refuse to stop preaching *Acts 4:1-23*

Paul seized and imprisoned for doctrines *Acts 22:1-30*

James on equality of man *Jas 2:1-13*

John's sermon on "God is love" *1 John 4:1-21*

See also freedom, government, orbit, rebellion

REWARD

Enoch walks with God and is translated *Gen 5:18, 21-24, Heb 11:5*

Noah rewarded with a covenant *Gen 9:1-17*

For his faith in God Abraham gets a son *Gen 21:1-8*

Joseph is made governor of Egypt *Gen 41:1-46*

The good get sure rewards for obedience *Deut 28:1-14*

Caleb gets his share of Canaan *Josh 14:6-15*

Ruth's faithfulness rewarded *Ruth 2:1-23, 4:13-22*

David is made king of Judah and Israel *2 Sam 2:1-4, 5:1-5*

Solomon gives the baby to the unselfish mother *1 King 3:16-28*

Elijah is translated over death *2 King 2:1-11*

Gehazi accepts the reward refused by Elisha *2 King 5:15-27*

Mordecai is promoted after persecution *Esther 8:1-8*

Job restored to prosperity *Job 42:1-17*

David's song, "the happiness of the godly" *Psal 1:1-6*

David's song, "Bless the Lord, O my soul" *Psal 103:1-22*

The poor man who saved the city is forgotten *Eccl 9:13-18*

Daniel's authority increased after lions' den *Dan 6:1-28*

The Beatitudes, rewards for Christian qualities *Mat 5:1-12, Luke 6:17-26, 36*

Jesus heals woman with issue of

blood twelve years *Mat 9:20-22, Mark 5:25-34, Luke 8:43-48*

Peter commended for acknowledging Jesus is Christ *Mat 16:13-20, Mark 8:27-30, Luke 9:18-21*

Jesus' parable of laborers in the vineyard *Mat 20:1-16*

Bartimaeus' persistence rewarded *Mat 20:29-34, Mark 10:46-52*

Jesus' parable of sheep and goats *Mat 25:31-46*

Jesus' parable of the talents *Mat 25:14-30, Luke 19:11-28*

Jesus' victory over death followed by ascension *Mark 16:19, 20, Luke 24:50-53, Acts 1:6-12*

Mary's purity rewarded *Luke 1: 26-38*

Jesus' parable of the prodigal's elder brother *Luke 15:25-32*

See also devil, excellence, goodness, punishment, service, wage

RHETORIC

See eloquence, language, speech

RICHES

Abraham's property grows, Lot's too *Gen 13:1-18*

Isaac's holdings increase *Gen 26: 12-31*

Jacob and Esau both prosperous *Gen 33:1-11*

Joseph becomes master of Egypt and his part of the world's food supply *Gen 42:1-8*

Women permitted to inherit estate *Num 27:1-11, 36:5-13*

Israel prosperous enough to build temple *1 King 6:1-38, 7:1-51, 2 Chron 3:1-17, 4:1-22, 5:1-14*

Hezekiah shows all his treasure to Babylonians *2 King 20:12-21, Isa 39:1-8*

Job loses all his possessions *Job 1: 13-22, 2:1-10*

David's song, "the earth is the Lord's" *Psal 24:1-10*

The values of wisdom *Prov 3:13-26, 4:1-13, 8:1-36*

The vanity of human things *Eccl 1:1-18, 2:1-26*

Jesus describes true treasures *Mat 6:19-21*

Jesus tells how to regard material things *Mat 6:25-34, Luke 12:22-34*

Jesus tells rich young ruler how to have eternal life *Mat 19:16-30, Mark 10:17-31, Luke 18:18-30*

Jesus' parable of rich man and bigger barns *Luke 12:15-21*

Jesus' parable of rich man and beggar *Luke 16:19-31*

Jesus' visit to Zacchaeus who gives away part of his fortune *Luke 19:1-10*

Jesus heals nobleman's son *John 4: 46-54*

Jesus tells the source of his great works *John 5:17-47*

Paul converts a rich woman *Acts 16:7-15*

See also abundance, prosperity, treasure, wealth

RIGHTEOUSNESS

Enoch "walked with God" *Gen 5: 18, 21-24, Heb 11:5*

Noah promised safety because he was righteous *Gen 6:5-22*

Abraham asks about deliverance by righteousness *Gen 18:20-33*

Moses makes righteousness into laws *Exod 20:1-19, Deut 5:1-24*

Aaron wears Urim and Thummim of office as priest *Exod 28:29-36*

Jehoshaphat's good reign of reform *2 Chron 17:1-13, 19:4-11*

Josiah's good reign, idolatry destroyed *2 King 23:1-22, 2 Chron 34:1-8, 29-33*

Job's integrity tested *Job 1:13-22, 2:1-10*

David's song of the happiness of the righteous *Psal 1:1-6*

David's song on the safety of the godly *Psal 121:1-8*

The virtuous woman described *Prov 31:1-31*

Jesus' parable of builders on rock or sand *Mat 7:24-27, Luke 6:48, 49*

Jesus explains why he eats with publicans and sinners *Mat 9:10-13, Mark 2:13-17, Luke 5:27-32*

Jesus casts traders out of temple *Mat 21:12, 13, Mark 11:15-17, Luke 19:45, 46, John 2:13-25*

Jesus forgives sin before healing paralysis *Mark 2:1-12, Luke 5: 17-26*

Jesus' parable of Pharisee and publican *Luke 18:9-14*

Jesus urges impotent man he healed to sin no more *John 5:1-16*

See also character, conscience, justice

RIGHTS

God creates man with dominion *Gen 1:26, 27*

Freedom from bondage is God's will *Exod 3:9-12*

Rights of women to inheritance *Num 27:1-11, 36:5-13*

Moses offers choice of good or evil *Deut 30:11-20*

Three Jews in fiery furnace insist on right to worship *Dan 3:1-30*

Daniel and right to worship *Dan 6:1-28*

Jesus on the Golden Rule for actions *Mat 7:12-14, Luke 6:41, 42*

Jesus on keeping the sabbath *Mat 12:1-13, Mark 3:1-5, Luke 6:6-11*

Jesus' parable of laborers in vineyard and rights to just pay *Mat 20:1-16*

Jesus on the right to sit by his side *Mat 20:20-28, Mark 10:35-45*

Jesus' right to fair trial *Mat 27:1, 2, 11-14, Mark 15:1-5, Luke 23:1-5, John 18:28-38*

Jesus' parable of prodigal's right to use property *Luke 15:11-24*

Peter permits uncircumcised Gentile to join church *Acts 10:1-48, 11: 1-18*

James on the equality of man *Jas 2:1-13*

John on those who have rights to the tree of life *Rev 22:1-21*

Jesus' healings and the right to good health (*See* Part II, Jesus Christ: Great Works)

See also equality, freedom, liberty, man, woman

RIPENESS

God made man in his image *Gen 1:26, 27*

Enoch walked with God and was not *Gen 5:18, 21-24, Heb 11:5*

Moses ready for revelation of God *Exod 3:1-18*

Moses on Mt. Sinai for Ten Commandments *Exod 19:1-9, 20:1-19, Deut 4:1-15, 5:1-24*

Aaron's rod blossoms *Num 17:1-11*

Angel announces Samson's coming birth to his mother *Judg 13:1-25*

Angel announces Samuel's coming birth to his mother *1 Sam 1:1-28*

Elijah is translated by ascension *2 King 2:1-11*

Elisha takes on the mantle of Elijah *2 King 2:12-15*

Isaiah prophesies the coming of Messiah *Isa 7:10-16, 9:2-7*

Jesus' parable of the sower *Mat 13: 3-23, Mark 4:1-20, Luke 8:4-15*

Jesus' parable of wheat and tares *Mat 13:24-30, 36-43*

Jesus withers fig tree without fruit *Mat 21:18-22, Mark 11:12-14, 20-24*

Jesus at Gethsemane *Mat 26:30, 36-46, Mark 14:26, 32-42, Luke 22: 39-46*

Jesus' parable of seed, blade, ear *Mark 4:26-29*

Jesus' ascension *Mark 16:19, 20, Luke 24:50-53, Acts 1:6-12*

At twelve years, Jesus astounds rabbis *Luke 2:41-52*

Jesus on fields white to harvest *John 4:31-38*

John's vision of new heaven and earth *Rev 21:1-27*

John's vision of tree of life with twelve fruits *Rev 22:1-21*

See also maturity, perfection, readiness

RITUAL

Abraham almost sacrifices his son *Gen 22:1-19*

Aaron attempts atonement through the scapegoat *Lev 16:1-28*

Wise men start custom of Christmas gift giving *Mat 2:1-12*

Jesus puts Commandments on mental basis *Mat 5:21-37, Mark 9:38-50*

Jesus explains why his disciples do not fast *Mat 9:14-17, Mark 2: 18-22, Luke 5:33-39*

Pharisees object to Jesus' disciples eating corn on sabbath *Mat 12: 1-8, Mark 2:23-28, Luke 6:1-5*

Pharisees object to healing on sabbath *Mat 12:9-13, Mark 3:1-5, Luke 6:6-11*

Jesus reproves Pharisees for hypocrisy *Mat 23:1-39, Mark 12:38-40, Luke 20:45-47, John 8:33-59*

Jesus establishes communion sacrament *Mat 26:26-29, Mark 14:22-25, Luke 22:14-30, 1 Cor 11:23-25*

Jesus' parable of new wine in old bottles *Luke 5:36-39*

Jesus' teaching that God is Spirit and must be worshipped in spirit and in truth *John 4:1-30, 39-42*

Jesus heals the man waiting for an angel to stir the pool *John 5:1-16*

See also church, hypocrisy, idolatry, Pharisee, worship

RIVER

Rivers of Eden *Gen 2:9-17*

People cross over Jordan dry shod *Josh 3:1-17*

Elijah divides Jordan to cross over *2 King 2:1-11*

Elisha repeats miracle *2 King 2:12-15*

Ezekiel's vision of holy waters flowing outward to encompass the universe *Ezek 47:1-12*

John the Baptist at Jordan *Mat 3:1-12, Mark 1:1-8, Luke 3:1-18*

Baptism of Jesus by John in Jordan *Mat 3:13-17, Mark 1:9-11, Luke 3:21, 22*

The river of life *Rev 21:1-27*

See also water

ROCK

Moses strikes water from rock in wilderness *Exod 17:1-7, Num 20:1-13*

Moses talks with God on top of Mt. Sinai *Exod 19:1-9, Deut 4:1-15*

Joshua sets up twelve stones as a memorial for crossing Jordan into Promised Land *Josh 4:1-24*

Elijah communicates with God on mount *1 King 19:9-13*

David's song, "I will lift up mine eyes unto the hills" *Psal 121:1-8*

Isaiah's vision, "Look unto the rock" *Isa 51:1-12*

Micah's vision of mountain of the Lord's house *Mic 4:1-8, 13, Isa 2:1-5*

Jesus' parable of builders on rock or sand *Mat 7:24-27, Luke 6:48, 49*

Jesus' parable of sower on stony ground *Mat 13:3-23, Mark 4:1-20, Luke 8:4-15*

Jesus on mount of transfiguration *Mat 17:1-13, Mark 9:2-13, Luke 9:28-36*

Jesus' body placed in tomb of rock *Mat 27:57-66, Mark 15:42-57, Luke 23:50-56, John 19:31-42*

Jesus led to brow of hill to be cast down, escapes *Luke 4:28-31*

See also conviction, hardness, protection, stone, strength

ROD

Moses throws down his rod at God's command *Exod 4:1-9*

Aaron's rod blossoms and bears almonds *Num 17:1-11*

Egyptian sorcerers' rods swallowed up by Aaron's rod *Exod 7:1-12*

Moses holds rod over Red Sea *Exod 14:5-31*

Moses smites rock with rod and draws water *Exod 17:1-7, Num 20:1-13*

David's song, "Thy rod and thy staff they comfort me" *Psal 23:1-6*

Isaiah's vision of Messiah as rod out of the stem of Jesse *Isa 11:1-12*

The vision by John of the child who will rule with a rod of iron *Rev 12:1-17*

See also authority, discipline, offspring, power, punishment

ROMAN

Jesus heals centurion's servant *Mat 8:5-13, Luke 7:1-10*

Jesus sends Peter for tribute money *Mat 17:24-27*

Jesus examined before Pilate *Mat 27:1, 2, 11-14, Mark 15:1-5, Luke 23:1-5, John 18:28-38*

Jesus scourged and mocked by soldiers *Mat 27:27-32, Mark 15:16-20, John 19:1-16*

Priests pay guards to give false report of resurrection *Mat 28: 11-15*

Before Jesus, guards fall backwards *John 18:4-6*

Paul's sea voyage to Rome and shipwreck *Acts 27:1-44*

Paul's letters to Romans before arrival *Rom 15:1-21, 8:1-39*

See also city, soldier

RUIN

See destruction

RULE

Joseph appointed governor by Pharaoh *Gen 41:1-46*

Moses formulates the basis of all law *Exod 20:1-19, Deut 5:1-21*

Samuel resists people's demand for a king as ruler *1 Sam 8:1-22*

Samuel anoints Saul as king *1 Sam 10:1-8*

Josiah's good reign *2 King 23:1-22, 2 Chron 34:1-8, 29-33*

The coming of Christ's kingdom *Isa 2:1-5, 11:1-12, Mic 4:1-8, 13*

Daniel given increased authority after lions' den *Dan 6:1-28*

Jesus heals daughter of ruler of synagogue *Mat 9:18, 19, 23-26, Mark 5:22-24, 35-43, Luke 8:41, 42, 49-56*

A rich young ruler asks about eternal life *Mat 19:16-30, Mark 10:17-31, Luke 18:18-30*

Pilate asks Jesus if he is "King of the Jews" *Mat 27:1, 2, 11-14, Mark 15:1-5, Luke 23:1-5, John 18:28-38*

Jesus' parable of the good shepherd *John 10:1-18*

See also authority, doctrine, government, guidance, principle

RUTH (one of the judges)

See Part II, Ruth

S

SABBATH

God blesses the seventh day of creation *Gen 2:1-4*

Fourth Commandment of Moses *Exod 20:8-11*

Ezra reads Book of the law on the first day of seventh month *Neh 8:1-12*

Jesus on Son of man as Lord of sabbath *Mat 12:1-8*

Jesus' disciples pluck corn on sabbath *Mat 12:1-8, Mark 2:23-28, Luke 6:1-5*

Jesus heals withered hand on sabbath *Mat 12:9-13, Mark 3:1-5, Luke 6:6-11*

Jesus' body entombed early to avoid burial on the sabbath *Mat 27:57-66, Mark 15:42-57, Luke 23:50-56, John 19:31-42*

See also day, rest, ritual, worship

SACKCLOTH

See mourning, remorse, repentance

SACRAMENT

Abraham plans to sacrifice his beloved son *Gen 22:1-19*

Aaron attempts atonement through the scapegoat *Lev 16:1-28*

Aaron puts on Urim and Thummim of office *Exod 28:29-36*

David anointed by Samuel to be future king *1 Sam 16:1-13*

David's song, "Create in me a clean heart" *Psal 51:1-19*

Zechariah's vision of two anointed ones *Zech 4:1-14*

Baptism of Jesus by John *Mat 3: 13-17, Mark 1:9-11, Luke 3:21, 22*

Jesus anointed by a woman *Mat 26:6-13, Mark 14:3-9, Luke 7:36-50*

Jesus offers bread and wine *Mat 26:26-29, Mark 14:22-25, Luke 22: 14-30*

Jesus crucified *Mat 27:32-56, Mark 15:21-41, Luke 23:26-49, John 19: 17-30*

Jesus' parable of the prodigal son and repentance *Luke 15:11-24*

Jesus changed water to wine at marriage *John 2:1-11*

Jesus washes disciples' feet *John 13:1-20*

Jesus' last breakfast with his disciples *John 21:1-14*

Peter on baptism and resurrection *Acts 2:14-47*

Paul on atonement *Heb 10:1-39*

See also atonement, baptism, communion, marriage, purity, repentance, sacrifice

SACREDNESS

Cain and Abel conflict over sacrifice *Gen 4:1-16*

Moses at the burning bush *Exod 3:1-18*

Moses on Mt. Sinai *Exod 19:1-9, Deut 4:1-15*

Aaron wears Urim and Thummim of office *Exod 28:29-36*

Aaron and sons consecrated to priesthood *Lev 8:1-13*

Solomon builds a temple to God *1 King 6:1-38, 7:1-51, 2 Chron 3: 1-17, 4:1-22, 5:1-14*

He dedicates it *1 King 8:22-66, 2 Chron 6:1-42*

Isaiah's vision of blessed state of new Jerusalem *Isa 65:17-25*

Micah's vision of mountain of the Lord's house *Mic 4:1-8, 13, Isa 2:1-5*

Zechariah's vision of two olive trees *Zech 4:1-14*

Jesus converses with Samaritan at Jacob's well *John 4:1-42*

John's vision of the sealed book *Rev 5:1-14*

John's vision of the holy city foursquare *Rev 21:1-27*

See also consecration, dedication, Eucharist, holiness, sacrament, sacrifice

SACRIFICE

Cain and Abel sacrifice in different ways *Gen 4:1-16*

Abraham tempted to sacrifice Isaac *Gen 22:1-19*

Aaron atones with bull and goats *Lev 16:1-28*

David sacrifices Uriah to obtain his wife *2 Sam 11:1-27*

Jesus dies on the cross for mankind *Mat 27:32-56, Mark 15:21-41, Luke 23:26-49, John 19:17-30*

See also atonement, blood, cross, denial, giving, holiness, lamb, offering

SADNESS

See mourning, sorrow

SAFETY

Noah builds ark of safety to escape flood *Gen 6:5-22*

Jacob promised the safety of God's presence wherever he goes *Gen 28:11-22*

Moses gives people Commandments to protect them *Exod 20:1-19, Deut 5:1-24*

David refuses safety of Saul's armor *1 Sam 17:17-37*

Jehoshaphat advised the battle is God's *2 Chron 20:1-32*

Elisha besieged by army, is protected by angels *2 King 6:8-23*

Nehemiah rebuilds wall of Jerusalem *Neh 4:1-23*

David's song, "The Lord is my shepherd" *Psal 23:1-6*

David's song, "the secret place of the most High" *Psal 91:1-16*

Security of wisdom as strength *Eccl 9:13-18*

Isaiah's reassurance, "Fear not, I am with thee" *Isa 43:1-28, 44:1-24*

Isaiah's advice, "Look unto the rock" *Isa 51:1-12*

Ezekiel's vision of God's care of his flock *Ezek 34:1-31*

Ezekiel's vision of a protective army *Ezek 37:1-14*

Three Jews demonstrate safety in fiery furnace *Dan 3:1-30*

Daniel demonstrates safety in lions' den *Dan 6:1-28*

Jesus and family flee to Egypt and return *Mat 2:13-43, Luke 2:39, 40*

Jesus' parable of builders on rock and sand *Mat 7:24-27, Luke 6: 48, 49*

Jesus saves Peter in water *Mat 14: 22-33, John 6:15-21*

Jesus passing through enemies, delivers himself *Luke 4:28-31*

Paul is saved from shipwreck *Acts 27:1-44*

Eutychus saved from effects of accident *Acts 20:7-12*

See also accident, danger, protection, Saviour, security

SAINT

Enoch "walked with God" *Gen 5: 18, 21-24, Heb 11:5*

Abraham blessed by Melchizedek *Gen 14:8-20, Heb 6:20, 7:1-28*

The Lord talks with Moses *Exod 19:1-9, 33:7-23*

Moses' face concealed by veil *Exod 34:29-35*

Aaron wears Urim and Thummim of office *Exod 38:29, 30*

Aaron's rod blossoms *Num 17:1-11*

Elijah communicates with God *1 King 19:9-13*

Elijah translated *2 King 2:1-11*

Elisha takes Elijah's mantle *2 King 2:12-15*

The virtuous woman *Prov 31:1-31*

Isaiah tells what the Messiah will be like *Isa 53:1-12, 61:1-11, 62:1-12*

Daniel's vision of meeting with Gabriel *Dan 9:21-23, 10:4-21*

Jesus transfiguration *Mat 17:1-13, Mark 9:2-13, Luke 9:28-36*

Man with unclean spirit says he knows Jesus is "the Holy One of God." Jesus heals him *Mark 1:21-28, Luke 4:33-37*

Jesus' ascension *Mark 16:19, 20, Luke 24:50-53, Acts 1:6-12*

Jesus' parable of good Samaritan *Luke 10:25-37*

Jesus restores ear cut off by Peter *Luke 22:50, 51*

Jesus' parable of good shepherd *John 10:1-18*

Paul, Christians' worst enemy, healed by Ananias *Acts 9:10-22*

Paul's cost to establish church *2 Cor 11:21-33*

Paul's sermon, "Come out from among them and be ye separate" *2 Cor 6:1-18*

See also church, consecration, holiness, separation

SALVATION

Noah, the righteous, promised safety *Gen 6:5-22*

Abraham called by God to search for promised land *Gen 11:31, 32, 12:1-9*

Covenant with Abraham renewed with Isaac *Gen 26:1-5*

Salvation dependent on obeying Ten Commandments *Exod 20:1-19, Deut 5:1-24*

Moses gives choice of good or evil *Deut 30:11-20*

David's song, "the happiness of the godly" *Psal 1:1-6*

David's song, "God is our refuge and strength" *Psal 46:1-11*

David's song, "God, the preserver of man" *Psal 121:1-8*

Isaiah's promise of the Messiah *Isa 7:10-16, 9:2-7*

Zephaniah's promise of salvation *Zeph 3:14-17*

Jesus on salvation by deeds not words *Mat 7:21-23, Luke 6:46, 47*

Jesus' parable of lost sheep *Mat 18:12-14, Luke 15:1-7*

Jesus' parable of the sheep and goats *Mat 25:31-46*

Jesus' own salvation, the resurrection *Mat 28:1-8, Mark 16:1-8, Luke 24: 1-12, John 20:1-10*

Jesus' parable of the prodigal son *Luke 15:11-24*

Jesus' parable of unjust steward *Luke 16:1-14*

Zacchaeus restores all he owes *Luke 19:1-10*

Philip promises Ethiopian salvation *Acts 8:26-40*

Paul on spirit versus the flesh *Rom 8:1-39*

Paul on effects of grace *Eph 2:1-22*

Paul on faith as salvation *Heb 11: 1-40*

James' sermon on works as salvation *Jas 2:14-26*

See also Christ, faith, grace, justification, redemption, Saviour, security, sin

SAME

See identity

SAMSON (one of the judges)

See Part II, Samson

SAMUEL (one of the judges)

See Part II, Samuel

SANCTIFICATION

See saint

SAND

Lord God creates Adam from dust *Gen 2: 6-8*
Jesus' parable of builders on rock or sand *Mat 7: 24-27, Luke 6: 48, 49*
Jesus writes in the sand *John 8: 1-11*
Jesus heals blind man and anoints eyes with clay *John 9: 1-41*

See also house, sea

SATAN

Serpent slanders God to Eve *Gen 3: 1-5*
Satan slanders Job to God *Job 1: 1-12*
Satan tempts Jesus *Mat 4: 1-11, Luke 4: 1-13*
Jesus on Satan and healing power *Mat 12: 22-30, Luke 13: 16*
Satan enters into Judas to betray Jesus *Mat 26: 14-16, Mark 14: 10, 11, Luke 22: 1-6*
Jesus foresees Peter possessed by Satan *Luke 22: 31-34*
Jesus sees Satan's fall *John 14: 4-24, Luke 10: 17-20*
Paul on armor against powers of darkness *Eph 6: 10-13*
Peter on the devil as a roaring lion *1 Pet 5: 1-11*
John warns against synogogue of Satan *Rev 2: 8-11*
John sees accuser cast down *Rev 12: 7-17*

See also adversary, devil, enemy, evil

SATISFACTION

Isaac, the child of promise, is born *Gen 21: 1-8*
Covenant with Abraham and Isaac renewed to Jacob *Gen 35 :9-15*
Moses supplies bread, meat and water in the wilderness *Exod 16: 1-36, 17: 1-7, Num 11: 1-15, 31, 32, 20 :1-13*
Aaron atones for sin by sacrifice *Lev 16: 1-28*
Claims of rights of women recognized *Num 27: 1-11, 36: 5-13*
Caleb's reward received at last *Josh 14: 6-15*
Deborah rejoices in God's victory *Judg 5: 1-20*
Hannah at last has a child *1 Sam 1: 1-28*
David's song, "how are the mighty fallen!" *2 Sam 1: 17-27*
Solomon dedicates the temple *1 King 8 :22-66, 2 Chron 6 :1-42*
His deeds are acknowledged by Queen of Sheba *1 King 10:1-12, 2 Chron 9: 1-12*
After building the wall people hear the book of the law *Neh 8: 1-12*
Job's condition is satisfactorily restored *Job 42: 1-17*
David's song, "The Lord is my shepherd" *Psal 23: 1-6*
David's song, "Rejoice in the Lord" *Psal 33: 1-22, 66: 1-20, 100: 1-5*
David's song, "Bless the Lord, O my soul" *Psal 103: 1-22*
David's song, "praise the Lord for his goodness" *Psal 107: 1-43*
Micah's vision of glory of the church *Mic 4: 1-8, 13, Isa 2: 1-5*
John the Baptist sends to Jesus for proof of Christ *Mat 11: 2-19, Luke 7: 18-35*
Jesus feeds 5000—twelve basketsful left over *Mat 14:15-21, Mark 6:35-44, Luke 9: 12-17, John 6: 5-14*
Jesus' parable of rich fool and bigger barns *Luke 12: 15-21*
Jesus' parable of the true vine *John 15: 1-17*
John's vision of new heaven and earth *Rev 21: 1-27*

See also atonement, contentment, debt, fulfillment, retaliation

SAVE

Noah builds ark *Gen 6: 5-22*
Abraham helps Lot escape *Gen 14: 8-20*

Lot protects two angel visitors from mob *Gen 1:14*

Isaac saved from sacrifice by angel *Gen 22: 1-19*

Joseph saves his family from famine *Gen 46: 2-7*

Moses leads people across Red Sea *Exod 14: 5-31*

Deborah saves her country from invasion *Judg 4:1-17*

Gideon expels Midianites *Judg 7: 1-25*

Elisha raises Shunammite's son *2 King 4: 8-37*

Jehoshaphat repels invaders *2 Chron 20:1-32*

Esther saves her people from persecution *Esther 5:1-14*

David's song, "God is our refuge and strength" *Psal 46:1-11*

Isaiah's vision of Messiah as Saviour *Isa 40:1-31, 45:1-13, 18-25, 51:1-12*

Jesus' parables:

wheat and tares *Mat 13:24-30, 36-43*

lost sheep *Mat 18:12-14, Luke 15: 1-7*

sheep and goats *Mat 25:31-46*

good Samaritan *Luke 10:25-37*

temple to be raised in three days *John 2:19-22*

good shepherd *John 10:1-18*

Jesus saves woman taken in adultery *John 8:1-11*

Jesus raises Lazarus after four days *John 11:1-46*

Paul saves Eutychus after fall *Acts 20:7-12*

Paul on salvation by faith *Heb 11: 1-40*

James on salvation by works *Jas 2:14-26*

See also danger, deliverance, healing, protection, rescue, safety, Saviour

SAVIOUR

Abraham rescues his nephew, Lot *Gen 14:8-20*

Joseph saves his brothers from famine *Gen 42:1-8*

Moses saves his people *Deut 32:1-47*

Esther saves her people *Esther 6:1-14, 7:1-10*

David's song, "The Lord is my shepherd" *Psal 23:1-6*

David's song, "God is our refuge and strength" *Psal 46:1-11*

A poor wise man saves his city *Eccl 9:13-18*

Isaiah's vision of Messiah's kingdom *Isa 11:1-12*

Jesus heals withered hand *Mat 12: 9-13, Mark 3:1-5, Luke 6:6-11*

Jesus saves Peter from the waves *Mat 14:22-33, John 6:15-21*

Jesus' parable of lost sheep *Mat 18: 12-14, Luke 15:1-7*

Jesus enters Jerusalem to applause *Mat 21:1-11, 14-17, Mark 11: 1-11, Luke 19:29-44, John 12:12-19*

The Christ, whose son is he? *Mat 22:41-46, Mark 12:35-37, Luke 20: 41-44*

Jesus on signs of Christ's coming *Mat 24:1-41*

Jesus raises son of widow of Nain *Luke 7:11-17*

Jesus' parable of the piece of money *Luke 15:8-10*

Jesus heals nobleman's son of fever *John 4:46-54*

Jesus on Christ *John 7:14-40*

Jesus saves adultress *John 8:1-11*

Jesus' parable of good shepherd *John 10:1-18*

Paul on Jesus is the Messiah *Acts 13:16-52*

Paul on resurrection *1 Cor 15:1-58*

Paul explains why we obey Christ *Heb 2:1-18*

See also Jesus, safety, salvation, save, security

SCARCITY

See abundance, lack, need, poverty, supply

SCIENCE

"Let there be..." God's knowing creates universe *Gen 1:1-31*

Man gives names to everything *Gen 2:18-20*

Moses sees the nature of God at burning bush *Exod 3:1-18*

Moses offers basis of all law *Exod 20:1-19, Deut 5:1-24*

Solomon chooses understanding

above all else   *1 King, 3:5-15,
2 Chron 1:7-12*

To Elijah the nature of God un-
folds   *1 King 19:9-13*

Elisha asks for a double portion of
Elijah's spirit   *2 King 2:1-11*

Job hears the infinite speak to man
Job 38:1-41

The values of wisdom   *Prov 3:13-
26, 4:1-13, 8:1-36*

Jesus lays down laws of Christian
living   *Mat 5:1-12, Luke 6:17-26,
36*

Jesus' parable of builders on rock
or sand   *Mat 7:24-27, Luke 6:48, 49*

Jesus controls elements   *Mat 8:23-27,
Mark 4:35-41, 6:45-52, Luke 8:
22-25*

Jesus' control over time   *Mat 17:1-
13, Mark 9:2-13, Luke 9:28-36*

Jesus' resurrection overcomes death
*Mat 28:1-8, Mark 16:1-8, Luke 24:
1-12, John 20:1-10*

Jesus walks on water   *Mark 14:22-
33, John 6:15-21*

At Jesus' birth laws of human generation are set aside again   *Luke
1:26-38*

At twelve years Jesus talks with
rabbis   *Luke 2:41-52*

Jesus as the light of the world   *John
1:1-14, 8:12-32*

Jesus explains basis of his great
works   *John 5:17-47*

Jesus says truth makes free   *John
8:12-32*

Jesus promises to send the Spirit
of truth   *John 14:1-31*

John's vision of river and tree of
life   *Rev 22:1-21*

See also knowledge, law, truth,
understanding, wisdom

SCOURGE

See punishment

SCRIPTURE

Ten Commandments—first writing
of God's law   *Exod 20:1-19, Deut
5:1-24*

Moses reviews God's care of Israel
Deut 32:1-47

Book of the law read to people
Neh 8:1-12

Daniel interprets handwriting on
wall   *5:1-31*

Jesus' transfiguration shows unity
of gospel, law and prophets   *Mat
17:1-13, Mark 9:2-13, Luke 9:28-36*

At twelve years Jesus astonishes
rabbis with his view of scriptures
Luke 2:41-52

John's vision of sealed book   *Rev
5:1-14*

John's vision of angel with book
Rev 10:1-11

John's vision of his book of prophecy
Rev 22:1-21

Jesus' contributions to scripture
(*See* Part II, Jesus Christ)

Disciples' contributions to scripture
(*See* Part II, James, John, Paul,
Peter, Philip, Stephen)

See also Bible, gospel, logos, testament, word

SEA

Firmament divides waters from
waters   *Gen 1:6-10, 20-22*

The flood lifts up the ark   *Gen 7:
1-24*

People pass throught the Red Sea
Exod 14:5-31

David's song, "Whither shall I flee
from thy presence?"   *Psal 139:
1-24*

Ezekiel's vision of the holy waters
Ezek 47:1-12

Jesus calms seas   *Mat 8:23-27, Mark
4:35-41, 6:45-52, Luke 8:22-25, John
6:21*

Swine drowned in sea   *Mat 8:30-34*

Jesus addresses multitude out of
boat on lake   *Mat 13:1, 2, Mark
4:1, 2, Luke 5:1-3*

Jesus walks on sea, Peter tries it
Mat 14:22-33, John 6:15-21

After resurrection, Jesus has breakfast on shore with his disciples
Mat 28:16-18, John 21:1-14

Jesus sees Peter's net filled at sea
Luke 5:1-11, John 21:1-11

Paul shipwrecked on way to Rome
Acts 27:1-44

John's vision of angel with left foot
on sea   *Rev 10:1-11*

See also danger, infinity, ship, water

SEAL

Daniel sealed into lions' den with king's seal *Dan 6:1-28*

John's vision of sealed book *Rev 5:1-14*

See also key, signs, symbols

SEARCH

God calls Abraham to find promised land *Gen 11:31, 32, 12:1-9*

Joseph's brethren come to Egypt to find food *Gen 42:1-8*

Caleb and Joshua scout the land of Canaan *Num 13:1-33, 14:1-11, 23-39, Deut 1:19-38*

Rahab and the spies in Jericho *Josh 2:1-24*

Nehemiah surveys the city *Neh 2:1-20*

Jotham's parable of trees finding a king *Judg 9:1-15*

Job searches for the nature of God *Job 2:11-3, 4:1—37:24*

Jonah tries to find a way to avoid obeying *Jonah 1:1-17, 2:1-10, 3:1-10*

Jesus' parables:

the pearl of great price *Mat 13:45, 46*

the dragnet *Mat 13:47-50*

the lost sheep *Mat 18:12-14, Luke 15:1-7*

the lost coin *Luke 15:8-10*

Jesus heals woman who searched twelve years for healing *Mat 9:20-22, Mark 5:25-34, Luke 8:43-48*

Jesus heals woman bowed together 18 years *Luke 13:11-17*

Jesus heals impotent man who searched 38 years for health *John 5:1-16*

See also healing, scripture, truth

SECOND COMING

Jesus prophesies *Mark 13:5-27, 14:57-62*

Jesus on signs of his coming *Mat 24:1-31*

Jesus' parable of the fig tree leafing *Mat 24:32, 33, Mark 13:28, 29*

Jesus on kingdom of God and second coming *Luke 17:20-37*

Jesus promises to send the "Spirit of truth" *John 14:1-31*

Jesus at ascension promises return *Acts 1:6-12*

Disciples at Pentecost *Acts 2:1-13*

Paul preaches Holy Ghost to Ephesians *Acts 19:1-10*

John's vision of new heaven and earth *Rev 21:1-27*

See also Christ, comforter, Pentecost, truth, understanding

SECRET

A veil conceals Moses' face *Exod 34:29-35*

David's song, "the secret place of most High" *Psal 91:1-16*

Elijah finds God in the still, small voice *1 King 19:9-13*

Jesus on benevolence in secret *Mat 6:1-4*

Jesus on fasting in secret *Mat 6:16-18*

Jesus tells why he speaks in parables *Mat 13:10-17, 34, 35, Mark 4:10-12, 33, 34*

Jesus' parable of leaven hidden in meal *Mat 13:33, Luke 13:20, 21*

Jesus' parable of treasure buried in field *Mat 13:44*

See also key, revelation, seal

SECURITY

Noah builds ark *Gen 6:5-22*

Abraham asks number of righteous needed to deliver city *Gen 18:20-33*

Jacob learns of God's ever-presence *Gen 28:10-22*

Moses is promised God's presence *Exod 3:9-12*

Moses orders people forward through Red Sea *Exod 14:5-31*

David refuses Saul's armor *1 Sam 17:17-37*

Elisha, besieged, knows he is surrounded by defending army *2 King 6:8-23*

Nehemiah repairs wall of Jerusalem *Neh 4:1-23*

Job asks why should the good man suffer *Job 3:1-26*

David's song, the happiness of the godly *Psal 1:1-6*

David's song, "The Lord is my shepherd" *Psal 23:1-6*
David's song, "God is our refuge and strength" *Psal 46:1-11*
David's song, "the secret place" *Psal 91:1-16*
David's song on the safety of the godly *Psal 121:1-8*
David's song, "Whither shall I flee" *Psal 139:1-24*
Is wisdom more secure than strength? *Eccl 9:13-18*
Isaiah's vision of lion and lamb dwelling together *Isa 11:1-12*
Isaiah's vision of a quiet habitation *Isa 33:20-24*
Isaiah's vision, "Comfort ye!" *Isa 40:1-31*
Isaiah's vision, "Fear not" *Isa 43:1-28, 44:1-24*
Daniel in lions' den *Dan 6:1-28*
Zephaniah's vision of salvation promised *Zeph 3:14-17*
Jesus' parables:
builders on rock and sand *Mat 7:24-27, Luke 6:48, 49*
wise virgins who provided oil *Mat 25:1-13*
temple to be rebuilt in three days *John 2:19-22*
the true vine *John 15:1-17*
Jesus controls storms *Mat 8:23-27, Mark 4:35-41, 6:45-52, Luke 8:22-25*
Jesus walks on water *Mat 14:22-33, John 6:15-21*
Jesus tells how to inherit eternal life *Mat 19:16-30, Mark 10:17-31, Luke 10:25-28, 18:18-30*
Paul's sermon on Jesus' resurrection proving ours *1 Cor 15:1-58*
Paul's sermon on qualities that are a Christian's armor *Eph 6:10-17*

See also defense, promise, protection, safety, salvation

SEED

God's covenant with Noah, "Be fruitful, and multiply" *Gen 9:1-17*
Abraham is promised he will bring forth a nation *Gen 15:1-21*
Jesus' parables:
the sower *Mat 13:3-23, Mark 4:1-20, Luke 8:4-15*
the mustard seed *Mat 13:31, 32, Mark 4:30-32, Luke 13:18, 19*

the seed, blade, ear *Mark 4:26-29*

See also children, farming, harvest, reaping, sowing

SEEK

See search

SEER

Abraham called by God to seek promised land *Gen 11:31, 32, 12:1-9*
Jacob learns of God's ever-presence *Gen 28:10-22*
Joseph's dreams of future *Gen 37:1-36, 39:21-23, 40:1-23, 41:1-46*
Moses at burning bush *Exod 3:1-18*
Moses talks with God and receives Ten Commandments *Exod 19:1-9, 20:1-19, Deut 4:1-15, 5:1-21*
A prophet promised *Deut 18:15-22*
Samuel called by God *1 Sam 3:1-10, 19-21*
Samuel anoints David king *1 Sam 16:1-13*
Elijah and the fire of heaven *1 King 18:17-40*
Elijah and the still small voice *1 King 19:9-13*
Elisha takes the mantle of Elijah *2 King 2:12-15*
The values of wisdom *Prov 3:13-26, 4:1-13, 8:1-36*
The vanity of human things *Eccl 1:1-18, 2:1-26*
All mortal events within time not eternity *Eccl 3:1-15*
The calling of Isaiah to speak *Isa 6:1-13*
The prophecy of Messiah *Isa 7:10-16, 9:2-7*
Isaiah's vision of peaceable kingdom *Isa 11:1-12*
Ezekiel's vision of holy waters *Ezek 47:1-12*
Daniel's meeting with angel Gabriel *Dan 9:20-23, 10:4-21*
Micah's vision of the glory of the church *Mic 4:1-8, 13, Isa 2:1-5*
Zechariah's vision of candlestick fed by two olive trees *Zech 4:1-14*
Jesus explains why he speaks in parables *Mat 13:10-17, 34, 35, Mark 4:10-12, 33, 34*

Jesus' parable of wheat and tares
Mat 13:24-30, 36-43

Jesus' parable of the leaven *Mat 13:33, Luke 13:20, 21*

Jesus heals the daughter of the Syrophenician *Mat 15:21-28, Mark 7: 24-30*

Jesus overcomes time *Mat 17:1-13, Mark 9:2-13, Luke 9:28-36*

Jesus foretells his own death and resurrection *Mat 17:22, 23, 20:17-19, 26:20-25, 31-36, Mark 9:30-32, 10:32-34, 14:18-21, Luke 9:43-45, 18:31-34, 19:47, 48, 22:21, 22, John 12:20-50, 13:21-35*

Jesus' parable of Pharisee and publican *Luke 18:9-14*

Jesus' sermon on unity and eternity of Christ *John 8:12-59*

Jesus promises Holy Ghost *John 14:1-31*

John's vision of new heaven and earth *Rev 21:1-27*

See also future, present, prophet, sight

SELECTION

Esau, Isaac's choice, loses blessing to Jacob *Gen 27:1-44*

Joseph appointed governor *Gen 41: 1-46*

Moses selected by God to lead people out *Exod 3:9-12*

Moses charges Joshua with leadership *Deut 31:7-23, Josh 1:1-9*

Samuel anoints David to be king *1 Sam 16:1-13*

Elijah selects Elisha as disciple *1 King 19:19-21*

God calls Isaiah to speak of Messiah *Isa 6:1-13*

Jesus assembles apostles *Mat 4:17-22, Mark 1:14-20, Luke 5:1-11, John 1:35-42*

Jesus points out true treasures *Mat 6:19-21*

Jesus' parable of wheat and tares *Mat 13:24-30, 36-43*

Jesus' parable of pearl of great price *Mat 13:45, 46*

Jesus selects Peter to lead *Mat 16:13-20, Mark 8:27-30, Luke 9:18-21*

Zebedee's wife requests special favors *Mat 20:20-28, Mark 10:35-45*

Jesus' parable of sheep and goats *Mat 25:31-46*

Crowd offered Barabbas or Jesus *Mat 27:15-26, Mark 15:6-15, Luke 23:13-23, John 18:39, 40*

Mary selected to be mother of Jesus *Luke 1:26-38*

Jesus selects impotent man at pool to be healed *John 5:1-16*

Disciples elect Matthias *Acts 1:15-26*

Ananias informed that Paul is a chosen vessel *Acts 9:10-22*

Paul's teaching to put off old man, put on new *Col 3:1-17*

See also choice, election

SELF

Man as God's image *Gen 1:26, 27*

Man from dust *Gen 2:6-8*

Enoch "walked with God; and he was not," self-translated *Gen 5: 18, 21-24, Heb 11:5*

Abram and Sarai receive new natures *Gen 17:1-8, 15-21*

Jacob's name changed to Israel *Gen 32:24-32, 35:9-15*

David's song, "What is man?" *Psal 8:1-9*

David's song, "Create in me a clean heart" *Psal 51:1-19*

David's song, "My soul longeth" *Psal 84:1-12*

Jesus' parable of unclean spirit and seven others *Mat 12:43-45, Luke 11:24-26*

Jesus on the Christ, "whose son is he?" *Mat 22:41-46, Mark 12:35-37, Luke 20:41-49*

Jesus' parable of rich man and bigger barns *Luke 12:15-21*

Jesus' parable of the unjust steward *Luke 16:1-14*

Jesus' parable of the temple to be raised in three days *John 2:19-22*

Jesus' great works have their source in the Father *John 5:17-47*

Jesus is one with the Father *John 10:22-42*

Jesus is the Christ *John 7:14-40*

Jesus on humility *John 13:12-20*

Paul's self-revealings *2 Cor 12:1-19*

James on how to bear our cross *Jas 1: 1-27*

See also ego, I Am, identity, nature

SELF-CONDEMNATION

Adam hides *Gen 3: 6-24*
Jacob wrestles with angel *Gen 32: 24-31*
David repents *2 Sam 12: 1-23*
Jonah repents *Jonah 1: 1-17, 2: 1-10*
Jesus heals Gadarene of insanity *Mat 8: 28-34, Mark 5: 1-20, Luke 8: 26-39*
Peter denies Jesus *Mat 26: 57, 58, 69-75, Mark 14: 66-72, Luke 22: 54-62, John 18:13-18, 25-27*
Judas hangs himself *Mat 27: 3-10, Acts 1: 15-20*
Jesus heals man with unclean spirit *Mark 1: 21-28, Luke 4: 33-37*
Jesus' parable of two debtors *Luke 7: 36-50*
Jesus' parable of the prodigal son *Luke 15: 11-24*
Jesus' parable of the Pharisee and publican *Luke 18: 9-14*
Zacchaeus restores what he took *Luke 19: 1-10*
Paul's self-revealings and thorn in the flesh *2 Cor 12:1-19*

See also guilt, judgment, regret, repentance

SELF-RIGHTEOUSNESS

Cain asks, "Am I my brother's keeper?" *Gen 4: 1-16*
Samuel declares Saul unfit *1 Sam 15: 7-26*
Uzziah's pride results in destruction *2 Chron 26: 1-23*
Isaiah's vision of fall of Babylon *Isa 14: 4-8, 12-17, 25-27*
Jesus' parable of the laborers in the vineyard *Mat 20: 1-16*
Jesus castigates Pharisees and lawyers *Mat 23: 1-39, Mark 12: 38-40, Luke 11: 37-54, John 8: 33-59*
Jesus' parable of the prodigal's elder brother *Luke 15: 25-32*
Jesus' parable of the Pharisee and publican *Luke 18: 9-14*
Jesus saves woman taken in adultery *John 8: 1-11*

Paul persecutes the Christians *Acts 8: 1-4, 9: 1-9*

See also leprosy, Pharisee

SENSES

Adam and Eve eat fruit of tree of knowledge of good and evil *Gen 3: 1-7*
Esau sells his birthright for pottage *Gen 25: 24-34*
Jacob wrestles and receives new name *Gen 32: 24-32*
The golden calf and sensuality *Exod 32: 1-24*
In wilderness people remember the good living of Egypt *Num 11: 1-15*
Samson betrayed by senses *Judg 16: 4-30*
Daniel refuses a portion of the king's meat *Dan 1: 1-28*
Jesus on fruits and trees, good and corrupt *Mat 7: 15-20, Luke 6: 43-45*
Jesus heals the blind *Mat 9:27-31, Mark 8: 22-26, John 9: 1-41*
Jesus' parable of the unclean spirit and seven others *Mat 12: 43-45, Luke 11: 24-26*
Jesus' parable of the wheat and tares *Mat 13: 24-30, 36-43*
Jesus heals deaf *Mark 7: 32-37*
Jesus asks if they follow him just for the loaves and fishes *John 6: 26-48*
Jesus removes Thomas' doubts *John 20: 19-29*
Paul healed of blindness *Acts 9: 10-22*
Paul on Spirit versus the flesh *Rom 8: 1-39*

See also body, hearing, materialism, sight, spirituality, taste, touch

SENSUALITY

The beguiling first lie of the forbidden fruit *Gen 3: 1-7*
Joseph resists Potiphar's wife *Gen 39: 1-20*
The golden calf worship *Exod 32: 1-24*
Samson and Delilah *Judg 16: 4-30*

David and Bathsheba *2 Sam 11:1-27*

The pride of women *Isa 3:16-26*

Jesus saves the adulteress *John 8: 1-11*

Paul's sermon on Spirit versus the flesh *Rom 8:1-39*

See also body, flesh, lust, materialism, senses

SENTINEL

Moses raises a serpent of brass in the camp *Num 21: 4-9*

Samuel as boy serves in the temple *1 Sam 3: 1-10*

Elijah's servant watches sky while he prays for rain *1 King 18:41-46*

Jesus' parable of the wise and foolish virgins *Mat 25:1-13*

Jesus at Gethsemane *Mat 26:30, 36-46, Mark 14:26, 32-42, Luke 22: 39-46*

Simon and Anna wait in temple for Christ *Luke 2:21-38*

Jesus' parable of the watchful servant *Luke 12:35-40*

Jesus Christ as the light of the world *John 1:1-14, 8:12-32*

The lame man watching for the moving of the waters *John 5:1-16*

See also guard, soldier, war, watch

SEPARATION

Adam and Eve driven out of Eden *Gen 3:22-24*

Abraham sends Hagar and Ishmael away *Gen 21:9-21*

Joseph sold into Egypt by his brothers *Gen 37:1-36*

Bathsheba's child dies *2 Sam 12:13-23*

Jeremiah foretells restoration after captivity *Jer 29:8-14*

Jesus' parables:
wheat and tares *Mat 13:24-30, 36-43*
the sheep and goats *Mat 25:31-46*
the man taking a long journey *Mark 13:34-37*
the lost sheep *Mat 18:12-14, Luke 15:1-7*

the lost coin *Luke 15:8-10*

the prodigal son *Luke 15:11-24*

Jesus restores daughter to Jairus *Mat 9:18, 19, 23-26, Mark 5:22-24, 35-43, Luke 8:41, 42, 49-56*

Jesus restores her son to widow of Nain *Luke 7:11-17*

Paul's advice to come out and be separate *2 Cor 6:1-18*

See also divorce, loss, parting, saint

SERAPHIM

Cherubims stand guard at gate of Eden *Gen 3:22-24*

Bites of fiery serpent healed by image *Num 21:4-9*

Isaiah's vision of God's glory surrounded by seraphims *Isa 6:1-13*

Four beasts (living beings) around throne *Rev 4:1-11*

See also angel, serpent, wings

SERMON

Moses on counting your blessings *Deut 8:1-20*

Moses on obedience *Deut 11:1-32*

Moses on warnings on idolatry and necromancy *Deut 13:1-18*

Moses on forbidden abominations *Deut 18:9-14*

Moses on the Messiah to come *Deut 18:15-22*

Moses on offering of first fruits *Deut 26:1-19*

Moses on the blessings of obedience *Deut 28:1-14*

Moses on choosing good or evil *Deut 30:11-20, Josh 24:1-25*

Moses on being strong and of a good courage *Deut 31:7-23, Josh 1:1-9*

Isaiah on "Comfort ye!" *Isa 40:1-31*

Isaiah on "Arise, shine" *Isa 60:1-5*

Peter on meaning of Christianity *Acts 2:14-47*

Peter speaks on healing *Acts 3: 12-26*

Paul on the Unknown God *Acts 17:15-34*

Paul's sermon on Adam versus Christ *Rom 5:1-21*

Paul on Spirit versus flesh *Rom 8: 1-39*

Paul on charity *1 Cor 13: 1-13*
Paul on Christian's armor *Eph 6: 10-17*
Paul on the new man *Col 3: 1-17*
Paul on faith *Heb 11: 1-40*
James on how to bear our cross *Jas 1: 1-27*
Peter calls on Christ the chief cornerstone *1 Pet 2: 1-25*
Jesus' sermons (*See* Part II, Jesus Christ: Teachings)

See also ministry, persuasion, preaching, teaching

SERPENT

The serpent beguiles Eve *Gen 3: 1-5*
Moses' rod becomes a serpent *Exod 4: 1-9*
Aaron's rod swallows sorcerers' *Exod 7:1-12*
Bites of fiery serpents healed *Num 21: 4-9*
Jesus' advice to be wise as serpents *Mat 10: 5-16*
Jesus instructs how to take up serpents *Mark 16: 15-18*
Jesus instructs how to tread on serpents *Luke 10: 17-20*
Paul bitten by viper *Acts 28: 1-6*
Great red dragon in John's vision *Rev 12: 1-17*

See also dragon, evil, fear, lie, malpractice, wisdom

SERVANT

Sarah gives her servant to Abraham *Gen 16: 1-16*
Joseph, a servant in the house of Potiphar *Gen 39: 1-20*
Gehazi, the servant of Elisha *2 King 5: 15-27*
Jesus parables:
  two servants awaiting their lord *Mat 24:42-51*
  the watchful servants *Luke 12: 35-40*
  the faithful steward *Luke 12: 41-48*
  the unjust steward *Luke 16: 1-14*
  the servant before he sups *Luke 17:7-10*

Jesus heals the centurion's servant *Mat 8: 5-13, Luke 7: 1-10*
The disciples contend who shall be greatest *Mat 18: 1-11, Mark 9: 33-37, Luke 9: 46-50*
Jesus washes his disciples' feet *John 13: 1-20*

See also bondage, employment, master

SERVICE

Joseph, a good slave in Egypt *Gen 39: 1-6*
Oppression of Israelites in Egypt *Exod 1: 8-14*
Rewards promised for service *Deut 28: 1-14*
Caleb's reward for faithful service *Josh 14: 6-15*
Solomon conducts dedication service *1 King 8: 22-66, 2 Chron 6: 1-42*
David's song on the happiness of the godly *Psal 1: 1-6*
David's song, "The Lord is my shepherd" *Psal 23: 1-6*
David's song, on the safety of the godly *Psal 121: 1-8*
Isaiah called to speak *Isa 6: 1-13*
Jonah at first refuses to serve *Jonah 1: 1-17*
Jesus' parables:
  laborers in the vineyard *Mat 20: 1-16*
  two sons ordered to work *Mat 21:28-32*
  two servants awaiting their lord *Mat 24:42-51*
  ten virgins *Mat 25: 1-13*
  talents *Mat 25: 14-30, Luke 19: 11-28*
  watchful servants *Luke 12: 35-40*
  the faithful steward *Luke 12:41-48*
  the unjust steward *Luke 16: 1-14*
  the servant who serves before he sups *Luke 17:1-10*
Jesus outlines disciples' service to man *Mat 10: 5-42, Mark 6: 7-13, Luke 9: 1-6*
Jesus teaches that no one looking back is fit for the kingdom *Luke 9: 57-62*
Jesus charges Peter, "Feed my sheep" *John 21: 12-19*

Matthias elected to serve as apostle *Acts 1: 15-26*

Seven deacons chosen to serve *Acts 6: 1-4*

Paul designated a chosen vessel *Acts 9: 10-22*

Paul on the hardships of his ministry *Acts 20: 17-38*

See also devotion, duty, master, ministry, servant, stewardship, worship

SEX

See sensuality

SHAME

Adam replies to God's question, "Where art thou?" *Gen 3: 6-24*

Saul destroys himself *1 Sam 31: 1-13, 1 Chron 10:1-14*

David repents his actions *2 Sam 12: 1-10*

Jonah's prayer after disobedience *Jonah 2: 1-10*

Peter weeps after denying Jesus *Mat 26: 57, 58, 69-75, Mark 14: 66-72, Luke 22: 54-62, John 18: 13-18, 25-27*

Judas hangs himself *Mat 27: 3-10, Acts 1: 15-20*

Jesus fills Peter's net to his consternation *Luke 5: 1-11*

Jesus' parable of the prodigal son *Luke 15: 11-24*

Jesus' saves woman taken in adultery *John 8: 1-11*

Jesus charges Peter three times because of his neglect of duty *John 21: 12-19*

See also disgrace, fear, guilt

SHEEP

Abel offers first fruits of the flock *Gen 4: 1-16*

Abraham and Lot's flocks grow *Gen 13: 1-18*

Abraham sacrifices a ram instead of his son *Gen 22: 1-19*

Moses institutes Passover lamb *Exod 11: 4-10, 12: 1-14, 21-41, Deut 16: 1-22*

David's song, "The Lord is my shepherd" *Psal 23:1-6*

Ezekiel's vision of God's care over his flock *Ezek 34:1-31*

Jesus heals withered hand and compares man with sheep *Mat 12:9-13*

Jesus' parable of lost sheep *Mat 18:12-14, Luke 15:1-7*

Jesus' parable of sheep and goats *Mat 25:31-46*

Jesus' birth announced to shepherds *Luke 2:8-20*

Jesus' parable of good shepherd *John 10:1-18*

Jesus' last instruction to Peter, "Feed my sheep" *John 21:12-19*

John's vision of Lamb opening the sealed book *Rev 5:1-14*

See also faith, humility, innocence, lamb, purity

SHELTER

Noah builds the ark *Gen 6:5-22*

Lot shelters two angels from the mob *Gen 19:1-14*

Rahab shelters the spies in Jericho *Josh 2:1-24*

David promises to build a house for God *2 Sam 7:1-29*

Solomon builds the temple *1 King 6:1-38, 7:1-51, 2 Chron 3:1-17, 4: 1-22, 5:1-14*

Elijah lives in a cave *1 King 19: 1-8*

The Shunammite builds a room for Elisha *2 King 4:8-16*

David's song, "God is our refuge and strength" *Psal 46:1-11*

David's song, "our dwelling place" *Psal 90:1-17*

David's song, "the secret place of the most High" *Psal 91:1-16*

Jesus' parable of builders on rock or sand *Mat 7:24-27, Luke 6:48, 49*

Jesus controls the elements *Mat 8:23-27, Mark 4:35-41, 6:45-52, Luke 8:22-25*

Jesus' parable of temple to be raised in three days *John 2:19-22*

Jesus on Christ, the good shepherd *John 10:1-30*

Jesus on comfort in tribulation *John 16:1-33*

See also building, defense, home, protection, refuge

SHEPHERD

See sheep

SHIELD

Goliath's shield described　*1 Sam 17:1-16*

David tries Saul's armor　*1 Sam 17:17-37*

David's song about God, "a sun and shield"　*Psal 84:1-12*

Paul describes the Christian's armor which includes the shield of faith　*Eph 6:10-17*

See also armor, defense, protection, shelter

SHIP

Noah builds ark against flood　*Gen 6:5-22*

Jonah cast out of ship at sea　*Jonah 1:1-17*

Disciples leave ships to follow Jesus　*Mat 4:17-22, Mark 1:14-20, Luke 5:1-11*

Jesus in ship controls weather　*Mat 8:23-27, Mark 4:35-41, Luke 8:22-25*

Jesus addresses multitude from vessel on lake　*Mat 13:1, 2, Mark 4:1, 2, Luke 5:1-3*

Jesus causes ship to arrive at destination instantly　*Mark 6:45-52, John 6:21*

After fishing all night, Peter is told to let down his nets　*Luke 5:1-11, John 21:1-11*

Paul shipwrecked on voyage to Rome　*Acts 27:1-44*

See also ark, sea, travel

SICKNESS

See healing

SIGHT

Moses' eye not dim　*Deut 34:1-11*

Elisha prays to open young man's eyes　*2 King 6:8-23*

Isaiah's vision of Messiah's redemption of blind　*Isa 35:1-10*

Jesus on letting your light shine so men can see your good works　*Mat 5:13-16, Luke 8:16-18*

Jesus' parable of mote and beam　*Mat 7:1-5, Luke 6:37-42*

Jesus heals two blind men　*Mat 9:27-31*

Jesus heals man both blind and dumb　*Mat 12:22-30, Luke 11:14-23*

Jesus tells why he speaks in parables　*Mat 13:10-17, 34, 35, Mark 4:10-12, 33, 34*

Jesus heals Bartimaeus　*Mat 20:29-34, Mark 10:46-52*

Jesus heals blind man in two stages　*Mark 8:22-26*

Jesus heals blind beggar　*Luke 18:35-43*

Jesus heals man born blind　*John 9:1-41*

Ananias heals Paul's blindness　*Acts 9:10:22*

John's vision of new heaven and earth　*Rev 21:1-27*

See also eye, insight, vision

SIGNS

Noah releases the raven and dove　*Gen 8:1-22*

The rainbow appears to Noah　*Gen 9:12-17*

Joseph's boyhood dreams of supremacy　*Gen 37:1-36*

Joseph interprets Pharaoh's dream　*Gen 42:1-46*

Moses turns aside to see burning bush　*Exod 3:1-18*

God transforms Moses' rod and leprosy　*Exod 4:1-9*

Aaron's rod swallows sorcerers' rods　*Exod 7:1-12*

Passover causes release from bondage　*Exod 11:4-10, 12:1-14, 21-41, Deut 16:1-22*

Pillars of cloud and fire guide　*Exod 13:20-22, Num 9:15-23*

Red Sea passed through　*Exod 14:5-31*

Song of Moses reviews signs　*Exod 15:1-19*

Manna and quails in wilderness　*Exod 16:1-36, Num 11:1-15, 31, 32*

Water from a rock　*Exod 17:1-7, Num 20:1-13*

Moses' hands upheld　*Exod 17:8-16*

Golden calf represents idolatry　*Exod 32:1-24*

Aaron's rod blossoms *Num 17:1-11*

Moses' song of deliverance reviews signs *Deut 32:1-47*

Joshua and people cross Jordan *Josh 1:10-18*

Walls of Jericho fall *Josh 6:1-27*

Gideon demands three signs *Judg 6:19-40*

Samson's miraculous birth *Judg 13: 1-25*

Elisha takes Elijah's mantle and crosses Jordan *2 King 2:12-15*

Daniel and handwriting on wall *Dan 5:1-31*

Jonah and the whale *Jonah 2:1-10*

John the Baptist sends to Jesus for proof of Christ *Mat 11:2-19, Luke 7:18-35*

Pharisees request a sign from Jesus *Mat 12:38-45, 16:1-4, Mark 8:10-13, Luke 11:16, 29-32*

Jesus reminds disciples of his great works *Mat 16:5-12, Mark 8: 13-21*

Jesus foretells his second coming *Mat 24:1-41, Luke 17:20-37*

Jesus' resurrection *Mat 28:1-8, Mark 16:1-11, Luke 24:1-12, John 20:1-18*

The descent of the Holy Ghost *Acts 2:1-13*

Peter and John, released from prison, cause signs and wonders *Acts 4:24-37*

All Jesus' healings and great works (*See* Part II, Jesus Christ: Great Works)

See also dreams, forerunner, idea, symbols

SIMILITUDE

See image, likeness

SIMPLICITY

God creates perfect universe *Gen 1:1-31*

Joseph interprets Pharaoh's dream and solves problem *Gen 41:1-46*

David refuses armaments and uses sling *1 Sam 17:38-52*

Solomon offers to divide the baby *1 King 3:16-28*

Elisha makes permanent peace *2 King 6:8-23*

David's song, the happiness of the godly *Psal 1:1-6*

David's song, "The Lord is my shepherd" *Psal 23:1-6*

David's song, "Rejoice in the Lord" *Psal 66:1-20, 100:1-5*

The poor wise man who saves his city *Eccl 9:13-18*

Daniel refuses king's meat *Dan 1: 1-21*

Jesus' sermon on qualities that make a Christian *Mat 5:1-12, Luke 6: 17-26, 36*

The Lord's Prayer *Mat 6:5-15, Mark 11:25, 26, Luke 11:1-4*

Jesus heals Peter's mother-in-law *Mat 8:14-17, Mark 1:25-34*

Jesus' parable of the sower *Mat 13: 3-23, Mark 4:1-20, Luke 8:4-15*

Jesus blesses little children *Mat 19:13-15, Mark 10:13-16, Luke 18: 15-17*

The birth of Jesus *Luke 2:1-20*

Jesus' parable of the good Samaritan *Luke 10:25-37*

Jesus' parable of the true vine *John 15:1-17*

John's sermon, "God is love" *1 John 4:1-21*

See also innocence, purity

SIN

The first lie: that the knowledge of good and evil is desirable *Gen 3:1-5*

Cain ruptures brotherhood of man by murder *Gen 4:1-16*

Egotism of the tower of Babel *Gen 11:1-9*

Jacob's duplicity to obtain his brother's blessing *Gen 27:1-44*

The golden calf—worship of sensuality *Exod 32:1-24*

Sin uncovered after failure to take the city of Ai *Josh 7:1-26, 8: 14-21*

Samson's betrayal by Delilah *Judg 16:4-30*

Saul consults familiar spirit *1 Sam 28:3-20*

Nathan uncovers David's sin *2 Sam 12:1-10*

Gehazi's greed punished *2 King 5: 15-27*

Uzziah's pride punished *2 Chron 26:1-23*

The pride of women exposed by Isaiah *Isa 3:16-26*

Isaiah's vision of fall of Babylon *Isa 14:4-8, 12-17, 25-27*

Jeremiah's vision of good and bad figs *Jer 24:1-10*

Jonah's disobedience to God *Jonah 1:1-17, 2:1-10*

Jesus puts Moses' commandments on mental basis *Mat 5:17-48, Mark 9:38-50, Luke 6:17-36*

Jesus tells why he eats with sinners *Mat 9:10-13, Mark 2:13-17, Luke 5:27-32*

Jesus' reply on what defiles a man *Mat 15:1-20, Mark 7:1-23*

Jesus' parable of the lost sheep *Mat 18:12-14, Luke 15:1-7*

Jesus' parable of the lack of a wedding garment *Mat 22:1-14*

Jesus' parable of the sheep and goats *Mat 25:31-46*

Judas settles the price to betray Jesus *Mat 26:14-16, Mark 14:10, 11, Luke 22:1-6*

Jesus tells paralytic his sins are forgiven *Mark 2:1-12, Luke 5:17-26*

Jesus' parable of the two debtors *Luke 7:36-50*

Jesus' parable of the prodigal son *Luke 15:11-24*

Jesus heals ten lepers and tells them to go to priests *Luke 17:11-19*

Zacchaeus restores what he has taken *Luke 19:1-10*

Jesus heals impotent man and tells him to sin no more *John 5:1-16*

Jesus saves adultress and tells her to sin no more *John 8:1-11*

Jesus heals man born blind, saying neither he nor his parents sinned *John 9:1-41*

Paul's sermon relates sin and death *Rom 5:1-21*

Paul's sermon on Spirit versus the flesh *Rom 8:1-39*

Paul's sermon on the Christian's armor *Eph 6:10-17*

Paul describes enemies of truth *2 Tim 3:1-17*

James on temptations and trials *Jas 1:1-27*

John's vision of war with the dragon *Rev 12:1-17*

See also conscience, corruption, disobedience, error, evil, failure, fallen man

SINCERITY

Joseph tells his dreams to his brothers *Gen 37:1-36*

Song of Moses *Exod 15:1-19, Deut 32:1-47*

Moses heals his sister who opposed him *Num 12:1-16*

Balaam refuses to curse Israelites *Num 22:1-41, 23:1-30, 24:1-25*

Moses encourages his successor *Deut 31:7-23, Josh 1:1-9*

David visits army and accepts challenge *1 Sam 17:17-37*

Solomon asks God for understanding to govern *1 King 3:5-15, 2 Chron 1:7-12*

David's song, the happiness of the godly *Psal 1:1-6*

David's song, "The Lord is my shepherd" *Psal 23:1-6*

David's song, "Create in me a clean heart" *Psal 51:1-19*

The virtuous woman *Prov 31:1-31*

Isaiah called to speak word *Isa 6:1-13*

Daniel refuses king's portion and eats pulse *Dan 1:1-21*

Woman with issue of blood confesses her healing *Mat 9:20-22, Mark 5:25-34, Luke 8:43-48*

Peter acknowledges Jesus as Christ *Mat 16:13-20, Mark 8:27-30, Luke 9:18-21*

Jesus heals unbelief in the father of the epileptic boy *Mat 17:14-21, Mark 9:14-29, Luke 9: 27-43*

Jesus' parables:

two sons ordered to work *Mat 21:28-32*

servants awaiting their lord *Mat 24:42-51*

two debtors forgiven *Luke 7:36-50*

good Samaritan *Luke 10:25-37*

faithful steward *Luke 12:41-48*

the Pharisee and the publican *Luke 18:9-14*

Peter and John speak the word with boldness *Acts 4:1-23*

Peter accepts Gentiles *Acts 10:1-48, 11:1-18*

Paul describes his hardships *2 Cor 11:21-33*

Paul's charge to the faithful *2 Tim 4:1-8*

Paul on the substance of religion *Heb 11:1-40*

James on faith without works *Jas 2:14-26*

John's sermon, "God is love" *1 John 4:1-21*

See also faith, honesty, hypocrisy, purity, truth

SKEPTICISM

See doubt

SKILL

Joseph's ability to interpret dreams *Gen 37:1-36, 39:21-23, 40:1-23, 41: 1-46*

Moses' great works *Exod 4:1-9, 14: 5-31, 16:1-36, 17:1-7*

David's skill with slingshot *1 Sam 17:38-52*

The prophecy of the healing skill of Christ *Isa 42:1-12, 16, 18, 61:1-11, 62:1-12*

Jesus' parable of builders on rock or sand *Mat 7:24-27, Luke 6:48, 49*

Jesus at twelve years holds attention of rabbis *Luke 2:41-52*

Jesus' parable of temple to be raised in three days *John 2:19-22*

The Master's great works and healing ability (*See* Part II, Jesus Christ: Great Works)

See also ability, art, science, talent

SKIN DISEASE

Moses sees leprosy as an illusion *Exod 4:1-9*

After talking with God, Moses' face shone *Exod 34:29-35*

Moses heals his sister of leprosy *Num 12:1-16*

Elisha heals Naaman *2 King 5:1-14*

Gehazi's greed punished with leprosy *2 King 5:15-27*

Job's boils disappear *Job 42:1-34*

David's song, "Bless the Lord . . . who healeth all thy diseases" *Psal 103:1-22*

Jesus heals man's leprosy *Mat 8: 1-4, Mark 1:40-45, Luke 5:12-16*

Jesus on what defiles a man *Mat 15:1-20, Mark 7:1-23*

Jesus heals ten men of leprosy *Luke 17:11-19*

See also leprosy

SLAVERY

Sarah gives her bondwoman to Abraham *Gen 16:1-16*

Joseph sold into slavery in Egypt *Gen 37:1-36*

Moses sees Israelites oppressed in Egypt *Exod 1:8-14*

Bricks without straw *Exod 5:7-19*

Passover and release from bondage *Exod 11:4-10, 12:1-14, 21-41, Deut 16:1-22*

Elisha saves widow's two sons from bondage *2 King 4:1-7*

Queen Esther helps captives in Persia *Esther 3:1-15, 4:1-17*

The misery of captivity *Psal 137:1-9*

Jeremiah promises restoration to freedom *Jer 29:8-14, 31:1-14, 31-34*

Daniel refuses king's portion and eats pulse *Dan 1:1-21*

Paul on bondage to law of sin and death *Rom 7:1-25*

See also bondage, captivity

SLEEP

Lord God causes deep sleep in Adam in order to remove rib and make Eve *Gen 2:21-25*

Jacob dreams of God's presence *Gen 28:10-22*

David spares Saul's life while asleep *1 Sam 24:1-22, 26:1-25*

Elijah dreams he is eating *1 King 19:1-8*

Jesus heals Jairus' daughter who he says is asleep *Mat 9:18, 19, 23-26, Mark 5:22-24, 35-43, Luke 8:41, 42, 49-56*

Jesus' parable of wheat and tares which enemy sowed while men slept *Mat 13:24-30, 36-43*

Jesus' parable of servants awaiting *Mat 24:42-51*

At Gethsemane the disciples fall asleep *Mat 26:30, 36-46, Mark 14: 26, 32-42, Luke 22:39-46*

Jesus' parable of the unwilling friend *Luke 11:5-13*

Jesus' parable of watchful servants *Luke 12:35-40*

Jesus discusses whether Lazarus is asleep or dead *John 11:1-46*

Eutychus falls from window when asleep *Acts 20:7-12*

See also dreams, hypnotism, rest

SOBER

See abstinence, earnestness

SOLDIER

Egyptian soldiers pursue people to Red Sea *Exod 14:5-31*

Gideon defeats army with 300 picked men *Judg 7:1-25*

Goliath's challenge *1 Sam 17:1-16*

David's surprise tactics *1 Sam 17: 38-52*

Uriah put in front line to kill him *2 Sam 11:1-27*

Elijah and the captains of fifty *2 King 1:3-15*

Nehemiah arms workers who are repairing the wall *Neh 4:1-23*

David's song, "the secret place of the most High" *Psal 91:1-16*

Army is raised by the resurrection of dry bones *Ezek 37:1-14*

Jesus heals centurion's servant *Mat 8:5-13, Luke 7:1-10*

Jesus scourged and mocked by soldiers *Mat 27:27-31, Mark 15:12-20, John 19:1-16*

Guard paid to give false report of resurrection *Mat 28:11-15*

Jesus heals soldier's ear cut off *Luke 22:50, 51*

Cornelius, the centurion, accepted by Peter *Acts 10:1-48*

Paul's sermon on the Christians' armor *Eph 6:10-17*

See also armor, leader, war

SOLOMON (son of David)

See Part II, Solomon

SON OF GOD

God makes man in his image *Gen 1:26, 27*

Lord God makes man of dust *Gen 2:6-8*

Fourth man in fiery furnace like Son of God *Dan 3:19-26*

Jesus on cross mocked by priests *Mat 27:41-45, 54*

The reason for Jesus' crucifixion *John 19:5-7*

John's purpose in writing his gospel *John 20:30, 31*

Paul's first preaching on Christ the Son of God *Acts 9:17-21*

Paul on knowledge of the Son of God *Eph 4:1-13*

Paul compares Melchizedek and Christ *Heb 7:1-5, 15-22*

John declares we are the sons of God *1 John 3:1-3*

See also Christ, Jesus, man

SON OF MAN

Ezekiel calls himself Son of man *Ezek 37:1-28*

Daniel's vision of one like the sons of men *Dan 9:20-23, 10:4-21*

Jesus calls himself the Son of man:

in contrast with John the Baptist's ways *Mat 11:16-20*

in asking Peter who he really is *Mat 16:13-20, Mark 8:27-30, Luke 9:18-21*

in foreseeing his betrayal *Mat 17:22, 23, Mark 9:30-32, Luke 9: 43-45*

in foretelling the second coming *Mat 24:1-41, Mark 13:1-37, Luke 21:5-36*

in asking Judas why he betrays with a kiss *Luke 22:48*

in urging his disciples to lift up the Son of man *John 8:23-30, 12:31-34*

See also Jesus

SONGS

Song of Moses *Exod 15:1-19, Deut 32:1-47*

Song of Deborah for victory *Judg 5:1-20*

Song celebrating David's victory over Goliath *1 Sam 18:6-9*

David's song, "how are the mighty fallen" *2 Sam 1:17-27*

David's psalm of thanksgiving *2 Sam 22:1-51, 1 Chron 16:17-36, Psal 137: 1-9*

Some of David's psalms summarized (*See* psalm)

Song of songs *Song Sol 1:1—8:14*

See also music, psalm

SONSHIP

God creates man his image *Gen 1: 26, 27*

Lord God creates Adam a man of dust *Gen 2:6-8*

Abraham is tempted to sacrifice his son *Gen 22:1-19*

Jacob competes for Isaac's blessings *Gen 27:1-44*

Moses says Israelites are God's chosen people *Deut 7:6-11*

Relation between Elijah and his disciple, Elisha *2 King 2:1-15*

Hosea's vision of Israel as a child *Hos 11:1-4*

At Jesus' baptism, voice declares his sonship *Mat 3:13-17, Mark 1:9-11, Luke 3:21, 22*

Jesus teaches prayer, "Our Father" *Mat 6:5-15, Mark 11:25, 26, Luke 11:1-4*

Jesus on "the Son of Man is Lord of the sabbath" *Mat 12:1-8*

Peter acknowledges Jesus as Son of God *Mat 16:13-20, Mark 8:27-30, Luke 9:18-21*

Jesus heals epileptic boy *Mat 17:14-21, Mark 9:14-29, Luke 9:37-43*

Zebedee's wife requests preference for her sons *Mat 20:20-28, Mark 10:35-45*

Jesus' parable of two sons ordered to work *Mat 21:28-32*

Jesus' parable of husbandmen who refused to pay rent *Mat 21:33-46, Mark 12:1-12, Luke 20:9-19*

Jesus on "Christ, whose son is he?" *Mat 22:41-46, Mark 12:35-37, Luke 20:41-44*

Jesus raises son of widow of Nain *Luke 7:11-17*

Jesus' parable of prodigal and elder brother *Luke 15:11-32*

Jesus is the Christ *John 7:14-40*

Paul on Jesus as the Messiah *Acts 13:16-52*

See also children, disciple, offspring

SONS

Adam's two sons fight *Gen 4:1-16*

Isaac is almost sacrificed by his father *Gen 22:1-19*

Jacob buys Esau's birthright *Gen 25:24-34*

Isaac blesses Jacob instead of Esau *Gen 27:1-44*

Joseph receives the coat of many colors *Gen 37:1-36*

Joseph forgives his brothers *Gen 43:1, 2, 45:1-11*

Jacob prophesies the future of his twelve son *Gen 49:1-28, Deut 33: 1-29*

Midwives ordered to drown Hebrew sons *Exod 1:15-22*

The parable of Gideon's son, Jotham *Judg 9:1-15*

Samuel inspects Jesse's sons, anoints David *1 Sam 16:1-13*

Jonathan, Saul's son, befriends David *1 Sam 18:1-16*

David befriends Jonathan's son *2 Sam 9:1-13*

David charges his son, Solomon, with the government *1 Chron 22:6-19, 23:1, 28:2-10, 20*

Elijah raises widow's son *1 King 17:17-24*

Elisha raises Shunammite's son *2 King 4:8-37*

Zebedee's wife asks preference for her two sons *Mat 20:20-28, Mark 10:35-45*

Jesus' parable of the two sons ordered to work *Mat 21:28-32*

Jesus raises son of widow of Nain *Luke 7:11-17*

Jesus' parable of the prodigal son and his brother *Luke 15:11-32*

Jesus heals nobleman's son who is absent *John 4:46-54*

John's vision of the woman and the man child *Rev 12:1-17*

See also children, family, parent

SORROW

Elijah helps destitute widow *1 King 17:1-16*

Elijah restores widow's dead son *1 King 17:17-24*

Elisha helps destitute widow *2 King 4:1-7*

Elisha restores widow's dead son *2 King 4:8-37*

Nehemiah's sorrow at state of Jerusalem *Neh 1:1-11*

Job expresses his woe *Job 3:1-26*

David's song, "Why art thou cast down, O my soul" *Psal 42:1-11*

David's song, "God is our refuge and strength" *Psal 46:1-11*

David's song, "Make a joyful noise" *Psal 66:1-20, 100:1-5*

David's song, "Let the redeemed of the Lord say so" *Psal 107:1-43*

Isaiah's vision of Messiah as man of sorrows *Isa 53:1-12*

The Last Supper *Mat 26:26-29, Mark 14:22-25, Luke 22:14-30, 1 Cor 11: 23-25*

Jesus at Gethsemane *Mat 26:30, 36-46, Mark 14:26, 32-42, Luke 22: 39-46*

Mary Magdalene weeps Easter morn, but her joy returns *Mat 28: 9, 10, Mark 16:9-11, Luke 24:1-12, John 20:11-18*

Jesus raises son of widow of Nain *Luke 7:11-17*

See also adversity, grief, mourning, pain, regret

SOUL

Lord God breathes into Adam's nostrils the breath of life *Gen 2:6-8*

Jacob wrestles with the angel *Gen 32:24-32*

Moses' face concealed by veil after talking with God *Exod 34:29-35*

Elijah taken to heaven *2 King 2: 1-11*

David's song, "Why art thou cast down, O my soul" *Psal 42:1-11*

David's song, "Create in me a clean heart" *Psal 51:1-19*

David's song, "My soul longeth... for the courts of the Lord" *Psal 84:1-12*

David's song, "our dwelliing place" *Psal 90:1-17*

David's song, "Bless the Lord, O my soul" *Psal 103:1-22*

Jesus' parable of the lost sheep *Mat 18:12-14, Luke 15:1-7*

Jesus' parable of the talents *Mat 25:14-30, Luke 19:11-28*

Jesus' parable of the rich man and bigger barns *Luke 12:15-21*

Jesus' parable of rich man and beggar at gate *Luke 16:19-31*

Jesus tells Nicodemus he must be born again *John 3:1-21*

Paul on Spirit versus flesh *Rom 8: 1-39*

Paul on putting on the new man *Col 3:1-17*

See also conscience, heart, immortality, life, man, spirit, substance

SOUND

People shout together at Jericho *Josh 6:1-27*

Gideon blows a trumpet *Judg 7: 1-25*

Jehoshaphat's army led by singers *2 Chron 20:1-32*

Elijah finds God in a still, small voice *1 King 19:9-13*

David's song, "Make a joyful noise" *Psal 66:1-20, 100:1-5*

At Jesus' baptism, noise from heaven *Mat 3:13-17, Mark 1:9-11, Luke 3: 21, 22*

Jesus calms boisterous wind *Mat 8: 23-27, Mark 6:45-52, John 6:15-21*

Sound of rushing wind at descent of Holy Spirit *Acts 2:1-13*

Paul hears sound of Jesus' voice *Acts 9:1-9*

See also ear, hearing, music, voice

SOURCE

God creates man as image *Gen 1: 26, 27*

Adam's origin in Lord God Jehovah *Gen 2:6-8*

Abraham to be father of nations *Gen 15:1-21*

Jacob prophesies future of his twelve sons — the children of Israel *Gen 49:1-48, Deut 33:1-29*

Moses originates basis of all law *Exod 20:1-19, 5:1-24*

Moses informs they are chosen people *Deut 7:6-11*

David's song, "What is man?" *Psal 8:1-9*

David's song, "the fountain of life"
Psal 36:1-12
David's song, "our dwelling place"
Psal 90:1-17
Isaiah promises birth of Messiah *Isa
7:10-16, 9:2-7*
Jesus accused of healing by Beelze-
bub *Mat 12:22-30, Mark 3:22-30,
Luke 11:14-23*
Jesus feeds thousands *Mat 14:15-21,
15:32-39, Mark 6:35-44, 8:22-26,
Luke 9:12-17, John 6:5-14*
Jesus on the "Christ, whose son is
he?" *Mat 22:42-46, Mark 12:35-
37, Luke 20:41-44*
Jesus serves the original communion
*Mat 26:26-29, Mark 14:22-25, Luke
22:14-30*
Peter's net filled *Luke 5:1-11, John
21:1-11*
Jesus changes water to wine *John
2:1-11*
Jesus tells source of his great works
John 5:17-47
Jesus' parable of vine and branches
John 15:1-17

See also beginning, cause, origin

SOWING

Jesus' parables:
the sower *Mat 13:3-23, Mark 4:1-
20, Luke 8:4-15*
the wheat and tares *Mat 13:24-
30, 36-43*
the mustard seed *Mat 13:31, 32,
Mark 4:30-32, Luke 13:18, 19*
the seed, blade, ear *Mark 4:26-29*

See also harvest, reaping, seed

SPACE

God creates entire universe and
finds it good *Gen 1:1-31*
Lord God creates man from dust and
finds him bad *Gen 2:6-8, 3:1-24*
Enoch walks with God and is trans-
lated *Gen 5:18, 21-24, Heb 11:5*
Noah builds an ark with rooms in it
Gen 6:5-22
Abraham's strife with Lot over liv-
ing room *Gen 13:1-18*
Jacob, wandering, is assured of
God's ever-presence *Gen 28:10-20*

Solomon builds temple *1 King 6:1-
38, 7:1-51, 2 Chron 3:1-17, 4:1-22,
5:1-14*
David's song, "The heavens declare
the glory" *Psal 19:1-14*
David's song, "The earth is the
Lord's" *Psal 24:1-10*
David's song, "our dwelling place"
Psal 90:1-17
David's song, "Whither shall I go
from thy spirit" *Psal 139:1-24*
Jonah and the whale *Jonah 2:1-10*
Jesus, master of space, moves ship
across lake instantly *Mark 6:45-51
John 6:21*
Jesus' parable, new wine in old bot-
les *Luke 5:36-39*
Jesus' parable of rich fool and big-
ger barns *Luke 12:15-21*
Jesus' parable of temple to be raised
in three days *John 2:19-22*
Jesus heals nobleman's son without
being present *John 4:46-54*
Jesus' body, after resurrection, ap-
pears in room without going
through doors *John 20:19-23*

See also allness, body, infinity, ever-
presence, spirit, time

SPEECH

A talking serpent tells the first lie
Gen 3:1-5
Moses complains of his speaking
ability *Exod 4:10-17*
Moses talks with God *Exod 3:1-18,
19:1-9, 33:7-23*
Jesus heals dumb *Mat 9:32-35*
Jesus heals blind and dumb man
Mat 12:22-30, Luke 11:14-23
Jesus' group healings *Mat 15:29-31*
Jesus heals deaf and dumb *Mark
7:32-37*
Father of John the Baptist loses
speech and recovers it *Luke 1:
5-25, 57-80*
Jesus heals dumb *Luke 11:14-23*
At Pentecost everyone hears speak-
ers in his own language *Acts
2:1-13*
Paul heals the soothsayer *Acts 16:
16-18*

See also dumbness, eloquence, tongue

SPINAL DISORDER

Woman bowed together 18 years
Luke 13:11-17

SPIRIT

God creates man in his image   *Gen 1:26, 27*

Enoch "walked with God: and he was not"   *Gen 5:18, 21-24, Heb 11:5*

God reveals his nature to Moses   *Exod 3:1-18*

Jesus on oneness with the Father   *John 10:22-42*

Jesus speaks with Moses and Elias   *Mat 17:1-13, Mark 9:2-13, Luke 9:28-36*

Jesus' resurrection   *Mat 28:1-8, Mark 16:1-8, Luke 24:1-12, John 20: 1-10*

Jesus casts out unclean spirit   *Mark 1:21-28, Luke 4:33-37*

Jesus' ascension   *Mark 16:19, 20, Luke 24:50-53, Acts 1:6-12*

Jesus tells woman, "God is a Spirit"   *John 4:1-30, 39-42*

Jesus promises the Holy Spirit   *John 14:1-31*

At Pentecost descent of Comforter   *Acts 2:1-13*

Paul on Spirit versus the flesh   *Rom 8:1-39*

Paul on the letter and the Spirit   *2 Cor 3:4-18*

Paul on fruits of the Spirit   *Gal 5:1-26*

See also ever-presence, God, Holy Spirit (Ghost), power, purity, soul, wind

SPIRITUALITY

Early man lived to advanced age   *Gen 5:1-32*

Enoch walks with God and is translated   *Gen 5:18, 21-25, Heb 11:5*

Abram and Sarai receive new names   *Gen 17:1-9, 15-22*

Jacob wrestles with angel and receives new name   *Gen 32:24-32*

Moses talks with God face to face   *Exod 33:7-23*

Veil conceals Moses' face   *Exod 34:29-35*

People set apart as God's own chosen   *Deut 7:6-11*

The Lord calls Samuel   *1 Sam 3:1-10*

Solomon requests understanding to judge people   *1 King 3:5-15, 2 Chron 1:7-12*

Isaiah called to speak   *Isa 6:1-13*

Jesus walks on water   *Mat 14:22-33, John 6:15-21*

Jesus' ascension   *Mark 16:19, 20, Luke 24:50-53, Acts 1:6-12*

Jesus turns water to wine   *John 2:1-11*

Jesus heals man born blind   *John 9:1-41*

Jesus' parable of the true vine   *John 15:1-17*

John's vision of new heaven and earth   *Rev 21:1-27*

See also heaven, morality, reality, renewal, soul, spirit

SPOKESMAN

See prophet

STANDARDS

God created man in his image   *Gen 1:26, 27*

Moses gives basis of all laws   *Exod 20:1-19, Deut 5:1-24*

Moses tells people they are chosen by God   *Deut 7:6-11*

Elisha asks for double portion of Elijah's spirit   *2 King 2:1-15*

David's song, the happiness of the godly   *Psal 1:1-6*

David's song, "What is man?"   *Psal 8:1-9*

David's song, "God is our refuge and strength"   *Psal 46:1-11*

Isaiah foretells the Christ—what he is like   *Isa 53:1-12*

Three Jews refuse to worship image set up in plain   *Dan 3:1-30*

Micah's vision of mountain of the Lord's house   *Mic 4:1-8, 13, Isa 2:1-5*

Jesus lists qualities that make a a Christian   *Mat 5:1-12, Luke 6:17-26, 36*

Jesus gives John proof of the Christ   *Mat 11:2-19, Luke 7:18-35*

Jesus heals dumb man, Pharisees say, by Beelzebub *Mat 12:22-30, Luke 11:14-26*

Jesus tells the rock on which he will build his church *Mat 16:13-20, Mark 8:27-30, Luke 9:18-21*

Jesus' parable of wise and foolish virgins *Mat 25:1-13*

Jesus' parable of good Samaritan *Luke 10:25-37*

Jesus as the light of the world *John 1:1-14, 8:12-32*

Jesus on the unity and eternity of the Christ *John 8:12-59*

Paul on charity *1 Cor 13:1-13*

Paul's teaching that Jesus' resurrection is our resurrection *1 Cor 15:1-58*

John's vision of new heaven and earth *Rev 21:1-27*

See also idea, perfection

STATE

See nation

STATUS

Abraham grows rich *Gen 13:1-18*

Abram and Sarai receive new names *Gen 17:1-9, 15-22*

Joseph made governor *Gen 41:1-46*

Aaron receives Urim and Thummim of his new office *Exod 28:29-36*

The chosen people set apart as God's own *Deut 7:6-11*

David made king of Judah and Israel *2 Sam 2:1-4, 5:1-5*

Solomon's deeds acknowledged by Queen of Sheba *1 King 10:1-12, 2 Chron 9:1-12*

Elisha takes up mantle of Elijah *2 King 2:12-15*

Jesus explains his oneness with the Father *John 10:22-42*

Jesus says a prophet is without honor in his own country *Mat 13:53-58, Mark 6:1-6, Luke 4:22-24, John 4:43-45*

Zebedee's wife asks preference for her sons *Mat 20:20-28, Mark 10:35-45*

All men seek Jesus; his fame increases *Mark 1:35-39, 45*

Disciples argue who shall be greatest *Luke 22:24-30*

Jesus' teaching that he is Christ *John 7:14-40*

See also fame, law, symbols

STATUTE

See commandment, law

STEADFASTNESS

Enoch walked with God and was not *Gen 5:18, 21-24, Heb 11:5*

Noah was righteous in his generation *Gen 6:5-22*

Abraham willing to sacrifice his son to God *Gen 22:1-19*

Joseph resists his master's wife *Gen 39:1-20*

Ruth loyal to her mother-in-law *Ruth 1:1-22*

The Shunammite refuses to complain *2 King 4:8-37*

David's song, "The Lord is my shepherd" *Psal 23:1-6*

Jeremiah in Babylon prison buys a field in Israel *Jer 32:2, 6-27, 37-44*

Ezekiel's vision of God's care for his flock *Ezek 34:1-31*

Job never loses his integrity *Job 1:13-22, 2:1-10*

Three Jews refuse to worship image *Dan 3:1-30*

Daniel prays despite threat of lions' den *Dan 6:1-28*

Jesus' parables:

the servants awaiting lord *Mat 24:42-51*

the watchful servants *Luke 12:35-40*

the faithful steward *Luke 12:41-48*

the good shepherd *John 10:1-18*

Jesus washes his disciples' feet *John 13:1-20*

Paul's hardships to establish church *2 Cor 11:21-33*

Paul on faith *Heb 11:1-40*

Paul preaches on the example left by Jesus *Heb 12:1-29*

James on how to bear our cross *Jas 1:1-27*

See also faith, persistence, resolution

STEALTH

Jacob obtains the blessing intended for his brother   *Gen 27: 1-44*
Moses gives basis of all law   *Exod 20:1-19, Deut 5:1-24*
David steals Uriah's wife   *2 Sam 11: 1-27*

See also commandment, covetousness

STEWARDSHIP

Adam put in Eden to dress it and keep it   *Gen 2: 15-17*
Joseph manages Potiphar's estate   *Gen 39: 1-6*
Solomon builds temple   *1 King 6: 1-38, 7: 1-51, 2 Chron 3: 1-17, 4: 1-22, 5: 1-14*
Solomon dedicates temple   *1 King 8: 22-66, 2 Chron 6: 1-42*
David's charge to Solomon to build temple   *1 Chron 22: 6-19, 23: 1, 28: 2-10, 20*
David accepts liberal offerings to build temple   *1 Chron 29:6-19*
Cyrus proclaims rebuilding of temple   *Ezra 1: 1-11*
Rebuilding of temple starts   *Ezra 3: 8-13*
Adversaries block rebuilding   *Ezra 4: 1-5*
Work taken up again   *Ezra 6: 1-3, 7, 8, 14, 15*
Nehemiah hears of Jerusalem's misery   *Neh 1: 1-11*
Nehemiah surveys the city ruins   *Neh 2: 1-20*
Nehemiah repairs wall   *Neh 4: 1-23*
Conspiracy to halt work fails   *Neh 6: 1-19*
David's song, "Fret not thyself because of evildoers"   *Psal 37:1-40*
The virtuous woman   *Prov 31: 1-31*
Micah's vision of victorious church   *Mic 4: 1-8, 13, Isa 2: 1-5*
Malachi urges tithing   *Mal 3: 10, 4: 1, 2*
Jesus' parables:
  the sower   *Mat 13: 3-23, Mark 4: 1-20, Luke 8 :4-15*
  the unmerciful debtor   *Mat 18: 23-35*
  the hiring of laborers for the vineyard   *Mat 20:1-16*
  the two sons ordered to work   *Mat 21:28-32*
  the husbandmen who refuse to pay rent   *Mat 21:33-46, Mark 12:1-12, Luke 20:9-19*
  the two servants who await their lord   *Mat 24:42-51*
  the talents   *Mat 25: 14-30, Luke 19:11-28*
  the watchful servants   *Luke 12: 35-40*
  the faithful steward   *Luke 12: 41-48*
  counting the cost of building   *Luke 14:25-33*
  the unjust steward   *Luke 16: 1-14*
  the rich man and beggar   *Luke 16:19-31*
  the servant who serves   *Luke 17: 7-10*
Jesus instructs disciples and sends them out   *Mat 9: 36-38, 10: 1-42, Mark 3: 13-21, 6: 7-13, Luke 9: 1-6*
Jesus helps Peter with fishing   *Luke 5: 1-11, John 21: 1-11*
Disciples return and report   *Luke 9: 10, 11*
Jesus washes disciples' feet   *John 13: 1-20*
Jesus charges Peter with his work   *John 21: 12-19*
Peter inquires about John's future   *John 21: 20-24*
Paul, a chosen vessel, healed of mental and physical blindness   *Acts 9: 10-22*
Paul's hardship to establish church   *2 Cor 11: 21-33*
James on faith without works   *Jas 2: 14-26*

See also employment, office, responsibility, service

STEPHEN (the martyr)

See Part II, Stephen

STONE

Jacob uses stone for a pillow and dreams   *Gen 28: 10-22*
David uses stones from brook to kill Goliath   *1 Sam 17: 38-52*
Simon's name changed to Peter (rock)   *Mat 16: 13-20, Mark 8: 27-30, Luke 9: 18-21*

Stone rolled away from Jesus' tomb
Mat 28: 1-8, Mark 16: 1-8, Luke 24: 1-12, John 20: 1-10

Stephen, the first martyr, is stoned
Acts 7: 51-60

Paul is stoned to death but recovers
Acts 14: 19, 20

See also conviction, foundation, hardness, kill, rock

STORM

Noah prepares for the flood *Gen 6: 5-22*

Elijah in wind, earthquake, and fire on mount *1 King 19: 9-13*

David's song, "The heavens declare the glory" *Psal 19: 1-14*

David's song, "Whither shall I go?" *Psal 139: 1-24*

Jesus controls storm at sea *Mat 8: 23-27, 14: 22-33, Mark 4: 35-41, 6: 45-52, Luke 8: 22-25, John 6: 15-21*

Storm at crucifixion *Mat 27: 50-53*

Paul's ship caught in storm on way to Rome *Acts 27: 1-44*

See also elements, sea, ship, weather

STRAIGHTWAY

Abraham called by God begins search for promised land *Gen 11: 31, 32, 12: 1-9*

Moses puts hand into bosom again and leprosy is healed *Exod 4: 1-9*

Paul and Silas sing hymns in prison and doors open *Acts 16: 19-40*

All Jesus' healings and great works were immediate (*See* Part II, Jesus Christ: Great Works)

See also immediate, present, time

STRANGER

Ruth enters Israel as a foreigner *Ruth 1: 1-22, 2: 1-23*

Widow takes care of Elijah, a stranger *1 King 17: 8-16*

Wise men from East seek King of the Jews to worship *Mat 2: 1-12*

Jesus heals Syrophenician's daughter *Mat 15: 21-28, Mark 7: 24-30*

Jesus' parable of the good Samaritan *Luke 10: 25-37*

Jesus heals ten lepers but only the Samaritan turns back to express gratitude *Luke 17: 11-19*

Peter accepts conversion of foreigner *Acts 10: 1-48, 11: 1-18*

See also foreigner, Gentile

STRENGTH

Moses complains of inability *Exod 3: 9-12*

Moses delegates authority to conserve strength *Exod 18: 13-27*

Caleb describes his 40 years in wilderness *Josh 14: 6-15*

Samson loses his strength *Judg 13: 1-25, 16: 4-30*

Goliath's strength frightens army *1 Sam 17:1-16*

David's song, "God is our refuge and strength" *Psal 46: 1-11*

Daniel refuses king's portion and eats pulse *Dan 1: 1-21*

Jesus heals Peter's mother-in-law; she gets up and serves them *Mat 8: 14-17, Mark 1: 29-34*

Jesus heals paralytic let down through roof *Mark 2: 1-12, Luke 5: 17-26*

Jesus heals impotent man *John 5: 1-16*

Paul's hardships to establish church *2 Cor 11: 21-33*

See also endurance, energy, omnipotence, power

STRIFE

See struggle

STRUCTURE

Noah builds the ark *Gen 6:5-22*

Tower of Babel *Gen 11: 1-9*

David promises a house for God *2 Sam 7:1-29*

Solomon builds temple *1 King 6: 1-38, 7: 1-51, 2 Chron 3: 1-17, 4: 1-22, 5: 1-14*

Shunammite builds addition to her house for Elisha *2 King 4: 8-17*

David is told his son will build temple *1 Chron 17: 1-27*

David receives liberal offerings for temple *1 Chron 29: 6-19*

Zerubbabel starts rebuilding of temple *Ezra 3: 8-13*

Work on temple blocked, then starts again *Ezra 6: 1-3, 7, 8, 14, 15, 7: 11-26*

Nehemiah reconstructs the wall of Jerusalem *Neh 4: 1-23*

Micah's vision of the mountain of the Lord's house *Mic 4: 1-8, 13, Isa 2: 1-5*

Jesus' parables:

the builders on rock or sand *Mat 7:24-27, Luke 6:48, 49*

the seed, blade, ear *Mark 4: 26-29*

the rich fool and bigger barns *Luke 12:15-21*

counting the cost of building a tower *Luke 14:25-33*

the temple to be raised in three days *John 2:19-22*

Jesus' body is resurrected *Mat 28: 1-8, Mark 16: 1-8, Luke 24: 1-12, John 20: 1-10*

Paul's teaching to put on the new man *Col 3:1-17*

See also building, body, cornerstone

STRUGGLE

Abraham's strife with Lot settled *Gen 13: 1-18*

Lot shelters two angels from mob *Gen 19: 1-14*

Isaac's herdsmen strive over wells *Gen 26: 12-31*

Jacob wrestles with angel *Gen 32: 24-32*

Aaron competes with Egyptian sorcerers *Exod 7: 1-12*

Aaron and Hur uphold Moses' hands during battle *Exod 17: 8-16*

Deborah defeats invaders *Judg 4: 1-17*

Gideon defeats army *Judg 7: 1-25*

David kills Goliath *1 Sam 17: 38-52*

Elijah competes with 450 prophets of Baal *1 King 8: 17-40*

Hezekiah repels invaders *2 King 18: 17-37, 19: 1-37, 2 Chron 31: 20, 21, 32: 1-23, Isa 36: 1-22, 37: 1-38*

Jehoshaphat marches to war relying on God *2 Chron 20: 1-32*

Nehemiah defeats conspiracy against building the wall *Neh 6: 1-19*

Esther saves her people from persecution *Esther 3: 1-15, 4: 1-17, 6: 1-14*

David's song, "God is our refuge and strength" *Psal 46: 1-11*

David's song, "the secret place of the most High" *Psal 91: 1-16*

Jesus heals issue of blood, a problem for twelve years *Mat 9:20-22, Mark 5: 25-34, Luke 8: 43-48*

Jesus conflicts with Pharisees, scribes and lawyers *Mat 12: 1-8, 22-37, Mark 3: 22-30, Luke 11: 37-54*

Jesus' parable of husbandmen who refuse rent *Mat 21:33-46, Mark 12: 1-12, Luke 20: 9-19*

Jesus at Gethsemane *Mat 26: 30, 36-46, Mark 14: 26, 32-42, Luke 22: 39-46*

Peter's net easily filled *Luke 5: 1-11, John 21:1-11*

Jesus' parable of prodigal's struggle with sin and repentance *Luke 15: 11-24*

Peter cuts off Malchus' ear in duel *Luke 22: 50, 51*

Jesus heals impotent man at pool 38 years *John 5: 1-16*

Paul attacked by idol makers *Acts 19: 23-29*

Paul's hardships to establish church *2 Cor 11:21-33*

Paul's self-revealings *2 Cor 12: 1-19*

Paul on putting on the new man *Col 3: 1-17*

Paul on enemies of the truth *2 Tim 3: 1-17*

James on trials *Jas 1: 1-27*

John's vision of war in heaven *Rev 12: 1-17*

See also competition, effort, persistence, trials, war

STUDY

Moses turns judging over to others *Exod 18: 13-27*

Moses anoints Aaron and his sons for priesthood *Lev 8: 1-13*

Eldad and Medad also prophesy in the camp *Num 11: 16-30*

Moses prepares Joshua for leadership *Deut 31: 7-23, Josh 1: 1-9*

Ruth follows her mother-in-law
Ruth 1: 1-22, 2: 1-23

Samuel as apprentice to Eli   *1 Sam
3: 1-10*

Elisha asks for a double portion of
Elijah's spirit   *2 King 2: 1-15*

Nehemiah surveys city and decides
to rebuild wall   *Neh 2: 1-20*

Job's dialogues with friends explore
nature of God   *Job 4: 1—37:34*

The values of Wisdom   *Prov 3: 13-
26, 4: 1-13, 8: 1-36*

Mortal life is vain   *Eccl 1: 1-18, 2:
1-26*

All mortal events within time framework   *Eccl 3:1-15*

Daniel reads the handwriting on the
wall   *Dan 5: 1-31*

Disciples request Jesus to teach
them to pray   *Mat 6: 5-15, Mark
11: 25, 26, Luke 11: 1-4*

Jesus instructs twelve disciples to
heal and preach   *Mat 9:36-38, 10:
1-42, Mark 3:13-21, Luke 9:1-6, 10,
11*

Jesus explains why he speaks only
in parables   *Mat 13: 10-17, 34, 35,
Mark 4: 10-12, 33, 34*

Jesus walks on water, Peter tries it
Mat 14: 22-33, John 6: 15-21

Jesus heals epileptic boy after disciples fail   *Mat 17: 14-21, Mark 9:
14-29, Luke 9: 37-43*

Jesus instructs 70 disciples   *Luke
10: 1-24*

Jesus opens scriptures to two disciples   *Luke 24: 13-35*

Jesus' parable of vine and branches
John 15: 1-17

Paul's advice to his disciples   *2 Tim
2: 1-26, 4: 1-8, 1 Thess 5: 1-28*

James on how to bear our cross
Jas 1: 1-27

Jesus' discourses with disciples (*See*
Part II, Jesus Christ: Teachings)

See also book, disciple, preparation,
teaching

SUBSTANCE

God creates the perfect universe
Gen 1: 1-31

Enoch walked with God and was
translated   *Gen 5: 18, 21-24, Heb
11: 5*

Esau sells his birthright for pottage
Gen 25: 24-34

Moses sees rod and leprosy transformed   *Exod 4: 1-9*

Moses gives Ten Commandments,
the substance of all law   *Exod 20:
1-19, Deut 5: 1-24*

God's promises to faithful   *Deut 28:
1-14, 11: 1-32*

Ruth goes from privation to substance   *Ruth 1:1-22, 2:1-23, 4:1-22*

Elijah sees the real nature of God
1 King 19: 9-13

David receives liberal offerings to
build temple   *1 Chron 29: 6-19*

Job hears the nature of God   *Job
38: 1-41*

David's song, the happiness of the
godly   *Psal 1: 1-6*

David's song, "What is man?"   *Psal
8: 1-9*

David's song, "The earth is the
Lord's"   *Psal 24: 1-10*

David's song, "the fountain of life"
Psal 36: 1-12

Daniel refuses king's portion and
eats only pulse   *Dan 1: 1-21*

Zechariah's vision of candlestick fed
by two olive trees   *Zech 4: 1-14*

Jesus on true treasures   *Mat 6: 19-
21*

Jesus' parable of builders on rock or
sand   *Mat 7: 24-27, Luke 6: 48, 49*

Jesus walks on the water, Peter
tries also   *Mat 14: 22-33, John 6:
15-21*

Jesus' body is resurrected   *Mat 28:
1-8, Mark 16: 1-8, Luke 24: 1-12,
John 20: 1-10*

Jesus' parable of the prodigal son
who wasted substance   *Luke 15:
11-24*

Jesus' parable of temple to be raised
in three days   *John 2: 19-22*

Thomas doubts but is convinced
John 20: 19-29, Luke 24: 36-49

Paul on Spirit versus the flesh
Rom 8: 1-39

Paul on faith, the substance of religion   *Heb 11:1-40*

John's sermon "God is love"   *1 John
4: 1-21*

John's vision of new heaven and
new earth   *Rev 21: 1-27*

See also body, faith, reality, supply, treasure, wealth, wisdom

SUCCESS

God creates perfect universe and man in his image *Gen 1:1-31*

Noah builds ark and saves all with him *Gen 6:5-22, 9:1-17*

Joseph becomes governor of Egypt and saves his family *Gen 41:37-46, 43:1, 2, 45:1-11, 25-28*

Moses' song of triumph *Exod 15:1-19, Deut 32:1-47*

Jericho falls to Joshua *Josh 6:1-27*

Deborah's song of triumph *Judg 5:1-20*

Gideon with 300 men puts enemy host to rout *Judg 7:1-25*

David crowned king of both kingdoms *2 Sam 2:1-4, 5:1-5*

Solomon dedicates temple he built *1 King 8:22-66, 2 Chron 6:1-42*

Elijah's translation over death *2 King 2:1-11*

Elisha's healing ability illustrated by Naaman *2 King 5:1-14*

Nehemiah rebuilds the wall *Neh 4:1-23*

Esther saves her people *Esther 6:1-14, 7:1-10*

David's song, "Praise the Lord for his goodness" *Psal 107:1-43*

Daniel saved from the lions *Dan 6:1-28*

Jesus' resurrection and ascension *Mat 28:1-8, Mark 16:1-8, 19, 20, Luke 24:1-12, 50-53, John 20:1-10, Acts 1:6-12*

All men seek Jesus; his fame increases *Mark 1:35-39*

Seventy disciples return to report success *Luke 10:17-24*

Jesus' parable of the unwilling friend *Luke 11:5-13*

Jesus' parable of the judge and the widow *Luke 18:1-8*

Signs and wonders cause church growth *Acts 4:24-37*

Paul on the prize for a race *1 Cor 9:24-27*

See also fortune, fulfillment, prosperity, triumph

SUCCESSION

The patriarchs lived to advanced age *Gen 6:5-22*

Moses charges Joshua with leadership *Deut 31:7-23, Josh 1:1-9*

Elisha takes mantle of Elijah *2 King 2:1-15*

Peter acknowledges Jesus as Christ and is appointed to lead *Mat 16:13-20, Mark 8:27-30, Luke 9:18-21*

John the Baptist testifies Jesus is the Christ *John 1:15-34*

Jesus promises Holy Ghost *John 14:1-31*

Judas' place filled by election of Matthias *Acts 1:15-26*

Paul's teaching to put off old man, put on new *Col 3:1-17*

Paul advises his disciple on carrying on the work *2 Tim 2:1-26*

John's vision of the new heaven and new earth *Rev 21:1-27*

SUFFERING

Jacob tortured by fear of his brother *Gen 32:1-32*

Grief and poverty of Ruth and Naomi *Ruth 1:1-22, 2:1-23*

Envy and failure cause self-destruction of Saul *1 Sam 31:1-13, 1 Chron 10:1-14*

David's and Bathsheba's child dies *2 Sam 12:13-23*

The Shunammite woman's heroism in suffering *2 King 4:8-37*

Asa diseased in his feet *2 Chron 16:11-14*

Job's woe *Job 1:13-22, 2:1-10, 3:1-26*

David's song, "Why art thou cast down?" *Psal 42:1-11*

David's song, "God is our refuge and strength" *Psal 46:1-11*

Isaiah foretells suffering of Messiah *Isa 53:1-12*

Ezekiel on hereditary pains *Ezek 18:1-32*

Jesus heals epileptic boy *Mat 17:14-21, Mark 9:14-29, Luke 9:37-43*

Jesus at Gethsemane *Mat 26:30, 36-46, Mark 14:26, 32-42, Luke 22:39-46*

Jesus scourged and mocked *Mat 27: 27-31, Mark 15: 16-20, John 19: 1-16*

Jesus crucified *Mat 27: 32-56, Mark 15:21-41, Luke 23:26-49, John 19: 17-30*

Jesus heals woman bowed together 18 years *Luke 13:11-17*

Jesus' parable of prodigal son *Luke 15:11-24*

Stephen stoned *Acts 7:51-60*

Paul's hardships to establish church *2 Cor 11:21-33*

James' sermon how to bear our cross *Jas 1:1-27*

See also cross, grief, pain, punishment, torment

SUGGESTION

Serpent suggests first lie to Eve *Gen 3:1-5*

Cain acts on suggestion to be rid of competition *Gen 4:1-16*

Jacob's mother shows him how to deceive his father *Gen 27:1-44*

Joseph resists his master's wife's suggestion *Gen 39:1-20*

Worship of golden calf introduced to people *Exod 32:1-24*

Saul consults familiar spirit *1 Sam 28:3-20*

David destroys Uriah for his wife *2 Sam 11:1-27*

Hezekiah shows his treasures *2 King 20:12-21, Isa 39:1-8*

Nehemiah foils conspiracy to interrupt rebuilding of the wall *Neh 6:1-19*

David's song, "Fret not thy self because of evildoers" *Psal 37:23-40*

The temptations of Jesus *Mat 4: 1-11, Mark 1:12, 13, Luke 4:1-13*

Jesus accused of casting out devils by Beelzebub *Mat 12:22-30, Mark 3:22-30, Luke 11:14-23*

Jesus' reply on what defiles a man *Mat 15:1-20, Mark 7:1-23*

Jesus heals Syrophenician's daughter of devil *Mat 15:21-28, Mark 7:24-30*

The rulers conspire against Jesus *Mat 26:1-5, Mark 14:1, 2*

Jesus casts out unclean spirit *Mark 1:21-28, Luke 4:33-37*

Paul describes enemies of the truth *2 Tim 3:1-17*

John's vision of dragon warring with woman *Rev 12:1-17*

See also hypnotism

SUN

God creates sun *Gen 1:14-19*

Sun and moon stand still at Ajalon *Josh 10:6-15*

David's song, "God is a sun and shield" *Psal 84:1-12*

John's vision of woman clothed with sun *Rev 12:1-17*

See also idolatry, light, soul, symbol, worship

SUNDAY (first day)

See sabbath

SUPERSTITION

Moses preaches against idolatry and necromancy *Deut 13:1-18*

The idol Dagon falls and breaks before the Ark of the Lord *1 Sam 5:1-5*

At Endor Saul consults familiar spirit *1 Sam 28:3-20*

Elijah contests with prophets of Baal *1 King 18:17-40*

Mortal life is vain *Eccl 1:1-18, 2: 1-26*

Paul heals soothsayer *Acts 16:16-18*

Paul's sermon on Unknown God *Acts 17:15-34*

Paul attacked by idol makers *Acts 19:23-29*

Paul's sermon, "Come out ... and be ye separate" *2 Cor 6:1-18*

Paul's description of non-Christians *2 Tim 3:1-17*

Paul heals cripple and is worshipped as Jupiter *Acts 14:11-18*

See also idolatry, ignorance, necromancy, magnetism

SUPPER

At feast Daniel reads handwriting on wall *Dan 5:1-31*

Jesus eats with publicans and sinners *Mat 9:10-13, Mark 2:13-17, Luke 5:27-32*

The Last (Lord's) Supper *Mat 26: 26-29, Mark 14:22-25, Luke 22:14-30*

Jesus eats with disciples after resurrection *Mark 16:12, 13, Luke 24: 13-49, John 20:19-23, 1 Cor 15:15*

Jesus dines with a Pharisee *Luke 7:36-50*

Jesus' parable of chief seats *Luke 14:7-14*

Jesus' parable of guests at great supper *Luke 14:15-24*

Jesus' parable of when the servant sups *Luke 17:7-10*

Jesus turns water into wine at wedding feast *John 2:1-11*

Jesus has supper with Lazarus whom he raised from the dead *John 11: 55-57, 12:1, 2, 9-11*

Paul on the Lord's supper *1 Cor 11:20-25*

See also communion, evening, feast

SUPPLY

Abraham's riches grow, strife with Lot *Gen 13:1-18*

Hagar and son saved in wilderness *Gen 21:9-21*

Isaac's strife between herdsmen over wells *Gen 26:12-31*

Joseph interprets Pharaoh's dream of famine *Gen 41:1-46*

Joseph's brethren come to Egypt for food *Gen 42:1-8*

Manna and quails in wilderness *Exod 16:1-36, Num 11:1-15, 13, 32*

Moses gets water from rock *Exod 17:1-7, Num 20:1-13*

Ruth gleans in the field of Boaz *Ruth 2:1-23*

Elijah fed by ravens and widow of Zarephath *1 King 17:1-16*

Elijah prays for rain *1 King 18: 41-46*

Elijah fed in a dream *1 King 19:1-8*

Elisha supplies water for an army *2 King 3:16-20*

Elisha and the widow's pot of oil *2 King 4:1-7*

Elisha feeds 100 men with 20 barley rolls *2 King 4:42-44*

Elisha prophesies incredible plenty *2 King 6:24, 25, 7:1-18*

Jehoiachin's continual allowance *2 King 25:27-30*

David gets liberal offerings to build temple *1 Chron 29:6-19*

David's song, "The Lord is my shepherd" *Psal 23:1-6*

Isaiah's vision of desert that blossoms *Isa 35:1-10*

Zechariah's vision of candlestick fed by two olive trees *Zech 4:1-14*

Jesus' parable of sower *Mat 13:3-23, Mark 4:1-20, Luke 8:4-15*

Jesus feeds 5000, then 4000 *Mat 14:15-21, 15:32-39, Mark 6:35-44, 8:1-10, Luke 9:12-17, John 6:5-14*

Jesus sends Peter for tribute money from mouth of fish *Mat 17:24-27*

Jesus' parable of talents *Mat 25:14-30, Luke 19:11-28*

Peter's net filled *Luke 5:1-11, John 21:1-11*

Jesus' parable of lost coin *Luke 15:8-10*

Jesus turns water into wine *John 2:1-11*

Jesus on the bread of life *John 6:26-65*

Paul on abundance *2 Cor 8:11-15, 9:6-15*

See also abundance, income, increase, money, prosperity, substance, success

SUPPORT

A helpmate for Adam created *Gen 2:21-25*

Moses' hands upheld by Aaron and Hur *Exod 17:8-16*

Moses encourages his successor *Deut 31:7-23, Josh 1:1-9*

Barak supports Deborah *Judg 4: 1-17*

Ruth aids her mother-in-law *Ruth 1:1-22*

Jonathan befriends David *1 Sam 18:1-16*

Elisha walks with Elijah *2 King 2:1-11*

Jehoshaphat supported by the prophet Jahaziel *2 Chron 20:1-32*

Isaiah supports King Hezekiah *2 Chron 31:20, 21, 32:1-23, Isa 36:1-22, 37:1-38*

Mordecai and people supported by Queen Esther *Esther 6:1-14, 7: 1-10*

Job's friends are no help *Job 2:11-13, 4:1-12*

David's song, "God is our refuge and strength" *Psal 46:1-11*

Peter commended for acknowledging Jesus as Christ *Mat 16:13-20, Mark 8:27-30, Luke 9:18-21*

All men seek Jesus; his fame increases *Mark 1:35-39, 45*

Twelve disciples return reporting success *Luke 9:10, 11*

Seventy disciples return reporting success *Luke 10:17-24*

Jesus' parable of good Samaritan *Luke 10:25-37*

John the Baptist testifies that Jesus is Christ *John 1:15-34*

Jesus' parable of good shepherd *John 10:1-18*

Holy Ghost descends to support Christians *Acts 2:1-13*

Peter and John continue signs and wonders *Acts 4:24-37*

Philip heals many *Acts 8:5-8*

Paul's teaching that Jesus' resurrection proves ours *1 Cor 15: 1-58*

Paul's hardships to establish Christ's church *2 Cor 11:21-33*

See also courage, defense, foundation

SUPREMACY

Abraham willing to sacrifice his son to God *Gen 22:1-19*

Joseph appointed governor of Egypt *Gen 41:1-46*

Moses takes God's word as basis of all law *Exod 20:1-19, Deut 5:1-24*

Solomon dedicates temple to God *1 King 8:22-66, 2 Chron 6:1-42*

Elijah translated over death *2 King 2:1-11*

Jehoshaphat shows that the battle is God's *2 Chron 20:1-32*

The infinite speaks to Job *Job 38: 1-41*

David's song, "the secret place of the most High" *Psal 91:1-16*

David's song on God, the preserver of man *Psal 121:1-8*

Three Jews preserved in fiery furnace *Dan 3:1-30*

Daniel saved in lions' den *Dan 6: 1-28*

Jesus' sermon on oneness with Father *John 10:22-42*

Jesus feeds 5000 *Mat 14:15-21, Mark 6:35-44, Luke 9:12-17, John 6:5-14*

Jesus walks on water *Mat 14:22-33, John 6:15-21*

Jesus' resurrection *Mat 28:1-8, Mark 16:1-8, Luke 24:1-12, John 20:1-10*

Angels announce birth of Jesus *Luke 2:8-20*

Jesus Christ as the light of the world *John 1:1-14*

Jesus heals man born blind *John 9:1-41*

John's vision of God's throne *Rev 4:1-11*

See also dominion, greatness, omnipotence, perfection

SURGERY

Lord God removes a rib from Adam and makes Eve *Gen 2:21-25*

Jesus heals withered hand *Mat 12: 9-13, Mark 3:1-5, Luke 6:6-11*

Jesus' wounded body is restored and raised *Mat 28:1-8, Mark 16:1-8, Luke 24:1-12, John 20:1-10*

Jesus heals woman bowed together *Luke 13:11-17*

Peter and John heal man lame from birth *Acts 3:1-11*

See also deformity, injury, medicine

SWORD

The Cherubims guard the way of the tree of life with a flaming sword *Gen 3:22-24*

"The sword of the Lord, and of Gideon," the war cry *Judg 7:1-25*

Goliath's sword is of no avail *1 Sam 17:1-16, 38-52*

David refuses Saul's armor and trusts God *1 Sam 17:17-37*

Nehemiah arms workers while building the wall *Neh 4:1-23*

War will be no more with the coming of the Messiah *Mic 4:1-8, 13, Isa 2:1-5*

Peter cuts off Malchus' ear and Jesus heals it Luke 22:50, 51
Paul on the Christian's armor Eph 6:10-17
John's vision of man on white horse with sharp sword Rev 19:11-21

See also armor, authority, decision, power, war

SYMBOLS

The rainbow as a token of the covenant Gen 9:12-17
Abram and Sarai receive new names Gen 17:1-9, 15-22
The burning bush, a symbol of indestructibility Exod 3:1-18
Moses' rod Exod 4:1-9, 17:1-7, Num 20:1-13
Aaron's rod Exod 7:1-12, Num 17:1-11
Pillars of cloud and fire illustrate God's guidance Exod 13:20-22, Num 9:15-23
Moses sets up a serpent of brass in wilderness Num 21:4-9
Zechariah's vision of candlestick fed by two olive trees Zech 4:1-14
The cross Mat 27:37-56, Mark 15:21-41, Luke 23:26-49, John 19:17-30
The ark as a symbol of faith Heb 11:7
John's vision of the city foursquare Rev 21:10-27

See also idea, idolatry, parable, signs

SYNAGOGUE

Jesus on hypocrites praying in synagogue Mat 6:1-5
The Roman centurion who built a synagogue Mat 8:5:13, Luke 7:1-10
Jesus teaches in the synagogue on sabbath Mark 1:21-28, Luke 4:33-37
Jesus at twelve years questions rabbis in synagogue Luke 2:41-52
Jesus' parable of Pharisee and publican praying Luke 18:9-14
Paul preaches in synagogue Acts 14:1-6
Paul disputes in synagogue Acts 17:17-23

See also congregation, worship

SYSTEM

God creates complete universe and calls it good Gen 1:1-31
Moses shows God as basis of all law Exod 20:1-19, Deut 5:1-24
Jesus explains how to heal a hard case Mat 17:14-21, Mark 9:14-29, Luke 9:37-43
Jesus instructs 70 disciples Luke 10:1-24
Jesus tells source of his great works John 5:17-47
Jesus promises spirit of truth will tell disciples all John 14:1-31
At Pentecost Holy Spirit descends Acts 2:1-13
Peter's sermon on how the lame man was healed Acts 3:12-18

See also body, mind, order, science

T

TABERNACLE

See church, temple

TALENT

Joseph's business ability, interpreter of dreams Gen 39:1-6, 41:1-46
Moses' communication with God Exod 3:1-18, 19:1-9, 20:1-19, 33:7-23
The wisdom of Solomon as a judge 1 King 3:5-28
Elijah as a spiritual seer 1 King 19:9-13
Elisha's healing abilities 2 King 4:8-37, 5:1-14
David as song writer Psal 23:1-6, 91:1-16
Isaiah's vision as a prophet Isa 6:1-13
Daniel's ability to interpret Dan 2:1-49, 4:1-27, 5:1-31
Jesus' parable of the talents Mat 25:14-30, Luke 19:11-28
Paul's ability at church building Acts 11:19-26, 2 Cor 11:21-33
Paul on the source of spiritual gifts 1 Cor 12:1, 4-11
Jesus' talents as a healer and miracle-worker (See Part II, Jesus Christ: Great Works)

Jesus as a preacher (*See* Part II, Jesus Christ: Teachings)

See also ability, power, skill

TASTE

Moses makes bitter water of Marah sweet *Exod 15:22-27*
Israelites remember the taste of foods in Egypt *Num 11:1-15*
Elisha nullified poison tasted in pottage *2 King 4:38-41*
The body and blood of Christ at the Last Supper *Mat 26:26-29, Mark 14:22-25, Luke 22:14-30, 1 Cor 11: 23-25*
Jesus' parable of the rich man who wanted water in hell *Luke 16: 19-31*
Jesus' host complimented on the taste of his wine *John 2:1-11*

See also, food, mind, senses, wine

TAXES

Joseph collects a portion of all the good harvest *Gen 41:46-49*
Liberal offerings are made to David to build the temple *1 Chron 29: 6-19*
Jesus sends Peter to obtain tribute money from the fish *Mat 17:24-27*
Jesus on paying tribute to Caesar *Mat 22:15-22, Mark 12:13-27, Luke 20:20-26*
The widow's mite *Mark 12:41-44, Luke 21:1-4*
Mary and Joseph go to Bethlehem to be taxed *Luke 2:1-7*
Jesus' parable of the Pharisee and publican *Luke 18:9-14*
Jesus visits a publican and he returns exhorted money *Luke 19: 1-10*

See also duty, tithing

TEACHING

Eve takes lessons from the serpent *Gen 3:1-5*
Moses teaches Israel the law *Exod 20:1-19, Deut 5:1-24*
Elijah prepares Elisha for his mantle *2 King 2:1-15*

The infinite speaks to Job *Job 38:1-41*
The value of wisdom *Prov 3:1-13, 3:13-26, 8:1-36*
Zechariah's vision of candlestick fed by two olive trees *Zech 4:1-14*
Parables and teachings of Jesus *(See* Part II, Jesus Christ: Parables, Teachings)
Jesus instructs twelve and sends them out *Mat 9:36-38, 10:1-42, Mark 3:13-21, 6:7-13, Luke 9:1-6, 10, 11*
Jesus teaches how epileptic boy is healed *Mat 17:14-21, Mark 9:14-29, Luke 9:37-43*
Jesus teaches relation between sickness and sin *Mark 2:1-12, Luke 5:17-26*
At twelve years, Jesus impresses the rabbis *Luke 2:41-52*
Jesus instructs 70 disciples *Luke 10:1-24*
Jesus as the light of the world *John 1:1-14, 8:12-32*
Jesus instructs Peter for benefit of all disciples *John 21:12-19*
Peter on the meaning of Christianity *Acts 2:14-47*
Peter on healing *Acts 3:12-26*
Paul on charity *1 Cor 13:1-13*
Paul on Christian precepts *1 Thess 5:1-28*
Paul on advice to his disciple *2 Tim 2:1-26*
Paul's charge to the faithful *2 Tim 4:1-8*
Paul on the nature of faith *Heb 11:1-40*
James on how to bear our cross *Jas 1:1-27*
John's sermon on God is love *1 John 4:1-21*

See also disciple, education, instruction, knowledge, preaching, study

TEMPERANCE

Adam and Eve eat forbidden fruit *Gen 3:6-24*
Cain kills Abel *Gen 4:1-16*
Joseph resists his master's wife *Gen 39:1-20*

Moses warns against abominations *Deut 18:9-14*

Gideon refuses to be king *Judg 8: 22, 23*

David resists harming Saul *1 Sam 24:1-22, 26:1-25*

Elisha returns captives to their homes *2 King 6:8-23*

Daniel refuses king's portion of meat and wine *Dan 1:1-21*

Jesus is tempted *Mat 4:1-11, Mark 1:12, 13, Luke 4:1-13*

Jesus puts Mosaic law on mental basis *Mat 5:21-48, Mark 9:38-50*

Jesus saves adultress, then advises her to sin no more *John 8:1-11*

Paul's teaching to come out from among them and be separate *2 Cor 6:1-18*

Paul's teaching to put on the new man *Col 3:1-17*

See also abstinence, appetite, food, forgiveness, moderation, wine

TEMPERATURE

Isaiah's vision that desert will blossom *Isa 35:1-10*

Three Jews in fiery furnace *Dan 3:1-30*

Jesus heals Peter's wife's mother of fever *Mat 8:14-17, Mark 1:29-34*

Jesus heals nobleman's son of fever while absent from him *John 4: 46-54*

See also fever, heat

TEMPLE

David's promise to build a house for the Lord *2 Sam 7:1-29*

Solomon builds the temple *1 King 6:1-38, 7:1-51, 2 Chron 3:1-17, 4:1-22, 5:1-14*

Solomon dedicates the temple *1 King 8:22-66, 2 Chron 6:1-42*

David receives liberal offerings for the proposed temple *1 Chron 29: 6-19*

Zerubbabel has the king announce rebuilding of the temple *Ezra 1:1-11*

Zerubbabel starts to rebuild *Ezra 3:8-13*

Adversaries block rebuilding *Ezra 4:1-5*

Work starts up again *Ezra 6:1-3, 7, 8, 14, 15*

Jesus casts traders out of temple *Mat 21:12, 13, Mark 11:15-17, Luke 19:45, 46, John 2:13-25*

Jesus foretells destruction of the temple *Mat 24:1-14, Mark 3:1-37, Luke 21:5-36*

Jesus heals man in synagogue *Mark 1:21-28, Luke 4:33-37*

Simon and Anna in temple meet Jesus *Luke 2:21-38*

Jesus' parable of counting the cost of building *Luke 14:25-33*

Jesus' parable of the Pharisee and publican in the temple *Luke 18:9-14*

Jesus' parable of the temple to be raised in three days *John 2:19-22*

Peter and John heal lame man laid at gate of temple *Acts 3:1-11*

Paul's teaching that "ye are the temple of God" *1 Cor 3:13-17, 6: 19, 20, 2 Cor 6:14-18*

John's vision of new heaven and earth with no temple *Rev 21:1-27*

See also body, building, church, house

TEMPTATION

Adam and Eve succumb *Gen 3:1-5*

Abraham tempted to sacrifice his son *Gen 22:1-19*

Joseph resists his master's wife *Gen 39:1-20*

Samson succumbs to temptation and is betrayed *Judg 16:4-30*

David is tempted to kill Uriah *2 Sam 11:1-27*

Ahab and Naboth's vineyard *1 King 21:1-27*

David's song, "Create in me a clean heart" *Psal 51:1-19*

Daniel refuses King's meat and wine *Dan 1:1-21*

Jesus is tempted *Mat 4:1-11, Mark 1:12, 13, Luke 4:1-13*

Judas settles the price of betrayal *Mat 26:14-16, Mark 14:10, 11, Luke 22:1-6*

Jesus' parable of the prodigal son *Luke 15:11-24*

Jesus saves the adultress *John 8: 1-11*

Paul on the Christian's armor *Eph 6:10-17*

James on temptations and trials *Jas 1:1-27*

See also abstinence, appetite, armor, devil, evil, serpent, trial

TEN COMMANDMENTS

See commandment

TENETS

Lord God forbids fruit of tree of knowledge of good and evil *Gen 2:9-17, 3:1-5*

Moses and Ten Commandments *Exod 20:1-19, Deut 5:1-24*

Moses says abominations are forbidden *Deut 13:1-18, 18:9-14*

David's song, "The Lord is my shepherd" *Psal 23:1-6*

Isaiah's vision of Christ's kingdom— "war no more" *Isa 2:1-5, Mic 4: 1-8, 13*

Jesus gives qualities of a Christian *Mat 5:1-12, Luke 6:17-26, 36, 12: 22-34*

Jesus explains healing of woman because of faith *Mat 9:20-22, Mark 5:25-34, Luke 8:43-48*

Jesus' disciples must be able to heal *Mat 9:36-38, 10:1-42, Mark 3:13-21, 6:7-13, Luke 9:1-6, 10, 11, 10:1-24*

Jesus explains faith healing to father of boy he heals *Mat 17:14-21, Mark 9:14-21, Luke 9:37-43*

The need for persistent prayer *Luke 11:5-13, 18:1-8*

Jesus teaches man must be born again *John 3:1-21*

Jesus is the Christ *John 7:14-40*

The need for abiding in Christ *John 15:1-17*

Jesus tells Peter, "Feed my sheep" *John 21:12-19*

Paul on qualities that protect *Eph 6:10-17*

Paul teaches put off old, put on new man *Col 3:1-17*

James' sermon of the equality of man *Jas 2:1-13*

See also commandment, doctrine, law

TEST

See trials

TESTAMENT

See covenant, will

TESTIFY

Moses asks for evidence that he has seen God *Exod 3:9-12, 4:1-9*

Song of Moses describes gratitude for deliverance *Exod 15:1-19*

Caleb and Joshua's report differs from that of other scouts *Num 13:1-33, 14:1-11, 23-39, Deut 1:19-38*

Song of Moses tells of God's care of Israel *Deut 32:1-47*

Song of Deborah rejoices in God's victory *Judg 5:1-20*

David's song of thanksgiving *2 Sam 22:1-51, 1 Chron 16:17-36*

David's song, "The Lord is my shepherd" *Psal 23:1-6*

David's song, "The earth is the Lord's" *Psal 24:1-10*

David's song, "Make a joyful noise" *Psal 66:1-20, 100:1-5*

David's song, "Bless the Lord, O my soul" *Psal 103:1-22*

David's song, "Let the redeemed . . . say so" *Psal 107:1-43*

David's song on God, the preserver of man *Psal 121:1-8*

Hosea's testimony of God's care of his child *Hos 11:1-4*

Voice says Jesus is His beloved son *Mat 3:13-27, 17:1-13, Mark 1:9-11, 9:2-13, Luke 3:21, 22, 9:28-36*

Woman who touched Jesus' hem admits her healing *Mat 9:20-22, Mark 5:25-34, Luke 8:43-48*

Jesus points to healing as proof of Christ *Mat 11:2-19, Luke 7:18-35*

Peter acknowledges Jesus as Christ *Mat 16:13-20, Mark 8:27-30, Luke 9:18-21*

Simon and Anna testify that the baby Jesus is the Christ *Luke 2:21-38*

Twelve disciples report success *Luke 9:10, 11*

Seventy disciples report success *Luke 10:17-24*

John acknowledges Jesus as Christ *John 1:15-34*

Jesus acknowledges Father as source of great works *John 5:17-47*

Man born blind gives legal witness to his healing *John 9:1-41*

Thomas affirms the resurrection of the body *John 20:24-29*

Peter and John speak the word with boldness *Acts 4:1-23*

Paul reports his healing *Acts 22: 1-30, 26:1-32*

See also evidence, fact, gratitude, witness

TEXTBOOK

See book

THANKSGIVING

Song of Moses describes gratitude for deliverance *Exod 15:1-19, Deut 32:1-47*

Moses on the rewards of obedience *Deut 28:1-14*

Joshua sets up memorial for deliverance *Josh 4:1-24*

David's song of thanksgiving *2 Sam 22:1-51, 1 Chron 16:17-36*

Liberal offerings to David for temple *1 Chron 29:6-19*

Jehoshaphat sends singers before army *2 Chron 20:1-32*

David's song, "Make a joyful noise" *Psal 66:1-20, 100:1-5*

David's song, "Bless the Lord" *Psal 103:1-22*

David's song, "praise the Lord" *Psal 107:1-43*

Nebuchadnezzar's insanity healed and he is grateful *Dan 4:28-37*

Malachi urges tithing *Mal 3:10, 4: 1, 2*

The woman, healed by touching Jesus' hem, admits her healing *Mat 9:20-22, Mark 5:25-34, Luke 8:43-48*

Jesus watches widow cast in her mites *Mark 12:41-44, Luke 21:1-4*

Heavenly host rejoices at Jesus' birth *Luke 2:8-20*

Jesus heals ten lepers, one returns *Luke 17:11-19*

Jesus gives thanks *before* raising Lazarus *John 11:1-46*

Paul and Silas, in prison, sing praises *Acts 16:19-40*

Paul on rejoicing *Phil 4:1-23*

See also acknowledge, gratitude, praise, testify

THEOLOGY

God creates the spiritual universe *Gen 1:1-31*

Lord God creates man of dust *Gen 2:6-8*

Abraham discusses deliverance by righteousness *Gen 18:20-33*

Moses' revelation of God's nature *Exod 3:1-18*

Moses' revelation of God's law *Exod 20:1-19*

People set apart as God's own *Deut 7:6-11*

Elijah's revelation of God's nature *1 King 19:9-13*

Job's revelation of God's nature *Job 38:1-41*

David's song of God's ever-presence *Psal 139:1-24*

Isaiah's Messiah concept *Isa 7:10-16, 9:2-7*

Jesus on the qualities that make a Christian *Mat 5:1-12, Luke 6:17-26, 36*

Jesus tells how to communicate in prayer *Mat 6:5-15, Mark 11:25, 26, Luke 11:1-4*

Jesus on the mission of disciples to preach and heal *Mat 28:16-20, Mark 16:15-18*

Jesus explains meaning of love thy neighbor *Luke 10:25-37*

Jesus tells process of sin and repentance *Luke 15:11-24*

Peter on resurrection and baptism *Acts 2:14-47*

Paul's teaching that Jesus' resurrection proves ours *1 Cor 15:1-58*

John's revelation of God's nature as love *1 John 4:1-21*

See also religion, revelation, science, teaching, truth

THINKING

God creates universe by thinking it *Gen 1:1-31*

Abraham's dialogue on the righteous man and the city *Gen 18: 20-33*

Abraham's temptation to sacrifice his son *Gen 22:1-19*

Jacob's wrestling leads to new name *Gen 32:24-32*

Joseph solves the problem of feast and famine *Gen 41:1-46*

Gideon develops a winning strategy *Judg 7:1-25*

Solomon selects proper values *1 King 3:5-15, 2 Chron 1:7-12*

Elijah arrives at the nature of God *1 King 19:9-13*

Esther considers whether she will risk helping her people *Esther 3:1-15, 4:1-17*

Job's dialogues with his friends *Job 2:1-13, 4:1-21*

David's song, "What is man?" *Psal 8:1-9*

Daniel refuses king's meat and wine *Dan 1:1-21*

The temptations of Jesus *Mat 4:1-11, Mark 1:12, 13, Luke 4:1-13*

Jesus heals insanity *Mat 8:28-34, Mark 5:1-20, Luke 8:26-39*

Jesus' reply on what defiles a man *Mat 15:1-20, Mark 7:1-23*

Jesus at Gethsemane *Mat 26:30, 36, 46, Mark 14:26, 32-42, Luke 22: 39-46*

Jesus heals mental derangement *Mark 1:21-28, Luke 4:33-37*

Jesus' maturity of thought at twelve years acknowledged by rabbis *Luke 2:41-52*

Jesus' parable of prodigal son *Luke 15:11-24*

Jesus' parable of rich man and beggar *Luke 16:19-31*

Jesus' parable of Pharisee and publican *Luke 18:9-14*

Peter changes his mind about Gentiles *Acts 10:1-48, 11:1-18*

Paul on inward versus outward man *2 Cor 4:14—5:21*

Paul on putting off old man, putting on new *Col 3:1-17*

John exposes thoughts of the churches *Rev 1:4-20, 2:1-29, 3: 1-22*

See also creation, idea, imagination, mind, reflection, wisdom

THIRST

Hagar and Ishmael thirst in the desert *Gen 21:9-21*

Moses makes bitter water sweet *Exod 15:22-27*

Moses obtains water from a rock *Exod 17:1-7, Num 20:1-13*

Gideon selects the men who lap water *Judg 7:1-25*

Waters of city healed by Elisha *2 King 2:16-22*

Elisha supplies water for large army *2 King 3:16-20*

David's song, "the fountain of life" *Psal 36:1-12*

Jesus says one of the qualities of a Christian is to thirst after righteousness *Mat 5:1-12, Luke 6:17-26, 36*

Jesus' parable of new wine in old bottles *Luke 5:36-39*

Jesus makes water into wine *John 2:1-11*

Jesus at Jacob's well, to obtain drink, offers living water to woman of Samaria *John 4:1-42*

John's vision of the river of the water of life *Rev 22:1-21*

See also appetite, water

THRESHOLD

See door

THRONE

Joseph next to the throne of Pharaoh *Gen 41:25-46*

David made king of combined kingdoms *2 Sam 2:1-4, 4:1-5*

John's vision of God's throne *Rev 4:1-11*

See also authority, crown, dominion, king, majesty, power

TIME

God creates universe in successive days *Gen 1:1-31, 2:1-5*

Early man lived to advanced age *Gen 5:1-32*

Sun and moon stand still *Josh 10: 6-15*

All mortal events within time framework *Eccl 3:1-15*

Jesus heals issue of blood after twelve years of ill-health *Mat 9:20-22, Mark 5:25-34, Luke 8: 43-48*

Jesus is risen after three days *Mat 28:1-8, Mark 16:1-8, Luke 24: 1-12, John 20:1-10*

Jesus causes ship to be across lake instantly *Mark 6:45-52, John 6:21*

Jesus mature at twelve years *Luke 2: 41-52*

After fishing all night Peter's net is filled at once *Luke 5:1-11, John 21:1-11*

Jesus heals woman bowed together 18 years *Luke 13:11-17*

Jesus' parable of the temple to be raised in three days *John 2:19-22*

Jesus heals impotent man 38 years at pool *John 5:1-16*

The unity and eternity of the Christ ("Before Abraham was, I am") *John 8:51-59*

Jesus raises Lazarus dead four days *John 11:1-46*

John's vision of new heaven and earth with time no longer *Rev 21:1-27*

See also age, day, eternity, present, year

TITHING

Joseph reserves grain in time of good harvest *Gen 41:28-46*

David receives liberal offering for the temple *1 Chron 29:6-19*

Malachi's promise for tithing *Mal 3:10, 4:1, 2*

Jesus gives Golden Rule for actions *Mat 7:12-14*

Jesus sends Peter for tribute money from fish's mouth *Mat 17:24-27*

Jesus reproves tithe of mint and anise without weightier matters *Mat 23:1-24*

Jesus comments on the widow's mite *Mark 12:41-44, Luke 21:1-4*

See also duty, gratitude, taxes

TONGUE

Moses complains of his speaking ability *Exod 4:10-17*

Eldad and Medad prophesy in the camp *Num 11:16-30*

Balak employs Balaam to curse Israelites *Num 22:1-41, 23:1-30, 24: 1-25*

David's song, "Make a joyful noise" *Psal 66:1-20, 100:1-5*

David's song, "Let the redeemed... say so" *Psal 107:1-43*

Isaiah is called to speak *Isa 6:1-13*

Jesus heals dumb man *Mat 9:32-35*

Jesus heals man blind and dumb *Mat 12:22-30, Luke 11:14-23*

Jesus heals group *Mat 15:29-31*

Prayer must be persistent *Luke 11:5-13, 18:1-8*

John the Baptist tells how Jesus' preaching differs from his *John 3:22-36*

Descent of Holy Ghost; they speak with tongues *Acts 2:1-13*

Paul on God, the source of all abilities *Eph 4:1-32*

See also language, speech

TORMENT

See torture

TORTURE

Joseph is put into a pit by his brothers *Gen 37:1-36*

Oppression of Israel in Egypt *Exod 1:8-14, 5:7-19*

Job asks why the good man should suffer *Job 3:1-26*

David's song, "Why art thou cast down?" *Psal 42:1-17*

Isaiah foresees the trial of the man of sorrows *Isa 53:1-12*

Three Jews put into fiery furnace *Dan 3:1-30*

Daniel in lions' den *Dan 6:1-28*

Jesus relieves the anguish of Jairus by healing his daughter *Mat 9: 18, 19, 23-26, Mark 5:22-24, 35-43, Luke 8:41, 42, 49-56*

Jesus relieves anguish of Syrophenician by healing her daughter *Mat 15:21-28, Mark 7:24-30*

Jesus relieves anguish of the father by healing the epileptic boy *Mat 17:14-21, Mark 9:14-29, Luke 9: 37-43*

Jesus at Gethsemane *Mat 26:30, 36-46, Mark 14:26, 32-42, Luke 22:39-46*

Jesus scourged and mocked *Mat 27:27-31, Mark 15:16-20, John 19:1-16*

The crucifixion *Mat 27:32-56, Mark 15:21-41, Luke 23:26-49, John 19:17-30*

Jesus' parable of rich man and beggar *Luke 16:19-31*

Stephen stoned to death *Acts 7:51-60*

Paul's hardships while establishing church *2 Cor 11:21-33*

See also devil, pain, persecution, suffering

TOUCH

Precious ointment on Jesus' head *Mat 26:6-13, Mark 14:3-9*

Jesus touches tongue and ears and heals deaf and dumb man *Mark 7:32-37*

Jesus touches bier and raises widow's son *Luke 7:11-17*

Jesus anointed by woman *Luke 7:36-50*

Jesus anoints eyes and heals blind *John 9:1-41*

Jesus washes disciples' feet *John 13:1-20*

Jesus asks Magdalene not to touch him *John 20:11-18*

Jesus permits Thomas to examine his wounds *John 20:24-29*

See also senses

TRADE

Abraham's riches grow, causing strife with Lot *Gen 13:1-18*

A proper wife is found for Isaac *Gen 24:1-67*

Joseph as slave causes prosperity to his master *Gen 39:1-7*

All the trades combine to build Solomon's temple *1 King 6:1-38, 7:1-51, 2 Chron 3:1-17, 4:1-22, 5:1-14*

The widow sells her miraculous supply of oil *2 King 4:1-7*

Elisha predicts drop in price of flour *2 King 6:24, 25, 7:1-18*

Jesus gives Golden Rule for actions *Mat 7:12-14*

Jesus casts traders out of temple *Mat 21:12, 13, Mark 11:15-17, Luke 19:45, 46, John 2:13-25*

Paul's rule of abundance for all *2 Cor 8:11-15, 9:6-15*

See also business, calling, profit, work

TRADITION

Lord God made man from dust *Gen 2:6-8*

Serpent deceived Eve *Gen 3:1-5*

Early man lived to advanced age *Gen 5:1-32*

The passover instituted in Egypt *Exod 11:4-10, 12:1-14, 21-41, Deut 16:1-22*

Aaron receives Urim and Thummim of office *Exod 28:29-36*

Atonement through scapegoat *Lev 16:1-28*

Isaiah predicts the coming of Messiah *Isa 7:10-16, 9:2-7*

Isaiah predicts treatment of Messiah on arrival *Isa 53:1-12*

Jesus endorses baptism *Mat 3:13-17, Mark 1:9-11, Luke 3:21, 22*

Jesus starts communion at Last Supper *Mat 26:26-29, Mark 14:22-25, Luke 22:14-30, 1 Cor 11:23-25*

Birth of Jesus and Christian tradition *Luke 2:1-7*

Jesus establishes Christian healing *(See* Part II, Jesus Christ: Great Works)

See also doctrine, knowledge, inherit, Pharisee

TRANSFIGURATION

Moses' face veiled *Exod 34:29-35*

Elijah taken to heaven in chariot of fire *2 King 2:1-12*

Jesus on mount with Moses and Elijah *Mat 17:1-13, Mark 9:2-13, Luke 9:28-36*

See also Jesus, space, time, voice

TRANSFORMATION

Abram and Sarai given new names by God *Gen 17:1-9, 15-22*

Lot's wife becomes pillar of salt *Gen 19:1, 15-29*

Joseph, the governor of Egypt, not recognized by his brothers *Gen 43: 1, 2, 45: 1-11, 25-28*

Moses' face changed by talking with God *Exod 34: 29-35*

David's song, "How are the mighty fallen!" *2 Sam 1: 17-27*

Nehemiah hears of Jerusalem's misery *Neh 1: 1-11*

Isaiah's vision of no more war *Isa 1: 1-12*

Jonah finally obeys God *Jonah 3: 1-10*

Micah's vision of the glory of the church *Mic 4: 1-8, 13, Isa 2: 1-5*

Jesus heals withered hand *Mat 12: 9-13, Mark 3: 1-5, Luke 6: 6-11*

Jesus' parable of the mustard seed *Mat 13: 31, 32, Mark 4: 30-32, Luke 3: 18, 19*

Jesus' parable of leaven *Mat 13: 33, Luke 13: 20, 21*

Jesus' transfiguration on mount *Mat 17: 1-13, Mark 9: 2-13, Luke 9: 28-36*

Jesus' parable of prodigal son *Luke 15: 11-24*

Jesus' parable of rich man and beggar *Luke 16: 19-31*

Paul no longer persecutor of Christians *Acts 8:1-4, 9:1-22*

Paul urges mental transformation *Rom 12: 1, 2*

John's vision of new heaven and earth *Rev 21: 1-27*

See also change, character, conversion, heart

TRANSLATION

Enoch walked with God and was not *Gen 5: 18, 21-24, Heb 11: 5*

Elijah taken to heaven in whirlwind *2 King 2: 1-11*

Jesus' transfiguration *Mat 17: 1-13, Mark 9: 2-13, Luke 9: 28-36*

Jesus' ascension *Mark 16: 19, 20, Luke 24: 50-53, Acts 1: 6-12*

At Pentecost everyone speaks in his own language but all hear in own native tongue *Acts 2: 1-12*

John's vision of the sealed book that only the lamb could open *Rev 5: 1-14*

See also eternity, language, life

TRAVEL

Abraham begins his wandering search for promised land *Gen 11: 31, 32, 12: 1-9*

Jacob flees his homeland *Gen 28: 10-22*

Joseph goes to Egypt *Gen 37:1-36*

Jacob and all his children emigrate to Egypt *Gen 46: 2-7*

Israelites cross Red Sea into wilderness *Exod 14: 5-31*

After wandering they cross Jordan into promised land *Josh 3: 1-17*

Naomi leaves Israel for Moab and returns *Ruth 1: 1-22, 2: 1-23*

David's song, "Whither shall I go from thy spirit?" *Psal 139: 1-24*

Jonah takes ship to Tarshish and returns to Nineveh *Jonah 1:1-17, 2: 1-10, 3: 1-10*

Wise men follow star *Mat 2: 1-12*

The flight to Egypt *Mat 2: 13-23, Luke 2: 39, 40*

Jesus transports the ship immediately to destination *Mark 6: 45-52, John 6: 21*

Jesus' parable of the man taking a long journey *Mark 13: 34-37*

Mary and Joseph go to Bethlehem *Luke 2: 1-7*

The trip to Jerusalem at twelve years of age *Luke 2:41-52*

Jesus' parable of good Samaritan *Luke 10: 25-37*

Philip goes to Gaza and baptizes an Ethiopian *Acts 8: 26-40*

Paul shipwrecked on voyage to Rome *Acts 27: 1-44*

See also sea, ship

TREACHERY

See betrayal

TREASON

Rebekah and Jacob deceive Isaac *Gen 27: 1-44*

People worship golden calf *Exod 32: 1-24*

Miriam and Aaron speak against Moses *Num 12: 1-16*

Jonathan rebels against his father, King Saul   *1 Sam 14: 24-32*

Absalom rebels against his father, King David   *2 Sam 15: 1-23*

Jesus' parable of farmers who killed the son of the landlord   *Mat 21: 33-45, Mark 12: 1-12, Luke 20: 9-19*

Judas sets price to betray Jesus   *Mat 26: 14-16, Mark 14: 10, 11, Luke 22: 1-6*

See also betrayal, duplicity, government

TREASURE

Hezekiah shows all his treasure to ambassadors from Babylon, and his country is attacked   *2 King 20: 12-21, Isa 39: 1-8*

Wise men bring gifts to Jesus   *Mat 2: 1-12*

Jesus on true treasures   *Mat 6: 19-21*

Jesus' parable of householder's treasures   *Mat 13:51, 52*

Jesus discusses precious ointment used to anoint him   *Mat 26: 6-13, Mark 14: 3-9, John 12: 3-9*

See also money, substance, wealth

TREATMENT

Abraham heals Abimelech and wife of barrenness   *Gen 20: 1-7, 17*

God shows Moses how to handle fear and disease   *Exod 4:1-9*

Elijah raises dead boy   *1 King 7: 17-24*

The Shunammite is a good patient   *2 King 4: 8-37*

Elisha specifies exactly the right treatment for Naaman   *2 King 5: 1-14*

David's songs:

    "the fountain of life"   *Psal 36: 1-12*

    "God is our refuge and strength"   *Psal 46:1-11*

    the Lord who heals and redeems   *Psal 103:1-22*

    "Let the redeemed . . . say so"   *Psal 107:1-43*

Jesus heals servant without being present with him   *Mat 8: 5-13, Luke 7: 1-10*

Jesus comments on healing on the sabbath   *Mat 12: 9-13, Mark 3: 1-5, Luke 6: 6-11*

Jesus explains a difficult case to his disciples   *Mat 17: 14-21, Mark 9: 14-29, Luke 9: 37-43*

Jesus compares healing sin and sickness   *Mark 2: 1-12, Luke 5: 17-26*

Jesus heals blind man in two treatments   *Mark 8: 22-26*

Jesus' parable of two debtors forgiven   *Luke 7: 36-50*

Jesus' parable of good Samaritan   *Luke 10: 25-37*

Jesus' parable of temple to be raised in three days   *John 2: 19-22*

Jesus explains source of great works   *John 5: 17-47*

Jesus expresses confidence before raising Lazarus   *John 11: 1-46*

Peter on healing   *Acts 3: 12-26*

Paul's teaching to put off old man, put on new   *Col 3: 1-17*

John's sermon, "God is love"   *1 John 4: 1-21*

See also demonstration, medicine, patient, proof

TREE

Trees of Eden   *Gen 2: 9-17*

Tree of knowledge of good and evil   *Gen 2: 16, 17, 3: 1-5*

Jotham's parable of the trees   *Judg 9: 1-15*

Absalom killed by a tree   *2 Sam 18: 6-33*

Elijah flees to juniper tree   *1 King 19: 1-8*

Jeremiah's vision of good and bad figs   *Jer 24: 1-10*

Daniel interprets king's dream of a tree   *Dan 4: 1-27*

Zechariah's vision of two olive trees   *Zech 4: 1-14*

Jesus' parable of mustard seed   *Mat 13: 31, 32, Mark 4: 30-32, Luke 13: 18, 19*

Jesus withers the barren fig tree   *Mat 21: 18-22, Mark 11: 12-14, 20-24*

The crucifixion on the accursed tree   *Mat 27: 32-56, Mark 15: 21-41, Luke 23: 26-49, John 19: 17-30*

Jesus' parable of barren fig tree   *Luke 13: 6-9*

Zacchaeus climbs a tree to see better
Luke 19: 1-10
John's vision of tree of life   Rev
22: 1-21

See also life, plant, symbols

TRIALS

Abraham's faith tried in sacrifice of
his son Gen 22: 1-19
Jacob wrestles with angel all night
Gen 32: 24-32
Joseph triumphs after succession of
trials Gen 37: 14-36, 39: 1-23, 41:
1-46
Israelites tried in wilderness Exod
16:1-36, 17:1-7, Num 11:1-15, 20:
1-13, 21:4-9, 31, 32
Moses cautions people to remember
trials Deut 8: 1-20
Ruth and Naomi survive repeated
blows Ruth 1:1-22, 2:1-23
Elijah discouraged by fortunes
1 King 19:1-8
Elisha raises Shunammite's son
2 King 4:8-37
Esther helps her persecuted people
Esther 5:1-14
Job's trials planned and executed
Job 1: 1-22, 2: 1-10
David's song, "Why art thou cast
down?" Psal 42: 1-11
David's song, "God is our refuge and
strength" Psal 46: 1-11
Isaiah's vision of man of sorrows
Isa 53: 1-12
Three Jews in fiery furnace Dan
3: 1-30
Daniel in lions' den Dan 6: 1-28
Jonah's prayer in trouble Jonah 2:
1-10
Jesus' temptations Mat 4: 1-11,
Mark 1: 12, 13, Luke 4: 1-13
Jesus heals woman of issue of blood
twelve years Mat 9 :20-22, Mark 5:
25-34, Luke 8 :43-48
Jesus' parable of lost sheep Mat
18: 12-14, Luke 15: 1-7
Jesus on trial before Pilate Mat
27: 1, 2, 11-14, Mark 15: 1-5, Luke
23:1-5, John 18:28-38
Jesus' crucifixion Mat 27: 32-56,
Mark 15: 21-41. Luke 23: 26-49,
John 19: 17-30

Jesus' parable of prodigal son Luke
15: 11-24
Jesus' teaching on bread of life
eliminates some followers John
6: 26-71
Peter and John on trial before coun-
cil Acts 4: 1-23
Stephen's trial Acts 6: 5-15
Paul on his trials as a Christian
Acts 20: 17-38
Agabus warns Paul of trials ahead
Acts 21: 8-15
Paul defends himself before Agrip-
pa Acts 26: 1-32
Paul's hardships to establish church
2 Cor 11: 21-33
James on how to bear our cross Jas
1 :1-27

See also cross, hardness, probation,
proof, purity, suffering, temptation

TRIBES

See children of Israel

TRIBUTE

See taxes

TRINITY

Moses defines the nature of God as I
Am Exod 3: 1-18
Isaiah predicts the coming of Christ
Isa 7: 10-16, 9: 2-7
Jesus explains oneness with Father
John 10: 22-42
Jesus ascends Mark 16: 19, 20, Luke
24: 50-53, Acts 1: 9-13
Jesus promises the arrival of the
Holy Spirit John 14: 1-31
Holy Spirit descends at Pentecost
Acts 2: 1-13
Paul on the unity of all Eph 4:1-32

See also comforter, father, Holy
Spirit (Ghost), sons

TRIUMPH

Song of Deborah for victory over
Sisera Judg 5: 1-20
Procession of David's victory 1 Sam
18: 6-16
David crowned 2 Sam 2: 1-4, 5: 1-5

Queen of Sheba acknowledges Solomon's success *1 King 10:1-12,* *2 Chron 9:1-12*

Jehoshaphat says the battle is God's *2 Chron 20: 1-32*

Nehemiah repairs wall *Neh 4: 1-23*

Esther victorious, Haman hanged *Esther 6: 1-14, 7: 1-10*

Job is restored *Job 42: 1-17*

David's songs of rejoicing *Psal 33: 1-22, 66: 1-20, 100: 1-5*

Wise men visit babe in manger *Mat 2: 1-12*

Jesus calms wind and sea *Mat 8: 23-27, Mark 4: 35-41, 6: 45-52, Luke 8: 22-25, John 6: 21*

Jesus enters Jerusalem to hosannas *Mat 21: 1-11, 14-17, Mark 11: 1-11, Luke 19: 29-44, John 12: 12-19*

Jesus is risen from tomb and death *Mat 28:1-8, Mark 16:1-8, Luke 24: 1-12, John 20:1-10*

Jesus raises Lazarus from death *John 11: 1-46*

Signs and wonders cause church growth *Acts 4:24-37*

Paul on the prize for a race *1 Cor 9:24-27*

John's vision of new heaven and earth *Rev 21: 1-27*

See also crown, success, victory

TROUBLE

See adversity

TRUST

Noah builds ark to save his household *Gen 6:5-22*

Abraham trusts God to lead him *Gen 11: 31, 32, 12: 1-9*

Isaac trusts his father *Gen 22: 1-19*

People follow pillars of cloud and fire *Exod 13:20-22, Num 9:15-23*

People walk through Red Sea *Exod 14: 5-31*

Gideon develops faith in God *Judg 6: 19-40*

David does not trust Saul's armor *1 Sam 17:17-37*

Elisha heals Shunammite's son *2 King 4:8-37*

Jehoshaphat relies on Lord in battle *2 Chron 20: 1-32*

David's songs:

"The Lord is my shepherd" *Psal 23:1-6*

"God is our refuge and strength" *Psal 46:1-11*

"the secret place of the most High" *Psal 91:1-16*

Jeremiah buys a field while in prison *Jer 32: 2, 6-27, 37-44*

Three Jews in fiery furnace *Dan 3: 1-30*

Daniel in lions' den *Dan 6:1-28*

Woman with issue of blood touches Jesus' hem *Mat 9: 20-22, Mark 5: 25-34, Luke 8: 43-46*

Jesus reminds disciples of his great works *Mat 16: 5-12, Mark 8: 13-21*

Jesus heals epileptic boy despite unbelief *Mat 17: 14-21, Mark 9: 14-29, Luke 9: 37-43*

On Jesus' word Peter lets down his net once more *Luke 5: 1-11*

Paul's sermon on abundance *2 Cor 8: 11-15, 9: 6-15*

See also belief, confidence, doubt, faith, reliance

TRUTH

God creates spiritual universe *Gen 1: 1-31*

Abram and Sarai get new names *Gen 17: 1-9, 15-22*

Moses' revelation of nature of God *Exod 3: 1-18*

Moses and the basis of all law *Exod 20: 1-19, Deut 5: 1-24*

Elijah sees true nature of God *1 King 19:9-13*

Ezekiel's vision of holy waters *Ezek 47: 1-12*

John the Baptist questions Jesus *Mat 11: 2-19, Luke 7: 18-35*

Jesus' parable of the leaven *Mat 13: 33, Luke 13: 20, 21*

Jesus as the light of the world *John 1: 1-14, 8: 12-32*

Jesus says the truth makes free *John 8: 12-32*

Jesus promises the spirit of truth *John 14: 1-31*

Jesus' parable of the true vine *John 15: 1-17*

Pilate asks, "What is truth?" *John 18: 28-38*

Paul on Jesus as the Messiah *Acts 13: 16-52*

See also Christ, fact, God, leaven, reality, sincerity

TURN

See conversion

TWELVE

Jacob prophesies future of his twelve sons *Gen 49: 1-28, Deut 33: 1-29*

Joshua sets up twelve stones as memorial *Josh 4:1-24*

Jesus chooses twelve disciples *Mat 4:17-22, Mark 1:14-20, Luke 5:1-11, John 1: 35-51*

Jesus heals Jairus' daughter at twelve years old *Mat 9:18, 19, 23-26, Mark 5: 22-24, 35-43, Luke 8: 41, 42, 59-56*

Jesus heals twelve years issue of blood *Mat 9:20-22, Mark 5:25-34, Luke 8:43-48*

Jesus promises his disciples twelve thrones *Mat 19: 27-30*

Jesus at twelve years stays in Jerusalem *Luke 2:41-52*

Thomas not with twelve disciples at resurrection *John 20: 19-29*

See also apostle, Jacob, children of Israel

TYRANNY

Egyptians oppress Israelites *Exod 1: 8-14, 5: 7-19*

Pursuit of people by Egyptian soldiers *Exod 14: 5-31*

Isaiah's vision of fall of Babylon *Isa 14: 4-8, 12-17, 25-27*

Mary, Joseph and Jesus flee Herod to Egypt *Mat 2: 13-23, Luke 2: 39, 40*

Caiaphas, the high priest, urges council to put Jesus to death *John 11: 47-54*

Peter and John rebel against priests *Acts 4: 1-23*

Angels war with dragon *Rev 12: 1-17*

See also authority, government, power

U

UNBELIEF

See doubt

UNCIRCUMCISION

See circumcision

UNCLEAN

See defile, purity

UNCONSCIOUS

Lord God puts Adam to sleep, makes Eve from a rib *Gen 2: 21-25*

Jacob dreams of communicating with God *Gen 28: 10-22*

Joseph as dream interpreter *Gen 39: 21, 23, 40: 1-23, 41: 1-46*

Elijah's revelation of God as still, small voice *1 King 19: 9-13*

Jesus raises Jairus' daughter from death *Mat 9: 18, 19, 23-26, Mark 5: 22-24, 35-43, Luke 6: 41, 42, 49-56*

Jesus heals epileptic boy *Mat 17: 14-21, Mark 9: 14-29, Luke 9: 37-43*

Disciples sleep at Gethsemane *Mat 26: 30, 30-46, Mark 14: 26, 37-42. Luke 22: 39-46*

Jesus is risen after entombment *Mat 28:1-8, Mark 16:1-8, Luke 24:1-12, John 20:1-10*

Jesus raises son of widow of Nain *Luke 7: 11-17*

Jesus raises Lazarus dead four days *John 11:1-46*

See also consciousness, death, dream, sleep

UNCOVER

Moses exposes fear and sickness as illusion *Exod 4:1-9*

Joshua uncovers sin at city of Ai *Josh 7:1-26, 8:14-21*

Saul's unfitness to be king exposed *1 Sam 15:7-26*

Jonathan's rebellion uncovered *1 Sam 14:24-35*

Nathan uncovers David's sin with Bathsheba *2 Sam 12:1-10*

Gehazi's greed punished *2 King 5:
15-27*

Hezekiah's unwise trust results in
loss of kingdom *2 King 20:12-21,
Isa 39:1-8*

Uzziah's pride exposed by leprosy
2 Chron 26:1-23

Nehemiah uncovers conspiracy *Neh
6:1-19*

Esther exposes plot to persecute her
people *Esther 6:1-14, 7:1-10*

Isaiah and the pride of women *Isa
3:16-26*

Isaiah foretells that hypocrisy will
be punished *Isa 29:11-24, 30:1-3,
20, 21*

Sins of Pharisees exposed *Mat 23:
1-39, Luke 11:37-54*

Jesus' parables:
  the wise and foolish virgins *Mat
  25:1-13*
  the talents *Mat 25:14-30, Luke
  19:11-28*
  the sheep and goats *Mat 25:31-46*
  the lost coin *Luke 15:8-10*
  the rich man and beggar *Luke
  16:19-31*
  the Pharisee and publican *Luke
  18:9-14*

Judas' betrayal exposed *Mat 27:3-
10, Acts 1:15-20*

Paul, healed of blindness, sees what
he has done wrong *Acts 9:10-22*

Paul describes the enemies of the
truth *2 Tim 3:1-17*

John's vision of the Lamb who opens
the book *Rev 5:1-14*

See also discovery, light, reason, revelation

UNDERSTANDING

Enoch "walked with God; and he
was not" *Gen 5:18, 21-24, Heb
11:5*

Joseph interprets Pharaoh's dream
and solves it *Gen 41:1-46*

Moses begins to learn God's nature
Exod 3:1-18

Moses begins to learn God's law
Exod 20:1-19, Deut 5:1-24

Solomon's dream and request for understanding *1 King 3:5-15, 2 Chron
1:7-12*

Elijah sees the nature of God *1 King
19:9-13*

Elijah is translated *2 King 2:1-11*

Job learns the nature of God *Job
38:1-41*

The value of wisdom *Prov 3:13-26,
4:1-13, 8:1-36*

Jesus explains why he speaks in
parables only *Mat 13:10-17, 34,
35, Mark 4:10-12, 33, 34*

Peter recognizes that Jesus is Christ
*Mat 16:13-20, Mark 8:27-30, Luke
9:18-21*

At twelve years Jesus converses with
leading rabbis *Luke 2:41-52*

Jesus imparts to disciples his understanding of the healing power
Luke 10:1-16

Jesus' parable of temple to be raised
in three days *John 2:19-22*

Jesus explains the source of his
great works *John 5:17-47*

At Pentecost the disciples begin to
understand Christianity from the
spirit of truth *Acts 2:1-13*

Paul on wise and foolish things
1 Cor 1:17—2:16, 3:18-23

John's teaching that God is love
1 John 4:1-21

John's vision of the Lamb who can
open the sealed book *Rev 5:1-14*

See also intelligence, knowledge,
mind, omniscience, reason, sight,
vision

UNFOLDMENT

God creates the universe in successive days *Gen 1:1-31*

God lays out his plan for Abraham's
seed *Gen 15:1-21*

Joseph's boyhood dreams come true
Gen 37:1-36, 43:1, 2, 45:1-11, 25-28

Jacob foretells his children's future
Gen 49:1-28, Deut 33:1-29

Moses reviews the escape from
Egypt *Deut 32:1-47*

God reveals himself and his plan
to Gideon *Judg 6:19-40, 7:1-25*

How Ruth, the foreigner, became the
great grandmother of David *Ruth
1:1-22, 2:1-23, 4:1-22*

How David became king of Israel
and Judah *1 Sam 16:1-13, 17:38-
52, 2 Sam 2:1-4, 5:1-5*

Elijah learns the nature of God
1 King 19:9-13

Elijah moves towards translation
2 King 2:1-11
Nehemiah builds the wall *Neh 1:
1-11, 2:1-20, 4:1-23*
Job's troubles and solution *Job 2:
1-13, 38:1-41, 42:1-17*
Isaiah's vision and prophecy *Isa
6:1-13, 7:10-16, 9:2-7*
Jonah's disobedience and reform
Jonah 1:1-17, 2:1-10, 3:1-10
Jesus heals Gadarene by causing the
trouble to be self-seen *Mat 8:28-
34, Mark 5:1-20, Luke 8:20-39*
John the Baptist sends to Jesus for
proof of Christ *Mat 11:2-19, Luke
7:18-35*
Peter acknowledges Jesus as Christ
*Mat 16:13-20, Mark 8:27-30, Luke
9:18-21*
Jesus talks with Moses and Elijah
*Mat 17:1-13, Mark 9:2-13, Luke
9:28-36*
Crucifixion (seeming failure) to
resurrection *Mat 27:32-56, 28:1-8,
Mark 15:21-41, 16:1-8, Luke 23:26-
49, 24:1-12, John 19:17-30, 20:1-10*
Jesus ascends *Mark 16:19, 20, Luke
24:50-53, Acts 1:9-13*
Jesus' parable of the prodigal son
Luke 15:11-24
Jesus promises the Holy Spirit *John
14:1-31*
Holy Spirit descends *Acts 2:1-13*
Saul, the persecutor of Christians,
becomes Paul *Acts 8:1-4, 9:1-22*
Peter accepts Gentiles in church
Acts 10:1-48, 11:1-18

See also expansion, open, progress,
revelation

UNITY

God makes man his image and like-
ness *Gen 1:26, 27*
Enoch "walked with God; and he
was not" *Gen 5:18, 21-24, Heb
11:5*
Jacob hears of God's ever-presence
Gen 28:10-22
Joseph united with his family *Gen
43:1, 2, 45: 1-11, 25-28*
The chosen people set apart as God's
own *Deut 7:6-11*
The people all shout together and
Jericho falls *Josh 6:1-27*

Gideon's 300 men act in concert
Judg 7:1-25
Jonathan befriends David *1 Sam
18:1-16*
David unites kingdoms of Judah and
Israel *2 Sam 2:1-4, 5:1-5*
Nehemiah builds because the people
had a mind to work *Neh 4:1-23*
David's song, "The Lord is my shep-
herd" *Psal 23:1-6*
David's song, "Whither shall I go
from thy spirit?" *Psal 139:1-24*
God's care over his flock *Ezek 34:
1-31*
Voice from heaven when Jesus is
baptized *Mat 3:13-17, Mark 1:
9-11*
Jesus on oneness with the Father
John 10:22-42
Jesus talks with Moses and Elijah
*Mat 17:1-13, Mark 9:2-13, Luke 9:
28-36*
Jesus' parable of prodigal's elder
brother *Luke 15:25-32*
Jesus says great works have source
in Father *John 5:17-47*
Jesus on unity and eternity of Christ
John 8:12-59
Jesus' parable of the true vine and
branches *John 15:1-17*
Paul on the unity of all *Eph 2:
1-15, 4:1-23*

See also ever-presence, harmony, infinity, monotheism, oneness, whole

UNIVERSE

God creates the spiritual universe
Gen 1:1-31
A material view of creation *Gen
2:6-25, 3:1-24*
The flood covers the earth *Gen 7:
1-24*
Job hears the voice of the infinite
Job 38:1-41
David's songs:
"The heavens declare the glory"
Psal 19:1-14
"The earth is the Lord's and the
fulness thereof" *Psal 24:1-10*
"Whither shall I flee from thy
presence?" *Psal 139:1-24*
The vanity of human things *Eccl
1:1-18, 2:1-26*
Change of time and seasons *Eccl
3:1-15*

Isaiah foretells the coming of Christ's kingdom *Isa 2:1-5, Mic 4:1-8, 13*
Isaiah foretells Christ's peaceable kingdom *Isa 11:1-12*
Ezekiel sees truth flow out encompassing the universe *Ezek 47:1-12*
Jesus' parables:
the leaven *Mat 13:33, Luke 13: 20, 21*
the marriage feast *Mat 22:1-14*
the great supper *Luke 14:15-24*
Jesus heals groups of people *Mat 4:23-25, 12:14-21, 14:14, 34-36, 15: 29-31, 19:1, 2, Mark 3:6-12, 6:53-56, Luke 4:40-44, 6:17-19*
Philip heals many *Acts 8:5-8*
Peter accepts conversion of all Gentiles *Acts 10:1-48, 11:1-18*
Paul on creation *Rom 1:17-25*
Paul on the unity of all *Eph 4: 1-32*
John sees a new heaven and earth *Rev 21:1-27*

See also allness, creation, earth, everpresence, heaven, oneness, power, whole

UNKNOWN

Abraham searches for promised land *Gen 11:31, 32, 12:1-9*
Pillars of cloud and fire lead the people *Exod 13:20-22, Num 9: 15-23*
Caleb and Joshua report their visit to Canaan *Num 13:1-23, 14:1-11, 23-39, Deut 1:19-38*
God makes himself known to Gideon by signs *Judg 6:19-40*
A prophet without honor in his own country *Mat 13:53-58, Mark 6: 1-6, Luke 4:22-24, John 4:43-45*
Jesus' parable of rich man and beggar *Luke 16:19-31*
Paul on the Unknown God *Acts 17:15-34*

See also God, ignorance, stranger

UNREALITY

In a mist the Lord God creates man from dust *Gen 2:6-8*
Abraham is tempted to sacrifice his son *Gen 22:1-19*

Moses sees serpent and leprosy disappear instantly *Exod 4:1-9*
Atonement by means of the scapegoat *Lev 16:1-28*
Fear of giants in promised land delays entrance 40 years *Num 13: 1-33, 14:1-11, 23-29, Deut 1:19-38*
David's songs:
"How are the mighty fallen!" (their power proved unreal) *2 Sam 1:17-27*
"Fret not thyself because of evildoers" *Psal 37:23-40*
"Why art thou cast down?" *Psal 42:1-11*
Mortal life is vain *Eccl 1:1-18, 2: 1-26*
Isaiah's vision of the desert blossoming *Isa 35:1-10*
Ezekiel's vision of children's teeth on edge *Ezek 18:1-32*
Daniel interprets king's dream of great image *Dan 2:1-49*
Jesus on no thought for material life *Mat 6:25-34, Luke 12:22-34*
Jesus proves death unreal *Mat 28: 1-8, Mark 16:1-8, Luke 24:1-12, John 20:1-10*
Jesus' parable of prodigal son *Luke 15:11-24*
Jesus heals ten men of leprosy *Luke 17:11-19*

See also delusion, dream, error, illusion, imagination, materialism

UNREST

People complain to Moses *Exod 16:1-36, Num 11:1-15, 31, 32*
Miriam and Aaron stir up people against Moses *Num 12:1-16*
Elijah hears still small voice *1 King 19:9-13*
Jesus stills storm *Mat 8:23-27, Mark 4:35-41, 6:45-52, Luke 8:22-25, John 6:21*
Jesus enters Jerusalem *Mat 21:1-11, 14-17, Mark 11:1-11, Luke 19: 29-44, John 12:12-19*
Jesus' parable of husbandmen who refuse to pay rent *Mat 21:33-46, Mark 12:1-12, Luke 20:9-19*
Jesus on unrest of nations *Mat 24: 1-41, Mark 13:1-37, Luke 21:5-36*
An idol maker stirs up the people against Paul *Acts 19:23-29*

See also rebellion, revolution

UNSELFISHNESS

Abraham offers Lot his choice of land *Gen 13:1-18*

Moses heals the sister who spoke against him *Num 12:1-16*

Ruth stays with her mother-in-law *Ruth 1:1-22*

Esther saves her people at risk of her crown *Esther 5:1-14*

The virtuous wife and mother *Prov 31:1-31*

The crucifixion *Mat 27:32-56, Mark 15:21-41, Luke 23:26-49, John 19: 17-30*

Jesus' parable of good Samaritan *Luke 10:25-37*

Jesus' parable of good shepherd *John 10:1-18*

Jesus washes disciples' feet *John 13:1-20*

John's last instruction to Peter *John 21:12-19*

Paul on charity *1 Cor 13:1-13*

Paul's hardships to establish church *2 Cor 11:21-33*

James on how to bear our cross *Jas 1:1-27*

John's teaching that God is love *1 John 4:1-21*

See also forgiveness, generosity, love, self

UPRIGHT

God sees Noah righteous before him *Gen 6:5-22*

Joseph does not lower his standards for his master's wife *Gen 39:1-20*

Moses and Ten Commandments — basis of all law *Exod 20:1-19, Deut 5:1-24*

Job's integrity *Job 1:13-22, 2:1-10*

David's songs:
  "What is man?" *Psal 8:1-9*
  "Why art thou cast down?" *Psal 42:1-11*
  "Create in me a clean heart" *Psal 51:1-19*
  the safety of the godly *Psal 121: 1-8*

The virtuous woman and wife *Prov 31:1-31*

Isaiah's inspiration to be Christlike *Isa 60:1-5*

Jesus overcomes temptation *Mat 4: 1-11, Mark 1:12, 13, Luke 4:1-13*

Jesus puts Mosaic commands on mental basis *Mat 5:21-48*

Jesus on what defiles *Mat 15:1-20, Mark 7:1-23*

Jesus' parable of sheep and goats *Mat 25:31-46*

Jesus on the Pharisees *Mat 23:1-39, Luke 12:1-15*

Jesus heals woman bowed together *Luke 13:11-17*

Jesus' parable of Pharisee and publican *Luke 18:9-14*

Peter and John heal lame man *Acts 3:1-11*

Paul heals cripple *Acts 14:8-10*

Paul urges to come out and be separate *2 Cor 6:1-18*

See also character, conscience, morality, righteousness

USHER

Lot shelters two angels from the mob *Gen 19:1-14*

Moses hands upheld by Aaron and Hur *Exod 17:8-16*

Aaron and sons anointed by Moses *Lev 8:1-13*

Elisha escorts Elijah until taken up *2 King 2:1-15*

Hezekiah shows all his treasure *2 King 20:12-21, Isa 39:1-8*

Jesus' parables:
  the unclean spirit and seven others *Mat 12:43-45, Luke 11:24-26*
  the servants awaiting their lord *Mat 24:42-51*
  the wise and foolish virgins *Mat 25:1-13*
  the good Samaritan *Luke 10:25-37*
  the faithful steward *Luke 12:41-48*
  the chief seats at wedding *Luke 14:7-14*
  the rich man and beggar at the gate *Luke 16:19-31*
  the servant who serves before he sups *Luke 17:7-10*

Andrew finds his brother Simon and ushers him to Jesus *Mat 4: 17-22, Mark 1:14-20, Luke 5:1-11, John 1:35-42*

Jesus heals centurion's servant on pleading of friends *Mat 8:5-13, Luke 7:1-10*

Jesus appoints Peter and gives him keys to heaven *Mat 16:13-20, Mark 8:27-30, Luke 9:18-21*

Precious ointment poured on Jesus' head *Mat 26:6-13, Mark 14:3-9*

Jesus casts traders out of temple *John 2:13-25*

Jesus promises spirit of truth will come before his second coming *John 14:1-31*

Paul and Silas convert their jailor *Acts 16:19-40*

See also calling, church, disciple, door

UZZIAH (one of the kings)

See Part II, Uzziah

V

VALLEY

Joseph's brethren cast him into pit *Gen 37:1-36*

People pass through walls of Red Sea *Exod 14:5-31*

Gideon defeats enemy host in valley *Judg 7:1-25*

David calls to Saul across valley *1 Sam 26:1-25*

David's song, "The Lord is my shepherd" *Psal 23:1-6*

Jesus at Gethsemane *Mat 26:30, 36-46, Mark 14:26, 32-42, Luke 22:39-46*

Jesus' parable of rich man and beggar *Luke 16:19-31*

See also darkness, death, depression, humility, meekness

VALUE

God saw all he had made and called it good *Gen 1:30, 31*

Lord God curses ground from which he made Adam *Gen 3:17-24*

Cain asks, "Am I my brother's keeper?" *Gen 4:1-16*

Abraham tempted to sacrifice his son *Gen 22:1-19*

Esau sells his birthright for pottage *Gen 25:24-34*

Joseph overcomes temptations *Gen 39:1-20*

Song of Moses praises God for deliverance *Exod 15:1-19, Deut 32:1-47*

Moses shows value of obedience *Deut 11:1-32, 28:1-14*

Joshua sets up memorial for crossing Jordan *Josh 4:1-24*

Ruth chooses to stay with Naomi *Ruth 1:1-22*

Samuel changes from Saul to David *1 Sam 15:7-26, 16:1-13*

Elisha chooses a double portion of spirit *1 King 2:1-15*

Solomon chooses understanding as highest good *1 King 3:5-15, 2 Chron 1:7-12*

Rehoboam turns from father's counselors to his young friends *1 King 12:1-18, 2 Chron 10:1-19*

Elijah values most the still small voice *1 King 19:9-13*

Esther decides to risk her crown to save her people *Esther 5:1-14*

Job maintains his integrity *Job 1:13-22, 2:1-10*

David's song, "What is man?" *Psal 8:1-9*

David's song, "Bless the Lord, O my soul" *Psal 103:1-22*

The happy value of wisdom *Prov 3:13-26, 4:1-13, 8:1-36*

The nature of a good wife and mother *Prov 31:1-31*

Mortal life is vain *Eccl 1:1-18, 2:1-26*

Wisdom is better than might *Eccl 9:13-18*

The pride of women is vain *Isa 3:16-26*

Three Jews refuse to worship image *Dan 3:1-30*

Daniel refuses to change his prayers *Dan 6:1-28*

Jesus parables:
the builders on rock and sand *Mat 7:24-27, Luke 6:48, 49*

the wheat and tares *Mat 13:24-30, 36-43*

the treasure in field *Mat 13:44*

the pearl of great price *Mat 13:45, 46*

the two debtors forgiven *Luke 7:36-50*

the rich fool and bigger barns *Luke 12:15-21*

the prodigal son *Luke 15:11-24*

Wise men visit King of the Jews *Mat 2:1-12*

Voice from heaven at baptism of Jesus *Mat 3:13-17, Mark 1:9-11*

Disciples leave nets immediately to follow Jesus *Mat 4:17-22, Mark 1:14-20, Luke 5:1-11, John 1:35-42*

Jesus rejected by people at Nazareth *Mat 13:53-58, Luke 4:14-32*

Jesus' mother and brethren wait outside *Mat 12:46-50*

Jesus admonishes Peter for urging Jesus to avoid the cross *Mat 16:21-28, Mark 8:31-38, Luke 9:20-27*

Voice from heaven at transfiguration *Mat 17:1-13, Mark 9:2-13, Luke 9:28-36*

Jesus blesses little children *Mat 19:13-15, Mark 10:13-16, Luke 18:15-17*

Jesus approves the widow's mite *Mark 12:41-44, Luke 21:1-4*

Seventy disciples report success of instructions *Luke 10:1-24*

Jesus' teaching on taking no thought for material things *Luke 12:25-34*

Jesus visits Zacchaeus and he is transformed *Luke 19:1-10*

Disciples debate who shall be greatest *Luke 22:24-30*

Jesus casts traders out of temple *John 2:13-25*

Peter permits conversion of Gentiles *Acts 10:1-48, 11:1-18*

Paul on Adam versus Christ *Rom 5:1-21*

Paul on Spirit versus flesh *Rom 8:1-39*

Paul preaches about thinking on good things *Phil 4:1-23*

Paul urges putting on new man *Col 4:1-17*

James on equality *Jas 2:1-13*

John's vision of new heaven and earth *Rev 21:1-27*

See also excellence, goodness, importance, money, praise, worth

VANITY

Tower of Babel's attempt to reach heaven *Gen 11:1-9*

Balaam says that it is in vain to curse Israelites *Num 22:1-41, 23:1-30*

Rehoboam consults old men, then his friends *1 King 12:1-18, 2 Chron 10:1-19*

Elisha heals Naaman's pride *2 King 5:1-14*

Uzziah's heart lifted up to destruction *2 Chron 26:1-23*

David's song, "Fret not thyself because of evildoers" *Psal 37:23-40*

Mortal life vain *Eccl 1:1-18, 2:1-26*

Body culture in vain *Isa 3:16-26*

Daniel interprets dream of great image *Dan 2:1-49*

Jesus on subject of Pharisee *Mat 23:1-39, Luke 11:37-54*

Jesus' parable of rich fool and bigger barns *Luke 12:15-21*

Jesus' teaching on take no thought for material things *Luke 12:22-34*

Jesus' parable of chief seats at wedding *Luke 14:7-14*

See also ego, nothingness, pride

VEIL

A mist arises and the Lord God begins creation *Gen 2:6-8*

Jacob disguises himself to deceive his father *Gen 27:1-44*

After talking with God, Moses veils his face *Exod 34:29-35*

At crucifixion the veil of the temple is split *Mat 27:32-56, Mark 15:21-41, Luke 23:26-49, John 19:17-30*

Paul's teaching about glory from the Old Testament veil of Moses to the open face of Christ *2 Cor 3:4-18*

See also body, flesh, secret

VENGEANCE

Cain kills Abel *Gen 4:1-16*

Sarah has Hagar and her child put out into wilderness *Gen 21:9-21*

Jacob fears his brother's revenge *Gen 32:1-32*

David's revenge balked by Abigail *1 Sam 25:2-42*

Elisha restores peace by preventing revenge by the King of Israel on his enemies *2 King 6:19-23*

Jesus' parable of husbandmen who refuse to pay rent *Mat 21:33-46, Mark 12:1-12, Luke 20:9-19*

Peter cuts off Malchus' ear, Jesus restores it *Luke 22:50, 51*

See also injury, justice, punishment

VICE

See evil, sin

VICTORY

Abraham in the war of kings *Gen 14:8-20*

Moses' hands upheld during battle *Exod 17:8-16*

Jubilee year proclaimed *Lev 25:9-17*

Jericho falls *Josh 6:1-27*

Sisera defeated *Judg 4:1-17*

The sword of Gideon *Judg 7:1-25*

David and Goliath *1 Sam 17:38-52*

Elijah translated over death *2 King 2:1-11*

Sennacherib repulsed *2 King 18:17-37, 19:1-27, 2 Chron 31:20, 21, 32:1-23*

Jehoshaphat says that the battle is God's *2 Chron 20:1-32*

Esther saves her people *Esther 6:1-14, 7:1-10*

A poor wise man saves the city *Eccl 9:13-18*

Christ's peaceable kingdom *Isa 11:1-12*

Daniel and lions' den *Dan 6:1-28*

Jesus calms wind and seas *Mat 8:23-27, Mark 4:35-41, Luke 8:22-25*

Transfiguration over time and space *Mat 17:1-13, Mark 9:2-13, Luke 9:28-36*

Resurrection *Mat 28:1-8, Mark 16:1-8, Luke 24:1-12, John 20:1-10*

Ascension *Mark 16:19, 20, Luke 24:50-53, Acts 1:6-12*

Seventy disciples return and report success *Luke 10:17-24*

Jesus' parable of the prodigal son *Luke 15:11-24*

Paul on prize for a race *1 Cor 9:24-27*

James' sermon, how to bear our cross *Jas 1:1-27*

War in heaven, dragon defeated *Rev 12:1-17*

See also crown, success, triumph

VIGILANCE

Moses exhorts to obedience *Deut 6:1-25, 11:1-32, 28:1-14*

Elisha faithful to his master *2 King 2:1-15*

Nehemiah foils conspiracy *Neh 6:1-19*

Zechariah's vision of candlestick fed by two olive trees *Zech 4:1-14*

Jesus' parables:

the unclean spirit and seven others *Mat 12:43-45, Luke 11:24-26*

the servants awaiting their lord *Mat 24:42-51*

the wise and foolish virgins *Mat 25:1-13*

the man taking a long journey *Mark 13:34-37*

the watchful servants *Luke 12:35-40*

the faithful steward *Luke 12:41-48*

Jesus at Gethsemane *Mat 26:30, 36-46, Mark 14:26, 32-42, Luke 22:39-46*

Jesus orders disciples to watch for second coming *Mat 24:1-41*

Angels announce Jesus' birth to watching shepherds *Luke 2:8-20*

In temple Simon and Anna call him Christ *Luke 2:21-38*

Jesus heals man at pool watching for moving of waters *John 5:1-16*

John's letters to seven churches *Rev 1:4-20, 2:1-29, 3:11-22*

See also awakening, danger, watch

VINE

Jotham's parable of the trees *Judg 9:1-15*

Every man sits under his vine *1 King 4:25, Mic 4:4*

Isaiah's parable of vine and wild grapes *Isa 5:1-8*

Jesus' parable on vine and branches *John 15:1-17*

See also Christ, wine

VIOLENCE

Cain murders Abel *Gen 4:1-16*

Sisera invades *Judg 4:1-17*

David arranged Uriah's death *2 Sam 11:1-27*

Elijah destroys 450 prophets of Baal *1 King 18:17-40*

Two captains of 50 destroyed by fire *2 King 1:3-15*

Sennacherib invades *2 King 18:17-37, 19:1-27, 2 Chron 31:20, 21, 32:1-23*

Haman persecutes the Jews *Esther 3:1-15, 4:1-17*

Jews thrown into fiery furnace *Dan 3:1-30*

Jesus heals the epileptic boy *Mat 17:14-21, Mark 9:14-29, Luke 9:37-43*

Jesus casts traders out of temple *Mat 21:12, 13, Mark 11:15-17, Luke 19:45, 46, John 2:13-25*

Jesus' parable of husbandmen who refuse to pay rent *Mat 21:33-46, Mark 12:7-12, Luke 20:9-19*

Jesus is scourged and mocked *Mat 27:27-31, Mark 15:16-20, John 9:1-16*

The crucifixion *Mat 27:32-56, Mark 15:21-41, Luke 23:26-49, John 19:17-30*

Signs at the crucifixion *Mat 27:50-53*

Jesus delivers himself from the mob *Luke 4:28-31*

Jesus' parable of good Samaritan *Luke 10:25-37*

Caiaphas urges council to put Jesus to death *John 11:47-54*

Paul's hardships in establishing the church *2 Cor 11:21-33*

See also destruction, force

VIRTUE

Enoch "walked with God ... and he was not" *Gen 5:18, 21-24, Heb 11:5*

Noah, the righteous promised safety *Gen 6:5-22*

Abram and Sarai receive new names for walking with God *Gen 17:1-9, 15-22*

God's promises to Abraham are renewed to Isaac *Gen 26:1-5*

Jacob approved by the angel *Gen 32:24-32*

Joseph resists Potiphar's wife *Gen 39:1-20*

Moses talks with God face to face *Exod 33:7-23*

Aaron's rod blossoms *Num 17:1-11*

Gideon refuses to be king *Judg 8:22, 23*

Ruth is loyal to Naomi *Ruth 1:1-22*

David and Goliath *1 Sam 17:38-52*

Solomon selects understanding *1 King 3:5-15, 2 Chron 1:7-12*

Elijah hears God's voice *1 King 19:1-8*

Elisha disarms Syrians and frees them *2 King 6:8-23*

Josiah's good reign *2 King 23:1-22, 2 Chron 34:1-8, 29-33*

Jehoshaphat's good reign *2 Chron 17:1-13, 19:4-11*

Esther saves her people *Esther 5:1-14*

Job never loses his integrity *Job 1:13-22, 2:1-10*

The virtuous woman and wife *Prov 31:1-31*

A poor wise man saves the city *Eccl 9:13-18*

Isaiah is called to prophecy *Isa 6:1-13*

Daniel in the lions' den *Dan 6:1-28*

Jesus' parables:

the wise and foolish virgins *Mat 25:1-13*

the talents *Mat 25:14-30, Luke 19:11-28*

the good Samaritan *Luke 10:25-37*

the good shepherd *John 10:1-18*

Jesus on the qualities that make a Christian *Mat 5:1-12, Luke 6:17-26, 36*

Jesus heals the servant of the good centurion *Mat 8:5-13, Luke 7:1-10*

Jesus approves Peter's acknowledgement that he is Christ *Mat 16:13-20, Mark 8:27-30, Luke 9:18-21*

Jesus at Gethsemane *Mat 26:30, 36-46, Mark 14:26, 32-42, Luke 22:39-46*

Jesus on the unity and eternity of Christ *John 8:12-59*

Jesus raises Lazarus *John 11:1-46*

Peter's shadow heals sick in streets *Acts 5:12-16*

See also chastity, courage, excellence, goodness, justice, morality, purity, temperance, wisdom

VISION

Abraham entertains angels *Gen 18:1-18*

Jacob sees angels ascending and descending ladder   *Gen 28:10-22*

Joseph interprets dream and envisions solution   *Gen 41:1-46*

Moses sights the burning bush   *Exod 3:1-18*

Moses promises a prophet to come   *Deut 18:15-22*

Joshua meets "captain of the host" Sun and moon stand still at Ajalon   *Josh 10:6-15*

Elisha sees Elijah taken up in chariot of fire   *2 King 2:1-11*

Job's nightmare of fear   *Job 4:13-21*

Isaiah's vision of God's glory   *Isa 6:1-13*

Isaiah's prophecy of Messiah   *Isa 7:10-16, 9:2-7*

Isaiah's vision of Christ's peaceable kingdom   *Isa 11:1-12*

Isaiah's vision of desert that blossoms   *Isa 35:1-10*

Isaiah's vision of blessed state of new Jerusalem   *Isa 65:17-25*

Ezekiel's vision of holy waters flowing outward   *Ezek 47:1-12*

Daniel's vision of meeting Gabriel   *Dan 9:20-23, 10:4-21*

Micah's vision of glory of the church   *Mic 4:1-8, 13, Isa 2:1-5*

Zechariah's vision of candlestick fed by two olive trees   *Zech 4:1-14*

Jesus restores vision to blind   *Mat 9:27-31, 12:22-30, 20:29-34, Mark 8:22-26, 10:46-52, Luke 18:35-43, John 9:1-41*

Jesus seen ascending   *Mark 16:19, 20, Luke 24:50-53, Acts 1:9-13*

Paul sees Jesus   *Acts 9:1-9*

Peter's vision of the great sheet   *Acts 11:1-18*

Peter imprisoned, released by angel   *Acts 12:1-17*

Paul's visions   *2 Cor 12:1-19*

John's revelations   *Rev 4:1-11, 5:1-14, 6:1-17, 10:1-11, 12:1-17, 21:1-27, 22:1-21*

See also dream, imagination, insight, revelation, sight

VOICE

The serpent speaks to Eve   *Gen 3:1-5*

Voice of God speaks out of burning bush   *Exod 3:1-18*

The Lord talks with Moses face to face   *Exod 33:7-23*

The people shout together and walls of Jericho fall   *Josh 6:1-27*

The Lord calls Samuel as a child   *1 Sam 3:1-10*

Elijah identifies God as a still small voice   *1 King 19:9-13*

Book of the law read to the people   *Neh 8:1-12*

Job hears the voice of thunder   *Job 38:1-41*

David's song, "Let the redeemed of the Lord say so"   *Psal 107:1-43*

The voice of John the Baptist crying in wilderness   *Mat 3:1-12, Mark 1:1-8, Luke 3:1-18*

Voice from heaven speaks of Jesus   *Mat 3:13-17, 17:1-13*

Satan speaks to Jesus   *Mat 4:1-11, Luke 4:1-13*

Jesus heals dumb   *Mat 9:32-35, 12:22-30, 15:29-31, Mark 7:32-37, Luke 11:14-23*

Zacharias loses his voice and regains it   *Luke 1:5-25, 57-86*

See also expression, songs, sound, speech, tongue

VOW

See promise

W

WAGES

Ruth gleans in the field of Boaz   *Ruth 2:1-23*

Jesus' parable of laborers in the vineyard   *Mat 20:1-16*

See also employment, labor, money, reward, work

WAITING

Noah sends raven and dove for signs to go forth   *Gen 8:1-22*

Noah sees the rainbow at last   *Gen 9:12-17*

God's promises to Abraham   *Gen 15:1-21*

People delay entrance to promised land 40 years   *Num 13:1-33, 14:1-11, 23-39, Deut 1:19-38*

Elijah flees and awaits next move
1 King 19:1-8
Elisha follows Elijah until he departs for heaven *2 King 2:1-11*
The Shunammite affirms health of her son *2 King 4:8-37*
Nathan reveals to David that he will not build the Lord's house, but that his son, Solomon, will *1 Chron 17:1-27*
Job patiently awaits his restoration *Job 2:1—37:24*
David's song, "Why art thou cast down?" *Psal 42:1-11*
Jeremiah's promise — the captivity will be turned in 70 years *Jer 29:8-14*
Jesus heals the woman with issue of blood twelve years *Mat 9:20-22, Mark 5:25-34, Luke 8:43-48*
Jesus heals the woman bowed together 18 years *Luke 13:11-17*
Jesus heals the impotent man waiting at the pool for 38 years *John 5:1-16*
Jesus' parables:
the wheat and tares *Mat 13:24-30, 36-43*
the mustard seed *Mat 13:31, 32, Mark 4:30-32, Luke 13:18, 19*
the leaven *Mat 13:33, Luke 13:20, 21*
the faithful steward *Mat 24:42-51, Luke 12:41-48*
the wise and foolish virgins *Mat 25:1-13*
the seed, blade, ear *Mark 4:26-29*
the watchful servants *Luke 12:35-40*

See also hope, patience, time, watch

WAKE

See awakening

WALKING

Enoch "walked with God" *Gen 5:18, 21-24, Heb 11:5*
Abraham and Sarah walking before God *Gen 17:1-9, 15-22*
People walk through Red Sea *Exod 14:5:31*
People walk through Jordan *Josh 3:1-17*

Elijah divides Jordan and walks over *2 King 2:8*
Elisha divides Jordan and walks over *2 King 2:1-15*
King sees four forms walk in midst of fiery furnace *Dan 3:1-30*
Hosea's vision of teaching a child to walk *Hos 11:1-4*
Jesus walks on water, Peter tries it *Mat 14:22-33, John 6:15-21*
Levite and priest walk by on the other side *Luke 10:25-37*
Jesus heals lameness *John 5:1-16*
Peter and John heal lame man *Acts 3:1-11*
Paul heals lame *Acts 14:8-10*
Paul's teaching to walk in the spirit *Rom 8:1-39*

See also life, spirit, path, way

WALL

A wall of water enables people to walk through Red Sea *Exod 14:5-31*
Walls of Jericho fall down *Josh 6:1-27*
Nehemiah repairs wall *Neh 4:1-23*
Paul let down over wall of Jerusalem in basket *Acts 9:23-31*

See also defense, protection, resistance

WANT

See lack, poverty

WAR

Abraham joins war of kings *Gen 14:8-20*
Moses' hands upheld by Hur and Aaron *Exod 17:8-16*
City of Jericho falls *Josh 6:1-27*
Sisera defeated *Judg 4:1-17*
Gideon defeats Midianites *Judg 7:1-25*
David visits battlefront and kills Goliath *1 Sam 17:1-52*
Asa victorious in war *1 King 15:9-24, 2 Chron 14:1-7*
Elisha, besieged by army of Syria, settles the war *2 King 6:8-23*
Invasion of Sennacherib repelled *2 King 18:17-37, 19:1-27, 2 Chron*

31: 20, 21, 32: 1-23, Isa 36: 1-22, 37: 1-38

Jehoshaphat—the battle is God's *2 Chron 20:1-32*

A poor wise man saves his city *Eccl 9: 13-18*

Isaiah's vision of war no more *Isa 2: 1-5*, *Mic 4: 1-8, 13*

Ezekiel's vision of the resurrection of the army *Ezek 37: 1-14*

Jesus' parable on counting the cost of making war *Luke 14: 25-33*

Paul on weapons of warfare *2 Cor 10: 3-5*

War in heaven *Rev 12: 1-17*

See also competition, enemy, peace, soldier, struggle, sword

WATCH

Noah watches for the return of the dove *Gen 8: 1-22*

Nehemiah sets watchers during repair of wall *Neh 4: 1-23*

Ezekiel's vision of God's care for his flock *Ezek 34: 1-31*

Habakkuk's watch on tower waiting for vision *Hab 2: 1-3*

Jesus' parables:

the servants awaiting their lord *Mat 24:42-51*

the wise and foolish virgins *Mat 25:1-13*

the man on a long journey *Mark 13:34-37*

the watchful servants *Luke 12: 35-40*

the faithful steward *Luke 12: 41-48*

Jesus tells how to watch for his second coming *Mat 24: 1-41*

Vigil at Gethsemane *Mat 26: 30, 36-46, Mark 14: 26, 32-42, Luke 22: 39-46*

Shepherds watch flocks by night *Luke 2: 8-20*

In temple Simon and Anna watch for Christ *Luke 2: 21-38*

Jesus heals lame man watching by pool 38 years *John 5: 1-16*

Paul and Silas, imprisoned, sing hymns *Acts 16: 19-40*

See also affirmation, awakening, denial, guard, night, protection, sentinel, time, vigilance

WATER

Waters divide in creation *Gen 1: 6-8*

The flood and Noah *Gen 7: 1-24*

Hagar's thirst supplied in wilderness *Gen 21: 9-21*

Isaac settles strife between herdsmen over wells *Gen 26: 12-31*

People pass through Red Sea *Exod 14: 5-31*

Waters of Marah made sweet *Exod 15: 22-27*

Moses delivers water from rock in desert *Exod 17: 1-7, Num 20: 1-13*

People pass through Jordan *Josh 3: 1-17*

Elijah prays for rain *1 King 18: 41-46*

Elijah divides water of Jordan to pass over *2 King 2: 7-9*

Elisha divides water of Jordan to pass over *2 King 2:12-15*

Elisha heals water of city *2 King 2: 16-22*

Elisha supplies water for an army *2 King 3: 16-20*

Naaman the leper refuses to bathe in Jordan *2 King 5: 1-14*

Elisha makes iron axehead swim *2 King 6:1-7*

David's song, "Whither shall I go from thy spirit?" *Psal 139: 1-24*

Ezekiel's vision of holy waters encompassing the universe *Ezek 47: 1-12*

Jonah cast into sea by sailors *Jonah 1: 1-17, 2: 1-10*

Jesus baptized in Jordan *Mat 3: 13-17, Mark 1: 9-11, Luke 3: 21, 22*

Jesus calms elements *Mat 8: 23-27, Mark 4: 35-41, Luke 8: 22-25*

Jesus and Peter walk on water *Mat 14: 22-33, John 6: 15-21*

Jesus transports ship to destination *Mark 6: 45-52, John 6: 21*

Jesus fills Peter's net *Luke 5: 1-11, John 21: 1-11*

Jesus heals man of edema *Luke 14: 1-6*

Jesus changes water to wine *John 2: 1-11*

At Jacob's well Jesus asks a drink and promises living water *John 4: 1-42*

Jesus heals impotent man at pool 38 years *John 5: 1-16*

Jesus washes disciples' feet *John 13: 1-20*
Philip finds water to baptize Ethiopian *Acts 8: 26-40*
Paul is shipwrecked *Acts 27: 1-44*
John's vision of angel standing on sea *Rev 10: 1-11*

See also baptism, purity, rain, sea, thirst

WAY

Jacob receives promise of God's presence wherever he goes *Gen 28: 10-22*
Moses' reluctance to lead the way overcome *Exod 3: 9-12*
Moses reveals Ten Commandments *Exod 20:1-19, Deut 5:1-24*
Moses on how to be righteous *Deut 6: 1-25, 8: 1-20, 11: 1-32, 13: 1-18, 18: 9-14, 26: 1-19, 28: 1-14, 30: 11-20*
The Lord calls Samuel *1 Sam 3: 1-10*
David's charge to Solomon *1 Chron 22: 6-19, 23: 1, 28: 2-10, 20*
Elisha quits his plowing *1 King 19: 19-21*
David's song, the happiness of the godly *Psal 1: 1-6*
David's song, "the secret place of the most High" *Psal 91: 1-16*
The way of the virtuous woman *Prov 31: 1-31*
Isaiah foretells what Christ will be like *Isaiah 53: 1-12*
Daniel refuses to change his diet *Dan 1: 1-21*
Jesus' parables:
  the rich fool and bigger barns *Luke 12:15-21*
  the prodigal son *Luke 15: 11-24*
  the rich man and beggar *Luke 16:19-31*
  the true vine *John 15: 1-17*
Jesus outlines qualities that make a Christian *Mat 5: 1-12, Luke 6: 17-26, 36*
Jesus' teaching to let your light shine *Mat 5: 13-16, Luke 8: 16-18*
Jesus on the Golden Rule *Mat 7: 12-14*
Jesus sends his disciples to heal and preach *Mat 10: 5-42, Mark 6: 7-13, Luke 9: 1-6*

Peter acknowledges Jesus as Christ *Mat 16: 13-20, Mark 8: 27-30, Luke 9: 18-21*
Jesus enters Jerusalem for last time *Mat 21: 1-11, 14-17, Mark 11: 1-11, Luke 19: 29-44, John 12: 12-19*
Jesus at Gethsemane *Mat 26: 30, 36-46, Mark 14: 26, 32-42, Luke 22: 39-46*
Jesus sends out 70 disciples *Luke 10: 1-24*
Jesus on no thought for material life *Luke 12: 22-34*
Jesus on Christ the door and good shepherd *John 10: 1-30*
Jesus' sermon, "I am the way" *John 14: 1-31*
Paul changes his way of life *Acts 9: 1-22*

See also Christ, Christian, life, opportunity, path, plan, progress

WEALTH

Abraham's riches grow, strife with Lot *Gen 13:1-18*
Jacob and Esau both attain wealth *Gen 33: 1-11*
Hezekiah shows his treasures to the enemy *2 King 20: 12-21, Isa 39: 1-8*
The vanity of human wealth *Eccl 1: 1-18, 2: 1-26*
Jesus' teaching, "seek ye first" *Mat 6: 25-34, Luke 12: 22-34*
A rich young ruler asks about eternal life *Mat 19: 11-30, Mark 10: 17-31, Luke 18: 18-30*
Jesus' parable of the talents *Mat 25: 14-30, Luke 19: 11-28*
Precious ointment poured on him *Mat 26: 6-13, Mark 14: 3-9*
Jesus' parable of the rich fool *Luke 12: 15-21*
Jesus' parable of rich man and beggar *Luke 16: 19-31*
Jesus visits Zacchaeus *Luke 19:1-10*
Paul on source of supply for all *2 Cor 8: 11-15, 9: 6-15*

See also abundance, possessions, property, riches, treasure

WEAPONS

Flaming sword guards tree of life *Gen 3: 23, 24*

David refuses armor and relies on sling *1 Sam 17:17-52*

David takes spear from Saul's bolster *1 Sam 26:1-25*

Nehemiah arms his builders of the wall *Neh 4:1-23*

Jesus killed on the cross *Mat 27: 32-56, Mark 15:21-41*

Peter cuts guard's ear with sword *Luke 22:50, 51*

Jesus uses whip to cast traders out *John 2:13-25*

Paul on weapons of our warfare *2 Cor 10:3-5*

Paul on Christian's armor *Eph 6: 10-17*

John's vision of two-edged sword *Rev 1:13-16, 19:11-15*

See also disarmament, peace, sword, war

WEARY

Hagar and her son lost in wilderness *Gen 21:9-21*

People hunger in the wilderness *Exod 16:1-36, Num 11:1-15, 31, 32*

Aaron and Hur hold up Moses' hands when weary *Exod 17:8-16*

Moses weary with judging *Exod 18:13-27*

Elijah discouraged and tired *1 King 19:1-8*

Job expresses his woe *Job 3:1-26*

David's song, "the secret place of the most High" *Psal 91:1-16*

Isaiah on how to run and not be weary *Isa 40:28-31*

Jesus heals woman twelve years with issue of blood *Mat 9:20-22, Mark 5:25-34, Luke 8:43-48*

Jesus' parable of lost sheep *Mat 18: 12-14, Luke 15:1-7*

Jesus at Gethsemane *Mat 26:30, 36-46, Mark 14:26, 32-42, Luke 22: 39-46*

The crucifixion *Mat 27:32-56, Mark 15:21-41, Luke 23:26-49, John 19: 17-30*

Jesus heals paralytic let down through roof *Mark 2:1-12, Luke 5:17-26*

Jesus' parable of servant who serves *Luke 17:7-10*

Paul's advice to strengthen the Christians *2 Tim 2:1-26*

James' sermon on how to bear our cross *Jas 1:1-27*

See also body, fatigue, spirit

WEATHER

Noah and the flood *Gen 7:1-24*

Noah sees rainbow *Gen 9:12-17*

Sun and moon stand still at Ajalon *Josh 10:6-15*

God controls the dew for Gideon *Judg 6:19-40*

Elijah prays for rain *1 King 18:41-46*

Elijah in earthquake and wind *1 King 19:9-13*

Job hears of God's control of the weather *Job 37:1-24*

David's song, "The heavens declare the glory" *Psal 19:1-14*

Jonah in storm at sea *Jonah 1:1-17*

Jesus' parable of builder on rock or sand *Mat 7:24-27, Luke 6:48, 49*

Jesus calms wind and seas *Mat 8: 23-27, Mark 4:35-41, Luke 8:22-25*

Signs at crucifixion *Mat 27:45-56*

Jesus calms tempest on sea *Mark 6:45-52, John 6:21*

Paul shipwrecked in storm at sea *Acts 27:1-44*

See also elements, storm, temperature, wind

WEDDING

A proper wife is found for Isaac *Gen 24:1-67*

Esther preferred by king and made queen *Esther 2:5-23*

Jesus' parable of the marriage feast and wedding garment *Mat 22:1-14*

Jesus' parable of chief seats at the wedding *Luke 14:7-14*

Jesus changes water to wine at the wedding *John 2:1-11*

See also bride, husband, marriage, wife

WHEAT

Joseph stores grain in good years *Gen 41:46-49*

Joseph's brethren go to Egypt for grain *Gen 42: 1-8*

Ruth gleans in the field of Boaz *Ruth 2: 1-23*

Elisha prophesies drop in price of flour *2 King 6: 24, 25, 7: 1-18*

Daniel prefers pulse to king's portion of food *Dan 1: 1-21*

Disciples pluck corn on sabbath *Mat 12: 1-8, Mark 2: 23-28, Luke 6: 1-5*

Jesus' parable of sower *Mat 13: 3-23, Mark 4: 1-20, Luke 8: 4-15*

Jesus' parable of wheat and tares *Mat 13: 24-30, 36-43*

Jesus feeds 5000 *Mat 14:15-21, Mark 6: 35-44, Luke 9: 12-17, John 6: 5-14*

Jesus' parable of seed, blade, ear, full corn *Mark 4: 26-39*

See also bread, food

WHOLE

God creates man in his image and likeness *Gen 1: 26, 27*

Jacob wrestles and receives a new name *Gen 32:24-32*

Moses' revelation of God as I Am That I Am *Exod 3: 1-18*

Elijah translated over death *2 King 2: 1-11*

Job restored to former status *Job 42: 1-17*

David's songs:
"What is man?" *Psal 8: 1-9*
"The Lord is my shepherd" *Psal 23:1-6*
"The earth is the Lord's, and the fulness thereof" *Psal 24:1-10*

The complete woman and wife *Prov 31: 1-31*

Jesus on oneness with the Father *John 10: 22-40*

Jesus restores withered hand "whole," like as the other *Mat 12: 9-13, Luke 3: 1-5, 6: 6-11*

Jesus' parable of lost sheep *Mat 18: 12-14, Luke 15: 1-7*

The resurrection *Mat 28: 1-8, Mark 16: 1-8, Luke 24: 1-12, John 20: 1-10*

Jesus restores Malchus' ear, cut off by Peter *Luke 22: 50, 51*

Paul's teaching to put on the new man *Col 3: 1-17*

See also perfection

WICKED

Serpent deceives Eve *Gen 3: 1-24*

Cain kills Abel *Gen 4: 1-16*

Moses denounces abominations *Deut 18: 9-14*

Ahab takes Naboth's vineyard *1 King 21:1-27*

Conspiracy against Nehemiah fails *Neh 6: 1-19*

Haman is hanged on gallows he built for Jews *Esther 6: 1-14, 7: 1-10*

David's song, "Fret not thyself . . . because of evildoers" *Psal 37: 23-40*

David's song, "the secret place of the most High" *Psal 91: 1-16*

Isaiah threatens workers in the dark *Isa 29: 11-24, 30: 1-3, 20, 21*

Jesus' temptations *Mat 4:1-11, Mark 1: 12, 13, Luke 4: 1-13*

Jesus accused of healing by Beelzebub *Mat 12: 22-30, Mark 3: 22-30, Luke 11: 14-23*

Jesus' parable of debtor unmerciful to fellows *Mat 18: 23-35*

Jesus casts traders out of temple *Mat 21: 12, 13, Mark 11: 15-17, Luke 19: 45, 46, John 2: 13-25*

Jesus' parable of husbandmen who refuse to pay rent *Mat 21: 33-46, Mark 12: 1-12, Luke 20: 9-19*

Jesus' parable of sheep and goats *Mat 25: 31-46*

Rulers conspire against Jesus *Mat 26: 1-5, Mark 14: 1, 2*

Judas settles price to betray Jesus *Mat 26: 14-16, Mark 14: 10, 11, Luke 22:1-6*

Jesus casts out unclean spirit *Mark 1: 21-28, Luke 4: 33-37*

Jesus delivers himself from destroyers *Luke 4: 28-31*

Jesus castigates the Pharisees *Luke 11: 37-54, Mat 23: 1-39*

Paul describes enemies of the truth *2 Tim 3: 1-17*

John's vision of dragon and the woman *Rev 12:1-17*

See also evil, morality, sin, wrong

WIDOW

Ruth and Naomi *Ruth 1: 1-22*

Elijah fed by widow of Zarephath *1 King 17: 8-16*

Elisha and widow with pot of oil
2 King 4: 1-7

David's song, "Why art thou cast down?" *Psal 42: 1-11*

Jesus approves widow's mite *Mark 12: 41-44, Luke 21: 1-4*

Jesus restores son of widow of Nain *Luke 7: 11-17*

Jesus' parable of judge and the widow *Luke 18: 1-8*

See also husband

WIFE

Eve created from Adam's rib *Gen 2: 21-25*

Wives enter ark *Gen 7: 1-7*

New names for Abram and Sarai *Gen 17: 1-9, 15-22*

A proper wife is found for Isaac *Gen 24: 1-67*

Joseph resists Potiphar's wife *Gen 39: 1-20*

Ruth becomes the wife of Boaz *Ruth 2: 1-22, 4: 13-22*

David takes Bathsheba, the wife of Uriah *2 Sam 11: 1-27*

The virtuous wife and mother *Prov 31: 1-31*

Zebedee's wife asks preference for her sons *Mat 20: 20-28, Mark 10: 35-45*

See also bride, husband, marriage wedding

WILDERNESS

Abraham sends Hagar out into wilderness *Gen 21:9-21*

Moses finds burning bush in wilderness *Exod 3:1-18*

People follow Moses into wilderness *Exod 16:1-36, Num 11:1-15, 31, 32*

Moses heals bites of fiery serpents *Num 21:4-9*

Elijah flees, lives in cave *1 King 19:1-8*

Isaiah predicts desert will blossom *Isa 35:1-10*

Ministry of John the Baptist in wilderness *Mat 3:1-12, Mark 1:1-8, Luke 3:1-18*

The temptations of Jesus after forty days and nights in the wilderness *Mat 4:1-11, Mark 1:12, 13, Luke 4:1-13*

Philip baptizes Ethiopian in wilderness *Acts 8:26-40*

See also desert

WILL

Adam and Eve eat forbidden fruit *Gen 3:6-24*

Jacob and Rebekah deceive Isaac *Gen 27:1-44*

Moses delivers God's law *Exod 20: 1-19, Deut 5:1-24*

Miriam and Aaron speak against Moses *Num 12:1-16*

Balaam refuses to curse whom God has blessed *Num 22:1-41, 23:1-30, 24:1-25*

Gideon refuses to be king *Judg 8: 22, 23*

Samuel learns to listen to voice of God *1 Sam 3:1-10*

David takes Bathsheba and kills her husband *2 Sam 11:1-27*

Rehoboam turns from his father's counselors *1 King 12:1-18, 2 Chron 10:1-19*

Job bows to will of God *Job 1:13-22, 2:1-10*

David's song, "the earth is the Lord's" *Psal 24:1-10*

Daniel refuses king's portion of meat and wine *Dan 1:1-21*

Three Jews refuse to worship an image *Dan 3:1-30*

Daniel conflicts with law of Medes and Persians *Dan 6:1-28*

Jonah disobeys God's directions *Jonah 1:1-17, 2:1-10, 3:1-10*

Jesus teaches prayer, "Thy will be done" *Mat 6:5-15, Mark 11:25, 26, Luke 11:1-4*

Jesus heals leper with "I will; be thou clean" *Mat 8:1-4, Mark 1: 40-45, Luke 5:12-16*

Jesus' parable of two sons *Mat 21: 28-32*

Jesus' parable of husbandmen who refuse to pay rent *Mat 21:33-46, Mark 12:1-12, Luke 20:9-19*

Jesus at Gethsemane *Mat 26:30, 36-46, Mark 14:26, 32-42, Luke 22: 39-46*

At Jesus' birth, the angel song "good will toward men" *Luke 2:8-20*

Jesus' parable of prodigal son *Luke 15:11-24*

See also ambition, appetite, control, disobedience, hypnotism, purpose, sin

WILLING

Noah builds the ark *Gen 6:5-22*
Abraham starts search for promised land *Gen 11:31, 32, 12:1-9*
Abraham and Lot willing to separate *Gen 13:1-18*
Isaac and Abraham both willing to sacrifice *Gen 22:1-19*
Moses at first reluctant to lead people *Exod 3:9-12*
Deborah willing to defend people *Judg 4:1-17*
Gideon asks signs of God *Judg 6: 19-40*
Ruth willing to stay with Naomi *Ruth 1:1-22*
Samuel willing to talk with God *1 Sam 3:1-10*
David accepts Goliath's challenge and runs to meet him *1 Sam 17: 1-52*
Solomon determines real mother by her willingness to sacrifice *1 King 3:16-28*
Elisha leaves his plowing *1 King 19:19-21*
Elijah ready for translation over death *2 King 2:1-11*
Willing givers offer liberal offerings for temple *1 Chron 29:6-19*
Esther tries to save her people *Esther 5:1-14*
Job accepts trials *Job 1:13-22, 2: 1-10*
David's song, "The Lord is my shepherd" *Psal 23:1-6*
A virtuous woman *Prov 31:1-31*
The disciples leave their nets when called *Mat 4:12-22, Mark 1:14-20, Luke 5:1-11, John 1:35-42*
Jesus heals leper with "I will; be thou clean" *Mat 8:1-4, Mark 1:40-45, Luke 5:12-16*
Jesus' parable of good Samaritan *Luke 10:25-37*
Jesus' parable of unwilling friend *Luke 11:5-13*
Paul's teaching to put on the new man *Col 3:1-17*

See also readiness, will

WIND

Red Sea driven back by strong east wind *Exod 14:5-31*
Elijah finds God not in the wind, but a still small voice *1 King 19:9-13*
Jesus' parable of builders on rock or sand *Mat 7:24-27, Luke 6:48, 49*
Jesus calms wind at sea *Mat 8:23-27, Mark 4:35-41, Luke 8:22-25*
At Pentecost there is a mighty wind *Acts 2:1-13*
Paul in windstorm at sea, shipwrecked *Acts 27:1-44*

See also elements, spirit, storm, weather

WINE

Daniel refuses to defile himself with the king's wine *Dan 1:1-21*
Jesus' parable of new wine in old bottles *Luke 5:36-39*
Jesus turns water to wine at wedding *John 2:1-11*

See also blood, inspiration

WINGS

God creates winged fowl of air *Gen 1:20-23, 30, 31*
The seraphims with six wings each *Isa 6:1-13*
The four living beings guarding throne are winged *Rev 4:1-11*
John's vision of woman escaping dragon with wings of eagle *Rev 12:1-17*

WINNING

Abraham in war of kings *Gen 14: 8-20*
The song of Moses for victory *Deut 32:1-47*
Jericho falls to Joshua *Josh 6:1-27*
Song of Deborah for victory *Judg 5:1-20*
Gideon defeats the Midianites *Judg 7:1-25*
David and Goliath *1 Sam 17:38-52*
Elisha besieged, disarms enemy *2 King 6:8-23*

Hezekiah defeats Sennacherib, invader *2 King 18:17-37, 19:1-27, 2 Chron 31:20, 21, 32:1-23*

Jehoshaphat finds the battle is God's *2 Chron 20:1-32*

Esther saves her people *Esther 5: 1-14, 6:1-14, 7:1-10*

Three Jews survive fiery furnace *Dan 3:1-30*

Daniel survives lions' den *Dan 6: 1-28*

Jesus' parable of wise and foolish virgins *Mat 25:1-13*

The resurrection *Mat 28:1-8, Mark 16:1-8, Luke 24:1-12, John 20:1-10*

The ascension *Mark 16:19, 20, Luke 24:50-53, Acts 1:6-12*

Seventy disciples return to report success *Luke 10:1-24*

Jesus' parable of rich man and beggar *Luke 16:19-31*

Paul on prize for a race *1 Cor 9: 24-27*

Paul's cost of establishing church *2 Cor 11:21-33*

Paul on rejoicing *Phil 4:1-23*

John's vision of new heaven and earth *Rev 21:1-27*

See also victory, success

WISDOM

Joseph solves problem that none of Pharaoh's wise men could *Gen 41:1-46*

Judges appointed to help Moses *Exod 18:13-27*

Moses reveals basis of all law *Exod 20:1-19, Deut 5:1-24*

Solomon's dream and choice of understanding *1 King 3:5-15, 2 Chron 1:7-12*

Solomon and wisdom in human relations *1 King 3:16-28*

Elisha asks for a double portion of Elijah's spirit *2 King 2:1-15*

The wisdom of Proverbs *Prov 3: 13-26, 4:1-13, 8:1-38*

The wise men seek out the Christ child *Mat 2:1-12*

Jesus on the qualities of a Christian *Mat 5:1-12, Luke 6:7-26, 36*

Jesus' prayer *Mat 6:5-15, Mark 11: 25, 26, Luke 11:1-4*

Jesus' parable of wise and foolish virgins *Mat 25:1-13*

At twelve years, Jesus amazes rabbis *Luke 2:41-52*

Nicodemus visits Jesus at night *John 3:1-21*

Paul on wise and foolish things *1 Cor 1:17—2:16, 3:18-23*

John's vision of the sealed book *Rev 5:1-14*

See also insight, knowledge, omniscience, science, understanding

WITNESS

God creates man and the universe as his image *Gen 1:1-31*

Enoch "walked with God" and was translated over death *Gen 5:18, 21-24*

Moses at burning bush wants evidence for the people *Exod 3:9-12*

In the wilderness, manna *Exod 16: 1-36, Num 11:1-15, 31, 32*

In the wilderness, water *Exod 17: 1-7, Num 20:1-13*

Miriam and Aaron speak against Moses *Num 12:1-16*

Aaron's rod blossoms *Num 17:1-11*

Gideon asks signs of God *Judg 6:19-40*

Queen of Sheba comes to see wonders of Solomon *1 King 10:1-12, 2 Chron 9:1-12*

Elijah sees nature of God *1 King 19:9-13*

The Shunammite insists that all is well, and her son is healed *2 King 4:8-37*

Naaman is astonished to see himself healed of leprosy *2 King 5:1-14*

Jehoshaphat urged to stand still and see the salvation of the Lord *2 Chron 20:1-32*

David's songs:

"The heavens declare the glory" *Psal 19:1-14*

"The earth is the Lord's" *Psal 24:1-10*

"Let the redeemed . . . say so" *Psal 107:1-43*

The Preacher says all mortal life is vain *Eccl 1:1-18, 2:1-26*

Isaiah is called to speak *Isa 6:1-13*

Isaiah foretells the Messiah *Isa 7: 10-16, 9:2-7*

Jesus' parable to judge ourselves and not others *Mat 7:1-5, Luke 6:37-42*

Disciples amazed at calming of seas by Jesus *Mat 8:23-27, Mark 4:35-41, Luke 8:22-25*

Jesus heals withered hand in midst of enemies *Mat 12:9-13, Mark 3:1-5, Luke 6:6-11*

Ascension of Jesus *Mat 16:19, 20, Luke 24:50-53, Acts 1:9-13*

Risen Jesus seen by 500 men and women *Mat 28:16-20, Mark 16:15-18, 1 Cor 15:6, 7*

Jesus casts out unclean spirit *Mark 1:21-28, Luke 4:33-37*

Risen Jesus seen by Magdalene *Mark 16:9-11, John 20:11-18*

Risen Jesus seen by two disciples at Emmaus *Mark 16:12, 13, Luke 24:13-35, 1 Cor 15:15*

Jesus heals man born blind *John 9:1-41*

Risen Jesus seen by apostles (Thomas absent) *John 20:19-23*

Risen Jesus seen by apostles (Thomas present) *John 20:24-29*

Risen Jesus seen by apostles at Galilee breakfast *John 21:1-14*

Risen Jesus seen by James and all apostles *Acts 1:1-8*

Paul's sermon on the cloud of witnesses who saw Jesus *Heb 12:1-29*

James' sermon on faith without works *Jas 2:14-26*

John's vision of new heaven and earth *Rev 21:1-27*

See also eye, martyr, proof, testify

WOMAN

Woman made in image and likeness of God *Gen 1:26, 27*

Eve made from Adam's rib *Gen 2:21-25*

Sarai gets new name "walking with God" *Gen 17:1-9, 15-22*

Potiphar's wife tries to seduce Joseph *Gen 39:1-20*

Miriam speaks against Moses *Num 12:1-16*

Daughters of Zelophehad establish some rights for women *Num 27:1-11, 36:5-13*

Deborah leads her people against the invader *Judg 4:1-17*

Delilah betrays Samson *Judg 16:4-30*

Ruth stays with Naomi *Ruth 1:1-22*

Samuel's miraculous birth by Hannah *1 Sam 1:1-28*

Abigail's gentleness pacifies David *1 Sam 25:2-42*

Queen of Sheba visits Solomon *1 King 10:1-12, 2 Chron 9:1-12*

Elisha heals Shunammite's son *2 King 4:8-37*

Queen Esther saves her people *Esther 5:1-14, 6:1-14, 7:1-10*

The virtuous woman *Prov 31:1-31*

The pride of woman *Isa 3:16-26*

Jesus heals Peter's mother-in-law *Mat 8:14-17, Mark 1:29-34*

Jesus heals woman of issue of blood *Mat 9:20-22, Mark 5:25-34, Luke 8:43-48*

Jesus heals Syrophenician's daughter *Mat 15:21-28, Mark 7:24-30*

Jesus' parable of the wise and foolish virgins *Mat 25:1-13*

Risen Jesus seen by Mary Magdalene *Mark 16:9-11, John 20:11-18*

Jesus heals woman bowed together *Luke 13:11-17*

Peter raises Tabitha *Acts 9:36-43*

John's vision of woman clothed with sun *Rev 12:1-17*

See also birth, gentleness, intuition, love, man, mother, purity, wife

WONDER

Abraham and Sarah amazed they will have a son *Gen 15:1-21*

People astonished at manna *Exod 16:1-36, Num 11:1-15, 31, 32*

Aaron's rod blossoms *Num 17:1-11*

Gideon sees signs from God *Judg 6:19-40*

Isaiah's vision of Messiah *Isa 7:10-16, 9:2-7*

King amazed that three Jews survive fiery furnarce *Dan 3:1-30*

King amazed that Daniel is preserved in lions' den *Dan 6:1-28*

Disciples amazed when Jesus calms storm *Mat 8:23-27, Mark 4:35-41, Luke 8:22-25*

People astonished that Jairus' daughter is raised *Mat 9:18, 19, 23-26, Mark 5:22-24, 35-43, Luke 8:41, 42, 49-56*

Jesus talks with Elias and Moses
*Mat 17:1-13, Mark 9:2-13, Luke 9:
28-36*

Jesus arisen *Mat 28:1-8, Mark 16:
1-8, Luke 24:1-12, John 20:1-10*

Angels announce Jesus' birth to
shepherds *Luke 2:8-20*

Disciples return to report healing
success *Luke 10:1-24*

Risen Jesus astonishes Mary who
mistakes him for gardener *John
20:11-18*

Thomas sees risen Jesus *John 20:
24-29*

Signs and wonders in church growth
Acts 4:24-37

John's vision of new heaven and
earth *Rev 21:1-27*

See also doubt, signs

WORD

God promises Abraham a son *Gen
15:1-21*

Jacob hears of God's ever-presence
Gen 28:10-22

Moses gets God's word in form of
law *Exod 20:1-19, Deut 5:1-24*

Balaam has God's word to bless,
and cannot curse *Num 22:1-41,
23:1-30, 24:1-25*

The watchword of Israel *Deut 6:
1-25*

Samuel listens to God *1 Sam 3:1-10*

Elijah and the still small voice
1 King 19:9-13

Isaiah is called to speak God's word
Isa 6:1-13

Jesus' parable of the sower *Mat
13:3-23, Mark 4:1-20, Luke 8:4-15*

Seventy disciples sent to preach and
heal *Luke 10:1-24*

In the beginning was the Word
John 1:1-14

Jesus' teaching on the bread of life
John 6:26-65

John's vision of the sealed book
Rev 5:1-14

John's vision of the angel with the
book *Rev 10:1-11*

See also affirmation, Bible, bread,
gospel, idea, logic, testament,
tongue

WORK

Adam condemned to till the soil
Gen 3:17-19

Ruth gleans in the field for grain
Ruth 2:1-23

Solomon builds temple *1 King 6:
1-38, 7:1-51, 2 Chron 3:1-17, 4:1-22,
5:1-14*

Elijah prays for rain *1 King 18:41-46*

Elisha leaves his plowing to follow
Elijah *1 King 19:19-21*

Nehemiah rebuilds the wall *Neh
4:1-23*

Zerubbabel rebuilds the temple *Ezra
3:8-13, 4:1-15, 6:1-3, 7, 8, 14, 15*

Jesus' parables:
the builders on the rock or sand
Mat 7:24-27, Luke 6:47-49

the hiring of the laborers *Mat
20:1-16*

the two sons ordered to work *Mat
21:28-32*

the talents *Mat 25:14-30, Luke 19:
11-26*

the faithful steward *Luke 12:
41-48*

the cost of building a tower *Luke
14:25-33*

Jesus heals on sabbath day *Mat 12:
9-13, Mark 3:1-5, Luke 6:6-11*

Jesus instructs his disciples *Mat
28:16-20, Mark 16:15-18*

Jesus fills Peter's net *Luke 5:1-11,
John 21:1-11*

Jesus tells source of his great works
John 5:17-47

James on faith without works *Jas
2:14-26*

See also activity, business, employment, labor, office, profession

WORKS

See faith, great works, justification

WORLD

God creates perfect universe *Gen
1:1-31*

Lord God disappointed in world and
causes flood *Gen 6:5-22, 7:1-24*

Tower of Babel tries to reach heaven
Gen 11:1-9

Lot delivered by escape from Sodom
Gen 19:1, 15-29

David's song, "The earth is the Lord's" *Psal 24:1-10*

David's song, "Whither . . . from thy presence?" *Psal 139:1-24*

All mortal life vain *Eccl 1:1-18, 2: 1-26*

Mortal events within time framework *Eccl 3:1-15*

Isaiah's vision of the coming of Christ's kingdom *Isa 2:1-5, 11:1-12, Mic 4:1-8, 13*

Jesus' parables:

the sower *Mat 13:3-23, Mark 4: 1-20, Luke 8:4-15*

the wheat and tares *Mat 13:24-30, 36-43*

the leaven *Mat 13:33, Luke 13: 20, 21*

the rich fool *Luke 12:15-21*

Jesus and the temptations of the world *Mat 4:1-11, Luke 4:1-13*

Jesus' teaching on "Seek ye first" *Mat 6:25-34, Luke 12:22-34*

Jesus' teaching on a house divided *Mat 12:22-37, Mark 3:22-30, Luke 11:14-20*

Rich young ruler and eternal life *Mat 19:16-30, Mark 10:17-31, Luke 18:18-30*

Jesus as the light of the world *John 1:1-14, 8:12-32*

Paul on Spirit versus flesh *Rom 8:1-39*

Paul's teaching to put off old man, put on new *Col 3:1-17*

John's vision of new heaven and new earth *Rev 21:1-27*

See also earth, heaven, man, universe

WORSHIP

Cain and Abel worship differently *Gen 4:1-16*

Abraham willing to sacrifice his son *Gen 22:1-19*

Moses at burning bush takes off shoes *Exod 3:1-18*

Song of Moses *Exod 15:1-19, Deut 32:1-47*

Song of Deborah *Judg 5:1-20*

Dedication of Solomon's temple *1 King 8:22-66, 2 Chron 6:1-42*

Elijah listens to still small voice *1 King 19:9-13*

David's song, "Bless the Lord, O my soul" *Psal 103:1-22*

Micah's vision of mountain of the Lord's house *Isa 2:1-5, Mic 4:1-8, 13*

Wise men visit "King of the Jews" *Mat 2:1-12*

Jesus heals Syrophenician's daughter *Mat 15:21-28, Mark 7:24-30*

Precious ointment for Jesus *Mat 26:6-13, Mark 14:3-9*

Jesus heals man in temple *Mark 1:21-28, Luke 4:33-37*

Jesus at Jacob's well says God must be worshipped in spirit *John 4: 1-30, 39-42*

Mary anoints Jesus' feet *John 12: 3-8*

People worship Paul and Barnabas as gods *Acts 14:11-18*

Paul on the Unknown God *Acts 17: 15-34*

See also church, devotion, praise

WORTH

Man created as God's very image *Gen 1:26, 27*

Man created from dust *Gen 2:6-8*

Enoch walked with God and was translated over death *Gen 5:18, 21-24, Heb 11:5*

Noah deemed righteous by God *Gen 6:5-22*

Abraham's faith rewarded by God's promises *Gen 15:1-21*

New names for Abram and Sarai *Gen 17:1-9, 15-22*

Jacob promised God's presence in his travels *Gen 28:10-22*

Jacob valued as a prince and given new name *Gen 32:24-32*

Moses self-depreciation overcome *Exod 3:9-12, 4:10-17*

Aaron's spirituality demonstrated *Num 17:1-11*

Chosen people set apart as God's own *Deut 7:6-11*

Song of Moses estimates God's value *Deut 32:1-47*

Barak insists on Deborah's help *Judg 4:1-17*

Saul unfit so Samuel anoints David *1 Sam 15:7-26, 16:1-13*

Queen of Sheba acknowledges Solomon's deeds *1 King 10:1-12, 2 Chron 9:1-12*

Elijah is translated over death
2 King 2:1-11

David's song, "God is our refuge and strength" *Psal 46:1-11*

David's song, "Praise the Lord for his goodness" *Psal 107:1-43*

Jesus' parables:

the treasure buried in field *Mat 13:44*

the pearl of great price *Mat 13:45, 46*

the householder's treasures *Mat 13:51, 52*

the hiring of laborers for vineyard *Mat 20:1-16*

the talents *Mat 25:14-30, Luke 19:11-28*

the sheep and the goats *Mat 25:31-46*

the rich fool and his barns *Luke 12:15-21*

the chief seats at wedding *Luke 14:7-14*

Wise men worship "King of the Jews" *Mat 2:1-12*

Jesus' teaching "Seek ye first" *Mat 6:25-34, Luke 12:22-34*

Jesus urged to heal centurion's servant because he is worthy *Mat 8:5-13, Luke 7:1-10*

Jesus, a prophet without honor in his own country *Mat 13:53-58, Mark 6:1-6, Luke 4:22-24, John 4:43-45*

All men seek Jesus; his fame increases *Mark 1:35-39, 45*

Jesus Christ as the light of the world *John 1:1-14, 8:12-32*

Jesus' teaching that he is Christ *John 7:14-40*

Jesus' teaching on unity and eternity of Christ *John 8:12-59*

See also value, wealth

WOUND

Isaiah's vision of wounded Messiah *Isa 53:1-12*

Jesus heals woman of issue of blood *Mat 9:20-22, Mark 5:25-34, Luke 8:43-48*

Crucifixion and spear thrust *Mat 27:32-50, Mark 15:21-41, Luke 23:16-49, John 19:17-30*

Jesus' parable of good Samaritan *Luke 10:25-37*

Jesus restores Malchus' ear cut off by Peter *Luke 22:50, 51*

Thomas examines Jesus' wounds after resurrection *John 20:24-29*

Vagabond exorcists wounded by patient *Acts 19:11-20*

Paul's hardships to establish church *2 Cor 11:21-33*

Paul's "thorn in the flesh" *2 Cor 12:1-19*

See also body, hurt, injury, pain, violence

WRATH

The Lord God condemns Adam and Eve *Gen 3:6-24*

Cain angry at his brother's success *Gen 4:1-16*

David's wrath pacified by Abigail's gentleness *1 Sam 25:2-42*

Naaman wrathful at conditions of Elisha *2 King 5:1-14*

Three cities excoriated by Jesus for disregarding his mighty works *Mat 11:20-30*

Jesus' parable of husbandmen who refused to pay rent *Mat 21:33-46, Mark 12:21-22, Luke 20:9-19*

Jesus casts out traders *Mark 11:15-17, John 2:13-25*

Jesus castigates Pharisees *Luke 11:37-54*

Jesus' parable of the prodigal's older brother *Luke 15:25-32*

Paul persecutes Christians *Acts 8:1-4*

See also anger, indignation

WRONG

The fall of Adam and Eve *Gen 3:6-24*

The first murder by Cain *Gen 4:1-16*

Joseph resists Potiphar's wife *Gen 39:1-20*

Samson betrayed by his sensuality *Judg 16:4-30*

Saul declared unfit by Samuel *1 Sam 15:7-26*

David takes Bathsheba by having her husband killed *2 Sam 11:1-27*

Asa turns away from God to physicians *2 Chron 16:11-14*

Job asks why the good man should suffer *Job 3:1-26*

David's song, "Fret not thyself because of evildoers" *Psal 37:23-40*

Isaiah's vision of workers in the dark *Isa 29:1-24, 30:1-3, 20, 21*

Jeremiah's vision of good and bad figs *Jer 24:1-10*

Ezekiel on heredity of bad characteristics *Ezek 18:1-32*

Jonah disobeys God *Jonah 1:1-17*

Jesus' parables:

the unmerciful debtor *Mat 18:23-35*

the husbandmen who refuse to pay rent *Mat 21:33-45, Mark 12:1-12, Luke 20:9-19*

the wedding garment *Mat 22:1-14*

the sheep and goats *Mat 25:31-46*

the prodigal son and his brother *Luke 15:11-32*

Jesus' teaching to take no thought for material life *Mat 6:25-34, Luke 12:22-34*

Disciples pluck corn on sabbath *Mat 12:1-8, Mark 2:23-28, Luke 6:1-5*

Jesus admonishes Peter *Mat 16:21-28, Mark 8:31-38, John 9:20-27*

Peter denies Jesus *Mat 26:57, 58, 69-75, Mark 14:66-72, Luke 22:54-62, John 18:13-18, 25-27*

Jesus heals impotent man and warns him to sin no more *John 5:1-16*

Jesus saves adulteress and warns "sin no more" *John 8:1-11*

Saul persecutes Christians *Acts 8:1-4*

Paul describes anti-Christians (enemies) *2 Tim 3:1-17*

See also error, morality, sin, wicked

Y

YEAR

Patriarchs lived hundreds of years *Gen 5:1-32*

Jeremiah promises restoration from captivity in 70 years *Jer 29:8-14*

At twelve years old Jesus goes to Jerusalem *Luke 2:41-52*

See also age, opportunity, renewal, time

Z

ZEALOUS

Noah builds the ark *Gen 6:5-22*

Abraham prepares to sacrifice his son *Gen 22:1-19*

Moses urges obedience *Deut 11:1-32, 28:1-14*

Caleb's reward for a lifetime of service *Josh 14:6-15*

Ruth leaves her own people to follow Naomi *Ruth 1:1-22*

Solomon's first choice—understanding *1 King 3:5-15, 2 Chron 1:7-12*

Elijah destroys 450 prophets of Baal *1 King 18:17-40*

Zerubbabel rebuilds temple *Ezra 3:8-13*

Nehemiah repairs wall of city *Neh 4:1-23*

Esther risks all to save her people *Esther 5:1-14*

David's songs:

"Create in me a clean heart" *Psal 51:1-19*

"My soul longeth" *Psal 84:1-12*

"our dwelling place" *Psal 90:1-17*

The virtuous woman *Prov 31:1-31*

The calling of Isaiah to speak *Isa 6:1-13*

The boy Daniel refuses king's favor *Dan 1:1-21*

Jesus' parables:

the mustard seed *Mat 13:31, 32, Mark 4:30-32, Luke 13:28, 29*

the leaven *Mat 13:33, Luke 13:20, 21*

the treasure in field *Mat 13:44*

the pearl of great price *Mat 13:45, 46*

the good Samaritan *Luke 10:25-37*

the barren fig tree *Luke 13:6-9*

The ministry of John the Baptist *Mat 3:1-12, Mark 1:1-8, Luke 3:1-18*

Jesus heals the daughter of the persistent Syrophenician *Mat 15:21-28, Mark 7:24-30*

Peter accepts Jesus as Christ *Mat 16:13-20, Mark 8:27-30, Luke 9:18-21*

Peter and John speak the word with boldness *Acts 4:1-23*

Paul, from ardent persecutor to ardent disciple *Acts 8:1-4, 9:1-22*

Paul's hardships to establish church *2 Cor 11:21-33*

See also devotion, inspiration

ZECHARIAH

See Part II, Zechariah

ZEPHANIAH

See Part II, Zephaniah

ZERUBBABEL

See Part II, Zerubbabel

ZION

Zerubbabel rebuilds temple *Ezra 3:8-13*

Nehemiah rebuilds wall *Neh 4:1-23*

Isaiah's vision of Jerusalem redeemed *Isa 52:1-15*

Jeremiah's promise of restored Israel *Jer 31:1-14, 31-34*

Zephaniah promises salvation to daughters of Zion *Zeph 3:14-17*

John's vision of New Jerusalem *Rev 21:1-27*

See also church, city, Jerusalem, mountain, temple

THE CHARACTER GUIDE

An alphabetical listing
of main characters
under which Bible stories
about each are classified

AARON

Appointed spokesman *Exod 4: 10-16*

Speaks with Israelites for Moses *Exod 4: 29-31*

Contest with Pharaoh's sorcerers *Exod 7: 10-13*

The passover with sacrificial lamb instituted *Exod 12: 1-14*

He preserves a pot of manna as a memorial *Exod 16: 33, 34*

With Hur, upholds Moses' weary arms during battle *Exod 17: 8-16*

Called into mount to see God *Exod 24: 9-17*

Aaron and sons consecrated *Exod 28: 1-4*

Wears Urim and Thummim of office *Exod 28: 29-36*

His descendants ordained forever *Exod 28: 40-43*

Burns incense at altar *Exod 30: 1-9*

Molds golden calf *Exod 32: 1-24, Deut 9: 13-21, Acts 7: 37-42*

He and sons anointed by Moses *Exod 30: 30-38, Lev 8: 1-13, Psal 133: 1-3*

He is forbidden wine or strong drink *Lev 10: 8-11*

The remains of the sacrifice are for the food of Aaron and his sons *Lev 10: 12-15*

Atonement through scapegoat *Lev 16: 1-28*

Jubilee year *Lev. 25: 9-17*

God's promises to the faithful *Lev 26: 1-20*

Aaron's benediction *Num 6: 22-27*

With sister Miriam rebels against Moses *Num 12: 1-16*

Begs Moses to heal his sister *Num 12: 11-13*

The rebellion of Korah who is swallowed by the earth *Num 16: 1-40*

Aaron makes atonement for the people and stays the plague *Num 16: 41-50*

Aaron's rod blossoms *Num 17: 1-11, Heb 9: 2-4*

The ointment that ran down Aaron's beard *Psal 133: 1-3*

Transfer of office to Eleazar and death *Num 20: 22-29, 33: 38, 39*

Contents of tabernacle include Aaron's rod *Heb 9: 2-4*

ABED-NEGO

One of three who refused to worship an image and are placed in a fiery furnace *Dan 3: 1-30*

ABIJAH

As son of Rehoboam, he defeats his father's old enemy Jeroboam *2 Chron 13: 1-20*

ABIMELECH

Beautiful woman he took is not Abraham's sister but his wife *Gen 20: 1-14*

Abraham heals him of barrenness *Gen 20: 15-18*

Isaac represents his wife as sister to deceive Abimelech *Gen 26: 6-11*

Abimelech's herdmen strive with Isaac over the wells *Gen 26: 12-33*

Abimelech, son of Gideon, is made king by slaughter of his brothers *Judg 9: 1-6*

His brother Jotham writes a parable of the trees about him *Judg 9: 7-21*

ABNER

As uncle of Saul he was present when David brought in the head of Goliath *1 Sam 17: 55-58*

He is taunted by David for not protecting King Saul *1 Sam 26: 5-25*

After Saul's death he sets up Ishbosheth as king of Israel to block David *2 Sam 2: 5-9*

At a truce with Joab **a** contest becomes a war *2 Sam 2: 12-17*

He is pursued by Asahel, Joab's brother, but kills him *2 Sam 2: 18-24*

Asks Joab for another truce *2 Sam 2: 25-32*

He quarrels with Ishbosheth over a concubine *2 Sam 3: 6-11*

He joins David and is feasted by him *2 Sam. 3: 12-21*

He is treacherously killed by Joab *2 Sam 3: 22-39*

ABRAHAM

God calls him; pilgrimage to promised land *Gen 11: 31, 32, 12: 1-9*

Because of famine he and Sarai go to Egypt. He says she is his sister *Gen 12: 10-20*

Returning from Egypt his riches grow; strife with Lot *Gen 13: 1-18*

Blessed by Melchizedek after war with kings to rescue Lot *Gen 14: 8-20, Heb 6: 20, 7: 1-28*

Promised a son; Canaan promised again *Gen 15: 1-21, Neh 9:7, 8, Psal 105:9*

His son Ishmael is born to Hagar, his wife's maid *Gen 16: 1-16, Gal 4: 22-31*

New names for Abram and Sarai *Gen 17: 1-9, 15-22*

Circumcision instituted *Gen 17:10-14, 22-27, Rom 4: 1-25*

Entertains angels and Sarah laughs at their promise *Gen 18: 1-18*

Righteous man and the city *Gen 18: 20-33*

Nephew Lot shelters two angels from mob *Gen 19: 1-14*

Lot escapes Sodom *Gen 19: 1, 15-29*

Abraham heals Abimelech and wife *Gen 20: 1-7, 17*

Isaac born *Gen 21: 1-8, Heb 11: 11*

Hagar sent away but saved *Gen 21: 9-21*

His faith is tested by the call to sacrifice son Isaac *Gen 22: 1-19, Heb 11: 8-11*

He buys a burial cave after Sarah's death *Gen 23: 1-20*

He sends servant to find a wife for son Isaac *Gen 24: 1-15*

At burning bush "I am the God of Abraham" *Exod 3: 3-6, Mark 12: 25, 26*

Jesus debates with the Pharisees on the subject of Abraham *John 8: 51-59*

Those with faith are the children of Abraham *Gal 3: 5-18*

Two sons of Abraham compared to two Jerusalems, bond and free *Gal 4: 22-31*

Parable of rich man and beggar *Luke 16: 19-31*

Paul speaks of Abraham *Rom 4:1-25*

Paul on Christians as the seed of Abraham *Gal 3: 1-29*

Paul on Abraham, Melchisedec, Christ *Heb 7: 1-28*

Paul on faith of Abraham *Heb 11: 8-19*

ABSALOM

He orders his half brother Amnon killed because his sister Tamar had been raped by Amnon *2 Sam 13: 1-39*

After five years' exile he is forgiven by King David his father *2 Sam 14: 1-33*

Absalom's beauty *2 Sam 14: 25, 26*

He steals the hearts of the people, rebels. David flees for his life. Absalom takes Jerusalem *2 Sam 15: 1-37*

Rebels debate their defeat of David *2 Sam 16: 15-23, 17: 1-14*

Spies reach David with Absalom's plan *2 Sam 17: 15-26*

He does battle with David's army *2 Sam 18: 1-8*

He is accidentally hanged by his beautiful hair and killed by Joab *2 Sam 18: 1-18*

David mourns Absalom excessively *2 Sam 18: 19-33*

David ceases mourning his son, the enemy of the people *2 Sam 19: 1-10*

David writes psalm during rebellion *Psal 3: 1-8*

ADAM AND EVE

Man from dust *Gen 2: 6-8*

Rivers and trees in Eden *Gen 2: 9-17*

Animals out of ground *Gen 2: 18-20*

Woman from a rib *Gen 2: 21-25*

Serpent deceives Eve *Gen 3: 1-5, 2 Cor 11: 2-4*

Fall and punishment *Gen 3: 6-24*

Birth of Cain *Gen 4: 1*

Birth of Abel *Gen 4: 2*

Birth of Seth *Gen 4: 25, 26*

Generations of Adam *Gen 5: 1-32*

Separation of Adam's sons *Deut 32: 7, 8*

Death by Adam but life by Christ *Rom 5: 12-21, 1 Cor 15: 20-26, 45-49*

Eve and the conduct of women *1 Tim 2: 9-15*

AGRIPPA

As king he visits Festus who tells him about Paul. He takes an interest in the case *Acts 25: 1-27*

Paul tells his life story and almost persuades him to be a Christian *Acts 26: 1-32*

AHAB

King of Israel he marries Jezebel who worships Baal *1 King 16: 28-34*

Because of his sins Elijah predicts a drought of three years *1 King 17: 1, 18: 1-16*

Elijah kills 450 priests of Baal *1 King 18: 17-40*

Elijah prays for rain for Ahab *1 King 18: 41-46*

Ahab successful in war with Syrians *1 King 20: 1-29*

Jezebel steals Naboth vineyard for Ahab *1 King 21: 1-29*

In battle Ahab disguises himself but is killed *1 King 22: 29-40*

Jehu anointed to supplant the family of Ahab *2 King 9: 1-10*

AMOS

He denounces Israel and foretells the judgment day of the Lord *Amos 5: 1-27*

The vision of the grasshoppers *Amos 7: 1-3*

The vision of the fire *Amos 7: 4-6*

The vision of the plumbline *Amos 7: 7-9*

The priest tells him to go back to Judah his own country *Amos 7: 10-17*

The vision of the basket of fruit *Amos 8: 1-3*

The vision of the Lord standing upon the altar *Amos 9: 1-10*

The final restoration to the promised land *Amos 9: 11-15*

ANANIAS

Heals and so converts Paul to a vessel of the Lord *Acts 9: 10-20*

ASA

In war supported by allies *1 King 15: 9-24, 2 Chron 14: 1-7*

Makes peace with Israel *2 Chron 15: 1-15*

Diseased in his feet and dies *2 Chron 16: 11-14*

BAAL

Gideon throws down altar to Baal *Judg 6: 25-32*

Elijah kills 450 prophets of Baal *1 King 18: 17-40*

Cult crushed by Jehu *2 King 10: 18-28*

Josiah made public worship of Baal to cease *2 King 23: 4, 5*

Baal denounced by Jeremiah because parents sacrifice children to him *Jer 19: 4, 5*

Jesus accused of healing by Beelzebub *Mat 12: 22-30, Mark 3: 22-30, Luke 11: 14-23*

BALAAM

Hired to curse Israelites *Num 22: 1-21*

His ass saves Balaam from destruction by angel *Num 22: 22-35*

He blesses Israelites on God's order
Num 23: 7-24

BARABBAS

Pilate offers to release Jesus or
Barabbas *Mat 27: 15-26, Mark 15:
6-15, Luke 23: 13-25, John 18: 39,
40*

BARNABAS

He brings Paul to Antioch where
converts are called Christians
Acts 11: 22-26
He and Paul bring relief to Judea
Acts 11: 27-30
He and Paul teach at Antioch and
are persecuted *Acts 13: 1-50*
After healing lame man, he and Paul
are worshipped as gods *Acts 14:
8-18*
He and Paul travel on together *Acts
14: 20-27, 15: 1-5*
He quarrels with Paul and travels
with Mark *Acts 15: 36-39*

BARTHOLOMEW

(see Nathanael)

BENJAMIN

Jacob keeps him home when ten
sons go to Egypt for food *Gen
42: 1-4*
Joseph demands ten return to Egypt
with Benjamin *Gen 42: 18-23*
Jacob is persuaded to send Benjamin
Gen 42: 36-38, 43: 1-13
Joseph reveals himself to Benjamin
and ten brothers *Gen 45: 1-4*

BILHAH

Rachel's maid is given to Jacob and
bears him Dan and Naphtali *Gen
30: 1-8*
Reuben commits incest with her
Gen 35: 22, 49: 4

BOAZ

Rich kinsman of poor Naomi *Ruth
2: 1*
Ruth gleans in his field *Ruth 2: 2-
17*

Naomi instructs Ruth how to get
his attention *Ruth 3: 1-18*
He buys the inheritance and marries
Ruth *Ruth 4: 1-22*

CAESAR

Jesus replies on tribute to Caesar
*Mat 22: 15-22, Mark 12: 13-17,
Luke 20: 20-26, 23: 1-5*
Augustus decrees a census *Luke
2: 1-7*
In reign of Tiberius John Baptist
begins to preach *Luke 3: 1-3*
Before Pilate Jesus charged with
rebellion against Caesar *John 19:
8-15*
Depression in Claudius' reign brings
Christians together *Acts 11: 27-30*
Paul's preaching contrary to decrees
of Caesar *Acts 17: 1-10*
Paul appeals to Caesar for judgment
Acts 25: 1-12, 21, 26: 32

CAIAPHAS

Conspires with chief priests to kill
Jesus *Mat 26: 1-3, John 11: 47-54*
Presides at trial of Jesus before
priests *Mat 26: 57-68, John 18: 13,
14, 19-24*

CAIN AND ABEL

The first murder *Gen 4: 1-16*
The faith of Abel *Heb 11: 1-4*
Abel's death compared to Jesus'
Heb 12: 22-29

CALEB

Scouts promised land with Joshua
*Num 13: 1-33, 14: 1-11, 23-39, Deut
1: 19-38*
Demands his share of Canaan *Josh
14: 6-15*

CHRIST

See Jesus Christ

CORNELIUS

He is converted by Peter *Acts 10:
1-48*

DAGON

He is offered thanks for capture of
Samson *Judg 16: 20-24*

Ark causes destruction of Dagon's
image *1 Sam 5: 1-11*

DANIEL

Hebrew boys refuse their portion
of king's meat and eat grain *Dan
1: 1-21*

Interprets king's dream of great
image *Dan 2: 1-49*

Three Hebrews refuse to worship
image; placed in fiery furnace
Dan 3: 1-30

Dream of great tree hewn down
Dan 4: 1-27

Prophesies insanity of Nebuchadnezzar *4: 28-37*

Reads handwriting on wall *Dan 5:
1-31*

Lions' den *Dan 6: 1-28*

Vision of meetings with Gabriel
*Dan 8: 15-19, 9: 20-23, 10: 4-21, 12:
1-4*

DAVID

David's grandfather is born *Ruth
4: 13-17*

Saul declared unfit by Samuel *1 Sam
15: 7-26*

David anointed by Samuel *1 Sam
16: 1-13*

Plays harp to calm Saul's troubled
spirits *1 Sam 16: 14-23*

As shepherd, slays lion and bear
1 Sam 17: 33-36

Goliath's challenge to army *1 Sam
17: 1-16*

David visits army; accepts challenge; refuses Saul's armor *1 Sam
17: 17-37*

Kills Goliath with slingshot *1 Sam
17: 38-52*

He carries the head of Goliath to
Saul *1 Sam 17: 53-58*

Jonathan befriends him; Saul envies
him and casts javelin *1 Sam 18:
1-16*

He becomes Saul's son-in-law for
200 Philistine foreskins *1 Sam
18: 17-30*

Saul urges his son and servants to
kill David *1 Sam 19: 1-7*

David playing harp escapes Saul's
javelin *1 Sam 19: 8-10*

Michal puts David's image in her
bed while he escapes *1 Sam 19:
11-18*

He flees to Samuel's house *1 Sam
19: 18-24*

Jonathan renews his pledge of love
for David *1 Sam 20: 1-17*

Jonathan arranges signal of three
arrows *1 Sam 20: 18-23, 35-42*

Jonathan defends David to Saul who
throws a javelin at his own son
1 Sam 20: 24-34

Hungry, David eats shewbred *1 Sam
21: 1-6, Mat 12: 1-8, Mark 2: 23-28*

Fleeing, David obtains Goliath's
sword *1 Sam 21: 7-10*

He feigns madness to the king of the
Philistines *1 Sam 21: 10-15*

He gathers a band of valiants *1 Sam
22: 1-5*

The priests that gave him the shewbread are killed by Saul *1 Sam
22: 6-23*

He saves Keilah from the Philistines
but is betrayed by them to Saul
1 Sam 23: 1-15

He renews his covenant with Jonathan but is betrayed again to Saul
1 Sam 23: 16-29

Spares Saul in cave at Engedi, cuts
off piece of his skirt *1 Sam 24:
1-22*

Pacified by Abigail's gentleness
1 Sam 25: 2-42

He marries Abigail and Ahinoam
1 Sam 25: 39-44

Again in Ziph, takes spear and cruse
from Saul's bolster *1 Sam 26: 1-25*

He flees to Gath and Saul stops
pursuit *1 Sam 27: 1-12*

Saul consults familiar spirit illegally
1 Sam 28: 3-25

Philistines refuse to let David help
them fight Saul *1 Sam 29: 1-11*

Returning home he finds his city
burned; he pursues and recovers
his wives and property *1 Sam 30:
1-25*

Death of Saul *1 Sam 31: 1-13, 2 Sam
1: 1-16, 1 Chron 10: 1-14*

David hears news of Saul's death and kills messenger *2 Sam 1: 1-16*

He laments on how the mighty have fallen *2 Sam 1: 17-27*

He is anointed king of Judah *2 Sam 2: 1-4*

A son of Saul is declared king by Abner and war begins *2 Sam 2: 5-32*

Amnon, Chileab, Absalom and Solomon are born *2 Sam 3: 1-5, 12: 24, 25, 1 Chron 3: 1-5*

Abner quarrels with his king *2 Sam 3: 6-11*

Abner revolts to follow David but Joab violates the truce and kills him *2 Sam 3: 12-39*

David hangs men who assassinated his enemy the son of Saul *2 Sam 4: 1-12*

Israel invites him to be their king; he reigns 40 years *2 Sam 5: 1-5, 1 Chron 11: 1-9*

He orders ark moved to his city but Uzzah steadies ark and dies *2 Sam 6: 1-11, 1 Chron 13: 1-14*

David dances before the ark, his wife critical *2 Sam 6: 12-23, 1 Chron 15: 25-29*

Promises to build a house for God *2 Sam 7: 1-29, 1 Chron 17: 1-27*

Shows kindness to Mephibosheth (son of Jonathan) *2 Sam 9: 1-13, 19: 24-30*

David's messengers to king Hanun are mistreated; war with Ammon *2 Sam 10: 1-19, 1 Chron 19: 1-19*

Takes Bathsheba, wife of Uriah *2 Sam 11: 1-27*

Nathan's parable of the one ewe lamb; David repents *2 Sam 12: 1-12*

Bathsheba's child dies *2 Sam 12: 13-23*

Solomon is born *2 Sam 12: 24, 25*

David's third son kills his first son *2 Sam 13: 23-29*

Absalom exiled *2 Sam 13: 30-39*

After five years David forgives Absalom *2 Sam 14: 1-33*

Absalom's conspiracy; he takes Jerusalem *2 Sam 15: 1-37*

Ziba rewarded by David *2 Sam 16: 1-4*

Shimei curses David *2 Sam 16: 5-13*

Rebels debate action *2 Sam 16: 15-23, 17: 1-26*

The battle with the rebels *2 Sam 18: 1-8*

Absalom's death *2 Sam 18: 6-33*

Runners carry tidings of victory *2 Sam 18: 19-33*

Excessive mourning for Absalom *2 Sam 18: 33, 19: 1-15*

Shimei is pardoned *2 Sam 19: 16-23, 1 King 2: 36-46*

Mephibosheth forgiven *2 Sam 19: 24-29*

David's gratitude for refuge with Barzillai *2 Sam 19: 31-40*

The new rebellion of Sheba of Israel from Judah *2 Sam 19: 41-43, 20: 1-22*

David releases seven sons of Saul to be hanged *2 Sam 21: 1-11*

David transfers bones of Saul and Jonathan to Saul's father's tomb *2 Sam 21: 12-14*

Four followers of David slay four giants *2 Sam 21: 15-22*

Psalm of thanksgiving *2 Sam 22: 1-51, 1 Chron 16: 7-36, Psal 18: 1-49*

Nathan reveals to David that his son shall build the Lord's house *1 Chron 17: 1-27*

Bathsheba and Nathan persuade David to select Solomon as successor *1 King 1: 1-53*

His charge to Solomon *1 Chron 22: 6-19, 23: 1, 28: 2-10, 20*

Liberal offerings to David for the temple *1 Chron 29: 6-19*

Sweet singer of Israel, he is credited with writing the basic Psalms *2 Sam 22: 1-51, 1 Chron 16: 7-36, Psal 1-Psal 150*

His last words *2 Sam 23: 1-5*

Exploits of his valiant men *2 Sam 23: 6-39, 1 Chron 11: 10-25*

He numbers the people and is punished with pestilence *2 Sam 24: 1-17, 1 Chron 21: 1-13*

He buys a threshingfloor, builds an altar and the plague is stayed *2 Sam 24: 18-25, 1 Chron 21: 14-30*

In old age a virgin found to keep him warm *1 King 1: 1-4*

He chooses between Adonijah and Solomon, helped by Bathsheba and Nathan *1 King 1: 5-37*

His son Solomon proclaimed king
and forgives his brother's usurpa-
tion *1 King 1: 38-53*

His last words to Solomon *1 King
2: 1-11*

He is revenged on Joab, put to
death by Solomon *1 King 2: 28-34*

Shimei who cursed him put to death
1 King 2: 36-46

Jesus called Son of David by blind
men he healed *Mat 9: 27-30, Mark
10: 47, 48, Luke 18: 38, 39*

Jesus heals blind and dumb, is called
son of David *Mat 12: 22, 23*

Jesus welcomed to Jerusalem, Ho-
sanna to son of David *Mat 21:
6-11*

Jesus questions Pharisees whether
Christ is the son of David *Mat
22: 41-46, John 7: 42*

Relation of Christ and David *Mat
22: 42-46, Mark 12: 34-37, Rom 1:
1-4*

Peter on the relation between David
and Christ *Act 2: 29-36*

DEBORAH

Defeats Sisera *Judg 4: 1-17*
Song of Deborah *Judg 5: 1-20*

DELILAH

Loved by Samson, she causes his
capture *Judg 16: 4-21*

DINAH

She is ravished by Shechem who
then offers her marriage *Gen
34: 1-12*

Shechem offers daughters of his
tribe for intermarriage *Gen 34:
13-24*

After agreeing Dinah's brothers kill
all Shechemites and take their
wives and possessions *Gen 34: 25-
31*

DORCAS

Raised from death by Peter *Acts 9:
36-42*

ELI

As high priest, he rebukes Hannah
then blesses her *1 Sam 1: 9-18*

A prophet complains to him about
his sons and his nepotism. He
predicts failure and poverty for
Eli's descendants *1 Sam 2: 27-36*

Samuel is his apprentice in the
temple *1 Sam 1: 24-28, 3: 1-10*

His sons are corrupt but he indulges
them *1 Sam 2: 12-17, 22-29*

The iniquity of his sons is exposed
to Samuel *1 Sam 3: 11-18*

His accidental death at 98 *1 Sam
4: 12-18*

His grandson Ichabod is then born
prematurely, causing the death of
the mother *1 Sam 4: 19-22*

ELIHU

Sets Job straight *Job 32: 1-22*

ELIJAH
(ELIAS)

Prophesies drought to King Ahab
1 King 17: 1-5

Ravens feed him; widow of Zara-
pheth feeds him *1 King 17: 3-16,
Luke 4: 25, 26*

Widow's son's sickness and death
healed *1 King 17: 17-24*

Elijah returns and assures Obadiah
that he will meet with King Ahab
1 King 18: 1-16

450 prophets of Baal slain *1 King
18: 17-40, Rom 11: 2-5, Luke 9:
52-56*

Prays for rain *1 King 18: 41-46,
Jam 5: 16-17*

Rests under juniper tree; is fed by
angel; lodges in cave *1 King 19:
1-10*

The still small voice *1 King 19: 9-13*

The Lord instructs him to anoint
two kings and a prophet *1 King
19: 14-18*

Finds Elisha plowing *1 King 19:
19-21*

On advice of a prophet Ahab repulses Syrians twice *1 King 20:
1-34*

Ahab takes Naboth's vineyard
1 King 21: 1-27

A prophet neglects to guard a prisoner safely *1 King 20: 35-43*

The prophets urge Ahab and Jehoshaphat to attack Syria but Ahab dies in the battle *1 King 22: 1-40*

Elijah prophesies death of king for turning in his sickness to Baalzebub to be healed *2 King 1: 1-8, 16-18*

Two captains of fifty destroyed by fire; third saved *2 Kings 1: 3-15*

Elijah taken to heaven in whirlwind *2 King 2: 1-11*

Water of Jordan divided *2 King 2: 1-18*

The spirit of Elijah rests on Elisha *2 King 2: 12-15*

Prophecy that Jezebel will be eaten by dogs comes true in the days of Elisha *2 King 9: 29-37*

His prophecy about death of Ahab's 70 sons comes true *2 King 10: 1-10*

Also family of king of Judah *2 King 10: 11-17*

Elijah prophesies plague because of king's misrule *2 Chron 21: 5, 12-15*

Pharisees ask John the Baptist if he is Elias *John 1: 19-28*

Angel Gabriel speaks of John the Baptist in the spirit of Elias *Luke 1: 11-17*

Jesus speaks of Elias *Luke 4: 25, 26, 9: 52-56*

Jesus compares John the Baptist to Elias *Mat 11: 11-15*

People think Jesus on the cross calls for Elias to help *Mat 27: 45-49*

Some say Jesus is Elijah returned *Mat 16: 13-17, Mark 6: 15, Luke 9: 7-9, 18-21*

Appears to Jesus on Mount of Transfiguration as representative of prophecy *Mat 17: 1-12, Mark 9: 2-13, Luke 9: 28-36*

ELIMELECH

Husband of Naomi. Died in Moab *Ruth 1: 1-3*

ELISHA

Disciple of Elijah *1 King 19: 16-21*

Takes up the mantle of Elijah and parts water of Jordan *2 King 2: 12-15*

Waters of city healed *2 King 2: 16-22*

He curses mocking children *2 King 2: 23-25*

Water supplied for large army *2 King 3: 16-20*

A widow's pot of oil multiplied *2 King 4: 1-7*

Shunammite's son healed *2 King 4: 8-37*

Poisoned pottage harmless *2 King 4: 38-41*

One hundred men fed *2 King 4: 42-44*

Naaman the leper healed *2 King 5: 1-14, Luke 4: 27*

Gehazi struck with leprosy for his greed *2 King 5: 15-27*

Elisha causes iron axe head to float *2 King 6: 1-7*

Besieged by Syrians; blinds them temporarily *2 King 6: 8-23*

Releases Syrians to return home *2 King 6: 19-23*

During the famine two women quarrel about eating their sons *2 King 6: 24-33*

Prophesies drop in price of flour (famine will end) *2 King 6: 24, 25, 7: 1-18*

Shunammite flees famine; returns to claim her property *2 King 8: 1-6*

Elisha prophesies death of king and accession to throne of the king's messenger, Hazael *2 King 8: 7-15*

He sends his messenger to anoint Jehu king in secret *2 King 9: 1-10*

After anointment by Elisha's order Jehu defeats two kings *2 King 9: 11-29*

Jehu causes Jezebel's death; her body eaten by dogs *2 King 9: 30-37*

Elisha foretells the symbol of the arrows shot by the king *2 King 13: 14-20*

He dies. When a man is buried in the same grave he is resurrected

to life by touching the bones of Elisha *2 King 13:20, 21*
Jesus refers to his healing of Naaman *Luke 4:27*

ENOCH

Son of Cain *Gen 4:17*
He walked with God and was translated *Gen 5:21-25, Heb 11:5*

EPHRAIM

Joseph's second son born *Gen 41:50-52*
Israel blesses him with right hand but first-born Manasseh with his left *Gen 48:1-22*
Ezekiel's vision of two sticks labeled Ephraim and Judah united *Ezek 37:15-28*
Hosea's vision of God teaching Ephraim to walk *Hosea 11:1-4*

ESAU

Twin of Jacob, red, hairy *Gen 25:24-26*
A hunter, he despised his birthright *Gen 25:27-34, Heb 12:15-24*
Old Isaac requests venison *Gen 27:1-4*
Esau returns with it too late to get blessing *Gen 27:30-40, Heb 11:20*
Esau plans to kill Jacob *Gen 27:41-44*
Esau displeases his father in selecting a wife *Gen 26:34, 35, 28:6-9*
Esau forgives Jacob years later *Gen 33:1-11*
Esau the father of the Edomites *Gen 36:43, Jer 49:8*
Descendants of Esau and Jacob continue the feud *Obad 1:8-18*

ESTHER

Mordecai's niece Esther is preferred by king and made queen *Esther 2:5-23*
Haman persecutes Jews; Esther promises to help them *Esther 3:1-15, 4:1-17*

Gives banquet to sue for her people's life *Esther 5:1-14*
Haman is hanged on gallows he built *Esther 6:1-14, 7:1-10*
Mordecai promoted and Jews released *Esther 8:1-8*

EVE

Her creation *Gen 2:21-25*
Beguiled by talking serpent *Gen 3:1-13, 2 Cor 11:3, 1 Tim 2:9-15*
Fig leaf aprons sewed *Gen 3:7*
Her punishment *Gen 3:15, 16*
Named by Adam *Gen 3:20*
Clothing made from skins *Gen 3:21*
Mother of Cain and Abel and Seth *Gen 4:1, 2, 25, 5:3, 4*

EZEKIEL

His vision of cherubims *Ezek 1:1-14*
His vision of the wheels *Ezek 1:15-25, 10:9-19*
His mission to speak unafraid to a rebellious people *Ezek 2:1-10, 3:15-23*
He eats the roll of prophecy *Ezek 3:1-14*
He recovers three times from dumbness *Ezek 3:25-27, 24:24-27, 33:20-24*
His symbol of the tile and iron pot for the siege of Jerusalem *Ezek 4:1-3*
Positions of the body and diets for the sins of Israel *Ezek 4:4-17*
He shaves his hair and beard and scatters it to indicate the dispersion *Ezek 5:1-5*
He prophesies a remnant will be saved after tribulation and the sword *Ezek 6:9-14, 14:22, 23*
His vision of the six men slaying in the city *Ezek 9:1-11*
His vision of the coals of fire *Ezek 10:1-8*
The stony heart and the heart of flesh *Ezek 11:16-25, 36:25-38*
The false proverb that every vision fails *Ezek 12:21-28*
His prophecy agains false prophets and prophetesses *Ezek 13:1-23*

He warns against idolatry *Ezek 14: 1-11*

His parable of the unfit vine *Ezek 15: 1-8, 19: 10-14*

His parable of the wretched infant *Ezek 16: 1-15*

His parable of the eagles and the vine *Ezek 17: 1-24*

He prophesies the Messiah as a tender twig of cedar *Ezek 17: 22-24*

His parable of the sour grapes *Ezek 18: 1-32*

His parable of the lion's whelps *Ezek 19: 1-9*

The symbol of dross in the furnace *Ezek 22: 13-22*

His parable of the two lewd women *Ezek 23: 1-49*

His parable of the boiling pot *Ezek 24: 1-14*

As a sign to all he refuses to mourn his wife *Ezek 24: 15-25*

The wreck of the gallant ship (fall of Tyre) *Ezek 27: 25-36*

His prophecy against false shepherds God's care of his flock *Ezek 34: 1-31, Mat 18: 12, 13, Luke 15: 3-6, John 10: 1-16*

An army resurrected from dry bones *Ezek 37: 1-14*

His prophecy of union of two sticks (Israel and Judah) *Ezek 37: 15-28*

God's judgment against Gog of the land of Magog *Ezek 38: 1, 2, 14-18, 21-23, Rev 20: 7-10*

His vision of a man measuring the new temple in Jerusalem *Ezek 40: 1-5*

His vision of the waters of life and health issuing from the temple *Ezek 47: 1-12*

EZRA

He is commissioned by Artaxerxes to gather a second group of exiles in Babylon for return to Jerusalem *Ezra 7: 11-28*

He refuses military escort for the journey, depends on God for safety, they arrive *Ezra 8: 21-23, 31, 32*

He makes them put away their heathen wives *Ezra 10: 1-17*

After Nehemiah rebuilds the wall Ezra reads the book of Moses' law in the street *Neh 8: 1-12*

FELIX

As governor of Judea, tries Paul accused by high priest *Act 24: 1-23*

With his wife trembles as Paul preaches Christ *Act 24: 22-26*

Leaves Paul in prison for successor to decide *Act 24: 27*

FESTUS

Successor to Felix tries Paul who appeals to Caesar *Act 25: 1-12*

He entertains King Agrippa by exhibiting Paul *Acts 25: 13-27, 26: 1-32*

GABRIEL

Sent to Daniel, the man greatly beloved *Dan 8: 15-19, 9: 20-23*

Sent to Zacharias, father of John the Baptist *Luke 1: 5-25*

Sent to Mary, mother of Jesus *Luke 1: 26-38*

GEHAZI

He lays Elisha's staff on the dead boy *2 King 4: 1-37*

Greedy for reward he follows Naaman, gets clothes, and contracts leprosy *2 King 5: 20-27*

When surrounded by enemies Elisha causes him to see the defending heavenly host *2 King 6: 8-18*

He tells the king all the great works of Elisha *2 King 8: 1-6*

GIDEON

Angel of Lord sends him to deliver Israel from Midianites *Judg 6: 6-18*

Three signs from God: Kid and unleavened cakes, altar of Baal overthrown, fleece of wool *Judg 6: 19: 40*

Enemy host defeated by surprise with 300 men *Judg 7: 1-25, Heb 11: 32*

In hot pursuit the men of Succoth refuse to feed his army *Judg 8: 6-9, 13-17*

Refuses to be king *Judg 8: 22, 23*

He celebrates victory by making an ephod from enemy earrings *Judg 8: 24-27*

Parable of trees by Gideon's son Jotham *Judg 9: 1-15*

GOLIATH

His description *1 Sam 17: 1-8*

His challenge and Israel's fear *1 Sam 17: 8-16*

David accepts the challenge and kills him *1 Sam 17: 17-52*

David as a fugitive picks up Goliath's sword *1 Sam 21: 8-10*

HABAKKUK

His description of God *Hab 1: 12, 13*

How he listens to God with faith *Hab 2: 1-4, 14, 29*

HAGGAI

He revives rebuilding the temple *Haggai 1: 1-15*

On the greater glory of the future church *Haggai 2: 1-9*

Blessings result from decision to rebuild *Haggai 2: 10-19*

His prophecy of restoration of Davidic kings *Haggai 2: 20-23*

HANNAH

She prays for a child *1 Sam 1: 1-11*

Eli rebukes her *1 Sam 1: 9-18*

Samuel, her son, is dedicated to the Lord *1 Sam 1: 19-28*

Her song of gratitude *1 Sam 2: 1-11*

She makes her son a little coat to worship in *1 Sam 2: 18-20*

Because she dedicated Samuel, she has three more sons and two daughters *1 Sam 2: 20, 21*

HAZAEL

God directs Elijah to anoint him king over Syria *1 King 19: 14-17*

Elisha prophesies that he will assassinate the king, take the throne and war against Israel *2 King 8: 7-15, 28*

Hazael bribed by king from attacking Jerusalem *2 King 12: 17, 18*

HEROD

Wisemen called by him to locate the Christ child *Mat 2: 1-9*

He kills all children under two in Bethlehem *Mat 2: 16-19*

On his birthday, he beheads John the Baptist *Mat 14: 3-12, Mark 6: 17-29, Luke 3: 19, 20*

He fears Jesus is John the Baptist arisen again *Mat 14: 1, 2, Mark 6: 14-16, Luke 9: 7-9*

Jesus calls him a fox *Luke 13: 31-33*

He questions Jesus as prisoner and returns him to Pilate *Luke 23: 6-12*

He persecutes the early Christians *Acts 12: 1-6, 19*

His miraculous death *Acts 12: 20-23*

Paul pleads his case before the king *Acts 25: 24-27, 26: 1-8*

HEZEKIAH

He becomes king of Judah and destroys idols *2 King 18: 1-8, 2 Chron 29: 1-36, 30: 20, 31: 20, 21*

He buys off the first attack of Sennacherib of Assyria with silver and gold *2 King 18: 13-16*

The captains of Sennacherib return to start a rebellion against Hezekiah *2 King 18: 17-37, 2 Chron 32: 1-19, Isa 36: 1-21, 37: 6-13*

He turns to Isaiah for help *2 King 19: 1-7, 2 Chron 32: 20, Isa 37: 1-5*

He prays and is promised victory *2 King 19: 8-34, Isa 37: 15-35*

Epidemic causes death in army of Assyrians and Sennacherib is assassinated *2 King 19: 35-37, 2 Chron 32: 21-23, Isa 37: 36-38*

His boil healed by Isaiah and his life lenghened *2 King 20: 1-7, 2 Chron 32: 24-26*

He asks a sign of Isaiah, who moves the shadow of the dial back 10 degrees *2 King 20: 8-11*

He unwisely shows his possessions to Babylonians and Isaiah predicts the captivity to Babylon *2 King 20: 12-21, 2 Chron 32: 27-33*

HIRAM

He befriends David, the new king and supplies material to build his house *2 Sam 5: 10-12*

Solomon appeals to him for materials to build a temple *1 King 5: 1-18*

He is dissatisfied with the six cities Solomon gives him as reward *1 King 9: 10-14*

HOSEA

When Israel was a child, he was loved by God *Hos 11: 1-4*

ISAAC

Stranger predicts unique birth *Gen 18: 1-19*

Isaac is born *Gen 21: 1-8*

His mother and Hagar quarrel over their sons *Gen 21: 8-14*

Sacrifice planned by Abraham but ram is substituted *Gen 22: 1-19, Heb 11: 17, Jam 2: 21*

A wife is found for him *Gen 24: 1-67*

Twins Esau and Jacob are born *Gen 25: 19-26, Rom 9: 7-14*

Promise to Abraham renewed to Isaac *Gen 26: 1-5, Gal 4: 28*

Strife between herdsmen over wells *Gen 26: 12-31*

Deceived by son Jacob who obtains the blessing intended for his first son Esau *Gen 27: 1-44, Heb 11: 20*

ISAIAH

Coming of Christ's kingdom; wars will cease *Isa 2: 1-5, 22, Mic 4: 1-8, 13*

Pride of women *Isa 3: 16-26*

Parable of wild grapes *Isa 5: 1-8*

Vision of God's glory and the prophet's call *Isa 6: 1-13*

Syria and Israel attack Jerusalem but Isaiah foretells their fall *Isa 7: 1-9*

Christ child prophesied *Isa 7: 10-16, 9: 2-7*

Christ's peaceable kingdom *Isa 11: 1-12*

A song of thanksgiving *Isa 12: 1-6*

Fall of Babylon *Isa 14: 4-8, 12-17, 25-27*

A strength to needy *Isa 25: 1-12*

A song of confidence in God *Isa 26: 1-15*

A sure foundation is laid; precept upon precept *Isa 28: 9-17*

Wisdom of men shall perish *Isa 29: 11-24, 30: 1-3, 20, 21*

Benefits of being good *Isa 33: 20-24*

Desert shall blossom *Isa 35: 1-10*

Isaiah urges resistence by Hezekiah *Isa 36: 1-22, 37: 1-38*

Isaiah heals King Hezekiah of boils *Isa 38: 1-22, 2 King 20: 1-11*

He foretells Hezekiah's defeat *Isa 39: 1-8*

Comfort offered to the people *Isa 40: 1-31*

Protection from fear *Isa 41: 8-22*

Office of the Christ *Isa 42: 1-12, 16, 18*

Fear not in troubled times *Isa 43: 1-28, 44: 1-24*

Saviour will make crooked places straight *Isa 45: 1-25*

Christ a light to the Gentiles *Isa 49: 6-23*

Look to creator *Isa 51: 1-12*

Awake, awake to salvation *Isa 52: 1-15*

Man of sorrows *Isa 53: 1-12*

Comfort for afflicted Gentiles *Isa 54: 1-6, 11-17*

Every one that thirsteth may come *Isa 55: 1-13*

The Lord answers every cry, defines fasting *Isa 58: 1-14*

Lord's hand is not shortened *Isa 59: 1-21*

Arise, shine, for the Gentiles glorify the church *Isa 60: 1-22*

Christ's works prophesied *Isa 61: 1-11, 62: 1-12*

His power to save *Isa 63: 7-19*

Blessed state of new Jerusalem *Isa 65: 17-25*

One church as the mother of all *Isa 66: 9-23*

Preaching of John the Baptist foretold by Isaiah *Mat 3: 1-3, John 1: 19-28, Luke 3: 1-6*

Prophecy about the Messiah fulfilled *Mat 4: 12-16, 8: 16, 17, 12: 14-21, 13: 10-17, 15: 7-10, John 12: 37-41*

Jesus in synagogue reads from Isaiah *Luke 4: 16-22*

Philip converts the eunuch who reads Isaiah *Acts 8: 26-40*

Paul quotes Isaiah *Acts 28: 23-29, Rom 9: 26-33, 10: 16-20, 15: 11-13*

ISCARIOT (see Judas Iscariot)

ISH-BOSHETH

Abner makes this son of Saul king of Israel for seven years *2 Sam 2: 8-11*

After a truce, 12 young men from each side destroy each other *2 Sam 2: 12-17*

Ish-bosheth quarrels with Abner over Saul's concubine *2 Sam 3: 1-11*

Abner deserts to David and is treacherously killed by Joab *2 Sam 3: 12-39*

Ish-bosheth assassinated and his head brought to David *2 Sam 4: 1-12*

David reigns over both kingdoms *2 Sam 5: 1-5*

ISHMAEL

His mother an Egyptian given to Abraham hears a description of her coming child *Gen 16: 1-16*

He is circumcised by Abraham *Gen 17: 15-27*

He and his mother are cast into wilderness by order of Sarah *Gen 21: 1-21*

He and Isaac bury their father *Gen 25: 8-10, 17, 18*

His daughter becomes wife of his nephew Esau *Gen 28: 6-9*

ISRAEL (see Jacob)

JACOB

Jacob and Esau are born twin sons of Isaac and Rebecca *Gen 25: 19-26, Rom 9: 7-14*

Buys Esau's birthright with pottage *Gen 25: 24-34*

Deceives Isaac and obtains Esau's blessing *Gen 27: 1-38*

Esau plans to kill Jacob after his father dies; Jacob flees to his uncle *Gen 27: 41-45, 28: 1-5*

Rebecca and Isaac discuss a marriage for Jacob *Gen 27: 46, 28: 1-5*

Dream of angels on ladder *Gen 28: 10-22*

Jacob earns Rachel by seven years labor *Gen 29: 1-20*

On the wedding night Laban substitutes Leah for Rachel *Gen 29: 21-30*

The sons of Jacob are born *Gen 29: 32-35, 30: 24, 35: 16-20*

Barren Rachel gives her maid to Jacob *Gen 30: 1-8*

Leah trades her mandrakes to Rachel for a night with Jacob *Gen 30: 14-21*

Jacob deals sharply with his father-in-law when they separate *Gen 30: 25-43*

Laban overtakes Jacob but lets him go with a blessing *Gen 31: 1-55*

On Jacob's return to Canaan, wrestles with adversary and receives new name *Gen 32: 1-32, 35: 9-15*

Esau forgives him *Gen 33: 1-11*

His son Reuben commits incest with his concubine Bilhah *Gen 35: 21, 22*

Makes Joseph a coat of many colors *Gen 37: 1-5*

Sends sons to Egypt for corn *Gen 42: 1-8*

He finally consents to let Benjamin go *Gen 43: 1-15*

Emigrates to Egypt with his family *Gen 45: 25-28*

In a dream Jacob gets God's direction to go live in Egypt *Gen 46: 1-7*

He is re-united with Joseph *Gen 46: 28-34*

With Joseph's influence, Jacob's

family given land of Goshen *Gen 47: 1-12, 27-31*

He adopts Joseph's two sons *Gen 48: 1-22*

Calls sons; gives prophecy about their tribes *Gen 49: 1-28, Deut 33: 1-29*

Age, death and burial details *Gen 50: 1-21*

Jesus asks a drink at Jacob's well *John 4: 5-14*

JAIRUS

Jesus raises his dead daughter *Mat 9: 18, 19, 23-26, Mark 5: 22-24, 35-43, Luke 8: 41, 42, 49-56*

JAMES (son of Alpheus)

He is among 12 disciples taught to heal by Jesus *Mat 10: 1-8*

He supports Paul that Gentiles need not be circumcised *Acts 15: 1, 2, 12-22, Gal 2: 7-10*

He gets a report from Paul on progress among the Gentiles *Acts 21: 17-20, Gal 1: 19*

He sees the arisen Jesus *1 Cor 15: 7*

His epistle writes of temptations and trials *Jas 1: 1-27*

He writes on equality of man *Jas 2: 1-13*

He comments on faith without works *Jas 2: 14-26*

He warns of the tongue *Jas 3: 1-18*

JAMES (son of Zebedee)

He is called by Jesus to be an apostle *Mat 4: 17-22, Mark 1: 14-20*

He asks to sit at right hand of Christ *Mat 20: 20-28, Mark 10: 35-45*

He urges Jesus to destroy by fire an inhospitable Samaritan village *Luke 9: 51-56*

He asks Jesus about the second coming *Mark 13: 1-6*

He was present at the following events in Jesus' life:

At draught of fishes *Luke 5: 10*
When Peter's wife's mother was healed *Mark 1: 29*

At raising of Jairus' daughter *Mark 5: 37, Luke 8: 51*

At transfiguration *Mat 17: 1, Mark 9: 2, Luke 9: 28*

At Gethsemane *Mat 26: 37, Mark 14: 33*

At second draught of fishes after resurrection *John 21: 1-11*

He is martyred by Herod *Acts 12: 1-3*

JEHOIACHIN

Defeated by Nebuchadnezzar and his people taken into captivity *2 King 24: 8-16*

As captive king, is well treated in Babylon *2 King 25: 27-30, Jer 52: 31-34*

JEHOSHAPHAT

His goodness includes education of the people in the book of the law *2 Chron 17: 1-13*

He allies with Ahab in war *2 Chron 18: 1-8*

Ahab disguises himself in battle but dies *2 Chron 18: 28-34*

Jehu the prophet rebukes his alliance with the ungodly Ahab *2 Chron 19: 1-3*

He sets up good judges and justice in his kingdom *2 Chron 19: 4-11*

He fears attack by three nations and prays *2 Chron 20: 1-13*

The prophet advises him to stand still and see the salvation of the Lord *2 Chron 20: 14-19*

Singers lead into battle and the enemy defeats itself *2 Chron 20: 20-32*

He builds a navy which is wrecked *2 Chron 20: 33-37*

JEHU

God tells Elijah to anoint him king of Israel *1 King 19: 15-17*

Elisha sends an assistant to anoint him *2 King 9: 1-10*

He leads conspirators to Jezreel, kills Joram son of Ahab *2 King 9: 11-29*

He orders Jezebel's death *2 King 9: 30-37*

He has Ahab's 70 sons beheaded *2 King 10: 1-10*

Feigning worship of Baal, he gathers the priests of Baal and kills them *2 King 10: 18-28*

JEPHTHAH

To mispronounce the password "Shibboleth" means death *Judg 12: 1-7*

JEREMIAH

He tells God he is too young to be a prophet *Jer 1: 4-10*

His vision of the almond tree and the seething pot *Jer 1: 11-19*

He complains Judah has left God for idols *Jer 2: 5-13, 19, 26-28*

He warns of the sword of Babylon on the unrepentant *Jer 4: 1-14*

He compares God with the folly of idolatry *Jer 10: 1-16*

He compares trust in God with trust in man *Jer 17: 5-14*

The example of the potter and the clay *Jer 18: 1-6*

His prophecies cause him to be struck by the governor and imprisoned *Jer 20: 1-6*

Discouraged by persecution he curses the day he was born *Jer 20: 14-18*

He advises people to accept captivity of Nebuchadnezzar rather than death *Jer 21: 4-10*

He promises the remnant a Messiah to feed the flock *Jer 23: 1-6, 33: 14-18*

False prophets do not have the word of the infinite God *Jer 24: 1-10*

Symbolic baskets of good figs and bad *Jer 24: 1-10*

His letter to Jews already in captivity *Jer 29: 1-14*

He predicts the restoration of Israel to Jerusalem *Jer 30: 1-24*

Both Israel and Judah shall be redeemd *Jer 31: 1-34, 33: 1-13*

To back up his promise while in prison, he buys a field in his home town *Jer 32: 1-27, 37-44*

He urges freedom of slaves (to help defense?) *Jer 34: 1-11*

He tests abstinence of house of Rechabites compared to Jews *Jer 35: 1-19*

He dictates book. Part of it is read to the king who burns it *Jer 36: 1-26*

He dictates the book again *Jer 36: 27-32*

His prophecy that Chaldeans would return causes him to be put in prison *Jer 37: 1-21, 38: 1-13*

He predicts his deliverance when the city falls *Jer 39: 15-18*

The king visits his cell for advice *Jer 38: 14-28*

Jerusalem falls, is burned, people and king captives *Jer 39: 4-10, 52: 8-30*

Jeremiah released from prison *Jer 39: 9-14*

Given the choice of going to Babylon he remains *Jer 40: 1-6*

He advises the remaining people to stay in Judah, not go to Egypt *Jer 42: 1-22*

They refuse, go to Egypt and take Jeremiah with them *Jer 43: 1-7*

He predicts defeat of Egypt by Babylon — but Jews are safe *Jer 46: 24-28*

He writes another book on God's judgment of Babylon; Seraiah reads it at Babylon and sinks it in the Euphrates *Jer 51: 59-64*

His poem on the Lord's mercies *Lament 3: 19-36*

He bewails Jerusalem's pitiful state *Lament 4: 1-12*

JEROBOAM

Ahijah tears his garment in twelve pieces and hands back ten *1 King 11: 26-39*

He escapes Solomon; goes to Egypt *1 King 11: 40-43*

When Solomon dies he leads the rebellion against his son Rehoboam *1 King 12: 1-19*

As king he forbids the people to worship at Jerusalem, sets up a golden calf *1 King 12: 19-33*

At the altar of the calf his hand dries up; a man of God heals it *1 King 13: 1-10*

The man of God is taken home by

a prophet in Bethel *1 King 13: 11-22*

When he leaves the prophet's house the man of God is killed by a lion *1 King 13: 23-32*

Still disobedient, Jeroboam sends his wife to Abijah, because his son is sick *1 King 14: 1-20*

He is attacked by Abijah next king of Judah, and is defeated *2 Chron 13: 1-20*

JERUBBAAL (see Gideon)

JESSE

The grandson of Ruth *Ruth 4: 17*

He introduces seven sons to Samuel who is looking to anoint a king to replace Saul *1 Sam 16: 1-13*

He sent provisions to three army sons by David, his youngest *1 Sam 17: 14-22*

Isaiah predicts the Messiah as a rod out of the stem of Jesse *Isa 11: 1, 10, Rom 15: 12*

JESUS CHRIST: Parables

Hiding candle under a bushel *Mat 5: 14-16, Mark 4: 21, Luke 8: 16*

New wine in old bottles and new cloth in old garment *Luke 5: 36-39*

Mote and beam *Mat 7: 1-5, Luke 6: 37-42*

Builders upon rock and upon sand *Mat 7: 24-27, Luke 6: 48, 49*

Two debtors forgiven *Luke 7: 36-50*

Temple to be raised in three days *John 2: 19-22*

Sower and seeds *Mat 13: 3-23, Mark 4: 1-20, Luke 8: 4-15*

Wheat and tares *Mat 13: 24-30, 36-43*

Seed, blade, ear, full corn *Mark 4: 26-29*

Mustard seed *Mat 13: 31, 32, Mark 4: 30-32, Luke 13: 18, 19*

Leaven *Mat 13: 33, Luke 13: 20, 21*

Treasure hid in field *Mat 13: 44*

Pearl of great price *Mat 13: 45, 46*

Dragnet *Mat 13: 47-50*

Householder's treasures *Mat 13: 51, 52*

Lost sheep *Mat 18: 12-14, Luke 15: 1-7*

Debtor unmerciful to his fellow-servant *Mat 18: 23-35*

Good Samaritan *Luke 10: 25-37*

Chief seats at wedding *Luke 14: 7-14*

The unwilling friend *Luke 11: 5-13*

Unclean spirit returns with seven others *Mat 12: 43-45, Luke 11: 24-26*

Rich fool who built bigger barns *Luke 12: 15-21*

Good Shepherd *John 10: 1-18*

Watchful servants *Luke 12: 35-40*

Faithful steward *Luke 12: 41-48*

Barren fig tree *Luke 13: 6-9*

Door shut by the master *Luke 13: 22-30*

Those bidden to a great supper *Luke 14: 15-24*

Counting cost of building tower or making war *Luke 14: 25-33*

Lost coin *Luke 15: 8-10*

Prodigal son *Luke 15: 11-24*

Elder brother *Luke 15: 25-32*

Unjust steward *Luke 16: 1-14*

Rich man and beggar *Luke 16: 19-31*

Servant who serves his master before he sups *Luke 17: 7-10 (Luke 6: 40)*

Unjust judge and widow *Luke 18: 1-8*

Pharisee and publican *Luke 18: 9-14*

Hiring laborers for vineyard *Mat 20: 1-16*

Two sons ordered to work *Mat 21: 28-32*

Talents *Mat 25: 14-30, Luke 19: 11-28*

Husbandmen refuse to pay rent *Mat 21: 33-46, Mark 12: 1-12, Luke 20: 9-19*

Marriage feast and wedding garment *Mat 22: 1-14*

Fig tree leafing *Mat 24: 32, 33, Mark 13: 28, 29, Luke 21: 29-33*

Man taking long journey *Mark 13: 34-37*

Two servants who await their lord's coming *Mat 24: 42-51*

Wise and foolish virgins *Mat 25: 1-13*

Sheep and goats *Mat 25: 31-46*

True vine *John 15: 1-17*

JESUS CHRIST: Great Works

Water into wine; Problem: supply *John 2: 1-11*

Nobleman's son healed; Problem: fever *John 4: 46-54*

Peter's net filled; Problem: supply *Luke 5: 1-11*

Unclean spirit cast out of man in temple; Problem: mental derangement *Mark 1: 21-28, Luke 4: 33-37*

Delivers himself by passing through midst of enemies; Problem: escape *Luke 4: 28-31*

Peter's mother-in-law healed; Problem: fever *Mat 8: 14-17, Mark 1: 29-34, Luke 4: 38*

Man healed of leprosy; Problem: skin disease *Mat 8: 1-4, Mark 1: 40-45*

Paralytic let down through roof; Problem: paralysis *Mat 9: 2-8, Mark 2: 1-12, Luke 5: 17-26*

Infirm man at pool of Bethesda; Problem: lameness *John 5: 1-16*

Withered hand; Problem: deformity *Mat 12: 9-13, Mark 3: 1-5, Luke 6: 6-11*

Centurion's (Gentile's) servant healed of palsy; Problem: paralysis *Mat 8: 5-13, Luke 7: 1-10*

Son of widow of Nain raised; Problem: death *Luke 7: 11-17*

Man both blind and dumb; Problem: sight and speech *Mat 12: 22-30, Luke 11: 14-23*

Wind seas calmed; Problem: control of elements *Mat 8: 23-27, Mark 4: 35-41, Luke 8: 22-25*

One or two men from the tombs of the Gadarenes; Problem: insanity *Mat 8: 28-34, Mark 5: 1-20, Luke 8: 26-39*

Swine drowned in sea; Problem: evil self-destroyed *Mat 8: 30-34*

Woman diseased with issue of blood twelve years; Problem: hemorrhage *Mat 9: 20-22, Mark 5: 25-34, Luke 8: 43-48*

Jairus' daughter raised; Problem: death *Mat 9: 18, 19, 23-26, Mark 5: 22-24, 35-43, Luke 8: 41, 42, 49-56*

Two blind men healed; Problem: sight *Mat 9: 27-31*

Mute man speaks at Capernaum; Problem: speech *Mat 9: 32-35*

Five thousand men and their families fed; Problem: supply *Mat 14: 15-21, Mark 6: 35-44, Luke 9: 12-17, John 6: 5-14*

Walks on sea; saves Peter who tries it; Problem: dominion over elements *Mat 14: 22-33, John 6: 15-21*

Windstorm calmed; ship at destination at once; Problem: control of weather, time and space *Mark 6: 45-52, John 6: 21*

Syrophoenician woman's daughter (Gentile) healed of a devil; Problem: mental derangement *Mat 15: 21-28, Mark 7: 24-30*

Deaf man with speech impediment; Problem: hearing and speech *Mark 7: 32-37*

Four thousand men and families fed; Problem: supply *Mat 15: 32-39, Mark 8: 1-10*

Blind man healed in two treatments; Problem: sight *Mark 8: 22-26*

Transfiguration on mountain; Problem: control over time; Christ's unity with law and prophecy *Mat 17: 1-13, Mark 9: 2-13, Luke 9: 28-36*

Epileptic boy cured after disciples fail; Problem: epilepsy *Mat 17: 14-21, Mark 9: 14-29, Luke 9: 37-42*

Tribute money from mouth of a fish; Problem: supply *Mat 17: 24-27*

Man born blind; Problem: sight *John 9: 1-41*

Dumb man healed (Pharisees claim devils cast out by Beelzebub); Problem: speech *Luke 11: 14-23*

Woman bowed together 18 years; Problem: spinal disorder *Luke 13: 11-17*

Man healed of dropsy; Problem: dropsy or edema (excess fluid in abdomen) *Luke 14: 1-6*

Ten men of leprosy; Problem: skin disease *Luke 17: 11-19*

Lazarus raised; Problem: death *John 11: 1-46*

Blind beggar (while Jesus enters Jericho); Problem: sight *Luke 18: 35-43*

Blind Bartimaeus (leaving Jericho);
Problem: sight *Mat 20: 29-34,
Mark 10: 46-52*

Fig tree withered; Problem: control
of nature *Mat 21: 18-22, Mark 11:
12-14, 20-24*

Guards fall backwards; Problem:
deliverance from military power
John 18: 4-6

Malchus' ear restored; Problem:
amputation *Luke 22: 50, 51*

Signs at crucifixion; Problem: nature manifests turmoil *Mat 27:
50-56*

Resurrection (body raised from
tomb); Problem: death *Mat 28:
1-8, Mark 16: 1-8, Luke 24: 1-12,
John 20: 1-10*

Risen Jesus appears to Mary; Problem: death *Mat 28: 9, 10, Mark
16: 9-11, Luke 24 13-49, John 20:
11-18*

Other appearances after resurrection; Problem: control of body
in probationary period before ascension *Mat 28: 16-20, Mark 16:
12-18, Luke 24: 13-49, John 20:
19-29, 21: 1-25, Acts 1: 1-8, 1 Cor
15: 5-8*

Enters room through closed doors;
Problem: material obstacle *John
20: 26*

Great haul of fish by casting on
right side; Problem: supply *John
21: 1-11*

Ascension; Problem: translation to
spirit *Mark 16: 19-20, Luke 24:
50, 53, Acts 1: 9-12*

Group Healings

Heals all manner of sickness; Problem: divers diseases, torments,
lunacy and palsy *Mat 4: 23-25,
Luke 4: 40-44*

Great multitudes follow him; Problem: many healed *Mat 12: 14-21,
Mark 3: 6-12*

Heals by touch of hem of garment;
Problem: all that were diseased
Mat 14: 14, Mark 6: 53-56

Heals all who touched him; Problem: variety of ills *Luke 6: 17-19*

Multitudes come to mountain; Prob-

lem: dumb, maimed, lame, blind,
and many others *Mat 15: 29-31*

Heals multitude beyond Jordan;
Problem: great numbers of sick
Mat 19: 1, 2

JESUS CHRIST: Other Events

Birth and Childhood

Genealogy *Mat 1: 1-17, Luke 3: 23-
38*

Birth of John the Baptist announced
to Elisabeth *Luke 1: 5-25*

Birth of Jesus announced to Mary
Luke 1: 26-38

Mary's visit to Elisabeth *Luke 1:
39-56*

Birth of John the Baptist *Luke 1:
57-80*

Angel appears to Joseph; the child's
name ordered *Mat 1: 18-25*

Virgin birth of Jesus *Luke 2: 1-7*

Angels' song and announcement of
birth to shepherds; they visit babe
Luke 2: 8-20

In temple Simon and Anna call him
Christ. He is circumcised and
named Jesus *Luke 2: 21-38*

Led by star, wisemen visit King of
the Jews *Mat 2: 1-12*

Flight to Egypt, and later return
Mat 2: 13-23, Luke 2: 39-40

At twelve years he goes to Jerusalem
with family *Luke 2: 41-52*

Three-Year Public Ministry

Ministry of John the Baptist *Mat
3: 1-12, Mark 1: 1-8, Luke 3: 1-18*

Jesus Christ as the light of the
world *John 1: 1-14*

John testifies that Jesus is the
Christ *John 1: 15-34*

Baptism of Jesus by John *Mat 3:
13-17, Mark 1: 9-11, Luke 3: 21, 22*

The temptations *Mat 4: 1-11, Mark
1: 12, 13, Luke 4: 1-13*

Jesus visits Zabulon and fulfills
Isaiah's prophecy *Mat 4: 12-16*

Peter, Andrew, James and John
called, Matthew too *Mat 4: 17-22,
9: 9, Mark 1: 14-20, Luke 5: 1-11,
John 1: 35-42*

Philip and Nathaniel called *John 1 : 43-51*

All men seek him, increasing his fame *Mark 1 : 35-39*

Nicodemus visits him at night *John 3 : 1-21*

John the Baptist tells how Jesus' preaching differs from his own *John 3 : 22-36*

At Jacob's well he converses with woman of Samaria *John 4 : 1-30, 39-42*

Preaches at Nazareth and is rejected by them *Luke 4 : 14-32*

Scribe volunteers to follow him *Mat 8 : 18-22*

Chooses twelve disciples, instructs them and sends them to heal and preach *Mat 9 : 36-38, 10 : 1-42, Mark 3 : 13-21, Luke 6 : 13-19*

In doubt, John the Baptist sends to Jesus for proof of Christ *Mat 11 : 2-19, Luke 7 : 18-35*

While dining with Pharisee, Jesus is anointed by woman *Luke 7 : 36-50*

With the twelve, makes a second circuit *Luke 8 : 1-3*

Disciples pluck corn on sabbath *Mat 12 : 1-8, Mark 2 : 23-28, Luke 6 : 1-5*

Accused of casting out devils by Beelzebub when healing *Mat 12 : 22-30, Mark 3 : 22-30, Luke 11 : 14-23*

Pharisees request a sign from him *Mat 12 : 38-45, Luke 11 : 16, 29-32*

Mother and brothers wait for him *Mat 12 : 46-50, Mark 3 : 31-35, Luke 8 : 19-21*

Addresses multitude out of vessel on lake *Mat 13 : 1, 2, Mark 4 : 1, Luke 5 : 1-3*

Eats with publicans and sinners *Mat 9 : 10-13, Mark 2 : 13-17, Luke 5 : 27-32*

Why disciples don't fast *Mat 9 : 14-17, Mark 2 : 18-22, Luke 5 : 33-39*

Speaks only in parables *Mat 13 : 10-17, 34, 35, Mark 4 : 10-12, 33, 34*

Prophet without honor in his own country *Mat 13 : 53-58, Mark 6 : 1-6, Luke 4 : 22-24, John 4 : 43-45*

Twelve sent forth with instructions

to preach and heal *Mat 10 : 5-42, Mark 6 : 7-13, Luke 9 : 1-6*

Herod mistakes Jesus for John the Baptist *Mat 14 : 1-13, Mark 6 : 14-29, Luke 9 : 7-9*

People follow him like sheep *Mark 6 : 30-34*

The twelve return to Jesus *Luke 9 : 10, 11*

His reply on what defiles a man *Mat 15 : 1-20, Mark 7 : 1-23*

Again Pharisees require sign *Mat 16 : 1-4, Mark 8 : 10-13*

Disciples reminded by him of his great works *Mat 16 : 5-12, Mark 8 : 13-21*

Peter acknowledges Jesus as the Christ *Mat 16 : 13-20, Mark 8 : 27-30, Luke 9 : 18-21*

Foretells his own death and admonishes Peter *Mat 16 : 21-28, Mark 8 : 31-38, Luke 9 : 20-27*

Again foretells his death and resurrection *Mat 17 : 22, 23, Mark 9 : 30-32, Luke 9 : 43-45*

Disciples dispute who shall be greatest *Mat 18 : 1-11, Mark 9 : 33-37, Luke 9 : 46-50*

Seventy instructed and sent forth *Luke 10 : 1-16*

Seventy return and report success *Luke 10 : 17-24*

Martha complains to him about her sister *Luke 10 : 38-42*

After sermon on bread of life many disciples leave him *John 6 : 66-71*

He sets his face toward Jerusalem and death *Luke 9 : 51-56, John 7 : 1-13*

No one looking back is fit for the kingdom *Luke 9 : 57-62*

Debates at festival of tabernacles; they try to seize him *John 7 : 14-53*

Saves woman taken in adultery *John 8 : 1-11*

Says he is the light of the world and the truth will make free *John 8 : 12-32*

Reproves Pharisees; they try to stone him *John 8 : 33-59*

Teaches disciples the Lord's Prayer *Luke 11 : 1-4*

At feast of dedication they again try to stone him *John 10 : 22-42*

Caiaphas urges council to put Jesus to death *John 11: 47-54*

Warns Herod he, Jesus, must continue to cure *Luke 13: 31-35*

On the kingdom of God and the second coming *Luke 17: 20-37*

Concerning divorce *Mat 19: 3-12, Mark 10: 2-12*

Blesses little children *Mat 19: 13-15, Mark 10: 13-16, Luke 18: 15-17*

Rich young ruler asks how to inherit eternal life *Mat 19: 16-30, Mark 10: 17-31, Luke 18: 18-30*

Again foretells his death and resurrection *Mat 20: 17-19, Mark 10: 32-34, Luke 18: 31-34, 19: 47, 48*

Zebedee's wife requests seats next to him for her sons *Mat 20: 20-28, Mark 10: 35-45*

Visit to Zacchaeus *Luke 19: 1-10*

Has supper with Lazarus whom he raised *John 11: 55-57, 12: 9-12*

Head and feet anointed by Mary, Martha's sister *John 12: 3-8*

The Last Passover Week

Enters Jerusalem on an ass *Mat 21: 1-11, 14-17, Mark 11: 1-11, Luke 19: 29-44, John 12: 12-19*

Casts traders out of temple *Mat 21: 12, 13, Mark 11: 15-17, Luke 19: 45, 46, John 2: 13-25*

Fig tree without fruit is withered *Mat 21: 18-22*

Chief priests ask by what authority he acts *Mat 21: 23-27, Mark 11: 27-33, Luke 20: 1-8*

They seek to destroy him but fear the people *Mark 11: 18, 19*

Pays tribute to Caesar *Mat 22: 15-22, Mark 12: 13-17, Luke 20: 20-26*

On remarriage and resurrection *Mat 22: 23-33, Mark 12: 18-27, Luke 20: 27-40*

Which is the great commandment? *Mat 22: 34-40, Mark 12: 28-34*

The Christ, whose son is he? *Mat 22: 41-46, Mark 12: 35-37, Luke 20: 41-44*

Reproves scribes and Pharisees *Mat 23: 1-39, Mark 12: 38-40, Luke 20: 45-47*

Widow casts in her mite *Mark 12: 41-44, Luke 21: 1-4*

Foretells own death; calls for confession of faith *John 12: 20-50*

Foretells destruction of temple and Jerusalem *Mat 24: 1-41, Mark 13: 1-37, Luke 21: 5-36*

Rulers conspire against him *Mat 26: 1-5, Mark 14: 1-2*

Precious ointment poured on his head by woman *Mat 26: 6-13, Mark 14: 3-9*

Judas settles price to betray him *Mat 26: 14-16, Mark 14: 10, 11, Luke 22: 1-6*

Apostles prepare passover *Mat 26: 17-19, Mark 14: 12-16, Luke 22: 7-13*

The last supper *Mat 26: 26-29, Mark 14: 22-25, Luke 22: 14-30, 1 Cor 11: 23-25*

Who shall be greatest? *Luke 22: 24-30*

Washes disciples' feet *John 13: 1-20*

Foretells his betrayal *Mat 26: 20-25, Mark 14: 18-21, Luke 22: 21, 22, John 13: 21-35*

Peter vows never to deny him *Mat 26: 31-35, Mark 14: 27-31, Luke 22: 31-34, John 13: 36-38*

Queries disciples about lack *Luke 22: 35-38*

Gethsemane—agony in the garden *Mat 26: 30, 36-46, Mark 14: 26, 32-42, Luke 22: 39-46*

Betrayed and made prisoner *Mat 26: 47-56, Mark 14: 43-54, Luke 22: 47-53, John 18: 1-12*

Peter denies him *Mat 26: 57, 58, 69-75, Mark 14: 66-72, Luke 22: 54-62, John 18: 13-18, 25-27*

Priests and council condemn him *Mat 26: 59-68, Mark 14: 55-65, Luke 22: 63-71, John 18: 19-24*

Examined by Pilate *Mat 27: 1, 2, 11-14, Mark 15: 1-5, Luke 23: 1-5, John 18: 28-38*

Judas hangs himself *Mat 27: 3-10, Acts 1: 15-20*

Jesus sent to Herod and returned to Pilate *Luke 23: 6-12*

Crowd offered Barabbas or Jesus *Mat 27: 15-26, Mark 15: 6-15, Luke 23: 13-25, John 18: 39, 40*

Scourged and mocked *Mat 27: 27-31, Mark 15: 16-20, John 19: 1-16*

The crucifixion *Mat 27: 32-56, Mark*

15: 21-41, Luke 23: 26-49, John 19:
17-30

Gives John care of his mother *John
19: 25-27*

Body taken down and buried *Mat
27: 57-66, Mark 15: 42-47, Luke 23:
50-56, John 19: 31-42*

The watch at the sepulcher *Mat
27: 62-66*

Resurrection and Ascension

Resurrection *Mat 28: 1-8, Mark 16:
1-8, Luke 24: 1-12, John 20: 1-10*

Seen by Mary Magdalene *Mark 16:
9-11, John 20: 11-18*

Guard paid to give false report *Mat
28: 11-15*

Seen by two on road to Emmaus
*Mark 16: 12, 13, Luke 24: 13-35,
1 Cor 15: 15*

Seen by apostles; Thomas absent
*Mark 16: 14, Luke 24: 36-49, John
20: 19-23, 1 Cor 15: 5*

Again seen by apostles; Thomas
present *John 20: 24-29*

Seen in Galilee by eleven apostles;
breakfasts with them *Mat 28: 16-
18, John 21: 1-14*

Thrice charges Peter to feed his
sheep *John 21: 12-19*

Peter inquires about John's future
John 21: 20-24

He is seen by 500 *1 Cor 15: 6*

Seen by James and then by all apostles *Acts 1: 1-8, 1 Cor 15: 7*

He is seen ascending to heaven
*Mark 16: 19, 20, Luke 24: 50-53,
Acts 1: 9-13*

JESUS CHRIST: Teachings

Man must be born again *John 3:
1-21*

God is Spirit and must be worshipped spiritually *John 4: 1-30,
39-42*

Reap—harvest is now *John 4: 31-38*

Sermon on Mount

Beatitudes—qualities that make a
Christian *Mat 5: 1-12, Luke 6:
17-26, 36*

Let your light shine before men
Mat 5: 13-16, Luke 8: 16-18

His mission: to Christianize the
law *Mat 5: 17-20*

Some Mosaic commandments put
on a mental basis *Mat 5: 21-32,
Mark 9: 38-50*

Expansion of Third Commandment *Mat 5: 33-37*

On treatment of enemies *Mat 5:
38-48, Luke 6: 27-36*

Benevolence in secret *Mat 6: 1-4*

The Lord's Prayer *Mat 6: 5-15,
Mark 11: 25, 26*

Fast in secret *Mat 6: 16-18*

True treasures *Mat 6: 19-21*

Impossible to serve God and mam-
mon *Mat 6: 22-24*

Disregard material things; seek
ye first the kingdom *Mat 6: 25-
34*

Judge not others *Mat 7: 1-5, Luke
6: 37-40*

Prayer of true petition *Mat 7:
6-11*

Golden Rule for actions *Mat 7:
12-14*

Know men by their fruits *Mat 7:
15-20, Luke 6: 43-45*

For salvation, deeds not words
Mat 7: 21-23, Luke 6: 46, 47

House on rock compared to house
on sand *Mat 7: 24-29, Luke 6:
48, 49*

His great works have their source
in the Father *John 5: 17-47*

Son of man is lord of the sabbath
Mat 12: 1-8

Same as Sermon on Mount *Luke
6: 17-49*

Three cities excoriated for disregarding his mighty works *Mat
11: 20-24*

Gospel revealed to babes *Mat 11: 25-
27, Luke 10: 21, 22*

"...my yoke is easy..." *Mat 11:
28-30*

Eulogy of John the Baptist *Mat
11: 7-15, Luke 7: 24-30*

A house divided *Mat 12: 22-37,
Mark 3: 22-30, Luke 11: 14-20*

"Who is my mother? and ... brethren?" *Mat 12: 46-50*

The charge to preach and heal *Mat
10: 5-42, Mark 6: 7-13, Luke 9: 1-6*
"I am the bread of life" *John 6:
26-65*
What defiles?—a reproof *Mat 15:
1-20, Mark 7: 1-23*
Humility (of little child) *Mat 18:
1-22, Mark 10: 13-16*
Handling of aggressions *Mark 9:
33-50*
Jesus is the Christ *John 7: 14-40*
Eternity of the Christ *John 8: 12-
59*
Christ is the door and the Good
Shephred *John 10: 1-33*
Oneness with the Father *John 10:
22-42*
Instructions to preach and heal
Luke 10: 1-16
Effective prayer *Mat 6: 5-15, Mark
11: 22-26, Luke 11: 1-13*
A prophet is without honor in his
own country *Mat 13: 53-58, Mark
6: 1-6, John 4: 43-45*
Castigations of Pharisees and law-
yers *Luke 11: 37-54*
Leaven of Pharisees, hypocrisy;
covetousness *Luke 12: 1-15*
No thought for material life; signs
of the times *Luke 12: 22-34, 49-59*
Do not offend but forgive; increase
of faith *Luke 17: 1-6*
Faith in Christ *John 12: 44-50*
Denouncing scribes and Pharisees
Mat 23: 1-39
Signs of Christ's coming *Mat 24:
1-44*
Humility *John 13: 12-20*
The Holy Ghost promised *John 14:
1-31*
Vine and branches *John 15: 1-27*
Comfort against tribulation *John
16: 1-33*
Prayer for disciples and their dis-
ciples *John 17: 1-26*
Coming resurrection *Mat 26: 31-35*
Expounds scriptures about Christ
Luke 24: 13-32, 45
Go and teach *Mat 28: 16-20, Mark
16: 15-18*

JETHRO

Moses shepherds the flock of his
father-in-law *Exod 3: 1-3*

He gives Moses permission to return
to Egypt *Exod 4: 18-20*
Moses tells Jethro of the peoples
miraculous escape from Egypt
Exod 18: 1-12
Jethro suggests to Moses the delega-
tion of authority as judge *Exod
18: 13-26*

JEZEBEL

Elijah kills 450 prophets of Baal
who ate at her table *1 King 18:
4, 13, 19-40*
She swears to kill Elijah *1 King
19: 1-3*
She brings false witnesses against
Naboth who is stoned *1 King 21:
1-16*
Elijah denounces her and Ahab
1 King 21: 17-27, 2 King 9: 4-10
Jehu has her thrown out the window
to her death *2 King 9: 30-39*
Elijah's prophecy that she will be
eaten by dogs comes true *2 King
9: 35, 36*

JOAB

He meets Abner head of Israel army
but war flares; his brother Asahel
is killed by Abner *2 Sam 2: 1-32*
Abner deserts to David but Joab
kills him treacherously *2 Sam 3:
17-30*
When David was crowned, Joab his
nephew is made commander of
the army *2 Sam 8: 14-16*
David sends a letter by Uriah that
Joab arrange Uriah's death in the
battle *2 Sam 11: 14-25*
Joab arranges Absalom's return to
court *2 Sam 14: 1-24*
Absalom complains to him and sets
his barley field afire *2 Sam 14:
28-33*
In Absalom's last battle against
David Joab dispatches Absalom
2 Sam 18: 9-17
Joab rebukes the king's excess
mourning and Amasa is put in
Joab's place *2 Sam 19: 1-13*
Joab treacherously stabs Amasa
2 Sam 20: 4-13

A woman stops the Sheba revolt for Joab *2 Sam 20: 16-22*

David forces Joab to sin by numbering the people *2 Sam 24: 1-9, 1 Chron 21: 1-5*

Joab supports Adonijah for king as David nears death *1 King 1: 5-7*

David selects Solomon as successor and instructs him to execute Joab *1 King 2: 5, 6*

He is killed in the tabernacle of refuge *1 King 2: 28-34*

JOB

Prologue in heaven *Job 1: 1-12*

The first trials (loss) *Job 1: 13-22*

Troubles completed (pain) *Job 2: 1-10*

Woe expressed *Job 3: 1-26*

Dialogues with friends *Job 2: 11-13, 4: 1—Job 37: 24*

The nightmare *Job 4: 13-21*

Job contrasts his former prosperity with his wretchedness *Job 29: 1—Job 31: 40*

Elihu's speeches *Job 32: 1—Job 37: 24*

Voice from the whirlwind *Job 38: 1—Job 41: 34*

Epilogue: restorations to Job *Job 42: 1-17*

James on patience cites Job *Jam 5: 7-11*

JOEL

He describes the terrible effects of a locust plague *Joel 1: 1-20, 2: 1-11*

He promises restoration and renewed spirit *Joel 2: 12-32*

The valley of decision on the day of the Lord *Joel 3: 11-18*

JOHN (the Apostle)

Called by Jesus from his trade as fisherman *Mat 4: 21, 22, Mark 1: 19, 20, Luke 5: 10*

He witnesses Jesus' healing of Peter's mother-in-law *Mat 8: 14-17, Mark 1: 29-34, Luke 4: 38*

He helps his partner with miraculous draught of fishes *Luke 5: 1-11*

He rebukes one healing in Jesus' name *Luke 9: 49, 50*

Urges fire from heaven on a village that rejected Jesus *Luke 9: 52-56*

Witnesses Jesus raising Jairus' daughter *Mark 5: 37, Luke 8: 51*

Witnesses transfiguration *Mat 17: 1, Mark 9: 2, Luke 9: 28*

John's mother requests that he sit at Jesus' right hand in heaven *Mat 20: 20-28, Mark 10: 35-45*

With Jesus in Garden *Mat 26: 37, Mark 14: 33*

At Last Supper *John 13: 23*

Present at Jesus' trial before the high priest *John 18: 13-16*

From the cross Jesus gave John the care of his mother Mary *John 19: 25-27*

Ran with Peter to the tomb *John 20: 1-10*

The purpose of John's gospel *John 20: 30, 31*

Present when risen Jesus appeared on shore of Galilee *John 21: 12-14*

Jesus talks about John's future *John 21: 22*

With Peter heals man lame from birth *Acts 3: 1-11*

He and Peter imprisoned *Acts 5: 18*

Sent with Peter to Samaria *Acts 8: 14*

On God is love *1 John 4: 1-21*

Letters to seven churches *Rev 1: 4-20, 2: 1-29, 3: 1-22*

Door opened in heaven *Rev 4: 1-11*

Sealed book *Rev 5: 1-14*

Four horsemen *Rev 6: 1-17*

Angel with little book *Rev 10: 1-11*

Woman with child threatened by dragon *Rev 12: 1-17*

New heaven and new earth *Rev 21: 1-27*

River and tree of life *Rev 22: 1-21*

JOHN THE BAPTIST

Coming birth announced to each of his parents *Luke 1: 5-25*

Birth, how he got his name *Luke 1: 57-80*

Ministry of repentance in wilderness *Mat 3: 1-12, Mark 1: 1-8, Luke 3: 1-18, Mal 3: 1*

Points to Jesus as the Christ *John 1: 29-37, 6: 32-36, 10: 37-42, Acts 13: 23-25*

Baptizes Jesus *Mat 3: 13-17, Mark 1: 9-11, Luke 3: 21, 22*

Tells how Jesus' preaching differs from his own *John 3: 22-36*

Jesus baptizes more disciples than John *John 4: 1-3*

Doubts Jesus is the Christ; asks proof *Mat 11: 2-19, Luke 7: 18-35*

Jesus praises John as the wayshower of Christ *Mat 11: 2-15, 17: 12, 13, 21: 32, Mark 11: 32, Luke 20: 6*

Beheaded, at request of a woman he accused of adultery *Mark 6: 17-30, Luke 3: 19, 20*

Herod thinks Jesus is John the Baptist returned to earth *Mark 6: 14-16*

Jesus compares the coming Holy Ghost with John's baptism *Acts 1: 4, 5, 11: 15-17*

JONAH

Sent to Nineveh, he disobeys and flees in opposite direction to sea *Jonah 1: 1-3*

To calm storm, he is cast overboard by sailors *Jonah 1: 4-17*

Prayer in fish's belly *Jonah 2: 1-10, Mat 12: 40*

Former instruction now obeyed *Jonah 3: 1-10, Mat 12: 41*

The parable of Jonah's pity for the gourd and God's pity for Nineveh *Jonah 4: 4-11*

Jesus compares himself to Jonah *Mat 12: 38-41*

Jesus refuses to give a sign; they know the sign of Jonah *Mat 16: 1-4*

JONATHAN

Jonathan and one man cause an army of Philistines to flee *1 Sam 14: 1-23*

Eats during pursuit of enemy in disobedience to king *1 Sam 14: 24-45*

Befriends David *1 Sam 18: 1-16*

Signals David by three arrows to escape *1 Sam 20: 1-42*

Death at battle of Gilboa *1 Sam 31: 1-13, 1 Chron 10: 1-14*

David laments death of Jonathan and Saul *2 Sam 1: 17-27*

Jonathan's son Mephibosheth helped by David *2 Sam 9: 1-13*

JOSEPH (son of Jacob)

After a dozen years of marriage Rachel bears a son *Gen 30: 22-24*

Coat of many colors; father's favorite *Gen 37: 1-3*

Boyhood dreams; sold into slavery in Egypt *Gen 37: 4-28*

His brothers report death by wild beasts *Gen 37: 29-35*

Potiphar's wife resisted *Gen 39: 1-20*

Dreams interpreted in prison *Gen 39: 21-23, 40: 1-23*

Pharaoh's dream of the famine *Gen 41: 1-46*

As governor Joseph lays up food in the seven plenteous years *Gen 41: 47-57*

Brothers search for food in Egypt *Gen 42: 1-8*

They return with food and their money without recognizing Joseph *Gen 42: 9-38*

They go again with Benjamin for more food *Gen 43: 1-34*

To delay their return Joseph accuses Benjamin of stealing his silver cup and will not let him return *Gen 44: 1-17*

Judah pleads for Benjamin's release for the sake of Jacob *Gen 44: 18-34*

Joseph reveals himself *Gen 45: 1-11*

Jacob and all his children emigrate to Egypt *Gen 45: 25-28, 46: 2-7*

Pharaoh invites Joseph's entire family to live in Egypt *Gen 45: 12-24*

Joseph sets aside the land of Goshen for his family to live as shepherds *Gen 46: 28-34*

He presents his brothers and father to Pharaoh *Gen 47: 1-12*

Joseph collects for food during famine, people's money, their cattle, their land. He taxes one-fifth of all produce *Gen 47: 13-26*

His father asks to be buried back in Canaan *Gen 47: 27-31, 49: 29-33*

Joseph and his two sons visit his dying father and are accepted as "children of Israel" *Gen 48: 1-5*

His father blesses the younger boy with his right hand *Gen 48: 5-22*

Jacob prophesies the future of his twelve sons *Gen 49: 1-28*

Joseph buries his father in Canaan *Gen 50: 1-14*

Joseph's brothers fear his vengeance again *Gen 50: 14-25*

He lives to be 110 years old *Gen 50: 22-26*

Bones of Joseph, carried through the wilderness, are buried in Shechem *Josh 24: 32*

Stephen reviews life of Joseph *Acts 7: 9-18*

JOSEPH (husband of Mary)

Genealogy *Mat 1: 1-16*

Angel informs him of coming birth of Jesus *Mat 1: 18-25*

Takes Mary to Bethlehem *Luke 2: 1-7*

Shepherds find him near babe in manger *Luke 2: 8-16*

Warned by angel, flees with mother and child to Egypt *Mat 2: 13-23*

At circumcision Joseph marvels at what Simeon says about Jesus *Luke 2: 21-33*

Takes Jesus at twelve years to Jerusalem *Luke 2: 41-52*

Jesus not accepted in Nazareth because they knew him as the son of Joseph their local neighbor *Luke 4: 16-28, John 1: 45, 6: 38-43*

JOSEPH (of Arimathea)

Obtains body of Jesus and puts it in his own tomb *Mat 27: 57-61, Mark 15: 42-47, Luke 23: 50-56, John 19: 38-42*

JOSHUA

Joshua prevails over Amalek while Moses' hands are upheld *Exod 17: 8-16*

He is an observer when Moses ascended Sinai and returned to destroy the golden calf *Exod 24: 13, 32: 17*

As one of 70 elders he asks Moses to forbid prophecy by Eldad and Medad *Num 11: 16-30*

Scouts the promised land *Num 13: 1-33, 14: 1-11, 23-39, Deut 1: 19-38*

Given command by Moses *Num 27: 15-23, Deut 3: 28, 31: 3, 22, 23, 34: 9, Josh 1: 1-9*

He is appointed to divide the promised land to the tribes *Num 34: 16-29, Josh 18: 10*

Orders crossing of Jordan *Josh 1: 10-18*

Rahab and spies in Jericho *Josh 2: 1-24*

Jordan crossed *Josh 3: 1-17*

Joshua sets up twelve stones *Josh 4: 1-24*

He circumcises those born in the wilderness *Josh 5: 1-9*

Meets captain of host *Josh 5: 10-15*

Jericho falls *Josh 6: 1-27*

Failure to take Ai on first attempt *Josh 7: 1-26*

New stratagem takes Ai *Josh 8: 1-29*

Joshua reads the law of Moses to the people *Josh 8: 30-35*

His neighbors by deceit make a league with Joshua *Josh 9: 1-27*

Sun and moon stand still at Ajalon *Josh 10: 6-15*

He captures five kings and executes them *Josh 10: 16-27*

Rewards Caleb with his share of Canaan *Josh 14: 6-15*

The Lord orders Joshua to appoint six cities of refuge *Josh 20: 1-9*

Exhorts people to obedience *Josh 23: 1-16*

Warns to choose between good and evil (review of blessings received) *Josh 24: 1-25*

Joshua dies at 110 *Josh 24: 29-31*

The vision of Joshua the high priest clothed in filthy garments *Zech 3: 1-10, 6: 9-15*

JOSIAH

Signs at his birth *1 King 13: 1-10*

His father assassinated and he

begins reign at age eight *2 King 21: 23-26, 22: 1, 2, 2 Chron 33: 21-25, 34: 1-7*

In repairing the temple they find the book with Mosaic law *2 King 22: 3-13, 2 Chron 34: 8-21*

He has the book read to the people and they act against idolaters *2 King 23: 1-25, 2 Chron 34: 29-33*

A prophetess assures him of a peaceful reign *2 King 22: 13-20, 2 Chron 34: 21-28*

He renews the passover service *2 Chron 35: 1-19*

He is killed in the war against Egyptian invaders *2 King 23: 29, 30, 2 Chron 35: 20-27*

JOTHAM

His parable of the trees condemns his half brother *Judg 9: 1-15, 56, 57*

JUDAH (4th son of Israel)

He proposes his brothers sell Joseph instead of kill him *Gen 37: 26-28*

Tamar wife of Judah's son when left a widow becomes mother of two more sons of Judah *Gen 38: 6-30*

He goes surety with his father for Benjamin's safe return from Egypt *Gen 43: 1-15*

He pleads with Joseph to allow Benjamin's return from Egypt and offers himself as hostage *Gen 44: 18-34*

He is selected by his father to lead the way to Goshen *Gen 46: 28*

Jacob passes by three oldest sons to bless Judah *Gen 49: 3-10*

David of tribe of Judah crowned king *2 Sam 7: 13-16, 1 Chron 17: 12, 14, 23*

Jesus the "son" of David was of the tribe of Judah *Mat 1: 1-17, Heb 7: 14*

JUDAS ISCARIOT

Appointed keeper of apostles' money *John 12: 6, 13: 29*

Questions cost of ointment used to anoint Jesus *Mat 26: 6-13, Mark 14: 3-9*

Betrays Jesus for 30 pieces of silver *Mat 26: 14-16, Mark 14: 10, 11, Luke 22: 1-6*

Identified by Jesus at Last Supper *Mat 26: 20-25, Mark 14: 18-21, Luke 22: 21, 22, John 13: 21-35*

At Gethsemane, he identifies Jesus with a kiss *Mat 26: 47-50*

Attempts to return money then hangs himself *Mat 27: 3-10, Acts 1: 15-20*

Peter claims David in Psalm 69: 25 foretold death of Judas *Acts 1: 16, 20*

JUDE

He condemns false teachers *Jude 1: 4-19*

On the duty of true Christians *Jude 1: 20-25*

JULIUS

This centurion takes Paul as a prisoner to Rome *Acts 27: 1-3*

He saves Paul from death by the soldiers *Acts 27: 39-44*

LABAN

He gives his sister in marriage to Isaac *Gen 24: 1-67*

He gives asylum to Jacob, his sister Rebecca's son *Gen 27: 41-46, 28: 1-5*

He deceives Jacob by giving him the undesired Leah as wife *Gen 29: 15-26*

He is outwitted by Jacob *Gen 30: 25-43*

Jacob leaves Laban with Rachel who takes her father's image *Gen 31: 17-24*

Laban overtakes Jacob but makes a covenant with him to part in peace *Gen 31: 25-55*

LAZARUS (of Bethany)

He is sick and dies *John 11: 1-14*

His sisters Mary and Martha witness his raising *John 11: 15-46*

Many Jews come to supper with Jesus at Bethany to see the raised Lazarus *John 12: 1-9*

The Jews plot to kill him as well as Jesus *John 12: 10, 11*

LEAH

She marries Jacob by substitution for Rebecca *Gen 29: 16-30*

She bears first four sons of Jacob's twelve *Gen 29: 31-35*

She trades her mandrakes to Rebecca for a night with Jacob *Gen 30: 14-16*

LOT

He journeys with Abraham to promised land *Gen 12: 1-5*

Strife between his herdmen and those of Abraham *Gen 13: 1-9*

He chooses the plain of Jordan. Leaves Abraham the promised land *Gen 13: 10-18*

He is taken prisoner in war of kings *Gen 14: 1-16*

He gives asylum to two angels *Gen 19: 1-11*

He flees from Sodom; wife turns to salt *Gen 19: 15-26, Luke 17: 26-37*

His daughters with child by him *Gen 19: 30-38*

LUKE

He travels with Paul from Asia to Macedonia in Greece *Acts 16: 10-12*

He travels with Paul from Troy to Jerusalem *Acts 20: 5, 6, 37, 38, 21: 1-8, 15*

Again with Paul to Rome; shipwrecked on way *Acts 27: 1-44, 28: 1-16*

He dedicates the Gospel to a Roman knight Theophilus *Luke 1: 1-4*

MALACHI

Foretells Messiah *Mal 3: 1-6*

Urges tithing; promises rewards *Mal 3: 10, 4: 1, 2*

Foretells coming of forerunner of Messiah *Mal 4: 4-6*

MALCHUS

His right ear cut off but healed *Mat 26: 49-51, Luke 22: 47-53, John 18: 7-12*

MANOAH

An angel foretells his son Samson's birth *Judg 13: 2-14*

He sacrifices and the angel ascends in the flame *Judg 13: 15-23*

MARK

He was with Paul *Acts 12: 25, 13: 1, 5*

Paul and Barnabas quarrel over him *Acts 15: 36-40*

In Rome with Paul *Col 4: 10, 2 Tim 4: 11*

When released from prison Peter goes to the house of Mark's mother *Acts 12: 12*

Author of 2nd Gospel *Mark 14: 51, 52*

MARTHA

Complains to get sister's help *Luke 10: 38-42*

Talks of immortal life of her brother *John 11: 17-31*

Hears Jesus say he is the resurrection and the life *John 11: 23-28*

Witnesses raising of her brother *John 11: 38-46*

Serves supper to Jesus *John 12: 1, 2*

MARY (Jesus' mother)

Espoused to Joseph, found with child by Holy Spirit *Mat 1: 18-25*

Angel annunciation *Luke 1: 26-38*

Visit to Elisabeth *Luke 1: 39-56*

Hymn of thanksgiving *Luke 1: 46-55*

Journey to Bethlehem; birth of child there *Luke 2: 1-7*

Shepherds come to see child *Luke 2: 8-20*

Messiahship of her son confirmed by Simeon *Luke 2: 21-38*

Flight to Egypt *Mat 2: 13-18*

Return to Nazareth *Mat 2: 19-23, Luke 2: 39, 40*

Takes Jesus to Jerusalem when he
is twelve years old *Luke 2: 41-52*

Urges Jesus to turn water to wine
John 2: 1-10

She interrupts Jesus' teaching *Mat
12: 46-50, Mark 3: 31-35, Luke 8:
19-21*

Appears in Jerusalem at the cross
Mark 15: 40, 41

Jesus gives her to care of John
John 19: 25-27

MARY MAGDALENE

She (?) bathed Jesus' feet with
tears at a banquet *Luke 7: 36-50*

One of women at cross *Mat 27: 56,
Mark 15: 40, 41, John 19: 25*

Observed Jesus' burial *Mat 27: 61*

Discovers body of Jesus missing on
morning of resurrection *John 20:
1, 2*

Jesus appears first to her *Mark
16: 9, John 20: 11-18*

MARY OF BETHANY (sister of Martha and Lazarus)

Martha complains about her *Luke
10: 38-42*

At raising of Lazarus *John 11: 1-46*

Anoints Jesus' head and feet with
costly ointment *John 12: 3-8*

MATTHEW

He leaves his job as publican to
follow Jesus *Mat 9: 9, Mark 2: 14,
Luke 5: 27*

He gives great feast with friends
for Jesus *Mat 9: 10-13, Mark 2:
15-17, Luke 5: 29-32*

He is listed among apostles *Mat
10: 3, Mark 3: 18, Luke 6: 15*

MELCHIZEDEK

As king of Salem (Jerusalem) he
brings bread and wine and blesses
Abraham *Gen 14: 17-20*

The Messiah will be a priest—king
like him *Psal 110: 1-5, Heb 5: 1-10,
6: 20*

Melchizedek is described by Paul
Heb 7: 1-13

Jesus compared to him *Heb 7: 14-28*

MEPHIBOSHETH

Son of Jonathan lamed by fall
2 Sam 4: 4

King David allows him to eat at his
table for life *2 Sam 9: 1-13*

His servant gets Mephibosheth's inheritance *2 Sam 16: 1-4*

David later divides the land *2 Sam
19: 24-30*

David spares Mephibosheth from a
hanging *2 Sam 21: 6-9*

MESHACH

One of three who refused to worship image and is thrown into
fiery furnace *Dan 3: 1-30*

MICAH

Mountain of the Lord's house
Micah 4: 1-8, 13, Isa 2: 1-5

The Messiah will come from a small
town *Micah 5: 1-5*

On true sacrifice *Micah 6: 6-9*

On general corruption *Micah 7: 1-8*

MANASSEH

He is born first son of Joseph *Gen
41: 51*

Jacob blesses him with left hand
and adopts him *Gen 48: 1-22*

MELZAR

He permits Daniel to eat grain
rather than defile himself with
the king's meat *Dan 1: 11-16*

MERCURIUS

Paul as chief speaker mistaken for
Greek god Mercury *Acts 14:11, 12*

METHUSELAH

Grandfather of Noah lives long life
Gen 5: 21-27, 1 Chron 1: 3

MICHAL

David earns this daughter of King
Saul by killing 200 Philistines
1 Sam 18: 17-30

She helps David escape through her window *1 Sam 19: 10-18*
Later they are reunited *2 Sam 3: 12-16*
She disapproves David's dancing in the streets *2 Sam 6: 12-23, 1 Chron 15: 29*
David gives her five sons to be killed *2 Sam 21: 6-9*

MICHAEL

The archangel has a message for Daniel *Dan 10: 13, 21*
He contends with the devil *Jude 9*
He and his army fight great red dragon *Rev 12: 7*

MIRIAM

She watches over baby Moses in ark *Exod 2: 4-8*
Her song when Egypt's army destroyed *Exod 15: 20, 21*
She and Aaron speak against their brother Moses *Num 12: 1-10, Deut 24: 9*
But Moses heals her of leprosy *Num 12: 11-15*

MORDECAI

He brings up his niece Esther *Esther 2: 5-7*
He saves the king's life exposing a plot *Esther 2: 21-23*
He refuses to bow down to Haman *Esther 3: 1-6*
A decree to destroy all Jews *Esther 3: 8-15*
He persuades Esther to help the Jews *Esther 4: 1-17*
Haman erects a gallows to hang him *Esther 5: 13, 14*
The king honors Mordecai *Esther 6: 6-14*
Haman hanged on the gallows prepared for Mordecai *Esther 7: 8-10*
Mordecai advanced *Esther 8: 1-8*
He lifts the oppression of the Jews *Esther 8: 9-17*
Under Mordecai the Jews slaughter their former enemies *Esther 9: 1-6*
He was next to the king in power *Esther 10: 1-3*

MOSES

Oppression of Israelites *Exod 1: 8-14*
Midwives ordered to drown sons *Exod 1: 15-22*
Birth and escape from death by the river *Exod 2: 1-10, Heb 11: 23*
Slays Egyptian and flees to wilderness *Exod 2: 11-15, Heb 11: 24*
Protects daughters of Jethro, marries one and becomes shepherd *Exod 2: 16-25*
Burning bush; the nature of God revealed *Exod 3: 1-18, Luke 20: 37*
Reluctance to lead overcome *Exod 3: 9-12*
Delivery from king of Egypt foretold *Exod 3: 16-22*
Rod and leprosy transformed *Exod 4: 1-9*
Complains of speaking ability *Exod 4: 10-17*
He returns to Egypt with his family *Exod 4: 18-23*
His wife circumcises his son reluctantly *Exod 4: 24-26*
Aaron joins him and they report to the people *Exod 4: 27-31*
He tells Pharaoh that God says let my people go *Exod 5: 1-6*
Israelite slaves have to make bricks without straw *Exod 5: 7-19*
God renews promises *Exod 5: 20-23, 6: 1-13*
Contest of Moses and Aaron with Egyptian sorcerers *Exod 7: 1-12, 2 Tim 3: 8, 9*
The ten plagues: blood, frogs, lice, flies, cattle, boils, hail, locusts, darkness, first-born slain *Exod 7: 14—Exod 12: 30*
Passover and release from bondage *Exod 11: 4-10, 12: 1-14, 21-41, Deut 16: 1-22*
Pillars of cloud and fire *Exod 13: 20-22, Num 9: 15-23, 1 Cor 10: 2*
Red Sea passed through *Exod 14: 5-31*
Song of Moses glorifying God *Exod 15: 1-19*
Waters of Marah made sweet *Exod 15: 22-27*
Manna in wilderness; quails *Exod*

16: 1-36, Num 11: 1-15, 31, 32, John 6: 32

Water from rock *Exod 17: 1-7, Num 20: 1-13*

Hands upheld during battle Exod *17: 8-16*

Jethro meets him and rejoices at events *Exod 18: 1-12*

Judges appointed to relieve Moses' burden *Exod 18: 13-27*

Talks with God on Mt. Sinai *Exod 19: 1-9*

The people stand at the foot of the mountain to meet with God *Exod 19: 10-25*

Ten Commandments; the basic constitution of monotheism *Exod 20: 1-19, Deut 5: 1-24*

The people ratify the Ten Commandments *Exod 24: 1-18*

The Urim and the Thummim put on Aaron's garments *Exod 28: 29-36*

Golden calf molded during absence *Exod 32: 1-24*

Moses orders killing of 3000 unruly idolaters *Exod 32: 25-35*

The Lord talks with Moses at the tabernacle door, face to face *Exod 33: 7-23*

Second tablets of stone *Exod 34: 1-8, Deut 10: 1-4*

The firstfruits belong to God *Exod 34: 18-28*

Veil conceals Moses' face *Exod 34: 29-35, 2 Cor 3: 7-15*

Moses consecrates Aaron and his sons *Lev 8: 1-13*

Moses institutes the sin offering and the scapegoat *Lev 16: 1-28*

The day of atonement *Lev 16: 29-34*

The jubilee *Lev 25: 9-17*

The blessings of obedience *Lev 26: 2-13*

The plagues of disobedience *Lev 26: 14-46*

Moses teaches Aaron how to bless the people *Num 6: 22-27*

The use of the silver trumpets *Num 10: 1-10*

Fire of the Lord burns complainers *Num 11: 1-3*

Remembering the good food of Egypt the people demand flesh to eat *Num 11: 4-15*

70 elders selected to share Moses' spirit *Num 11: 1-25*

Eldad and Medad prophesy in camp *Num 11: 26-30*

Miriam and Aaron rebel against Moses; her resultant leprosy healed by Moses *Num 12: 1-16*

Caleb, Joshua and others scout the land of Canaan *Num 13: 1-33, 14: 1-11, 23-39, Deut 1: 19-38*

Moses persuades the Lord to pardon the people's reluctance to enter promised land *Num 14: 11-23*

Murmurers will die in wilderness; only Caleb and Joshua shall enter promised land *Num 14: 23-39*

A man found gathering sticks on the sabbath is ordered stoned to death *Num 15: 32-36*

The earth swallows up the censer rebels agains Moses's authority *Num 16: 1-40*

Israelites healed of plague in wilderness *Num 16: 41-50*

Moses demonstrates Aaron's authority by the test of rods *Num 17: 1-11*

Bites of fiery serpents healed *Num 21: 4-9, John 3: 14*

Amorites refuse passage and are defeated, also Bashan *Num 21: 21-35*

Balaam refuses at first to help Balak turn back Moses *Num 22: 1-21*

Balaam's ass saves him *Num 22: 22-35*

God prevents Balaam from cursing Israel *Num 23: 5-30*

Balaam prophesies success of Israel and is dismissed by Balak *Num 24: 1-14, 25*

Balaam foretells the Messiah *Num 24: 15-19*

Phinehas the priest slays a man and whore together, to stay the plague *Num 25: 1-18*

Second census, only 2 men left from first numbering, Caleb and Joshua *Num 26: 63-65*

Daughters of Zelophehad sue for inheritance *Num 27: 1-11, 36: 5-13*

Lord tells Moses Joshua is his successor *Num 27: 12-23*

Reubenites and Gadites promise Moses to stay with others until all the land is possessed *Num 32: 1-42*

Aaron dies at 123 years *Num 33: 38, 39*

Moses asks to go into the land but is permitted only to see it *Deut 3: 24-29, 4: 21, 22, 32: 48-52, 34: 1-4*

He sets up three cities of refuge *Deut 4: 41-43, 19: 1-10*

Exhortations to obey God *Deut 4: 1-15, 6: 1-25*

The chosen people set apart *Deut 7: 6-11*

Warning to remember trials *Deut 8: 1-20*

Obedience urged again *Deut 10: 12-22, 11: 1-32*

Warnings against enticers to idolatry, necromancy *Deut 13: 1-18*

Duty of kings *Deut 17: 14-20*

Abominations forbidden *Deut 18: 9-14*

Another prophet promised; Christ foreshadowed *Deut 18: 15-22*

Offering first fruits *Deut 26: 1-19*

Blessings of obedience *Deut 28: 1-14*

He reminds of miracles *Deut 29: 1-17, 29*

Farewell address on choice for good or evil *Deut 30: 11-20*

Lord informs Moses he will not enter promised land but Joshua will lead *Num 27: 12-23*

Moses charges Joshua with leadership *Deut 31: 7-23, Josh 1: 1-9*

Song of deliverance *Deut 32: 1-47, Rev 15: 3*

Blessing of each tribe *Deut 33: 1-29*

He dies and is buried *Deut 34: 5-12*

At 120 years his eyesight and strength still good *Deut 34: 7*

At transfiguration he appears representing Old Testament law and talks with Jesus *Mat 17: 1-13, Mark 9: 2-13, Luke 9: 28-36*

Victorious people sing the song of Moses *Rev 15: 1-3*

NAAMAN

As Commander delivers Syria but is a leper *2 King 5: 1*

His soldiers bring his wife a captive maid from Israel *2 King 5: 2-4*

Elisha refuses to see him but heals him *2 King 5: 5-14*

Naaman is converted to Jehovah but permitted to perform his secular duties before the god Rimmon *2 King 5: 17-19*

Elisha's servant accepts reward refused by Elisha and becomes leprous *2 King 5: 15-27*

Jesus refers to Naaman's healing *Luke 4: 27*

NABAL

Wealthy churlish husband of Abigail *1 Sam 25: 1, 2*

He refuses to help David *1 Sam 25: 3: 13*

Abigail pacifies David's anger *1 Sam 25: 14-35*

On his death the widow marries David *1 Sam 25: 36-42*

NABOTH

He refuses to sell his inherited vineyard to King Ahab *1 King 21: 1-4*

Jezebel arranges Naboth's death *1 King 21: 5-16*

Elijah prophesies Ahab's punishment *1 King 21: 17-27*

Ahab's son killed in the field of Naboth *2 King 9: 21-26*

As prophesied, Jezebel eaten by dogs *2 King 9: 30-37*

NAHUM

Teaches the majesty of God *Nahum 1: 2-15*

Predicts fall of Nineveh *Nahum 3: 1-19*

NAOMI

Famine causes her family to move to Moab *Ruth 1: 1-5*

She returns to Bethlehem in Judah with Ruth alone *Ruth 1: 6-22*

Her kinsman marries Ruth and makes her ancestress of David *Ruth 4: 13-22*

NATHAN

His vision that David's son would build the temple *2 Sam 7: 1-13, 1 Chron 17: 1-27*

His parable of the ewe lamb accuses the king *2 Sam 12: 1-15*

He arranges the succession of Solomon as king *1 King 1: 1-53*

He kept the chronicles of kings *1 Chron 29: 29, 2 Chron 9: 29*

He and David instituted musical service in the sanctuary *2 Chron 29: 25-28*

NATHANAEL

He is called by Jesus although he questioned a Messiah from Nazareth *John 1: 45-51*

In boat with Peter at draught of fishes from Galilean lake *John 21: 1-8*

He (Bartholomew?) among twelve given power to heal and sent forth to preach *Mat 10: 1-42, Mark 3: 13-18*

He (Bartholomew?) among witnesses to the ascension *Acts 1: 9-14*

NEBUCHADNEZZAR

The prophecy of his conquest of Tyre *Ezek 26: 7-21*

He takes Jerusalem, carries king and many people off *2 King 24: 10-16, 2 Chron 36: 5-10, Dan 1: 1, 2*

He quells rebellion of king Zedekiah, burns the temple and carries back the rest of the people *2 King 25: 1-26, 2 Chron 36: 11-21, Jer 39: 1-14, 52: 1-30*

He invades Egypt *Ezek 29: 17-20, Jer 46: 1-26*

He is prophesied as an instrument of God's judgment *Jer 27: 1-9*

Orders certain children of Israel educated *Dan 1: 3-20*

His dream of great image interpreted by Daniel *Dan 2: 1-49*

Puts three Hebrews in fiery furnace *Dan 3: 1-30*

His dream of great tree interpreted by Daniel *Dan 4: 1-29*

His insanity prophesied by Daniel; sanity returns *Dan 4: 28-37*

NEHEMIAH

News of Jerusalem's misery *Neh 1: 1-11*

Permitted to return, he surveys the city *Neh 2: 1-20*

Begins repair of wall; builders armed *Neh 4: 1-23*

He restores property to the people, taken from them by their rulers *Neh 5: 1-19*

Conspiracy to halt building fails *Neh 6: 1-19*

Book of the Law read to people by Ezra *Neh 8: 1-12*

Capsule history of Jews leads to renewal of covenant *Neh 9: 1-38, 10: 28-39*

Sabbath day reforms and mixed marriage reforms *Neh 13: 14-31*

NICODEMUS

Comes at night to question Jesus *John 3: 1-21*

As a follower defends Jesus *John 7: 50-52*

Helps take Jesus' body down from cross *John 19: 39*

NIMROD

As son of Cush a mighty hunter *Gen 10: 8, 9*

He builds Babel *Gen 10: 10, 11: 1-9*

NOAH

Building the ark *Gen 6: 5-22, Heb 11: 7*

Entering the ark *Gen 7: 1-24*

The raven and the dove *Gen 8: 1-22*

The covenant repeated to Noah *Gen 9: 1-17*

The rainbow is the sign of the covenant *Gen 9: 12-17*

His vineyard and drunkenness *Gen 9: 19-27*

Jesus compares coming of Son of man to the flood *Mat 24: 34-41, Luke 17: 20-37*

OBADIAH

He hid 100 prophets in a cave to prevent persecution by king Ahab *1 King 18: 2-4, 13*

He objects to introducing Elijah to the king *1 King 18: 1-16*

The great prophet in his book in Scripture predicts the Day of the Lord is coming *Obadiah 8-18*

OBED

Son of Ruth and grandfather of David *Ruth 4: 17-22*

PAUL

Educated a Pharisee, was zealous *Acts 22: 3, 26: 4, 5*

His father attained Roman citizenship *Acts 16: 37, 22: 25-28*

Saul (Paul) consents to Stephen's death and persecutes the church *Acts 8: 1-4, 9: 1, 2*

Saul (Paul) commissioned to persecute, is stricken blind; talks with Jesus near Damascus *Acts 9: 1-9, 22: 4-9, 26: 9-15*

Healed of blindness by Ananias, baptized, preaches Christ *Acts 9: 10-22*

Jews watch gates to kill him; is let down over wall in basket *Acts 9: 23-31*

Goes back to Jerusalem and spends 15 days with Peter *Gal 1: 18-20*

With Barnabas, establishes church at Antioch, now called Christian *Acts 11: 19-26*

He blinds a false prophet *Acts 13: 1-13*

Sermon on lineage of Christ and salvation by Jesus *Acts 13: 16-43*

At Antioch Jews expel him and he turns to the Gentiles *Acts 13: 44-52*

Heals cripple while preaching at Lystra *Acts 14: 8-10*

People worship him and Barnabas as gods *Acts 14: 11-18*

Is stoned but recovers *Acts 14: 19, 20*

Dissension about circumcision, Peter supports Paul *Acts 15: 1-35*

Paul quarrels with Barnabas *Acts 15: 36-41*

Converts Lydia *Acts 16: 7-15*

Damsel soothsayer healed *Acts 16: 16-18*

He and Silas imprisoned; earthquake opens doors; they convert jailor *Acts 16: 19-40*

Followed by persecutors from Thessalonica to Berea *Acts 17: 1-15*

At Athens, preaches on the unknown God *Acts 17: 15-34*

At Corinth lives with Aquila, a tent-maker; in a vision God tells Paul to speak out *Acts 18: 1-11*

Apollos competes with Paul in good works *Acts 18: 24-28, 1 Cor 1: 11-13, 3: 1-10*

Preaches Holy Ghost to Ephesians *Acts 19: 1-10*

Vagabond exorcists attempt to imitate his work *Acts 19: 11-20*

An idol silversmith contends with him *Acts 19: 23-29*

Eutychus falls from upper window but is healed *Acts 20: 7-12*

Sermon on trials as a Christian *Acts 20: 17-38*

He visits Philip and four daughters *Acts 21: 8, 9*

Agabus warns him not to go to Jerusalem *Acts 21: 8-15*

Soldiers save him from the mob *Acts 21: 26-34, 23: 9-35*

Is seized but gives sermon on how he was converted *Acts 21: 33-40, 22: 1-30*

His vision predicts he will bear witness in Rome *Acts 23: 11*

Almost convinces Felix *Acts 24: 22-26*

Before Festus Paul appeals to Caesar *Acts 25: 1-21*

Defends himself before King Agrippa *Acts 26: 1-32*

Voyage to Rome; delivered from shipwreck *Acts 27: 1-44*

On Malta, viper bite is healed *Acts 28: 1-6*

On Malta, Publius' father healed of hemorrhage *Acts 28: 7-10*

Paul preaches at Rome *Acts 28: 23-29*

On the power of the gospel *Rom 1: 16-25*

On judging others and being judged by God *Rom 2: 1-29*

On Abraham's faith *Rom 4: 1-25, Gal 3: 6-18*

Adam vs. Christ *Rom 5: 12-21*

On escape from the wages of sin and death *Rom 6: 1-23*

The law of sin vs. the law of God *Rom 7: 14-25*

Spirit vs. flesh *Rom 8: 1-39, Gal 5: 16-25*

On transforming to a life of purity and self-denial *Rom 12: 1-21*

On love, the fulfilling of the law *Rom 13: 7-14*

On the wise and the foolish *1 Cor 1: 17-31, 3: 18-23*

On manner of his preaching *1 Cor 2: 1-16*

On factions in the church *1 Cor 3: 1-17*

On prize for a race *1 Cor 9: 24-27*

Describes the Last Supper *1 Cor 11: 23-29*

On spiritual gifts *1 Cor 12: 1-31*

On charity (love) *1 Cor 13: 1-13*

On Christ's resurrection; the proof that we, too, shall rise again *1 Cor 15: 1-58*

On comfort and consolation *2 Cor 1: 1-10*

On the letter and the spirit *2 Cor 3: 2-18*

On outward and inward man *2 Cor 4: 14 to 5: 21, Eph 4: 17-25*

On separating from unbelievers *2 Cor 6: 1-18*

On giving and receiving *2 Cor 8: 11-15, 9: 6-15*

On spiritual warfare *2 Cor 10: 3-5*

Hardships to establish church *2 Cor 11: 21-33*

His self-revealings and thorn in the flesh *2 Cor 12: 1-10*

On justification by faith and not by works *Gal 2: 14-21, Eph 2: 8, 9*

Outward observance of the Jewish law contrasted to trust in Christ *Gal 3: 2-29, 5: 2-14*

On Abraham's two sons, by a bond-woman and by a freewoman *Gal 4: 22-31*

On fruits of the flesh and of the Spirit *Gal 5: 16-26*

The effect of grace on Christians *Eph 2: 1-22, Col 1: 9-13*

Prayer for church members *Eph 3: 14-21*

On the elements of the church body,

Christ the head *Eph 4: 1-16, Col 1: 13-23*

On Christian discipline, putting off the old man to be renewed *Eph 4: 17-32, Col 3: 9, 10*

The light of Christian life awakens *Eph 5: 1-20*

Husband and wife a symbol of Christ and church *Eph 5: 21-33*

On family relations *Eph 6: 1-9, Col 3: 18-25, 4: 1*

On the Christian's armor *Eph 6: 10-17*

On the mind of Christ *Phil 2: 1-15*

On the example of Paul trying to apprehend Christ *Phil 3: 8-17*

On rejoicing; things to think on *Phil 4: 1-9*

On the Christian's risen life and duties *Col 3: 1-17*

How to prepare for the Second Coming of Christ *1 Thess 5: 1-28*

On how soon Christ will come again *2 Thess 2: 1-17*

His advice to a disciple *2 Tim 2: 1-26*

His description of enemies of the truth *2 Tim 3: 1-17*

His charge to fight the good fight *2 Tim 4: 1-8*

He asks Philemon to forgive a run-away slave *Philemon 1-25*

Why Christ is supreme to the Hebrew Christian *Heb 1: 1-14*

Jesus as a priest after the order of Melchisedec *Heb 7: 1-28*

On O. T. atonement and that of Jesus Christ *Heb 10: 1-22*

On faith as substance and evidence *Heb 11: 1-40, 12: 1-3*

On the chastening of the Lord *Heb 12: 1-15*

PETER

Peter selected by Jesus *Mat 4: 17-22, Mark 1: 14-20, John 1: 35-42*

Net filled after fishing all night; net breaks *Luke 5: 1-11*

His wife's mother healed of fever *Mat 8: 14-17, Mark 1: 29-34, Luke 4: 38, 39*

Present when woman in crowd is healed by touching Jesus *Luke 8: 43-48*

Present at healing of Jairus' daughter *Mark 5:35-43, Luke 8: 49-56*

Is among twelve disciples taught by Jesus to preach and heal *Mat 10:1-42, Mark 3:13-21*

Walks on water to Jesus *Mat 14: 22-33*

Questions about what defiles a man *Mat 15:10-20*

Is first to acknowledge Jesus as Christ *Mat 16:13-20, Mark 8:27-30, Luke 9:18-21*

Name changed by Jesus from Simon Bar-jona to Peter (or Cephas or the Rock) *Mat 16:16-18*

Rebuked for urging Jesus to avoid the cross *Mat 16:21-28, Mark 8: 31-38*

At the transfiguration *Mat 17:1-13, Mark 9:2-13, Luke 9:28-36*

Gets tribute money from fish's mouth *Mat 17:24-27*

He notes the fig tree has withered Mark 11:12-14, 20, 21

Questions Jesus about his second coming *Mark 13:1-27*

Questions Jesus how many times one should forgive *Mat 18:21, 22*

Asks Jesus to whom the parable of the steward applies *Luke 12:35-48*

Sent with John to prepare the Passover *Luke 22:7-13*

Refuses to let Jesus wash his feet; then accepts *John 13:1-20*

Vows never to deny Jesus *Mat 26: 31-35, Mark 14:27-31, Luke 22: 31-34, John 13:36-38*

Asleep at Gethsemane *Mat 26:36-45, Mark 14:32-41*

Cuts off Malchus' ear *Luke 22:50, 51*

Denies Jesus when arrested *Mat 26: 57, 58, 69-75, Mark 14:66-72, Luke 22:54-62, John 18:13-18 25-27*

Day of resurrection *Mat 28:1-8, Mark 16:1-8, Luke 24:1-12, John 20:1-10*

An angel message from Jesus *Mark 16:7*

Returns to his occupation of fishing at Galilee *John 21:1-14*

Great draught of fishes and breakfast with Jesus *John 21:4-14*

Finally instructed by Jesus *John 21:12-19*

Inquires about John's future *John 21:20-24*

Election of Mathias to replace the apostle Judas Iscariot *Acts 1: 15-26*

Descent of promised Holy Spirit (Ghost) *Acts 2:1-13*

Peter's sermon on resurrection and baptism *Acts 2:14-47*

With John heals man lame from birth *Acts 3:1-11*

Sermon on healing *Acts 3:12-26*

He and John tried before council for preaching *Acts 4:1-23*

Their successful release causes signs and wonders in church growth *Acts 4:24-37*

He exposes hypocrisy toward God of Ananias and Sapphira; their death follows *Acts 5:1-11*

His shadow heals sick in streets *Acts 5:12-16*

Imprisoned again, released by angel; Gamaliel intercedes for him *Acts 5:17-42*

Seven deacons chosen *Acts 6:1-4*

He goes to Samaria to help Philip preach *Acts 8:14-18*

Rebukes Simon the sorcerer for his offer to buy the power of the Holy Ghost *Acts 8:14-24*

Aeneas healed of paralysis *Acts 9: 32-35*

Tabitha (Dorcas) raised from death *Acts 9:36-43*

Accepts conversion of Cornelius, a Roman Gentile *Acts 10:1-48*

Defends his acceptance of the Gentiles by relating his vision of great sheet *Acts 11:1-18*

Imprisoned by Herod; angel releases him *Acts 12:1-17*

His two letters to the churches from Rome *1 Peter, 2 Peter*

Receives Paul as minister in fellowship to Gentiles *Gal 1:18-20, 2: 1-10*

He is rebuked by Paul and persuaded that Gentiles need not be circumcised *Gal 2:11-21*

PHARAOH

At time of Abraham, Sarah is taken into the Pharaoh's household *Gen 12:10-20*

At time of Jacob, the Pharaoh appoints Joseph governor *Gen 41: 37-46*

At time of Moses, the Pharaoh blocks exodus of people temporarily; ten plagues *Exod 4:14 to 12:30*

Sends army to pursue them; it perishes in Red Sea *Exod 14:5-31*

At time of Solomon, the Pharaoh gives him one of his daughters to wife *1 King 3:1-3*

At time of Hezekiah, he is warned from an alliance with Pharaoh *2 King 18:19-21*

At time of Josiah, the Pharaoh invades Assyria *2 King 23:29, 30*

At time of Jeremiah, prophecy that Nebuchadnezzar will overthrow Egypt *Jer 46:1-12*

At time of Ezekiel, desolation of Egypt predicted *Ezek 29:1-12*

PHILEMON

Paul asks forgiveness by Philemon of his runaway slave Onesimus *Philemon 10-25*

PHILIP (the Apostle)

Called by Jesus to follow him *John 1:43-48*

Present at feeding of 5000; questions that it can be done *John 6:1-14*

Ushers in some Greeks who wish to interview Jesus *John 12:20-22*

Asks Jesus to show disciples the Father *John 14:1-11*

Was with apostles in upper chamber after the ascension *Acts 1:9-14*

PHILIP (the Evangelist)

He is appointed deacon to help the apostles *Acts 6:1-6*

Many healed by him in Samaria *Acts 8:5-8*

He converts and baptizes Simon the sorcerer *Acts 8:9-13*

Simon offers to buy power of Holy Ghost (Spirit) *Acts 8:14-25*

Ethiopian eunuch baptized *Acts 8: 26-40*

Paul visits his house; meets his four daughters who prophesy *Acts 21: 8, 9*

PILATE

He orders blood of some Galileans mingled with their sacrifices *Luke 13:1*

As governor he cross-examines Jesus *Mat 27:1, 2, 11-14, Mark 15:1-5, John 18:28-38, 19:8-12*

He sends Jesus to Herod who returns him *Luke 23:6-12*

He offers mob choice of Jesus or Barabbas *Mat 27:15-23, Mark 15: 6-15, Luke 23:13-25, John 18:39, 40*

He orders crucifixion but washes his hands of responsibility for it *Mat 27:24-26*

He writes a title for cross; Jews object *John 19:19-22*

He releases body of Jesus for burial *Mat 27:57-60, Mark 15:42-46, Luke 24:50-56, John 19:38-42*

He permits a guard to watch the tomb *Mat 27:62-67*

POTIPHAR

He buys Joseph as a slave and makes him overseer *Gen 39:1-4*

He accepts his wife's accusations of Joseph and orders him to prison *Gen 39:16-20*

PUBLIUS

Chief man at Malta lodges Paul and shipwrecked sailors *Acts 28:7*

His father healed by Paul *Acts 28: 8-10*

RAB-SHAKEH

Sent by king of Assyria to stir up rebellion against Hezekiah of Jerusalem *2 King 18:17-37, 19: 1-8, Isa 36:2-22, 37:1-8*

RACHEL

She meets Jacob at the well *Gen 29: 9-12*
To marry her Jacob serves seven years and then Laban substitutes her older sister on the wedding night *Gen 29: 15-27*
Jacob obtains her after seven more years *Gen 29: 27-30*
She begs for children like her sister Leah *Gen 30: 1, 2*
She offers her maid to Jacob *Gen 30: 3-8*
She sells the service of Jacob to Leah for Reuben's mandrakes *Gen 30: 14-21*
God hears her prayers and Joseph is born *Gen 30: 22-24*
She steals her father's images on leaving him *Gen 31: 13-19, 27-35*
She bears Benjamin *Gen 35: 16-18, 24*
Her death and burial *Gen 35: 18-20, 48: 7, 1 Sam 10: 2*
Weeping for her children, refuses to be comforted *Jer 31: 15-17, Mat 2: 16-19*

RAHAB

She assists the spies of Israel to escape *Josh 2: 1-24*
She and her family are spared when Jericho falls *Josh 6: 17-25*
Her faith in Israel commended *Heb 11: 31, Jas 2: 25*

REBEKAH

A wife found for Isaac *Gen 24: 1-67*
Esau and Jacob, the twins, born *Gen 25: 19-26, Rom 9: 7-14*
She passes as Isaac's sister *Gen 26: 6-11*
With Jacob plots deceit on blind Isaac *Gen 27: 1-44*
To escape Esau she sends Jacob to her brother Laban *Gen 27: 42-46*

REHOBOAM

Son of Solomon ascends throne of Judah *1 King 11: 43, 14: 21-27, 2 Chron 9: 31*
Consults his father's counselors, then follows advice of his own friends *1 King 12: 1-18, 2 Chron 10: 1-19*
Invaded by Egypt and punished *1 King 14: 25-28, 2 Chron 12: 1-12*
Wars with Jeroboam of Israel *1 King 12: 16-24, 14: 29, 30, 2 Chron 13: 7*

REUBEN

Born son of Leah *Gen 29: 32*
He brings mandrakes to his mother *Gen 30: 14-21*
Commits incest with Jacob's concubine Bilhah *Gen 35: 21, 22, 49: 3, 4*
Saves Joseph from death by suggestion to sell him into slavery *Gen 37: 21-30*
Offers Jacob his two sons as hostage for Benjamin *Gen 42: 37*
Jacob prophesies Reuben's future *Gen 49: 1-4*

RUTH

Returns with Naomi to Israel *Ruth 1: 1-22*
Her devotion to her mother-in-law and conversion *Ruth 1: 14-19*
Gleans in field of Boaz *Ruth 2: 1-23*
Becomes mother of Obed, grandfather of David *Ruth 4: 1-22*

SAMSON

Angel foretells his birth to his mother *Judg 13: 1-25*
The angel predicts that he will not drink wine nor cut his hair *Judg 13: 3-5*
Samson kills a lion with his hands, later finds honey and bees in the carcass *Judg 14: 5-14*
His wife divulges his riddle about the lion and honey to his enemies *Judg 14: 1-4, 12-18*
He is denied his wife and burns the corn with firebrands tied to foxes *Jud 15: 1-8*
He slaughters Philistines with a jawbone *Judg 15: 9-17*
Dying of thirst God supplies him a fountain *Judg 15: 18-20*

He escapes from the harlot's house at Gaza and takes the gate of the city with him *Judg 16: 1-3*

Delilah betrays him; his blindness and death *Judg 16: 4-30*

SAMUEL

Miraculous birth *1 Sam 1: 1-28*

His mother's song of thanksgiving *1 Sam 2: 1-10*

Lord calls him at twelve years of age *1 Sam 3: 1-10, 19-21*

His vision of the punishment of the house of Eli *1 Sam 3: 11-18*

The ark of the Lord captured by the Philistines causes the destruction of the image of Dagon *1 Sam 5: 1-12*

The ark is returned to Israel with gift offerings *1 Sam 6: 1-16*

Samuel prays for Israel and they defeat Philistines *1 Sam 7: 1-11*

A judge of Israel *1 Sam 7: 12-17*

He makes his corrupt sons judges *1 Sam 8: 1-3*

Resists people's demand for king *1 Sam 8: 4-22*

Anoints Saul to be king *1 Sam 9: 10, 10: 1-8*

Saul prophesies *1 Sam 10: 9-27*

Samuel's integrity as judge and ruler *1 Sam 12: 1-5*

He causes thunder and rain as a sign against the rebels *1 Sam 12: 15-19*

Saul declared unfit to be king *1 Sam 13: 11-15, 15: 7-26*

Saul tears Samuel's mantle *1 Sam 15: 27-35*

Anoints David as future king *1 Sam 16: 1-13*

Shelters David when fleeing Saul *1 Sam 19: 18-24*

His death and lament *1 Sam 25: 1*

Called up by witch to speak with Saul *1 Sam 28: 3-20*

SANBALLAT

He and Tobiah oppose the repair of Jerusalem by Nehemiah *Neh 2: 10, 4: 1-8, 6: 1-14*

SARAH

She is Abrahm's half-sister but marries him *Gen 11: 27-30, 20: 12*

In Egypt she is represented as her husband's sister *Gen 12: 9-20*

As she is childless she gives her handmaid Hagar to Abraham *Gen 16: 1-16*

Name changed from Sarai, a child promised *Gen 17: 15-22, Rom 4: 19, 9: 9, Heb 11: 11*

She laughs at news *Gen 18: 1-18*

In Gerar she passes again as Abraham's sister *Gen 20: 1-16*

Isaac born to her *Gen 21: 1-8*

In jealousy she causes Abraham to cast out Hagar and her child *Gen 21: 9-21, Gal 4: 22-31*

She lives to be 127 years old *Gen 23: 1, 2*

Her son Isaac marries Rebekah and brings her home to Sarah's tent *Gen 24: 67*

SAUL

He searches for the lost asses *1 Sam 9: 1-27, 10: 1, 2*

Anointed king by Samuel *1 Sam 10: 1-8, 17-27, 11: 10-15*

Prophesies *Sam 10: 9-27*

He relieves the siege of Jabesh *1 Sam 11: 1-15*

He usurps Samuel's place at sacrifice *1 Sam 13: 8-15*

Only his enemies have secret of iron *1 Sam 13: 19-23*

His son wins the battle of Michmash *1 Sam 14: 1-23*

He threatens death to his son for disobedience *1 Sam 14: 24-30, 43-46*

Neglects to slay Amalekites, Samuel decides him unfit *1 Sam 15: 7-26*

He rips Samuel's mantle *1 Sam 15: 27-35*

Calmed when David plays harp *1 Sam 16: 14-23*

Frightened by Goliath's challenge *1 Sam 17: 1-16*

Offers David his armor *1 Sam 17: 32-40*

David brings him the head of Goliath *1 Sam 17: 55-58*

Envies David *1 Sam 18: 1-16*
Offers David his daughter for 100 foreskins *1 Sam 18: 17-30*
He urges his son to kill David *1 Sam 19: 1-7*
He casts javelin at David playing harp *1 Sam 19: 8-10*
Michal puts David's image in her bed to save his life from her father *1 Sam 19: 11-18*
He pursues David to Samuel's house *1 Sam 19: 18-24*
Jonathan helps David escape his father's wrath *1 Sam 20: 1-42*
Saul slays the priests of Nob because they helped David *1 Sam 22: 9-23*
In wilderness of Ziph David is pursued and escapes *1 Sam 23: 16-29*
Pursues David, spared by David in cave *1 Sam 24: 1-22*
He is spared again by David; blesses him *1 Sam 26: 1-25*
Consults witch of Endor contrary to his own decree *1 Sam 28: 3-20*
Death on own sword *1 Sam 31: 1-13, 1 Chron 10: 1-14*
Report of death to David *2 Sam 1: 1-16*
Lamented by David *2 Sam 1: 17-27, 1 Chron 10: 13*

SENNACHERIB

Invades Judah twice *2 King 18: 13-37, 2 Chron 32: 1-20, Isa 36: 1-22*
Plague destroys his army. He is slain by his sons *2 King 19: 35-37, 2 Chron 32: 21-23, Isa 37:21-38*

SHADRACH

One of three who refused to worship an image and are placed in a fiery furnace *Dan 3: 1-30*

SHAPHAN

The scribe who read the Book of the Law to Josiah *2 King 22: 3-13*

SHEBA

Visits Solomon to confirm report of his greatness *1 King 10: 1-13*

SHEM

With Japheth protects his father Noah and is blessed *Gen 9: 18-27*

SHIMEI

He cursed king David as the enemy of Saul *2 Sam 16: 1-14*
He is later pardoned by David *2 Sam 19: 16-23*
Solomon puts him to death *1 King 2: 36-46*

SHUNAMMITE

Great woman whose son Elisha raised from death *2 King 4: 8-37*
She flees famine; returns to claim her property *2 King 8: 1-5*

SILAS

Imprisoned with Paul they pray and sing until an earthquake opens the door *Acts 16: 19-40*

SIMEON

Second son of Leah and Jacob *Gen 29: 31-35*
He slays the people of Shechem because their prince ravished his sister Dinah *Gen 34: 1-31*
He is left with Joseph as a hostage for Benjamin *Gen 42: 24-38*
Jacob's prophecy about him *Gen 49: 5-7*
A man of Jerusalem prophesies that the babe Jesus is the Christ *Luke 2: 25-35*
James refers to the prophecy of the Gentiles *Acts 15: 13, 14*

SIMON (Bar-jona)

See PETER

SISERA

Captain for Jabin; defeated by Deborah *Judg 4: 1-17*
Killed in his sleep by a woman *Judg 4: 18-24*

SOLOMON

Nathan prophesies about him *2 Sam 7: 12-17, 1 Chron 17: 11-17*

Son of David and Bathsheba *2 Sam 12: 24, 25, 1 King 1: 13, 17, 21*

Nathan and Bathsheba manipulate his succession *1 King 1: 1-53*

David's charge to Solomon *1 Chron 22: 6-19, 23: 1, 28: 2-10, 20*

He takes throne of Israel *1 King 1: 11-48, 2: 12, 1 Chron 23: 1, Eccl 1: 12*

He puts his previously forgiven brother to death for a request to marry their father's concubine *1 King 2: 13-25*

Anointed king second time *1 Chron 29: 22*

Solomon's dream and request for understanding *1 King 3: 5-15, 2 Chron 1: 7-12*

Dividing the baby *1 King 3: 16-28*

Builds temple *1 King 6: 1-38, 7: 1-51, 2 Chron 3: 1-17, 4: 1-22, 5: 1-14*

Dedication of temple and blessing of congregation *1 King 8: 22-66, 2 Chron 6: 1-42*

Covenant renewed with him after building temple *1 King 9: 1-9*

Visit by Queen of Sheba *1 King 10: 1-13, 2 Chron 9: 1-12, Luke 11: 31*

Builds his own palace *1 King 3: 1, 7: 1, 8, 9: 10, 2 Chron 7: 11, Eccl 2: 1-26*

Vineyards, orchards, pools *Eccl 2: 4-6*

The splendor of his court *1 King 10: 5-9, 12, 2 Chron 9: 3-8, Eccl 2: 9, Mat 6: 29, Luke 12: 27*

Commerce of *1 King 10: 11, 12, 22, 28, 29*

Affluent wealth (achieved by excess taxation) *1 King 10: 10, 14, 15, 23, 27, 12: 1-18*

700 wives, 300 concubines *1 King 11: 3, 4*

His wives' idolatry is punished in the next generation *1 King 11: 3, 4, 9-14*

Gifts to King Hiram *1 King 9: 10-13*

He is credited with the book of Proverbs *Prov 1: 1*

Credited (probably falsely) with book of Ecclesiastes *Eccl 1: 1*

Credited (probably falsely) with Song of Solomon *Song 1: 1*

His raiment compared to lilies of the field *Mat 6: 28-34, Luke 12: 27-34*

Jesus says a greater than Solomon is here *Mat 12: 38-42*

STEPHEN

His miracles and trial as deacon *Acts 6: 5-15*

Sermon of defense *Acts 7: 1-53*

Is stoned to death *Acts 7: 54-60*

TABITHA (Dorcas)

Raised from death by Peter *Acts 9: 36-42*

TAMAR

Widow of Judah's son; she becomes mother of two boys by Judah *Gen 38: 6-30*

Sister of Absalom, abused by her half brother Amnon *2 Sam 13: 1-20*

Because of this crime Absalom arranges Amnon's death *2 Sam 13: 21-39*

TERAH

He becomes father of Abraham *Gen 11: 26, 27*

He takes Abraham and others towards promised land but dies partway *Gen 11: 31, 32, Josh 24: 1-3*

THEOPHILUS

Luke addresses his gospel to him *Luke 1: 1-4*

Luke addresses The Acts to him *Acts 1: 1*

THOMAS

Called by Jesus *Mat 10: 3, Mark 3: 8, Luke 6: 15, Acts 1: 13*

Offers to die with Jesus *John 11: 16*

Asks Jesus the way he will go *John 14: 1-7*

Doubts report Jesus is risen *John 20: 24, 25*

Convinced when Jesus appears again
John 20: 26-30

Goes back to his trade as fisher
John 21: 1-8

Is present at breakfast on the shore
John 21: 14-19

TIBERIAS

Sea of Galilee renamed after this
Roman Emperor *John 6: 1*

TIMOTHY

He was converted by Paul *1 Cor 4:
17, 1 Tim 1: 2*

As a child instructed in O. T. *2 Tim
1: 5, 3: 15, Acts 16: 1*

He is circumcised after conversion
Acts 16: 2, 3

He accompanies Paul's journeys
Acts 17: 14, 15, 1 Thes 1: 1

He is advised by Paul's epistles
1 Tim and 2 Tim

TITUS

Converted but refuses to be circumcised *Gal 2: 3-5*

Paul sends him as deputy to Corinth
2 Cor 2: 13, 7: 6, 13

Paul writes him in Crete with advice
on his ministry there *Titus 1, 2, 3*

TOBIAH

Conspires with Sanballat and Ge-
shem against the rebuilding of
Jerusalem by Nehemiah *Neh 2:
10, 4: 1-8, 6: 1-14*

TYCHICUS

Advance man for Paul *Acts 20: 4*

Delivered epistles to Ephesians and
Colossians *Eph 6: 21, Col 4: 7*

TYRANNUS

Offered Paul the use of his school
at Ephesus for preaching *Acts
19: 9*

URIAH

One of David's mighty men *2 Sam
23: 39, 1 Chron 11: 41*

To possess Uriah's wife, Bath-sheba,
David arranges his death in the
front line *2 Sam 11: 1-27, Mat 1: 6*

UZZAH

He steadies the ark and is struck
dead *2 Sam 6: 3-11, 1 Chron 13:
7-14*

UZZIAH (Azariah)

He strengthened Judah *2 Chron 26:
6-8*

His heart lifted up to destruction
2 Chron 26: 9-23

VASHTI

As queen she is divorced for refusing to show herself at his feast
Esther 1: 1-22, 2: 1-4

ZACCHEUS

Jesus dines at his house and conversion ensues *Luke 19: 1-10*

ZACHARIAS

Father of John Baptist struck dumb
by angel *Luke 1: 5-25*

When his child is born he recovers
and prophesies *Luke 1: 57-79*

ZEBEDEE

Father of James and John left in
his ship by his sons *Mark 1: 19,
20*

His wife asks Jesus for special con-
sideration of his sons *Mat 20:
20-28*

ZEBULON

Sixth son of Leah and Jacob *Gen
30: 19, 20, 35: 23*

Went to Egypt with Jacob and his
family *Exod 1: 3*

Israel blesses him in connection with the sea *Gen 49: 13, Deut 33: 18, 19*

Jesus goes through the land of Zebulon to fulfill the prophecy of Isaiah (9: 1) about the Messiah *Mat 4: 12-16*

ZECHARIAH

Vision of the messengers on red horses watching over the earth *Zech 1: 7-17*

Vision of the four horns that scattered the Jews *Zech 1: 18-21*

Vision of the man with the measuring line to rebuild Jerusalem *Zech 2: 1-13*

Vision of the high priest and Satan; the purifying of the church *Zech 3: 1-10, 6: 9-15*

Vision of candlestick fed by two olive trees *Zech 4: 1-14*

Vision of the flying roll *Zech 5: 1-4*

Vision of evil personified by a woman *Zech 5: 5-11*

Vision of the four chariots *Zech 6: 1-8*

The vision of restored Jerusalem *Zech 8: 1-23*

ZEDEKIAH

Appointed king by Nebuchadnezzar he revolts to ally with Egypt *2 King 24: 17-20, 2 Chron 36: 11-13, Ezek 17: 11-21*

He imprisons Jeremiah for denouncing him *Jer 37: 11-21*

He asks Jeremiah's help but the prediction is destruction *Jer 38: 14-28*

He is taken captive to Babylon, blinded *2 King 25: 1-10, 2 Chron 36: 17-20, Jer 39: 1-14*

ZELOPHEHAD

He dies without sons but Moses permits his five daughters to inherit *Num 27: 1-11, 36: 5-13*

ZEPHANIAH

He rejoices at restoration of Zion *Zeph 3: 14-17*

ZERUBBABEL

Cyrus proclaims rebuilding of temple *Ezra 1: 1-11*

Zerubbabel sets up the altar first *Ezra 3: 1-7*

Rebuilding the temple starts *Ezra 3: 8-13*

Adversaries block the work *Ezra 4: 1-15*

Work starts up again *Ezra 6: 1-3, 7, 8, 14, 15*

Letter of Artaxerxes to Ezra *Ezra 7: 11-26*

Zechariah encourages him to rebuild the temple *Zech 4: 4-10*

ZERUIAH

Sister of David, mother of David's three greatest warriors *2 Sam 2: 18, 16: 9, 10, 19: 22, 23*

ZIBA

As servant of Mephibosheth he betrays him to David *2 Sam 16: 1-4*

After David's victory Mephibosheth gets back half of Ziba's possessions *2 Sam 19: 17-30*

ZILPAH

Maidservant to Leah; given by Leah to Jacob as secondary wife; she bears him two sons, Gad and Asher *Gen 30: 9-13*

ZIPPORAH

Daughter of Jethro marries Moses *Ex 2: 16-22*

She opposed circumcision but acquiesces *Ex 4: 18-26*

She tells Jethro all God had done for Moses *Ex 18: 1-12*

ZOPHAR

Tries to comfort Job by rebuking him *Job 11: 1-20*

CPSIA information can be obtained
at www.ICGtesting.com
Printed in the USA
LVHW021954220222
711733LV00004B/85